# MOON

# PUERTO VALLARTA

**JUSTIN HENDERSON & BRUCE WHIPPERMAN**

# PUERTO VALLARTA

Bahía de Banderas

To Hotels Rosita and Buenaventura →

Malecón

HIDALGO

CAFÉ DES ARTISTES/
COSTANTINI WINE BAR ▾

LANDMARK HOTEL

CARRANZA

PIPILA

LEONA VICARIO

PASEO DE ORDAZ

GALERIA
DE OLAS

ZTAI

BANORTE

LA CANTINA

ORTIZ DE DOMINGUEZ

JUAREZ

ABASOLO

ALDAMA

DAVANNA
YOGA

HOTEL LOS
CUATRO VIENTOS &
CHEZ ELENA RE

F. CARRANZA

MIRAMAR

VILLA DAVID

CASA KIMBERLY

CENTRO CULTURAL
RIO CUALE

CENTRO CULTURAL
VALLARTENSE

LA DOLCE VITA ▾

HARD ROCK CAFÉ ▾

THE ZOO ▾

MORELOS

LAS PALOMAS ▾

HILO

GALERIA
PACIFICO

CASA DE
FENG SHUI

CORONA

GALERIA
UNO ▾

MAJOLICA

GALERIA
LA INDEGENA

DAVID'S
B&B ●

ITURBIDE

PLANETA
VEGETARIANO ●

GRINGO
GULCH

BIKE MEX/
ECORIDE

CASA DEL
PUENTE

PLAZA JOHN HUSTON

LE BISTRO ▾

CHEEKY MONKEY ▾

OCEANO
BAR ▾

QUERUBINES

GALEANA

OLE
TAPETES

MINA

BARCELONA ▾
TAPAS

BANCOMER

JEWELRY
FACTORY

PRESIDENCIA
MUNICIPAL

BANCO INVERLAT

CATHEDRAL

HACIENDA
SAN ANGEL

EXPEDICIONES
CIELO ABIERTO

OPEN SKY
EXPEDITIONS

HSBC

MUNICIPAL
CRAFTS MARKET

ZARAGOZA

LOS ARCOS
AMPHITHEATER ★

Plaza De
Armas

TOURIST
INFORMATION

BUSTAMENTE
GALLERY

GUERRERO

BANAMEX

PEYOTE
PEOPLE

LIBERTAD

CURVAS
PELIGROSAS

CRAFT
STALLS

RIVER

BANCOMER

GALERIA
VALLARTA

ALBERTO'S
JEWELRY

CAFÉ
CANELA

RODRIGUEZ

HOTEL
ENCINO/SUITES
PLAZA DEL RIO

ENCINO

VITEA ▾

GALERIA
TESOROS

HOTEL RIO

PUEBLO VIEJO ▾

ANTHROPOLOGY

IGNACIO VALLARTA

INDIGENOUS
ART MUSEUM ★

THE MALECÓN ▾

Plaza A
Serdán

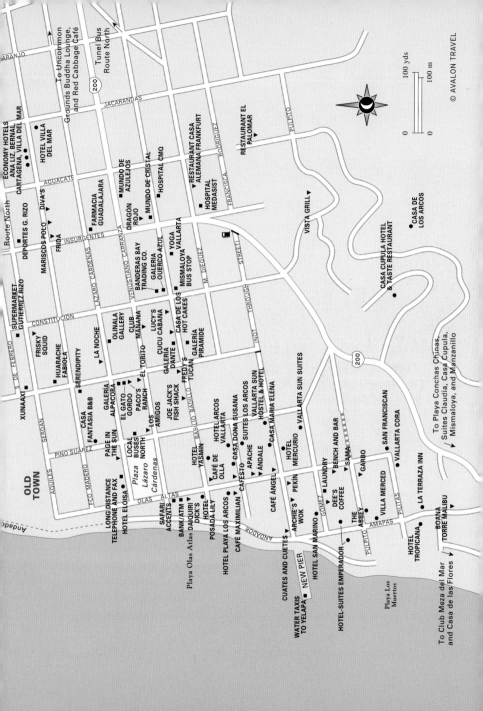

OLD TOWN

Playa Olas Atlas

To Uncommon
Grounds Buddha Lounge,
and Red Cabbage Café

Tunel Bus
Route North

Route North

ARANJO

JACARANDAS

AGUACATE

INSURGENTES

CONSTITUCIÓN

5 DE FEBRERO

SERDAN

AQUILES

PINO SUAREZ

FCO MADERO

OLAS ALTAS

ANDADOR

VENUSTIANO CARRANZA

LAZARO CARDENAS

BASILIO BADILLO

GOMEZ

PULPITO

AMAPAS

PILITAS

M. DIEGUEZ

FRANCISCA

RODRIGUEZ

PULPITO

INTO THROUGH STREET

ECONOMY HOTELS
ANA LIZ, BERNAL,
CARTAGENA, VILLA DEL MAR

HOTEL VILLA
DEL MAR

DEPORTES G. RIZO

DIVA'S

FRIDA

MARISCOS-POLO

SUPERMARKET
GUTIÉRREZ RIZO

FRISKY
SQUID

HUARACHE
FABIOLA

SERENDIPITY

LA NOCHE

CASA
FANTASIA B&B

PAGE IN
THE SUN

GALERÍA
ALPACORA

LOCAL
BUSES
NORTH

FARMACIA
GUADALAJARA

MUNDO DE
AZULEJOS

DRAGON
ROJO

MUNDO DE CRISTAL

HOSPITAL CMQ

RESTAURANT CASA
ALEMANA FRANKFURT

HOSPITAL
MEDASIST

RESTAURANT EL
PALOMAR

BANDERAS BAY
TRADING CO.

GALERIA
QUERCO-AZUL

YOGA
VALLARTA

MISMALOYA
VALLARTA
BUS STOP

VISTA GRILL

CASA CUPULA HOTEL
& TASTE RESTAURANT

CASA DE
LOS ARCOS

OLINALA
GALLERY

CLUB
MAÑANA

EL TORITO

LUCY'S

CASA DE LOS
HOT CAKES

GALERÍA
PIRAMIDE

CUCU CABANA

GALERIA
DANTE

FREDY'S
TUCAN

EL GATO
GORDO

PACO'S
RANCH

JOE JACK'S
FISH SHACK

LOS
AMIGOS

HOTEL
YASMIN

CAFÉ DE
OLLA

CAFESTO

APACHE

ANDALE

HOTEL ARCOS
VALLARTA

CASA DOÑA SUSANA

SUITES LOS ARCOS

VALLARTA SUN
HOSTEL & HOTEL

CASA MARIA ELENA

VALLARTA SUN SUITES

HOTEL
MERCURIO

BENCH AND BAR

SAMA

GARBO

SAN FRANCISCAN

VALLARTA CORA

VILLA MERCED

LA TERRAZA INN

CAFÉ ÁNGEL

ARCHIE'S
WOK

PEKIN

DEE'S
COFFEE

LAUNDRY

THE
ABBEY

HOTEL
TROPICANA

BORIA
TORRE MALIBU

SAFARI
ACCENTS

BANK/ATM

DICK'S

DAIQUIRI

POSADA LILY

HOTEL

CAFÉ MAXIMILIAN

HOTEL PLAYA LOS ARCOS

HOTEL ELOISA

LONG DISTANCE
TELEPHONE AND FAX

CUATES AND CUETES

WATER TAXIS
TO YELAPA

NEW PIER

HOTEL SAN MARINO

HOTEL-SUITES EMPERADOR

Playa Los
Muertos

To Club Meza del Mar
and Casa de las/Flores

To Playa Conchas Chinas,
Suites Claudia, Casa Cupula,
Mismaloya, and Manzanillo

Plaza
Lázaro
Cárdenas

Andador

200

200

200

© AVALON TRAVEL

0        100 yds
0        100 m

# Contents

# Discover
# Puerto Vallarta

Puerto Vallarta and its surrounding areas have long had die-hard fans. From the wild, undeveloped southern coast to the colorful beach towns of the northern shores, it's plain to see why visitors return year after year. Gold beaches embrace the calm waters of the Bay of Banderas, one of the largest, deepest bays in the world. This aquatic haven is home to myriad species, a source of both abundant seafood and diverse recreational activities. It shelters Puerto Vallarta from storms and provides a protected habitat for endangered sea turtles and whales that give birth on its shores and in its warm waters each year.

Nestled into a verdant valley, Puerto Vallarta is rich with resources. Fertile farmlands, tropical fruit orchards, and blue agave fields surround the area, giving rise to craggy, volcanic mountains. In petite coves and along sweeping seashores, small settlements provide a glimpse into what Puerto Vallarta used to be.

While Old Town, or Zona Romántica, as it is called, retains its rustic charm, Vallarta has grown into a modern city complete with posh discos, upscale designer boutiques, modern cinemas, and even a few small casinos. This transition has brought new prosperity and opportunity to the residents.

The heart of Puerto Vallarta remains in Old Town and the lively Malecón that runs along the shoreline. Along the Malecón you'll find endless entertainment, from sand sculptures and living statues to clowns and musicians. It comes alive at night as people congregate to watch the sunset and later enjoy the live entertainment, delicious street food, and ever-entertaining people-watching that are always available.

There's something for everyone in the greater Puerto Vallarta region: from the spunky beach town of Barra de Navidad to the tranquil and time-less San Blas; slumbering fishing hamlets to the exclusive communities of the rich and famous; surf towns to wild beaches so removed that you can only reach them by sea. The diversity of the area attracts more people each year, many who return again and again. Join them. You'll discover your own special place in this magical region by the sea.

# Planning Your Trip

## ▶ Where To Go

### Puerto Vallarta

Puerto Vallarta is divided north and south by the gentle, vine-swathed Río Cuale, which ripples from its foothill canyon. The old town north and south of the river retains much of its original charm, especially south of the river in the Avenida Olas Altas district and the adjacent Playa los Muertos. In spite of a few massively overbuilt hotels and apartment buildings, the appeal continues to the south, along the villa-decorated Conchas Chinas headland, past the bay-shore villages of Mismaloya (and the nearby offshore Los Arcos giant rocks snorkeling/scuba sanctuary), and farther south, to petite Boca de Tomatlán shoreline village.

North of the Río Cuale, the old town spreads uphill to the meandering lanes of Gringo Gulch, the bayfront Los Arcos amphitheater, and the airy Malecón shoreline promenade. Farther north, the beach boulevard passes through the Zona Hotelera lineup of world-class hotels along golden-sand Playa de Oro, continuing past the plush Marina condohome district and golf course to the airport at the town limits.

## If You Have . . .

**A LONG WEEKEND:** Stick to Puerto Vallarta proper and enjoy Old Town, the Malecón, and the local beaches. Snorkel at Los Arcos, pet a lion cub at the zoo, or go bird- and butterfly-watching at the botanical gardens.

**A WEEK:** Stay close by, but check out the beach at Boca de Tomatlán, or grab a water taxi and visit Yelapa. Don't skip the pie.

**TWO WEEKS:** Head north and explore Bucerías, Punta Mita, Sayulita, or San Pancho for an overnight or two without getting too far away. Do some surfing or stand-up paddling. Visit the *tianguis* (flea market) in La Peñita, beachcomb in Lo de Marcos, or join the party at Rincón de Guayabitos. Take a half-day hike to see the petroglyphs and waterfalls at Alta Vista.

**LONGER:** The world is your oyster. For funky beach town ambience, hit Barra de Navidad for a few nights, and then work your way up the coast through the wild beaches of Costalegre. Love history, farmlands, and cool mountain air? Hit San Sebastián, Mascota, or Talpa. For a mix of both great beaches and historical significance, head to San Blas for fun surf and great jungle hiking and sightseeing.

Los Arcos, on the south end of the Malecón in Puerto Vallarta

## Around the Bay of Banderas

There are many wonderful things to do and see around the Bay of Banderas. Bucerías lies along the northern shoreline, followed by Punta Mita and coral-strewn Playa Anclote, all great places for sunbathing, surfing, and snorkeling. Excursions to wildlife-rich offshore Islas Marietas are a popular adventure as well.

Visitors find even more in the cool Sierra Cuale, a trio of invitingly old-world colonial-era towns, not far east of Puerto Vallarta. San Sebastián, curled around a precious little plaza, offers comfy country inns and old gold mines to explore. Mascota adds tasty home-cooked country food and museums. Nearby, picturesque Talpa is a pilgrimage town, home of the miraculous Virgin of Talpa, that affords a fine museum and good restaurants.

## Sayulita and the Riviera Nayarit

For years, the Nayarit Coast has been one of Puerto Vallarta's best-kept secrets. Visitors come to enjoy the gorgeous beaches, good surfing, snorkeling, wildlife-watching, and charming country-Mexico ambience.

Moving north, the highlights include hot surf town Sayulita, sleepy San Francisco, and precious Chacala. Finally comes San Blas, famous for bird-watching, wildlife viewing, and occasional world-class surfing. Beyond San Blas is the idyllic automobile-free Mexcaltitán, an island village where an excellent museum tells the island's fascinating story.

## Barra de Navidad and the Jalisco Coast

For travelers yearning to follow the path less traveled, the Jalisco Coast may be just the ticket. From Puerto Vallarta, it stretches more than 100 miles south, traversing pine-tufted mountains, deserty savanna, lush tropical forest, and seemingly endless pristine golden strands.

On the three broad bays that indent the Jalisco Coast—Bahía de Chamela, Bahía de Tenacatita, and Bahía de Navidad—a few villages, including Perula, El Super, and La Manzanilla, provide a modicum of food, lodging, and services for the growing trickle of travelers seeking a Mexican paradise.

A number of splendidly isolated boutique hotels sprinkle the Jalisco Coast. If you enjoy being pampered in the wilderness, this is the place.

Many travelers' Jalisco Coast journeys wind down at the drowsy far southern twin resorts of Melaque and Barra de Navidad, where they enjoy lots of sun, golden sand, and sparkling Pacific sunsets.

a perfect day in downtown Barra de Navidad, where the mermaids play

# ▶ WHEN TO GO

The most popular time to visit Puerto Vallarta is high season (Christmas-Easter), when the days are warm and dry and the nights are cool. With exception of the actual holidays, this is when prices are highest and the hotels most crowded.

Travelers looking for lower costs and less crowds should visit before Christmas, from about late October. The weather is still lovely, and there's no shortage of hotel rooms or deals.

True bargain hunters and surfers looking for less-crowded waves should visit in summer. Days are steamy and hot, but the evenings are cooled by spectacular thunderstorms, washing away the dust and presenting brilliant evening light shows. Summer is low season, and savvy visitors can take advantage of discounts on everything from hotels to massages.

To catch the best cultural events, visit during the first two weeks of December during the celebration of the Virgin of Guadalupe. Streets are closed off, and nightly processions of floats, folkloric dancers, and musicians head to the cathedral. If you are a foodie, don't miss Restaurant Week in mid-May. The best restaurants in Puerto Vallarta offer prix fixe meals under $25.

Puerto Vallarta's cathedral

flying performers on Puerto Vallarta's Malecón

## ▶ BEFORE YOU GO

No vaccinations are necessary when heading to Mexico for your vacation. During the rainy summer months there is an abundance of mosquitoes, some of which carry dengue, an unpleasant but rarely fatal tropical virus. Dengue shouldn't be a concern unless you are staying in rural areas, close to standing water.

Keep the tourist visa you receive when traveling into Mexico. You will face fines if you try to leave without it. If you are traveling from or through the United States, you will need a valid passport to return from Mexico.

If you plan on traveling with your pet, make sure you have current health records and a rabies vaccination (given within 30 days of your arrival). Few hotels are pet friendly, so it's best to check in advance.

# The Best of Puerto Vallarta

For the most intimate view of Puerto Vallarta, stay in a comfortable hotel within close walking distance of the colorful Old Town sights, cafés, restaurants, and shops. If you opt to stay in the north-end Hotel Zone or the Marina, you can easily hail a taxi ($5-8) or hop a local bus to go where the action is. If it's your thing, be sure to reserve seats ahead for a Fiesta Mexicana show.

Those who want a full dose of urbanity with their beach time should stick to Puerto Vallarta, either downtown or Old Town, since this puts you within easy reach of the city's best restaurants and nightlife while also keeping you close to the beach and bay. If you're looking to really chill out, however, you might consider staying up at the north end of the

Hotel Zone, or even in Nuevo Vallarta, and cabbing or busing in to "the big city" for day trips or nights on the town. And if a beach-front city isn't on your agenda except as a pass-through, why not spend a night or two in Vallarta at the beginning or end of your travels and head north to Sayulita or south to Cabo Corrientes for the rest of your trip?

Wherever you stay, be sure and take at least one leisurely promenade down the Puerto Vallarta Malecón at sunset or in the early evening. This is simply a great urban beachfront experience.

## Day 1

The majority of flights arrive at the Puerto Vallarta airport in the late afternoon. After customs and transportation to your hotel, that doesn't leave much time for sightseeing, and who wants to rush out after a long day of travel anyway?

Change out of your travel clothes and into some casual beach attire; grab your camera, your travel companions, and maybe

view of Vallarta and the bay

a book; and head down to a beach restaurant and dig your toes into the sand. Order a tropical drink and some fresh guacamole, then people-watch and decompress until you catch your first brilliant Vallarta sunset. Take a dozen pictures to impress your friends. Ahhhh, isn't that better?

After drinks and chips, you probably won't be very hungry, so stroll along the Malecón and nibble on crepes, tacos, and fresh fruit from the food stands as the mood strikes. Check out the central Plaza de Armas and watch the concert (or the clowns) at the adjacent shoreline Los Arcos amphitheater.

Things start picking up at the dance clubs around midnight, so head over to Mandala or the Zoo to get your groove on and work off those margaritas.

## Day 2

Who can resist the beach on your first full day? Head out and start beach exploring. Start at the seafront park just north of the Río Cuale and stroll south over the river bridge and continue along the seashore *andador* (walkway) along Playa los Muertos. Walk out on the new pier to see what's biting, or grab a lounge chair at any of the restaurants and beach clubs. There's plenty of people to watch, friends to make, and margaritas to drink!

Still have the urge to explore? Head south by local Mismaloya or Boca bus (from the corner of Constitución and Basilio Badillo). Visit Mismaloya, and then head back into town to watch the sunset at one of many establishments along the famous Malecón. Or, if you prefer, continue south a few miles past Mismaloya to the unmissable Le Kliff Restaurant, overlooking the ocean, on the right.

Later, hit one or more of the nightclubs on the Malecón. Now closed to auto traffic, the Malecón is party central, especially during spring break but pretty much year-round. The old standards—Hilo, the Zoo—still rock, and now a couple of relative

Feed the flamingos at the Puerto Vallarta Zoo.

# A Perfect Day for Romance

sunset at Yelapa

Ask any of the hundreds of brides, grooms, and honeymooning couples who visit each year, and they'll tell you that Puerto Vallarta is the place for romance. Swaying palms on golden beaches, moonlit walks along the shore, and brilliant Pacific sunsets make the Bay of Banderas the perfect backdrop for weddings, anniversaries, engagements, or just a quick romantic getaway. The following are suggestions for a perfect romantic day in Puerto Vallarta.

Start your morning with breakfast on your balcony. Order room service and start the day relaxed and unhurried while watching the waves together. When you're ready, get dressed and hail a cab to **Playa los Muertos.** From there, enjoy an hour boat ride, viewing the magnificent mansions and villas that line the shore on your way to **Yelapa.**

If it's still early in the day, hike to the waterfall or take a horseback ride into the jungle. When you return, have a light lunch (and a slice of pie) at one of the beachfront restaurants. Go ahead and swim, sunbathe, or buy some trinkets from the local vendors, and then catch a return boat back to the pier.

On your way back to your hotel, recharge with a **couple's massage** at a local spa. Tables are set up side by side so you and your sweetie can enjoy the relaxing and healing powers of massage together. For a real treat, buy a package at one of the hotel spas to enjoy steam rooms, sauna, massage, and total pampering. Once back at your hotel, rest for a while before getting dressed for dinner.

There are any number of restaurants along the Malecón where you can watch a spectacular sunset, but **Vista Grill, Barcelona Tapas,** and **Restaurant Chez Elena** are elevated and offer a panoramic view of the city as well. Share a dessert and a kiss as the evening fireworks light up the sky at about 10.

If you've still got it in you, head out to **La Bodeguita del Medio** or **J&B** for some salsa dancing, or stop by a **La Playa** liquor store and pick up a bottle of Chambrule sparkling wine for a moonlit stroll along the beach. End your perfect day with a kiss at midnight, your feet buried in the sand and the warm waters of the bay lapping at your ankles.

newcomers—Mandala, La Vaquita—have totally amped up the Malecón party options.

## Day 3

You've done the beaches, and now it's time to hit the water. Take a relaxing day cruise for snorkeling at Los Arcos and a waterfall swim at either Quimixto or idyllic Yelapa on the Bay of Banderas's jungly southern shore. Don't miss the pie ladies of Yelapa.

Head back into town for dinner, and then do a little nightclub hopping along the Malecón (or seek out more conversation-friendly entertainment at either Ándale pub or Garbo in the Olas Altas district). Tired of techno and dance music? Hit Club Roxy for some raucous rock and roll.

## Day 4

After all of the previous activity, it may be best simply to rest for a day. Or if you prefer, head for an out-of-town adventure at Punta Mita or Sayulita village (an hour by bus north of town). There you can stroll, boogie board, and maybe try your hand at surfing.

If you are taking a break from the sun and surf today, head south and make a stop at the Puerto Vallarta Zoo to cuddle a lion cub and/or the Vallarta Botanical Gardens to view their amazing collection of orchids and the picturesque grounds. Both are excellent for nature photography and bird-watching.

Tonight, head north for some killer salsa dancing at J&B.

## Day 5

Part of your last day will be spent picking up mementos of your trip and handicrafts for the folks back home. Head down to the Isla Cuale and check out the wares for sale in the many shops and stalls. If you can handle the heat, head into the Mercado Municipal just down-hill from the bridge. Grab some Mexican vanilla, organic coffee, or colored glassware for affordable and useful gifts.

For the rest of your day, schedule a special tour such as horseback riding or a whale-, dolphin-, or bird-watching excursion to the Islas Marietas. Don't miss your last Puerto Vallarta sunset!

a bougainvillea-draped doorway at the Vallarta Botanical Gardens

If you've still got one more night of partying left, spend it like a local at the dive bar La Cantina. Just mind your manners, because things can get pretty rowdy.

## Exploring Sayulita and the Nayarit Coast

I've yet to meet a day-tripper on excursion from Puerto Vallarta to Sayulita who didn't want to stay overnight. Sayulita (and San Pancho, five minutes north) both have that effect on people. You get there, and you do not want to leave. It's less than an hour from the Puerto Vallarta airport, but you'll feel like you have entered another world.

### DAY 1

Zip up from Vallarta to Sayulita by local bus for about $2 (a rental car will just be a parking headache, and it is an expensive cab ride). The ride from the airport to Sayulita by local bus is roughly an hour; from downtown, probably 90 minutes, depending on traffic. As soon as you get into Sayulita, head to the plaza, and you'll quickly see what the buzz is about. Sayulita is small, lively, and colorful, stocked with hordes of interesting characters, dozens of great restaurants ranging from taco carts to gourmet dining rooms, and an array of interesting shops selling all manner of offbeat, chic, and unique merchandise. And then there's the beach and the surf, and the surfers, paddleboarders, kayakers, and swimmers at play on the shore and in the waves.

Find a room soon if it's high season. Charming, reasonably priced quarters can be rented at the Hotelito Los Sueños on the north side, or the Petit Hotel Hafa downtown. If you want to go super low-budget, check out the hostels; there are several. If you want to go high-end, the designer Villa Amor, at the south end of the town beach, and the

exquisitely rustic Hotel Playa Escondida, five minutes' drive south of town, are great lodging options.

Stay up late at one of several ultralively late-night bars, such as Don Pato, the Sayulita Public House, or Club Camaron.

### DAY 2

Now that you've familiarized yourself with the scene, on the second day take a surfing or paddleboarding lesson. Spend half the day on the water and the other half on the beach, watching one of the more interesting beach scenes in Mexico play out. It's a real circus. In the evening, sample fare from the fish-taco carts or one of the dozen-plus taco stands, or head across the bridge to Tacos on the Street (makers of the best tacos in Mexico, some say) and finish up with one of their great desserts.

### DAY 3

Head up from Sayulita to San Pancho by cab (around $10 for the 5- to 10-minute drive is the going rate) and have the cabbie drop you somewhere not too far in from the entrance to town. From here you can spend an hour or two sauntering toward the sea down Avenida Tercer Mundo, taking in the many cool shops, restaurants, bars, and coffeehouses along the way. Be sure and check out the quirky furniture, glassware, and crafts made from recycled materials on sale at Entreamigos Community Center, the local community and recycling center. When you reach the beach, stroll south and have a look at the estuary, almost always busy with hundreds of birds. Beware of swimming if there is any surf at all—San Pancho's waters are often dangerous. Have a drink and/or lunch at one of the beachside restaurants, then head back to Puerto Vallarta—or back to Sayulita for some remedial yoga before you return to the big city.

# Highlights of Gay Puerto Vallarta

cocktail hour on Playa los Muertos

When you arrive in Puerto Vallarta, make sure to pick up a copy of the excellent *Gay Guide Vallarta* or visit their website, **www.gayguide-vallarta.com,** for a wealth of information on Puerto Vallarta's many gay-friendly establishments and events. Also recommended is **www.discoveryvallarta.com,** one of the city's best websites for gay travelers.

## BEACHES

There are plenty of free palapas in the general area of the famous Blue Chairs resort at **Playa los Muertos,** the stretch of sand most popular with the gay community. Most hotels and beach clubs are happy to let you use their lounge chairs and facilities with a minimum food or drink purchase of about $20 worth of pesos. Whether you are looking forward to making new friends or just people-watching, Playa los Muertos is the place to be.

## ACCOMMODATIONS

Hotels catering to gay travelers can be found all over Old Town. Gay-owned **Casa Fantasia B&B** offers a soothing haven from the busy streets and beaches of the Zona Romántica. This three-house hacienda-style B&B is spacious yet welcoming.

One of the most beautiful and eccentric of all Vallarta hotels is **Casa Cúpula,** contained in three side-by-side houses and a modern new lobby building, joined by winding stairways and paths. Casa Cúpula is considered one of the best gay-friendly guesthouses in Puerto Vallarta. It's also home to **Taste,** one of Puerto Vallarta's finest gourmet restaurants.

## NIGHTLIFE

There is nightlife aplenty in gay Vallarta. For a wild time of it, check out **C.C. Slaughter's,** which has an ambient martini lounge on one side and a raucous, multilevel dance club on the other.

For a low-key night, check out the neighborhood piano bar **Garbo,** a popular after-work place for locals that has cheerful waiters and a friendly, mixed crowd.

Try one of the neighborhood bars in the Zona Romántica, such as Frida, Diva's, La Noche—or all of them. **Frida** is a nice, quiet hangout with cheap drinks and a fun atmosphere. Relaxed **Diva's** is a great place to go alone or with friends early in the evening before hitting the nearby dance clubs. **La Noche** offers quiet corner booths for conversation or a romantic drink as well as more central seating for more social groups.

## TOURS

Ocean Friendly Whale Watching is a good choice for trips catering to the gay community. The whales come to Puerto Vallarta every year to either mate or give birth, and it's likely that you'll get to see some amazing mating behavior from these massive mammals.

If you really want to experience gay life on the water, choose one of the **gay tours** available, perhaps to one of the private beaches along the south coast. **Diana's Tours** has always focused on and catered to gay and lesbian tourists, but its "straight-friendly" tours remain open to everybody.

## Exploring the Jalisco Coast

Should you find three or four days in cosmopolitan Puerto Vallarta to be enough (stateside city dwellers might find the crowds, cars, and ambient city noise all too familiar), hit the road for a trip down the Jalisco Coast. You can get very far away from it all in just a few hours, heading south out of Puerto Vallarta.

### DAYS 1-3

Drive or bus to El Tuito, up in the mountains on Cabo Corrientes. From here, head west to Tehualmixtle or Playa Mayto. The road to the Cabo Corrientes coast was nearly finished as of this writing, so the going should be relatively smooth and not too time-consuming. Figure on roughly 90 minutes driving time, depending on if and when the road is really completed (and hopefully not washed away by the next rainy season). At the end of the road, the beaches are gorgeous, empty,

and endless, with potentially great surfing, fishing, beachcombing, and just plain chilling out. There are sweet, inexpensive little hotels along this stretch of coast. Try the Hotel Mayto, or the El Rinconcito Hotel just down the road, with its inexpensive air-conditioned rooms, general store, and restaurant with pool table. If you are on a low budget, a bus ride followed by two or three nights at these two hotels would serve as a fine excursion.

On the other hand, if you plan ahead, rent a car, make a reservation, and can afford a one- or two-night fling in the land of rustic luxury, by all means book a room at the Hotelito Desconocido. This strikingly well-designed outpost of ecoluxury is surely one of the most beautiful, isolated, and distinct lodgings on the entire Pacific coast of Mexico. It's an amazing place to unwind, and you might even get to help send some baby turtles into the sea!

Burros, near Punta Mita, offers challenging surfing waves.

# Surfing and Stand-Up Paddleboarding

Surfing and stand-up paddleboarding (SUP) enthusiasts can find plenty of action in the Puerto Vallarta region. The best surfing conditions customarily occur during winter, but swells hit various spots around Banderas Bay year-round, providing good surf somewhere in the area almost any time of year.

Several great local spots, north and south of Puerto Vallarta, include the following. If you're paddleboard surfing, you can find waves at any of these beaches (don't attempt to learn surfing on a paddleboard in big waves!). If it's flat, just go for a paddle.

## Bay of Banderas

### NORTH SHORE

Burros, La Lancha, Anclote, and El Faro offer good beginner, intermediate, and advanced breaks along the shore near Punta Mita. There are other spots along this stretch of bay, but these four are the most well-known.

- Burros (intermediate to advanced): Features an interesting jungle hike in and a pretty beach.

- La Lancha (beginner, intermediate, and advanced): Offers a fun, gentle surfing wave (that gets big and fast when the swell is on) and one of the bay's most beautiful beaches.

- Anclote (beginner, intermediate, and advanced): Easily accessible, supergentle, user-friendly wave; great for beginning surfers and paddleboarders (and intermediate and advanced surfers when the swell is big).

- El Faro (advanced intermediate to advanced): The legendary "lighthouse" of 1970s surf lore; fast, fun, tubular, and powerful, but hard to get to, fickle, and not for beginners.

### SOUTH SHORE

- Quimixto (intermediate breaks): Approachable by boat only; a good fast beach break; long- or shortboards; in front of a small resort village.

## Nayarit Coast

- Sayulita (beginning, intermediate, and advanced): A crowded, lively break, great for beginners at the south end, while the rivermouth lefts and rights are good for better surfers.

- Aticama and Santa Cruz (intermediate): These are rocky point breaks, both lefts, directly in front of the small towns they are named for.

- Matanchén (great for beginners): Endless, soft, fun point break waves on shallow sand bottom; occasionally gets big and even more endless.

- Stoner's Point (advanced): Can be a fantastic wave but is very fickle; big, powerful, and fast enough to be for advanced surfers only.

## Jalisco Coast

- Ipala and Las Peñitas (intermediate to advanced): On the Cabo Corrientes coast south of Tehualmixtle; hard-breaking beach-break waves; better for shortboards.

- Playa el Tecuán and Arroyo Seco (beginner to advanced): Hard-breaking beach-break waves; better for shortboards.

- Playa la Manzanilla (intermediate to advanced breaks): Beach break in front of the town; can be good on a strong swell; long- and shortboards fine.

- Barra de Navidad (beginning and intermediate): At the jetty; fun, easygoing in-town wave for everybody; better for longboards.

# At Play in the Bay

There are many ways to have fun in Bahía de Banderas, from the simple pleasure of taking a swim in warm, buoyantly salty water to more time-consuming and expensive diversions such as whale-watching and scuba diving. Hey, it's the Pacific Ocean, and it is one big, thrill-filled and exciting adventure, however you choose to go in.

## Scuba Diving and Snorkeling

While Puerto Vallarta might not have the aquamarine waters of the Caribbean, it does offer a wide variety of aquatic life that ranges from rainbow-colored tropical fish to jaw-dropping giant manta rays that grow as large as 25 feet across. Puerto Vallarta has two marine life preserves, Los Arcos

and Islas Marietas, both of which offer fantastic diving and snorkeling opportunities. More advanced divers can do the amazing wall dive at Los Arcos, where the continental shelf drops more than 1,800 feet down, or partake in a night dive when the predators like lobsters and octopuses come out to feed.

## Whale-Watching

December-March marks the return of the humpback whales to the Bay of Banderas for their annual mating and birthing. Whale-watching trips usually leave early in the morning and get back midday. You'll have an opportunity to get up close and personal with these magnificent beasts, plus, if you are lucky, you'll see all kinds of mating behavior, such as tail slapping, breaching, and maybe even the mating itself! Just be sure to pick a licensed and ethical company when you book your tour.

The grottoes beneath Los Arcos provide the finest snorkeling and diving in Bahía de Banderas.

# Best Hideaways

Majahuitas Resort

There are all kinds of hotel experiences to be had in the Puerto Vallarta region. For those who really just want to get away from it all and do nothing in beautiful isolation, here are a few options.

- **Hotelito Desconocido** (Jalisco Coast), two hours south of Puerto Vallarta, is hands down one of the most beautiful hotels in Mexico, and it's about as far away from it all as you can get.

- **Majahuitas Resort** (Bay of Banderas), on the beach between Yelapa and Quimixto, can only be reached by boat. It's a perfect getaway with fantastic views of the bay stretching north to Punta Mita.

- **Hotel Playa Escondida** (Nayarit Coast), five minutes, two miles, and a million light years south of Sayulita, features its own little beach and cove; a fabulous spa; a few dozen individually designed, luxuriously rustic guest rooms; and a lush, verdant setting that is about as romantic as can be.

- **Tailwind Outdoor** (Nayarit Coast), a couple of miles north of San Pancho up a seasonal dirt road, offers tents on platforms and *palapa*-roofed casitas flanked by pools and yoga platforms. All are beautifully sited in a hillside jungle tumbling down to a beautiful, isolated beach.

- **Hotel Rincón del Cielo** (Nayarit Coast), on the hill above the beach at Punta Raza, is way off the beaten path (and the grid, having its own solar and propane power sources) and offers access to the long, empty Playa Punta Raza and its neighboring, bird-filled lagoon. This fabulous beach is slated for development, but nothing is going on to date. It is fenced, gated, and guarded, but it's open to guests of the hotel. Imagine a five-mile beach with no one on it. It's yours.

a crowded day at Playa Punta Raza

# Best Beaches

Although a "best" beach for some folks might be horrible for others, many people would agree that a good, all-purpose beach should have convenient bus or car access, somewhere to stay and eat, gentle surf with no more than mild undertow, and also be safe for boogie boarding and swimming.

## Best All-Purpose Beaches

Beginning on Puerto Vallarta's south side, Playa los Muertos is the hands-down favorite. It's long enough that you can spread out if you don't wish to join the throngs of beachgoers, but it also has all of the amenities you could want, including beach clubs, restaurants, and bars.

Out of town, the south-side best beaches are at Mismaloya and Boca de Tomatlán. On the north side of town, the best beach is made up of the Hotel Zone strip between the Hotel Sheraton and the Hotel Krystal, ending just before the Terminal Maritima (cruise-ship terminal). There's plenty of public access spots, all marked with signs on the main highway. You are usually welcome to grab a chair in front of any hotel or restaurant as long as you plan on ordering from their bar or restaurant.

On the bay's northwest side, Playa Bucerías is a favorite for calm surf and family-friendly conditions. The beach gets more crowded at the southern end due to the presence of an oversized resort complex. Farther away, on the Bay of Banderas's northwest side, are petite and very busy Playa Manzanillo (at the Hotel Piedra Blanca) and Playa Anclote at Punta Mita, with good *palapa* restaurants, snorkeling and surfing nearby, and excursions to offshore Islas Marietas. If you don't mind carrying a surfboard in (nonsurfers are not allowed under current Punta Mita Development Corporation policy), La Lancha is one of the prettiest beaches in all of Banderas Bay. You can also get there by boat from Playa Anclote.

Another favorite beach, on the Nayarit Coast, is gemlike Playa Chacala, whose golden sand curves gently around its intimate, palm-tufted half-moon bay.

The first best beach south on the Jalisco Coast is at family-friendly Perula, on islet-decorated Chamela Bay. Farther south, find Playa Boca de Iguanas (trailer park). Finally, those who want it all—good hotels, restaurants, and drowsy, country-Mexico tranquility—choose Melaque.

## Best Wildlife Beaches

On the Nayarit Coast, the beaches at San Francisco and Punta Raza both are fed by estuaries. This means superb bird-watching, and you may even get to see some of the indigenous species, like crocodiles, turtles, or coatis. The beaches are steep, often with thunderous waves and strong undertow. San Francisco has beach restaurants and amenities, but Punta Raza only has just one small hotel near the south end.

For pristine isolation, wildlife-watching (egg-laying turtles in the fall), surf fishing, tent camping, and a small hotel with restaurant and clean facilities, no place could be finer than Playa Platanitos, just north of Las Varas on the way to San Blas.

Also very lovely and worthwhile is the local country beach haven of Playa El Naranjo, north of Rincón de Guayabitos-La Peñita. It offers *palapa* restaurants, a near-level beach with little undertow, surfing breaks, a mangrove lagoon, crocodiles, plenty of birds, and lots of palm-shaded room for RV or tent camping. This beach is not accessible during the rainy season, as the road turns into a mud wallow.

## Best Hidden Beaches

South of Puerto Vallarta, venture off-road to Playa Mayto, accessible from Highway 200 at El Tuito. You'll need a Jeep or a public minivan to navigate the 3 miles of paved road followed by 15 or so miles of dirt road. Playa Mayto is a three-mile-long golden-sand beach good for virtually all beach diversions and is home to a pair of comfortable, moderately priced hotels, both with restaurants and one with a pool.

Playa los Muertos stretches south from the Río Cuale.

There's always something going on at Mismaloya Beach.

Alternatively, go a mile farther south to Tehualmixtle fishing cove, with restaurants and a rustic hotel; add fishing, snorkeling, and scuba diving (with your own equipment) to the family-friendly beach activities.

## Most Beautiful Beaches

Gem of gems, Playa Careyes sits on its own petite half-moon bay and offers *palapa* restaurants, turtle-watching, surf fishing, fishing trips, and more. A few miles farther, de facto wildlife refuge Playa el Tecuán offers everything: a long pristine strand perfect for beachcombing, powerful rollers for advanced surfers, great surf fishing, and even bird- and wildlife-watching in your own kayak on the Tecuán lagoon. The beach has no facilities, however, so bring everything.

# PUERTO VALLARTA

It is easy to see how Puerto Vallarta (pop. 256,000) inspired the imaginations of location scouts looking for an evocative setting for John Huston's movie *The Night of the Iguana.* The lush, verdant jungle and the rolling foothills of the Sierra Madre make for a spectacular backdrop, not just for the movies but for life as well.

© DONNA DAY

# HIGHLIGHTS

LOOK FOR ◖ TO FIND RECOMMENDED SIGHTS, ACTIVITIES, DINING, AND LODGING.

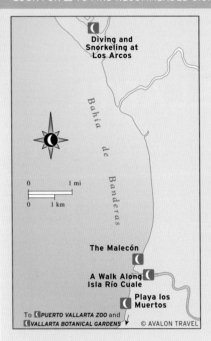

◖ **A Walk Along Isla Río Cuale:** Take in crafts stalls; sidewalk artists; quaint, swaying suspension bridges; and the John Huston statue. En route, stop for lunch at a riverside restaurant or one of the view *fondas,* upstairs at the Mercado Municipal (page 31).

◖ **The Malecón:** Take an early-evening stroll along this waterfront promenade, highlighted by quirky sculptures along the way. Start out at the Los Arcos amphitheater, and continue north, taking your pick of diversions from the parade of lively clubs, bars, shops, and restaurants (page 33).

◖ **Puerto Vallarta Zoo:** Feed the animals and have your photo taken with lion and jaguar cubs (page 36).

◖ **Vallarta Botanical Gardens:** With 20 acres of trees, flowers, birds, and butterflies, plus a fine little restaurant, a small museum and store, and a swimmable river, this makes for a great way to spend a day out in the country (page 38).

◖ **Playa los Muertos:** Its strand of yellow sand, gentle waves, and lack of undertow make Playa los Muertos a good spot for wading and swimming. Watch the fisherfolk bring in their daily haul, or catch the sunset and a margarita at a beachfront restaurant (page 39).

◖ **Diving and Snorkeling at Los Arcos:** Los Arcos Marine Sanctuary, offshore from Mismaloya, is a magnet for both vacationers and fish. The vacationers snorkel while watching the droves of fish graze the seaweed and coral (page 43).

The pearl of the Mexican Pacific, Puerto Vallarta radiates with the same rare intensity as the gemstone. As miners from inland pueblos traveled to the coastline in search of a spot to send their salt by sea to coastal Mexican towns, they came upon the paradise that is now Puerto Vallarta. What they found was perfection: loamy soil fertilized by the many rivers that feed into the sea, cream-colored beaches that stretched endlessly along the edge of Bahía de Banderas, and protection from even the worst storms of the Pacific Ocean.

Even today, despite its rapid growth from tiny village to tourist mecca, Puerto Vallarta retains the magic that those miners must have felt as they looked into the Edenic valley. With its mild temperatures year-round (excepting the rainy-season heat of August-September), stunning white gold beaches, and a dazzling array of exciting recreational opportunities, it is easy to see what draws tourists back to the Bay of Banderas time and time again.

The centerpiece of Puerto Vallarta is the Bay of Banderas, one of the deepest and largest natural bays in the world. Visitors plumb its mysterious depths on scuba trips, delight

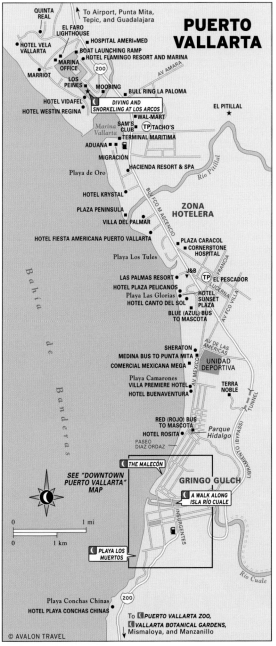

**PUERTO VALLARTA**

QUINTA REAL
To Airport, Punta Mita, Tepic, and Guadalajara
EL FARO LIGHTHOUSE
HOTEL VELA VALLARTA
HOSPITAL AMERI+MED
BOAT LAUNCHING RAMP
HOTEL FLAMINGO RESORT AND MARINA
MARINA OFFICE
200
AV AMARA
MARRIOT
LOS PEINES
MOORING
BULL RING LA PALOMA
HOTEL VIDAFEL
HOTEL WESTIN REGINA
DIVING AND SNORKELING AT LOS ARCOS
EL PITILLAL
WAL-MART
Marina Vallarta
SAM'S CLUB
TP TACHO'S
TERMINAL MARITIMA
ADUANA
MIGRACIÓN
HACIENDA RESORT & SPA
Río Pitillal
Playa de Oro
HOTEL KRYSTAL
BLVD FCO M ASCENCIO
ZONA HOTELERA
PLAZA PENINSULA
VILLA DEL PALMAR
HOTEL FIESTA AMERICANA PUERTO VALLARTA
PLAZA CARACOL
CORNERSTONE HOSPITAL
Playa Los Tules
AV FRANCIA
Bahía
LAS PALMAS RESORT
J&B
TP EL PESCADOR
HOTEL PLAZA PELICANOS
AV LUCERNA
Playa Las Glorias
HOTEL SUNSET PLAZA
HOTEL CANTO DEL SOL
AV FCO VILLA
BLUE (AZUL) BUS TO MASCOTA
de
SHERATON
AV DE LAS AMÉRICAS
MEDINA BUS TO PUNTA MITA
AV MÉXICO
UNIDAD DEPORTIVA
COMERCIAL MEXICANA MEGA
Playa Camarones
TERRA NOBLE
VILLA PREMIERE HOTEL
HOTEL BUENAVENTURA
TUNNEL
Banderas
RED (ROJO) BUS TO MASCOTA
HOTEL ROSITA
Parque Hidalgo
LIBRAMIENTO (BYPASS)
PASEO DIAZ ORDAZ
THE MALECÓN
SEE "DOWNTOWN PUERTO VALLARTA" MAP
GRINGO GULCH
A WALK ALONG ISLA RÍO CUALE
INSURGENTES
0      1 mi
0      1 km
PLAYA LOS MUERTOS
Río Cuale
Playa Conchas Chinas
200
HOTEL PLAYA CONCHAS CHINAS
To PUERTO VALLARTA ZOO,
VALLARTA BOTANICAL GARDENS,
Mismaloya, and Manzanillo
© AVALON TRAVEL

in its abundance of brightly colored tropical fish on snorkeling tours, and, several times a year, compete for the biggest tuna and marlin in international sportfishing tournaments. Surfers, paddleboarders, and swimmers frolic in the beautifully shaped waves that break along its shores. The bay is also home to sea turtles and dolphins. Each year, from November through March, humpbacks and other whales arrive to mate or give birth to calves in its sheltered waters.

The Bay of Banderas also provides a plethora of fresh seafood that is available in every restaurant, from the rustic *palapa* huts lining the beaches to the high-end gourmet restaurants that dot the hillsides on winding cobblestone streets above Vallarta's city center. Puerto Vallarta attracts international talent to its many exquisite restaurants and is host to an annual gourmet festival. One thing is certain: Vallartenses (residents of Puerto Vallarta) love good food.

In fact, it may just be the Vallartenses that make Puerto Vallarta truly special. Perhaps nowhere else in Mexico will you experience the feeling of warmth and welcoming you find in Puerto Vallarta. With their homes tucked in between art galleries and souvenir shops, the residents will greet you with a smile and a "*buenas noches*" as they sit outside enjoying an evening breeze. In many areas, you will meet the artisans themselves and experience the pride and joy they take in creating their art and crafts.

This guide provides a road

map for residents and visitors alike, whatever their passions. From the well-known and well-loved Zona Romántica and Isla Cuale to lesser-known hamlets and everything in between, Puerto Vallarta, like the pearl, is a rare and beautiful treasure to be discovered.

## PLANNING YOUR TIME

Part of the beauty of Puerto Vallarta is the tremendous variety of activities available for a wide range of interests. With so many choices, prioritization is key. On an average weeklong trip, there is just too much to do and see for all but the most determined travelers, especially if relaxation is on the agenda. However, there are two things not to be missed during your trip: spending some time on or in the lovely Bay of Banderas and dining at a few of the incredible restaurants scattered throughout the city.

Shopping enthusiasts will find innumerable boutiques and shopping centers, many offering authentic Mexican art and handicrafts. Art lovers can spend a couple of days exploring the variety of fine art galleries and viewing the sculpture and architecture of the city. Adventurers can tromp through the jungle on foot, horseback, or ATV, or even fly through the treetops on one of the many canopy tours. Of course, scuba divers and snorkelers will be delighted with the unusual mix of tropical fish and other aquatic life. Surfers, paddleboarders, and kiteboarders will find plenty of spots in the bay and beyond to ride the waves and wind.

Evenings can be spent dining with your feet in the sand at one of the many beachfront restaurants, or viewing the glittering lights of the bay from one of the hillside restaurants perched above the city. Afterward, take a stroll down into town and join the Vallartenses on their evening promenade along the seaside Malecón, with its entertaining array of sculptures, street performers, and artists. Later, when the clubs start picking up (after about 11pm), you can shake your moneymaker at any number of discos and bars that line the street.

### Beyond the Town Limits

Those in town for only a few days or a few

a Puerto Vallarta street leading to the ocean

© ELENA ELISSEEVA/123RF

hours will probably want to spend their time in Puerto Vallarta proper, but if you can spare the time, take a short trip out of town. One possibility is Mismaloya, a lovely beach just 15 minutes south (made less lovely by the presence of a massive all-inclusive hotel, but still a charming getaway). Enjoy swimming in the calm cove or relaxing on one of the lounge chairs offered by the beach restaurants while dining on fresh shrimp and sipping a margarita. If you're a movie buff, walk along a pathway to peer into the now closed set of **John Huston's** *The Night of the Iguana.* Or skip the cinematic nostalgia and swim over to the rocky outcropping for some excellent snorkeling. If the oversized hotel scares you off, get back on the bus and find another stretch of sand. There are several along this route that offer more seclusion, if no lounge chairs or cocktails. On the way back, stop at **Le Set** for a cocktail and appetizer and enjoy the spectacular view of the bay. Alternately, should you have more time, continue farther south to the **Vallarta Botanical Gardens** (www.vbgardens.org), where you can view a wide variety of tropical plants, including a wonderful display of Mexican orchids. Take in the flora, enjoy the birds and butterflies, check out the gift shop and museum, have lunch in the flower-bedecked Hacienda de Oro restaurant, and then stroll down for a swim in the river before heading back to town. Should you take this particular plunge, figure 45 minutes total travel time in each direction.

For more out of town adventure, take one of the many **water taxis** from the brand-new pier at Playa los Muertos to the charming villages of **Quimixto, Las Ánimas,** or **Yelapa** on the south shore of the bay. While there, take a hike, drench yourself in a waterfall, sun on the beach, and enjoy a good seafood lunch at a beachfront *palapa* restaurant. The more athletic traveler can start at the small fishing village of **Boca de Tomatlán** (past Mismaloya, before the botanical gardens) and take a moderately challenging hike along the water and through the jungle to Las Ánimas, stopping at some superb hidden beaches along the way. The trailhead is just over the suspension bridge and heads south along the coastline. Water taxis to Yelapa also depart from Boca de Tomatlán.

## Farther North, South, and Inland

Farther afield, you could spend a day (or two or three, with overnights) busing or driving to beach towns not far north of Puerto Vallarta, such as **Punta Mita,** for lunch, sunning, swimming, and maybe surfing or stand-up paddleboarding; or visit **Sayulita** or **San Francisco** (known as San Pancho to the locals) for the same.

Consider heading farther north and spending two or three more days enjoying the scenic beauty of the northern coast and visiting less touristy havens such as **Chacala** or **San Blas.**

You can also meander farther south, where you'll find wild, mostly deserted beaches of unparalleled beauty on the far reaches of **Cabo Corrientes,** charming beach towns such as **La Manzanilla,** and the tranquil resort towns of **Melaque** and **Barra de Navidad.**

Another kind of adventure can be found in the mountains inland from Vallarta, where the towns of **San Sebastián, Mascota,** and **Talpa** showcase a distinctly different part of Mexico. Up in these horse country highlands you can explore old silver mines and organic coffee plantations, hike in the mountains, take horseback or mountain bike rides, visit a church with a miraculous story behind it, and spend a night or two in a grand hacienda hotel or a rambling country inn.

## ORIENTATION

Puerto Vallarta is long and narrow, stretching from the Riviera-like Conchas Chinas condo headland at the south end to the marina district at the north end. In between, you'll encounter the popular **Playa los Muertos** and the intimate old **Río Cuale** neighborhood, joined across the river by the busy (but mostly beachless) central **Malecón** lined with shopping and restaurants and always bustling with activities. To the north, the beaches resume again at **Playa Camarones** and continue past the **Zona Hotelera** (Hotel Zone) string of big resorts to the Terminal Maritima dock, where several times a week behemoth cruise ships dock and let forth a stream of daytime tourists. The city technically ends at the international **airport,** although continuing past that, you will pass a naval base on the left and then find the working-class neighborhood of **Las Juntas,** other residential neighborhoods, and roadside commerce of all kinds. Beyond and to the west, across the Río Ameca, lie the newer, upscale hotel and residential beachfront zones of **Nuevo Vallarta.**

Nuevo Vallarta lies in Nayarit, a state distinct from Jalisco, home to Puerto Vallarta, and many new visitors do not realize its distance from the city when booking their stay. While Nuevo Vallarta and the southern part of Nayarit formerly were in a different time zone than Puerto Vallarta and the airport (leading to many a missed flight), in 2010 that time zone border was moved farther north and now lies on the northern border of the Bahía de Banderas municipality near the beach town of Lo De Marcos. Now, the northern Nayarit towns of

Old Town's cobbled streets lead down to Playa los Muertos.

Chacala and San Blas are on Nayarit (mountain standard) time, while the towns south of Lo De Marcos, including San Pancho, Sayulita, and Punta Mita, are on Puerto Vallarta (central standard) time, an hour later.

One basic thoroughfare serves the entire beachfront. Officially **Bulevar Francisco Medina Ascencio,** it changes names three times as it conducts express traffic south past the Zona Hotelera. Narrowing, it first becomes the cobbled **Avenida México;** then becomes the closed-to-automobiles, pedestrians-only **Paseo Díaz Ordaz** along the seafront Malecón, lined with tourist restaurants, clubs, and shops; and changing finally to **Avenida Morelos** and turning back into an automobile road before it passes the Presidencia Municipal (city hall) and central plaza.

**Isla Río Cuale,** the tree-shaded, midstream island where the city's pioneers built their huts, marks the change from **El Centro** (which is how people refer to downtown Puerto Vallarta) to **Zona Romántica,** also known as **Old Town,** and formally designated Colonia Emiliano Zapata. It is in this neighborhood that many of the unusual shops and art galleries are located and visitors can idle away the hours shopping. This is also home to the majority of the gay-friendly clubs, bars, and shops.

## HISTORY
### Before Columbus
For centuries before the arrival of the Spanish, the coastal region that includes present-day Puerto Vallarta was subject to the kingdom of Xalisco, centered near the modern Nayarit town of Xalisco, near Tepic. Founded around AD 600, the Xalisco civilization was ruled by chiefs who worshipped a trinity of gods: foremost, Naye, a legendary former chief elevated to a fierce god of war; the more benign Teopiltzin, god of rain and fertility; and wise Heri, the god of knowledge.

Recent archaeological evidence indicates another influence: the Aztecs. It seems they left Náhuatl-speaking colonies along the southern Nayarit coastal valleys during their centuries-long migration to the valley of Mexico.

## Conquest and Colonization

Some of those Aztec villages still remained when the Spanish conquistador Francisco Cortés de Buenaventura, nephew of Hernán Cortés, arrived on the Jalisco-Nayarit coast in 1524.

In a broad, mountain-rimmed valley, an army of 20,000 warriors, their bows decorated with colored cotton banners, temporarily blocked the conquistador's path. The assemblage was so impressive that Cortés called the fertile vale of the Río Ameca north of present-day Puerto Vallarta the Valle de las Banderas (Valley of the Banners). Thus the great bay later became known as the Bahía de Banderas.

The first certain record of the Bay of Banderas itself is in the log of conquistador Don Pedro de Alvarado, who sailed into the bay in 1541 and disembarked (probably at Mismaloya) near some massive sea rocks. He named these Las Peñas, and they're undoubtedly the same as the present Los Arcos rocks that draw daily boatloads of snorkelers and divers.

For 300 years the Bay of Banderas slept under the sun. Galleons occasionally watered there, and a few pirates hid in its jungle-fringed coves waiting for them.

## Independence

The rebellion of 1810-1821 freed Mexico, and a generation later, as with many of Mexico's cities, the lure of gold and silver led to the settlement of Puerto Vallarta. Enterprising merchant Don Guadalupe Sánchez made a fortune here—ironically, not from gold, but from salt for ore processing, which he hauled from the beach to the mines above the headwaters of the Río Cuale. In 1851 Don Guadalupe built a hut and brought his wife and children. Their tiny trading station grew into a little town, Puerto de Las Peñas, at the mouth of the river.

Later, the local government founded the present municipality, which, on May 31, 1918, officially became Puerto Vallarta, in honor of the celebrated jurist and former governor of Jalisco, Ignacio L. Vallarta (1830-1893).

However, the Cuale mines eventually petered out, and Puerto Vallarta, isolated, with no road to the outside world, slumbered again.

## Modern Puerto Vallarta

But it didn't slumber for long. Passenger planes began arriving sporadically from Tepic and Guadalajara in the 1950s, and a gravel road was pushed through from Tepic in the 1960s. The international airport was built, the coast road was paved, and tourist hotels sprouted on the beaches. Perhaps most notably, in 1963, director John Huston, at the peak of his creative genius, arrived with Richard Burton, Elizabeth Taylor, Ava Gardner, and Deborah Kerr to film *The Night of the Iguana*. Huston, Burton, and Taylor stayed on for years, waking Puerto Vallarta from its long doze. It hasn't slept since.

# Sights

Puerto Vallarta has an abundance of wonderful things to see, from the beautiful sculptures that line the beachfront, to the natural beauty of its beaches and bay. Those who sequester themselves inside their resort miss out on much of what Puerto Vallarta has to offer.

## ◀ A WALK ALONG ISLA RÍO CUALE

Start at the **Museo Río Cuale** (www.tiendadel-museo.com, 9am-2pm and 3pm-6pm daily, free admission), a joint government-volunteer effort near the downstream or western tip of Isla Río Cuale. Inside is a fine three-room collection of pre-Columbian ceramics excavated in Jalisco, Nayarit, and Colima, including some especially attractive female sculptures and some charming representations of Colima's famously fetching dogs. The museum's website illustrates a number of for-sale examples.

Head upstream beneath the bridge and enjoy the shady *paseo* of shops and restaurants. For

© JUSTIN HENDERSON

**Suspension bridges connect Isla Río Cuale with downtown.**

the local English-language newspapers, all of which are available online as well as on paper.

A few more steps upstream at a small plaza stands the headquarters and auditorium of the city-sponsored **Centro Cultural Cuale.** On the left side of the courtyard are the Centro Cultural's graphic and fine arts courses. (A schedule of courses open to the general public is posted by the Centro Cultural's office by the auditorium, open 10am-2pm and 4pm-7pm Monday-Saturday.)

Walk a few steps farther upstream to the boulder-strewn far point of the island, where you can enjoy the airy river panorama: clear (in dry season) rushing water framed by great riverbank trees, verdant canyon ramparts, and distant cloud-capped mountains.

## EL PITILLAL

For those looking for a sample of the truly authentic Mexico that still slumbers behind the glitz of the now cosmopolitan tourist city of Puerto Vallarta, El Pitillal will transport you directly there. Located only 3 miles (4.8 km) or so behind the massive Walmart-Sam's Club shopping center, and just north of Vallarta's Costco store and a pair of mega shopping malls, the petite and ever active central square of Puerto Vallarta's most populated neighborhood can be reached via a short cab or bus ride.

El Pitillal is home to many of the working people of Puerto Vallarta, and you will find that the businesses there cater to their needs instead of tourist desires. As a result, you can find incredible bargains and unusual wares tucked into the warren of streets and storefronts. Lining the streets surrounding the square are leather shops, jewelers, trinket stores, and a mishmash of clothing stores, restaurants, and hardware shops.

During the evening after most people are off from their day jobs of working in hotels and restaurants, the square comes alive, often with live music, assorted street vendors, and a clutch of delicious food stands where you can purchase fresh tamales, roasted corn on the cob, and tacos.

Spend some time admiring the church and

fun, stroll out on one of the two quaint suspension bridges over the river. Evenings, these are the coolest spots in Puerto Vallarta, as night air often funnels down the Cuale valley, creating a refreshing breeze along the length of the clear, tree-draped river.

Farther upstream, on the adjacent riverbank, stands the **Mercado Municipal Río Cuale,** a honeycomb of stalls stuffed with crafts from all over Mexico. Continue past the upriver bridge (Av. Insurgentes) to **Plaza John Huston,** marked by a pensive bronze likeness of the renowned Hollywood director.

About 100 yards farther on, stop in at the small gallery of the **Centro Cultural Vallartense,** a volunteer organization that conducts art classes, sponsors shows of promising artists, and sometimes invites local artists to meet the public and interested amateurs for informal instruction and idea exchange. Ask the volunteer on duty for more information or see the community events listings in *PV Mirror, Vallarta Tribune,* or *Banderasnews.com,*

# IF YOU ARE . . .

- **an animal lover:** Visit the Puerto Vallarta Zoo.
- **a water enthusiast:** Snorkel or dive at Los Arcos and Las Marietas.
- **a daredevil:** Try the zip lines at Los Veranos.
- **a bird-watcher:** Take a trip to the Vallarta Botanical Gardens.
- **a foodie:** Don't miss the International Gourmet Festival and Restaurant Weeks.
- **a romantic:** Enjoy sunset cocktails at Le Kliff.
- **a spa junkie:** Indulge in a massage at the Grand Velas Spa.
- **a sports nut:** Go for a bucket of shrimp and the game at El Torito.
- **an angler:** Take a fishing trip on the Bay of Banderas.
- **a shopaholic:** Head to the Mercado Municipal and the Galerías Vallarta.
- **an equestrian:** Try Rancho El Charro horseback riding excursions.
- **a surfer:** Go on a day trip to Punta Mita or Sayulita.
- **a family:** Experience a trip on the Marigalante Pirate Ship.
- **a bargain hunter:** Take a trip to El Pitillal.
- **a salsa dancer:** Spend a night dancing at J&B.

# ◖ THE MALECÓN

Several of Puerto Vallarta's other memorable sights lie along the water's edge, on or near the Malecón (seafront walkway). First, let the much-photographed belfry of the cathedral be your guide. Named **La Parroquia de Nuestra Señora de Guadalupe** for the city's patron saint, the church is relatively new (1951) and undistinguished except for the very unusual huge crown atop the tower. Curiously, it was modeled after the crown of the tragic 19th-century Empress Carlota, who went insane after her husband was executed.

Head across the main town square, the Plaza de Armas, flanked by the Presidencia Municipal on its north side, and Los Arcos (The Arches) amphitheater, marked by the arches picturesquely set at the seafront, at the beginning of the Malecón. Although interesting enough by day, Los Arcos frequently forms a backdrop for a colorful flurry of evening snack stalls, sidewalk arts and crafts, playful clowns, and free evening music and dance performances. From there, the Malecón stretches north along the seafront about a mile, toward the Zona Hotelera, which you can see along the curving beachfront. In 2011 the powers that be hit upon the brilliant idea of closing the Malecón to automobiles, immediately transforming it from a mixed-use, pleasant but often noisy promenade into an inspired strollers' delight.

Along with the wonderful views of the bay, a number of quirky modernistic sculptures, including several pieces added since cars were banned, highlight the Malecón; tourists often climb all over the elongated seats, ladders to the sky, and other oddly compelling works of art, eagerly shooting photos of each other. From November through April, Gary Thompson, director of **Galeria Pacifico** (with 30 years of experience in the Puerto Vallarta art world), offers a free two-hour walking tour of the public sculpture collection, well worth attending if you want to find out more about these strange, beautiful creations. The tour begins at the Millennium Sculpture by the Rosita Hotel at the north end, every Tuesday at 9:30am.

buying souvenirs, and then take a stroll over to the Río Pitillal. You won't need more than a few hours in Pitillal to get a glimpse of an entirely different side of Puerto Vallarta. You can dine at any one of the local *fondas* tucked back on the streets (look for one that is busy during mealtimes) or at **Mariscos Tino's** (Calle Avenida 333, tel. 322/225-2171), an original Pitillal favorite just a few blocks uphill from the square.

PUERTO VALLARTA

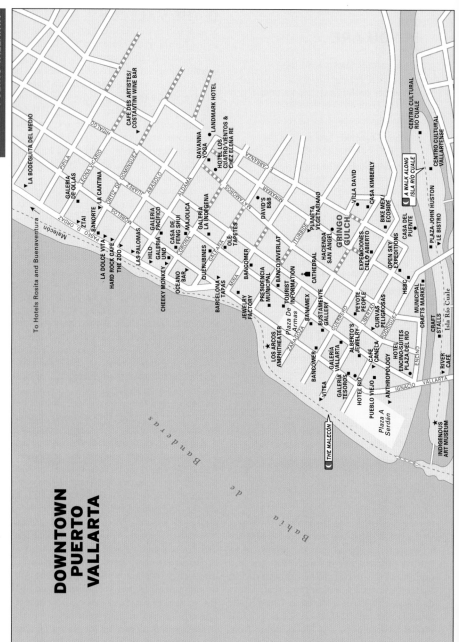

# DOWNTOWN PUERTO VALLARTA

Bahía de Banderas

To Hotels Rosita and Buenaventura

LA BODEGUITA DEL MEDIO

HIDALGO

PIPILA

LEONA VICARIO

ORTIZ DE DOMINGUEZ

JUAREZ

ABASOLO

ALDAMA

CARRANZA

MIRAMAR

MATAMOROS

GUERRERO

ITURBIDE

CAFÉ DES ARTISTES/
CONSTANTINI WINE BAR

LANDMARK HOTEL

DAVANNA
YOGA

HOTEL LOS
CUATRO VIENTOS &
CHEZ ELENA RE

GALERÍA
DE OLLAS

LA CANTINA

ZTAI

BANORTE

GALERÍA
PACÍFICO

CASA DE
FENG SHUI

MAJOLICA

GALERÍA
LA INDÍGENA

DAVID'S
B&B

PLANETA
VEGETARIANO

VILLA DAVID

CASA KIMBERLY

LA DOLCE VITA

HARD ROCK CAFÉ

THE ZOO

LAS PALOMAS

HILO

GALERÍA
UNO

CORONA

CARDENAS

OLÉ
TAPETES

BANCOMER

BANCO/INVERLAT

HACIENDA
SAN ANGEL

GRINGO
GULCH

BIKE MEX/
ECOBIKE

CASA DEL
PUENTE

CENTRO CULTURAL
RIO CUALE

A WALK ALONG
ISLA RÍO CUALE

PLAZA JOHN HUSTON

CENTRO CULTURAL
VALLARTENSE

LE BISTRO

CEO

CHEEKY MONKEY

OCÉANO
BAR

QUERUBINES

MINA

BARCELONA
TAPAS

JEWELRY
FACTORY

PRESIDENCIA
MUNICIPAL

ZARAGOZA

TOURIST
INFORMATION

CATHEDRAL

EXPEDICIONES
CIELO ABIERTO

OPEN SKY
EXPEDITIONS

HSBC

MUNICIPAL
CRAFTS MARKET

CRAFT
STALLS

Isla Río Cuale

LOS ARCOS
AMPHITHEATER

BANCOMER

Plaza De
Armas

BANAMEX

BUSTAMANTE
GALLERY

PEYOTE
PEOPLE

LIBERTAD

CURVAS
PELIGROSAS

RODRIGUEZ

ENCINO

RIVER
CAFÉ

VITEA

GALERÍA
VALLARTA

GALERÍA
TESOROS

HOTEL RÍO

PUEBLO VIEJO

ALBERTO'S
JEWELRY

CAFÉ
CANELA

ANTHROPOLOGY

Plaza A
Serdán

HOTEL
ENCINO/SUITES
PLAZA DEL RÍO

IGNACIO

VALLARTA

INDIGENOUS
ART MUSEUM

THE MALECON

Malecón

PASEO D. ORAOZ

MORELOS

Bahía de Banderas

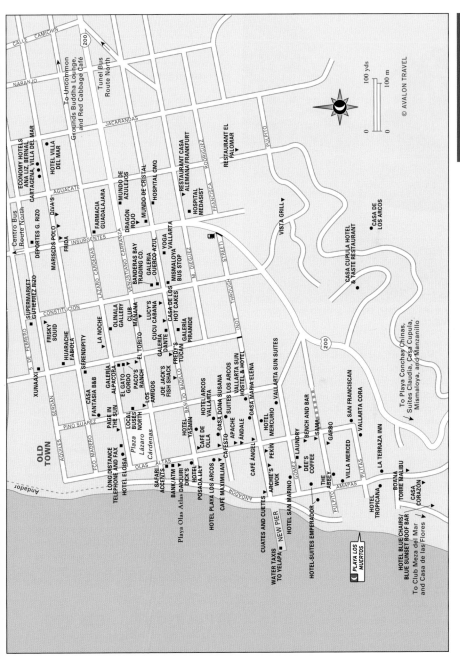

© AVALON TRAVEL

© DONNA DAY

a quiet morning on the pedestrians-only Malecón

Along with the artworks, you'll find street vendors, sand sculptors, and performers such as rock balancers and living statues. On the inland side of the Malecón you'll find blocks of storefronts, restaurants, discos, bars, and time-share salespeople. Beware of anyone asking how long you will be in town!

The Malecón action regularly climaxes in the evening, and especially Saturday around 10pm, when everyone in town seems to be out for a stroll. This is when the people-watching is at its best. Young people gather in groups to flirt, families take their evening constitutionals, and, of course, tourists from all over the world marvel at the sights. The disco scene spills out onto the Malecón, and everybody parties!

## TERRA NOBLE

A unique artistic oasis created by owner-artist Jorge Rubio, Terra Noble (tel. 322/223-0308, www.terranoble.com, 9am-4pm Mon.-Sat., free admission) blends into the jungle perfectly on a hilltop above the middle of town. It's an art and healing center offering workshops, a traditional *temescal* sweat lodge experience, and spa treatments, including a delicious chocolate body treatment. The view from the top is amazing, a panoramic vista of the entire city and bay. Terra Noble spreads downhill through a tropical deciduous forest at the western edge of the Agua Azul Nature Reserve. Villa Kenya, on-site, is available for rent and is family and pet friendly. Rates start at about $300 per night for two, three, or four persons, with a three-night minimum. For architectural details of the unique villa, handcrafted by clay sculptor Suzy Odom from a design by Jorge Rubio, see the Terra Noble feature story in *Architectural Digest*, July 1996. The buildings and landscaping suggest an organic blend of Spanish architect Antonio Gaudi, pueblo style, African sculpture, and a host of other influences.

Besides its singular buildings and enchanting landscapes, Terra Noble is a serious healing center. A variety of treatments are available from a single massage to an all-day experience in the open-air treatment rooms, each graced with amazing views. Terra Noble is a favorite for weddings and special events, and the spa can handle groups of up to nine people at once.

Regardless of whether you get the full treatment, Terra Noble is worth a visit, if for nothing more than a look around and a picnic (pack a lunch). Contact Terra Noble ahead of time to verify hours. Get there by car, taxi, or any local bus that follows the *libramiento* (bypass road) through the hills east of town. Follow the side road, signed Par Vial Zona Centro, about 100 yards south of the summit tunnel (not the short tunnel at the south end), on the west (ocean) side of the *libramiento*. After about a half mile curving uphill, you'll see the Terra Noble entrance sign—an old car body, transformed into a sculpture—on the side of the road.

## ◀ PUERTO VALLARTA ZOO

Head south out of Puerto Vallarta on the main highway, and you'll arrive at a pair of hidden

© JUSTIN HENDERSON

sculptured signage at the entrance to Terra Noble

treasures tucked back into the jungle: the Puerto Vallarta Zoo and the Vallarta Botanical Gardens.

The Zoologico de Vallarta (Camino al Eden 700, Mismaloya, tel. 322/228-0501 or 322/228-0955, www.zoologicodevallarta. com, 10am-7pm daily, $10) is a beautifully sited zoo that climbs the hill up into the jungle-draped canyon behind Mismaloya, about 7 miles (11.5 km) from Puerto Vallarta. Here, for an extra $5 visitors can purchase a small bag of food to feed the animals. The bag contains five different foods along with a handy chart of which animals eat what. Unlike American zoos, the Puerto Vallarta Zoo has no plexiglass or safety moats, except between you and the predatory cats such as the jaguars; the animals are right there for you to see and touch. Toss peanuts to the monkeys on the island or hand-feed the flamingos that wade in the water at arm's reach. The ostriches are probably the scariest to feed because they're so bizarre looking up close, but they're remarkably gentle as they peck away at your open

palm. You can even feed animal crackers to the sweet-tempered black bears. Hand-feeding a giraffe is an intense experience, and here you're free to try it.

The zoo, which was once private, does brisk business in trading big-cat cubs with other zoos, which is why throughout most of the year, there are cubs for you to hold and play with. For another $10, you can spend 10 minutes getting your picture taken or frolicking with a month-old white tiger or jaguar cub. While some of the enclosures seem cramped, the staff members at the zoo are always working hard to improve conditions. They can only do that with the support of visitors and the community.

The zoo offers a selection of one-hour guided tours, each driven by a theme such as local flora and fauna, endangered species, mammals, reptiles, insects, and so on. You can plan in advance by looking over the themes at the website, so you know what you're getting into when you sign up for a tour. The tours are $15 for one person, $8 per person for two, $6 per person for three, $5 per person for four.

© JUSTIN HENDERSON

Villa Kenya at Terra Noble, an architectural enchantment

## VALLARTA BOTANICAL GARDENS

About 7 miles (11.5 km) farther south from the Puerto Vallarta Zoo, past the gorgeous Le Kliff Restaurant, **Boca de Tomatlán,** and **Chico's Paradise,** lie the Vallarta Botanical Gardens (Hwy. 200, Km 24, tel. 322/223-6182, www. vbgardens.org, 9am-5pm daily, closed Mon. May-Nov., $5), 20 acres of jungle property (half of these acres were formerly overgrazed cattle pasture) that contain more than 3,000 different species of plants, including hundreds of strikingly beautiful and colorful flowers. There are several trails worth exploring, all well marked with signage identifying varied species of plants. Wind your way through the blue agave hills where more than 6,000 of these cacti grow, or meander through the butterfly and flower gardens, where bilingual signs explain some of the interesting ways that plants, insects, and birds interact in this part of the world. (Make sure to bring your binoculars and camera.) Check out the amazing Mexican orchid collection, housed along with a vast array

of other exotic flora in greenhouses adjacent to the Hacienda del Oro visitors center. This elegantly beautiful two-story structure, draped in bougainvillea and other flowering vines, houses a small museum, a store with arts and crafts and books for sale, and a charming little restaurant with a great view over the grounds down toward a river.

After you've spent some time wandering the grounds and perhaps had lunch or a snack, feel free to stroll down to the river and, if it's a hot day, take a swim. This is the same river that flows through Chico's Paradise a little ways downstream, and you'll find the same inviting, rock-lined natural swimming pools here. Don't be surprised if a chattering flock of parakeets comes by to see what you are up to.

## CHICO'S PARADISE

At kilometer marker 20 (about 12.5 mi/20 km from Vallarta), you'll find the Chico's turnout. What Chico's (tel. 322/473-0413, 10am-8pm daily) offers is gorgeous natural scenery—rock pools, waterfalls, rapids, and jungle

© JUSTIN HENDERSON

feeding a giraffe at the Puerto Vallarta Zoo

vines—with assorted bridges and pathways linking it all together, and to the restaurant and the zip line nearby. The natural water features are beautiful, and the place has been unintrusively organized to take advantage of the scene without overdoing it. There are lovely natural pools for swimming. The zip line comes well recommended for good, fast scenic zips (about $50). The food is hit-and-miss, and pricey, with entrées averaging around $25. In other words, unless you absolutely have to stop here and take a swim (you can experience the same river just upstream at the botanical gardens), have a look and then head to the gardens, where you'll find more compelling scenery, if not swimming, and better food.

# Beaches

The beaches along the Bay of Banderas are truly wonderful. Long stretches of golden sand line the Puerto Vallarta area while they are spun into white gold just south of town at Las Gemelas. There are beaches that are right for anyone; secluded and empty beaches lie to the north and south, while the perfect for people-watching Playa los Muertos is at the heart of the action.

## ◖ PLAYA LOS MUERTOS
Easily the most popular beach in Puerto Vallarta, Playa los Muertos is the strand of yellow sand that stretches for a mile south of the Río Cuale. This is the best beach for people-watching and making new friends, as there are always people fishing, sunbathing, strolling, and just enjoying the beautiful weather. Vacationers in this area range from mild to wild, so this might not be the best beach choice for conservative types.

There are many beach clubs and restaurants lining Los Muertos, and most establishments allow you the use of their lounge chairs with a minimal food or beverage purchase.

## FAMILY FUN

Mexico is a very child-friendly country; indeed, children are practically revered by men and women alike. Holidays like Children's Day (April 30) and Mother's Day (May 10) are widely celebrated with fiestas and parties, plus presents for the honored guests. On Mother's Day, moms can expect to be greeted with hugs and congratulations, even from barely known acquaintances.

Children adapt very easily to Mexico and will soon make friends with the Mexican children in your neighborhood or at your hotel, despite any language barriers. Don't be surprised when your young child is teaching you Spanish words and phrases at the end of your trip. Bringing along some toys to share or inexpensive gifts like coloring books and crayons is an excellent way to help shyer children make new friends.

If you are traveling with small children, often the large resorts are the way to go. They have special areas with shallow swimming pools for the children, plus kids' clubs and daily activities where the children can interact with others in their age group. Some of the best child-friendly resorts are the **Hotel Krystal** (Av. de las Garzas s/n, tel. 322/224-0202, toll-free Mex. tel. 01-800/903-3300, toll-free U.S. tel. 888/726-0528, toll-free Can. tel. 866/299-7096, fax 322/226-0738, www.nh-hotels.com) and the **Hotel Buenaventura** (Av. México 1301, tel. 322/226-7000, toll-free Mex. tel. 01-800/713-2888, toll-free U.S. tel. 888/859-9439, fax 322/222-3546, www.hotelbuenaventura.com.mx).

There are many tours and activities that children can enjoy, from the **Marigalante Pirate Ship** (Paseo Diaz Ordaz No. 770-21, tel. 322/223-0309, www.marigalante.com.mx), which is good for older children but can be scary for some small children, to swimming with the dolphins at **Vallarta Adventures** (tel. 322/297-1212, toll-free U.S. tel. 888/303-2653, www.vallarta-adventures.com). Other popular activities for children include zip-line tours, horseback riding for the older children, and snorkeling for children of all ages.

If you're willing to venture a little farther north, spend a day at **Splash Waterpark** (tel. 322/297-0708, $10 adults, $8 kids, 10am-7pm daily, rides 11am-6pm), next to Highway 200 immediately to the right as you get off the highway at the first Nuevo Vallarta exit. They have rides, slides, games, pools, and a swimming with the dolphins feature. There is plenty of fast food available.

If you've got little animal lovers in your group, you can't miss the **Puerto Vallarta Zoo** (Camino al Eden 700, Mismaloya, tel. 322/228-0501, www.zoologicodevallarta.com, $10), where you can feed many of the animals, including giraffes, flamingos, and zebras. For a small fee you can even hold and play with lion and jaguar cubs (seasonal) while you get your photo taken.

Feeding your children shouldn't be too rough depending on how picky they are. Most restaurants are happy to provide quesadillas, chicken fingers, and other kid-friendly cuisine even if they don't have a kids' menu.

If you are traveling with small children, you might want to take advantage of **Lots for Tots** (tel. 322/209-1740, www.lotsfortots-mexico.com), which offers a selection of rental equipment. Owner Anjalla Berttall provides delivery of every type of baby gear imaginable—including strollers, playpens, cribs, and even diapers and baby food—right to the door of your hotel or condo before you arrive.

**Fishing** is great off the rocks on the south end of the beach. *Lisa* (mullet), *sierra* (mackerel), *pargo* (snapper), and *torito* are commonly caught anywhere along close-in beaches.

Gentle waves and lack of undertow make Playa los Muertos generally safe for wading and good for swimming beyond the close-in breakers. The same usually feeble breakers, however, eliminate Los Muertos for bodysurfing, boogie boarding, or surfing, although most days a contingent of teenage boogie boarders can be seen catching waves at the north end of the beach,

© JUSTIN HENDERSON

Playa los Muertos

just offshore of the mouth of the Cuale. You can watch them doing their 360-degree flips in the waves from a perch atop the bridge spanning the river's mouth.

## PLAYA CONCHAS CHINAS

Playa Conchas Chinas (Chinese, or "Curly," Shells Beach) is not one beach but a series of small sandy coves dotted by rocky outcroppings beneath the condo-clogged hillside that extends for about a mile south of Playa los Muertos. A number of streets and driveways lead to the beach from the Manzanillo Highway 200 (the extension of Insurgentes) south of town. Drive, take a taxi, or ride one of the many minibuses marked Mismaloya or Boca that leave from the corner of Constitución and Calle Basilio Badillo, just below Insurgentes, or hike along the tide pools from Los Muertos.

Fishing off the rocks is good here; the water is usually clear enough for snorkeling, and there are plenty of fish to be viewed among the rocks. Bring your own gear, however, as there's none for rent. The many rocks, both visible

and hidden underwater, and the usually gentle waves make any kind of surfing very doubtful.

## BEACHES JUST SOUTH OF TOWN

Beach lovers can spend a month of Sundays poking around the many little beaches south of town. Drive, take a taxi, or hop a Mismaloya or Boca minibus from the corner of Calle Basilio Badillo and Constitución.

Just watch out the window, and when you see a likely spot, ask the driver to stop. Say "*Pare* (PAH-ray) *por favor.*" The location will most likely be one of several lovely *playas:* **El Gato** (Cat), **Los Venados** (Deer), **Los Carrizos** (Reeds), **Punta Negra** (Black Point), **Garza Blanca** (White Heron), or **Gemelas** (Twins).

Although many of these little sand crescents have big hotels and condos looming over them, it doesn't matter because beaches are public in Mexico up to the high-tide line. There is always some path to the beach used by local folks. Just ask "*¿Dónde está el camino* (road,

PUERTO VALLARTA

© JUSTIN HENDERSON

boats moored on the Mismaloya River

path) *a la playa?*" and someone will probably point the way.

## MISMALOYA AND LOS ARCOS

If you ride all the way to Playa Mismaloya, you will not be disappointed, despite the oversized Hotel Barceló crowding the beach. Follow the dirt road just past the hotel to the intimate little curve of sand and lagoon where the cool, clear Mismaloya stream meets the sea. A rainbow of fishing *lanchas* (boats) and a few Jet Skis lie afloat in the river mouth in front of a line of beachside *palapa* restaurants. You can rent a boat and snorkeling gear here for about $10 per person, gear included, and head out to Los Arcos for an underwater adventure.

Continue past the *palapas* to the ruins of the movie set of *The Night of the Iguana*. Aside from their use in the film, the rooms behind those now-crumbling stucco walls served as lodging, dining, and working quarters for the dozens of crew members who camped here for eight busy months in 1963. For movie and pop culture buffs, it's a strangely compelling archaeological

site, just 50 years old but definitely "ancient" in contemporary cultural time.

Stop for food or a drink at the **Restaurant las Gaviotas** *palapas* across the river. A big fish fillet plate, any style, with all the trimmings is $8, or consider breakfast eggs from the restaurant's own hens.

For another kind of cinematic adventure at Mismaloya, consider heading up to the *Predator* movie site, formerly the ecoadventure site known as El Eden. This minor action classic was shot here, and the "set," as it were, is now a destination complete with movie helicopter wreckage, a restaurant, a set tour, a jungle hike, and a bunch of zip lines that will send you flying down a mountainside at 50 miles per hour (80 kilometers per hour) through the jungle, dodging whatever alien beasts are lurking therein. The creek that flows through is gorgeous, and there are plenty of places to swim here and also downstream at the restaurant called Capomo Paraiso. To reach this destination, go east or inland on the dirt road just north of the Mismaloya bridge—this is the same road that you take to the Puerto Vallarta Zoo. After passing the zoo entrance, keep going on the dirt road, which can get pretty gnarly. Call ahead, especially in the rainy season, to see what kind of wheels you might need, or just book the trip on a tour to play it safe. If you book online, **Vallarta Tour Center** (toll-free Mex. tel. 01-800/681-1858, toll-free U.S. tel. 888/558-3330, www.vallartatourcenter.com) offers a good discount on the zip-line fee from $81 to $71 for kids and from $106 down to $81 for adults. The road is rough, and it feels like a long way, but it's not—the zoo entrance is 0.4 mile (0.6 km) from the highway, Capomo Paraiso is 0.9 mile (1.4 km) farther, and the entrance to the movie set is another mile (1.6 km). Even if the movie means nothing to you, it's a beautiful spot, and the zip lines are spectacular.

Fishing, especially casting from the rocks beneath the waterfront movie set, is great at Mismaloya. Every other kind of beach activity can be enjoyed here as well, except that the waves are usually too gentle for surfing and boogie boarding.

## Diving and Snorkeling at Los Arcos

North, offshore beyond the Mismaloya cove, rise the green-brushed Los Arcos sea rocks, a federal underwater park and ecopreserve. The name comes from the arching grottoes that channel through the bases of some of the rocks. Los Arcos Marine Sanctuary is one of the best snorkeling grounds around Puerto Vallarta. Get there by hiring a boat and snorkeling gear at Mismaloya. These are informal arrangements handled on the beach, in person, and should cost around $10 per person, snorkeling gear included. Another option is to join one of the tours out of Marina Vallarta. Serious snorkelers be warned: Some of these Los Arcos tours out of Marina Vallarta are more about drinking tequila and partying than about snorkeling, so if you are looking for a real snorkeling experience, be sure and shop around. Also, make sure you go on a sunny day, and/or after any morning haze or clouds have burned off; underwater viewing is infinitely superior with bright sun

shining through the water. Along with everything else, the folks at **Vallarta Adventures** (Paseo de las Palmas, Nuevo Vallarta, tel. 322/297-1212, toll-free U.S. tel. 888/303-2653, www.Scuba-Vallarta.com) run a great scuba diving program, with lessons available for everyone from the age of 8 up; they hit all the good dive sites around the bay, including Los Arcos. There are several other companies offering similar packages, so shop around.

Snorkeling at Los Arcos is a Puerto Vallarta "must-do." Swirling bunches of green algae and branching ruddy corals attract schools of grazing parrot, angel, butterfly, and goat fish. Curious pencil-thin cornet fish may sniff you as they pass, while big croakers and sturgeon will slowly drift, scavenging along the coral-littered depths.

Similarly, scuba diving at Los Arcos is fantastic for experienced and beginner divers alike. There are shallow reefs to dive as well as the more challenging wall dive of the Devil's Canyon, the lip of the continental shelf that plummets down about 1,800 feet (548.6 m). Los Arcos is also where night dives take place, allowing brave divers to experience the magic of phosphorescent algae, sleeping fish, and night predators like the octopus and lobster at their most active. Marina Mismaloya offers one- and two-tank Los Arcos dives for $60 and $90.

## BEACHES FARTHER SOUTH

Three miles (4.8 km) south of Mismaloya is **Boca de Tomatlán,** a tranquil country village overlooking a broad strip of yellow sand and a small river-mouth lagoon with fishing boats bordering a petite blue bay. *Palapa* restaurants supply enough food and shade for days of easy relaxation.

If you decide to linger, contact Agustín Bas, a personable English-speaking Argentinian expatriate. He and his partner, Marjorie Torrance, offer lodging in their gorgeous two-bedroom, three-bath jungle bayfront **Casa Tango** (tel. 322/224-7398, U.S. tel. 310/494-9970, www.tangorentals.com, click on Vacation Rentals). Low-season (May-Sept.) tariffs run about $80 per day, $560 weekly ($120 and $790 high season Oct.-Apr.) for up to six, including airport pickup. Agustín and Marjorie also offer many other vacation rentals and personalized guided snorkeling, fishing, horseback, and other tours, specializing in the verdant Bay of Banderas southern shoreline.

You can continue by *colectivo* water taxi (about $6 pp each way) to the pristine paradises of Las Ánimas, Quimixto, and Yelapa farther south. **Las Ánimas** has seafood, *palapas,* an idyllic beach, and snorkeling; the same is true for **Quimixto,** which also has a waterfall nearby for splashing, and sometimes has a good surfing wave as well.

**Yelapa,** a settlement nestled below lush palm-crowned hills beside an aquamarine cove, is home to perhaps a hundred local families and a small colony of expatriates. For visitors, it offers a glimpse of South Seas life as it was before the automobile. Since Yelapa is accessible only by sea, residents get around on foot or horseback (although there are a few ATVs around these days, cruising the cobblestone trails). A waterfall cascades through the tropical forest above the village, and a string of *palapa* restaurants lines the beach. If you're up for a hike, another waterfall can be found upstream, about an hour and a half away. This waterfall walk will reveal some colorful examples of rustic backcountry living, Mexican-style.

One of the highlights of Yelapa is the pie. Yelapa's pie ladies roam the beaches until about 4pm daily, selling freshly baked pies (and slices) to people on the beach. The pie is fantastic and comes in yummy flavors like chocolate, fresh coconut, lime, and mango. A hefty slice will run you about $2, so don't forget your wallet.

If you are the kind of traveler who likes to try crazy new things, how about flying with the vultures? Seriously. Hang gliding is big in Yelapa, with thermal winds blowing off the ocean at predictable speeds and times of day, and there are pilots here who will take you 2,000 feet (609.6 m) up into the sky on a tandem flight. Try **Ascenso Libre** (tel. 322/209-5174, U.S. tel. 801/707-0508, ask for Brad, brad@paraglideutah.com, info@ascensolibre.mx, www.ascensolibre.mx) to book a flight, or

find them when you get there (Yelapa is a very small town). The cost is about $120 per flight, and if you are an adventurous soul, I would say it's well worth it. This is not parasailing—your pilot might use a boat to get aloft, but once you are, you and the pilot are on your own, riding the thermals with, yes, the vultures.

Lodging is available through either hotels or rental homes, with the majority of the property in Yelapa being for rent. Try the *palapa*-roofed cabanas of the rustic **Hotel Lagunita** (tel. 322/209-5055 or 322/209-5056, www.hotel-lagunita.com, $70 d low season, $120 high). The Lagunita, run by a friendly, droll expat New Yorker named Luke Donoghue, also has a great three-meal restaurant right on the beach and a pretty, rock-lined swimming pool. Reservations are especially recommended during the winter high season. For a high-end ecoresort experience, visit the unique **Verana** resort (toll-free U.S. tel. 866/687-9358, www.verana.com, starting at $320 d plus meal plan), perched high up on the hill overlooking the bay. To reach the resort, guests must make the 25-minute hike while their luggage is delivered by burro up the mountain. Once there, the view is incredible, but the property is still etched into the hillside, so this is not a good choice for the unathletic or infirm. While the meal plan is mandatory ($80 d pp) and drinks are not included, you will not be disappointed by the food, which is flavorful, fresh, and inspired. Verana has two spas, one on-site at the resort and a day spa down below near the water line. Either one is well worth a visit.

## NORTH-END (ZONA HOTELERA) BEACHES

These are Puerto Vallarta's cleanest, least-crowded in-town beaches, despite the many hotels that line them. Beginning at the Hotel Rosita at the north end of the Malecón, **Playas Camarones, Las Glorias, Los Tules,** and **de Oro** form a continuous 3-mile (4.8-km) strand to the marina. Stubby rock jetties about every quarter mile have succeeded in retaining a 50-yard-wide strip of golden sand most of the way.

The sand is grainy, midway between coarse and fine. The waves are usually gentle, breaking right at the water's edge, and the ocean past the breakers is fairly clear (10- or 20-foot visibility) and blue. Stormy weather occasionally dredges up clam, cockle, limpet, oyster, and other shells from the offshore depths.

Fishing by pole, net, or simply line is common along here. Surfing, bodysurfing, and boogie boarding, however, are not, although there are often good waves near the Pitillal river mouth just north of the Holiday Inn. A nearby public access has made this the surf spot of choice for a small crew of local Puerto Vallarta surfers and boogie boarders. All other beach sports, especially the high-powered variety, are available at nearly every hotel along the strand.

Farther north, along the shore past the Terminal Maritima-Marina Harbor entrance, the beach narrows to a seasonally rocky strip at the oceanfront of a row of big resort hotels.

Should you be staying somewhere other than the beach, rest assured that for now, there is plenty of free beach access in Puerto Vallarta. If you are driving, most free access points in the hotel zone offer parking, and where there is parking, there is usually someone to watch and wash your car for a small fee.

Almost all of the beachfront hotels offer two types of passes for nonguests. The most basic is usually a facilities pass, allowing you use of towels, the pool, gym, and beach for the day. These normally run in the $10-20 range. If the hotel is all-inclusive, then the pass is more expensive but allows for unlimited food and national drinks (think well liquor) normally between the hours of 10am to 5pm or 6pm. Those passes run from as little as $20 per person (at the Krystal) up to $150 per person (for the exquisite Grand Velas Hotel and its gourmet restaurants).

## BEACH HIKES

A pair of good close-in hikes are possible. For either of them, don't forget a sun hat, sunscreen, bug repellent, a shirt, and some light shoes. On the south side, walk from Playa los Muertos about 1.5 miles (2.4 km) along the little beaches and tide pools to Playa Conchas Chinas. Start at either end and take half a day to swim, snorkel, sun, and poke among the rocks.

The more ambitious can hike the entire 3-mile (4.8-km) beach strip from the northern end of the Malecón to the marina. If you start by 9am, you'll enjoy the cool of the morning with the sun at your back. Stop along the way at the showplace pools and beach restaurants of hotels such as the Sheraton, the Canto del Sol, the Fiesta Americana Vallarta, and the Krystal. Walk back, or opt for a return by taxi or city bus.

## WATER TAXIS

Puerto Vallarta visitors can also reach the southern beaches of Quimixto, Las Ánimas, and Yelapa from Puerto Vallarta itself. You have a couple of options: fast water taxis or one of several all-day tourist cruises. The water taxis (about $20 round-trip), which allow you more time at your destination, customarily leave Playa los Muertos by the pier three times in the morning, at about 9:30am, 11am, and 11:30am high season (11am and 11:30am low season), with multiple departures in the afternoon as well. There are also departures from Marina Vallarta and from the beach at Hotel Rosita. In the afternoon, they return twice, at around 4pm and 4:30pm high season (but once only, at around 4pm, low season). The morning departures allow about three hours for lunch and swimming at either the Quimixto or Yelapa waterfalls or beaches. The schedule can be loose (you can check the current schedule at www.vallartainfo.com), so you should confirm departure times at both ends either at the beach or through any of the many tour operators in town. Many people offer tickets for the water taxi or will steer you to someone who does. A third option is to take a taxi, bus, or car to Boca de Tomatlán. Water taxis also depart hourly to Yelapa from Boca and return several times daily. You'll cut half an hour off water taxi time departing from Boca, so on a windy, choppy day, especially if you're prone to seasickness, it's not a bad option.

The more leisurely tourist cruises, including those aboard luxury catamarans (with onboard lunch), leave around 9am (returning by mid- to late afternoon) from the Terminal Maritima (cruise ship dock) on the north-side marina harbor complex.

# Sports and Recreation

Some people believe that the weather in Puerto Vallarta is too hot for sports, but that's not necessarily the case, especially since water sports couldn't be more perfect during the warm midday, while jogging, tennis, and golf are best enjoyed in the early mornings and late afternoons. Whatever the case, Puerto Vallarta affords plenty of opportunities for exercising your bliss, particularly if you are of the ocean-loving persuasion. In Bahía de Banderas and beyond, you'll find waves, wind, and usually warm water—a perfect combination.

## WATER SPORTS
### Swimming, Kayaking, Surfing, and Boogie Boarding
While Puerto Vallarta's calm waters are generally safe for swimming and kayaking, they are often too tranquil for surfing, bodysurfing, and boogie boarding. However, surfable waves are almost always in evidence at the Río Cuale river mouth, just north of Playa los Muertos, where a gang of local boogie boarders is out daily. There is also surf at the mouth of the Río Pitillal, just north of the Holiday Inn in the Zona Hotelera. But the better waves are farther out, at Quimixto to the south and the many breaks along Bahía de Banderas's northern shores—El Tizate, Pools, Burros, La Lancha, Anclote, El Faro, the Cove, and the other, less-known spots hidden between these.

Kayaking enthusiasts will find one- and two-person kayaks available at most of the hotels on the beach, usually free of charge or for a small fee, for use by hotel guests.

### Stand-Up Paddleboarding, Sailboarding, and Kiteboarding
Stand-up paddleboarding (SUP) has taken off here, as it has everywhere, not so much in Vallarta itself but farther afield, especially in Bucerías, Punta Mita, and Sayulita, where you'll find plenty of shops renting and selling paddleboards of all shapes and sizes. For those interested in learning or at least trying a wonderful new sport that offers a chance to get out on the water in a quiet, natural way (no motors involved), get a great core workout, and possibly ride the waves, I can enthusiastically recommend a lesson in stand-up paddleboarding.

Sailboarding's glory days disappeared with the arrival of kiteboarding, which has supplanted sailboarding as the most exciting way for an individual to ride the wind on the water. There are still a few sailboards for rent at some of the hotels in the zone, but by no means can you assume your hotel will have them available. Bucerías is the consistently windiest spot in Bahía de Banderas, with thermal winds predictably hitting almost every afternoon, and Adam Finer's **Pacific Paddle** (tel. 322/123-3034 or 329/298-1057, www.pacificpaddle.net) has both kiteboards and sailboards for rent or sale at the shop, a block in from the beach on Lazaro Cardenas in Bucerías. They also rent and sell stand-up paddleboards.

The following are some sample prices (from Pacific Paddle in Bucerías) for renting gear and learning the aforementioned water sports. SUP lessons range from $45 per person for a group of eight up to $90 for an individual private lesson. Boards with paddles can be rented for $10 an hour, $40 per day, or $200 per week. Kiteboarding lessons start with a $45 30-minute intro and range up to a nine-hour course for $599, which will get you seriously started in the sport. Tours and excursions are also on offer. The Marietas Islands SUP Tour starts with a 9am departure from Bucerías to El Anclote by car, and then a ride out to the islands by boat

# LEARNING TO WALK ON WATER

Like all things relating to surfing, **stand-up paddleboarding,** the fastest-growing water sport in the world, started in Hawaii. A few decades back, beachboy surf instructors at Waikiki began standing up in their outrigger canoes in order to take pictures of their surfing students. Then, around the turn of the 21st century, several Hawaiian surfers, including world-renowned big-wave rider Laird Hamilton, began stand-up paddling as a way to train for surfing competitions when the surf was flat. Soon they started catching waves on their paddleboards, and a new water sport was born.

Stand-up paddleboarding (SUPping) is now hugely popular in most surfing towns, including those around Puerto Vallarta. There are shops in Bucerías, Punta Mita, and Sayulita. SUPpers outnumber surfers at Punta Mita these days, and there are plenty of them at all the surf spots in the Vallarta region.

SUPping has evolved into two sports, or even three, although many people practice at least two of them at the same time. One is flat-water paddling, which you can do anywhere—on a lake, a flat ocean, a river, anywhere with water worth exploring or crossing. What's great about it, aside from the core workout, is the changed perspective it gives you. Since you are standing on the board, you can see down into the water, and much farther across the water, than you do when lying on a surfboard or paddling a kayak.

The second is paddleboard racing, with stand-up competitors paddling longer, thicker, and more pointed paddleboards designed to cut through the water ultra-fast and smooth.

Finally, there is surfing on a paddleboard, which is done pretty much like regular surfing except you can use the paddle to catch the wave and to get extra speed while riding, and also to maneuver, executing turns that would be impossible to pull off on a surfboard. Like regular surfing, SUP surfing has a huge range of board types—short boards, long boards, thick boards, thin boards; single, double, triple, and quad fin setups. In other words, all the same mix you see in surfboards.

Give it a try on a calm day. Unless you already know how, do yourself and everybody else in the water a favor and don't try to surf on your SUP—just enjoy the paddling. One valid complaint traditional surfers have about the SUP invasion is that too many people get on them and think that if they can paddle without falling down, they can surf. Trust me, they can't. Surfing is an incredibly difficult sport to learn. Stand-up paddleboarding on flat water is not, but it is hugely fun, a great workout, and a wonderful way to experience the lovely waters of coastal Nayarit and Jalisco, especially in Banderas Bay.

If you want to try surfing a paddleboard, go to Anclote at Punta Mita and take a lesson. The waves here are by far the most forgiving and easiest to learn on. Be sure to wear water shoes; there are some rocks on the bottom.

from El Anclote Beach. Once in the islands, the trip combines teaching paddleboarding technique with an exploration of the islands, a beach landing and snack, and some snorkeling. It is $95 per person, and I have to say, being a stand-up paddleboarder and a big fan of the Marietas, that this sounds like a fantastic way to experience the islands while learning your way around a stand-up paddleboard. Make sure you go when there is little or no wind or swell.

There are plenty of other shops with SUPs for rent, especially at El Anclote and in Sayulita. If you are at all serious about exploring the SUP experience, shop around, try a few different boards, and give it a go.

## Board Rentals

The following shops rent stand-up paddleboards and offer lessons (and even tours) as well; most also rent surfboards.

- In Bucerías, **Pacific Paddle** (tel. 322/123-3034 or 329/298-1057) rents and sells paddleboards, kiteboards, and sailboards and offers lessons in all three sports. **Coral Reef**

**Surf Shop** (tel. 329/298-0261) rents stand-up paddleboards, rents and sells surfboards and boogie boards, and does surf lessons and trips.

- In Sayulita, **Lunazul** (tel. 329/291-2009), **Get Up Stand Up** (tel. 322/118-9992), **El Tigre Surf School** (tel. 329/291-3267 or 322/131-8815), **Sayulita Surf School** (tel. 322/102-1032), **Patricia's Board Rentals** (tel. 329/291-2070), and several other shops offer surfboard and paddleboard rentals, sales, and lessons.

- In Punta Mita, **Mictlan** (tel. 322/134-3383), **La Escuelita Surf** (tel. 322/136-6755 or 322/205-5684), and **Pacific Paddle** (tel. 329/298-1057 or 322/123-3034) all offer paddleboard and surfboard rentals and lessons.

## Personal Watercraft, Waterskiing, and Parasailing

These are available right on the beach at a number of the north-side resort hotels, such as the Sheraton, Las Palmas Resort, Fiesta Americana Puerto Vallarta, and Krystal.

The same sports are also seasonally available south of Cuale on Playa los Muertos, in front of the Hotels Playa los Arcos and Tropicana. Expect to pay about $50 per half hour for a personal watercraft, $75 per hour for waterskiing, and $25 for a 10-minute parasail.

## Snorkeling and Scuba Diving

All of the local tour companies offer diving and snorkeling trips around the bay. The two largest, and by extension, most crowded, are **Vallarta Adventures** (Las Palmas 39, Sin Nombre Loc. Bucerías, Nuevo Vallarta, tel. 322/297-1212, toll-free U.S. tel. 888/303-2653, www.vallarta-adventures.com) and **Chico's Dive Shop** (Malecón at Díaz Ordaz 770, btwn. Pípila and Vicario, tel. 322/222-1895, www.chicosdiveshop.com, 8am-10pm daily).

For those who prefer a small group of usually fewer than 10 people, try **PV Scuba** (Dive Center, Hotel Villa Vera, Paseo de la Marina Sur No. 210, Marina Vallarta, tel. 322/306-0806, www.pvscuba.com). Dive instructor Alex Vega offers a full range of certifications from PADI Open Water to Divemaster. Those who have never tried diving before can book a Discover Scuba Diving class ($115), which includes a pool class and a two-tank open water dive. Because of the quality of the equipment, strong attention to detail and safety, and diving experience, PV Scuba is my personal choice when I dive in the Bay of Banderas. Also, be aware that some of the snorkeling tours are basically party boats to Los Arcos, with lots of drinking and carousing and not much serious snorkeling. If you're looking for quality underwater time, shop around, find a smaller or more serious company, and don't be afraid to ask questions and find out what the tour is really about—diving or drinking.

Another quality company that offers smaller personalized trips for those eschewing tequila-saturated cattle boat operations is **Local Divers** (Gavilan 104, tel. 322/221-6429, www.puertovallartadivers.com). Leslie and her husband, Nacho, consistently get great word-of-mouth referrals for offering small group trips and superb service, especially for dives around Nacho's hometown of Chimo, known for frequent sightings of giant Pacific manta rays.

**Los Arcos** marine park is wonderful for scuba or snorkeling, as are the gentle spots of **Majahuitas** and **Quimixto**. Divers looking for more advanced or challenging dives should check out **Chimo, Las Marietas,** or **El Moro.** For expert divers looking for an all-day adventure, popular fishing spot **La Corbeteña** is the place to see larger sea life, including, occasionally, a shark or two.

## DAY CRUISES

Tickets for the popular booze cruises are available nearly everywhere, but the best deal is to buy them directly at the Maritime Terminal. Beware of time-share sellers offering free tours and cruises in exchange for attending a time-share presentation. While free tickets are nice, with some haggling you can save enough money to buy your own tickets and then some. Booking online through the operator's website can also net you discounts. For all cruises, wear your bathing suit and bring a towel and lots of sunscreen. Beware of drinking too much free booze and spending time in the sun.

The most reliable of the tourist cruises are offered by **Cruceros Princesa** (tel. 322/224-4777, www.crucerosprincesa.com.mx). They operate three boats, which each follow separate routes. Itineraries do vary from time to time; call or check the website for current details and reservations. The package for all daytime cruises includes light breakfast, fish or chicken lunch, open beer-and-soft-drink bar, onboard live music show, and dancing for about $50 per person.

The roomiest boat is the *Princess Yelapa,* a triple-decked steel tub with space for hundreds. The route follows the south coastline, passing the Los Arcos sea rocks and continuing to idyllic Majahuitas for an hour of snorkeling. Later, at Yelapa, passengers disembark for about two hours to sun on the beach or hike to the waterfall (it can be reached by horseback, if desired). It is $42 per person.

Cruceros Princesa also runs the *Sarape,* a smaller motor cruiser accommodating around 60 people, for snorkeling at Los Arcos, continuing to Las Ánimas and Quimixto for a hike (or horseback ride), and swimming at a waterfall. It is $33 per person.

Other variations are offered by the *Princess Vallarta,* a scaled-down version of the *Princess Yelapa,* for snorkeling and wildlife viewing at the Islas Caletas and a stop at Las Ánimas on the Bay of Banderas's south shore. It is $42 per person.

For romantics, the *Princess Vallarta* also offers a 6pm-9pm sunset cruise, with snacks, open bar, and live music for dancing, for about $25 per person.

If you tend toward seasickness, fortify yourself with Dramamine before these cruises. Also note that destination disembarkation at Las Ánimas, Quimixto, and Yelapa is by motor launch and can be difficult for travelers with disabilities. On all these tours, children 3-5 are $4, while children 6-11 are half the adult price. The company also offers two daily whale-watching trips in season.

## BOATING

The superb 350-berth **Marina Vallarta** (P.O. Box 350-B, Puerto Vallarta, Jalisco 48300, tel. 322/221-0275, fax 322/221-0722) has all possible hookups, including certified potable water, metered 110- to 220-volt electricity, phone, fax, showers, toilets, laundry, dock lockers, trash collection, pump-out, and 24-hour security. It is surrounded by condominiums, tennis courts, a golf course, and dozens of shops and offices. Slip rates run around $0.90 per foot per day for 1-6 days, $0.73 for 7-29 days, $0.62 for 30 or more days, and $0.42 for three months prepaid, plus 16 percent tax on all rates.

You can also drop by the marina office, open 9am-5pm Monday-Friday and 9am-12:30pm Saturday. Get there from the airport boulevard, northbound, by turning left at the main marina turnoff (marked by the huge Neptune sculpture on the building to the left). Note that you usually but not always have to get over to the lateral road on the right in order to turn left in Mexico. Once you've made your left turn, bear right at the fork, onto Paseo Marina. Timón is the second street on the left. Turn in and find a place to park, and head into the marina on foot. The office faces into the marina waters from a spot behind the promenade near the foot of Ancla Street.

The marina also has a **public boat-launching ramp** where you can float your craft into the marina's sheltered waters for a nominal fee. If the guard isn't available to open the gate, call the marina office for entry permission. To get to the launch ramp, follow the street marked Proa, next to the faded pink-and-white Collage disco, one block south of the main Marina Vallarta entrance (below the monumental Neptune sculpture on the corner building).

There is another yacht club farther north in Nuevo Vallarta that serves that marina. **Vallarta Yacht Club** (Paseo de los Cocoteros, next door to the Paradise Village Resort, tel. 322/297-2222, www.vallartayachtclub.com) offers reciprocal arrangements with many yacht clubs around the world and offers nonmembers two free visits. Club amenities include a full-service staff, swimming pool, BBQ area, and member pricing at the very good and reasonably priced restaurant. The club emphasizes social activities and offers a junior sailing program. Members can participate in the several regattas and other events that take place throughout the year.

## Sailing

**Vallarta Sailing** (tel. 322/221-2244 or 322/221-3041, www.sailingvallarta.com), which operates from Marina Vallarta, takes parties out on sailing, fishing, or yachting excursions, as does **Vallarta Adventures** (tel. 322/297-1212, toll-free U.S. tel. 888/303-2653, www.vallarta-adventures.com) for $176 for two. There are dozens of boats out there offering sailing tours and cruises, and most have an office or a booking agent in Marina Vallarta. Your best bet is to walk around the marina and shop for prices and offers.

If you're seriously interested in learning to sail, check out **Captain (Robert) Kupps' Ocean Adventures** (cell tel. in Puerto Vallarta 044-322/779-7526, www.captainkupps.com), who,

in addition to taking you on a sailboat ride, offers comprehensive how-to-sail instruction. Another option is **J World** (tel. 322/226-6767, toll-free U.S. tel. 800/910-1101, www.sailing-jworld.com), which offers charters, sailing lessons, and certifications.

## SPORTFISHING

At their present rate of attrition, sailfish and marlin will someday certainly disappear from Puerto Vallarta waters. Some captains and participants have fortunately seen the light and are releasing the fish after they're hooked in accordance with IFGA (International Fish and Game Association) guidelines.

You can hire a *panga* (outboard launch) with skipper on the beach in front of several hotels, such as Los Arcos on Playa los Muertos; the Buenaventura and Sheraton on Playa los Camarones; the Plaza Pelícanos, Las Palmas Resort, and Fiesta Americana Puerto Vallarta on Playa las Glorias; and the Krystal on Playa de Oro. Expect to pay about $25 per hour for a two- or three-hour trip that might net you and

© ANTHONY ANEESE TOTAH JR/DREAMSTIME.COM

A sportfishing boat heads back to Puerto Vallarta as a storm approaches.

a few friends some jack, bonito, *toro,* or dorado for dinner. Ask your favorite local-style restaurant to fix you a fish banquet with your catch.

Another agency that rents sportfishing boats is **Team Redbone** (north end of the Malecón at 31 de Octubre, across from Hotel Rosita, tel. 322/222-1202, www.teamredbone.com), which has a dozen boats, ranging in size from 26 to 48 feet (7.9 to 14.6 m). They've set it up so you can pay from as little as $65 per person per day for a spot on a completely outfitted boat, if you don't mind making new friends. Check out the website and then talk to the manager, who is usually there 8am-noon and 4pm-8pm Monday-Saturday, and speaks fluent English.

A number of local English-speaking captains regularly take parties out on their well-equipped sportfishing boats. Alex Gómez, known as **Mr. Marlin** (tel. 322/221-0809, www.mrmarlin.com), record holder of the biggest marlin catch in Puerto Vallarta, acts as agent for more than 40 experienced captains. Prices begin at about $450 for a 36-foot boat and $600 for a 50-foot boat for a half day inside Banderas Bay, including bait, ice, and fishing tackle, and range up to $1,800 for a 12-hour day on a 50-foot boat with a 50-mile (80-km) range. Mr. Marlin also offers a boat sharing service if you want to cut costs and don't mind sharing the boat with others.

Alternatively, go **Fishing with Carolina** and Captain Juan (Muelle Los Peines, Marina Vallarta, tel. 322/224-7250, cell tel. 044-322/292-2953, www.fishingwithcarolina.com), who offer deep-sea fishing, sportfishing, whale-watching, and snorkeling expeditions on their fully equipped diesel boat. Two anglers go all day for $125 per person, three for $350.

Call Mr. Marlin if you'd like to enter the Puerto Vallarta **Sailfish Tournament** (tel. 322/221-0809, www.fishvallarta.com); it's been held annually since 1955 and takes place in November. The registration fee is steep, but it does include the welcome dinner and the closing awards dinner. The five grand prizes usually include automobiles. The biggest sailfish caught was a 168-pounder in 1957.

**Freshwater bass fishing** is also an option

at the lovely Cajón de las Peñas Reservoir, on your own or through the **Rancho Andrea** (Calle El Dique, Domicilio Conocido, Cajon de las Penas, tel. 322/225-8294, www.rancho-andrea.com), which offers both day tours and overnights with a stay at their hotel. Day tours are $200, and overnights with hotel are $250; both include all fishing gear and licensing, boat with guide, transportation to and from Puerto Vallarta, and meals and drinks.

## LAND SPORTS
### Bicycling
The serious bikers who run **Ecoride** (Miramar 382, tel. 322/222-7912, www.ecoridemex.com) offer several advanced bike trips that start in town on the Río Cuale, climb a few miles up the river, and then side trip off to waterfalls and villages. These tours range in price from about $45 to $60, times of 3.5-6 hours, and have varying degrees of difficulty. They also do a trip from El Tuito (get there by bus) down to Yelapa ($100) that sounds like a major thriller. Other options are offered by **Puerto Vallarta Tours** (Manuel Dieguiz 404, tel. 322/222-4935, toll-free Mex. tel. 01-800/832-3632, toll-free U.S./Can. tel. 866/217-9704 or 866/464-6915, www.puertovallartatours.net), including the Río Cuale ride (four hours, adults $52.50, kids $26), the Jungle Mountain Bike ride (four hours, adults $49.50, kids $27), and the more difficult Killer Donkey Ride (five hours, adults $57, kids not allowed).

### Tennis and Golf
The Tennis Club at the **Hotel Canto del Sol** (Jose Clemente Orozco 125, tel. 322/226-0123, 8am-10pm daily) rents eight courts—four outdoor clay, four indoor ($12/hr). A sign-up board is available for players seeking partners. Also available are massage, steam baths, equipment sales and rentals, and professional lessons ($40/hr).

The **Hotel Krystal** (Av. de las Garzas s/n, tel. 322/224-0202 or 322/224-2030) has several lighted courts for nighttime play ($15/hr). The Krystal club also offers equipment sales, rentals, and professional lessons ($20/hr). Other clubs, such as at the **Sheraton** (F. M. Ascencio 999, tel. 322/223-0404, 7:30am-dusk daily), also rent their courts to the public ($10/hr).

There are many championship and celebrity-designed golf courses in Puerto Vallarta and the Bay of Banderas. In fact, it's possible to play a different course every day of the week. The 18-hole, par-71 **Marina Vallarta Golf Course** (Pelícanos, Marina Vallarta, tel. 322/221-0073, www.marinavallartagolf.com), designed by architect Joe Finger, is one of Mexico's best. It is open to the public for $129 for morning, $98 for afternoon, which includes greens fee, caddy, and cart.

Alternatively, try **Vista Vallarta** (Circuito Universidad 653, tel. 322/290-0030, www.vistavallartagolf.com), with two 18-hole golf courses in the country, about 3 miles (4.8 km) east of the marina. Greens fees run about $183 for morning, $129 after 2pm. One course was designed by Tom Weiskopf, the other by Jack Nicklaus.

If you are staying in Nuevo Vallarta or don't mind the drive, you can take on **El Tigre** (Paseo Paraiso 800, Casa Club El Tigre, Paradise Village Golf & Country Club, Nuevo Vallarta, tel. 322/297-0773, www.eltigregolf.com)—an 18-hole, par-72 course, which while mostly flat makes use of water and sand to make things interesting. Many national and international tournaments take place at El Tigre. Green fees are $116 for morning and $80 for afternoon.

The green, palm-shaded 18-hole **Los Flamingos Golf Course** (Hwy. 200, Km 145, 8 mi/13 km north of the airport, tel. 329/296-5006, www.flamingosgolf.com.mx, 7am-5pm daily) offers an alternative. Open to the public, Los Flamingos services include carts, caddies, club rentals, a pro shop, restaurant, and locker rooms. The greens fee of $121 for morning and $77 for afternoon includes the cart.

Finally, if you're determined to play what has been called one of the top 10 golf courses in the world and includes the famous "Whale's Tale," the world's only natural island green, then head out to Punta Mita and spend a night at the **Four Seasons Resort** (Carretera Federal 200 Km. 19, Punta Mita, tel. 329/291-6000, www.fourseasons.com/puntamita/golf) or the **St. Regis Hotel** (Carretera Federal 200 Km. 19.5, Lote H-4, Punta Mita, tel. 329/291-5800) and play the Jack Nicklaus-designed **Pacifico** course; or try the adjacent **Bahia** course. These rank among the great golf courses in the world, but unfortunately they are available only to guests of the Four Seasons and the St. Regis hotels and members of the golf club. However, with one day's notice they will allow nonguests and nonmembers to play, subject to availability, for a greens fee that ranges from $450 up, but it can be discounted as much as 50 percent in the low season. This allows you to play the course and use the clubhouse for the day. Definitely worth a call if you need to kick that course off your bucket list.

## Horseback Riding

A pair of nearby ranches gives visitors the opportunity to explore the Puerto Vallarta region's gorgeously scenic tropical forest, river, and mountain country. Options include English or Western saddles, and rides range

© ANTHONY ANEESE TOTAH JR/DREAMSTIME.COM

El Tigre golf course

from two hours to a whole day to a whole week. Contact either **Rancho Ojo de Agua** (Cerrada de Cardenal 227, Fracc. Aralias, tel. 322/224-0607, www.mexonline.com/ranchojo.htm) or **Rancho El Charro** (Vincente Guerrero 456, tel. 322/224-0114 or 322/294-1689, www.ranchoelcharro.com).

Rancho Ojo de Agua tours include the twice-daily three-hour **La Aguatera Mountain Ride** into the higher reaches of the Sierra Madre overlooking the bay, priced at $60; the **La Aguatera Sunset Ride,** same trail and price; and the **Fascinating Waterfall Ride Into the Mountain,** which offers riders an opportunity to swim with their horses under a waterfall, and then ride down the back of the mountain to a small village for lunch; five hours, $78, kids over eight welcome. This ranch also offers English-style riding lessons. Internet reservations include a 10 percent discount.

Rancho El Charro offers several partial and full-day rides, as well as multiday adventures. Their three-hour **Tropical Forest Ride** includes a ride along a jungle river, with a stop for a swim by a waterfall and lunch at a mountainside restaurant ($61.50). The 5.5-hour **Natural Wonders Trail Ride** includes breakfast and lunch, trail ride with a guide discussing flora and fauna, and a stop for a swim by a waterfall ($81.50, children welcome). Their **All-Day Adventure Ride** includes two meals, waterfall swimming high in the jungle, and trail riding along a river. The multiday trips include everything from **Overnight Lost in the Jungle** for $350 to a weeklong adventure called **A Horseback Adventure Somewhere in Mexico,** which encompasses seven nights in luxury hotels and four days riding. This tour has a four person minimum, $2,700 per person, and is held in high season only. Sounds luxuriously wild!

## GYMS

Puerto Vallarta has a number of good exercise gyms. One of the best is the women-only **Total Fitness Gym** (Timón 1, Marina Vallarta, tel. 322/221-0770), offering 40 machines, complete weight sets, professional advice, and aerobics. Similar facilities and services are available for both sexes at the **Hola Puerto Vallarta** hotel and spa (Blvd. F. M. Ascencio, Km 2.5, tel. 322/226-4600, 750 pesos/about $57 per month, no daily fee use available). Many of the larger hotels in the hotel zone and Nuevo Vallarta have luxurious spas and well-equipped gyms available for day use.

Many hotels offer yoga classes, but the quality of the instructors at many resorts can be hit or miss. If you are interested in yoga while in Puerto Vallarta, try classes at **Yoga Vallarta** (Basilio Badillo 325, tel. 322/222-1706, www.yogavallarta.com), with several classes in yoga and Pilates offered every day. Their drop-in class fee is $10, about $70 for 10 classes; they also offer Zumba classes for $4. **Davanna Yoga** (Calle Matamoros 542, tel. 322/147-7008), up on the hill by Los Cuatros Vientos in El Centro, is another excellent yoga option. Both the interior and rooftop studios offer great views; this is the first yoga studio in Puerto Vallarta to be registered with the Yoga Alliance, and Davanna offers a full menu of classes and training sessions in various yoga styles. A single drop-in class is $12, $5 for kids. A 4-class drop-in card, valid for 3 months, is $40; 10 classes, $90, 12 classes, $100. They also offer private classes for individuals or groups for $60 for one hour, $150 for three one-hour sessions.

## SPORTING GOODS

Given the sparse and pricey local sporting goods selection, serious sports enthusiasts should consider packing their own equipment to Puerto Vallarta. A few stores carry some items. Among the most reliable is **Deportes Gutiérrez Rizo** (corner of Av. Insurgentes and A. Serdán, tel. 322/222-2595, 9am-7pm and 4pm-8:30pm Mon.-Sat.). Although fishing gear—rods, reels, line, sinkers—is its strong suit, it also stocks a general selection including sleeping bags, inflatable boats, tarps, pack frames, wet suits, scuba tanks, and water skis. For basic sporting or camping gear, you can also try one of the three Walmarts in Puerto Vallarta, or Costco (which even sells surfboards and stand-up paddleboards whenever they get

# SPAS, SPAS, SPAS!

The hot tub at Terra Noble offers a spectacular view of the Bay of Banderas.

Spa junkies might find that one of their favorite things about visiting Mexico is the low prices on spa treatments and massages. It's common to find specials at the dozens of spas throughout Puerto Vallarta, especially during low season (Apr.-Nov.). An hour massage at a discount spa will run you somewhere around $45/hour during high season and $30/hour during low. Make sure to ask about packages for multiple treatments to take advantage of further discounts, and don't forget a 10 percent tip if you receive good service.

For affordable spa treatments in a fairly bare-bones but clean, pleasant atmosphere, try **Massage Lily** (Carranza 235, tel. 322/222-1723, open daily) in the Zona Romántica, just a few blocks from the beach. In El Centro, diagonally from Pipi's restaurant, **Healing Hands** (Pipila 240, tel. 322/222-8441) is a good bet for a relaxing no-frills massage.

In the Vallarta Marina, you can get a little more upscale at **Day Spa Specialty Massage Clinic** (tel. 322/221-0176), a few doors west of the El Faro lighthouse. They offer good package deals, and the ambience is peaceful and relaxing, with private rooms and aromatherapy service.

For an unforgettable splurge, try one of the top spas in the world at the **Grand Velas Spa** (Av. Cocoteros 98 Sur, tel. 322/226-8045, www.vallarta.grandvelas.com), in Nuevo Vallarta. Expect to pay top dollar for a first-class experience at this luxury spa. Arrive an hour prior to your appointment to experience the full process of steam room, warm and cool dipping pools, foot hydrotherapy, and more. The treatment rooms are opulent, and most massages begin with a decadent foot cleansing ritual.

For truly luxurious, tropical spa experiences, there are two excellent choices. The first is the incomparable **Terra Noble** (Tulipanes 595, tel. 322/223-0308, www.terranoble.com), where your treatment room is open to the jungle and a magnificent panoramic view of the city and bay. Terra Noble offers massage, a divine Chocolate Body Treatment (among others), and a traditional Aztec steam bath. The second, **Verana Day Spa** (Yelapa, tel. 322/222.0878, www.verana.com), offers a great day package that includes round-trip transportation to the Yelapa-based spa from Boca de Tomatlán and three treatments (approximately US$120). Once on-site, you can spend the day enjoying the pool and other facilities as well as their fantastic spa restaurant. Single services are also available. If you want more than a day trip, you'll need to commit to the five-day minimum stay at the stunning Verana luxury resort at the top of the hill.

them in), or any one of the several Mega or Soriano supermarkets. These stories all sell everything from fishing poles to boogie boards, soccer balls, tents, snorkeling gear, backpacks, and almost anything else you might want or need for recreational activity. It's not exactly high-quality stuff, but it works. There are also a number of shops renting surfboards and paddleboards, especially in Sayulita and Punta Mita but also in Puerto Vallarta and Bucerías. Given the steep price of carrying surfboards on planes these days, renting on location is an economical option for a short trip. Surfboards rent for anywhere from $4 to $15 an hour, depending on the shop and the value/quality of the board, and $25 to $40 per day. Many shops also offer weekly rentals.

## TOURS
### Adventure Tours

A number of nature-oriented tour agencies lead off-the-beaten-track Puerto Vallarta-area excursions. **Vallarta Adventures** (tel. 322/297-1212, toll-free U.S. tel. 888/303-2653, www.vallarta-adventures.com) offers boat tours to the Islas Marietas wildlife sanctuary (sea turtles, manta rays, dolphins, whales, seabirds), airplane excursions, and a rugged all-day Mercedes-Benz truck ride (canyons, mountains, crystal streams, rustic villages) into the heart of Puerto Vallarta's backyard mountains. You can also book dolphin and sea lion encounters, zip-line tours, and other outdoor adventures. Discounts are available when booking online. With offices in Puerto Vallarta, Marina Vallarta, and Nuevo Vallarta, and kiosks in many hotels, this company basically does everything for everybody all over the region, so whatever your interest, they will likely have a tour available. Prices range from $75 per person ($50 kids) for a Marietas Islands Eco Discovery Tour up to $200 to be a dolphin Trainer for a Day. They do day trips, night tours, whale-watching, and dolphin encounters, with a fine selection designed especially for families.

The offerings of ecologically aware **Expediciones Cielo Abierto** (Open Sky Expeditions, 339 Guerrero, two blocks north of the riverside Mercado Municipal, tel. 322/222-3310, U.S./Can. tel. 866/422-9972, www.vallartawhales.com) include snorkeling around Punta Mita, hiking in the Sierra Cuale foothill jungle, bird-watching, cultural tours, dolphin encounters, and whale-watching. The whale-watching tour is the best in Puerto Vallarta, offering up-close and personal viewing of the whales from a semi-inflatable boat. The guides are all marine biologists and provide lots of interesting facts and trivia about the whales of Vallarta. They are sensitive to the whales and, unlike other tours, do not disclose the location of whale pods over the radio, limiting the number of boats viewing them at one time.

**Ocean Friendly Whale Watching** (Muelle Los Peines, Marina Vallarta, tel. 322/225-3774, www.oceanfriendly.com) is available for private tours or group trips and is also dedicated to responsible whale-watching. Marine biologist Oscar Frey is dedicated to spreading the word about responsible whale-watching and does extensive research on the humpback whales each year. You are sure to learn a lot you didn't know about whales on one of Oscar's tours. Prices are $95 for adults, $75 for kids, for half-day, small group (maximum 12 people) trips.

**Viva Tours** (Terminal Maritima, Marina Vallarta, tel./fax 322/224-0410, www.vivatours-vallarta.com) organizes a number of off-the-beaten-track adventures, including horseback riding, hiking, biking, fishing, and much more.

Finally, if you want to see a listing of all adventures possible in Puerto Vallarta, visit **Puerto Vallarta Tours** in person, on the phone, or best of all, online (Manuel Dieguiz 404, tel. 322/222-4935, toll-free Mex. tel. 01-800/832-3632, toll-free U.S./Can. tel. 866/217-9704 or 866/464-6915, www.puertovallartatours.net). This is the creation of Web-savvy agents Johann and Sandra, who offer discounted pricing on a long list of tour options, from booze cruises and golf to visits to remote Huichol mountain villages and hot-air ballooning.

### Jungle Canopy Tours

At **Canopy Tour Los Veranos** (tel. 322/223-0504, www.canopytours-vallarta.com, $79,

$58 for kids 6-12) you'll enjoy a bird's-eye view and plenty of thrills as you zip from tree to tree through the jungle on 14 separate zip-line cables totaling over 2 miles (3.2 km). Reach it by car or bus, via Highway 200 south, 3 miles (4.8 km) past Boca de Tomatlán. At Las Juntas y Los Veranos, turn right onto the dirt side road. Continue about a mile to Canopy Tour Los Veranos at the end of the road. There are several offices in and around Puerto Vallarta, so this is an easy trip to book.

Alternatively, **Vallarta Adventures** (tel. 322/297-1212, toll-free U.S. tel. 888/303-2653, www.vallarta-adventures.com, adults $79, children $56) offers perhaps the best of all canopy tours, at its camp nestled in the vine-hung tropical forest foothills along the road to San Sebastián. The actual canopy tour takes you through about 10 sturdy forest perches, via 100- or 200-yard cable rides from perch to perch in a total of about an hour and a half.

There are also canopy/zip-line tours available at the *Predator* movie set destination (formerly El Eden), up the road from the zoo; at the Sayulita Ziplines on the back road from Sayulita to Punta Mita; and at another called Canopy River reachable from a turn off the *libramiento* in Puerto Vallarta. This one is set up over the Río Cuale in the hills behind Old Town and is rumored to be the longest, biggest, and fastest zip-line tour of all. You can book most, at a discount, at the website www.canopytourspuertovallarta.com.

A note on zip lines: When these first came into being about 20 years ago, they were high-risk operations—nobody really knew what they were doing, and the braking systems were marginally functional. Unfortunately, accidents happened. Fortunately, lessons were learned, and today, while not foolproof, they're low-risk at worst. It's a little risk for a big rush, and loads of fun if you like flying through the jungle at high speed, dangling from a wire.

# Entertainment and Events

Puerto Vallarta is a town full of entertainments, most of them spontaneous. The glowing sunsets, the balmy evening sea breeze, the crowds of relaxed folks out and about, and the abundance of sidewalk stands, selling everything from paintings to popcorn, are sources of continuous impromptu diversions. Add to that the more formal entertainments, such as the Malecón-front nightclubs, Mexican fiesta tourist shows, quiet refined side-street bars, plus all the traditional festivals—Virgin of Guadalupe, Mexican Independence, Carnival, and much more—and there's enough to enjoy a party for every day you spend in Puerto Vallarta.

## NIGHTLIFE

The popularity of Puerto Vallarta's nightlife scene has given it an extra touch of sophistication that many other beach destinations don't share. There's something for everyone here: The offerings range from quiet neighborhood bars and numerous terraces with ocean-view tables to ultracool rooftop lounges and pounding dance clubs. Since Puerto Vallarta is a top destination for Mexicans and foreigners alike, you can expect to find an international clientele at many of the trendy nightspots.

For the visitor this means that a night out isn't the inexpensive fun it once was. It's much harder on the wallet these days, but on the other hand, you won't have any trouble finding a bartender who will pour you a wicked cosmopolitan or offer a lengthy martini or margarita menu with flavors that you hadn't dreamed existed. You'll need to dress up more than you might when clubbing in other beach destinations, but don't forget to wear comfortable shoes—there aren't just the long nights of dancing to consider, there are also the cobblestone streets. But some things are the same as the rest of Mexico: The action doesn't really start until after midnight.

The night scene isn't just for drinking and dancing anymore. In earlier decades, late-night

# PUERTO VALLARTA ON SCREEN

© JUSTIN HENDERSON

the entrance to the famous movie location of *The Night of the Iguana*

In the history of Puerto Vallarta, there is before **The Night of the Iguana,** and after. That melodramatic and brilliant 1964 classic, directed by John Huston from the play and screenplay by Tennessee Williams, made the city world famous, helped by the charismatic presences of its several stars, especially Richard Burton, holed up in his Gringo Gulch love nest with the woman many considered, at the time, to be the most beautiful in the world. That would be Elizabeth Taylor. In the 1960s, these two were gods, and everybody wants to play where the gods play. So naturally the paparazzi of the time were here chasing Liz and Dick. They took pictures, not just of the players but the playground, and so, for better or worse, Vallarta got discovered, and things have never been the same.

In 1987 another iconic character showed up in Vallarta to make a movie—a guy by the name of Schwarzenegger. Arnold, having perfected his deadpan tough-guy acting style, starred in an action flick called **Predator.** Like *Iguana,* this one was shot at Mismaloya, although in this case the cast and crew headed up the river into the jungle, where Arnold and friends fight first a bunch of nasty guerrillas and then a monstrous alien hunter/predator. Today the "set" is a tourist destination, with a location tour, a restaurant, and a zip-line ride.

In 2004 came **Puerto Vallarta Squeeze.**

Given that it starred several reasonably well-known actors—Scott Glenn, Harvey Keitel, and Craig Wasson—it's surprising that it went straight to video. The story's pretty good: Freelance hit man and ex-marine Scott Glenn hires a writer and his sexy wife (played by Mexican actress Giovanna Zacarias) to get him across the border. The plot thickens. Keitel, CIA operative, goes after them. Further thickening. Fun fact: The film is based on a novel by *Bridges of Madison County* scribe Robert James Waller.

A Stanley Kramer-directed dog from 1977, **The Domino Principle** was also shot in Vallarta, and it managed to waste the talents of a great cast including Gene Hackman, Candice Bergen, Mickey Rooney, and Richard Widmark.

There are others, most of which have disappeared into cinematic history. **Gunmen** is a low-budget comedy thriller with a surprisingly cool cast including Mario Van Peebles, Patrick Stewart, Christopher Lambert, and Ron Silver. Then there is **Deadly Swarm,** a 2003 horror movie about some deadly wasps that has attained the status of "so bad it's good." And last but far from least, there is **Beverly Hills Chihuahua** from 2008, with Jamie Lee Curtis, an utterly silly movie that I love in spite of its silliness, because there is lots of Mexican footage, including several minutes shot in my hometown of Sayulita.

dining options consisted of the corner taco stand or the other corner taco stand. Now the growing popularity of nightclubs with food on premises allows you more than just a toss-it-down snack. Whether it's sushi or tapas, it may be just what you needed to catch that second (or third) wind.

While the actual number of nightclubs is limited, nearly every restaurant on the Malecón offers either live or recorded music in the evenings. Restaurants like Ztai turn from restaurant to dance club around 11pm nightly.

As the hot spot for gay travelers in Mexico, Puerto Vallarta has seen an increase in the range and refinement of the gay nightlife choices as well. There are drag shows and friendly local bars, along with the pick-me-up, toss-me-down, shake-it-loose joints and strip clubs. The Zona Romántica, the area south of the Río Cuale in downtown Puerto Vallarta, is home to most of the area's gay bars. Of course, that doesn't mean that heterosexual singles or couples aren't welcome. In fact, several of the most fun bars in Puerto Vallarta are mixed crowds where the gay and straight mingle. With street-side coffee shops, restaurants, clubs, shops, and boutiques, it's also a great place to spend the evening just walking around the casual streets of the neighborhood.

All this sophistication doesn't mean that people looking for the serious party scene will be disappointed. Puerto Vallarta has a lot of raucous nightspots, especially along the Malecón during spring break and in late June, when school gets out. Whatever your taste, you're bound to find something fun. Just get out there: The night lasts forever and the sun comes up late in Vallarta.

## Bars and Lounges

On the Malecón, **Restaurant Las Palomas** (corner of Aldama, tel. 322/222-3675) is a place traditionalists often enjoy, featuring live marimba music 7pm-10pm and a mariachi guitar trio after that. The bar also has an authentic Mexican atmosphere and cuisine.

Italian restaurant **La Dolce Vita** (corner of Domínguez, tel. 322/222-3852,

10am-midnight daily in season), also on the Malecón, entertains dinner customers with live Latin and Cuban music. A popular favorite with the younger crowd is **Ztai** (Morelos 737, Centro, tel. 322/222-0306, www.ztai.com, 6pm-4am daily), which offers a quiet restaurant on one side and an open garden lounge on the other. Friday night is ladies night, with open bar and no cover charge for the females. Men pay 250 pesos (around $19). You can order from the full menu of international cuisine in the bar while you dance to the latest techno beats.

For that romantic tête-à-tête, there's simply no place like **Costantini Wine Bar** (Guadalupe Sánchez 740, Centro, tel. 322/222-3228, www.cafedesartistes.com, 6pm-1am daily). Its dark red interior with high-backed banquettes holds many hidden corners. There is usually live music in the evenings, piano and jazz. This is also a downtown hot spot for business cocktails and can be a fun gathering place for friends or coworkers.

In the same building, the bar at Café des Artistes has been redesigned and reopened as the Huichol-inspired **P'yote Lounge** (Guadalupe Sánchez 740, Centro, tel. 322/222-3228, www.cafedesartistes.com, 6pm-1am daily), offering Mexican-based tapas and martinis. Tequila's been done, and now it's on to mezcal, made into mezcalinis using high-end liquor (premium brands will be served at the bar). The artworks are Huichol or Huichol inspired, and the finishes, furnishings, and fabrics were created by Pineda Covalín, a Mexican fashion design company that uses traditional patterns, figures, and images from native Mexican cultures, in this case the Huichol. Have a seat and a mezcalini, and take a minute to contemplate the cosmos, Huichol version, in that amazingly colorful and evocative piece of art behind the bar.

Located just a block off the Malecón on Morelos, **La Cantina** (Morelos 709, Centro, tel. 322/222-1629, 11:59am-2am Sun.-Tues., 11:59am-4am Wed.-Sat.) is a popular hangout for the younger Mexican crowd and is known to get quite raucous at night. Bar altercations and people dancing on tables are not uncommon here. La Cantina is genuine and doesn't give a thought to tourists, since not many of them find their way here. The dark interior feels homey, and the canned music, which ranges from *banda* to mariachi to ballads, adds to the very Mexican ambience, while the high ceilings lend a 1940s-hacienda atmosphere.

For good food with your entertainment, try the longtime favorite **Restaurant El Torito** (corner of Vallarta and Carranza, tel. 322/222-3784, 10pm-5am nightly), where you can share a bucket of fresh shrimp among friends and catch all of the latest sports games on the TV.

A number of popular bars and nightspots entertain folks along Avenida Olas Altas. For example, many folks' nights wouldn't be complete without stopping in at the **Ándale** Mexican pub (Olas Altas 425, tel. 322/222-1054, open until around 2am), a quiet and respectable restaurant during the day and a rowdy, raucous bar known for its sing-alongs at night.

**Garbo** (Púlpito 142, Zona Romántica, tel. 322/229-7309, www.bargarbo-vallarta.com, 6pm-2am daily) is one of the most popular and fun bars in Puerto Vallarta. Located in the trendy Olas Altas area, Garbo caters to a mixed crowd of straight and gay men and women. You can sit at the bar and chat with the lively bartender and your neighbors, or find a quiet table in the corner and enjoy the nightly piano music. You'll find the clientele and staff very friendly and the drink list exquisite.

## Dance Clubs

When **Hilo** (Paseo Díaz Ordaz 588, Malecón, tel. 322/223-5361, 4pm-4am daily) opened across from the Malecón, the two-floor-high sculpture of a woman leaning out to peer toward the sea caused a sensation. The ocean-view tables here are great for a drink at sunset. A high second-floor mezzanine might cause vertigo, but climb up to find yourself above the very Mexican sculptures. The dance floor gets crowded with tourists sometime after midnight, and the music pounds into the night at this fun club. Like most dance clubs in this area, the music is extremely loud, so don't plan on having conversations without yelling.

Pronounced ho-ta-bei for the letters JB in Spanish, **J&B** (F. M. Ascencio 2043, Zona Hotelera, tel. 322/224-4616, www.jbdiscoclub. com, 10pm-6am daily, cover $9) offers the best ambience for dancing to Latin music with locals. (The club actually opens, at times, during the day and at 8pm for dance classes during the week. See www.tangobar-productions.com for information.) The night usually starts with DJ-spun music, but on weekends it alternates with live music. Try out your steps in salsa, rumba, merengue, cha-cha, tango, and more in this true community spot where most people get on the floor and dance. If you're part of a group, buy an entire bottle of liquor with mixers for a better deal. Even if you aren't a dancer, watching the incredible talent that dances here nightly can be a real treat.

Cuba staunchly holds its own in downtown Puerto Vallarta with **La Bodeguita del Medio** (Paseo Díaz Ordaz 858, Malecón, tel. 322/223-1585, 11am-1am daily), which serves up not only the best mojitos in town—the drink was invented at the original Bodeguita in Havana—but also the hottest live Latin music. The tiny dance floor doesn't deter reveling regulars. Revolutionary Cuba is reflected in the huge one-star flag that covers one wall, while the other walls are scribbled with notes, signatures, and epithets in pre-revolutionary style.

When you want to dance and conga line with strangers, the **Zoo** (Paseo Díaz Ordaz 630, Malecón, tel. 322/222-4945, www.zoobar-dance.com, 11am-6am daily) is the perfect spot to release inhibitions that were in hiding until a couple of tequila shots jolted them loose. A 200-pound costumed dancing gorilla may leap down from his perch in the window to meet you on the street to invite you in, where a party of tourists will most likely become your new best friends. The decor of mounted animal heads and other zoolike paraphernalia lives up to this nightspot's name.

The strip of Malecón that is home to the Zoo and Hilo has a couple of newer dance clubs as well. The Asian-themed **Mandala** (Paseo Díaz Ordaz 640, tel. 322/223-0977 or

322/120-4168, www.mandaladisco.com), next door to the Zoo, is drawing crowds of revelers, lured into the bright stroboscopic wonderland by a huge, multiarmed Buddha statue in the back of the room. Several levels of dance floor, blasting disco and house music, and plenty of free-flowing tequila keep the spirits high here. This trio of clubs—Mandala, the Zoo, and the newer **La Vaquita** (Paseo Díaz Ordaz 610, tel. 322/222-8281 or 322/111-3940), with its flying cow next door to Las Palomas Restaurant—together form a hundred-yard-long party zone (Hilo is in the next block) that pretty much spills out onto the Malecón as well these days, now that it is closed to traffic. It's a total party scene, but it doesn't feel scary or raunchy—there are too many grandmothers strolling the Malecón with their grandchildren to allow things to get out of hand. It's just good clean nightlife fun. And these newer clubs make it certain that downtown Vallarta will remain party central for the foreseeable future. Farther north in the Zona Hotelera, the once-hot nightclub called Christine failed, was totally remodeled and reopened as Hyde in 2011, failed again, and then opened again as Xtine. In 2012, the building went through another complete renovation and the spot reopened as **Xtine Garden** (Av. de las Garzas by the Hotel Krystal). Given the great location in the hotel zone, and the great big round room, it will probably come back to life. Worth a look, anyway, if you are out and about in the Zona Hotelera.

### Adult Clubs

Puerto Vallarta is host to a number of adult clubs, both gay and straight, and varying from the upscale to the raunchy. Several of the straight, more upscale ones can be found along Highway 200 near the entrances to Marina Vallarta. A popular favorite is the posh **Aquah** (F. M. Ascencio 2600, tel. 322/221-2071, 8pm-6am daily), although reports are the pressure to buy overpriced drinks (for yourself and whatever "lady friend" has landed in your lap) gets pretty intense at Aquah. A better, if pricey, choice is **Prestige Men's Club** (F. M. Ascencio

2033, tel. 322/225-6941, 8pm-6am daily). As a good rule of thumb, pay cash as you go, and do not run a tab to avoid surprises at the end of the night. Most clubs charge a cover fee (unless you are local with an ID or show up in a private car rather than a taxi) and offer VIP lounges and private back rooms. For visitors, the cover charge usually runs about $25 and includes 1-2 free national drinks. Less-pricey versions of these clubs can be found all over town. Generally speaking, cab drivers will know how to get you there, although they often take a fat commission for doing so, and you know that will be coming out of your pocket somewhere down the line.

## LIVE MUSIC

Free music concerts are often held at the bayside **Los Arcos** amphitheater. For more information on these and other live-music listings, check out the events calendars and nightlife pages in *Vallarta Today* or *Vallarta Tribune*.

Cover charges are not generally required at the hotel bars, many of which offer live music and dancing. Among the most reliable venues are the **Sheraton** (F. M. Ascencio 999, tel. 322/224-0202), the **Marriott Casa Magna** (Paseo de la Marina Norte 435, Marina Vallarta, tel. 322/226-0000), the **Fiesta Americana** (Blvd. F. M. Ascencio, Km. 2.5, tel. 322/226-2100), and the **Playa los Arcos** (Olas Altas 380, tel. 322/226-7100). Be sure to phone ahead to check programs.

Many Puerto Vallarta restaurants also offer live music accompaniment with your evening meal. For example, for Latin music try **La Palapa** (tel. 322/222-5225), on Playa los Muertos. For jazz, go to **Cuates y Cuetes** (tel. 322/222-9511), also on Playa los Muertos, or the **River Cafe** (tel. 322/223-0788) on Isla Río Cuale below the downstream Avenida Vallarta bridge.

Local rock bar **Club Roxy** (Ignacio Vallarta 217, tel. 322/223-2404) offers live and loud rock music nightly, often to a full house of locals and tourists. The dance floor is usually packed as the crowd rocks out to classic rock, Motown, and blues.

Los Arcos amphitheater

## TOURIST SHOWS

Visitors who miss real-life fiestas can still enjoy one of several local **Fiesta Mexicana** tourist shows, which are as popular with Mexican tourists as they are with foreigners. The evening typically begins with a sumptuous buffet of salads, tacos, enchiladas, seafood, and barbecued meats, and ends with flan and pastries for dessert. Then begins a nonstop program of music and dance from all parts of Mexico: a chorus of revolutionary *soldaderas* and their Zapatista male compatriots; raven-haired senoritas in flowing, flowered Tehuántepec silk dresses; rows of dashing Guadalajaran *charros* twirling their fast-stepping *chinas poblanas* sweethearts, climaxing with enough fireworks to swab the sky red, white, and green.

The 3.5-hour **Fiesta Mexicana Cerro Verde** takes place each Thursday at a ranch outside of town and includes round-trip transportation from three in-city pick-up spots, with a tour guide setting the stage en route. Once there, the show includes mariachi, roping acrobatics, horse dancing, piñatas, folkloric dancing,

fireworks, a full buffet feast, an open bar, and for those with strong stomachs, cockfighting. You can book this tour through most of the major tour companies, including Puerto Vallarta Tours (Manuel Dieguiz 404, tel. 322/222-4935, toll-free Mex. tel. 01-800/832-3632, toll-free U.S. tel. 866/217-9704 or 866/464-6915, www.puertovallartatours.net). This primarily Internet-based company offers a 10 percent online discount on the price ($72 adults, $52 children).

Another good tourist-show bet is at the **Sheraton** (F. M. Ascencio 999, tel. 322/226-0404), which also takes place on Thursday. The tariff for the show typically runs $75 per person with open bar. During holidays and the high winter season reservations are generally necessary; it's best to book through a travel or tour desk agent.

## MOVIES

A quartet of posh multiplex movie houses entertain residents and visitors to Puerto Vallarta these days. Movies change every Friday and cost about $4 per adult. The theaters, invariably located in large shopping centers, offer first-run American movies in both English and Spanish, with assorted subtitle options, along with made-in-Mexico movies and some international releases as well. These modern theaters are furnished with reclining seats and have excellent air-conditioning (a dark, air-conditioned movie theater can be a serious cheap thrill on a hot afternoon in Puerto Vallarta, believe me—but bring a sweater) and cheap treats. Multitheater complexes include **Cinépolis** (Francisco Villa 1642 in the Soriana shopping center, tel. 322/293-6763), in El Pitillal; **Cinemark** (in Plaza Caracol on the main highway, tel. 322/224-8927); **Cinemex,** also in a shopping center on the main highway (Galerìas Vallarta, tel. 322/221-0095); and **Cinemex Macro Plaza** (in the Centro Comercial Macro Plaza), also in El Pitillal. You can get movie listings from *Vallarta Today* or *Vallarta Tribune* newspapers or online at www.virtualvallarta.com or www.banderas-news.com.

## ARTS AND MUSIC COURSES

The private, volunteer **Centro Cultural Vallartense** (tel. 322/223-8214) periodically sponsors theater, modern dance, painting, sculpture, aerobics, martial arts, and other courses for adults and children. From time to time it stages exhibition openings for local artists, whose works it regularly exhibits at the gallery/information center at Plaza del Arte on Isla Río Cuale. For more information, look for announcements in the events pages of *Vallarta Today* or the *Vallarta Tribune,* or drop by and talk to the volunteer in charge at the Plaza del Arte gallery and information center, at the upstream end of Isla Río Cuale.

Sharing the Plaza del Arte is the **Centro Cultural Cuale** building and adjacent classrooms (tel. 322/223-0095), where, late weekday afternoons, you may hear the strains of students practicing the violin, guitar, piano, flute, and pre-Columbian instruments. Such lessons are open to the general public; apply in person during the late afternoon or early evening.

## FESTIVALS AND EVENTS

Puerto Vallarta residents enjoy their share of local fiestas. Preparations for **Semana Santa** (Easter week) begin in February, often with a **Carnival** parade and dancing on Shrove Tuesday, and continue for the seven weeks before Easter. Each Friday until Easter, you might see processions of people bearing crosses filing through the downtown for special Masses at neighborhood churches. This all culminates during Easter week, when Puerto Vallarta is awash with visitors, crowding the hotels, camping on the beaches, and filing in somber processions, which finally brighten to fireworks, dancing, and food on Domingo Gloria (Easter Sunday).

If you are looking for a relaxing vacation, Semana Santa is not the time to come to Puerto Vallarta. The beaches are literally covered with families camping, partying, and barbecuing from dusk to dawn, and the streets are lined with cars as thousands of Mexican nationals pour in from Guadalajara and other inland cities. While the festival atmosphere can be exciting and fun for some, the traffic, crowds, and resulting litter and noise can be overwhelming for others.

The town quiets down briefly until the **Fiesta de Mayo,** a countrywide celebration of sports contests, music and dance performances, art shows, parades, and beauty pageants.

On the evening of **September 15,** the Plaza de Armas (City Hall plaza) fills with tipsy merrymakers who gather to hear the mayor reaffirm Mexican independence by shouting the Grito de Dolores—"Long Live Mexico! Death to the Gachupines!"—under booming, brilliant cascades of fireworks.

Celebration again breaks out seriously during the first 12 days of December, when city groups—businesses, families, neighborhoods—try to outdo each other with music, floats, costumes, and offerings all in honor of Mexico's patron, the Virgin of Guadalupe. The revelry climaxes on **December 12,** when people, many in native garb to celebrate their indigenous origins, converge on the downtown church to receive the Virgin's blessing. If you miss the main **Festival of the Virgin of**

**Guadalupe,** you can still enjoy a similar but smaller-scale celebration in El Tuito a month later, on January 12.

Puerto Vallarta is also home to a number of annual events for locals and tourists alike. Two foodie favorites include the **Festival Gourmet** each November (www.festivalgourmet.com for dates) and **Restaurant Week** each May (www.virtualvallarta.com for dates). The Festival Gourmet is the pricier of the two, offering special culinary exhibitions and tastings as well as special menus at many of Puerto Vallarta's top restaurants featuring guest chefs from around the world. The more reasonable Restaurant Week in May also offers special prix fixe menus—but at the price points of $16 and $29 per person—and it's a no less delightful culinary experience.

# Shopping

Although Puerto Vallarta residents make few folk crafts themselves, they import tons of good—and some very fine—pieces from the places where they are made. Puerto Vallarta's scenic beauty has become an inspiration for a growing community of artists and discerning collectors who have opened shops filled with locally crafted sculptures, paintings, and museum-grade handicrafts gathered from all over Mexico. Furthermore, resort wear needn't cost a bundle in Puerto Vallarta, where a number of small boutiques offer racks of stylish, comfortable Mexican-made items for a fraction of stateside prices.

## ZONA ROMÁNTICA
The couple of blocks of Avenida Olas Altas and side streets around the Hotel Playa los Arcos are alive with a welter of T-shirt and *artesanías* (crafts) stores loaded with the more common items—silver, onyx, papier-mâché, pottery—gathered from all over Mexico.

A few shops stand out, however. On Avenida Olas Altas, a block north of Hotel Playa los Arcos, find **Safari Accents** (Olas Altas 224, tel. 322/223-2660, 10am-11pm daily). Inside, peruse a delightful trove of the baroque, including brilliant designer candles, angelic icons, bright metal-framed mirrors, a rainbow of glass lampshades, and gleaming candelabras.

Basilio Badillo is home to several fine galleries worth visiting. Start with the eclectic sculpture collection at **Galleria Dante** (Basilio Badillo 269, tel. 322/222-2477, fax 322/222-6284, www.galleriadante.com, 10am-5pm Mon.-Fri., 10am-2pm Sat.). *Exquisite* wouldn't be too strong a description of the many museum-quality pieces, from neoclassic to abstract modern. Head farther up the street to **Lucy's Cucú Cabaña** (Basilio Badillo 295, tel. 322/222-1220, 10am-6pm daily) to see a charming and colorful mix of authentic Mexican handicrafts. While you are there, pick up one of co-owner Gil Gevin's humorous books about life in Puerto Vallarta. He might even sign it for you if he's there.

Nearby on Ignacio Vallarta, stop into **Galería Alpacora** (Ignacio Vallarta 232, tel. 322/222-4179, 10am-8pm Mon.-Fri., 10am-1pm Sat.), where you will see some incredibly vibrant wall hangings and rugs imported from South America and made with alpaca wool. **Cuban cigars** are forbidden in the United States, but if you want to pick some up for your stay in Mexico, be sure to drop into **El Gato Gordo** (Ignacio Vallarta 226, tel. 322/223-5282, 10am-7pm Mon.-Sat., 1pm-8pm Sun.). If owner Rogelio isn't busy, he can give quite the lesson on how to spot a fake Cuban cigar.

Continue north on Vallarta to **Xunaaxi** (Ignacio Vallarta 139, tel. 322/222-2119, 9am-9pm Mon.-Sat.) for some great cotton clothing and fun, affordable Mexican handbags.

Occcupying a prime spot on busy Carranza a few doors up from Insurgentes is **Mundo de Azulejos** (Carranza 374, tel. 322/222-2675, fax 322/222-3292, www.talavera-tile.com, 9am-7pm Mon.-Fri., 9am-2pm Sat.). This lively, spacious store and tile factory offers a treasury of made-on-site tile and Talavera-style pottery

# SHOPPING FOR ARTS AND HANDICRAFTS

Puerto Vallarta has become an excellent place to shop for handicrafts, fine art, resort wear, and home furnishings. Both the large selection of goods and the reasonable prices add to the temptation to do all your holiday gift shopping in Puerto Vallarta, regardless of the season. For the more common, low-priced (but nevertheless attractive) items, be sure to visit the Mercado Municipal by the upstream Río Cuale bridge, preferably early in your tour.

Although virtually all Mexican handicrafts are available in Puerto Vallarta, most of the following stores are especially well stocked in certain categories.

## CLOTHING
For both resort wear and traditional clothes for women, head to **Luisa's** (Juárez 144, tel. 322/222-5042, 10am-8pm Mon.-Sat.) or **Querubines** (Juárez 501A, tel. 322/223-1727, 9am-9pm Mon.-Sat.).

## GLASS
You'll find some excellent selections of Mexican glass at **Safari Accents** (Olas Altas 224, tel. 322/223-2660, 10am-11pm daily) and **Mundo de Cristal** (Insurgentes 333, tel. 322/222-4157, 9am-7pm Mon.-Fri., 9am-2pm Sat.).

## HUICHOL ART
Some of the best Huichol art can be found at **Galería La Indígena** (Juárez 628, tel. 322/223-0800, 10am-8pm Mon.-Fri., 10am-6pm Sat., 11am-3pm Sun.) and **Peyote People** (Juárez 222, tel. 322/222-6268 or 322/222-2302, www.peyotepeople.com, 10am-8pm Mon.-Fri., 10am-6pm Sat.-Sun.).

## JEWELRY
Head to **Alberto's** (Juárez 185, tel. 322/222-8317, 10am-6pm Mon.-Sat.), **Cassandra Shaw** (Basilio Badillo 276, tel. 322/223-9734, 9am-9pm Mon-Sat., 10am-5pm Sun.), and **Fábrica de Joyería Regina** (Morelos 434, tel. 322/222-2487, 10am-10pm daily) for excellent selections of Mexican jewelry.

## LEATHER
You'll find fine leather goods at **Huarachería Fabiola** (Ignacio Vallarta 145, tel. 322/222-9154, 10am-9pm Mon.-Sat., 10am-3pm Sun.).

## METALWORK
**Safari Accents** and **Querubines** offer selections of beautiful metalwork.

## PAINTING
For Mexican paintings, head to **Galería Vallarta** (Guerrero 187, tel. 322/222-0290, 10am-9pm), **Galería Uno** (Morelos 561, tel. 322/222-0908, 10am-10pm Mon.-Sat.), and **Galería Pacífico** (Aldama 174 upstairs, tel. 322/222-1982, 10am-10pm daily).

## SCULPTURE
If you're looking for serious Mexican sculpture, head to **Galleria Dante** (Basilio Badillo 269, tel. 322/222-2477, 10am-5pm daily) and **Sergio Bustamante** (Juárez 275, tel. 322/223-1405, 10am-6pm daily).

## TILE AND CERAMICS
For tile and ceramics, check out **Mundo de Azulejos** (Carranza 374, tel. 322/222-2675, 9am-7pm Mon.-Fri., 9am-2pm Sat.), **Querubines, Galería de Ollas** (Corona 176, tel. 322/223-1045, www.galeriadeollas.com, 11am-6pm Mon.-Fri., 11am-2pm Sat.), and **Majolica Antica** (Corona 191, tel. 322/222-5118, 10am-8pm Mon.-Fri., 10am-5pm Sat., 10am-2pm Sun.).

## WOOD CARVINGS AND MASKS
**Olinala Gallery** (Lazaro Cardenas 274, tel. 322/222-4995, 10am-5pm Mon.-Sat.) and **Galería La Indígena** are good places to look for traditional word carvings and masks.

## WOOL WEAVINGS
You'll find a good selection of Mexican wool weavings at **Querubines.**

at reasonable prices. Unique, however, are the custom-made tiles—round, square, oval, inscribed, and fired as you choose—with which you can adorn your home entryway or facade. Look for the buses parked nearby—it's a stop on many Vallarta tours these days.

If you are looking for furnishings, either authentic or custom made, stop into **Banderas Bay Trading Company** (Constitucíon 319A, tel. 322/223-9871, www.banderasbaytradingcompany.com, 10am-6pm Mon.-Sat.), located by the fun-filled Blue Pig Gallery at Constitucíon 325. Here Tari and Peter Bowman have displayed their massive collection of Mexican furniture, art, and decor. The Bowmans, who also own Daiquiri Dick's, travel throughout Mexico, attending fairs and purchasing goods directly from the artisans.

For glassware, visit **Mundo de Cristal** (Insurgentes 333, tel. 322/222-4157, 9am-7pm Mon.-Fri., 9am-2pm Sat.) for a large, all-Mexico selection, including glasses, goblets, vases, mirrors, lamps, and much more, all at reasonable prices.

## ALONG THE RÍO CUALE

For the more ordinary, yet attractive, Mexican handicrafts, head any day except Sunday (when most shops are closed) to the **Mercado Municipal** (9am-7pm) at the north end of the Avenida Insurgentes bridge. Here, most shops begin with prices two to three times higher than the going rate. You should counter with a correspondingly low offer. If you don't get the price you want, always be prepared to find another seller. If your offer is fair, the shopkeeper will often give in as you begin to walk away. Theatrics, incidentally, are less than useful in bargaining, which should merely be a straightforward discussion of the merits, demerits, and price of the article in question.

The Mercado Municipal is a two-story warren of dozens upon dozens of shops filled with jewelry, leather, papier-mâché, T-shirts, and everything in between. The congestion can make the place hot; after a while, take a break at a cool river-view seat at one of the *fondas* (permanent food stalls) on the second floor.

It's time to leave when you're too tired to distinguish silver from tin and Tonalá from Tlaquepaque. Head downstream to the **Pueblo Viejo** complex (9am-7pm Mon.-Sat.) on Calle Augustín Rodríguez between Juárez and Morelos, near the Avenida Vallarta lower bridge. This mall, with individual stores rather than stalls, is less crowded but generally pricier than the Mercado Municipal. Some shopkeepers will turn their noses up if you try to bargain. If they persist, take your business elsewhere.

If, on the other hand, you're in the market for **huaraches,** cross the Avenida Vallarta (downstream river bridge) and continue to jewel-of-a-store **Huarachería Fabiola** (tel. 322/222-9154, 9am-9pm daily), near the northeast corner of Vallarta and Aquiles Serdán. Inside, find festoons of every kind of huarache seemingly conceivable, in sizes for everyone from giants to leprechauns and styles from the latest chic to rubber tire-soled models.

## EL CENTRO

A sizable fraction of Puerto Vallarta's best boutiques, galleries, and arts and crafts stores lie along the six downtown blocks of Avenida Juárez, beginning at the Río Cuale.

For original silver jewelry designed on-site, be sure to visit **Alberto's** (Juárez 185, tel. 322/222-8317, www.albertos.com.mx, 10am-8pm Mon.-Sat.), arguably Puerto Vallarta's top class-act jewelry store. Here, owner-artisan Jaime Ballesteros and his son Emersson carry on the Puerto Vallarta tradition begun by Jaime's late father, Roberto ("Alberto") Ballesteros. They offer a treasury of unique pieces, mostly crafted by Jaime and Emersson, taken from designs passed down through three generations. Considering their fine work, their prices are very reasonable. Unfortunately, there is another Alberto's down the street, so make sure you visit the original!

Across the street, curvy women can find a huge variety of bathing suits and some resort wear at **Curvas Peligrosas** (Juárez 178, tel. 322/223-5978, 10am-5pm Mon.-Fri., 11am-3pm Sat.). Owner Robina Oliver opened the store after taking a vacation and realizing that

a colorful streetside serape and blanket shop

none of the dozens of swimwear stores carried larger sizes. Curvas Peligrosas sizes run 6-36 (U.S. sizing).

A block up and around the corner at Guerrero 187 is **Galería Vallarta** (tel./fax 322/222-5125, 10am-6pm Mon.-Sat. low season, 10am-8pm Mon.-Sat. high season, Sun. by appointment only). The storefront gallery is no longer open, but the upstairs gallery with the entrance around the corner is still going strong. Through the years, arts and crafts lovers Barbara Peters and her late husband, Jean, collected so many Mexican handicrafts that they had to find a place to store their finds. Galería Vallarta, a small museum of singular paintings, ceremonial masks, lampshades, art-to-wear, and more, is the result. The entire collection is now contained in the upstairs gallery rooms.

Renowned Guadalajara resident and art impresario **Sergio Bustamante** has a gallery in Puerto Vallarta (Juárez 275, tel. 322/223-1405, 10am-9pm Mon.-Sat.). Bustamante is an eccentric yet highly successful commercial artist and one of a kind; it's hard to understand how a single artist could be so prolific. (The answer: He has a factory-shop full of workers who execute his fanciful, sometimes unnerving, studies in juxtaposition.) Bustamante's more modest faces on eggs, anthropoid cats, and double-nosed clowns go for as little as $200; the largest, most flamboyant works sell for $10,000 or more. Many consider his best work to be large-scale sculpture, and you can see one of his large, quirky pieces on the Malecón as well.

For something different, drop into **Peyote People** (Juárez 222, tel. 322/222-6268 or 322/222-2302, www.peyotepeople.com, 10am-8pm Mon.-Fri., 10am-6pm Sat.-Sun.) and take a look inside for some excellent Huichol crafts in this fair trade co-op. They offer authentic, handmade examples of the intricate artwork produced by the Huichol Indians, including the vibrant yarn art wall hangings and the painstaking bead work that the Huichol are known for. Information about the individual artists is available for many of the beautiful pieces they offer.

A few blocks farther on, at the northwest corner of Juárez and Galeana, an adjacent pair of stores, **Querubines** (Juárez 501A, tel. 322/223-1727, 9am-9pm Mon.-Sat. high season, 10am-6pm Mon.-Sat. low season) and **La Reja** (Juárez 501B, 10am-6pm Mon.-Sat. high season, 10am-2pm and 4pm-8pm Mon.-Sat. low season), display their excellent traditional merchandise—riots of papier-mâché fruit, exquisite blue pottery vases, gleaming pewter, clay trees of life, heavenly baroque reproductions, rich Oaxaca and Chiapas textiles, shiny Tlaquepaque hand-painted pottery—so artfully crafted they are simply fun to walk through.

For more Huichol work (these days the Huichol are represented by numerous galleries and shops all over Puerto Vallarta) as well as other folk arts, step into **Galería La Indígena** (Juárez 626, tel. 322/222-3007, 10am-8pm Mon.-Sat.) for a brilliant display of fine native ceremonial crafts. Here, you can appreciate bright Huichol yarn paintings and masks; Tarascan art from Ocumichu, Michoacán; Nahua painted coconut faces from Guerrero; a host of masks, both antique originals and new reproductions; pre-Columbian replicas; and Oaxacan fanciful wooden *alebrijes* (animal figures).

Recross Juárez and follow Corona downhill to ceramics gallery **Majolica Antica** (Corona 191, tel. 322/222-5118, 10am-8pm Mon.-Fri., 10am-5pm Sat., 10am-2pm Sun.), which uses the older name, after the Mediterranean island of Majorca. The celebrated Talavera pottery style, a blend of Moorish, Chinese, and Mediterranean traditions, originated on Majorca before migrating to Spain and Mexico. The later name, Talavera, comes from the town in Spain from which the potters, who eventually settled in Puebla, Mexico, emigrated. The personable owner/manager hand selects the pieces, all of which come from the Puebla family workshops that carry on the Talavera tradition. Prices reflect the high demand that the colorful, classic, elegant Talavera style has commanded for generations.

Downhill, at the corner of Corona and Morelos, is **Galería Uno** (Morelos 561, tel. 322/222-0908, www.mexonline.com/galeriauno.htm, 10am-8pm Mon.-Sat.), one of Puerto Vallarta's longest-established fine art galleries. The collection—featuring internationally recognized artists with whom the gallery often schedules exhibition openings for the public—tends toward the large, the abstract, and the primitive. Check their website for the exhibition schedule.

For a similarly excellent collection, step one block north and around the uphill corner of Aldama to **Galería Pacífico** (Aldama 174 upstairs, tel. 322/222-5502 or tel./fax 322/222-1982, 10am-8pm Mon.-Sat., by appointment only June 15-Sept. 15). Here, in an airy upstairs showroom, personable owner Gary Thompson offers a fine collection of paintings, prints, and sculptures of Mexican artists, both renowned and up-and-coming. The mostly realistic works cover a gamut of styles and feelings, from colorful and sentimental to stark and satirical. Gary often hosts Friday meet-the-artist openings, where visitors are invited to socialize with the local artistic community. He also leads the free Malecón Sculpture Walking Tour, starting from the Millennium Sculpture by the Hotel Rosita, 9:30am on Tuesday, November-April.

Open since 1998, Carolina Orozco's **Galería de Ollas** (Corona 176, tel. 322/223-1045, www.galeriadeollas.com, 11am-6pm Mon.-Fri., 11am-2pm Sat.) is dedicated to showing the pottery produced by artisans in the rural Chihuahuan village of Mata Ortiz. There are some 400 potters in this small town of 2,000 people, creating ceramics in a style derived from ancient techniques. The work is exquisite.

Finally, head a few blocks back south along Morelos to the **Fábrica de Joyería Regina,** or Regina Jewelry Factory (Morelos 434, on the Malecón, tel. 322/222-2487, 10am-10pm daily), for just about the broadest selection and best prices in town. Charges for the seeming acres of gold, silver, and jeweled chains, bracelets, pendants, necklaces, and earrings are usually determined simply by weight.

## ZONA HOTELERA

All along the hotel zone you will find tourist boutiques with trinkets and beachwear, but the majority of the shopping is in the form of shopping centers or malls. Unfortunately, due to high import taxes there aren't many deals to be had on merchandise in Puerto Vallarta's department stores. For groceries and housewares, visit Comercial Mexicana or locally owned Supermarket Gutiérrez Rizo. Comercial Mexicana's biggest local branch is the **Megastore** (tel. 322/222-7708 or 322/222-7709, 7am-10pm daily), 0.25 mile (0.4 km) south of the Hotel Sheraton. The other branch is at **Plaza Marina** (Hwy. 200, Km 6.5, a few blocks south of the airport, tel. 322/221-0053 or 322/221-0490, open same hours). Rizo's has a location in Zona Romántica at Aquiles Serdán and Constitución, although the arrival of Costco, multiple Walmarts, Megastores, and Soriano Supermarkets all over Vallarta has just about put Rizo out of business. They do have another less pricey store in Pitillal on Revolución, just west of the main street that passes by the church.

The popular if partially uninhabited **Plaza Península** (Francisco Medina 2485) houses a Starbucks, Chili's, and several other eateries (including the de Santos Restaurant); some upscale retail stores; and a small casino and sportsbook. There are also branches for most of the banks available in Mexico. Special events open to the public and music are common on weekend evenings.

Recent years have seen tremendous development in Puerto Vallarta, and with that the addition of an upscale mall, **Galerías Vallarta** (next door to Walmart, across from the cruise ship terminal, 11am-9pm daily), which houses a Liverpool department store. Inside the mall you can find a number of higher priced retail stores, several restaurants, a large movie theater, and even another casino and sportsbook.

Central to the Hotel Zone is **Plaza Caracol** (Hwy. 200, Km 2.5, www.plazacaracolpv.com), which houses another massive grocery store, Soriana. Inside the plaza are a number of small boutiques, nail salons, electronics stores, and eateries. Upstairs is a movie theater with a sweet little coffee shop just outside the entry, a food court featuring Mexican and American fast food joints, and an arcade for the kids. There are several other shopping malls in Vallarta these days (yes, even a Costco) back in the commercial sections of Fluvial Vallarta (a recently developed area east of the Zona Hotelera, just a few short blocks south of the heart of El Pitillal), and others can be found farther up Highway 200.

## MARINA DISTRICT

On the walkways and streets that encircle the Puerto Vallarta marina, and along the stretch of Highway 200 bordering the marina, you will find a number of large and small shops, spas, art galleries, and restaurants. Much of what's for sale is predictably tacky souvenir merchandise or modern appliances, furnishings, and housewares, here to supply the region's large and growing expat community, but there are a few diamonds in the rough, including **Galería EM** (Marina Las Palmas II, Local 17, Marina Vallarta, tel. 322/221-2228, 2pm-5pm Mon.-Sat.), where artist Mariano Pérez creates unique stained-glass art, beautiful crystal lenses encased in metal, and other treasures. You can also order custom stained-glass windows and doors.

# Accommodations

In Puerto Vallarta you can get any type of lodging you want at nearly any price. The location sets the tone, however. The relaxed, relatively tranquil but charming neighborhood south of the Río Cuale (especially around Avenida Olas Altas) has many budget and moderately priced hotels, apartments, and condos within easy walking distance of restaurants, shopping, and services. Virtually all hotels welcome guests regardless of race, religion, or sexual preference. A very few do not accept families with young children. Many of the best-buy small hotels are very close to, if not right on, lively Playa los Muertos. While no strict dividing line separates the types of available lodgings, hotels generally offer rooms with maximum service (front desk, daily cleaning, restaurant, pool, although budget hotels seldom have pools) but no kitchens for shorter-term guests, while apartments and condos virtually always offer multiple-room furnished kitchen units at greatly reduced daily rates for longer stays. If you're staying more than two weeks, you'll save money and also enjoy more of the comforts of home in a good apartment or condo rental. You can often find good deals and last-minute specials on popular rental sites like www.vrbo.com or on the Puerto Vallarta Craigslist website at http://pv.craigslist.org.

Bear in mind that the peso/dollar exchange rate is always in flux, and prices may vary from those listed as a result. Most of the prices in this guide are based on an exchange rate of 13 pesos to the U.S. dollar.

One thing to note is that in Mexico, the beds are hard. You may find little difference between beds at a $50 per night hotel versus a $200 per night hotel, save for the linens. At the higher-end hotels, they may offer egg-crate foam pads for the mattress, but if you are used to a soft mattress or are a sensitive sleeper, you should call ahead to make sure and skip the low-budget hotels.

## ZONA ROMÁNTICA
### Under $50

On Avenida Francisco I. Madero, just downhill from the corner of Jacarandas, stand Puerto Vallarta's most recommendable economy hotels. These bare-bulb—but respectable and clean—one-star hostelries have tiers of interior rooms with few amenities other than four walls, a shower bath (check for hot water), and a double bed. The prices, however, are certainly right. The best of the bunch are probably **Hotel Ana Liz** (Madero 429, tel. 322/222-1757, $25 s, $35 d) and **Hotel Bernal** (tel. 322/222-3605, $28 s, $33 d), next door. Also, you might check out **Hotel Cartagena** (Madero 426, tel. 322/222-6914, $28 s, $32 d), across the street.

Also especially worthy is the slightly pricier **Hotel Villa del Mar** (Madero 440, tel. 322/222-0785, www.hvilladelmar.com), whose longtime loyal patrons swear by it as the one remnant of Puerto Vallarta "like it used to be." The austere dark-wood lobby on the corner of Madero and Jacarandas leads to a double warren of clean upstairs rooms, arranged in interior and exterior sections. (Above that is a top-floor cluster of attractive budget-priced studio kitchenette apartments.) The 30 or so exterior-facing rooms (about $36 per day year-round) are generally the best, with nondeluxe but comfortable amenities including queen-size beds, traditional-style dark-wood decor, ceiling fans, more light and quiet, and in some cases even private street-view balconies. The less desirable interior-wing rooms (about $32 year-round), by contrast, have windows that line walkways around a sound-reflective, and therefore often noisy, interior tiled atrium, and guests must draw curtains for quiet and privacy. Rooms vary, so inspect a few before you decide. No TV, phones (there is one in the lobby for local and international calls), or pool are available, and credit cards are not accepted.

At the same economical price level but much closer to the beach and heart of Old Town, the **Hotel Posada Lily** (Basilio Badillo 109, tel.

322/222-0032, $30 s to $50 d high season) lies one short block from Playa los Muertos. The five-floor walk-up has fairly good-size rooms with two or three double or queen beds, ceiling fans or air-conditioning, color TV, baths with showers, and small outside patios with views of the water on the Basilio Badillo side.

## $50-100

The **Hotel Yasmín** (Basilio Badillo 168, tel. 322/222-0087, about $50 s, $60 d with fan, add $10 for a/c, year-round), at Pino Suárez, a block from the beach, offers another budget choice. The Yasmín's positives are its plant-festooned inner patio, a small pool, Wi-Fi, and Café de Olla, a good restaurant next door, although it can get noisy at night. The three stories of plain rooms are clean, but many are small. Inspect before you pay. You can compensate by renting one of the lighter, more secluded sunny-side upper rooms.

Just north of the Avenida Vallarta (downstream) bridge stands the renovated **Hotel Encino-Suites Plaza del Río** (Av. Juárez 122, tel. 322/222-0051 or 322/222-0280, toll-free U.S. tel. 866/352-3989, toll-free Can. tel. 800/649-9756, www.hotelencino.com). The lobby opens into a pleasant patio with tropical fountain, enfolded by tiers of 75 rooms that go for about $50 s, $56 d high season; ask for a low-season *paquete* (discount package). Inside, the rooms are tastefully decorated in blue and white, many with ocean or city-hill views. Twenty-four large, similarly appointed one- and two-bedroom kitchenette suites (about $75 low season, $101 high) are available in an adjoining building. The hotel climaxes at the rooftop pool and sundeck, where guests enjoy a panoramic view of the surrounding jungly hills above the white-stucco-and-tile Old Town, spreading to the blue, mountain-rimmed bay. Monthly rental discounts can run as much as 50 percent, and amenities include air-conditioning in rooms (no a/c in suites), phones, security boxes, and restaurant/bar.

A few blocks farther south on Playa los Muertos, the seven-story apartment-style **Hotel-Suites Emperador** (Amapas 114, tel. 322/222-5143, fax 322/222-1767, www.hotelemperadorpv.com) offers ocean-view lodgings at moderate prices. Although the hotel fronts the beach, it has no beach entrance nor beach facilities. It does, however, offer guests a small but inviting pool and patio half a block away. The hotel, in two sections (formerly Hotel Las Glorias and Suites Emperador, respectively) on opposite sides of Amapas, offers either hill views or ocean views, with air-conditioning, phones, TV, and free Wi-Fi with lobby computers for guests. High-season rates range from $77 d for a standard room to $287 d for a master suite. Credit cards are accepted.

Just north and east of the Avenida Insurgentes bridge is **Casa del Puente** (Av. Insurgentes, tel. 322/222-0749, U.S. tel. 415/513-5313, toll-free U.S./Can. tel. 888/666-9540, www.casadelpuente.com), tucked on the north riverbank upstream from a bridge-front sidewalk restaurant. Unfortunately, the restaurant was built on the site of the house's former garden, and so access to the hotel entry gate requires walking through the back of the restaurant. The elegant villa/home of Molly Stokes, grandniece of celebrated naturalist John Muir, Casa del Puente is a lovely home away from home. Antiques and art adorn the spacious, high-beamed-ceiling rooms, while outside its windows and around the decks great trees spread, tropical birds flit and chatter, jungle hills rise, and the river gurgles, hidden from the city hubbub nearby. Molly offers three lodging options: an upstairs river-view room with big bath and double bed ($45 d low season, $60 d high), a spacious one-bedroom/one-bath apartment ($50 d low, $90 d high), and a two-bedroom/two-bath apartment ($60 d low, $95 d high), with wireless Internet access. (Add 15 percent tax to all rates.) Discounts may be negotiated, depending upon season and length of stay. Reserve early for the winter season, as there are many annual returnees.

Renovations have boosted the venerable ◨ **Hotel Eloisa** (Calle Lázaro Cárdenas 170, tel./fax 322/222-6465, 322/222-0286, or 322/223-3650, www.hoteleloisa.com) from hohum to invitingly attractive. Find it two blocks south of the river, on the quiet, bus-free north (cul-de-sac) side of Plaza Lázaro Cárdenas. The hotel's five floors of approximately 75 rooms ($55 d low season, $75 d high for rooms and studios with ceiling fans; $10 more with a/c) and kitchenette suites ($20 more) enclose an appealingly light and airy inner atrium. Downstairs, past the small lobby, guests enjoy a modest restaurant/bar and a small but inviting pool patio. Upstairs, standard-grade rooms are decorated with white tile floors, pastel bedspreads, king-size (or a pair of double) beds, modern shower baths, and pleasingly traditional wood furniture and doors. Many rooms open to sunny balconies with a view of the plaza. Studios and suites are similarly decorated but larger, with kitchenettes, one or two bedrooms, and a living/dining room. A breezy rooftop sundeck with a view completes the attractive picture. All rooms have satellite TV and air-conditioning or fans (or both), and it's only a block from the beach. Discounts for long-term rentals are negotiable, and online prepaid bookings (credit cards accepted) can save you a bundle.

Another good choice, two blocks uphill from the beach in the heart of the Olas Altas neighborhood, is the **Vallarta Sun Hotel and Hostel** (Francisca Rodríguez 169, tel. 322/223-1523, www.vallartasunsuites.com, $68-85 d daily, $1,200/month year-round). Here, about 20 spacious rooms with balconies overlook a sunny pool patio. Inside, rooms are clean, attractive, and comfortable, with modern bathrooms and queen-size beds.

Right down the street from the Vallarta Sun is **Casa María Elena** (Francisca Rodríguez 163, tel. 322/222-0113, fax 322/223-1380, www. casamariaelena.com, $50 low season, $80 high). Here, seven attractive fan-only brick-and-tile units (four one-bedrooms, two large studios, one small studio) stand in a four-story stack on a quiet, cobbled side street just a block and a half from the beach. The immaculate, light, and spacious units have living room with TV, bedroom, Wi-Fi access, and modern kitchenettes (with toaster oven and coffeemaker). A one-week rental gets a 10 percent discount;

longer-term discounts are negotiable. The hotel also offers guests a 10 percent discount at its restaurant, **Cuates y Cuetes,** located on Playa los Muertos.

Vacationers who need beachfront ambience often pick the all-inclusive **Hotel San Marino** (Rodolfo Gómez 111, tel. 322/222-1555 or 322/222-3050, www.hotelsanmarino.com), right in the middle of the Playa los Muertos action. The San Marino's soaring *palapa* restaurant patio opens to an oceanfront pool and courtyard with a sundeck. Occupants of all 160 renovated, marble-floored, pastel-and-white rooms ($85 d low season, $95 d high) and suites ($100 d low season, $135 d high) enjoy city, mountain, or ocean views, with air-conditioning, cable TV, phones, and access to the bar and two restaurants.

A major Olas Altas neighborhood activity hub is the **Hotel Playa Los Arcos** (middle of the block btwn. Calles Basilio Badillo and M. Dieguez), a favorite of a generation of savvy American and Canadian winter vacationers. The Playa Los Arcos (Olas Altas 380, tel. 322/226-7100, 322/226-7101, or 322/226-7102, toll-free U.S. tel. 800/648-2403, toll-free Can. tel. 888/729-9590, www.playalosarcos.com) is the flagship of a triad that includes the nearby Casa Doña Susana and the apartments at Suites Los Arcos; it handles bookings for all three, and guests are welcome to enjoy all of the Playa Los Arcos's leisurely beachfront facilities.

All three of these lodgings have swimming pools and many comfortable, tastefully decorated, air-conditioned rooms with TV and phones; many rooms have small refrigerators. The mecca, however, is the bustling Playa Los Arcos, with its compact palm- and vine-decorated inner pool patio, restaurant with salad bar, live music every night, and beach chairs in the sand beneath shady palms or golden sun. The Hotel Playa Los Arcos's 175 economy-grade rooms rent from about $90 d low season to approximately $100 d high season. More spacious superior-grade rooms, some with ocean views, run about $117 d low season, $125 d high season; credit cards are accepted. Many guests pay much less by prebooking bargain air-hotel packages through travel agents or the Internet. There are also all-inclusive packages available. Moreover, during low season (May-mid-July, Sept., Oct., and sometimes Nov., and even Jan.) all three hotels often offer special promotions, such as a 20 percent senior discount, two kids under 12 free when sharing a room with parents, long-term discounts, or third night free.

The family-friendly █ **Hotel Tropicana** (Amapas 214, tel. 322/222-0912, www.hotel-tropicana.com, standard room $95 d low season, superior $20 more, with breakfast; add about 15 percent high season) is one of the plushest hotels on Playa los Muertos. Guests benefit from spacious rooms in a newer wing, an airy pool patio, and a flock of beachfront amenities—sundeck, restaurant, volleyball, and shady *palapas*—that spread all the way to the surf. Upstairs, virtually all of the comfortable, older semideluxe standard-grade rooms and the newer superior-grade deluxe rooms enjoy private balconies and ocean vistas. All rooms have air-conditioning and cable TV, and credit cards are accepted. It won't hurt to ask for a promotional price (*promoción*), especially weekdays and low season.

## Over $100

Back near Avenida Olas Altas, find the apartment-style **Suites Los Arcos** (on M. Dieguez, book through Hotel Playa Los Arcos, tel. 322/226-7100, 322/226-7101, or 322/226-7102, toll-free U.S. tel. 800/648-2403, toll-free Can. tel. 888/729-9590, www.playalosarcos.com, $113 d low season, $135 d high), with a long blue pool patio and an airy sitting area to one side of the lobby. Upstairs are 15 studio apartments, simply but attractively furnished in tile, wood furniture, and pastel-blue sofas and bedspreads. All have baths (some with shower bath), king-size beds, furnished kitchenette, air-conditioning, TV, and private balcony.

## EL CENTRO

Hotels generally get more luxurious and expensive the farther north of the Río Cuale you look. The far northern section, on the marina's ocean side, with a lineup of several big international chain hotels, is isolated several miles from downtown and has only a narrow beach, often with more rocks than sand. Most of the central part of downtown, which begins at the Río Cuale and stretches for about a mile north along the Malecón, has no good beach except at the far north end and is generally too noisy and congested for comfortable lodgings, with some exceptions.

## $50-100

One of the sprinkling of good downtown hotel options is the longtime **Hotel Los Cuatro Vientos** (Matamoros 520, tel./fax 322/222-0161 or 322/222-2831, www.chezelena.com), perched in the quiet hillside neighborhood above and a few blocks north of the main town church. The 16 rooms and suites are tucked in tiers above a flowery patio and Restaurant Chez Elena, and beneath a rooftop panoramic-view sundeck. The fan-only units are simply but attractively decorated in colonial style, with tile, brick, and traditional furniture and crafts. Rates (excluding Dec. 15-Jan. 6) run about $68 s or d, $78 for a suite October 15-June 15, $35 and $50 other times, with continental breakfast (during Oct.-June high season only) and a small pool; credit cards are accepted. Rooms vary, so check more than one before paying.

Located on the street behind the southern end of the Malecón is the **Rio Hotel** (Morelos 70, tel. 322/222-0366, www.hotelrio.com.mx, starting at $50 high season). The rooms are simple and clean, and the courtyard offers a nice swimming pool. Better yet, the popular **Coexist Café** is located here, a good, lively place to enjoy a happy hour drink or a traditional Mexican breakfast. The rooms include air-conditioning, telephones, and cable TV. Some rooms are available with kitchenettes for longer stays. It's a busy, loud location, but the price is hard to beat, and you're in the heart of the action of both the Romantic Zone and the Malecón.

At the north end of the Malecón stands one of Puerto Vallarta's popular old mainstays, the homey beachfront **Hotel Rosita** (Díaz Ordaz

901, corner of 31 de Octubre, tel./fax 322/223-2185, 322/223-2000, or 322/223-2151, www.hotelrosita.com). It's centered around a grassy, palm-shadowed ocean-view pool, patio, and restaurant, with plenty of space for relaxing and socializing. Most of the spacious rooms, of *típica* Mexican tile, white stucco, and wood, either look out to the ocean or down upon the tranquil patio scene, while some, to be avoided if possible, border the noisy, smoggy main street. An unfortunate, but probably necessary, wire security fence mars the ocean view from the patio. Egress to the nearest beach, Playa Camarón, is through a south-side gate. The Rosita's 115 rooms ($75-100 d low season, $95-140 high, depending on location) include fans or air-conditioning, security boxes, and a bar; credit cards are accepted.

## $100-150

The **Hotel Buenaventura** (Av. México 1301, tel. 322/226-7000, toll-free Mex. tel. 01-800/713-2888, toll-free U.S. tel. 888/859-9439, www.hotelbuenaventura.com.mx, $143 d), on the beach several blocks farther north, where the airport boulevard narrows as it enters Old Town, is one of Puerto Vallarta's few north-side close-in deluxe hotels. The lobby rises to an airy wood-beamed atrium and then opens toward the beach through a jungle walkway festooned with giant hanging leafy philodendrons and exotic palms. At the beachfront Los Tucanes Beach Club, a wide, palm-silhouetted pool patio borders a line of shade *palapas* along the creamy yellow-gray-sand beach. Most of the smallish rooms, decorated in wood, tile, and earth-tone drapes and bedspreads, open to petite, private ocean-facing balconies. The 236 rooms include air-conditioning, phones, buffet breakfast, restaurant, bar, and live music in season; all-inclusive plans add about $15-20 per person per day to the room rate. Credit cards are accepted.

## Over $150

Directly next door to the north is the sister property of the Buenaventura, the **Villa Premiere Hotel** (tel. 322/226 7040, www.

premiereonline.com.mx). The Villa Premiere is an adults-only hotel, with no one under 16 years of age admitted. The hotel has an elegant swimming pool with sundecks overlooking the beach, private lounge cabanas on the sand, and a fully equipped gym. The rooms are very comfortable and tastefully decorated in a kind of Mexi-contemporary style, with upscale luxuries including a pillow menu, aromatherapy selection, Jacuzzi-style tubs in many bathrooms, private view balconies, and plasma televisions. The hotel is very peaceful given its in-city location, with trickling fountains and staff masseuses on hand to give complimentary five-minute massages to guests. Rates begin at about $138 for the European plan during high season. Add an additional $90 per day per person for all-inclusive, which along with the Premiere's three restaurants (and 24-hour room service) includes the restaurants at the Buenaventura as well.

Only superlatives can possibly describe the ◖ **Hacienda San Ángel** (Miramar 336, tel. 322/222-2692, U.S. tel. 415/738-8220, fax 322/223-1941, www.haciendasanangel.com, $320-700 d high season), life project of personable owner-manager Janice Chatterton. She invites her guests to enjoy her Hacienda, once the house of celebrated actor Richard Burton, as their home away from home in Puerto Vallarta. Beginning in the early 1990s, Janice bought the three adjacent houses, which, with consummate design and decorative skill, she integrated into her present grand mansion.

Janice has spared little to adorn her abode with a heavenly choir of cherubs, saints, adored Madonnas, and a veritable museum of handsome old-world antique furnishings. She and her four-dog family invite visitors to enjoy any one of 14 uniquely designed and decorated suites, many with airy town and ocean vistas. All accommodations come with fans, air-conditioning, cable TV, DVD player, phone, continental breakfast, wireless Internet, and a load of luxurious extras, including a full-service gourmet restaurant and two lovely heated pools. Sorry, no children under 16. (You may also reserve at Hacienda San Ángel through

Mexico Boutique Hotels, toll-free Mex. tel. 01-800/508-7923, toll-free U.S./Can. tel. 800/728-9098, www.mexicoboutiquehotels. com.)

Superlatives of a more contemporary sort describe the **Landmark Hotel** (Calle Aldama 297, tel. 322/222-2870, www.landmarkhotelpv. com, $200-475 d high season), which opened in summer 2012 a few blocks up from the Malecón. This gleaming white hillside building with an attractive, art deco-esque feel to it, is reminiscent of the old hotels in Southern California built in the 1930s and 1940s. It's stylish without trying too hard. The hotel has a pair of fine restaurants: **The View,** with chef Oscar Galvan, former chef to the president of Mexico, and **O Wat Joi,** an Asian fusion dining room offering buffet-style dining. Rooms consist of eight luxurious, pricey, and elegant suites decked out in ultramodern white, black, and gray, with big windows offering spectacular city and bay views. While high-end hotels these days tend to be megasized and all-inclusive and out of town, this little in-town gem is a real boutique, a one-of-a-kind place with contemporary style to spare right in the heart of Vallarta. The hotel spa offers a range of massages, facials, and assorted therapies, as well as yoga and gym facilities.

## ZONA HOTELERA

Near the north end of the downtown Malecón, where the beach resumes at Playa Camarones, so do the beachfront hotels. They continue, dotting the tranquil, golden strands of Playa las Glorias, Playa los Tules, and Playa de Oro. On these beaches are the plush hotels (actually self-contained resorts) from which you must have wheels to escape to the shopping, restaurants, and piquant sights and sounds of old Puerto Vallarta.

Puerto Vallarta's plush hostelries vary widely, and higher tariffs do not guarantee quality. Nevertheless, some of Pacific Mexico's best-buy luxury gems glitter among the 20-odd hotels lining Puerto Vallarta's north-end Zona Hotelera beaches. The prices listed are rack rates—the highest prices paid by walk-in customers. Much cheaper—with as much as a 50 percent discount—airfare-lodging packages are often available, especially during low season, which runs roughly June through October, but is "lowest" in August and September. Get yourself a good buy by shopping around among hotels, the Internet, and travel agents several weeks before departure.

By 2012 most of the more luxurious, high-end all-inclusives were to be found farther north, in Nuevo Vallarta. In response, in the Zona Hotelera a minor frenzy of hotel building and rebuilding has been ongoing since 2011. Where this will end up remains to be seen, as several of these would-be posh new properties ran out of gas (money) before completion, leaving a few half-built hulks up and down the beach. But most got done, and there is at least one very posh, striking new property to add to the Zona Hotelera list: The Sunset Plaza.

### $50-100

At the far north end, just before the cruise-ship Terminal Maritima, stands the neocolonial **Hacienda Hotel and Spa** (Paseo de la Marina, tel. 322/226-6667, fax 322/226-6672, www.haciendaonline.com.mx, $50 d low season, $60 d high, all-inclusive). One of the Zona Hotelera's best-buy options, the Hacienda offers a load of amenities at moderate rates. Its 155 rooms, arranged in low-rise tiers, enfold a leafy green patio/garden, graced by a blue free-form pool and a slender, rustic shade *palapa*. On one side, water gurgles from a neo-antique aqueduct, while guests linger at the adjacent airy restaurant. The rooms are spacious, with high hand-hewn-beam ceilings, marble floors, and rustic-chic tile-and-brick baths, and include air-conditioning, phones, cable TV, and some wheelchair access. Credit cards are accepted. There are two drawbacks to this fine deal. One, guests must walk a couple of short blocks to the beach; and two, the hotel sits right on busy, noisy Highway 200, and you can hear it. Spa services, such as a *temescal* sauna, facials, many massage options, reflexology, and aromatherapy, are abundant but cost extra.

## $100-150

The majority of the hotels in the Hotel Zone will fall into this price range, especially if you book in advance online. You can often get airfare and lodging specials through travel websites that offer big discounts at resorts and usually include the all-inclusive package. One all-inclusive resort to consider is **Las Palmas by the Sea** (Blvd. F. M. Ascencio, Km 2.5, tel. 322/226-1220, fax 322/226-1268, www.laspalmasresort.com). Past the reception, an airy, rustic *palapa* shelters the lobby, which opens to a palmy beachside pool patio. Here on the wide, sparkling Playa las Glorias, opportunities for aquatic sports are at their best. The 225 rooms, with all food, drinks, and in-house entertainment, start at about $150 per person low season, $220 high; kids are discounted depending on their ages. Guests in most rooms enjoy private ocean-view balconies and comfortable semideluxe furnishings, with air-conditioning, phones, TV, restaurant, snack bar, bars, pool, and parking; credit cards are accepted. Check the website for promotional packages, such as kids under nine free, or third night free during times of low occupancy (Sept.-Nov. and May-June). European plans are also available for those not interested in the all-inclusive packages.

A couple of blocks farther south, the **Hotel Plaza Pelícanos** (Calle Diego Rivera 120, tel. 322/226-2700, toll-free Mex. tel. 01-800/509-0588, www.plazapelicanos.com.mx) consists of two properties, the Plaza Pelícanos Grand Beach Resort, directly on the beach, and the Plaza Pelícanos Club Beach Resort, across a small street. These Spanish-style, Mexican-owned hotels cater mostly to North American clientele during the winter, and Mexican tourists during national holidays, before Easter week, and in August. They share a website and a name but are different entities. Depending on which hotel you are booked in, the luxurious rooms overlook the patio, pool, gardens, or beach and ocean from small view balconies, and are tile floored, with decor in dark wood, white stucco, and blue and pastels. Rooms rent, all-inclusive only, for about $60 per person low

season, and $70 per person high season at the Club Resort, and $100 person low season, $125 per person high season at the Grand Resort, with air-conditioning, cable TV, pools, bars, restaurants, and parking.

Next door to the south, find the **Hotel Canto del Sol** (Jose Clemente Orozco 125, tel. 322/226-0123, ext. 4142, 4143, or 4144, fax 322/224-4437 or 322/224-5236, www.cantodelsol.com, $156 d, all-inclusive). During the high winter season, Hotel Canto del Sol bustles all day with tennis in the eight-court Tennis Club next door; aerobics, water polo, and volleyball in the big central pool; and parasailing, jet boating, and sailboarding from the golden Playa las Glorias. The luxurious but smallish rooms, decorated in soothing pastels, open to balconies overlooking the broad palm-decorated patio. All-inclusive packages cover all in-house food, drinks, and entertainment. Fourth night is often gratis, especially during the May-June and September-October low seasons. Amenities include air-conditioning, shows, water aerobics, tennis, kids' club, restaurants, bars, sauna, hot tub, exercise room, wheelchair access, and parking.

For another bountiful option, return a mile (1.6 km) north to the **Hotel Krystal** (Av. de las Garzas s/n, tel. 322/224-0202, toll-free Mex. tel. 01-800/903-3300, toll-free U.S. tel. 888/726-0528, toll-free Can. tel. 866/299-7096, fax 322/226-0738, www.nh-hotels.com, $91 d low season, $150 d high, two kids under 12 free). Stay here, and you get more than a mere hotel: This palmy, roomy, low-rise resort-village (one of the few Puerto Vallarta luxury resorts designed by and for Mexicans) is exactly what a Mexican Walt Disney would have built. Feast your eyes on the amenities spread over its 34 beachside acres: a flock of deluxe garden bungalows that open onto private pool patios, and a colonial-style aqueduct gushing water into a pool at the edge of a serene, spacious palm-shaded park. Guests who prefer a livelier environment can have it. Dancing, in season, goes on in the lobby or beside the huge meandering beachside pool, where the music is anything but serene. The Krystal's 460 deluxe rooms and suites include air-conditioning, phones, cable TV, 44 pools (no joke, though most of them are private, in-suite dipping pools), multiple restaurants, and all sports.

## Over $150

Half a mile (0.8 km) south, the ◖ **Hotel Fiesta Americana Puerto Vallarta** (Blvd. F. M. Ascencio, Km. 2.5, tel. 322/226-2100, toll-free U.S./Can. tel. 800/FIESTA-1 or 800/343-7821, fax 322/224-2108, www.fiestaamericana.com, $150 d low season, $250 d high, two kids under 12 free) is for many the best hotel in town. The vast lobby *palapa,* is an attraction unto itself. Its 10-story palm-thatch chimney draws air upward, creating a continuously cool breeze through the open-air reception. Outside, the high-rise rampart of ocean-view rooms overlooks a pool and garden of earthly delights, complete with a gushing pool fountain, water volleyball, swim-up bar, and in-pool recliners. Beyond spreads a wide strip of wave-washed yellow sand. Amenities include air-conditioning, TV, phones, all sports, aerobics, three restaurants, huge pool, three bars, wheelchair access, and parking.

Next door to the north, the all-inclusive **Hola Puerto Vallarta** (Blvd. F. M. Ascencio, Km 2.5, tel. 322/226-4600, toll-free Mex. tel. 01-800/327-0000, fax 322/224-4447, www.holapuertovallarta.com, $75 pp low season, $150 high, kids 7-11 $30, 12-17 $50) offers an attractive all-inclusive option for vacationers who enjoy lots of food, fun, and company. On a typical winter-season day, hundreds of fellow sunbathing guests line the rather cramped poolside, while a few steps away dozens more relax beneath shady beachfront *palapas.* Nights glow with beach buffet theme dinners—Italian, Mexican, Chinese, and more—for hundreds, followed by shows where guests often become part of the entertainment. The list goes on—constant food, open bars, complete gym and spa, tennis by night or day, scuba lessons, volleyball, water sports, free disco, golf privileges, stress therapy, yoga, aerobics galore—all included at no extra charge. If you want relief from the hubbub, you can always escape to the greener, more spacious Fiesta Americana poolside next door. The hotel's 320 rooms, all with private view balconies, are luxuriously decorated in pastels and include air-conditioning, cable TV, phone, and wheelchair access; credit cards are accepted. As is true with almost all of the hotels listed here, the best deals can be made by booking in advance through the hotel website.

Back down at the south end of the hotel zone, you can't miss the curving, three-colored modernist tower that houses the **Sunset Plaza Beach Resort & Spa** (Diego Rivera 121, tel. 322/226-2757, www.sunsetplaza.com.mx), a posh hotel that ups the ante for luxury in the neighborhood. With three pools, including an adults-only pool with built-in lounge chairs; air-conditioned gym; Wi-Fi everywhere; concierge and butler service; a pair of elevated, adults-only Jacuzzi decks; two restaurants and 24-hour room service; and a host of other amenities and luxurious touches, this hotel takes the all-inclusive concept to a new level. There are the basic rooms, and then multiple types of suite, including the Fitness Suites and Spa Suites, as well as Master Suites for couples or families. Each looks out over the beach and ocean, and has a private terrace, 32-inch flat-screen TV, complimentary Wi-Fi, air-conditioning, jetted bathtub, and an iPod dock in the alarm clock. The look is very contemporary, with granite countertops, modern artwork, and polished wooden furniture and finishes counterpointed by warm, bright colors and fabrics. Rates start at around $125 d and head way higher, depending on suite size, butler service, level of all-inclusiveness, and so on, but as always, booking through the website is the best way to get deals.

## SOUTH OF TOWN
## $50-100

Take a bus or drive the Manzanillo Highway 200 (the southward extension of Insurgentes) about a mile (1.6 km) south of town, and your reward will be the **Hotel Playa Conchas Chinas** (P.O. Box 346, Puerto Vallarta, Jalisco 48390, tel./fax 322/221-5230 or 322/221-5763,

# SPLENDID ISOLATION: RUSTIC LUXURY RETREATS

A sprinkling of secluded upscale miniresorts, perfect for a few days of quiet tropical relaxation, have opened in some remote corners of the Puerto Vallarta region. Being hideaways, they are not always easily accessible. But for those willing to make an extra effort, the rewards are rustically luxurious accommodations in lovely natural settings.

In order of proximity to Puerto Vallarta, first comes the minihaven **Majahuitas Resort** (tel. 322/293-4506, U.S. tel. 831/336-5036, www.mexicanbeachresort.com, or contact Mexico Boutique Hotels, toll-free U.S./Can. tel. 800/728-9098, www.mexicoboutiquehotels.com), tucked into a diminutive palm-shaded golden strand on the bay between Quimixto and Yelapa. Here, guests have their choice of seven uniquely decorated cabanas ($250-315 for two, meals included, low season, $375 high), including a honeymoon suite. Solar panels supply electricity, and a luxuriously appointed central house serves as dining room and common area. A spring-fed pool, sunning, snorkeling, and horseback and hiking excursions into the surrounding tropical forest provide diversions for guests. Get to Majahuitas by water taxi, from the beach at Boca de Tomatlán, accessible by car or the "Boca"-marked buses that leave Puerto Vallarta from the south-of-Cuale corner of Basilio Badillo, one block downhill from Insurgentes. It's closed in August and September, and kids under five are not allowed.

The following three splendidly isolated small resorts are tucked along the Jalisco Coast south of Puerto Vallarta and are road accessible from Highway 200.

Find **Hotelito Desconocido** (toll-free Mex. tel. 01-800/013-1313, toll-free U.S./Can. tel. 800/851-1143, www.hotelito.com, $340 d Apr. 15-Dec. 20 low season, $450 d high season, includes breakfast and all activities) basking on a pristine lagoon and beach two hours south of Puerto Vallarta. Here, builders have created a colony of thatched designer houses on stilts. From a distance, it looks like a native fishing village. However, inside the houses (called *palafitos* by their Italian creator), elegantly simple furnishings—antiques, plush bath towels, and artfully draped mosquito nets—set the tone. Lighting is by candle and oil lantern only. Roof solar panels power ceiling fans and warm showers. Outside, nature blooms, from squadrons of pelicans wheeling above the waves by day to a brilliant overhead carpet of southern stars by night. In the morning, roll over in bed and pull a rope that raises a flag, and your morning coffee soon arrives. For the active, a full menu, including volleyball, billiards, bird-watching, kayaking, and mountain biking, can fill the day. Reservations are strongly recommended.

About 30 miles farther south, the small sign at Kilometer 83 shows the way to **Las Alamandas** (toll-free U.S./Can. tel. 888/882-9616, www.alamandas.com), where Isabel Goldsmith, daughter of the late British tycoon Sir James Goldsmith, has created an idyllic isolated resort. Guests (28 maximum) enjoy accommodations that vary from luxuriously simple studios ($425 low season, $520 high) to entire villas that sleep six ($1,600 low season, $2,200 high), all with full breakfast. Activities include a health club, tennis, horseback riding, bicycling, fishing, and lagoon and river excursions.

Alternatively, you can enjoy isolation at more moderate rates at **Hotel Punta Serena** (reservations through Blue Bay Club Los Angeles Locos, tel. 315/351-5020, ext. 4013 or 4011, fax 315/351-5412, www.puntaserena. com, $170 d low season, $200 d high), perching on a high headland overlooking the blue Bay of Tenacatita. From the hotel lobby, walkways meander to the tile-roofed lodging units, spread over a palmy parklike garden. The lodging units themselves (all with a/c) are designer-spartan, in white and blue, with modern baths, high ceilings, and broad ocean vistas from view balconies.

Here you can enjoy it all: an adults-only romantic retreat, with all meals and in-house activities—a big blue ocean-view pool patio, sauna, sea-vista hot tub, gym, clothing-optional settings—included at no extra cost. Added-cost amenities include native Mexican *temescal* hot room, and massage and spa services.

www.hotelconchaschinas.com), which offers a bit of charm and luscious seaside ambience at moderate rates. The stucco-and-brick complex rambles several levels down a palm-shaded hillside (with dozens of stairs) to a petite pool patio overlooking an intimate cove on Conchas Chinas beach. Here, gulls soar, pelicans dive, palm trees sway, and sandy crescents nestle between tide pool-dotted sandstone outcroppings. The 19 lodgings themselves come in two grades. Studio superior rooms ($90 d low season, $110 d high) are spacious, decorated in Mexican traditional tile-brick and furnished in brown wood with kitchenette and tub bath; most have an ocean view. Studio deluxe grade ($115 d low, $130 d high) adds a bedroom, ocean-view patio/balcony, and a whirlpool tub. Amenities include air-conditioning, phones, and the romantic El Set sunset restaurant above (this is where the crew from *The Night of the Iguana* used to hang out, hence the name and movie souvenir decor) and a wonderful beachfront café below, perched practically in the water among the rocks and tide pools; there is no elevator or wheelchair access. Credit cards are accepted. Low-season discounts, such as one day free for a four-day stay or two days free for a one-week stay, are sometimes offered.

## Over $100

Two miles (3.2 km) south of Puerto Vallarta's southern edge, on Playa Las Estacas, you can enjoy the extravagant isolation of the **Dreams Puerto Vallarta Resort and Spa** (tel. 322/226-5000, toll-free U.S./Can. tel. 866/2DREAMS or 866/237-3267, fax 322/221-6000, www.dreamsresorts.com) at correspondingly extravagant prices. The region's first world-class hotel, the Dreams Puerto Vallarta (formerly the Hotel Camino Real) has aged gracefully. It's luxuriously set in a lush tropical valley, with polished wooden walkways that wind along a beachside garden intermingled with blue swimming pools. The totally self-contained resort on a secluded, seasonally narrow strip of golden-white sand offers a host of vacation delights: luxury-view rooms in the main tower (from $235 d high season, with lots of online deals available) or the Royal Beach Club (preferred) tower (about $70 more per adult), all in-house food and drinks, water sports, restaurants, bars, live music every evening, shows, and supervised children's activities for one all-inclusive price. Rooms in the Royal Beach Club tower have hot tubs and wheelchair access.

## APARTMENTS AND CONDOMINIUMS

Puerto Vallarta abounds with apartments and condominiums, mostly available for one week or more. Many of the best-buy Puerto Vallarta apartments and condos are concentrated in the colorful Olas Altas-Conchas Chinas south-side district, and high-season rates run from about $500 per month for modest studios to $1,000 and more for three-bedroom houses.

One of the most recommendable local apartment and condo rental agents is friendly **Bayside Properties** (Rodolfo Gómez 111, tel. 322/222-8148, fax 322/223-0898, www.baysidepropertiespv.com), in the heart of the Olas Altas district.

Other well-established south-of-Cuale rental agencies that you may find useful are **Tropicasa Realty** (Pulpito 145A, corner of Olas Altas, tel. 322/222-6505, fax 322/222-2555, www.tropicasa.com) and **Tango Rentals** (tel. 322/224-7398, U.S./Can. tel. 310/401-6752, toll-free U.S./Can. tel. 888/433-9057, www.tangorentals.com), run by personable Agustín Bas and his partner, Marjorie Torrance. They offer a wide range of vacation rentals, from modest condos to luxurious villas, especially in the intimate south-of-Cuale neighborhood.

Other apartments are rentable directly through local managers. The best place to look for rental homes and apartments is **Vacation Rentals by Owner** (www.vrbo.com) or the local Craigslist page under "Vacation Rentals" (http://pv.craigslist.org). If you are looking for longer-term housing or unfurnished places, try the local Spanish-language classified guide *Mano a Mano* (www.manoamano.com.mx), which comes out every Thursday and can be purchased at any local newsstand or OXXO convenience store.

# TRAILER PARKS AND CAMPING

Puerto Vallarta visitors enjoy two good trailer parks. The smallish palm-shaded **Trailer Park El Pescador** (Francia 143, tel. 322/224-2828) is two blocks off the highway on Francia at the corner of Lucerna, a few blocks north of the *libramiento* downtown bypass fork. The 65 spaces (four blocks from the Playa las Glorias) rent for about $24 per day, with one free day per week, one free week per month; it includes all hookups, including showers, toilets, long-distance phone access, and launderette. Pets are okay. The location in the pleasant Versailles neighborhood means luxury hotel pools and good restaurants are nearby. Long-term renters get huge discounts.

Farther out, but much more spacious, is **Tacho's Trailer Park** (P.O. Box 315, Puerto Vallarta, Jalisco 48300, tel. 322/224-2163), 0.5 mile (0.8 km) from Highway 200 on the road (Prisciliano Sánchez) that branches inland across the airport highway from the cruise-ship dock. Turn right off Highway 200 northbound just before Sam's Club/Walmart, and you'll find it on your left 0.5 mile (0.8 km) inland. Tacho's offers a large grassy yard with some palms, bananas, and other trees for shade. The 100 spaces run about $26 per day (one free week on a monthly rental), including all hookups and use of showers, toilets, laundry room, pool and *palapa,* and shuffleboard courts. Pads are paved, and pets are okay.

Other than the trailer parks, Puerto Vallarta has precious few campsites within the city limits. Plenty of camping possibilities exist outside the city, however. Especially inviting are the pearly little beaches, such as Las Ánimas, Quimixto, Caballo, and others that dot the wild coastline between Boca de Tomatlán and Yelapa. *Colectivo* water taxis regularly head for these beaches for about $6 per person each way from Boca de Tomatlán. Local stores at Quimixto, Las Ánimas, and Boca de Tomatlán can provide water (bring water purification tablets or filter) and basic supplies.

# Food

What a lot of people don't realize about Puerto Vallarta is that the city is home to a tremendous number of superb restaurants, and not just the regional specialties of fresh seafood and authentic Mexican food, but of all types. Home to two separate food events during the year, Puerto Vallarta is developing a well-deserved reputation for being a foodie town. From five-star dining to the local corner taco stand, there is something for everyone when it comes to dining in Puerto Vallarta.

Vacationers should avoid the all-inclusive plan at the local resort and opt instead to sample some of the regional fare, although in all fairness many all-inclusives in Vallarta, like everywhere else, are upping the quality of their menus in response to demand and competition. While it's easy to find traditional favorites that are common in U.S. restaurants, be sure to try more authentic Mexican food, such as the delicious *pozole,* a soup that you can find in nearly any Mexican restaurant, especially on weekends. Made from chicken or pork and cracked corn and topped with cabbage, cilantro, and onion, it can be as much as a meal as it is a soup.

## COFFEEHOUSES AND BREAKFAST
### Zona Romántica

Good coffee is plentiful in Puerto Vallarta, where many cafés roast from their own private sources of beans. The best coffeehouses are sprinkled around the Avenida Olas Altas area, just a block from Playa los Muertos. Here, coffee and book lovers get the best of both worlds at **Page in the Sun** (relocated to a spot overlooking the plaza at Lazaro Cardenas 179, tel. 322/222-3608, 7am-midnight daily). At Page in the Sun, longtimers sip coffee and play chess while others enjoy their pick of lattes, cappuccinos, ice cream, muffins, and walls of used paperbacks and magazines.

Around the corner and south a block or two on Olas Altas, the **Café San Ángel** (corner of Rodríguez, 8am-10pm daily, $3-5) is a good place to take a table and soak up the sidewalk scene. Here, you can enjoy breakfast, a sandwich, or dessert and good coffee in a dozen varieties.

**Cafesto** (Olas Altas and Dieguiz, 7am-11pm daily) is a lively little corner spot serving good java, pastries and such in the morning, and salads and sandwiches all day. Sit inside, or outside right in the midst of the Olas Altas action.

Across from the Hotel San Marino on Gomez, **Dee's Coffee** (7am-10:30pm daily) has excellent coffee; pastries including pies, cakes, cookies, and cinnamon rolls; as well as sandwiches, frappes, and juices all day. Tall café tables face the sidewalk out front, and a pleasant "library" with sofas and bookshelves offers a quieter option in the back.

For fancier offerings and refined ambience, go to the Old Europe-style **Café Maximilian** (380 Olas Altas, tel. 322/222-5058, 8am-midnight daily, closed Sun. in low season), on the sidewalk in front of Hotel Playa los Arcos.

For breakfast, **La Casa de Los Hot Cakes** (Basilio Badillo 289, btwn. Ignacio Vallarta and Constitución, tel. 322/222-6272, 8am-2pm Tues.-Sun., $4-6), skillfully orchestrated by personable travel writer turned restaurateur Memo Barroso, has become a Puerto Vallarta institution. Besides bountiful Mexican and North American breakfasts—orange juice or fruit, eggs, toast, and hash browns for about $5—Memo offers an indulgent list of pancakes. Try his nut-topped, peanut butter-filled O. Henry chocolate pancakes, for example. For lighter eaters, vegetarian and less-indulgent options are available. Memo's latest love is coffee. If you're lucky enough to be near La Casa de Los Hot Cakes at the right time, simply follow your nose to the source of the heavenly aroma of his roasting beans—premium estate-grown only, from Oaxaca, Chiapas, and Veracruz.

Enjoy an affordable and authentic Mexican breakfast at **Fredy's Tucán** (next door to Hotel Posada de Roger, on the corner of Basilio Badillo and Vallarta, tel. 322/223-0778, 8am-4am daily, $4-12). Fredy's is a favorite of locals and tourists alike, frequently voted "best breakfast" in Puerto Vallarta. Although they do serve lunch and dinner as well as have a full bar, breakfast is the favorite and is served until 2:30pm daily.

## El Centro

Just behind the Blockbuster video on Highway 200 is **Café Canela** (Lucerna 107, tel. 322/293-5423), where you can enjoy a variety of coffee drinks in a comfortable lounge setting. Those missing their home-brew chain coffeehouses will find **Starbucks** on the south side of the downtown plaza, in Peninsula Plaza, and at the top of the escalator in the Galerias Vallarta mall. There are also several coffee bars in Plaza Caracol.

## Marina

Along the walkway surrounding the marina, you will find one coffee shop that serves light meals and freshly made coffee drinks. **The Coffee Cup** (tel. 322/221-2517) also houses some beautiful art. Customers are invited to use the free computers and Internet available. **Starbucks** is here as well, in the ground floor of the luxury Nima Bay condo project that now dominates the marina entrance, breaking a number of zoning regulations and visually diminishing the formerly grand statues of Neptune and the mama and baby whales.

**Café Organico** can be found just north of the marina on Timón, with organic coffees and pastries.

## STALLS AND SNACKS
### Zona Romántica

A number of food stalls concentrate along Avenida Constitución, Francisco Madero, and Pino Suárez just south of the Río Cuale; several others cluster on the side-street corners of Avenida Olas Altas a few blocks away.

One of the stalls, the **Calamar Aventurero** (The Frisky Squid, tel. 322/222-6479, 9am-7pm Mon.-Sat., $2-6), has become a very popular open-air seafood restaurant. It's located at the corner of Aquiles Serdán and Constitución.

# NOPAL

If you visit any supermarket while in Puerto Vallarta, you are sure to see a stand laden with cactus pads while in the produce section. You'll also see cactus being prepared and sold in outdoor markets, from street vendors, and on menus of local restaurants. This cactus is called nopal, but you might know it better as prickly pear.

Nopal is common in its native homeland of Mexico, but it's also very popular in the Southwestern United States (where it's commonly used in jelly and margaritas). It has been a part of Mexican cuisine since long before the Spanish arrived in Mexico, and it is thought that the Aztecs may have named Tenochtitlán (place of the cactus), now Mexico City, after the hearty plants that were so important to the ancient civilization.

Once the pads of the nopal have been cut, they are called *nopalitos* and are used in a variety of dishes, including *huevos con nopal* and *tacos de nopales*. You'll also find it in salads and mixed into other dishes with other vegetables.

Because nopal is so high in fiber and nutrients, it has been investigated since the 1990s for its curative properties. It's said that nopal can lower cholesterol, reduce arterial plaque, and help with certain liver problems, diabetes, and even colon cancer.

Choose from smoked marlin tacos, ceviche, fish burritos, and much more.

Some of the most colorful, untouristed places to eat in town are, paradoxically, at the tourist-mecca Mercado Municipal on the Río Cuale, at the Avenida Insurgentes bridge. The *fondas* (7am-6pm daily) tucked on the upstairs floor (climb the street-side staircase) specialize in steaming home-style soups, fish, meat, tacos, moles, and chiles rellenos ($2-4). Point out your order to the cook and take a seat at the cool, river-view seating area.

## El Centro

Although food stalls are less numerous north of the Río Cuale, you can fill up quite well with the sprinkling of evening taco, hot dog, and sweet corn (*elote*) stands around the downtown plaza.

Alternatively, try **Tuti Fruti** *lonchería* (Allende 220 by Juárez, tel. 322/222-1068, 8am-11pm Mon.-Sat., $3-4), an inviting nook for a refreshing snack, especially while sightseeing or shopping around the Malecón. You could even eat breakfast, lunch, and dinner there, starting with juice and granola or eggs in the morning, a *torta* and a *licuado* during the afternoon, and an *hamburguesa* for an evening snack.

**Pepe's Tacos** (Honduras 173, across from the Pemex gas station, tel. 322/223-1703, 1pm-6am daily) has long been rumored to have the best *tacos al pastor* in Puerto Vallarta. This casual Mexican restaurant offers many other delicious dishes, all at a reasonable price, but make sure to try the tacos. *Tacos al pastor* are made from a slow roasted rotisserie pork and served with a bit of roasted pineapple, onions, and cilantro. Top with fresh salsa. At less than $1 a taco, a family can have a very affordable lunch here. Pepe's is also open late at night and is a great place to grab some tacos on the way home from the clubs.

Directly next door to Pepe's is **El Tacón de Marlin** (corner of Honduras and Peru), where seafood lovers cannot miss the *robalo con camaron* burrito: a large flour tortilla stuffed with bacon-wrapped marlin and fresh shrimp ($7). Tacón de Marlin has two other locations as well; one is directly across from the airport on the main highway and great to stop into before you hop on a flight home.

## Marina

While in the marina, be sure to stop at **Marisma Fish Taco** on the corner of Popa, behind Plaza Neptune. Enjoy crispy, fresh tacos made from deep-fried shrimp, dorado, or calamari and wash it down with a frozen lemonade to keep you cool. The tacos are served with lettuce, mayo, and four salsas to pick from.

Marisma's serves other Mexican food as well, but you can't go wrong with the tacos, which are some of the best in town.

## RESTAURANTS

If you're coming to Puerto Vallarta mainly for its gourmet offerings, avoid, if possible, September and October, when some of the best restaurants are closed.

### Zona Romántica

**The Café de Olla** (Basilio Badillo 168, tel. 322/223-1626, 9am-11pm Wed.-Mon., $6-10) serves affordable and delicious Mexican breakfast, lunch, and dinner. During high season it will be recognizable by the flock of evening customers waiting by the door. Café de Olla serves Mexican food the way it's supposed to be, starting with enough salsa and *totopos* (chips) to make appetizers irrelevant. Your choice comes next—either chicken, ribs, and steaks from the street-front grill or the savory *antojitos* platters piled with tacos, tostadas, chiles rellenos, or enchiladas by themselves or

all together in the unbeatable *plato mexicano*. Prepare by skipping lunch and arriving for an early dinner to give your tummy time to digest it all before bed.

**Archie's Wok** (Francisca Rodríguez 130, btwn. Av. Olas Altas and the beach, tel. 322/222-0411, 2pm-11pm Mon.-Sat., $8-15) is the founding member of a miniature "gourmet ghetto" that is flourishing in the Olas Altas neighborhood. The founder, now deceased, was John Huston's longtime friend and personal chef. However, Archie's widow, Cindy Alpenia, carries on the culinary mission. A large local following swears by her menu of vegetables, fish, meat, and noodles. Favorites include Thai coconut fish, barbecued ribs hoisin, and spicy fried Thai noodles. Make up a party of three or four, and each order a favorite to share. Arrive early—there's usually a line by 7:30pm for dinner. Visa is accepted.

Next door to Archie's Wok, **Restaurant Pekíng** (F. Rodríguez 136, tel. 322/222-2264, noon-10pm daily, $6-8) adds a new, refined version of Chinese cooking to Puerto Vallarta's

view over Old Town from a hilltop restaurant

already rich gastronomic treasury. Perhaps the promise of "the only Chinese-born chef in Puerto Vallarta" is its secret to success, but the food, whether a light lunch of spring rolls and wonton soup or a dinner of stir-fried scallops, kung pao chicken, and a whole fish, is bound to please.

If you are looking for the best Baja-style fish tacos in Puerto Vallarta, look no further than **Joe Jack's Fish Shack** (Basilio Badillo 212, tel. 322/222-2099, noon-1am daily). This deceptively small-looking restaurant offers a fun, casual atmosphere and two-for-one mojitos in various flavors during happy hour. The fish taco plate is massive ($9) and offers three huge pieces of breaded fish (or you can have it grilled) on flour tortillas. Joe Jack's also has all-you-can-eat fish-and-chips on Friday. If the downstairs bar is too crowded, don't worry; they have a second level for dining as well.

For some of the best seafood in Vallarta, try **Mariscos Polo's** (Francisco Madero 376, btwn. Insurgentes and Aguacate, tel. 322/306-8944, noon-10pm Wed.-Mon., $10-15). Here you will find a dazzling array of seafood dishes to choose from, including garlic octopus, fish fillet with mushrooms and white wine, coconut shrimp, and shrimp ceviche. The food is fresh and delicious, and the service is impeccable.

Another good place to feast is **Hacienda Alemana Frankfurt** (Basilio Badillo 378, one-half block uphill from Insurgentes, tel. 322/222-2071, 11am-10pm daily), the closest thing to a German *biergarten* south of New Braunfels, Texas. It's the brainchild of master chef Michael Pohl, who started out with a budget hotel in 1995 (which he still operates) and expanded to a garden restaurant a few years later. Besides all of the German favorites, such as smoked pork chops with sauerkraut, Wiener schnitzel, bratwurst ($8-13), and melt-in-your-mouth *apfel strudel,* Michael also offers popular French, Italian, and vegetarian specialties. If you can manage to skip lunch, go for the best of all, Michael's all-out effort—a genuine Bavarian buffet (about $18, served 6pm-10pm Mon., Wed., and Sat., Nov.-Apr.; call to confirm).

Tucked back along the Río Cuale is hidden favorite **Red Cabbage Café** (Rivera del Río 204a, tel. 322/223-0411, www.redcabbagepv. com, 5pm-11pm, $10-20). A small restaurant decorated with a vibrant and eclectic mix of Frida Kahlo-themed decor, its menu is focused on items that were served at Frida Kahlo and Diego Rivera's wedding feast. Everything is superb, but the *chiles en nogada* and chicken mole are widely recognized as divine. The restaurant is smoke free and cash only. If you are looking for truly authentic Mexican food at a reasonable price, don't miss the Red Cabbage.

A number of good restaurants offer both leisurely ambience and good food right on the bank of the Río Cuale. Moving upstream, start at the **River Café** (tel. 322/223-0788, www. rivercafe.com.mx, 9am-10pm daily), beneath the downstream Avenida Vallarta bridge. The owners have earned a solid reputation with a gorgeously tranquil streambank location, tasty international-style cuisine, and attentive service. Here, breakfast, lunch and sandwiches, and supper (ribs, fish, and Mexican specialties $14-25) are equally enjoyable. During the day, especially when there are cruise ships in port, you will find large groups and families enjoying the restaurant. Relaxing instrumental music afternoons and subdued jazz evenings complete the River Café's attractive picture.

For indulgently rich but good food and a luxuriously leafy atmosphere, the showplace **Le Bistro Jazz Cafe** (Isla Río Cuale 16A, tel. 322/222-0283, 9am-11:30pm Mon.-Sat., $10-20) is tops, just upstream from the Avenida Insurgentes bridge. The atmosphere is European and elegant, and decidedly more upscale and refined than the River Café. The river gurgles past outdoor tables, giant-leafed plants festoon a glass ceiling, and jazz CDs play so realistically that you look in vain for the combo. Try the *roles supremo* ($9) as an appetizer, and if there's room, the chicken crepes are delicious ($11).

For a great beachfront option for breakfast, lunch, or dinner, you can't go wrong with **Daiquiri Dick's** (Olas Altas 314, tel. 322/222-0566, www.ddpv.com, 9am-11pm daily, lunch $8-15). Dine outside on the beachfront patio and watch the people enjoying Playa los Muertos. The restaurant is spacious, with a comfortable but upscale atmosphere. Daiquiri Dick's often has live music, whether it's a mariachi band in the evenings or the soft sounds of live harp music during Sunday brunch.

With the 2011 opening of **Taste** (129 Callejon de la Igualdad, tel. 322/223-2484, 9am-5pm and 6pm-11pm Mon.-Sat., 10am-2pm Sun., $8-20), Puerto Vallarta gained another fabulous dining spot. Located at the lovely, immaculate, and imaginatively designed Hotel Casa Cupula (but fully intended as a destination restaurant in itself), Taste offers diners full or half portions of dishes from four distinct cuisines: American, Mexican, South American, and Asian. The idea is to try a taste of this, a taste of that, with many choices to make a meal. The spacious, high-ceilinged dining room is invitingly lovely, with warm, creamy yellow walls; a wonderful collection of light fixtures, artwork, and decorative objects; and patio seating on an intimate little deck tucked amid the hotel's lush gardens. Why not indulge in a taste of Cantonese dim sum, Peruvian ceviche, and Cajun chicken at a single dinner? Taste is also open for breakfast, lunch, and Sunday brunch.

Your stay in Puerto Vallarta would not be complete without sunset cocktails and dinner beneath the stars at one of Puerto Vallarta's south-of-Cuale hillside-view restaurants. Of these, the **Vista Grill** (formerly Señor Chico's, Púlpito 377, tel. 322/222-3570, 5pm-11pm daily, reservations recommended, $10-25) continues as a visitor favorite for its romantic atmosphere and airy town and bay view. Soft guitar solos, flickering candlelight, pastel-pink tablecloths, balmy night air, and the twinkling lights of the city below are virtually certain to make your Puerto Vallarta visit even more memorable. It's best to get there by taxi. If you drive yourself, turn left at Púlpito, the first left turn possible uphill past the gasoline station as you head south on Highway 200 out of town. After about two winding blocks, you'll see the Vista Grill on the left as the street tops

a rise. Winter nights it's best to bring a sweater or jacket. The offshore breeze by 9pm may be a bit cool.

## El Centro

Within the bustle of the Malecón restaurant row stands the longtime favorite **Las Palomas** (Malecón at Aldama, tel. 322/222-3675, 8am-10pm Mon.-Sat., 9am-5pm Sun., $5-12). Soothing suppertime live marimba music and graceful colonial decor beneath a towering big-beamed ceiling afford a restful contrast from the sidewalk hubbub just outside the door. Both the breakfasts and the lunch and dinner entrées (nearly all Mexican-style) are tasty and bountiful.

Good macrobiotic and vegan cuisine is getting a foothold in Puerto Vallarta in a number of locations. For a very worthy choice, go to **Planeta Vegetariano** (Iturbide 270, near the corner of Hidalgo, tel. 322/222-3073, 8am-10pm daily, $6), located downtown near the north side of the church. The very affordable buffet mixes a cold salad bar with hot options like soups, curries, and other delicious veggie dishes. The owners (with just 10 tables) have achieved renown with a healthy and delicious offering for Puerto Vallarta's growing cadre of health-conscious visitors and locals. It's easy to imagine some visitor-devotees eating all their meals there and being amply rewarded. It is a self-serve restaurant, so pay in advance and then help yourself.

Another great lunch spot is the ocean-front bistro **Vitea** (on the Malecón, corner of Libertad, tel. 322/222-8703, 8am-midnight daily, breakfast $5-12, lunch $5-15, dinner $7-20). Vitea offers great people-watching and great service. They have a delicious French onion soup and grilled vegetable sandwich, among other Mediterranean-inspired dishes. The atmosphere is upscale casual, so no beachwear!

Perched on the hill with a great view of the bay is ◖ **Barcelona Tapas** (Matamoros and 31 de Octubre, just up from Woolworth's, tel. 322/222-0510, www.barcelonatapas.net, noon-11:30pm daily, individual tapas $4-15, tapas to share $15-25). An authentic Spanish tapas restaurant, Barcelona offers fantastic service and superb food. In addition to tapas, hungry diners can try the seafood paella ($24) or the chef's surprise tasting menu, six courses selected by the chef including soup, salad, hot and cold tapas, and dessert ($33). Be sure to grab one of the coupons available on the Barcelona website for a discount on your meal or a free dessert. Note that you must climb four flights of stairs to dine here, but the view is worth it!

There's a trio of romantic hillside dining options, listed from north to south. Start out one evening at the striking castle-tower of chef Thierry Blouet's (C **Restaurant Café des Artistes** (Guadalupe Sánchez 740 at Leona Vicario, tel. 322/222-3228 or 322/222-3229, www.cafedesartistes.com, 6pm-11:30pm daily, reservations mandatory, latest at 10:30pm, entrées $10-30, most around $20) that rises above the surrounding neighborhood. Only romantics need apply. Candlelit tables, tuxedoed servers, gently whirring ceiling fans, soothing live neoclassical melodies, and gourmet international cuisine all set a luxurious tone. You might start with your pick of soups, such as chilled cream of watercress or cream of prawn and pumpkin, and continue with a salad, perhaps the smoked salmon in puff pastry with avocado pine nut dressing. For an entrée, choose honey- and soy-glazed roast duck or shrimp sautéed with cheese tortellini and served with a carrot custard and a spinach-basil puree. The building also houses the gorgeous Huichol-inspired P'yote Lounge.

Higher up the slope is longtime favorite **Restaurant Chez Elena** (Matamoros 520, tel. 322/222-0161, www.chezelena.com, 6pm-10pm daily, reservations recommended, closed Aug.-Sept., $8-14), on a quiet side street a few blocks above and north of the downtown church. Soft live guitar music and flickering candlelight in a colonial garden terrace set the tone, while a brief but solid Mexican-international menu, augmented by an innovative list of daily specialties, provides the food. On a typical evening, you might be able to choose between entrées such as *cochinita pibil*

(Yucatecan-style shredded pork in sauce, $9), banana leaf-wrapped Oaxacan tamales ($6), or dorado fillet with cilantro in white sauce ($14). Chez Elena guests often arrive early for sunset cocktails at the rooftop panoramic-view bar and then continue with dinner downstairs.

Finally, highest on the hill, treat yourself to dinner at Puerto Vallarta's most uniquely private restaurant, at the elegant, boutique 15-room **Hacienda San Ángel** (Miramar 336, tel. 322/222-2692 or 322/221-2277, 6pm-10pm). Personable owner Janice Chatterton initially created her restaurant for her in-house guests but now extends her invitation to all lovers of fine fusion Mexican-continental-North American cuisine. Some of her favorite recommendations include, for starters, smoked salmon carpaccio ($14) and/or pan-seared scallops with arugula salad ($14). Continue with shrimp coconut cream soup ($10) and climax it all with stuffed chile poblano, packed with shrimp, with a lemon risotto ($30). For more of her suggestions, visit www.haciendasanangel.com.

## Zona Hotelera

(C **Restaurant de Santos** (freestanding in the center of Peninsula Plaza, Blvd. F. M. Ascencio, tel. 322/221-3090, 5pm-2am daily, reservations strongly recommended, $6-23) moved up from El Centro into the Peninsula Plaza a few years ago, when they heard the Malecón was closing to cars (sending all the traffic into their street), but it still carries on in the same high style. The room is spacious, airily contemporary but with plenty of old-world decorative touches to keep it grounded in a traditional way. The atmosphere is lively and often crowded, with live music on the main floor. This is a restaurant where the crowds gather in the later evening, so for early diners, reservations are not required. There are many tasty items to choose from on the menu at de Santos, but the spicy lobster ravioli is particularly good. The ambience is relaxed and peaceful during the early evening, but after 11 when the crowds start arriving, the soft music is replaced by loud DJs. The upstairs lounge is quite a scene after midnight.

## Marina

A well-established dining option in the marina is **Gazebo** (Condominios Marina Golf, Local C-3, tel. 322/221-3700, 6pm-11pm daily, $4-12), where most nights you will be enticed in by the owner himself. Gazebo offers one of the best deals for dinner in the surrounding area, a three-course affair for about $22. The regular menu offers an array of Italian and Mexican dishes as well as fresh seafood.

With two locations to choose from, carnivores can pick their favorite to enjoy a festival of meat at **Brasil** (tel. 322/221-5027, 2pm-11pm daily, $20). Brasil has locations in the Romantic Zone (Carranza and Vallarta) and the marina. At this traditional Brazilian steak house, the meat doesn't stop coming until you say so. The price includes unlimited servings of grilled meats and a large selection of side dishes brought to your table by waiters. The meats range from chicken wings to cuts of tender filet mignon, and all are delicious.

Tucked away in the warren of shops and offices a few dozen yards east of the Lighthouse, **El Salon de Lupita** (no phone, 8am-6pm daily, $1-5) is the real deal for good, cheap tacos and other Mexican delights. Nothing is over $5, and the tacos are a dollar apiece.

You might think you're in Marina del Rey rather than Marina Vallarta, walking into the vast, airy, and light environs of the **Sonora Grill** (behind Starbucks in the Nima Bay condo project at Paseo de la Marina 121, tel. 322/221-2134, 1pm-midnight Sun.-Wed., 1pm-2am Thurs.-Sat., $20-35), so packed is the place with stylish strivers and successful operators of both sexes, all looking each other and the menu over. A glass wall brings the outside in and the inside out, as does extensive patio seating. This is a great place to see and be seen, and indulge in some hearty meat eating, although the feel is not exactly authentic Mexico. But then again, there is a Starbucks next door.

Across the street from the faded Collage disco with the bowling alley in back, on the street to the boat launch in the marina, you'll find the much-loved seafood joint called **Ocho Tostadas** (corner of Calle Quilla and Proa, Local 28-29, tel. 322/209-1508 or 322/209-1780, www.ochotostadas.com, 11am-6pm Mon.-Sat., $2-10). According to some, they make the best shrimp cocktails, the best ceviche, and the best shrimp empanadas in the entire Vallarta area, which can be enjoyed indoors or outdoors. Low-budget decor, cheap beer, no frills: The whole production is low-cost. It's all about great, inexpensive seafood, but the servings are generous. Closing time coincides with when they run out of food.

## SUPERMARKETS, BAKERIES, AND ORGANIC GROCERIES
### Zona Romántica

For imported foods and favorites from back home, try locally owned **Supermarket Gutiérrez Rizo** (Constitución and Vallarta, just south of the Río Cuale, tel. 322/222-0222 or 322/222-6701, 6:30am-10pm daily), a remarkably well-organized dynamo of a general store. Besides vegetables, groceries, socks, spermicide, and sofas, it stocks one of the largest racks of English-language newspapers and magazines (some you'd be hard-pressed to find back home) outside of Mexico City. A note of caution: This market has fallen on hard times since the arrival of all the supermarkets. Last time I checked, there was a sign in the window that said, "Contrary to rumors, we are not going out of business, and we would appreciate your business." It's kind of sad since this was an institution, but the half-empty shelves up and down many of the aisles were not very inviting.

There are now at least a half dozen large supermarkets in Puerto Vallarta, including Sorianos, Megas, Walmarts, and one Costco. They all have just about everything for sale, including Mexican products by the thousands as well as plenty of imports from north of the border. They all have extensive sections devoted to fruits and vegetables, just like American supermarkets, and most have at least a small organic produce section as well as bakeries with plentiful fresh breads and pastries. While these markets lack the charm of small independent shops, the bakeries, for example, carry a lot of good, fresh stuff and should not be dismissed out of hand as too "American." They are very Mexican in what they sell and how they sell it. Do be careful buying "fresh" meat and chicken in these markets, however, as it often sits out in the open for far too long.

### Zona Hotelera

On the north side of town, **Panadería los Chatos** (8am-8pm Mon.-Sat.) offers a fine selection at three locations: in the Hotel Zone (Fco. Villa 359, tel. 322/223-0485) across from the Hotel Sheraton, farther north in the marina (tel. 322/221-2540), and out by the airport (Blvd. F. M. Ascencio 7390, tel. 322/223-0485).

# Puerto Vallarta for Gay Travelers

Puerto Vallarta has long been popular with gay and lesbian travelers, many of whom end up purchasing homes and returning year after year. There is a large and vibrant gay community within Zona Romántica, making it easy for newcomers to make friends and feel welcome when visiting for the first time. While Zona Romántica is where the majority of the gay-friendly and gay-owned businesses reside, its popularity is not exclusive to the gay community. Indeed, all visitors will find plenty to do and see when visiting this quaint and charming area, from live music and art galleries to rooftop parties and after-hours dance clubs.

While most of the gay bars and accommodations are located in Zona Romántica, don't feel as though you must limit your choices to that area. Indeed, gay and lesbian travelers are generally welcomed with open arms throughout Puerto Vallarta. Despite the conservative and religious beliefs of many of the residents, Vallartenses are very live and let live in their approach to differences, whether it's someone of another race, religion, or sexual orientation. Still, it is best to remember that culturally, Mexico is conservative, and over-the-top displays of public affection will be frowned upon whether it is of the gay or heterosexual variety.

## RECREATION AND ENTERTAINMENT
### Gay Tours

There's a variety of tours and cruises to select from throughout the city, so don't feel restricted to only those that cater to gay and lesbian travelers. However, if you are looking for an exclusively gay tour, there are several great ones. The online **www.gogaypuertovallarta.com** offers a variety of exciting tours, including the Jungle Adventure, which packages a zip-line canopy tour, lunch, a waterfall hike, and a tequila tasting. The same company also has an El Tuito Hacienda and Horseback Tour and a Río Cuale Adventure Tour.

**Diana's Tours** (Los Muertos Pier, tel. 322/222-1510, www.dianastours.com, US$80) has always focused on and catered to gay and lesbian tourists, but its "straight-friendly" tours remain open to everybody. Thursday is the main day for the cruise, but during high season they may offer Friday tours as well.

Marine biologist Oscar Frey of **Ocean Friendly Whale Watching** (Muelle Los Peines, tel. 322/225-3774, www.oceanfriendly.com) is available for private tours catering to gay and lesbian travelers. While most other tours are gay friendly, there's nothing wrong with having a professional gay guide who is dedicated to responsible whale-watching and research. He specializes in groups, so if you have one, call him first. You are sure to learn a lot you didn't know about whales on one of Oscar's tours, and he's also an expert photographer, so if you ask nicely, you may be able to take home some beautiful photos.

**Boana Horseback Riding** (Boana Torre Tour Desk, Amapas 325, tel. 322/222-0999, www.boana.net/tours.htm, US$40) is a great way to get to know the area beyond

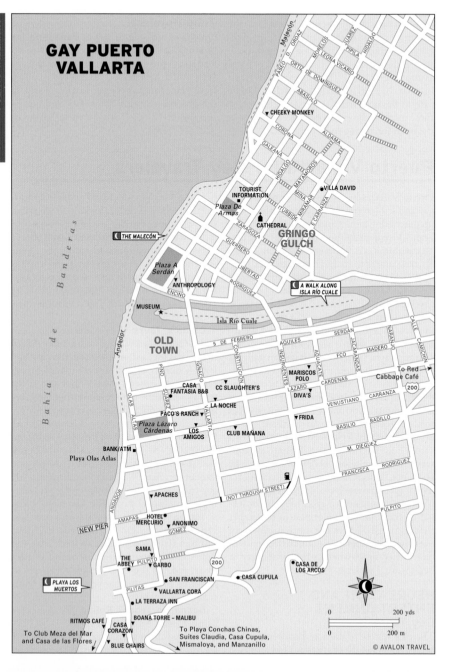

# GAY PUERTO VALLARTA

Malecón

PASEO D. ORDAZ

MORELOS

LEONA VICARIO

JUÁREZ

PÍPILA

HIDALGO

ORTIZ DE DOMÍNGUEZ

ABASOLO

CHEEKY MONKEY

NARANJO

CORONA

ALDAMA

GALEANA

HIDALGO

MATAMOROS

TOURIST INFORMATION

MINA

VILLA DAVID

Plaza De Armas

ITURBIDE

MIRAMAR

E. CARRANZA

THE MALECÓN

ZARAGOZA

CATHEDRAL

GRINGO GULCH

GUERRERO

Plaza A Serdán

LIBERTAD

ANTHROPOLOGY

RODRÍGUEZ

A WALK ALONG ISLA RÍO CUALE

ENCINO

MUSEUM

Isla Río Cuale

Andador

Bahía de Banderas

OLD TOWN

5 DE FEBRERO

CONSTITUCIÓN

AQUILES

SERDÁN

JACARANDAS

MADERO

NARANJO

CALLE CAMICHIN

PINO

IGNACIO

INSURGENTES

AGUACATE

FCO

CÁRDENAS

To Red Cabbage Café

200

MARISCOS POLO

CASA FANTASIA B&B

CC SLAUGHTER'S

LÁZARO

DIVA'S

SUÁREZ

LA NOCHE

VENUSTIANO

CARRANZA

PACO'S RANCH

VALLARTA

FRIDA

BASILIO

BADILLO

Plaza Lázaro Cárdenas

OLAS ALTAS

LOS AMIGOS

CLUB MAÑANA

BANK/ATM

M. DIEGUEZ

Playa Olas Atlas

FRANCISCA

RODRÍGUEZ

(NOT THROUGH STREET)

APACHES

ANDADOR

PULPITO

AMAPAS

HOTEL MERCURIO

ANONIMO

NEW PIER

GÓMEZ

SAMA

PULPITO

THE ABBEY

GARBO

200

CASA DE LOS ARCOS

SAN FRANCISCAN

CASA CUPULA

PLAYA LOS MUERTOS

PILITAS

VALLARTA CORÁ

LA TERRAZA INN

RITMOS CAFÉ

BOANA TORRE – MALIBU

CASA CORAZÓN

To Club Meza del Mar and Casa de las Flores

BLUE CHAIRS

To Playa Conchas Chinas, Suites Claudia, Casa Cupula, Mismaloya, and Manzanillo

0          200 yds

0          200 m

© AVALON TRAVEL

© JUSTIN HENDERSON

the Blue Chairs, set up for breakfast

the highway, bars, and beaches—once you go beyond the beaten track, the lushness of the jungle is breathtaking. Take a scenic afternoon ride along the river and into the hills. Their tour includes transportation to their mountain ranch, snacks, and drinks.

**Unique ATV Tours** (429-B Basilio Badillo, tel. 322/223-6182, www.uniqueatvtours.net) can arrange tours for groups or private parties to some little-known areas in the mountains and jungle, or you can swing through the trees on a zip-line tour with **Canopy Chico's** (Hwy. 200, Km 20, Las Juntas, Cabo Corrientes, tel. 322/222-0501) at the luscious Los Veranos zip-line site.

Whether or not you're staying at the Blue Chairs Beach Resort, the **Blue Chairs Concierge** (Malecón 4, tel. 322/222-5040, www.bluechairs.com) is more than happy to help you find the gay tour or outing you're looking for to pass the time, get to know the area, or just meet new friends. They can arrange for anything from home-visit massages to horseback rides.

## Beach Clubs

The most popular and well-known beach club and resort within the international gay community is the **Blue Chairs Beach Resort** (Malecón 4, tel. 322/222-5040, toll-free U.S./Can. tel. 866/514-7969, www.bluechairs.com), perched on the south side of breezy Playa los Muertos. During the busy winter season, you can join the hotel's buzz of activity, starting with a friendly crowd that congregates in the hotel's famous beachfront blue chairs, and continuing with anything from bingo and karaoke to laughing with the crowd at drag shows and theme parties up on the rooftop terrace.

Adjacent to the Blue Chairs is **Ritmos Beach Café** (tel. 322/222-1371, www.ritmoscafe.com), which offers live music in the afternoons and evenings, and a fine continental menu all day long.

Since opening in 2010, the **Lido Beach Club** (Malecón 167, tel. 322/170-4984) has become one of the popular spots along Playa los Muertos. Featuring a full-service European breakfast in high season and an eclectic international menu year-round, the club offers towel service, fine dining options, and no pressure to spend lots of money in order to avoid chair fees. It's Los Muertos! Pull up a lounge chair and have a ball!

## Dance Clubs

One of the most popular gay discos, Club Paco Paco is now under new management and has changed its name—to **Paco's Ranch** (Ignacio Vallarta 237, tel. 322/222-8147, 6pm-6am daily)—as well as its location, but you'll still find the same fun-loving clientele. It's one of the oldest gay bars and clubs in Puerto Vallarta, offering several bars and dance floors, including a rooftop bar and outside terrace. Here you can dance until the wee hours of the morning to a mix of techno, hip-hop, and disco. There are late-night drink specials and drag shows on the weekend.

**Anonimo** (Gómez 157, no phone) is a stylish, popular little spot just off Olas Altas with great (meaning low) drink prices and plenty of opportunity for conversation.

**C.C. Slaughter's** (Lazaro Cardenas 254, tel. 322/222-3412) has been a hit since opening in 2011. No wonder, with an ambient martini lounge on one side and a raucous, multilevel dance club on the other, complete with go-go dancers overhead. It's frequented by both locals and tourists.

**Antropology** (Morelos 101, Centro, 9pm-4am daily) is a men-only strip club offering shows nightly, so if you're in the mood for eye candy, this is the place to go. There's a busy upstairs bar as well as a quieter rooftop bar if you prefer conversation. There's no cover charge.

## Events

Puerto Vallarta is home to a number of popular annual events for the gay community. **Women's Week** takes place in February each year (see www.vallartaheat.com for more information on dates) and draws a huge lesbian crowd for some fun in the sun. Like most weeklong events, there are scheduled activities to choose from as well as lodging packages from participating venues.

Still going strong after a dozen-plus years is the **Annual Latin Fever** weekend, which usually takes place over the American Thanksgiving holiday in November.

At the end of January, you will find **Steve Buczek's Annual Leather and Bear Week** (www.beefdip.com) in full effect. You can check out the action at the website. Scheduled events include pool parties, booze cruises, beach dance parties, and adventure tours like zip lines and ATVs. Special lodging and airfare packages are available to those registered for the event.

## FOOD AND DRINK

A comfortable street-side neighborhood bar, **Apaches** (Olas Altas 439, Zona Romántica, tel. 322/222-5235, apaches2000@yahoo.com, 4pm-1am Mon.-Sat.) is a favorite with both gay and lesbian patrons as well as a straighter crowd. This lesbian-owned establishment always treats you like you matter. While it sometimes might be a bit dusty around the edges, it's always a great place to spend the afternoon or evening.

**Los Amigos** (Venustiano Carranza 239, Zona Romántica, tel. 322/222-7802, www.losamigosbar.com, 6pm-4am daily) caters to a slightly more mature and sometimes blue-collar crowd. The cantina atmosphere and the friendly service convince patrons to stick around this laid-back neighborhood hangout, despite the draw of two popular gay hangouts nearby. Daily specials offered 6pm-8pm include 20-peso (US$1.50) cocktails and 10-peso (US$0.80) beers.

Primarily serving the guests of the Blue Chairs Resort, **Blue Sunset Roof Bar** (Hotel Blue Chairs Resort, Zona Romántica, tel. 322/222-5040, www.bluechairs.com, 7pm-11pm daily) is nevertheless accessible by elevator to the passing public. If you don't already have the event calendar from their website or the latest *Gay Guide,* ask about the entertainment—frequently a visiting chanteuse or reigning drag queen will put on a show on the weekends during the busy season. In addition to live entertainment, this popular hangout

© JUSTIN HENDERSON

**Apaches is a long-time favorite in Old Town.**

always has something going on, from bingo to karaoke. This is a favorite spot for nightly sunset viewing.

**The Cheeky Monkey** (Corona at the Malecón, tel. 322/222-8938, www.cheeky-monkeypv.com, noon-4am daily) is the only gay-owned restaurant and bar located on the popular Malecón in downtown Vallarta. Climb to the third floor after locating the side-door on Corona, just in from the corner of Paseo Díaz Ordaz. It's a mixed crowd, so there's no problem with bringing your straight friends along. Don't expect a wild, raunchy evening here. Instead enjoy the food, people-watching, and $2 margaritas.

With lipstick-red interiors adorned with black-and-white Hollywood glossies from earlier days, the quiet and relaxed **Diva's** (Fco. Madero 388, Zona Romántica, tel. 322/222-7774, www.divaspv.com, 6pm-2am daily) is a great place to go alone or with friends early in the evening before hitting the nearby dance clubs. The drinks are good, and the service is at your elbow without being in your face. You

don't have to worry about offending anyone if you don't feel like chatting up the loyal crowd of regulars. This is a great place to go if you prefer conversation over pounding techno. You may have to search for the bar, however, as it's nearly hidden on a side street.

**Frida** (Insurgentes 301, Zona Romántica, no phone, www.fridaunbar.com, 1pm-2am daily) relocated to a great two-story corner location, but it's still a nice, quiet bar—a good place to go with old friends. The pool table takes your mind off the drink in your hand, but the jukebox can sometimes make it difficult to talk. Beer is the beverage of choice and rugged jeans are the preferred attire among the crowd here, primarily older locals and their young friends. Cheap drinks and a fun atmosphere make Frida's an enjoyable hangout.

There are few places like **Garbo** (Púlpito 142, Zona Romántica, tel. 322/229-7309, www.bar-garbo.com, 6pm-2am daily), where you can sit and chat with friends in comfort or flirt with your neighbor with ease in the same breath. A regular spot for many local professionals, usually during happy hour, Garbo's gives you space and respect, but you're always welcome to join the party. Sit at the high bar or find a quiet four-top with chairs or banquettes. Weekends and evenings bring the added benefit of live music, usually on piano, which often results in rousing sing-alongs. The mixed crowd, charming servers, and superb martini menu make Garbo's a don't-miss venue and a favorite of locals and tourists alike.

**La Noche** (Lázaro Cárdenas 257, Zona Romántica, tel. 322/222-3364, www.lanochepv.com, 6pm-3am daily, opens later off-season) offers quiet corner booths for conversation or a romantic drink as well as more central seating for more social groups. The dimly lit air-conditioned interior removes you from the busy world, and the music is enjoyable and not overbearing. Sexy videos play on the wall-mounted TVs throughout this petite bar. At this hangout for a crowd neither too young nor too veteran, you'll find a great drink menu, friendly service, and nightly specials, plus lots of delicious eye candy.

When you're wandering around and just want to sit down and put up those feet, stop in at **Sama** (Olas Altas 510, Zona Romántica, tel. 322/223-3182, 5pm-2am Tues.-Sun.), a sidewalk cocktail bar with shaded tables and nibbles to eat in case you're hungry. Service is quick and friendly, and the drinks are good and strong. You'll find Sama quite popular with the young crowd.

Overstuffed couches, large bronze sculptures of goddesses, and a breezy interior cooled by huge fans give the **Uncommon Grounds Buddha Lounge** (Lázaro Cárdenas 625, Zona Romántica, tel. 322/223-3834, www.uncommon-grounds.com, 4pm-close Tues.-Sun.) a comfortable feel. Stop in for a drink and chat with the owners, a vivacious lesbian couple from New Jersey who fell in love with Vallarta—these friendly women give this popular spot its character. Daily drink specials include such toothsome selections as raspberry mojitos and mango margaritas. This is a good place to go either to meet friends for a drink early in the evening or to get to know someone

new. If you're going to be in town for a while, sign up for their email event listings.

Tucked back along the Río Cuale is hidden favorite **Red Cabbage Café** (Rivera del Río 204a, tel. 322/223-0411, 5pm-11pm daily, $9-20). A small restaurant decorated with a vibrant and eclectic mix of Frida Kahlo-themed decor, its menu is focused on items served at Frida Kahlo and Diego Rivera's wedding feast. Everything is superb, but the *chiles en nogada* and chicken mole are widely recognized as divine. The restaurant is smoke free and cash only.

## ACCOMMODATIONS

Puerto Vallarta offers a wide variety of gay-friendly hotels, villas, and B&Bs. All of the properties listed in this section advertise in the local gay media, and the majority, if not all, are gay owned. Many are located in the Zona Romántica, an appealing gay-friendly neighborhood south of the Río Cuale in downtown Puerto Vallarta. Of course, just because a hotel or resort isn't listed here doesn't mean that you won't be welcome. Many gay and lesbian visitors book their first trip into the hotel zone, which is comprised mostly of large beach resorts. Once they realize that the majority of gay bars and clubs are south of the Río Cuale, they usually stay in that part of town for their next trip. There's a wide variety of places to choose from in all different price points, so whether you are looking specifically for a gay hotel or just want to be away from the big resorts, Zona Romántica has something for you.

### $50-100

Climb the hill to find your private apartment-like room at **La Terraza Inn** (Amapas 299, Amapas, tel. 322/223-5431, www.terrazainn.com, $55-62 d low, $92-99 d high), a friendly gay-owned inn just a block up from Playa los Muertos on Amapas. Upper terrace rooms have a bit of a view beyond the high-rise in front, but each of the 10 rooms is spacious and comfortable and has a terrace complete with lounge furniture for sunning. Some rooms have kitchenettes. Guests also have access to the inn's laundry, Wi-Fi, dining services, and on-call massage service. Pets are allowed, and, in fact, if you leave your window open, neighborhood cats may just pop in for a peek. All of the rooms have ceiling fans, but if you are visiting during the steamy summer, make sure you book a room with an air conditioner. A breakfast café is available on the lower floor.

When a carefree vacation is on the horizon, the young and restless choose the men-only **Vallarta Cora** (Pilitas 174, Zona Romántica, tel. 322/222-6085, www.vallartacora.com, $75-105 d high, special rates by email), which has earned a well-deserved reputation as a party place. The four-story white stucco tower houses 14 clean tiled rooms with basic amenities, living room, dining room, kitchenette, air-conditioning, balcony, and oval-shaped bathtub. There are also small safes to store your valuables. The happening pool area is open to the public for weekly pool parties, while the hot tub can accommodate up to 60 people, all clothing optional. Two-for-one happy hours and the behind-the-bar steam room keep this place hopping. Wi-Fi is available throughout the premises.

Back downhill in the Olas Altas neighborhood, on a quiet uphill side street, stands the modest but well-managed gay and lesbian resort **Hotel Mercurio** (Francisca Rodríguez 168, tel./fax 322/222-4793, www.hotel-mercurio.com, $60 s or $78 d low season, $98 s or $128 d high). The small lobby leads to an intimate leafy pool patio, enclosed by three tiers of rooms simply decorated in rustic wood, tile, and stucco, with TV, air-conditioning, and shower bath; credit cards are accepted. During times of low occupancy, the Mercurio sometimes offers promotions, which you can read about online on their website. Although the Mercurio is gay friendly, straight visitors are welcome, too, but it's adults only, so no one under 18 is allowed on-site.

Directly above the Playa los Muertos south shoreline, the breezy plant-decorated room tiers of ◀ **Casa Corazón** (Amapas 326, tel./fax 322/222-6364, toll-free U.S./Can. tel. 866/648-6893, www.casacorazonvallarta.

com, small rooms $37 s, $53 d low season, $48 s, $100 d high; large rooms with kitchenette can be rented by the month) stair-step down its beachfront hillside. Tucked on one of the middle levels, a homey open-air restaurant (breakfast included in room rate) and adjacent soft-couch lobby with a shelf of used paperbacks invite relaxing, reading, and socializing with fellow guests. No TVs, ringing phones, or buzzing air conditioners disturb the tranquility; the people and the natural setting—the adjacent lush garden and the boom and swish of the beach waves—set the tone. The 42 rooms, while not deluxe, are varied and comfortably decorated with tile, brick, and colorful native arts and crafts. Guests in some of the most popular rooms enjoy spacious, sunny ocean-view patios. While not gay owned, it is certainly gay friendly and is a much more family-oriented atmosphere than some of the other hotels in the area. Check the website for specials.

## $100-150

The modern 10-floor tower of **Boana Torre-Malibu** (Amapas 325, Zona Romántica, tel. 322/222-6695 or 322/222-0999, www.boana.net, $40-70 d low, $65-130 d high) offers special rates for longer stays, giving you the option of experiencing condo living right in the Zona Romántica just across from the gay beach at Playa los Muertos. You can take virtual tours of almost all of the units from their website, because they do vary in style and amenities. All apartments have one bedroom (one unit has two bedrooms), a separate kitchen, living area with balcony, and air-conditioning, and guests have access to what is called "gay Vallarta's largest pool." The on-site travel agency will book tours and day cruises for you, although finding something to do shouldn't be a problem here—the location puts you within easy walking distance of the best restaurants, coffee shops, and bars. It's billed as a "straight-friendly" condo-hotel, so all are welcome.

**Casa de las Flores** (Calle Santa Barbara 359, Zona Romántica, tel. 322/120-5242, U.S. tel. 510/763-3913, www.casadelasflores-spv.com, $80-300 d low, $100-500 d high,

$150-600 d holiday) is a much-photographed quirky bed-and-breakfast that allows pets and children. This property has a rambling, homey atmosphere with some air-conditioned rooms, Internet access, fully equipped kitchen and bar, dipping pool for the main house, housekeeping service, and cable TV. Located within walking distance of Playa los Muertos, the casa offers impressive views of the bay from its terraces. While not focused solely on the gay community, Las Flores is gay owned. Long-term rates are available May-October, and the minimum stay at any time is seven nights.

The interior-focused **Casa Fantasia B&B** (Pino Suárez 203 at Francisco Madero, Zona Romántica, tel. 322/223-2444, www.mexonline.com/casafantasia.htm, $70-90 d low, $140-175 d high) offers a haven from the busy streets and beaches of the Zona Romántica. With more than 10,000 square feet (929 sq m) of space, this three-house hacienda-style B&B is handsomely decorated with antiques and art. Gay and lesbian couples are the preferred guests of choice, and unregistered guests are not allowed into the rooms. The champagne happy hour and full breakfast at the sunny poolside are de rigueur. Full breakfast is served daily. Only a block from the beach, this gay-owned guest house is spacious yet welcoming.

The deluxe men-only, clothing-optional **Villa David** (Galeana 348, Gringo Gulch, tel. 322/223-0315, toll-free U.S. tel. 877/832-3315, www.villadavidpv.com, rooms $93 d low season, $109 high; larger suites $119 d low, $139 d high) is the only gay lodging choice in the tony Gringo Gulch area. It offers an inviting and homelike atmosphere. Villa David's 10 rooms enfold an intimate, leafy tropical pool patio overlooking panoramic vistas of Puerto Vallarta, bay, and mountains. The rooms, decorated with 19th-century-style traditional hardwood furniture, embellished with reading lamps and handmade bedspreads, likewise all enjoy bay views. All rooms and suites have private baths, fans, and air-conditioning, and include a hearty buffet breakfast. Other amenities include a common kitchen and living room with TV and DVD player, in-house wireless Internet, rooftop viewing deck, and a hot-tub deck with bar. Guests enjoy easy walking access to both Río Cuale and Malecón sights, galleries, shops, and restaurants.

## Over $150

Forty-two rooms and 12 suites make up **Abbey Hotel Vallarta** (Púlpito 138, Zona Romántica, tel. 322/222-8445, www.abbeyhotelvallarta.com.mx, $58-129 d low, $160-240 d high), a modern tower-style hotel right by the gay beach in the Zona Romántica and just around the corner from local hot spots like Garbo. All rooms are invitingly furnished, with immaculate tile floors, modern hardwood furniture, and private town- or ocean-view balconies. Amenities include an in-room safety deposit box, air-conditioning, telephone, cable TV, and high-speed Internet access. Suites include kitchenettes and a large living room with dining area. Other on-site offerings include a reserved beach area, swimming pool, and Jacuzzi as well as restaurant and bar. For an additional charge, VIP airport pickup, in-room massage, and your choice of local tours and outings, including a private Abbey Sailboat Tour, are also available.

When you need to feel the comfort and services of the international gay community, head to the **Blue Chairs Beach Resort** (Malecón 4, tel. 322/222-5040, toll-free U.S./Can. tel. 888/790-5264, www.bluechairs.com), perched on the south side of breezy Playa los Muertos. Gay owned since 1998, the hotel, which advertises itself as the world's largest gay-and-lesbian beachfront resort, is a six-story stack of about 40 comfortably furnished rooms and suites, many with private sea-view balconies. During the busy winter season, you can join the hotel's buzz of activity, starting with a friendly crowd that congregates in the hotel's famous beachfront blue chairs, and continuing with anything from bingo and karaoke to laughing with the crowd at drag shows and theme parties. Lodging prices vary, from the most economical room with partial ocean view (about $134 s or d low season, $150 s or d high), to a kitchenette junior suite with ocean view ($181 s or d low season and $197 s or d high), to, at the top of the scale, a one-bedroom ocean-view villa ($230 s or d low, $246 s or d high); add $44 low season or $52 high season for each additional person after the first two. All rates include breakfast. All lodgings come with private baths, fans, air-conditioning, and cable TV, as well as use of the rooftop restaurant and pool.

The ever-popular **Casa Cúpula** (Callejon de la Igualdad 129, Zona Romántica, tel. 322/223-2484, www.casacupula.com, $160-279 d low, $195-310 d high, suites $275-375) is considered one of the best gay-friendly guest houses in Puerto Vallarta. Nestled on a steep, cobbled side street above the Conchas Chinas beaches just south of Old Town, Casa Cúpula is contained in three side-by-side houses and a modern lobby building joined by winding stairways and paths. The hotel contains 21 rooms and suites, each individually designed in styles ranging from eccentric to eclectic to ultramodern cool, with eye-catching artwork, chic furniture, and bathing facilities to die for. The hotel also has a small gym with plentiful iron to pump, two pools, a jetted hot tub seating seven, a rooftop deck, a bar, and a five-bedroom villa next door that is rentable in its entirety or by the room. Casa Cúpula is also home to **Taste,** one of Puerto Vallarta's finest gourmet restaurants, named the best new restaurant in 2011 by readers of *Vallarta Lifestyles Magazine.* If you don't stay there, at least splurge on a meal.

**Casa de Los Arcos** (Hortensias 168, Alta Vista, tel. 322/222-5990, www.casadelosarcos. com, $100-200 d low, $150-275 d high, weekly rates), a four-casita hillside villa, allows the option of renting the entire place for groups of family or friends, or, when available, renting a separate casita. Each casita features its own living room, dining area, kitchen, and private terrace with air-conditioning in the closed areas. The house is fully staffed Monday-Saturday; the cook is available Sunday for an extra charge. What's great about this residence is that you and a group of friends can all stay in one place, but you'll have your privacy when you need it, as well as large common living areas. The atmosphere has a very Mexican flavor, and the open-air *palapa* roof and private terraces will help you relax. Well-behaved pets are welcome. This spectacular-view property sits high above Conchas Chinas and Old Town; you'll need a car or taxi to go anywhere.

A boutique condo-hotel located right in the Zona Romántica, the **San Franciscan Resort & Gym** (Pilitas 213, Zona Romántica, tel. 322/222-6473, www.san-franciscan.com, $98-140 d low, $130-285 d high; four-bedroom suites $270 d low, $360 d high) offers a protected haven with 20 rooms and easy access to any of the services outside the gates. The five floors host five types of suites, including four-bedroom suites that can accommodate groups of up to six or eight. Amenities and services include free Internet access; no rate increase for regular registered customers for 10 years; air-conditioning; kitchens with microwaves, cookware, silverware, and china; and just about anything else to make your stay comfortable, including a complete free-weight gym. The San Franciscan also has a comedy club on the premises. Adults only; no pets.

## Real Estate Brokers

**Bayside Properties** (Rodolfo Gómez 111, tel. 322/222-8148, www.baysidepropertiespv.com), a gay-friendly rental and real estate sales operation owned by two women, handles many of the downtown and south-side apartments and condominiums.

The gay-friendly **Timothy Real Estate Group** (Ignacio Vallarta 130, tel. 322/223-5300, U.S. tel. 310/356-6514, toll-free U.S. tel. 877/204-7730, toll-free Can. tel. 877/382-4106) is one of the largest property sales and management companies in Vallarta, and it handles everything from rentals of apartments to sales of small condos and enormous villas, and everything in between.

Home mortgages are increasing in popularity among both foreign buyers and local residents. Gay-owned **Mexlend** (Insurgentes 441, tel. 322/222-7377, www.mexlend.com) is one of the leading lenders and can arrange for loans on many property types anywhere in Mexico. They offer both U.S.-dollar loans and peso loans for Mexican nationals or expats who decide to live and work in Mexico full time.

One of the partners of **Paradise Properties** (Atún 118, Las Gaviotas, tel. 322/224-5416, www.paradisepropertiespv.com) is gay; this agency focuses on personal service in sales and rentals.

The founder and many of the staff of **PVRPV** (Pino Suarez 210, Zona Romántica, tel. 322/222-0638, U.S./Can. tel. 206/388-3703, toll-free U.S./Can. tel. 877/462-7720, www.pvrpv.com) are gay. This busy, successful operation offers an extensive list of rental properties of all types and features a top-notch, easy-to-use online reservation system.

The founding partner of extremely successful **Tropicasa** (Púlpito 145-A, Zona Romántica, tel. 322/222-6505, www.tropicasa.com) is an active member of the gay community as well as the president of the local real estate association and the local Make-A-Wish Foundation.

# Information and Services

Since Puerto Vallarta is an up-to-date city, information is as close as your hotel telephone (or, if you don't speak Spanish, your hotel desk clerk) or one of the hundreds of publicly available Internet connections. A plethora of banks with ATMs, street telephones, Internet stores, pharmacies, doctors, hospitals, and much more are available, ready to smooth your Puerto Vallarta visit.

## TOURIST INFORMATION OFFICES

The downtown tourist information office (tel. 322/223-2500, ext. 230 or 232, fax ext. 233, 8am-7pm Mon.-Sat., 9am-2pm Sun.) is on the northeast corner of the central plaza. They provide assistance and information, and dispense whatever maps, pamphlets, and copies of *Vallarta Today* and *Puerto Vallarta Lifestyles* they happen to have.

## PUBLICATIONS

New books in English are not particularly common in Puerto Vallarta, nor are newspapers in English (since they are widely available online). However, there are several English-language papers published locally in print and/or online. *Vallarta Today* (tel. 322/221-1777 or 322/116-8480, www.vallartatoday.com), *Vallarta Tribune* (tel. 322/226-0829, www.vallartatribune.com), and the *PV Mirror* (www.pvmirror.com) are all informative tourist papers (all with complete online editions as well) and handed out free at the airport and travel agencies, restaurants, and hotels all over town (contact them directly if you can't find a copy). Besides detailed information on hotels, restaurants, and sports, they include a local events and meetings calendar and interesting historical, cultural, and personality feature articles.

*Puerto Vallarta Lifestyles* (Calle Timón 1, tel. 322/221-0106, 9am-7pm Mon.-Fri.), the quarterly English-language magazine, features unusually detailed and accurate town maps as well as an overwhelming number of real estate ads. Refer to the dining guide in the magazine for a peek at the menus of Vallarta's most upscale restaurants. Other useful information includes art gallery listings and usually profiles of outlying areas. If you cannot find a copy at the airport or your hotel, contact *Lifestyles* directly or pick one up at their office in the marina.

Also very useful is the class-act **Gay Guide Vallarta** that lists many gay/lesbian and gay-friendly hotels, restaurants, real estate offices, and bars and nightclubs, plus a calendar and much more. Visit the website, www.gayguide-vallarta.com, or pick up a copy at one of their advertisers, notably the Blue Chairs Beach Resort (tel. 322/222-2176 or 322/222-5040) on Playa los Muertos, south end, or contact the editor (tel. 322/222-7980, editor@gayguide-vallarta.com).

The **Puerto Vallarta Library** (Francisco Villa 1001 in Colonia Los Mangos, director Ricardo Murrieta tel. 322/224-9966 or Jimmie

Ellis tel. 322/222-1478, 9am-9pm Mon.-Fri., 9am-5pm Sat.), built and now operated by the volunteer committee Pro Biblioteca Vallarta, has accumulated a sizable English and Spanish book collection. Get there by taxi or car; it's several blocks along Villa, which runs at a diagonal north and inland at the sports field across the airport boulevard from the Hotel Sheraton. Or take a bus marked Pitillal and Biblioteca. You will need picture ID and a local address to get a library card, which takes one day.

You can find new English-language books at the **NV Bookstore** upstairs in Paradise Village and at its other location on Basilio Badillo by Joe Jack's Fish Shack. These two stores specialize in yachting paperwork, immigration photography (thus the Paradise Village location near the consulate), and a small but excellent selection of English-language books. You will also find both books and magazines in English at Costco. However, the easiest way to get "new" novels or books in English is to see if your hotel has an informal exchange library. Almost every hotel lobby or bar or coffee shop these days has at least one or more shelves full of paperbacks left behind by guests, where other guests are usually welcome to exchange their own books for someone else's. Although these informal libraries can be weighted toward romance novels and mainstream pop beach reads, you're almost sure to find something you haven't read and probably want to.

## MONEY

Banking has come to the Olas Altas district, with the branch of **Banorte** (Av. Olas Altas 246, btwn. Basilio Badillo and Carranza, tel. 322/222-4040, 9am-5pm Mon.-Fri.). After hours, use its ATM. Banorte also has a branch on the Malecón (Paseo Diaz Ordaz 690, tel. 322/222-4040, 9am-5pm Mon.-Fri., 9am-2pm Sat.). ATMs are everywhere in Puerto Vallarta, and you won't have trouble finding one. However, ATM fraud is rampant as well, and so people are advised to use ATMs inside banks, Cashola-brand ATMS (better security), or ATMs that are in very well-lit, well-trafficked places. Be careful, don't give away

your PIN, and change the PIN frequently if you are on an extended trip.

Most downtown banks cluster along Juárez, near the plaza. One exception is **HSBC** (tel. 322/222-0027 or 322/222-0277, 8am-7pm Mon.-Sat.), on Libertad, corner of Carranza, just north of the Insurgentes bridge and open the longest hours of all.

Another option is **Banamex** (Zaragoza 176, at Juárez, south side of the town plaza, tel. 322/226-6110). For money exchange, go to the special booth (9am-4pm Mon.-Fri., 10am-2pm Sat.) to the left of the bank's main entrance.

If the lines at Banamex are too long, try **Scotiabank** (Juárez 374, half a block north of the plaza, tel. 322/222-2745 or 322/223-1221, money exchange hours 9am-5pm Mon.-Fri.) or **Bancomer** across the street (corner of Juárez 450 and Mina, tel. 322/222-1919 or 322/222-3501, 8:30am-4pm Mon.-Fri.). All of these banks have other branches and/or ATMs around town; finding cash is easy, but to say it again for emphasis, ATM fraud has become a major problem in the Puerto Vallarta area, and people are advised to use ATMs with caution.

Additionally, scores of little *casas de cambio* (exchange windows) dot the cobbled Old Town streets, especially along the south end of the Malecón downtown, and along Avenida Olas Altas and Insurgentes south of the Río Cuale. Although they generally offer about $2 per $100 less than the banks, they compensate with long hours, often 9am-9pm daily. In the big hotels, cashiers will generally exchange your money at rates comparable to the downtown exchange booths.

## COMMUNICATIONS

Puerto Vallarta has a number of branch post offices, although my experience with Mexico's international mail service—slow, slow, slow—leads me to advise using email and/or Skype. The main *correo* (Mina 188, tel. 322/223-1360, 9am-5pm Mon.-Fri., 9am-1pm Sat.), with secure Mexpost mail service, is downtown, two blocks north of the central plaza, just off Juárez. There's a branch at the Edificio Maritima (Maritime Building), near the cruise-ship dock (tel. 322/224-7219, 8am-2pm Mon.-Fri., 9am-1pm Sat.), but the airport has lost its post office branch; deposit postcards and letters in the airport mailbox (*buzón*).

To keep in touch by **telephone,** the cheapest and often most convenient option is to simply buy a cell phone for the duration of your trip. You can get one for around $40, buy some minutes, and you're all set. You will find Tel-cel stores and kiosks everywhere in Puerto Vallarta and in most Mexican towns. If you don't have a phone, call from your hotel. Lacking a hotel (or if you don't like its extra charges), go to one of the many *casetas de larga distancia* (long-distance telephone offices), sprinkled all over town.

Puerto Vallarta has a flock of public **Internet** cafés. Ask your hotel desk clerk for the closest one, although the hotel itself will probably have Internet in the lobby if not in your room as well—these days most hotels have Wi-Fi, even the smaller ones. However, if you should need an Internet café, in Old Town the **Café Vayan** (Olas Altas 350, tel. 322/222-0092) has several computers with Internet available for a nominal fee, and Wi-Fi for free if you bring your own and order something. They're open 7am-11pm daily; have an extensive, moderately priced three-meal menu; and have sidewalk and interior seating.

Many locations offer free wireless Internet services, from bars and restaurants to the local shopping centers. If you have your laptop, you probably aren't far from a free signal. **Starbucks** in Plaza Peninsula, in the Nima Bay condo building in the marina, and downtown in the *zocalo* (town square) all offer free Internet with purchase.

## HEALTH AND EMERGENCIES

If you need emergency care, go to one of the Puerto Vallarta hospitals that have 24-hour service: **Amerimed** (on the highway outside the marina at Blvd. F. M. Ascencio 3970, tel. 322/226-2080), **Medasist** (south of Cuale at Dieguez 360, tel. 322/223-0656), and **San Javier** (also near the marina at Blvd. F. M. Ascencio 2760, tel. 322/226-1010).

If, however, you prefer to go to one of Puerto Vallarta's newer hospitals, with a load of diagnostic equipment and a raft of specialists to use it, go to **Cornerstone Hospital** (tel. 322/226-3700), behind Plaza Caracol at Los Tules 136. Alternatively, go to the respected **Hospital CMQ** (Centro Médico Quirúrgico, Basilio Badillo 365, btwn. Insurgentes and Aguacate, tel. 322/223-1919 ground floor or 322/223-0011 second floor), south of the Río Cuale.

For an American-trained English-speaking doctor, Puerto Vallarta visitors enjoy the services of at least two IAMAT (International Association for Medical Assistance to Travelers) doctors: Consult either Dr. Alfonso Rodríguez (Lucerna 148, tel. 322/293-1991) or Dr. Mark Engleman (founder of the Amerimed Hospital, on the airport boulevard, in the marina, tel. 322/226-2080).

Pamela Thompson's firm, **Health Care Resources Puerto Vallarta** (tel. 322/222-9638, www.healthcareresourcespv.com), will connect you with virtually any kind of doctor you might need or care to see, any time of year, in the Puerto Vallarta area. For both travelers and expat residents, its website is the place to go for information about anything from emergencies to cosmetic surgeries.

For round-the-clock prescription service, call or go to the well-stocked 24-hour **Farmacia Guadalajara** (on the Av. Insurgentes corner of Av. Lázaro Cárdenas, south of Cuale, tel. 322/222-0101). Other branches of Farmacia Guadalajara can be found at P. Sanchez 123 (tel. 322/225-8735) and 24 de Febrero 258 (tel. 322/225-5770). Alternatively, try one of the five branches of **Farmacia CMQ,** such as south of Cuale (Basilio Badillo 367, tel. 322/222-1330 or 322/222-2941) or on the north side (Peru 1146, tel. 322/222-1110).

Furthermore, a legion of loyal customers swears by the diagnostic competence of Federico López Casco, of **Farmacia Olas Altas** (Av. Olas Altas 465, tel. 322/222-2374), two blocks south of Hotel Playa Los Arcos, whom they simply know as "Freddy." Although he's a pharmacist and not a physician, his fans say he is a wizard at recommending remedies for their aches and pains.

For **police** emergencies, call the emergency number—060 or 066, or 080 from cell phones, or 322/290-0507 or 322/290-0512. In case of **fire,** call the *bomberos*—the fire department (tel. 322/224-7701).

## IMMIGRATION, CUSTOMS, AND CONSULATES

If you need an extension to your tourist card, you can get a total of 180 days at the local branch of **Instituto Nacional de Migración.** Present your existing tourist card at the office next to the Pemex gas station (upstairs at street number 2755, tel. 322/224-7653 or 322/224-7970, fax 322/224-7719, 9am-1pm Mon.-Fri.), or the office at the airport (tel. 322/221-1380 or 322/221-1325, open 24 hours daily). If you lose your tourist card, go to Migración with your passport or identification and some proof of the day you arrived in Mexico, such as a copy of the original permit or your airplane ticket.

Both the U.S. and Canadian consulates have moved out of downtown. They have retained their local Puerto Vallarta telephone numbers, however. The **U.S. consulate,** which issues passports and does other essential legal work for U.S. citizens, is located on the main Nuevo Vallarta beachfront boulevard (Plaza Paraíso, Paseo de los Cocoteros 85, 2nd Fl., tel./fax 322/222-0069 or 322/223-0074, 8:30am-12:30pm Mon.-Fri.). In an emergency after hours, call the U.S. Consul General in Guadalajara (tel. 333/268-2100 or 333/268-2200).

The **Canadian honorary consul,** who has moved to the Peninsula Plaza (Plaza Peninsula, Local Sub F, Blvd. F. M. Ascencio 2485, tel. 322/293-0098 or 322/293-0099, fax 322/293-2894, 9am-1pm Mon.-Fri.), provides similar services for Canadian citizens. In an emergency or after hours, call the Canadian Embassy in Mexico City (toll-free Mex. tel. 01-800/706-2900).

## SPANISH INSTRUCTION

The **University of Guadalajara Study Center for Foreigners** (Libertad 105, tel. 322/223-2082, fax 322/223-2982, www.cepe.udg.mx)

offers one-, two-, and four-week total-immersion Spanish-language instruction, including home stays with local families. Other programs can be found through various online websites, including www.spanish-school.com.mx/puerto-vallarta, www.amerispan.com/language_schools/Mexico/Puerto_Vallarta, and www.donquijote.org/english/la/puerto-vallarta.asp. Once you're in town, ask around; you'll probably find a class offered in your hotel or somewhere nearby.

## VOLUNTEER WORK

A number of local volunteer clubs and groups invite visitors to their meetings and activities. Check with the tourist information office or see the events calendar and directory pages in *Vallarta Today* or *Vallarta Tribune.* Another good place to look for volunteer opportunities is the website www.vallartainfo.com/puerto-vallarta-notices.html.

The International Friendship Club, or **Club Internacional de la Amistad** (Parian del Puente office complex, Local 13, P.O. Box 604, Puerto Vallarta, Jalisco 48350, tel. 322/222-5466, www.pvmexico.com, 8:30am-12:30pm Mon.-Fri.), an all-volunteer service club, sponsors a number of health, educational, and cultural projects. It welcomes visitors to the (usually second Monday) monthly general membership meeting. For more information, see the events calendar section of *Vallarta Today,* the directory page of the *Vallarta Tribune,* or drop by the office behind the HSBC bank, above the north bank of the Río Cuale Avenida Insurgentes (upper) bridge.

The **Ecology Group of Vallarta** (tel. 322/112-2679), a group of local citizens willing to work for a cleaner Puerto Vallarta, welcomes visitors to its activities and regular meetings.

The **Refugio Infantil Santa Esperanza, A.C.** (R.I.S.E.) shelters children under 14 years of age who have been sent there by DIF, a government agency devoted to protecting children. The refuge is always in need of volunteers, and interested people are welcome to take a tour. Email volunteer coordinator Christian Larson (risevoluntario@gmail.com) to look into this opportunity. Tours can be arranged by Luis Cardona (luiscardona13@hotmail.com) or Chris Amo (chris@cshf-us.org).

The **S.O.S. Animal** (tel. 322/227-5519 or 322/221-0078) protection association is working to humanely reduce the number of stray and abandoned animals on Puerto Vallarta streets. Call for more information, or see the directory page of the *Vallarta Tribune.*

**Children of the Dump** (tel. 322/223-4311, www.childrenofthedumpvallarta.org), a local nonprofit that has been working for more than 10 years on improving education and providing assistance for the children in Puerto Vallarta's poorest neighborhood, is always in need of classroom helpers or teachers. For those willing to commit to several months of time, a small stipend is available. Children of the Dump also offers free tours of the neighborhoods surrounding the municipal dump. During the tours you will see how the other side of Puerto Vallarta lives, participate in the hot lunch program, and meet the children who attend the **School of Champions,** the free after-school program for children ages 5-13. Tours can be arranged through Arthur Fumerton via the organization's phone number or website.

# Getting There

Dozens of air departures, hundreds of long-distance buses, and a good paved highway network speed thousands of travelers to and from Puerto Vallarta daily.

## BY AIR

Several major carriers connect Puerto Vallarta by direct flights with U.S. and Mexican destinations.

**Aerocalafia Airlines** (flight information tel. 322/222-0486 or 322/222-9581, reservations toll-free Mex. tel. 01-800/560-3949) connects with Los Cabos.

**Aeroméxico** (tel. 322/224-2777) flights connect daily with Los Angeles (through Guadalajara), Tijuana, Guadalajara, Acapulco, León, Monterrey, and Mexico City.

**Alaska Airlines** (reservations toll-free Mex. tel. 01-800/426-0333) flights connect with Los Angeles, San Francisco, and Seattle; for arrival and departure information, call the airport (tel. 322/221-1350 or 322/221-2610).

**American Airlines** (tel. 322/221-1927) flights connect with Dallas-Fort Worth and Chicago seasonally.

**Aviacsa** airlines (flight information tel. 322/221-3095 or 322/221-2624, reservations toll-free Mex. tel. 01-800/735-5396) connects with Mexico City.

**Continental Airlines** (tel. 322/221-1025 or toll-free Mex. tel. 01-800/900-5000) flights connect with Houston, San Francisco, Los Angeles, New York, and Chicago.

**Frontier Airlines** (toll-free U.S. tel. 800/432-1359, www.frontierairlines.com) flights connect with Denver, Kansas City, and Chicago.

**United Airlines** (flight information tel. 322/222-3264, reservations toll-free Mex. tel. 01-800/003-0777) flights connect with San Francisco and Los Angeles through Houston.

**U.S. Airlines** (flight information tel. 322/221-1333, reservations in Mexico toll-free U.S. tel. 800/428-4322) flights connect with Phoenix and Los Angeles.

**West Jet** (toll-free U.S. tel. 888/937-8538) charter flights connect with several Canadian cities (Toronto, Winnipeg, Saskatoon, Regina, Calgary-Edmonton, and Vancouver), mostly during the winter. **Other charters** that connect with Puerto Vallarta from a number of U.S. cities seasonally are USA 3000, Funjet, Transmeridian, and Apple Vacations. Contact a local travel agent.

## Airport Arrival and Departure

Air arrival at Puerto Vallarta Airport (code-designated PVR, officially Gustavo Díaz Ordaz International) is generally smooth and simple. After the cursory (if any) customs check, arrivals can avail themselves of two 24-hour ATMs and a money-exchange counter open 9am-6pm daily. The airport virtually doubled in size with a new terminal wing completed in 2011 and now sports an international-style array of shops, restaurants, and duty-free stores. A lineup of car rental booths includes **Advantage** (tel. 322/221-1499), **Alamo** (tel. 322/221-1228), **Avis** (tel. 322/221-1112), **Budget** (tel. 322/221-1730), **Dollar** (tel. 322/221-1985), **Europcar** (tel. 322/209-0921), and **National** (tel. 322/221-1226). All that said, I find **Gecko Car Rentals** (tel. 329/298-0339, www.geckorentcar.com) to be the best in Puerto Vallarta (though they are located in Bucerías) because they don't try to sell you extra, expensive, and often unnecessary insurance. Plus they will deliver your car to you or you to your car, whichever works, and throw in board racks if you have surfboards. You might also save money with an air-and-car package or by reserving with a discount (such as AARP, AAA, senior, airline, credit card, or others) before you leave for Mexico.

**Transportation to town** is easiest by *colectivo* (collective taxi-van) or *taxi especial* (individual taxi). Booths sell tickets at curbside. The regulated *colectivo* fare runs about $6 per person to the northern hotel zone, $7 to the center of town, and $8 or more to hotels and hamlets south of town. Individual taxis (for up to four passengers) run about $15, $16, and $25 for the same rides.

Taxis to more distant northern destinations, such as Sayulita (30 mi/50 km), San Francisco (32 mi/53 km), Rincón de Guayabitos (39 mi/62 km), and San Blas or Tepic (100 mi/160 km), run about $50, $60, $108, and $170, respectively. A much cheaper alternative is to walk over the pedestrian bridge spanning Highway 200 outside the terminal and catch a northbound bus. Just make sure the bus is going to your destination—read the sign, or ask the driver or passengers onboard. Sayulita, for example, is 2 miles (3.2 km) from the highway, and buses headed up to Compostela or Tepic don't make that side trip to Sayulita.

**Airport departure** is as simple as arrival. Save by sharing a taxi with departing fellow hotel guests. Agree on the fare with the driver before you get in. If the driver seems too greedy, hail another taxi.

If you've lost your tourist card, arrive early and be prepared with a copy, or you may have to pay a fine unless you've gotten a duplicate through Migración. In any case, be sure to save enough pesos or dollars to pay your **departure tax** (unless your ticket already includes it—most if not all tickets do these days).

## BY CAR OR RV

Three road routes connect Puerto Vallarta north with Tepic and San Blas, east with Guadalajara, and south via Melaque-Barra de Navidad with Manzanillo.

To Tepic, **Mexican National Highway 200** is all asphalt and in good condition for most of its 104 miles (167 km) from Puerto Vallarta. Traffic is ordinarily light to moderate, except for some slow going around Tepic, and over a few low passes about 20 miles (32.2 km) north of Puerto Vallarta. Allow three hours for the southbound trip and half an hour longer in the reverse direction for the winding 3,000-foot climb to Tepic.

A shortcut connects San Blas directly with Puerto Vallarta, avoiding the oft-congested uphill route through Tepic. Heading north on Highway 200, at Las Varas turn off west onto Nayarit Highway 16 to Zacualpan and Platanitos, where the road continues through the coastal tropical forest to Santa Cruz village on the Bay of Matanchén. From there you can continue along the shoreline to San Blas. In the opposite direction, heading south from San Blas, follow the signed Puerto Vallarta turnoff to the right (south) a few hundred yards after the Santa Cruz de Miramar junction. Allow about three hours, either direction, for the entire San Blas-Puerto Vallarta trip.

The story is similar for Mexican National Highway 200 along the 172 miles (276 km) to Manzanillo via Barra de Navidad (134 mi/214 km). Trucks and a few potholes may cause slow going while climbing the 2,400-foot Sierra Cuale summit south of Puerto Vallarta, but light traffic should prevail along the other stretches. Allow about four hours to Manzanillo, three to Barra de Navidad, and the same in the opposite direction.

The Guadalajara route is nearly as easy. From Puerto Vallarta, follow Highway 200 as if to Tepic, but, just before Compostela (80 mi/129 km from Puerto Vallarta) follow the 22-mile (36-km) Guadalajara-bound *cuota* (toll) shortcut east, via Chapalilla. From Chapalilla, connect seamlessly east via **Mexican National Highway 15 D** *cuota autopista*. Although expensive (about $50 per car, much more for motor homes), the expressway is a breeze compared to the narrow, winding, and congested *libre* Highway 15. Allow around five hours at the wheel for the entire 214-mile (344-km) Guadalajara-Puerto Vallarta trip, either way (seven hours by the old *libre* route).

All of these roads, excepting perhaps the newest sections of the major toll roads, are best traveled by day. The basic rule of thumb is driving at night in Mexico is a bad idea for a number of reasons: bad lighting, unexpected potholes, unmarked construction zones, unmarked *topes* (speed bumps), drunk drivers, loose cows or horses, bike riders without lights—the usual suspects. Also, day and night there are many large, slow-moving trucks on the highways, and when they're going uphill, they go even slower; should you get stuck behind one on a two-lane road with no passing lane, don't get impatient and try to pass on a curve. Don't rush it, and take it slow and easy. There are already plenty of aggressive drivers out there.

## BY BUS

Many bus lines run through Puerto Vallarta. The major long-distance bus action is at the **Camionera Central** (Central Bus Station) about a mile north of the airport. Reservations and ticketing are efficiently computerized, and most major lines accept credit cards. The shiny, air-conditioned complex resembles an airline terminal, with a cafeteria, juice bars, a travel agency, a long-distance telephone and fax service, luggage storage lockers, a gift shop, and

a hotel reservation office (tel. 322/290-1014). The buses are usually crowded; don't tempt people with a dangling open purse or a bulging wallet in your pocket.

Mostly first- and luxury-class departure ticket counters line one long wall. First-class **Elite** and its parent **Estrella Blanca** (tel. 322/290-1001), with its affiliated lines Turistar, Futura, Transportes Norte de Sonora, and Transportes Chihuahenses, connect the entire northwest-southeast Pacific Coast corridor. Northwesterly destinations include La Peñita (Rincón de Guayabitos), Tepic, San Blas, Mazatlán, and all the way to Nogales or Mexicali and Tijuana on the U.S. border. Other departures head north, via Tepic, Torreón, and Chihuahua to Ciudad Juárez, at the U.S. border. Still others connect northeast, via Guadalajara, Aguascalientes, Zacatecas, and Saltillo, with Monterrey, where quick connections are available with the east Texas border at Matamoros. In the opposite direction, departures connect with the entire southeast Pacific Coast, including Melaque-Barra de Navidad, Manzanillo, Playa Azul junction, Lázaro Cárdenas, Ixtapa-Zihuatanejo, and Acapulco (where you can transfer to Oaxaca-bound departures). Additionally, **Transportes Norte de Sonora** (TNS) departures connect north with San Blas via the coastal (Tepic bypass) shortcut.

Competing first-class line **TAP** (tel. 322/290-0119 or 322/290-1001), Transportes y Autobuses del Pacífico, provides about the same first-class northwest Pacific service as both Elite and Transportes Pacífico.

**Transportes Pacífico** (tel. 322/290-1008) offers first-class departures (for cash only) that also travel the northwest Pacific route, via Tepic and Mazatlán to Nogales, Mexicali, and Tijuana. Transportes Pacífico provides additional first-class connections east with Guadalajara and Mexico City direct, and others to Guadalajara by expressway shortcut (*corta*).

Transportes Pacífico also provides very frequent second-class daytime connections north with Tepic, stopping everywhere, notably Bucerías, Sayulita, Guayabitos, La Peñita, Las

Varas, and Compostela en route. The Bucerías bus fare should run less than $2, Sayulita $4, Guayabitos about $5, and Tepic or San Blas $7. (For San Blas, go by Transportes Norte de Sonora direct or Transportes Pacífico second-class and transfer at Las Varas.)

Affiliated lines **Autocamiones del Pacífico** and **Transportes Cihuatlán** (tel. 322/290-0994) provide many second-class and some first-class departures along the Jalisco coast. Frequent second-class connections stop at El Tuito, Tomatlán, El Super, Careyes, Melaque, Barra de Navidad, and everywhere in between. They also connect with Guadalajara by the long southern route, via Melaque, Autlán, and San Clemente (a jumping-off point for Talpa, Mascota, and San Sebastián). **Primera Plus,** its luxury-class line, provides a few daily express connections southeast with Manzanillo, with stops at Melaque and Barra de Navidad.

A separate luxury-class service, a subsidiary of Flecha Amarilla, also called **Primera Plus** (tel. 322/290-0716 or toll-free Mex. tel. 01-800/375-7587), also provides express connections southeast with Melaque, Barra de Navidad, Manzanillo, and Colima. Other such Primera Plus departures connect east with Lake Chapala and Guadalajara, continuing to Aguascalientes, Irapuato, Celaya, Querétaro, and León. Affiliated line **Autobuses Costa Alegre** provides frequent second-class connections southeast along the Jalisco coast, via El Tuito, El Super, Careyes, Melaque, Barra de Navidad, and all points in between.

Additionally, **ETN** (Enlaces Transportes Nacional, tel. 322/223-2999 or 322/290-0997) provides first-class departures connecting east with Guadalajara and Mexico City, offering continuing connections in Guadalajara with several Michoacán destinations.

# Getting Around

## BY BUS

Since nearly all through traffic flows along one long thoroughfare, Puerto Vallarta bus transportation is a snap. Puerto Vallarta is blessed by a large squadron of buses, operated by both private companies and bus drivers' cooperatives. They run north-south, beginning at their south-of-Cuale terminus on the east (Calle Pino Suárez) side of Plaza Lázaro Cárdenas. From Plaza Lázaro Cárdenas, all buses head north. Most of them (marked "Centro") pass through the downtown center northbound along Avenida Juárez. A few other buses, marked "Tunel," bypass the downtown center via a tunnel uphill, east of downtown, and continue along the foothill *libramiento* boulevard and rejoin the main-route buses on the northbound side of thoroughfare Bulevar Francisco Ascencio at the Zona Hotelera. From there, the major bus terminals (marked prominently on the bus windshields) are at Pitillal (at the north end of the Zona Hotelera), the marina, and the Las Palmas, Juntas, and Ixtapa suburbs, farther north.

The Puerto Vallarta bus system is a simple learn-as-you-go (no tourist passes, transit maps, nor set schedules) expanded version of the original village system of two generations ago. However, it's efficient and very safe, except perhaps for an occasional pickpocket when crowded. Be sure to keep your purse buttoned and your wallet secure in your waist belt.

Buses run daily between about 5:30am and 10pm, at two-minute intervals during peak hours, five-minute intervals nonpeak. Have enough coins (*monedas*) in hand to pay your 8- to 12-peso (around US$0.60-0.90) tariff to the driver, who can usually change small bills (but will not take dollars). All buses eventually return to their south-end terminus, at Plaza Lázaro Cárdenas a few blocks south of the Río Cuale. Northbound, from Plaza Lázaro Cárdenas, buses retrace their routes to one of several important stops scrawled across their windows. Destinations on the north side, from closest in to farthest north, are the Centro (town center, 1-2 mi/1.6-3.2 km, 5 minutes), Zona Hotelera (Hotel Zone, 3-5 mi/4.8-8 km, 10-15 minutes), Pitillal (5 mi/8 km, 15 minutes), Marina Vallarta (7 mi/11.3 km, 20 minutes), the airport (8 mi/12.9 km, 22 minutes), Camionera Central (long-distance bus station, 10 mi/16.1 km, 24 minutes), Las Palmas (11 mi/17.7 km, 25 minutes), Juntas (13 mi/20.9 km, 28 minutes), and Ixtapa (15 mi/24.1 km, 33 minutes). Since the buses headed to the destinations farthest north stop at all of the intermediate destinations, you can go everywhere you are likely to want to go by hopping on buses marked "Las Palmas," "Juntas," or "Ixtapa."

Hint: If you're headed to downtown north of the Río Cuale, be sure to take a "Centro"-marked bus (not a "Tunel"-marked bus that bypasses the town center by going through the tunnel and along the uphill *libramiento* bypass). On the other hand, from south of Cuale, if you want to get to north-side destinations (Zona Hotelera, marina, airport) in a hurry, you should take the "Tunel"-marked bus.

Two other **local bus terminals** serve Puerto Vallarta. For south-end destinations of Mismaloya and Boca de Tomatlán, catch one of the minibuses marked "Mismaloya" or "Boca" that leave from the south-of-Cuale corner of Constitución and Calle Basilio Badillo, just below Insurgentes.

On the other hand, for the northwesterly Bay of Banderas destinations of Bucerías, Cruz de Huanacaxtle, and Punta de Mita, go by **Autotransportes Medina** buses that you can conveniently catch either at their downtown north-side station (1410 Brasil, tel. 322/212-4732 or 322/222-7279) or on the main boulevard, northbound side, across from the Hotel Sheraton.

## BY CAR

Congestion and lack of parking space (or enough parking garages) reduce the desirability of doing much driving of your own car or a rental car around downtown Puerto Vallarta. Nevertheless, for excursions outside of town, a car adds flexibility, convenience, and economy over the price of a guided tour, especially if you share costs with other passengers. Expect to pay about $40-65 a day for the cheapest rental, including legally required liability insurance. Make sure you ask about insurance as many of the rental companies will try to sell you unnecessary extra insurance. Read the fine print. Car rental companies have booths at the airport.

If you're coming into town along the ingress boulevard from the north, follow the *libramiento* downtown bypass that forks left at the big Barra de Navidad sign over the boulevard. It leads you quickly to the less-congested south-of-Cuale Old Town neighborhood. There, either park your car and walk, or take a taxi. If you still insist on driving, go north along one-way Avenida Insurgentes, cross the Río Cuale bridge, bear left three blocks along Libertad, then right into the town center along Juárez, where you will eventually be able to find a parking place.

There are several parking garages now in place, although hours vary. Some are open 24 hours, and others close late at night. Be sure to check before you leave the garage. The garages are: Parque Hildalgo, at the northern end of the Malecón; Juárez parking garage, at the south end of the Malecón; and one more in Zona Romantía, under the Parque Lazaro Cardenas. Rates run about $1 an hour, and several restaurants and businesses offer parking validation for the Juárez garage (see cashier for a list). Due to the major construction that happens throughout the city, for large cars and trucks especially, parking in a garage is a smart choice.

## BY TAXI

Taxis are all private, convenient, safe, and relatively cheap (about $4-8 per trip within the city limits; verify rates at your hotel desk). Most taxi drivers will quote you the correct going rate. If not, bring him to his senses by hailing another taxi. Under any circumstances, don't get in until the price is settled. Most hotels have basic fares to the most popular destinations posted near their lobby doors, so you should know what to expect.

## WALKING AND BIKING

Walking is by far the best choice for getting around downtown Puerto Vallarta. The heart of the Old Town, north and south of the river, stretches barely a mile and a half (2.5 km), a 30-minute walk north-south, and a 0.5-mile (0.6 km) 10-minute walk east-west. Bicycles, while available for rent ($10/day) downtown, are not a very safe way to travel, given the many buses and fast drivers who either don't see or ignore bicycles. Moreover, bicycles are a burden in Puerto Vallarta's hilly Old Town neighborhoods.

# AROUND THE BAY OF BANDERAS

Once upon a time, Puerto Vallarta was *the* destination for tourists and snowbirds headed into central Pacific Mexico, but with the city's explosive development and limited space due to the buttress of mountains at its back, growth along the sandy northern shores of the Bay of Banderas was inevitable. Now many people skip the urban setting of Puerto Vallarta entirely, instead

© JUSTIN HENDERSON

# HIGHLIGHTS

LOOK FOR ◖ TO FIND RECOMMENDED SIGHTS, ACTIVITIES, DINING, AND LODGING.

Playa Anclote

Islas Marietas

*Bahía de Banderas*

San Sebastián

Puerto Vallarta

Laguna Juanacatlán

Mascota Museum and Casa de Cultura

Virgin of Talpa Basilica

0        20 mi

0    20 km

© AVALON TRAVEL

◖ **Playa Anclote:** Spend the day lounging on the beach, enjoying a surfing or stand-up paddleboarding lesson, or taking an excursion to the Islas Marietas for bird-, dolphin-, and whale-watching (page 125).

◖ **Islas Marietas:** An aquatic wonderland, this protected marine park provides myriad opportunities for swimming, snorkeling, scuba diving, and viewing rare blue-footed boobies (page 128).

◖ **San Sebastián:** This hidden mountain hamlet can be visited in a day by car or bus. Spend a few hours strolling the little plaza and the cobbled streets, as well as visiting the Hacienda Jalisco, a coffee farm, and perhaps an old gold mine (page 132).

◖ **Mascota Museum and Casa de Cultura:** Admire the Mascota Museum's lovingly displayed memorabilia collection and the Casa de Cultura's fascinating 3,000-year-old ceramics (page 142).

◖ **Laguna Juanacatlán:** Enjoy an overnight at the Sierra Lago Resort and Spa on the luscious spruce-tufted lakeshore (page 149).

◖ **Virgin of Talpa Basilica:** Visit the Virgin of Talpa in her basilica and the nearby museum. If possible, attend one of Talpa's four tumultuous annual festivals honoring the Virgin (page 150).

BAY OF BANDERAS

opting for the megaresorts of Nuevo Vallarta or the bucolic towns that ring the bay and nestle into the majestic mountain range that rises behind Vallarta.

In the smaller towns, the accommodations and services are fewer but tend to be more authentic and usually more affordable. The beaches are usually less crowded, and the outdoor recreational opportunities are more varied and exciting than those in the big city. These smaller towns offer a glimpse of what Puerto Vallarta might have been like before becoming a major tourist destination.

The golden northwestern beaches and boutique resorts of Bucerías, La Cruz de Huanacaxtle, and Punta Mita beckon within sight of downtown Puerto Vallarta. They decorate the long shoreline that curves north and west to the Bay of Banderas's farthest northern point, at Punta de Mita. With the onslaught of condominium complexes and megaresorts, it's difficult to believe that you can still find an empty stretch of beach to call your own along this well-trod shoreline, but with a little luck, and/or a boat with an open agenda and a willing captain, it's true. There's plenty of opportunity for surfing, sailing, snorkeling, fishing, stand-up paddleboarding, kiteboarding, and swimming,

BAY OF BANDERAS

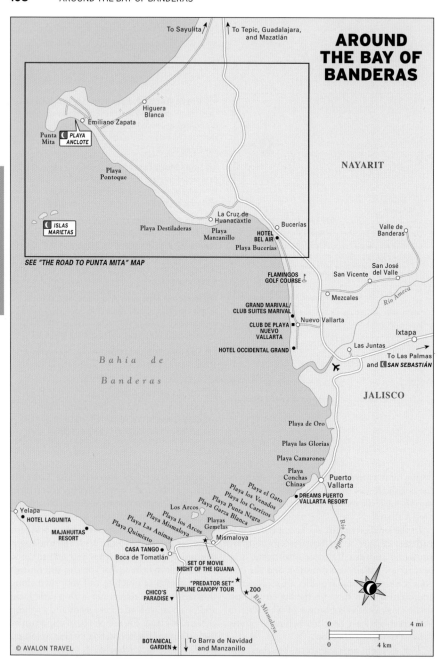

AROUND
THE BAY OF
BANDERAS

To Sayulita
To Tepic, Guadalajara,
and Mazatlán

Higuera
Blanca

Emiliano Zapata

Punta
Mita

PLAYA
ANCLOTE

NAYARIT

Playa
Pontoque

ISLAS
MARIETAS

La Cruz de
Huanacaxtle

Playa Destiladeras

Playa
Manzanillo

Bucerías

Valle de
Banderas

HOTEL
BEL AIR

Playa Bucerías

SEE "THE ROAD TO PUNTA MITA" MAP

FLAMINGOS
GOLF COURSE

San Vicente

San José
del Valle

Mezcales

Río Ameca

GRAND MARIVAL/
CLUB SUITES MARIVAL

CLUB DE PLAYA
NUEVO
VALLARTA

Nuevo Vallarta

Ixtapa

Las Juntas

To Las Palmas
and SAN SEBASTIÁN

HOTEL OCCIDENTAL GRAND

Bahía de
Banderas

JALISCO

Playa de Oro

Playa las Glorias

Playa Camarones

Playa
Conchas
Chinas

Puerto
Vallarta

Playa el Gato

Playa los Venados

Playa los Carrizos

DREAMS PUERTO
VALLARTA RESORT

Playa Punta Negra

Yelapa

HOTEL LAGUNITA

Los Arcos

Playa Garza Blanca

Playas
Gemelas

Playa los Arcos

MAJAHUITAS
RESORT

Playa Mismaloya

Río Cuale

Playa Las Animas

Mismaloya

Playa Quimixto

CASA TANGO

Boca de Tomatlán

SET OF MOVIE
NIGHT OF THE IGUANA

"PREDATOR SET"
ZIPLINE CANOPY TOUR

ZOO

CHICO'S
PARADISE

Río Mismaloya

0        4 mi

0        4 km

BOTANICAL
GARDEN

To Barra de Navidad
and Manzanillo

© AVALON TRAVEL

© KOKOPHOTO/ISTOCKPHOTO

fishing boats on a beach in Bucerías

BAY OF BANDERAS

north of Puerto Vallarta. There you can shop in the colorful warren of marketplace stalls near the town square, swim or beachcomb the several miles of burnt-sugar beaches, and end your day with crab enchiladas and a dazzling Pacific sunset at a beachfront restaurant like **Mar y Sol.**

With a day or two more, you might grab a room at one of the local hotels or B&Bs and stay awhile, or head a bit farther around the bay to **La Cruz de Huanacaxtle,** home to a beautiful marina that draws big boats, and big bucks, from up the coast. Here you might book a day trip on a catamaran and explore the Marietas, or have a picnic and snorkeling adventure at one of the bayside beaches unreachable by car or foot. Farther out on the coastal road that follows the bay's shoreline, the once pristine and isolated **Punta de Mita** has become host to a gated compound containing a slew of high-end luxury resorts and golf courses, but between La Cruz and Punta Mita there are still a couple of beaches available for public access, and more if you hire a boat. This stretch is well-known for its several excellent surf spots. If you want to chase some waves, splurge on a luxury room on the beach, or opt for one of the still affordable, more spartan hotels just off the beach, and see what the swells might bring you.

For Puerto Vallarta's **mountain country,** go by either bus, sturdy passenger car or SUV, or charter flight tour (very expensive). In one long day, you can visit **San Sebastián,** enjoy lunch, stroll around the village square, visit a historic hacienda or an old gold mine, and return to Puerto Vallarta.

If you have two or more days, you can continue on to **Mascota** for an overnight or two in one of its comfortable hotels. Stroll around the town, visit the **Raoul Rodríguez Museum** and the **Casa de Cultura,** and maybe camp on the pine-shaded shoreline of **Corinches Reservoir.** Spend another day visiting the picturesque villages of **Yerbabuena, Cimarrón Chico,** and **Navidad.** Alternatively, drive out in a different direction from Mascota and spend a day, maybe an overnight, at pristine high-sierra **Laguna Juanacatlán** and Sierra Lago Resort and Spa.

or just spending the day shopping and gallery hopping, and then winding down with a cool margarita under a beachside *palapa,* watching the waves break on the shores of the bay.

On the other hand, the Sierra Cuale, which rises to the east behind Puerto Vallarta's downtown streets, remains relatively untrafficked by tourists and offers unique opportunities for adventurous travelers. In and around the petite mountain-country towns of San Sebastián, Mascota, and Talpa you can explore old gold mines and picturesque hidden villages; camp or lodge at pine-shadowed lakes and streams; trek by foot or horseback through sylvan, wildlife-rich mountain valleys by day; and relax in comfortable small hotels and luxurious haciendas by night. All this awaits travelers who venture into Puerto Vallarta's backyard mountains.

## PLANNING YOUR TIME

To reach the **northwestern bay beaches,** follow Highway 200 north by car, bus, or tour. If you're on a short time budget, go for a day to **Bucerías,** a medium-size town just 25 minutes

With another day, continue on to the fascinating pilgrimage town of **Talpa.** Visit the **Virgin of Talpa Basilica,** adored by hundreds of thousands of yearly pilgrims.

## GETTING TO NUEVO VALLARTA, BUCERÍAS, AND PUNTA MITA

**Autotransportes Medina** (Brasil 1410, tel. 322/212-4732 or 322/222-7279) buses complete a flood of daily round-trips between Playa Anclote (Restaurant El Dorado terminal) and the Puerto Vallarta station, north of the Malecón. Buses leave every 7 minutes for Punta Mita (23 pesos, dollars not accepted) and every 10 minutes for Nuevo Vallarta (13 pesos, dollars not accepted). In Puerto Vallarta, walk or hire a taxi to the terminal, or catch the bus as it heads north along the airport boulevard through the Zona Hotelera. Stops en route include Nuevo Vallarta, Bucerías, La Cruz de Huanacaxtle, Piedra Blanca, and Destiladeras, but the driver will stop pretty much anywhere if you

ask. The last bus returns to Puerto Vallarta at about 9pm.

Taxis are available but expensive, with fares running as much as $75 or more for a one-way trip to Punta Mita. The shared white minivans are more affordable and can be waved down nearly anywhere on the highway. For a more leisurely or extended trip, a rental car would be a good investment (approx. $60 per day from the airport).

**Water taxi** service now links Puerto Vallarta (boarding at the half-finished pier on Playa los Muertos) with Nuevo Vallarta as well as La Cruz de Huanacaxtle and Marina Vallarta. There are departures 9am-5pm every hour on the half hour Monday, Wednesday, and Friday, on the hour Tuesday, Thursday, and Saturday, $14 one-way, $22 round-trip, about 30 minutes each way. The same guys (tel. 322/221-1863, ask for Captain George) also offer a wildlife tour in the swampy canals behind Nuevo Vallarta, where there are plentiful birds and iguanas, as well as more than a few crocodiles.

# Nuevo Vallarta

When planning a trip to Puerto Vallarta, new visitors sometimes book a room in Nuevo Vallarta, thinking that Nuevo Vallarta is part of or even close to Puerto Vallarta. This is not the case. Nuevo Vallarta lies 15-20 minutes north of the Puerto Vallarta Airport, which is already 15 minutes out of town. Nuevo Vallarta is located west of Highway 200, once you've crossed the river into the state of Nayarit. With few exceptions, there is little to do and see in Nuevo Vallarta outside of the mega beach resort complexes and golf courses. Nuevo Vallarta is a bit like the Disneyland version of Mexico or an outpost of Southern California. The streets are perfectly paved, the tropical landscaping is perfectly groomed, the gates are guarded, and most of the Mexicans one encounters are bilingual, extremely polite, and work in the resort or service industries. You'll find very

little to remind you of the more authentic Mexico that you will experience if you stay in less-controlled environments.

Let's face it: This is Resortlandia. There are now at least a dozen resort complexes in Nuevo Vallarta, most of them massive. The beachfront is lined with these giant hotels (or equally large condominiums) almost all the way to Bucerías, excepting a few vacant lots here and there. Most of them are mid-priced to high-end all-inclusives, with multiple restaurants, pools, spas, gyms, bars and sports bars, nightclubs, and everything else you could dream up and cram into a resort. But they are not quite cookie-cutter properties; there are variations in scale and quality. Truth is, these days many people like knowing exactly how much their vacation is going to cost, and one way to control cost is to go the all-inclusive route.

## GOLF

The centerpiece of Nuevo Vallarta is **El Tigre** (Paseo Paraiso 800, Casa Club El Tigre, Paradise Village Golf & Country Club, tel. 322/297-0773, www.eltigregolf.com), an 18-hole, par-72 course, which while mostly flat makes use of water and sand to make things interesting. Many national and international tournaments take place at El Tigre. Greens fee is $155 for morning and $100 for afternoon, high season, $125 morning, $86 afternoon, low season, including cart, bottled water, practice balls, and cold towels.

A bit farther north, the palm-shaded 18-hole **Los Flamingos Golf Course** (Hwy. 200, Km 145, 8 mi/13 km north of the airport, tel. 329/296-5006 from Puerto Vallarta, www.flamingosgolf.com.mx, 7am-5pm daily) offers an alternative to El Tigre. Open to the public, Los Flamingos services include carts, caddies, club rentals, a pro shop, restaurant, and locker rooms. The greens fees are $140 for morning and $90 for afternoon, high season, $111 morning, $76 afternoon, low season. My golfing friends proclaim Flamingos to be the most "Mexican" of all the golf courses in the Puerto Vallarta area, and by that I think they mean the least expensive, least pretentious, and most welcoming to visiting golfers.

## SAILING

**Vallarta Yacht Club** (Paseo de los Cocoteros, next door to the Paradise Village mall, tel. 322/297-2222, www.vallartayachtclub.com) has reciprocal arrangements with many yacht clubs around the world and offers nonmembers two free visits. Club amenities include a full-service staff, swimming pool, BBQ area, and a very good and reasonably priced restaurant, which offers the same menu to the public at about a 20 percent markup from members' prices. The club emphasizes social activities and offers a junior sailing program. Members can participate in the several regattas and other events that take place throughout the year.

For those looking to charter a sailboat or even take sailing lessons, **J World** (tel. 322/226-6767, toll-free U.S. tel. 800/910-1101, www.sailing-jworld.com) is in Paradise Village. Head through the gates and past the caged tigers, then down toward the water, to find their offices.

## SHOPPING

Other than the usual overpriced hotel gift stores and boutiques, and beach vendors, there isn't a lot of shopping in Nuevo Vallarta, save for the large **Paradise Village** mall (Paseo de los Cocoteros, 9am-6pm daily). Inside the mall you will find a number of fast food joints, restaurants, a midsized grocery store, and several bank branches. There are many shops to browse, and though the prices are not what you'd call south-of-the-border cheap, you'll find some interesting leather goods at Huante, Mexican wedding shirts at Guayaberass, jewelry and watches at Tesoro de Taxco, beach wear at Palo de Rosa and La Palapa, Asian decorative items at Lombok, and organic bath products at Bambu. There is also a factory tequila store, Casa Cofradia, and the Hikuri Huichol Gallery. But this is more like shopping American-style; unless you plan on skipping Puerto Vallarta, save your pesos for a trip into town.

## ACCOMMODATIONS

Nearly all of the hotel offerings in Nuevo Vallarta are expensive and/or all-inclusive. Most also offer time-shares. This means that you will be invited to a "welcome gathering" or a free tour of the hotel's time-share units and breakfast on at least one day during your stay. If you're not interested, simply decline the invitation, or grin and bear it, since these days many time-share salespeople will actually pay you a couple of hundred dollars just to show up. If not money, many hotels will offer free gifts for attending these presentations, and the quality of the gift is entirely dependent on the attendee's negotiating skills. Tough negotiators will walk out with cold, hard cash or, at the very least, a pair of expensive tour tickets.

According to salespeople who work in the Nuevo Vallarta market, the most aggressive time-share sellers work for the Mayan Group,

# BAY OF BANDERAS BY BOAT

Each year, thousands of people who visit Puerto Vallarta charter sailing or fishing boats, but hundreds of people sail and cruise down the Pacific Coast of Mexico to stay for a little or long while as well. The coastline is scenic, the waters calm, and Pacific Mexico is well-known for its wonderful sportfishing opportunities.

In addition to the fishing and recreational boating opportunities, there are boat shows, fishing tournaments, and sailing regattas. Find out additional information from the four marinas that serve the Puerto Vallarta and Bay of Banderas areas:

- **Marina Vallarta:** Quite possibly one of the largest marina complexes in Mexico, Marina Vallarta is set on almost 500 acres of land that includes a 500-slip marina, an 18-hole golf course, multiple fine hotels, and a marina-side Malecón with galleries, restaurants, spas, and boutiques. It's located just south of the Puerto Vallarta airport at the large statue of Neptune.

- **Marina Nuevo Vallarta:** Located in the tony Nuevo Vallarta area just over the border of Nayarit, the petite Marina Nuevo Vallarta (www.marinanuevovallarta.com) is another option for cruisers stopping off in the Bay of Banderas. It offers 80 berths and services like showers, electric, water, and Wi-Fi access.

- **Paradise Village Marina:** Paradise Village is home to a 200-slip marina (www.paradisevillagemarina.com), a luxury resort complex, and the **Vallarta Yacht Club.** Fuel is not available on-site; you must go to nearby Marina Vallarta for that, but there are plenty of opportunities for shopping, dining, and recreation.

- **Marina Riviera Nayarit:** Based in the growing village of **La Cruz de Huanacaxtle,** Marina Riviera Nayarit (www.marinarivieranayarit.com) is the newest marina in the Bay of Banderas area. While the 351-slip marina is complete, along with the yacht club, sky bar, and fuel station, there are still plans to add a five-star hotel, several condo towers, and retail commercial spaces to the complex.

which owns a massive chunk of beachfront territory at the south end of Nuevo Vallarta and is seemingly planning to build a hundred thousand time-share hotel rooms on their acreage (there are dozens of buildings done or under construction), along with a train to deliver guests to their Mayan racks from a centralized parking zone somewhere near Highway 200. This Mayan organization has a reputation for the hard sell; if you are heading to Nuevo Vallarta and don't want to be subjected to a sales pitch, it's best to avoid them.

No one wants to pay the rack rate on these hotels, so be sure to book in advance. Normally, you can get a good discount by purchasing a package or booking directly from the website of the hotel, where promotions and specials are listed.

One of Nuevo Vallarta's first world-class hotels is **Marival Resort & Suites** (Blvd. Nuevo Vallarta y Paseo Cocoteros, tel. 322/226-8200, toll-free Mex. tel. 01-800/774-6158, fax 322/297-0160, www.gomarival.com), a palmy Mediterranean-style French-Canadian-owned twin development. Its older (circa 1990) section, the **ClubSuites Marival,** sits beside the new, shinier **Grand Marival.** The day-use rate is $75 per person, 10am-5pm. The all-inclusive package here includes all the usual food, drink, and fun stuff, plus some extras: rock climbing, soccer, pool tables, Xbox, table tennis, and darts for teens; a kids' club with minigolf, movies, and camping nights; a renovated gym; and cooking and Spanish lessons daily. If you take a room in the Grand Marival, the all-inclusive food, lodging, and activities run about $212 per day for two in low season, $386 high. The Club section, being half a block from the beach, is cheaper by about $10 per person. If you reserve through an agent, be sure to ask for a package or promotional price. The hotel's own website offers all kinds of package deals—be sure and have a look. You'll pay extra for snorkeling, scuba diving, and fishing trips, but all other water sports are included.

A little ways south down the boulevard is the **Occidental Grand Nuevo Vallarta** (Paseo de los Cocoteros 18, tel. 322/226-9800, toll-free Mex. tel. 01-800/907-9500, toll-free U.S./Can. tel. 800/858-2258, fax 322/297-0082, www. occidental-hoteles.com), offering a similar all-inclusive vacation package for about $190 for two in low season, $240 high. Children are 50 percent off. Day passes are $55, evening passes $65. Bargain packages—which can cut your rack rate by as much as 50 percent—are often available by Internet reservation, through agents during nonpeak seasons, or if you book well in advance.

At the far north end of Nuevo Vallarta, on Flamingos Beach just a few hundred yards south of Bucerías, is the **Bel Air Collection Resort & Spa** (Blvd. Costero 800, tel. 322/226-1050, toll-free U.S. tel. 866/799-9097, www. belairvallarta.com), a smaller-scale (215 rooms) all-inclusive. Unfortunately it is crowded in on both sides by a pair of massive resorts, which has lessened the still-considerable appeal of this lush, beautifully designed property, with its two-story, glass-enclosed spa by the entrance, and infinity pool overlooking the beach. The rooms and suites are luxuriously romantic, with great bedding and pillows; the restaurants and bars offer gourmet fare and à la carte options on the all-inclusive plan. Rates start at around $94 low season, to $109 high season, European plan. The gourmet all-inclusive plans range up from $347. These prices are based on advance booking via Internet. This is the best of the smaller-scale all-inclusive hotels in Nuevo Vallarta, and though it's a bit farther away from Puerto Vallarta, the luxurious and tranquil ambience of the property more than compensates.

## FOOD

Outside of the hotels and the Paradise Village mall, there aren't many places to eat in Nuevo Vallarta, and, of course, the more authentic dining experiences are to be had in Puerto Vallarta. There are however, a few standouts. A couple of spots are tucked around the corner on a quiet street at the south end of the development—you have to go around the marina and skirt the edge of Grupo Mayan territory to find them. **Nopal Beach** (Blvd. de Nayarit 70, tel. 322/297-4568, 8am-11pm daily, $5-10), also known as Eddy's Place, is one of these hidden gems. With simple outdoor seating close to the marina waters and a casual menu of Mexican favorites, Nopal Beach is a favorite place for locals and tourists alike. For breakfast try the breakfast burrito, made with your choice of ingredients and wrapped inside a large flour tortilla. For lunch, grab some guacamole and chips, and the fish tacos. They often have live bands at night.

Just around the corner from Nopal Beach as you head back toward the highway is a pair of European-influenced gems, both with pleasant sidewalk seating, a wonderful amenity in this quiet neighborhood. First, try the French restaurant **Le Coin Des Amis** (Blvd. de Nayarit 400, tel. 322/297-7457, 3pm-10pm daily, $10-20), a bistro opened by Alsatian Frenchman Christian Ziss in 2011. With his ever-shifting menu of French classics (people rave about the duck à l'orange), Ziss hopes to attract some of the Mayans bored with the time-share experience, and whoever else happens by, by car or boat.

A perennial Nuevo Vallarta favorite is **Guido's Napoli** (Villa 5 s/n, Loc. 1, Blvd. de Nayarit, next door to Le Coin Des Amis, tel. 322/297-1061, www.guidos-vallarta.com.mx, 4pm-10:30pm daily, $7-15), where you can find authentic Italian food prepared by the owner/chef Guido Morelli. Guido offers a nice selection of pastas and Italian dishes, a good wine list, and fine service. They close for the low season in mid-May.

Outside in front of the Paradise Village mall are a couple of sweet little inside/outside spots for sandwiches, panini, pizza, soups, and smoothies. They share outdoor seating. One is called **Tuttopronto** (tel. 322/297-8071, 8am-8pm Mon.-Sat., $5-10), and the other is called **Fresca** (no phone, 7am-5pm daily, $4-12). The latter is slightly more health food oriented. Both places offer food that is well prepared, fresh, and very tasty.

The Nuevo Vallarta branch of **Ocho Tostadas** (Morelos 20, Náutico Turístico, tel. 322/297-7605, 11am-6pm daily, $1-15) offers the same fabulous seafood you'll find at the other Ocho Tostadas in Puerto Vallarta and Marina Vallarta. This is one little restaurant worth hunting down if you find yourself lost in Nuevo wondering where or what to eat. Ceviche tostadas for a dollar, stuffed shrimp, whole snapper, and fresh tuna are among the favorites with locals and visitors alike.

## CROCODILES

Should you have a rental car, be sure and take the kids to the **Cocodrilario** (no phone, 11am-6:30pm daily, 15 pesos/US$2 pp), accessible via a turnoff on the west side of Highway 200 between Bucerías and Mezcales. It's easy to miss the nameless, dusty little dirt road turnoff with the Cocodrilario sign at the side of the highway, but this throwback spot is well worth an hour or two of your time, especially with kids. Should the need to feed hit the kids, **Restaurant El Cora,** on-site, offers moderately priced seafood and other fare.

A mile and a half down the dirt road is a collection of animals—goats, geese, rabbits, *tejones*—tucked into pens and cages amid some ramshackle buildings and wooden walkways. The walkways are built over mangrove swamps that are the muddy homes of several crocodiles. The whole project, owned and operated by Jose Santos with permission from the federal environmental ministry, serves as a research center and sanctuary for the crocodiles, the mangrove swamp and estuary, and countless hundreds of sea- and shorebirds. This old-school, low-budget tourist attraction is what all of Nuevo Vallarta looked like just a few years ago.

# Bucerías

Bucerías (Place of the Divers) doesn't look like much from the highway, just a long stretch of low-rise commercial buildings, some in good shape, some not so good. There's nothing like a major highway running through the heart of a town to turn it into an eyesore, but looks are deceiving. Bucerías, as the signs proudly proclaim, is a nationally designated "Pueblo Magico," and if you look past the roadside commercial wasteland, you can still find the magic.

Bucerías is situated 12 miles (19 km) north of the Puerto Vallarta airport. En route you'll pass a couple of all-American big-box stores— first Home Depot, and then a few miles up the road, Walmart, the invader from Arkansas, in a vast, paved complex with an auto parts store and the Cevichería restaurant, both freestanding in the parking lot. Inside this airplane hangar-size Walmart complex, called Lago Real for reasons not immediately evident, is a Cinépolis multiplex cinema with first-run movies in Spanish and English, and along with the Walmart itself, a gaggle of other stores. Enter at your peril, although honestly, this Walmart—with the same amenities of air-conditioning and cheaply priced stuff as its U.S. cousins—is popular with the locals, and the Cevichería restaurant in the parking lot isn't bad. But don't stop; just head north, and soon you'll drive through the bustling one-stoplight town of Mezcales, then pass the next massive shopping development, anchored by the Mega grocery store, and a minute later you'll be in Bucerías (pop. 5,000), with its seemingly endless golden beach, clutch of wonderful restaurants, and comfortable lodging choices. Several places offer live music, and the town square often hosts events or small carnivals. There's even a weekly art walk in high season. Local people have long flocked to Bucerías on Sunday for beach play, as well as for fresh seafood from one of several beachfront *palapa* restaurants.

Bucerías is popular with retirees due to its inexpensive and quiet nature. A sizeable community of expats, including many Canadians, live here full time and run B&Bs, restaurants, or other small businesses. The town has developed continuously from its beginning as a fishing village of a few long dusty streets running parallel to the beach. Now as the space becomes more limited, Bucerías has started to spread to the north with the addition of several large condo complexes (a few of them unfortunately half finished and seemingly bankrupt), little strip malls, and suburban housing developments on the inland side of the highway. The largest and most popular addition to the area is the Mega, which sits just south of town on the main highway. Here residents and tourists alike do their shopping. Along with the supermarket, in the Mega complex you'll find banks, fast-food joints, and some specialty shops. On the access road into the Mega parking lot sits a small Tourist Information Office for the Riviera Nayarit. Everything available in this office can also be found online at www.rivieranayarit.com.

Despite its burgeoning popularity and the Americanization of Highway 200, much of the original charm of Bucerías remains: lots of old-fashioned local color, especially around the lively town-center market and the adjacent rickety midtown footbridge over the creek (that blocks through traffic and divides Bucerías into a pair of subvillages). On the south side of town, Lázaro Cárdenas has evolved into a lovely strolling street, with art galleries, bars, restaurants, and coffee shops clustered here and there, just a short block from the golden-white-sand beach.

## RECREATION

The ocean here offers beach-break waves perfect for swimming, bodysurfing, boogie boarding, and surf fishing. It isn't so great for surfing, as there is nothing much in the way of reefs or sandbars to shape the waves, but the calm morning water is great for paddleboarding and kayaking, and every afternoon, most of the year, the wind blows hard enough for great kiteboarding and sailboarding.

BAY OF BANDERAS

© OTTO DUSBABA /123RF

*Palapas* provide shade on a beach in Bucerías.

**Pacific Paddle** (Lázaro Cárdenas 86, tel. 322/123-3034 or 329/298-1057, www.pacificpaddle.net) rents and sells stand-up paddleboards, kiteboards, and sailboards and offers lessons in all three sports. Tours and excursions are on offer as well. Pacific Paddle also has a rental/lessons shop on the beach at Anclote, Punta Mita.

**Coral Reef Surf Shop** (Heroes de Nacozari 114, tel. 329/298-0261, www.coralreefsurfshop.com) rents stand-up paddleboards, rents and sells surfboards and boogie boards, and does surf lessons and trips.

Tent camping is customary on the beach, especially during the Christmas and Easter holidays.

## ENTERTAINMENT AND EVENTS
### Nightlife and Live Music

For what's pretty much a quiet little town, Bucerías does have a few venues for live music and nighttime socializing. In the evening the square downtown in front of the church comes alive with Mexican families, courting sweethearts, tourists, and teens all gathering in and around the gazebo to mix and mingle. Street vendors and food stands appear as if by magic around dusk, and sometimes the occasional musician or street performer will materialize to entertain the masses as well. This is definitely where the action is.

For those looking for the most popular bars, you'll usually find a good crowd at **The Shamrock Pub** (Av. México 22, tel. 329/298-3073), particularly on St. Patrick's Day.

Two blocks south, you will find **The Twisted Rose** (corner of Mexico and Hidalgo, tel. 322/146-3023), which offers live music on many nights as well as special events for holidays.

A lively nightclub located between these two is **The Luna Lounge** (Av. México 142, tel. 322/889-8391), offering all-you-can-eat BBQ feasts, DJ nights, live music, and drag shows on occasion.

On the south side of town is **El Gecko Pub** (Morelos 8, across from Casa Tranquila), a good place to stop for some billiards and a cold one. El Gecko is less of a tourist hangout and more of a worker's bar, so enjoy the local flavor.

## ACCOMMODATIONS
### North Side of Town

At the town's serene north end is the Playas de Huanacaxtle subdivision, with big flower-decorated villas owned by well-heeled Mexicans and North Americans. Sprinkled among the intimate, palm-shaded *retornos* (cul-de-sacs) are a number of good bungalow-style beachside lodgings. As you move southward from the north edge of town, the top-value accommodations begin with the **Vista Vallarta Suites** (Av. de los Picos 827, Playas de Huanacaxtle, tel. 329/298-0361, toll-free Mex. tel. 01-800/570-7292, toll-free U.S./Can. tel. 888/888-9127, www.vistavallartasuites.com, $195 d high season, $95 d low). Here, three stories of comfortably furnished stucco-and-tile apartments cluster intimately around a palm-tufted beachside pool and patio. Discounts may be negotiable for long-term rentals.

A block south, the family-style **Bungalows Princess** (Retorno Destiladeras, Playas de Huanacaxtle, tel. 329/298-0100 or 329/298-0110, fax 329/298-0068, www.bungalowsprincess.com, $55 and up) looks out on blue Bahía de Banderas. Their several two-story detached beachfront bungalows provide all the ingredients for a restful vacation for a family or group of friends. Behind the bungalows, beside an interior pool patio, a stone's throw from the beach, a motel-style lineup of rooms and one-, two-, and three-bedroom suites fill the economy needs of couples and small families. A total of 36 bungalows, suites, and rooms are available, all featuring TV with HBO, phone, and air-conditioning. Hotel amenities include desk service, a minimarket, and two pools. Credit cards are accepted.

Continuing south, nearby **Bungalows Los Picos** (Av. los Picos and Retorno Pontoque, Playas de Huanacaxtle, tel. 329/298-0470, fax 329/298-0131, www.lospicos.com.mx) shares the same palm-shadowed Bucerías beachfront. The rambling, Mexican family-style complex centers around a big inner pool patio, spreading shoreward to a second motel-style bungalow wing beside a breezy beachside pool area. There are plenty of room options, ranging from small singles ($48) to three-bedroom suites with kitchenettes ($230). All prices are subject to Internet and early reservation discounts.

## South Side of Town

On the south side of town near the beach (much of it lined with posh private homes), the inviting **Casa Tranquila** (Morelos 7A, tel. 329/298-1767, cell tel. 322/728-7519, www.casatranquila-bucerias.com, $55-70 d) is worth considering. Welcoming owners Patricia Mendez and Joann Quickstad offer five compact one-bedroom kitchenette apartments that open to a lovely tropical garden pool patio. All of the apartments are clean, comfortable, and individually decorated (in Aztec, Gringo, Vaquero, Suzie Wong, and Quimixto styles). Rates vary depending on season and whether you prefer air-conditioning or fan. Light sleepers should opt for the downstairs units, as the bar across the street can get noisy sometimes.

Attached to the hotel is **Gringo's Books & Coffee,** an excellent place for trading in your paperbacks and finding new beach reads. There are also a variety of books written by local authors or having to do with the subject of Mexico.

Around the corner, less than a block away, find the inviting **Hotel Palmeras** (Lázaro Cárdenas 35, tel./fax 329/298-1288, U.S./Can. tel. 647/722-4139, www.hotelpalmeras.com). It's located near restaurants, art galleries, and just a stone's throw from the beach, and you can easily spend a week here for an affordable tropical vacation. In the center of the hotel is a lushly landscaped pool area, and the rooms are clean and comfortable, especially the suites in the newer building. One-bedrooms in the old wing run about $35 low season, $85 high, two-bedrooms about $75 low, $120 high for four persons, all with air-conditioning, fans, and kitchenettes. The newer wing apartments, all either studios or one-bedroom, run about $65 low season, $100 high, all with

air-conditioning, fans, cable TV, and private patios or sitting areas. Amenities include lounge with satellite TV, wireless Internet, beach towels, and daily maid service. Everything is available by the month at reduced rates.

About four blocks farther south is the popular **Bungalows Arroyo** (Lázaro Cárdenas 500, tel./fax 329/298-0076, bungalowsarroyo@hotmail.com, $100 low season, $120 high). The dozen-odd roomy two-bedroom apartments are clustered beside a palmy swimming pool and garden a block from the beach. The units have king-size beds, private balcony, kitchen, and living and dining room. They're popular; get your winter reservations in months early. Discounts are available for monthly rentals.

For a wonderful B&B experience, try Brian and Sandi Barkwell's beautiful **Casa Cielito Lindo** (Calle Fibba 12, tel. 329/298-2440, www.waterfrontdreamvacations.com), located just a few blocks uphill from the beach. There are four lodging choices, the newest being the Mirador suite located on the third floor, with views of the ocean. The rooms are comfortable and well appointed, Mexican-style. High-season rates start at $125 per night for the Sunflower or Eclipse rooms and go up to $175 per night for the Palapa Retreat Suite, which includes a full kitchen. Some suites can be combined for larger groups, and there's a one-week minimum during the holiday season. The rates include a full, hot breakfast (you can opt out and save $15 per day) and access to the home's amenities, including the fourth-floor *palapa* for sunset viewing, the swimming pool, and the common areas. In residence are Sandi and Brian's treasured golden retrievers, so this is not a good choice for those with dog allergies. The entire house can be rented for $350 per day during the low season (May 15-Oct. 15, seven-night minimum).

## Trailer Parks and Camping

There aren't many options for trailer and RV camping in and near Bucerías; however, the **Altarose Rancho RV Park** (Valle de Banderas, Jalisco, tel. 322/148-7031, www.rvparkvallarta.com $20/day or $450/month) is located about 20 minutes east. In Bucerías, turn east on Avenue Estacion (at Famar Restaurant) and follow the highway about 7.5 miles (12 km) to Valle de Banderas. Bypass the town; when the highway turns right, you're there. Look for the white house with the red roof. This park offers country camping with a view of the mountains. Amenities include large lots with water, power, and sewer. Outdoor activities including volleyball, baseball, swimming, soccer, ATV rentals, and walking trails are available; services and supplies can be had in the nearby town, which is itself a pretty, charming little pueblo, serving as the administrative center for Bahía de Banderas as well as the heart of this rich agricultural valley.

## FOOD

A number of good restaurants serve Bucerías's cadre of discriminating diners. A large selection of them lie between the cross streets of Galeana and Morelos, along Calle Lázaro Cárdenas, the street that parallels the beach south of Puente de los Besos (Bridge of the Kisses). On the north side of the bridge along the beach you'll find a strip of popular seafood restaurants, all offering fresh fish and an opportunity to dip your toes into the sand and watch the sunset. Heading north on Avenida Mexico, you will find a number of more eclectic choices, from pizza to tapas.

One of the most popular south-side restaurants is **Sandrina's** (btwn. Galeana and Morelos, tel. 329/298-0273, www.sandrinas.com, 3pm-10:30pm Wed.-Mon., $8-15), just south of Hotel Palmera. The labor of love of Victoria, British Columbia, expatriates Andrew and Sandra Neumann, the restaurant offers a varied late lunch 3pm-6pm and dinner until 10:30pm, with a Mediterranean fusion menu offering plentiful Greek and Italian specialties (antipastos, salads, souvlaki, lasagna, pizzas) and exquisite mahimahi fish fillet dinners in a beautifully artistic inside-outside garden setting.

Especially popular and equally enjoyable for lunch or dinner, **Claudio's Meson Bay** (tel. 329/298-1634, 2pm-10pm daily) is a block

farther north on the beach side. Here you'll find superfresh catch-of-the-day fish, lobster, prawns, clams, and oysters ($8-14), plus a bountiful meat barbecue ($8-18) and a salad bar ($5). This all climaxes every Wednesday night with an overflowing all-you-can-eat barbecue ($12). There are also all-you-can-eat fish and shrimp barbecues on Monday ($15) and all-you-can-eat Mexican food and margaritas on Friday ($18).

After trying the aforementioned eateries, you might also check out a number of other reliably recommended restaurants in the same neighborhood. Located right on the beach, **Karen's Place** (Lázaro Cárdenas, at the end of Juárez, tel. 329/298-1499, 8:30am-10pm Mon.-Sat., 8:30am-3pm Sun., $5-12), in the big Costa Dorada condo complex, serves breakfast, lunch, early dinner, and Sunday champagne brunch under the shade of a large *palapa* and out on the beach. While all of the seatings here offer delicious food, the brunch is one of the best deals in town ($9 without alcohol, $14 with). The eggs Benedict is very good. Karen also has a tea and coffee house on the corner of Lázaro Cárdenas and Juárez.

A higher-end gourmet option along Lázaro Cárdenas is Massimo de Berardinis's chic, stylishly contemporary **Ristorante Adriatico** (Lázaro Cárdenas 162, tel. 329/298-6038, www.adriaticoristorante.com, 5pm-closing nightly, closed Mon. in low season), offering a classic Italian menu and a range of meat and fish dishes, great salads, and desserts served up in an open-air garden setting. He's getting raves from locals and tourists alike. Prices start at around $5 for appetizers and go to $20 for main courses, with plenty of options in between.

Across the street is another high-end option, **Mark's Bar & Grill** (Lázaro Cárdenas 56, tel. 329/298-0303, www.marksbucerias.com, 10am-10pm daily), a spacious, high-ceilinged inside-outside dining room with a Continental menu offering everything from seafood appetizers through pizzas, pastas, and main courses of meat and fish. Mark's recently garnered a Best Restaurant in Riviera Nayarit award.

Occasional live-music nights, a fun bar scene, and an art gallery next door enhance the ambience. Appetizers start around $4, soups and salads start at $5, main courses start around $16, pizzas $6, and pastas and risottos around $14. Reports are it's worth every penny.

Up the block, **Vera Bakery Cafe** (Lázaro Cárdenas 135, tel. 329/298-1962) has a great selection of home-baked breads, cakes, and pastries, and serves sandwiches and light snacks daily.

Back along Lázaro Cárdenas is the **Red Apple** (corner of Morelos, tel. 329/298-1235, 8:30am-10pm Mon.-Sat., 8am-4pm Sun., $5-15), an upstairs ocean-view *palapa* specializing in garlic shrimp, fajitas, and hearty *ranchero* breakfasts. If you are looking for a beer and a pool table, try the **El Gecko Pub** (half a block east on Morelos), where many of the local Mexican residents hang out. Just across the street is **Gringo's Books & Coffee,** run by Joann and Patricia of **Casa Tranquila.** Grab an espresso and fresh baked cookie while browsing through the extensive collection of used books.

On the other side of town, moving north from the plaza you'll find a beachfront row of Mexican seafood restaurants. Of all of the waterfront restaurants, **Mar y Sol** (Av. Pacifico, tel. 329/298-1914, 8am-10pm daily, $5-15) is a perennial personal favorite, with their spicy and delicious crab tacos and sparkling fresh-squeezed lemonade. The staff are friendly and competent, and have a good mastery of English. Grab some oysters on the half shell or BBQ ribs and enjoy the music from the traveling mariachis.

There is a series of eclectic dining choices along and around Avenida Mexico, the street running north from the square just past the church. Grab a slice of pizza at **Yo Yo Mo's** sports bar or a croissant and a cup of coffee around the corner at Guillaume Demay's wonderful **Delices de France** (Hidalgo 3, tel. 322/278-9638, www.delices-defrance.net, 8am-10pm Mon.-Sat.), a fine little bakery and coffee shop with simple café chairs and tables tucked into the back of a small food court. Demay and his crew make Viennese-style pastries, cakes, and classic French breads including sourdough.

**Tapas del Mundo** (corner of Av. México and Hildalgo, tel. 322/118-1795, www.tapasdelmundo.com, 7pm-11pm daily) offers a wide variety of tasty tapas for discerning guests. Enjoy the show as friendly owner/operator Jorge whips up his amazing Caesar salad from scratch, and make sure not to miss the Cuban sausage with white sauce. There's something for everyone on the menu, from sizzling garlic shrimp to the vegetarian potato cakes. Jorge also offers cooking classes. Once you've had your fill of tapas, head upstairs to **The Bar Above** to sample one of dessert master Buddy's mouthwatering chocolate soufflés and a Spanish coffee. Enjoy the view from the 4th-floor *palapa* while you watch the evening fireworks over the bay.

One stop worth making along the Highway 200 commercial slash through town is at the Bucerías branch of **Pie in the Sky** (Heroes de Nacozari 202, tel. 329/298-0838 or 329/298-1397, www.pieinthesky.com.mx), long recognized as the best expat bakery, and pretty much the best bakery overall, in the Vallarta region. As they've been around since the 1980s, they know what they're doing—and what they do are amazingly rich and flavorful cakes, pies, and baked goods of all sorts, much of it produced for special occasions. There is always great stuff on hand for walk-ins, however. With all the weddings and birthdays they cater, their products are pretty to look at, too. Their version of the traditional *tres leches* Mexican cake is definitely to die for. At least stop in for a coffee and a petits four. You won't regret it unless you're on a diet (this place is definitely not for dieters). Pull to the right onto the lateral at the first chance you get, heading north into Bucerías; you'll find your Pie on the right, almost immediately.

# La Cruz de Huanacaxtle

A day trip on the road to Punta Mita used to take you past white-sand beaches and waterfront *palapa* restaurants, but now you are more likely to be driving past construction sites and new condos. A short distance north of Bucerías the Punta Mita highway splits left (west) and passes over Highway 200. The first town you arrive at is the once-scruffy little village of La Cruz de Huanacaxtle, growing less scruffy every year thanks to the completion of the marina. The number of good restaurants is expanding, as are the lodging choices, but the beach isn't anything special. You'll find nicer sand and surf farther along the highway. However, those enamored of yachts, sailboats, and fresh fish might want to linger awhile.

Once hardly more than a flyspeck on a map, La Cruz, thanks to the marina, is becoming a popular vacation spot for those who find that even Bucerías has gotten too big for their taste. The marina has brought an upscale element to La Cruz; however, you'll find it's not yet nearly as spendy as Punta Mita or Sayulita. Some say that La Cruz is the next big thing to hit Riviera Nayarit.

Driving into town on the Punta Mita highway, however, you will not be impressed. The scene is scruffy and dusty, with randomly sited miscellaneous businesses, taco stands, gas stations, and so on—the usual roadside detritus. But after you get onto the lateral road on the right, make a left turn, and head into downtown La Cruz, the scene changes. It's a charming, sweet little town, and with the marina drawing more boaters every year, it's sure to get more charming and sweeter (and pricier, no doubt).

## CHARTER BOATING

There are several charter boat options available in the La Cruz marina, which is beginning to draw the multitudes of big shiny boats and well-heeled boaters that such marinas are intended to attract. This opens up a whole ocean of possibilities for day-tripping visitors. You can book a day fishing, sailing, whale-watching, or beach hopping on seagoing vessels ranging from small wooden pangas for local close-to-shore fishing to open-ocean motorized fishing cruisers to single-hulled yachts or twin-hulled catamaran sailboats for shoreline cruising or island hopping at the Marietas, an hour away. There are a number of gorgeous boats here, and many can be chartered.

One great option is the **Chica Locca** (booking office: Av. Revolución/Calle Delfín N44-C, Sayulita, tel. 329/291-2065, 322/101-9708, or 322/180-0597, U.S. tel. 323/952-3271, www.chicalocca.com), moored in the marina. Not just whale-watching goes on when you book a day trip on the *Chica Locca* (Crazy Woman); there is also snorkeling, diving, swimming, cruising the bay, touring the islands and hidden beaches—and having more fun than you can imagine packed into a single day. Motoring out of the marina, this colorful, comfortable catamaran, converted from sailing to motor cruising only, seats up to 60, with cushions, hammocks, and plenty of space and spots for lounging. You can party the day away, throw out a line and perhaps reel in a sleek dorado while the boat heads to the islands, ask the captain to swing over and park by one of the surf spots or inaccessible (from land) beaches along the Bahía de Banderas shore, and then enjoy some of the fabulous food provided by Sayulita's own Ruben's Deli.

One thing to consider: Family groups with kids have a different agenda than large crowds of tequila-crazed twentysomethings with partying on their minds. Things can get pretty wild at times on these day-tripping boats, so don't be afraid to ask who's going to be onboard.

This is all well and good, but during winter, when the boat comes upon the whales, something unbelievable and magical occurs: Everyone onboard becomes awestruck, staring, astounded, at the great, beautiful beasts at play in the water. It is simply astonishing to see a humpback whale as it passes beneath your boat

© DONNA DAY

BAY OF BANDERAS

**Fishing boats and pleasure yachts share the La Cruz marina.**

or breaches a hundred yards off the bow. If you are in Puerto Vallarta between December and April, take a whale-watching trip, on this boat or any other. It is an unforgettable thrill.

## SHOPPING

Whether you're buying or not, be sure and pay a visit to the La Cruz **Mercado del Mar,** the seafood market located on the working (fishermen's) side of the marina on Calle del Mar. (Turn toward the water on Atun, the first major left as you come into La Cruz from Highway 200. Go to the end, bear right, and soon you'll see Eva's Brickhouse Restaurant. The seafood market is to the right.) You'll see what comes out of the bay every day: hundreds of wonderfully fresh fish of every variety and size, including pompano, *huachinango* (red snapper), *sierra* (mackerel), *atún* (tuna), dorado (mahimahi), *langosta pacifico* (Pacific lobster), *ostiónes* (oysters), calamari, *pulpo* (octopus), and *lisa* (mullet). The variety is fascinating, and the price is right. You can buy great slabs of fresh tuna or a whole giant snapper wholesale. If you are

staying in a place with a cook and/or a kitchen, this is your chance to eat the freshest fish of your life.

## ACCOMMODATIONS

Your best option for accommodations outside of renting a house or condo might be the **La Cruz Inn** (Calle Marlin 36, tel. 329/295-5849, www.lacruzinn.com), where you can rent one of five available rooms for about $100 d year-round (one of the five goes for $80). The rooms are comfortable and tastefully decorated with carved wooden furniture and Mexican handicrafts. Four of the rooms have lovely outdoor kitchens and private patios. All rooms have both fans and air-conditioning. The rooms open onto a shared courtyard where guests can enjoy a swim in the pool, and there is an on-site restaurant, **Arriba,** that specializes in comfort food. Wi-Fi is available throughout the hotel.

Up on the hill on the inland side of the Punta Mita highway (turn right at the Chocolatl restaurant signs), the lovely little bed-and-breakfast called **Villa Bella** (Calle de Monte Calvario

12, tel. 329/295-5161 or 329/295-5154, toll-free U.S. tel. 877/273-6244, toll-free Can. tel. 877/513-1662, www.villabella-lacruz.com) offers spectacular views across the bay to Puerto Vallarta from almost every room and suite. The property contains four suites and two bedrooms in the main house, and two suites in the owner's house, with varying combinations of bedrooms, living rooms, and kitchens and kitchenettes available for rent. The individually named suites are beautifully designed and decorated with a contemporary Mexican feel, each in its own unique style. Rates include hearty, finely prepared breakfasts served on the poolside patio, and airport pickup service ($25 after 7pm). Bedrooms are $69 d, suites $149 or $169 d; rent the entire Main House, with its three suites, for $680 d, or the Owner's House, with the owner's apartment and one suite, for $335 d.

## FOOD

Whether or not you decide to stay overnight in La Cruz, there are several restaurants you won't want to miss. At **Frascati** (Av. Langosta 10, tel. 329/295-5154, 5pm-11pm daily, $11-20) diners can enjoy wood-fired pizzas or freshly made pasta with savory sauces. If you enjoy Alfredo sauce, this is the place to order it. The garden-like interior setting is beautiful, and the waiters are attentive without being overbearing.

If you are looking for the expat crowd, you can try **Philo's** (Calle Delfin 15, tel. 329/295-5068, 8am-1am Tues.-Sat., $3-12), which is as much a social club and community center as it is a restaurant (serving mostly pizza and salad) and rock and roll bar. It's especially popular with cruisers who dock at the nearby marina. There's live music on the weekends, and you never know when Philo and his band will grace the stage throughout the week. Pizza and ribs are the specialty, but the menu includes burgers, salads, and sandwiches as well.

Moved from Bucerías into a marina-side location, **Eva's Brickhouse** (Calle del Mar, Loc. 3, Marina de La Cruz, next to the seafood market, tel. 329/298-2238, cell tel. 322/141-3909, www.evasbrickhouse.com, 1pm-11pm

entrance to the fish market in La Cruz de Huanacaxtle

© DONNA DAY

daily, $15-25) has a solid reputation for serving great meat and seafood dishes. The La Cruz fish market is 50 yards away, so you know the catch is fresh. The bright, warm, open-air dining room, tucked under a large *palapa,* spills out onto a deck overlooking the marina. Eva and Kent are always there, running the kitchen, dining room, and bar, chatting everybody up. The menu is short and simple, with a few appetizers and salads, followed by steak, ribs, chicken, and a couple of fish dishes.

Arguably the most popular and well-known dining option in La Cruz is **Tacos on the Street** (Calle Huachinango 9, 5pm-11pm Wed., Sat., and Sun.). This casual restaurant is in front of a local family's house and serves tacos and quesadillas. Some say these are the best tacos in Mexico. Seating is outside at plastic tables and chairs, and guests are welcome to bring their own beer or wine. Soft drinks and Jamaica water are available. Make sure to grab a piece of flan for dessert.

Development along the road toward Punta Mita includes a large condo project called Alamar, located in a couple of towers on the inland side of the highway. The project includes a very posh private beach club across the highway at Playa Manzanillo, and adjacent to this beach club is the open-to-the-public gourmet dining room **Sandzibar** (Carretera a Punta de Mita, Km 3, tel. 329/295-5697, www.sandzibar.com, 11am-midnight daily, $20), the third restaurant opened by chef Bernard Guth, whose two Puerto Vallarta restaurants, Trio and Vitea, have been popular fixtures on the Vallarta dining scene for years. Sandzibar features a sophisticated multiethnic menu with Italian, French, Spanish, and Mexican influences. The open-air beachfront place is gorgeous, stylishly appointed with plenty of organically toned furnishings and verdant garden surroundings. It's sure to be a hit with the foodies of Bahía de Banderas.

## PLAYA MANZANILLO AND HOTEL PIEDRA BLANCA

Half a mile (at around Mile 2/Km 3) farther past the center of La Cruz, a side road to the left leads to beautiful Playa Manzanillo and the Hotel Piedra Blanca. The beach itself, a carpet of fine golden-white coral sand, stretches along a little cove sheltered by a limestone headland—thus Piedra Blanca (White Stone). This place was made for peaceful vacationing: snorkeling at nearby **Playa Piedra Blanca** on the opposite side of the headland; fishing from the beach, rocks, or by boat launched on the beach or hired in the La Cruz marina. If you go on holidays or weekends, be prepared for a crowd. This beach gets mobbed.

The **Hotel Piedra Blanca** (Alcatraz 36, Cruz de Huanacaxtle, tel. 329/295-5489 or 329/295-5493, reserva_hotelpblanca@hotmail.com) is an unpretentious family-managed resort. The best of the big, plain but comfortable suites offer upstairs ocean views. All the ingredients—a tennis court, a shelf of used paperback novels, and a rustic *palapa* restaurant beside an inviting beach-view pool and patio—are perfect for a season of tranquil relaxation. The 41 suites ($77 d high season, $50 d low season, 20 percent discount for stay of a week or more, $1,230 per month high season) have kitchenettes, air-conditioning, and cable TV; credit cards are not accepted.

Past Piedra Blanca, the highway winds for 12 miles (19 km) to Punta Mita through the bushy summer-fall green-jungle country at the foot of the Sierra Vallejo. Although pristine only a few years ago, this stretch is now pocked with condo and villa developments that unfortunately restrict access to the emerald-forested and coral-studded shoreline.

## PLAYA DESTILADERAS AND PUNTA BURROS

At Mile 5/Km 8 on the road to Punta Mita, you'll find Playa Destiladeras, a beach lover's heavenly mile of white sand. The intriguing name, *destiladeras,* originates with the fresh water dripping from the cliffs, collecting in freshwater pools right beside the ocean. Here, along the entire length of this inviting white-sand beach, waves roll in gently, providing good conditions for swimming, bodysurfing, and boogie boarding. When the swells get big (from the north in winter, from the south in summer, as a rule), the big waves crash in shallow water here, and it's dangerous for swimming or body surfing. That's when the serious surfers come out, up the beach. Surfing gets better as you get farther west, out to the break known as Veneros, where luxury housing overlooks the sand. Farther on, just before you reach the Palladium Hotel (an unfortunately oversized all-inclusive), you'll find the world-class surfing wave known as Punta Burros, or simply Burros. The left-breaking waves here are okay, but the rights, on a big swell, are fast, well shaped, and exciting to ride. This can be one of the best surfing waves in Nayarit on occasion.

Unfortunately, or fortunately if you are the developers or their clients, a huge development is under construction right on top of Destiladeras. This megadevelopment, called Nahui, will include homes, condos, timeshares, retail, restaurants, commercial space, possibly golf courses, possibly hotels. Those of us who live in the area aren't quite sure yet, but it is an overwhelming, oversized project. The long, beautiful beach at Destiladeras will seemingly remain open to the public, but it will not be the same. Not even close, and never again.

When they rebranded this coast the Riviera Nayarit, this apparently is a big part of what they had in mind: big money, big development, big projects.

## VILLA ANANDA

Well-heeled travelers in need of a retreat or a detoxification cleanse need look no further than Villa Ananda (tel. 322/134-6757, U.S. tel. 503/922-1712, www.villaananda.com), an Ayurvedic spa and yoga retreat located in a spacious, tastefully decorated contemporary house on the beach just east of the Punta Burros surf spot. (Two km/1.2 mi past the Costa Banderas development entrance, turn left at the first dirt road. Drive down to the cobblestone gate entrance. Villa Ananda is 0.5 km/0.3 mi from the entrance on the left. Watch for street signs for Villa Ananda.) Here, teacher and healer Mindy Reser, originally from Portland, Oregon, and her staff offer Ayurvedic treatments, *pancha karma* (also known as five actions, this is the core Ayurvedic method for cleaning and detox), and a weeklong program devoted to cleansing and detoxification in a serene, beautiful setting. Fortunately for those of us unable to scrape together the $4,500 for the seven-day program or $4,000 for the six-day program, Villa Ananda also offers daylong retreats that include massage, Ayurvedic therapies, exfoliation treatments, and all the rest of the pleasures such places can provide ($160-340). The three-hour Ananda Royal Experience ($340)—Ananda's signature experience—combines an herbal body exfoliant with aromatic steam, four-handed massage, Chakra Anointment, and Shirodhara. Sounds like a great way to while away an afternoon between bouts in the surf.

# Punta Mita

In the early 1990s, the Mexican government concluded a deal with private interests to build the Four Seasons resort development at Corral de Riscos, at the end of the Punta Mita highway. The idyllic Corral de Riscos inlet, however, was *ejido* (communally owned) land and base of operations for the local fishing and boating cooperative, Cooperativa Corral de Riscos. In 1995 the government moved the people, under protest, into modern housing beside a new anchorage at nearby Playa Anclote.

There is still no end to the development plans for this once isolated area, as new golf courses, hotels, and condo developments have sprung up along the repaved road to Sayulita as well as inside the Punta Mita gates. At approximately Mile 12 (Km 19) coming from La Cruz, a private gate on the right leads to a pair of high-priced, mostly private 18-hole golf courses; the Four Seasons Hotel; the St. Regis Hotel; and a number of condominium and freestanding residential developments—all of this pricey business distributed over an impressive amount of privatized and publicly inaccessible acreage. After the real estate bubble burst in 2008, some of the projects tanked—there are empty, not-quite-finished clusters of condos behind those high-security fences, along with the multimillion-dollar homes and luxury hotel rooms.

Despite the accumulation of high-end resorts and housing developments and the restricted access to the beaches of the area, Punta Mita, or at least Playa Anclote, can still feel like a funky beach town. There's a clutch of rustic economy hotels and affordable *palapa* restaurants amid the wealth of the new residents and visitors, keeping Punta Mita a viable option for traveling surfers looking to ride waves that can last for more than half a mile.

Punta Mita (actually Punta de Mita) encompasses the entire northwestern headland of the Bay of Banderas. Important sections include the Emiliano Zapata village on the bluff above the beach; Nuevo Corral de Riscos, the new town that the government built for the displaced *ejido* people, west of Emiliano Zapata; and the boat harbor and beachfront *palapa* restaurant strip called Playa Anclote, or simply "Anclote" by local folks. Outside the gates of the Punta Mita compound, about 2,000 people call this area home.

The hotel people are trying to erase Corral de Riscos, the lovely west-side fishing inlet and location of the original *ejido* village, from memory. "Corral de Riscos doesn't exist," they claim. The people who know the history carry it with them, for better or worse.

## ◖ PLAYA ANCLOTE

Head left, downhill, at the highway's end roundabout (Mile 13/Km 21, where you'll also find the second gated and guarded entrance to the Four Seasons and the rest of the compound) toward Playa Anclote (Anchor Beach), which gets its name from the galleon anchor once displayed at one of the beachside *palapa* restaurants. The beach itself is a half-mile-long curving strand of soft, very fine coral sand interspersed with beds of rocks and coral, and a few jetties that calm the waves for the boats

moored just offshore. The water is shallow for a long distance out, and the waves are gentle and slow. Those long, slow Anclote waves are great for beginners, stand-up paddleboarders and surfers alike. If you are considering a lesson or a try at either surfing or stand-up paddleboarding, this is a great place to jump in and give it a go. The bottom is rocky, so consider bringing water shoes.

Anclote's waves are great for learning, and when they get big, they're fun for experienced surfers as well. However, for those surfers seeking something more challenging, you can hire a boat at Anclote (don't be afraid to negotiate, and don't travel in a pack, as the other surfers will hate you) and head out to either the **Cove** (aka Bahía) or **El Faro** (The Lighthouse). These breaks are also within walking distance of Anclote, but it's a 20- to 30-minute walk—not bad going in, but after a couple of hours in the water, walking back carrying a surfboard is tough. There are also lots of urchins on the rocks, so should you decide to walk in, wear your sandals or water shoes. It's better to hire a boat and a surf guide. They need the work and can advise on swell and tide; they also can take you to the fun, beginner-friendly wave called **La Lancha,** a mile or so east of Anclote. Like Anclote, La Lancha is fun when the waves are small and more challenging when they get bigger, but surfers around Punta Mita will tell you that El Faro is the best wave in the neighborhood when the swell is big and coming from the right direction. Faro is an epic right point break, a legend from the early days of surfing in Mexico, and still, in spite of the crowds, an amazing wave when it works.

A few hundred yards downhill from the highway, to the left of the T at the bottom, stands the **Sociedad Cooperativa Corral del Risco** (Av. El Anclote, Manzana 17 No. 1 Corral del Risco, tel./fax 329/291-6298, www.puntamitacharters.com). This former fishing cooperative, now a tourism provider, offers a number of services, such as sightseeing and snorkel tours, and scuba diving at the Islas Marietas, 15 minutes offshore; fishing for good-eating dorado and tuna ($40/hr);

BAY OF BANDERAS

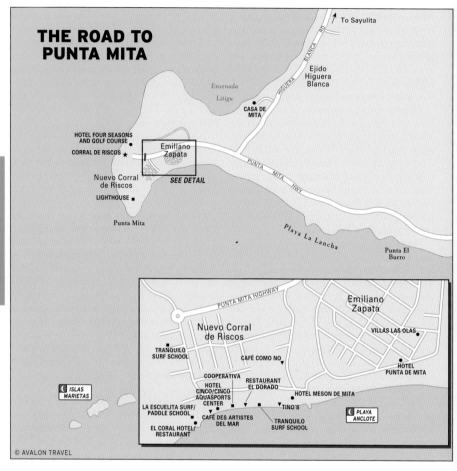

THE ROAD TO PUNTA MITA

© AVALON TRAVEL

whale-watching (Dec.-Mar.); and surf and stand-up paddleboard instruction.

There are a number of surf schools and excellent surf instructors at Anclote and in Punta Mita. One of the local heroes and probably the most experienced surf instructor is Josuá Villegas of **Tranquilo Surf Adventures** (Calle Pez Vela 130, NVO Corral del Risco, tel. 329/291-6475, cell tel. 322/142-1511). In addition to his home base up the hill in the village, Josuá has an office down across the avenue from the Cooperativa. Let me just say that when pop megastar Lady Gaga came to stay

and learn to surf at Punta Mita, the bilingual, superfriendly, and suave Josuá was her choice for surf instruction.

Another great surfing/stand-up paddleboarding instructor at Anclote is a man who goes by the name Oso Negro (Black Bear), who works out of the former Hotel des Artistes, now called Hotel Cinco. Famed surfer and stand-up paddler Gerry Lopez opened a small shop there, the **Cinco Aquasports Center** (tel. 329/291-5005), where he occasionally shows up to run paddleboarding clinics and help promote the sport. Oso Negro takes care of business when

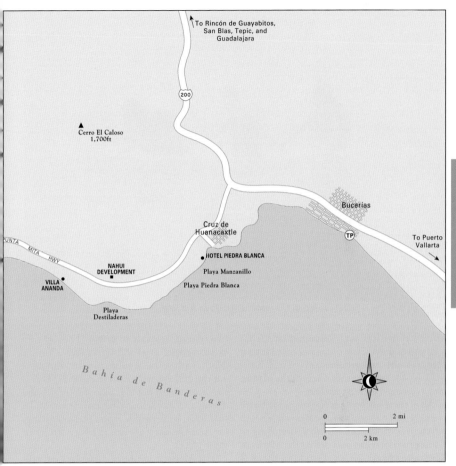

Gerry's not in town, and he's a gifted easygoing teacher who is very patient with kids and an extremely talented surfer in his own right. (Watching him ride waves on his stand-up paddleboard with his little dog Neptuno on board is Anclote entertainment at its local best.)

Alternatively, look up the veteran surf instructor and guide **Eduardo del Valle Ochoa** (Langostina 3, Cruz de Huanacaxtle, tel. 329/295-5087 or in Punta Mita 329/291-6633, www.acciontropical.com.mx), who welcomes visitors daily across the street from the Cooperativa office. Besides offering surfing lessons, Eduardo arranges sportfishing launches (Dec.-May, three hours, $150, including fishing tackle and bait) and snorkeling, wildlife-watching, and photography boat tours to the offshore wildlife sanctuaries of Islas Marietas. During a typical half-day trip, visitors may glimpse dolphins, sea turtles, and whales in season, as well as visit breeding grounds for brown and blue-footed boobies, Heermann's gulls, and other birds.

Another option is Antonio Ramirez's **La Escuelita Surf** school (Av. El Anclote, Nuevo Corral del Risco, tel. 329/136-6755), with an

© JUSTIN HENDERSON

**Three girls share a paddleboard in the waters off Playa Anclote.**

office behind El Coral Restaurant at the far west end of the Anclote restaurant row. He's got plenty of surf- and paddleboards, several boats available for trips to other waves or the islands, and a seasoned crew of teachers.

All of these surf schools also do paddleboard training and take visitors on all possible ocean adventures, from seasonal whale-watching to fishing to snorkeling and diving the Marietas. They also change places of work, so if one of the guys mentioned here isn't at the same shop, try another guy or another shop. If you show up at Anclote, there will be a boat, a guide, a teacher, and whatever boards or gear you need to get out in the water and have fun.

## ◖ ISLAS MARIETAS

Las Marietas Islands biosphere reserve and national park was originally made famous by **Jacques Yves Cousteau,** who studied the area because of the vast variety of species found there. Technically, Las Marietas is an archipelago, located 3 miles (4.8 km) from Punta Mita. This archipelago is formed by

two islands, volcanic in origin. The reefs are extensive and range 15-90 feet (4.6-27 m) in depth, with volcanic tubes running throughout the underwater area of the islands. This is the second most popular place for local scuba diving and snorkeling after Los Arcos. Make sure to go with a guide if you plan on diving, because the currents can get very strong in some places.

The Marietas are busy these days but still amazingly beautiful and unusual. Swim under a rock arch—watch out as the wave surge lifts you up toward the overhead rocks—into a cove with a tiny sand beach informally called Lover's Beach, with a sea cave nearby. Check out those manta rays and needle fish. The "reserve" part of the name means fishing is not allowed, thus there are many, many fish to look at. For ocean enthusiasts, this is a great trip. Inquire about water temperatures—though this is the tropics, the water can be cold in winter—and go on a clear, windless, sunny day for the best snorkeling.

People love these islands for the wildlife:

© DONNA DAY

La Lancha, with Punta Mita in the background

There are numerous species of coral, marine mammals, birds, and fish. Particularly, the islands are known for the large population of **blue-footed boobies,** found only here and in the Galapagos. There are sheltered areas for swimming and several small beaches for relaxing and sunbathing. Whether or not you dive or snorkel, the trip out to the island is worth it because you will very likely see dolphins, manta rays, and humpback whales (in season)—they tend to hang out around these islands.

## GOLF
Behind the gates and fences of the ultrasecure **Four Seasons** compound (Carretera Federal 200 Km. 19, tel. 329/291-6000, www.fourseasons.com/puntamita/golf), you'll find the pricey, world-class **Pacifico** and **Bahia** courses, worth the $450 greens fee if you're a golf nut determined to play one or both of these spectacular courses. For non-hotel guests, these courses are subject to availability. The fees are generally lower in low season. Call for a price when you're here.

## ACCOMMODATIONS
If you decide to stay, Punta Mita offers a number of comfortable, inexpensive accommodations. Upscale travelers spend $500 to $3,000-plus a day for luxury accommodations and access to a more private beach at the **Four Seasons** (www.fourseasons.com/puntamita) and the **St. Regis** (www.starwoodhotels.com/stregis/puntamita).

### Under $50
The downscale **Hotel Punta de Mita** (Hidalgo 5, Fracc. E. Zapata, tel. 329/291-6269, www.hotelpuntamita.com, $40, $50 with kitchen) overlooks the bay in Emiliano Zapata. Here, what you see is what you get: about 15 small, plain motel-style rooms around an inviting kid-friendly grassy pool patio. Amenities include air-conditioning, bunk beds for the kids, and hot showers.

Informal tent **camping** and **RV** parking around Punta Mita is possible, although increasing density makes this problematic; ask at the Playa Anclote restaurants if it's okay to camp under big trees at either end of the beach. Stores nearby and on the highway in Emiliano Zapata (commonly known as Punta Mita) a quarter-mile east can furnish the necessities, including drinking water. Camping is also available at **Hotel Mesón de Mita** (Av. Anclote, Corral de Riscos Nuevo, tel. 329/291-6330, mesondemita@yahoo. com.mx) on their grounds, where campers pay about $12 per person per day.

## $50-100

In the town of Emiliano Zapata, on the bluff above Playa Anclote, there are several choices for budget lodging. One of the best deals has got to be David Walsh's and Lisa Bombard's **Villas Las Olas** (Av. Alfonso Reyes Morelos, tel. 329/291-5337, U.S. tel. 310/734-6113, www.vrbo.com/112603). There are just four "rooms," but these are spacious one- and two-bedroom apartments with white tile floors, big windows, multiple beds, large bathrooms, full kitchens, satellite TV, high-speed Internet, and movie collections. The rates are $50 per day for two people, $10 extra per day per person for more than two. David has several dozen surfboards in all shapes and sizes available for rent; Lisa will cook the fish you catch. She also brings morning coffee, no matter the hour. They will send you to the best waves, best fishing captains, and the best restaurants and bars. This is a great little spot five minutes' walk from Anclote's beachfront restaurant row. If David happens to be playing a gig in one of the local bars while you're there, don't miss it. He's an excellent guitarist and plays Hendrix—well, almost like Hendrix.

If you must stay on the beach, you can do it, at Playa Anclote's first beachfront hotel, the **Hotel Mesón de Mita** (Av. Anclote, Corral de Riscos Nuevo, tel. 329/291-6330, mesondemita@yahoo.com.mx, $50 d low season, $65 d high). Owners offer 18 spacious, comfortably furnished rooms with shiny baths and air-conditioning. Some have ocean views, all overlooking the hotel's beach and pool patio. Camping is available for the price of $12 per person, and campers have use of the facilities, including the pool.

## Over $100

Increased visitor arrivals now support a sprinkling of mid- to high-end accommodations even outside the compound. Among the loveliest is ◖ **Casa de Mita** (Playa Cayero, tel. 329/298-4114 or 866/740-7999, fax 329/298-4112, www.casademita.com), formerly known as Casa Las Brisas. Owner Marc Lindskog personally makes sure that his guests enjoy the best of all possible tropical worlds: a breezy, usually deserted white-sand beach, gourmet cuisine, fine wines, spacious art- and antiques-decorated rooms, and plenty of peace and quiet, around an azure pool patio. For the active, Marc provides a universal gym station and optional fishing, horseback riding, surfing, golf, and more. All this for about $525-655 for two, high season, all lodging, food, and drinks included. You may also reserve Casa de Mita accommodations through Mexico Boutique Hotels (toll-free Mex. tel. 01-800/508-7923, toll-free U.S./Can. tel. 800/728-9098, www.mexicoboutiquehotels.com). Additional fees apply for stays of fewer than three nights. Note that this hotel is not in the Punta Mita village or on Anclote Beach but is rather on the south end of Litibu Beach, at a beach called Playa Cayero; this stretch is home to several private homes and a couple of other resorts, about 5-7 minutes' drive away on the other side of Punta Mita. There are no stores or restaurants or other "amenities." Unlike Anclote, sheltered inside the point of Punta Mita, Litibu Beach faces open ocean, and so the sea here can be rougher. On the other hand, unlike Anclote, the beach here is often completely deserted.

For an upscale beachfront resort right on the main Anclote beachfront strip, try the **Hotel Cinco** (Av. El Anclote 5, tel. 329/291-5005, toll-free Mex. tel. 01-866/628-2693, www.cincohotel.com), a condo-hotel formerly called Hotel des Artistes, with chef Thierry Blouet's **Café des Artistes del Mar** ensconced on the ground floor. The ownership is the same, and the restaurant is still intact, but the hotel has reinvented itself with a new name and a couple of new angles on the hospitality business. They still have several high-priced suites for rent. Up on the roof, a restaurant called Local Harvest, featuring a large, communal dining table, now serves breakfast and lunch based on a menu of fresh local foods, and cocktails may be had at the adjacent Barefoot Bar. The rooftop views are absolutely stunning. The one-bedroom ($495-585), two-bedroom ($710-840) and three-bedroom ($980) deluxe suites are spacious, decked out with fine contemporary furnishings, full kitchens, laundry rooms, and large ocean-facing terraces. There is style to spare throughout this project. The Cinco Aquasports Center, with legendary surfer and stand-up paddleboarder Gerry Lopez occasionally on hand to run wave-riding clinics, offers a full lineup of surfboards, paddleboards, and lessons; the fully equipped athletic club offers both daily and monthly memberships for non-hotel guests.

## FOOD

On the beachfront street, you'll find one of Playa Anclote's oldest and best seafood restaurants, 🄲 **El Dorado** (tel. 329/291-6296 or 329/291-6297, 9:30am-9:30pm daily, $5-25). Take a table in the airy upstairs ocean-view seating area. The menu is based on meat, poultry, and the bounty of superfresh snapper, scallops, oysters, and lobsters that local fisherfolk bring onto the beach.

There is no better place to while away a Sunday afternoon at Anclote than the venerable **El Coral** (Av. El Anclote, tel. 329/291-6332, www.hotelrestaurantelcoral.com, 8:30am-9pm daily, $5-20), which has been in business since the early 1980s. The slightly glitzy "Mexican Malibu" real estate office and snazzy entryway (the upstairs floors contain a small hotel) lend El Coral a hint of formality, but there's nothing formal once you're past the La Escuelita paddle-and surfboard rental shop inside. You'll find a TV high on one wall usually tuned to a soccer match, and a bunch of tables and chairs arrayed under a *palapa* and spilling out under ramadas and umbrellas a few steps above and down onto the narrow Anclote beach, with surf-touring and whale-watching pangas moored out front.

Gentle, perfect-for-beginners surf rolls in beyond the jetty to the right. Locals, Mexican families out from Vallarta for the day, and a motley crew of old gringo surfers and stand-up paddleboarders often spend entire days here, drinking margaritas, beer, and *limonadas,* and eating delicious whole grilled fish, ceviche, *pulpo al Diablo,* and a host of other moderately priced, superfresh seafood items between bouts with the waves. They even have an outdoor shower so you can wash the salt off before you sit down for lunch. Nobody minds if you sit at a table all day, drinking a single beer, and buying food from passing vendors. It's that kind of laid-back.

For something a bit fancier, try **Tino's Punta Mita** (Av. El Anclote 64, tel. 329/291-6473, 11am-9:30pm daily, $6-22), next door to El Dorado. At this outpost of this popular chain of restaurants, the food is just as delicious as it is in the original location in Pitillal. Here it's nearly all seafood, from marlin tacos and shrimp salad to mixed fish kebab and oysters.

A great addition to the Anclote dining scene is **Café Como No** (Av. la Pangas 14, tel. 329/291-6310, www.cafecomono.com, up to $6), up on the hill in Corral de Riscos, with the best *limonadas* and French fries in town, excellent tacos for under a buck, a cheeseburger to die for, and plenty of other options, nothing costing more than about six bucks. In other words, a great Mexamerican menu at reasonable prices. You can dine downstairs by the open kitchen or in a garden courtyard, or up on the roof under the stars, where the view of the bay goes on forever.

The second location of the popular high-end Puerto Vallarta restaurant **Café des Artistes** (Av. El Anclote 5, tel. 329/291-5415 for reservations, www.cincohotel.com, 5pm-10:30pm daily), with a "Del Mar" added to the name, is located off the lobby of the Hotel Cinco on the beach. Avant-garde seafood-based cuisine, an extensive wine list, and the luxurious setting make this a popular choice for a romantic dinner, special occasion, or just a night out to treat yourself.

# Into the Mountains

Although the little mountain enclaves of San Sebastián, Mascota, and Talpa are, as the bird flies, not very far from Puerto Vallarta, they are a world apart from the coast and very distinct from each other. All are accessible directly from Puerto Vallarta by highway or horseback, or light-airplane charter flights.

San Sebastián is a half-forgotten former mining town with a noble plaza and fine colonial-era houses and buildings, notably the Hacienda Jalisco, that appear as they did a century and a half ago. Some old mines, now in ruins, can still be visited, preferably in the company of local guides. Guides can also lead you on foot or horseback through verdant mountain country for day-trip explorations or to overnight campsites. There you can enjoy the sunset, relax around an evening campfire, savor the forest's quiet natural sounds, and marvel at the brilliance of a truly dark night sky.

Mascota, the hub of a rich farm valley, enfolded by lush pine- and oak-forested ridges, is a departure point for outdoor excursions and explorations of the idyllic villages of Yerbabuena, Cimarrón Chico, and Navidad, and the pristine high-sierra **Laguna Juanacatlán.**

Talpa, tucked in its own lush valley, is famous throughout Mexico for its colorful village ambience. Its towering baroque basilica and surrounding plaza are magnets for hosts of visitors who flock to pay respects to the adored **Virgin of Talpa,** one of the renowned Three Sisters virgins of Mexico.

## ◖ SAN SEBASTIÁN

San Sebastián's upland valley was the heartland of the Náhuatl- (Aztec-) speaking chiefdom of Ostoticpac, which translates roughly as "hollow in the highlands." The people, known as the Texoquines, worshipped the gods of sun and fertility, cultivated corn and cotton, and extracted gold and silver from local deposits. Although the Texoquines initially accepted Christianity peaceably, they later rose in revolt, possibly in reaction to the rapacious excesses of renegade conquistador Nuño de Guzmán. Then-governor Francisco Vásquez de Coronado, reinforced with soldiers from Guadalajara, marched from the Bay of Banderas into the mountain domain of Ostoticpac, and after a bloody campaign against a determined force of 5,000 warriors,

## THE FESTIVALS OF SAN SEBASTIÁN

The lovely mountain town of San Sebastián makes for a wonderful day or overnight trip from Puerto Vallarta. The several-hour drive on windy but well-paved roads is scenic, punctuated by breathtaking vistas and rolling fields of blue agave. Once you arrive, you may be surprised by the tranquil and timeless atmosphere of San Sebastián and the other small mountain towns. So whether you simply want to experience a wonderful cultural event or are looking for something more social to do during your visit, visiting during one of the many annual festivals is a great time to travel. Each of the mountain hamlets has its own festival calendar, so be sure to check the dates when planning your trip.

- **Festival of Patron San Sebastián Martyr:** January 19-21
- **San Sebastián Silver Festival:** Late May
- **Festival of the Virgin of the Asunción:** August 15
- **Mexican Independence Celebration:** September 15-16
- **Festival of the Virgin of the Rosary:** October 7
- **Festival of the Virgin of Guadalupe:** December 12

vanquished the Texoquines. The defeated people returned to their homes and fields, and during hundreds of years of Spanish-supervised peace they contributed their labor to the church and *hacendados*, who grew rich from cattle, gold, and silver.

One glance around the present plaza tells you that San Sebastián (pop. 700, elev. 5,250 ft/1,600 m) is unique. Once the most important mining town in the state of Jalisco, the hamlet seems near deserted and tranquil except when the tour buses from Puerto Vallarta arrive. If you wish to avoid the throngs of tourists, make your trip in the morning or late afternoon. The town's cobbled hillside plaza, lined with a steepled cathedral and dignified white buildings trimmed with deep purple highlights, and enclosing a correct Porfirian bandstand, presents a perfect picture of old-world gentility. Such a scene, incongruously tucked at the far end of a winding mountain road, requires explanation.

San Sebastián was once a seat of wealth and modern living, its population exploding during the early 1600s and maintaining decent numbers until the 1930s. The area, rich with gold and silver, gems, and agriculture employed more than 30,000 people until the mines closed. Now fewer than a thousand remain. Residents of San Sebastián—officially San Sebastián del Oeste (Saint Sebastian of the West) to distinguish it from a host of other similarly named towns—now earn a living in other ways. In addition to the traditional corn and cattle, local folks cultivate coffee, whose red berries they harvest from the acres of bushes that flourish beneath shady mountainside pine groves. Make sure to pick up some of the locally grown and roasted coffee at **La Quinta**, located on your left as you exit town.

## San Sebastián Plaza

The most important sights in San Sebastián are visible from the central plaza. The road into town from Puerto Vallarta comes in on the west side of the plaza. Far above the opposite side, the landmark mountain **La Bufa** (elev. 8,400 ft/2,560 m) crowns the eastern ridge.

Beyond the north edge of the plaza rises the town **church,** dedicated to San Sebastián, who is adored for his martyrdom in Rome in AD 288. The church, restored during the 1980s, replaced an earlier 17th-century structure destroyed in an 1868 earthquake. The main altar of the present church holds a pious, heavenward-gazing image of San Sebastián dedicated in 1882. Local folks celebrate the saint's martyrdom during their major local fiesta on January 20.

Near the northeast corner of the plaza, visit the **papelería** and general store of María Francisca Perez Hernández, the local poet who wrote "*La Caída de los Cedros,*" lamenting the chainsawing of old cedars that decorated the plaza before its renovation in 1984. Pamphlets of her poetry and the local history of chronicler-priest Gabriel Pulido Sendis are for sale inside.

## Sights Outside of Town

The road angling downhill past the northwest corner of the plaza marks the route to **La Quitería mine,** the most famous local dig site. About five miles (eight km) from town, at the end of a Jeep-negotiable dirt road, lie the ruins, all that remain of a mine that produced millions in gold and silver before closing around 1930. Stripped of machinery by local people, the mine has been reduced to bare walls, gaping processing pits, and great ore tailings.

Head out of town along the west (Puerto Vallarta) road; after about two downhill miles (three km), a signed gate on the right marks the driveway to **Hacienda Jalisco** (tel. 322/222-9638 or 322/107-7007), the lifelong project of American expatriate Bud Acord. Close the gate after you enter and continue another half mile to the Hacienda.

If, like some visitors, you arrive by plane, you won't be able to avoid seeing the Hacienda Jalisco, because the airstrip is on its land. Bud Acord moved into the dilapidated 1840-era estate during the late 1960s, and Hacienda Jalisco became host to dozens of celebrities over time, especially during the heyday of Puerto Vallarta in the 1970s and 1980s. Although Bud has passed on, the management of the guesthouse continues, and curious visitors can view historical memorabilia related to the mining operation, such as maps and accounting ledgers. The museum (9am-4pm Mon.-Sat., entrance fee $2.50) leads to a baronial *sala* and a porticoed veranda and flowery courtyard. Don't miss the opportunity to stay at least one night at Hacienda Jalisco.

## Shopping
For local handicrafts, stop by **La Primavera** (on the north side of the plaza, tel. 322/297-2856, 10am-3pm and 6pm-10pm daily). Friendly craftsperson Luz María Preciado crafts many of her offerings by hand, which include a big family of handmade dolls, embroidered pillows, sewing baskets, and *ponche de guayaba* (guava punch).

## Accommodations
San Sebastián's most distinguished lodging is ◖**Hacienda Jalisco** (reservations through Pamela Thompson in Puerto Vallarta, tel. 322/222-9638 or 322/107-7007, www.haciendajalisco.com), a mining-era hacienda that will make you feel as though you've stepped back in time. It's located out of town along the west (Puerto Vallarta) road; after about two downhill miles (three km), a signed gate on the right marks the driveway to the hacienda. The cavernous rooms, which include the Pamela and Fire Suites, each with two bedrooms and three beds, and the John Huston Suite, with a king-size bed, all have large baths, and the suites have private patios. They are decorated with antiques and are lit with oil lamps and individual fireplaces (as there is no electricity on-site). Unless there is a full moon, there is virtually no light in the country after sunset, so guests are encouraged to bring flashlights. Mosquito repellent is also highly recommended. Classic-movie buffs are especially welcome—as guests of the hacienda have included John Huston, Richard Burton, Elizabeth Taylor, and Ava Gardner. Hacienda Jalisco's high-season rates, including a hearty breakfast and dinner, run about

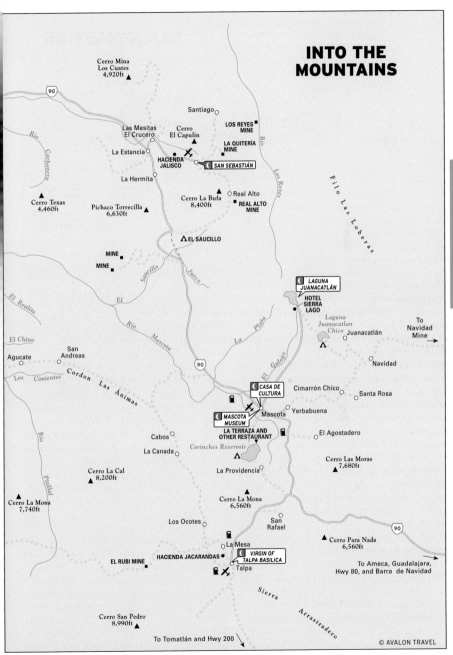

# INTO THE MOUNTAINS

BAY OF BANDERAS

Cerro Mina
Los Cuates
4,920ft

90

Santiago

Las Mesitas
El Crucero

Cerro
El Capulín

LOS REYES
MINE

La Estancia

LA QUITERÍA
MINE

HACIENDA
JALISCO

SAN SEBASTIÁN

La Hermita

Cerro Texas
4,460ft

Pichaco Torrecilla
6,630ft

Cerro La Bufa
8,400ft

Real Alto

REAL ALTO
MINE

EL SAUCILLO

MINE

MINE

Río Carbonera

Río Las Reyes

Filo Las Loberas

Saucillo

Jueco

El

Río Mascota

La Plata

LAGUNA
JUANACATLÁN

HOTEL
SIERRA
LAGO

Laguna
Juanacatlan
Chico

Juanacatlán

El Galope

To
Navidad
Mine

Navidad

El Realito

El Chino

Agucate

San
Andreas

Los Cimientos

Cordon Las Ánimas

90

CASA DE
CULTURA

Cimarrón Chico

Santa Rosa

Yerbabuena

MASCOTA
MUSEUM

Mascota

LA TERRAZA AND
OTHER RESTAURANT

El Agostadero

Cabos

La Canada

Corinches Reservoir

Cerro Las Moras
7,680ft

Río Pitillal

Cerro La Cal
8,200ft

La Providencia

Cerro La Mona
7,740ft

Cerro La Mona
6,560ft

Los Ocotes

San
Rafael

90

Cerro Para Nada
6,560ft

EL RUBI MINE

HACIENDA JACARANDAS

La Mesa

VIRGIN OF
TALPA BASILICA

Talpa

To Ameca, Guadalajara,
Hwy 80, and Barra de Navidad

Cerro San Pedro
8,990ft

Sierra

Arrastradero

To Tomatlán and Hwy 200

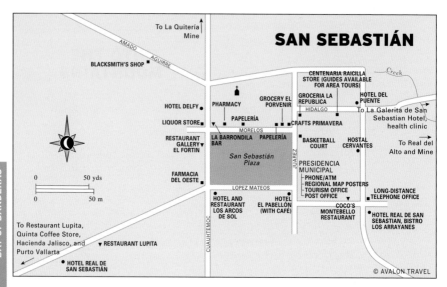

$63 per person per night, $50 per person with breakfast only. Pets and children under 12 are not allowed.

Another good option is **Hotel El Pabellón** (López Mateo 1, tel. 322/297-0200, $22 s, $39 d, $55 t), on the plaza. Here, you seem to be stepping into an earlier age. Past the entrance, a graceful *sala* leads to a patio garden of fragrant orange trees surrounded by doorways opening into spacious, high-ceilinged rooms; you can easily imagine that, long ago, El Presidente once slept here. The nine individually named rooms have private hot-water shower baths. The Café Montana El Pabellón, on the street side of the hotel, overlooks the square and serves lattes, cappuccinos, sandwiches, and pastries 9am-10:30pm daily.

On the southeast side of town, find the **Hotel del Puente** (Lerdo de Tejada 3, tel./fax 322/297-2834 or 322/297-2859, $12 s, $24 d, $36 t), a former family house that dates from not long after the town's founding in 1605, past the plaza corner adjacent downhill to the Presidencia Municipal. Here, the long-established Trujillo family has renovated an ancestral home and decorated it with handsome

rustic furniture, attractive tile highlights, and wall art. All seven rooms open to a quiet, sunny inner patio garden. Options include rooms, all with private baths and hot-water showers, with 1-5 beds.

Another budget choice on the same street is the quiet and cozy **Hostal de Cervantes** (Lerdo de Tejada 13, tel. 322/297-2902, $25 s, $35 d), where for you can get a simple but clean room with bath, TV, and, in some rooms, a hot tub. Some of the rooms in the back have a bit of a view, and there's an on-site restaurant and bar open all day for authentic Mexican cooking or sipping a cold beer. The hotel owners, the Cervantes Castellon family, also offer motorcycle rentals and horseback tours.

On the same street a few steps up the hill (behind the statue of the miner in the small triangular plaza) is the **Hotel Real de San Sebastián** (Lerdo de Tejada, tel. 322/297-3225, www.sansebastiandeloeste.com.mx, $55 d). The four-room hotel strives for a slightly posh, high-end feeling and sort of pulls it off.

A higher-end choice is **La Galerita de San Sebastián** (tel. 322/297-3040, www.lagalerita.com.mx, $150 d, with breakfast), a lovely

the San Sebastián plaza, with its elegant central bandstand

rustic stone-and-wood home on the northeast side of town, two blocks past Hotel del Puente. The owners offer three simply but invitingly decorated suites with bath and private patio. Breakfast is included, and Internet access and cable TV are provided.

Another pleasant option is the **Hotel and Restaurant Los Arcos De Sol** (López Mateos 15, tel. 322/297-2854 or 333/297-6038, about $15 s, $25 d), on the town plaza's southwest corner (on the right as you enter town), distinguished by its high, arch-decorated front porch. Here you can drink in the entire scene—plaza, church, mountain backdrop—by day, perched at a table in the café on that elevated porch, and sleep in an 18th-century room by night. The hotel's fortunate deviation from 18th-century furnishings is its clean rooms, with electric lights and private hot-water bathrooms. Rooms surround a homey hillside patio garden decorated with flowers and fruit trees, all overseen by the proficient management of owner Jesus Heliodoro Aquirre Dueñas.

## Food and Drink

For store-bought food, try the limited selections of either the grocery **Porvenir** (7am-11pm daily), on the north side of the plaza, or the small ramshackle corner produce and grocery store, **La Republica** (9am-2pm and 4pm-9pm Mon.-Sat.), half a block beyond the northeast plaza corner, past the basketball court. If you're going to need good fresh produce, best stock up, especially during the winter season, in either Puerto Vallarta or Mascota before departure.

Just about the most reliable of local low-cost restaurant choices is **Restaurant Lupita** (tel. 322/297-2903, 7am-11pm daily), about four blocks west of the plaza, on the left, along the Puerto Vallarta road out of town. The friendly, motherly owner cooks just what she would be cooking for her family—eggs, hotcakes, or pork chops for *desayuno* ($2-5) and a four-course *comida* of soup, rice, *guisado* (savory meat or chicken stew), and dessert ($4-5). Evenings, you can usually count on her hearty *pozole* (shredded chicken or pork over hominy

# THE HACIENDA TRAIL

Puerto Vallarta's **Rancho El Charro** (Francisco Villa 895, Fracc. Las Gaviotas, tel. 322/224-0114, www.ranchoelcharro. com) offers complete horseback package tours to and from San Sebastián, Talpa, and Mascota. Participants can sign on, with meals and lodging included, for about $2,200 per person for a seven-day trip. Other packages are available and start at about $150 per person, per day.

Tours typically include guided back-country riding and at least one night camping out on the trail. In addition to exploring San Sebastián, Mascota, or Talpa and neighboring villages, you'll enjoy swimming and hot-tubbing, hearty dinners and cozy evenings at comfortable haciendas and country inns, and, when available, local fiestas. At least one authoritative naturalist/guide accompanies the tour, enriching the experience with expert commentary on trailside flora and fauna.

If horseback riding isn't your thing or you aren't looking for an overnight adventure, try **Wildmex**'s (tel. 322/107-0601, www.wildmex.com) day tours from San Sebastián to Las Palmas (near Puerto Vallarta) via mountain bike. The tour includes transportation from Las Palmas to San Sebastián, bike rental, helmet, water, a guide, and snacks. It starts early in the morning, and the ride is about 5-6 hours in length. Rates start at $110 per person for two or more riders.

in broth), with chopped onions and cabbage, and crispy *totopos* (roasted corn tortillas) on the side ($3).

Alternatively, try **Restaurant El Fortín and Gallery** (on the west side of the plaza, tel. 322/297-2856, 9am-9pm Tues.-Sat.), whose welcoming owner has introduced Italian-Mexican fusion food to San Sebastián. Both inside and outdoor seating make this a nice choice for either escaping the heat of the day or people-watching in the square. Choices include tomato and vegetable salad ($5), cream

of *cuitlachoche* with red wine ($5), and red pepper and rosemary pasta ($8). The chicken curry here is surprisingly good.

For authentic Italian choices, go to **Coco's Montebello Restaurant** (tel. 322/297-2883, 2:30pm-10:30pm daily, except closed on alternate Mon. and Tues., about $15 including salad), a block east, past the plaza's southeast corner, and run by husband-wife team Walter Cappelli and Coco Gil. Here, you can have it all, including homemade breads, pastas, gnocchi, lasagna, good wine, and much, much more.

Before or after dinner, be sure to stop by town hangout **La Barrondila bar** (9am-midnight daily), at the northwest corner of the plaza. Join the locals and select from a dozen tequilas and the *raicilla* (mezcal liquor) of the bartender's nephew, lined up on the bar. Relax with some dominoes beneath the portico out front, and if hard liquor is not your thing, simply enjoy a cooling Corona and play a tune on their jukebox.

## Information and Services

San Sebastián's small *correo* (tel./fax 322/297-2888) is in the Presidencia Municipal (town hall), on the east side of the town plaza. For those without cell phones, there is a Ladatel card-operated **telephone** on the front wall of the Presidencia Municipal. There is also an **ATM** here, convenient since few local businesses take credit cards. Make sure to carry cash with you for dining and shopping particularly. Most of the hotels and other places in town have Wi-Fi these days; at times you can even get a free connection sitting in the plaza. The area's **tourism office** is also in the town hall; a great, informative poster-size map on the veranda will show you the way to just about anywhere you'll want to go in the area.

If you get sick, go to the local **Centro de Salud** (Health Clinic), about three blocks east, uphill, from the plaza. For minor illnesses, consult the town pharmacy, **Farmacia del Oeste** (tel. 322/297-2833, 11am-3pm and 5pm-10pm Mon.-Sat.), at the southwest plaza corner, adjacent to the Puerto Vallarta road.

© JUSTIN HENDERSON

**Organic coffee is grown and roasted in the San Sebastián region.**

One of the most highly recommended **guides** in town is English-speaking Obed Dueñas (tel. 322/297-2864), with a car. Also highly recommended, if you can supply the wheels, are a pair of competent Spanish-only-speaking guides (bring along someone to translate). They are Ramon Ramos Peña, who lives on the extension of Calle Hidalgo, about a kilometer east of the plaza, and blacksmith (*herrador*) Pedro González Traigos (Amado Aguirre 33), who leads visitors on explorations of local mines. Pedro gained his extensive practical knowledge from his father, a longtime blacksmith at the Quitería mine. A visit to Pedro's shop is worthwhile in itself; you may find him forging red-hot iron into horseshoes. (Perhaps Pedro could recommend someone to translate.)

Pamela Thompson, reservations manager of Hacienda Jalisco, also recommends a guide, Juan, who regularly shows Hacienda Jalisco guests and others to local interesting sights. These often include, besides the in-town sights, the La Quinta coffee farm and processing center, Santa Gertrudis Mine, and La Taberna *raicilla* (mezcal liquor) distillery. Contact Pamela (tel./fax 322/222-9638 or 322/226-1014, info@haciendajalisco.com or pmt15@hotmail.com), and she will forward your message to Juan. There are two employees of the Centenaria *raicilla* store, just past the basketball court off the plaza, who are also available as guides.

## Getting There

**By Bus:** Road and weather conditions permitting, a sturdy red (*rojo*) ATM (Autotransportes Guadalajara Talpa Mascota, www.talpamascota.com) bus connects Puerto Vallarta with the San Sebastián crossroad at La Estancia, continuing to Mascota and Talpa. It departs daily in the early morning, with an afternoon departure around 4:30pm from the north side of Puerto Vallarta's Parque Hidalgo, a couple of blocks north of the Malecón. Check the departure schedule and buy your reserved ticket ahead of time at the little store (tel. 322/222-4816, 9am-3pm and 6pm-9pm daily) at the corner of Argentina and Guadalupe Sánchez, two short blocks uphill, east of the bus stop. Under good conditions, the morning bus arrives at the San Sebastián stop around 9am, Mascota at 11am, and Talpa at 2pm. The daily morning return trip follows the reverse route, departing Talpa in the early morning (afternoon departure around 3pm), arriving in Mascota around 8am, San Sebastián (La Estancia) 10am, and finally in Puerto Vallarta about 1pm. Take drinks and food; little or nothing is available en route.

Note: The *rojo* bus does not go all the way into San Sebastián, but drops off and picks up passengers at the La Estancia crossing, about 7 miles (11.3 km) from town. Local trucks and taxis then ferry passengers to and from town, on a once-gnarly road that has been (mostly) cobbled and paved, and is now an easy ride, even in heavy weather.

Furthermore, a **van** customarily connects San Sebastián with Mascota. It leaves around 7am from the San Sebastián plaza and passes through La Estancia in time for passengers to meet the Puerto Vallarta-bound bus from Mascota. The van continues, arriving in Mascota around 9am. On the return trip it leaves Mascota around noon and arrives in San Sebastián around 2pm. This cost is about US$4.

**By Car:** Despite the ready bus access, driving your own car or a rented vehicle to San Sebastián on the all-weather highway, which is in good shape save for the occasional pothole, from Puerto Vallarta is even easier, and it affords you added independence and flexibility to boot. The direct route from Puerto Vallarta bypasses the small town of **Las Palmas,** inland, an hour northeast of Puerto Vallarta. Farther up the road, a gas station just past La Estancia on the road to Mascota has made worrying about filling the tank a thing of the past. To get on the correct road, drive north past the Puerto Vallarta airport along Highway 200. At the signed Highway 70 right turnoff to Ixtapa and Las Palmas a few miles north of the airport (keep your eyes peeled for a sign that says Guadalajara via Mascota, as this turnoff is in the midst of a very busy, at-times confusing multiroad junction), continue along the excellent (but slow; watch for speed bumps and potholes) paved road about 15 miles (24 km) to Las Palmas. Mark your odometer at the signed fork (where you continue straight ahead for San Sebastián and go left for Las Palmas town).

The highway continues smoothly (except for a few construction detours and/or mini-landslides, depending on the weather), winding uphill, providing stunning vistas of the valleys and mountains (the views from the long, gorge-spanning bridge just short of La Estancia are spectacular; be sure and take a photo break here) and passing a few hard-scrabble ranchos. There are a couple of places to make a pit stop along the way, including the occasional tequila distillery and roadside restaurant or two. At Mile 19 (Km 30), you reach **La Estancia** village crossing, with a restaurant and stores. Continue ahead for Mascota, or turn left for San Sebastián. At La Mesita rancho, at Mile 22 (Km 35), turn right for San Sebastián. At Mile 24 (Km 38), pass the Hacienda Jalisco signed gate on the left. Continue another mile to San Sebastián plaza, at Mile 25 (Km 40).

## MASCOTA

Mascota is a contraction of the Aztec name Mazocotlan (place of the deer and pines, a translation depicted by Mascota's traditional hieroglyph of an antlered deer head in profile beneath a three-limbed pine tree).

Although local gold and silver deposits drew early Spanish colonists, agriculture has proved to be the real treasure of Mascota. Its 4,300-foot (1,300-m) altitude brings a refreshingly mild, subtropical climate and abundant moisture to nurture a bounty of oranges, lemons, avocados, apples, grapes, and sugarcane in the surrounding farm valley. Even during the dry winter months, many fields remain lush, irrigated by the Río Mascota, which eventually meanders downhill through its deep gorge to join its sister stream, the Ameca, near Puerto Vallarta.

Mascota (pop. 13,000) is the metropolis

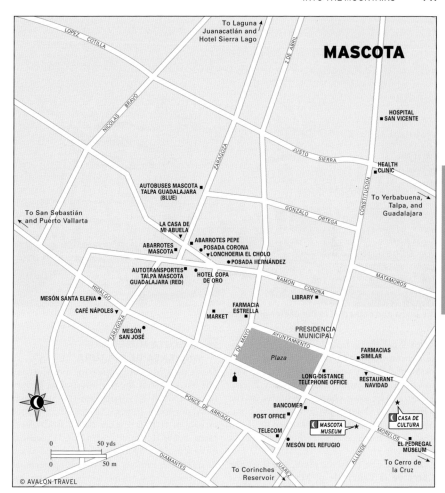

BAY OF BANDERAS

of Puerto Vallarta's mountains, offering such services as hotels, restaurants, markets, banks, doctors, and hospitals to local residents and visitors. It's the seat of the local *municipio* of the same name, which spreads beyond the Mascota Valley to a number of idyllic villages tucked away in their own remote emerald vales.

Quiet streets lined with original adobe homes, for the most part well maintained, lend the town an almost European old-world charm. The streets and town square are impeccably free of garbage and debris. Signs have been posted reminding residents to keep the town clean, and garbage receptacles can be found throughout the city. Now if only more towns would follow suit!

## Orientation and Sights

The town spreads out along roughly north-south and east-west lines from the central plaza. The Presidencia Municipal occupies the north side of the plaza; facing it, streets on your right run east, converging on Avenida Justo Sierra, which at the edge of town becomes the

© DONNA DAY

the plaza and cathedral in the center of Mascota

Talpa-Guadalajara road. In the opposite direction, running from the south side of the plaza past the church, Avenida Hidalgo heads west toward San Sebastián and eventually Puerto Vallarta. The town church, dedicated to the Virgen de los Dolores (Virgin of Sorrows), was begun around 1780 and not finished until 100 years later. It replaced an earlier church built in 1649.

Looking east from the plaza, you'll see the **Cerro de la Cruz,** site of Mascota's biggest yearly party, rising at the edge of town. On May 3, the national **Día de la Cruz** (Day of the Cross), nearly everyone climbs the hill for a high Mass, followed by picnicking, mariachis, and evening bonfires.

Late afternoon is a good time to make the 20-minute climb to the summit, where you can enjoy the cool breeze and the sunset view. On the hilltop, look north across the green valley to see a road winding over a forested ridge. This ridge conceals Mascota's gems—the picturesque hamlets of Yerbabuena, Cimarrón Chico, and Navidad.

## MASCOTA MUSEUM AND CASA DE CULTURA

Don't miss Mascota's museum (on Morelos, one block west of the southwest plaza corner, tel. 388/386-0189, 10am-2pm and 5pm-8pm daily, donation, 10 pesos suggested), the labor of love of retired teacher Raoul Rodríguez. Here, Señor Rodríguez, who gives a personal guided tour (in Spanish; bring a friend along to translate), exhibits his fascinating personal collection of Mascota memorabilia. Highlights include mementos of Mascota native daughter Ester Fernández, star of what has become the golden age of Mexican cinema. Other displays highlight the devotion of Mascota priest José María Roble, who was martyred during the Cristero rebellion of the late 1920s. A third section exhibits the oil paintings of noted Mascota landscape painter Gilberto Guerra.

The Mascota Casa de Cultura (Allende 115, tel. 388/386-2202, 10am-2pm and 4pm-7pm Mon.-Sat., 10am-2pm Sun., donation, 10 pesos suggested), half a block north of the museum, features a permanent exhibit of photos of some

© DONNA DAY

Mascota's graceful cathedral

is seriously weird stuff, oddly beautiful, visually compelling, and well worth a walk-through. Peña is also the proud author of a book on the history of Mascota, *La Historia de Mascota,* although it's only available in Spanish.

One other not-to-be-missed Mascota site is the abandoned, roofless church known as the **Templo de la Preciosa Sangre de Cristo.** This unfinished "ruin" is a garden, a sanctuary, and an archaeological wonder, with its open windows and roofless walls framing stirring vistas of mountains and sky. To this practicing non-Christian, this wreck of a cathedral building contains more spiritual energy than any church I've ever been in. You'll find it near the entrance to town (coming from Puerto Vallarta direction) on Calles Carranza and Lopez Cotillera. Stop for 10 minutes and stroll through. You won't regret it.

## Entertainment and Events

Other than an occasional public *baile* (dance), *corrida de toros* (bullfight), or *charreada* (rodeo), Mascota people rely on simple diversions. You can join them in a stroll around the town plaza on any evening (especially Sat. and Sun.) or a climb to the top of Cerro de la Cruz.

Mascota life heats up during a number of regionally important fiestas. **Fiestas Patrias** kick off around September 10 with the crowning of a queen, and merrymaking continues during a week of performances, competitions, and patriotic events. On September 13, folks gather to solemnly honor the bravery of the beloved Niños Héroes; then, two days later, fireworks paint the night sky above the plaza as the crowd joins the mayor in a shouted reenactment of Father Hidalgo's Grito de Dolores. Concurrent with the patriotic tumult, the festival of Mascota's patron, La Virgin de Dolores, continues with processions, pilgrimages, high Masses, and an old-fashioned carnival.

Besides participating in all of above, the nearby hamlets of Yerbabuena, Cimarrón Chico, and Navidad stage their own celebrations. Yerbabuena's patron saint is the Virgin of Guadalupe, and the town honors her with native costumes, folk dances, and processions

of the 12,000 petroglyphs discovered locally in 1999 and 2000. The rock carvings appear to represent rites of sun, water, and fertility. In three other rooms, a number of professionally arranged and labeled displays reveal a fascinating trove of handsome human- and animal-motif ceramic sculptures, dating from about AD 1000. All of these finds were excavated during recent years by a team led by Professor Joseph Mountjoy of the University of North Carolina.

For more history and perhaps something a little unusual, stop in at the **El Pedregal** museum (Morelos 64, hours vary, $2), where you can view photos from the town's history as well as an amazing variety of stone-covered objects. Here local author and craftsman Francisco Rodríguez Peña has worked for over 20 years to cover nearly everything in his home with rocks and pebbles. From old TVs to an entire bedroom set, the pieces are varied and fascinating. The other Mascota museums are worthy of visits, but this guy is a low-keyed fanatic, a man possessed by the need to cover absolutely everything he can lay his hands on with rocks. This

climaxing in a special Mass on December 19. Neighboring Cimarrón Chico celebrates its patron saint in a harvest-style fiesta September 20-29. Navidad honors patrons San Joaquín and Santa Ana with processions, dancing, and fireworks that climax on July 26.

## Accommodations

For a more bucolic lodging option that is still close to town, try the **Hotel Rancho La Esmeralda** (tel. 388/386-0953 or 388/101-2513, www.rancholaesmeralda.com.mx), which offers ranch-style accommodations of eight cabins and seven rooms in a country setting with a view of the surrounding mountains. Simple country furnishings make the rooms homey and comfortable. The cabins are a great deal for larger parties, as they each sleep up to six people and have fully equipped kitchenettes. Rooms are around $45 d and cabins $90-110 d, with various discounts and freebies for kids. The hotel has a nice swimming pool with a deck and grassy lawn surrounding, and also offers horseback and ATV tours of the bucolic countryside. To get to the hotel, follow the signs from the Pemex gas station as you enter town. Make a left from the main highway, and the hotel is ahead about 300 yards.

For lodging in the heart of the town, a trio of good small-town hotels line Calle Corona, two short blocks from the town plaza's northwest corner. Walk a block north to Corona, then west another block to the **Posada Corona** (Ramón Corona 72, tel. 388/386-0250, fax 388/386-0460, analuzsd@hotmail.com). Inside, past the immaculate tiled lobby, you'll probably meet the hotel's manager, Analuz Díaz, who carries on the mission of her late mother, "Cuca" Díaz. Most of their 17 rooms—very clean and comfortably furnished with twin or double beds, reading lamps, ceiling fans, and hot-water shower baths—line plant-decorated upstairs corridors. Rates run about $16 s and $30 d; add $5 for additional people. During the Talpa festivals (around Feb. 2, Mar. 10-19, May 12, and Sept. 10-19), rates are higher and reservations are mandatory.

Two doors east is the similarly clean and comfortably furnished **Posada Hernández** (Ramón Corona 66, tel. 388/386-0049, $16 d, $30 t). Efficiently managed by owner Esther Hernández, the hotel's 10 rooms surround a leafy, tranquil inner patio. A cabin suitable for up to 10 people is available for $64 per night.

Across the street stands the **Hotel Copa de Oro** (Ramón Corona 75, tel. 388/386-0016, $16 s, $26 d, $34 t). The front desk leads to an open-air interior courtyard, enclosed by ground- and upper-level floors of simply furnished but clean rooms. Owners have brightened up the hotel with paint, polish, and a sprinkling of new furnishings throughout. Expect higher rates during fiesta days.

Mascota's three deluxe hotels, two of which are historic buildings, stand near opposite sides of the central plaza. The more traditional of the three is ◖ **Mesón del Refugio** (Independencia 187, tel. 388/386-0767, mesondelrefugio@yahoo.com). The owners, working with Jalisco tourism's Haciendas and Casas Rurales promotion program, have renovated a distinguished Mascota hotel. The handsome result is 13 high-ceilinged, airy rooms on two floors around a tranquil, inviting inner patio. The rooms ($50 d) and suites ($75 d or t), furnished with designer-rustic tiled floors, hand-loomed bedspreads, handmade wood and leather furniture, original wall paintings and etchings, and bright Talavera-tiled bathrooms, complete the lovely picture. Some even larger, pricier suites have two or three beds and sleep up to six. Amenities include cable TV in the rooms and a bar downstairs.

On the opposite side of the plaza, consider spending your Mascota time in luxurious comfort in the **Mesón de Santa Elena** (Hidalgo 155, tel. 388/386-0313, www.mesondesantaelena.com). The hotel's 15 accommodations, which all enfold a graceful plant-bedecked interior patio, are elaborately decorated with handsomely crafted traditional furniture, decorator lamps, soft carpets, and shiny deluxe tiled baths. All this for a mere $55 d in a standard room; around $85 d for larger suites. Every room and suite has cable TV, and the hotel offers a rooftop panoramic-view terrace, restaurant, and comfortably furnished sitting rooms for resting and relaxing.

Half a block away is **Mesón de San José** (Hidalgo 165, tel. 338/386-1501 or 338/386-1502, www.mesonsanjose.com.mx, $35-70 d). Although, like Mesón del Refugio and Mesón de Santa Elena, this was a renovation of an existing structure, the rebuilding converted an old house into something nearly completely modern. Downstairs, past the reception and intimate smallish inner patio, is an inviting restaurant, furnished in luxurious shiny all-oak furniture. Upstairs, the 14 rustic-deluxe rooms are completely up-to-date, gleaming with new furnishings and fixtures. The owner's pride and joy is a room in the rear, with an expansive private patio commanding a panoramic over-the-rooftops mountain sunset view. For all this luxury, prices are reasonable.

For an unusually luxurious mountain-lake lodging option, consider the **Sierra Lago Resort and Spa** (tel./fax 322/224-9350, toll-free Mex. tel. 01-800/725-6277, toll-free U.S./Can. tel. 877/845-5247, www.sierralago.com, $380 d, $450 d, or $550 d, depending on room type) in Laguna Juanacatlán. A luxurious yet unpretentious hotel, it offers all-inclusive accommodations with a multitude of amenities in gorgeous alpine surroundings.

### Camping

Local camping opportunities are excellent at **Corinches Reservoir,** near Mascota. Here, authorities have built a fine facility, now known locally as La Terraza. For starters, you can enjoy bass and carp dinners from one of several lake-view *palapa* restaurants with mariachi entertainment Saturday and Sunday afternoons. Alternatively, you can enjoy your own picnic beneath one of several airy picnic shelters, complete with car pad, useable for self-contained RV parking and camping. Launch your own boat at a good boat ramp downhill, and swim in the cool, freshwater lake to your heart's content.

Moreover, wilderness camping is permitted all around the reservoir's gorgeous five-mile pine-and-oak-studded shoreline. Get there by car or taxi from the Mascota plaza, southeast

corner. Follow Calle Constitución south one block. Turn left on Juárez and follow the signs about three miles (five km) to Restaurant La Terraza on the lakeshore. There are now several other restaurants to choose from, as well as some private homes overlooking the lake. But the campsites remain in place, useable for no charge. The road from town is relatively flat dirt and gravel, ideal for easy mountain biking if that's on your agenda.

The surrounding mountains offer still more wilderness camping opportunities. Pine-bordered volcanic crater Lake Juanacatlán Chico, accessible from Navidad, is a good spot to set up a tent and enjoy a bit of fishing, swimming, and hiking.

### Food

The fruits and vegetables are local and luscious at the town **market** (Prisciliano Sánchez at the corner of Hidalgo), a block west of the plaza. For general groceries, go to the big **Abarrotes Mascota** at the corner of Corona and Degollado, a half block west of the Posada Corona. If it doesn't have what you want, Pepe Díaz, owner of **Abarrotes Pepe** (Corona 94, tel. 388/386-0374, 7am-3pm and 4pm-9pm Mon.-Sat., 7am-4pm Sun.), across the street, probably will.

Moreover, Mascota offers a bounty of regional sweets. Check out **Dulces de Mascota** (Ramón Corona 72, tel. 388/386-0049, 8am-3pm and 4pm-9pm Mon.-Sat., 8am-3pm Sun.), in front of Posada Hernández. Here, select from a delicious assortment (mango, guava, pineapple) of homemade *conservas* (jams), empanadas (fruit turnovers), and crisp locally famous *galletas* (cookies), plus much more.

Moreover, good coffee and pastries are plentiful in Mascota, at cozy family-style **Café Napoles** (corner of Hidalgo and Zaragoza, two blocks west of the plaza church, tel. 388/386-0051). Drop in for a savory cappuccino, mocha, or latte and a slice of cake (chocolate, mocha, *tres leches*) or a turnover (pineapple, banana, mango).

For good breakfasts or snacks, Cuca Díaz's nephew Chole runs the **Lonchería El Cholo**

(R. Corona, about three doors east of Posada Corona, tel. 388/386-0771, 7am-3pm and 7pm-10pm Mon.-Sat.).

Upstairs from Cholo, you'll find the **Cyber Gallo Internet Café** (Corona 70, tel. 388/386-1627 or 388/102-4822, 9am-2pm and 4pm-10pm daily), offering computer services.

For more serious eating, try restaurant ◖ **La Casa de Mi Abuelita** (corner of Corona and Zaragoza, tel. 388/386-1975, 8am-midnight daily, $2-7), a block north and a block west of the plaza. Owners and chefs at My Grandmother's House (which it really was) are very proud of their food, which is nearly exclusively hearty Mexican country fare. Here, you can feast on the specialties that you can't usually get north of the border. These include yogurtlike *jocoque,* a *chivichanga* (a thin burrito made with a corn tortilla), and a *chingadera* (like nachos, except with meat instead of cheese).

You're in for a treat at **Restaurant Navidad** (on Ayuntamiento, half a block east of the plaza's northeast corner, tel. 388/386-0469 or 388/386-0806, 7am-11pm daily), where you can find out if your favorite Mexican restaurant back home is making enchiladas, quesadillas, tacos, and burritos (*burros* here) authentically. At Restaurant Navidad, they're all good and all very correct. The cavernous space has two rooms of seating and an attached pizza restaurant in case you wish to try something other than Mexican food. A large plate of four crispy *flautas* and accompanying salad will run you about $4.

Agriculture is the main industry of the area, so be sure to stop into some of the many shops tucked into the warren of streets from the main square and purchase some regional products. Fresh cheese can be bought almost anywhere, as well as honey, fruit candies, and high-octane *raicilla,* also known as Mexican moonshine.

## Information and Services

Get the most pesos for your money at **Bancomer** (tel. 388/386-0387 or 388/386-1463, 8:30am-4pm Mon.-Fri.), on the southeast plaza corner. After hours, use the ATM.

Mascota's main health clinic is the first-rate government **Hospital Primer Contacto** (tel. 388/386-0174 or 388/386-1823), on Avenida Justo Sierra, the road to Guadalajara, on the northeast side of town. They have 24-hour emergency services and three doctors, a surgeon, a gynecologist, and a general practitioner on call. For serious illnesses and extraordinary diagnostic services, go either to Puerto Vallarta or one of the big Seguro Social Hospitals in Ameca or Tala, about 80 miles (128.7 km) east on the road to Guadalajara.

Find the town *biblioteca* on Ramón Corona at the corner of Constitución, behind the Presidencia Municipal. The *correo* (Independencia 156, tel. 388/386-0197, 8am-3pm Mon.-Fri.) is half a block south of the plaza's southeast corner. For public fax and money orders, go to **Telecom** (tel. 388/386-0022, 9am-3pm Mon.-Fri.), off the plaza's southeast corner, half a block south of Bancomer. As is true of many Mexican towns these days, Internet access is readily available in almost every restaurant and hotel, or can be found somewhere nearby.

## Getting There

**By Bus:** At least two bus lines serve Mascota. The best equipped is **Autotransportes Guadalajara Talpa Mascota** (ATM, www.talpamascota.com), known locally as the *rojo* (red) bus. It connects Mascota with Puerto Vallarta, Talpa, and Guadalajara. Tickets and departures in Mascota are available from the curbside *rojo* (ATM) bus station (Corona 79, tel. 388/386-0093), adjacent to the Hotel Copa de Oro.

Road and weather conditions permitting, a sturdy red ATM bus connects Puerto Vallarta with the San Sebastián crossroad at La Estancia, continuing to Mascota and Talpa. It departs daily in the early morning, with an afternoon departure around 4:30pm from the north side of Puerto Vallarta's Parque Hidalgo, a couple of blocks north of the Malecón. Check the departure schedule and buy your reserved ticket ahead of time at the little store (tel. 322/222-4816, 9am-3pm and 6pm-9pm daily) at the corner of Argentina and Guadalupe Sánchez, two short blocks uphill, east of the bus stop. Under good conditions, the morning bus arrives at the San Sebastián stop around 9am, Mascota at 11am, and Talpa at 2pm. The daily morning return trip follows the reverse route, departing Talpa in the early morning (afternoon departure around 3pm), arriving in Mascota around 8am, San Sebastián (La Estancia) 10am, and finally in Puerto Vallarta about 1pm. Take drinks and food; little or nothing is available en route.

Regular **van service** connects San Sebastián and Mascota. It starts out at the San Sebastián plaza daily in the early morning (check for the time locally). The return van departs from the *rojo* (ATM) station in Mascota at around 1pm, arriving at San Sebastián plaza around 3pm.

The competing **Autobuses Mascota Talpa Guadalajara** (known as the Autobus Azul, or Blue Bus) also connects Mascota with Guadalajara, Talpa, and Puerto Vallarta. Tickets and departure information are available at the small Mascota streetside station (corner of Cotilla and Zaragoza, tel. 388/386-1006), two blocks north of Corona.

**By Car:** Although buses are cheaper, driving will give you added mobility for exploring Mascota's scenic mountain country and hidden villages. The good, paved, all-weather 80-mile (128-km) route from Puerto Vallarta to Mascota is doable in about three hours under good conditions. From Puerto Vallarta, drive north past the Puerto Vallarta airport along Highway 200. At the signed Highway 70 right turnoff to Ixtapa and Las Palmas a few miles north of the airport (keep your eyes peeled for a sign that says Guadalajara via Mascota, as this turnoff is in the midst of a very busy, at-times confusing multiroad junction), continue along the excellent (but slow; watch for speed bumps and potholes) paved road about 15 miles (24 km) to Las Palmas. Mark your odometer at the signed fork, where you continue straight ahead for San Sebastián.

The highway continues smoothly (except for a few construction detours and/or mini-landslides, depending on the weather), winding uphill, providing stunning vistas of the valleys and mountains (the views from the long, gorge-spanning bridge just short of La Estancia are spectacular; be sure and take a photo break here) and passing a few hardscrabble ranchos. There are a couple of places to make a pit stop along the way, including the occasional tequila distillery and roadside restaurant or two. At Mile 19 (Km 30), you reach La Estancia village crossing, with a restaurant and stores. Continue straight ahead for Mascota. Set your odometer at the La Estancia crossing.

Two miles (three km) farther—you'll find a gas station along this stretch, should you need to fill your tank—pass through Ermita village; continue six more miles (nine km) uphill along a pine-and-oak-shaded ridge to a breezy view pass at Mile 8 (Km 13). A faint Jeep road heads left along the summit ridge to La Bufa peak and Real Alto village. Continue downhill, passing over El Saucillo Creek, at about Mile 11 (Km 18) and Palo Jueco Creek, about two miles farther on. Continue over a second oak-studded pass at around Mile 19 (Km 29). Then coast five miles (eight km) more downhill past a former fighting-cock farm on the left, at around Mile 24 (Km 43). Continue to the Mascota town limit (and gas station) about four miles (seven km) farther and, finally, the Mascota plaza at Mile 28 (Km 45).

Mascota has two **gas stations,** one on the west side, about a mile west of the Mascota plaza, and another on the east side, about three miles east of town on the Guadalajara-Talpa road.

## EXCURSIONS FROM MASCOTA

Having come as far as Mascota, you might enjoy spending some additional hours or a day or two poking around the idyllic trio of hamlets—Yerbabuena, Cimarrón Chico, and Navidad—and maybe taking in the great outdoors at the spruce-studded high-sierra crater lake, Laguna Juanacatlán. Photographers will happily capture the rolling fields and stunning vistas.

If you're driving, Laguna Juanacatlán requires a full day for the round-trip, but a single graded road safely negotiable by passenger car connects the three hamlets in a leisurely four- or five-hour 25-mile (40-km) round-trip from Mascota. Head out via Avenida Justo Sierra to the road fork at the east edge of Mascota town; the right branch heads to Talpa and Guadalajara, while the left fork proceeds to Yerbabuena, Cimarrón Chico, and Navidad. If you're traveling on foot (carry water), you'll find few, if any, public buses heading to Yerbabuena, Cimarrón Chico, and Navidad. You can probably catch a ride with one of the cars and trucks that often head along the road during the day. Stick out your thumb; if someone stops, offer to pay.

## Yerbabuena

The latter-day renown of Yerbabuena is the labor of love of its longtime resident and official municipal historian, Father Vidal Salcedo R.:

> Yerbabuena, idyllic and enchanted little nook, You stand apart from Mascota, the noble and lordly. Whoever ventures to

> thee and pauses at your door, You beckon through love, both given and received.

That sentiment, in Spanish, heads the pamphlet that Salcedo offers visitors who arrive at his **Quinta Santa María** *mini-museo* (mini-museum) not far from the town plaza. To get there, bear east at the street (16 de Septiembre) past the east side of the plaza, and continue a couple of blocks until you see a big mill wheel beneath a small forest of spreading tropical trees. Open during daylight hours, this informal museum has free admission.

If Salcedo is out, someone else—perhaps Hector, his nephew—will offer to guide you around the flowery grounds, which bloom with the fruits of Salcedo's eclectic, unconventional tastes. The ornaments Salcedo has distributed around the grounds range from pious marble images to rusting antique farm implements.

The grounds are scattered with small one-room buildings displaying Salcedo's painstakingly gathered collections. Highlights include indigenous archaeological artifacts, working

on the mountain road from Mascota to Talpa

models of an ore mill and cane crusher, an ancient typewriter, religious banners and devotional objects, a fascinating coin and bill collection, and a metal step-ramp once used with Mascota's first passenger planes that now leads to an upstairs garden gazebo.

## Cimarrón Chico

From Yerbabuena, head east again. Don't miss the antique country cemetery about a mile out of town. Next stop is Cimarrón Chico (Little Wild Place), the bucolic valley and hamlet about 6 miles (10 km) over the next ridge. Despite its name, Cimarrón Chico appears peaceful and picturesque. Adobe farmhouses, scattered about a sylvan mountain-rimmed hollow, surround a neat village center. The town's pride and joy is its diminutive picture-book **church** at the east edge of the village.

Another don't-miss local stop is the charmingly small and tidy *abarrotería* in the middle of the village. Drop in for good fresh fruits, vegetables, and Jumex brand canned juices. Enjoy a chat with friendly proprietor and community leader Juan López Sandoval. He's a good source of local information, including homes where you might stay overnight, camping spots, and guides for horseback or hiking excursions. He especially recommends that you arrive during the spring (Mar.-May) to enjoy the locally distilled *raicilla* (mezcal liquor).

There is one local place to stay. East of town, follow a road fork signed **Rancho Paraíso Cimarrón,** where you'll find a large guest cabana (large enough for a big family) and a small pool. For reservations, call ranch owner Martín Peña (tel. 200/124-7395), who can arrange your stay. The rates are $10 per person, per night.

Continue east, over another scenic pine-clad ridge, 4 miles (6.5 km) farther to Navidad. Along the way, notice the yellow lichen-daubed volcanic-chimney cliffs towering on the left halfway uphill. Also, at the ridgetop within sight of Navidad, note the cobbled road that forks left, uphill. It leads to the hamlet of Juanacatlán (3 mi/4.8 km, half an hour), as well as Laguna Juanacatlán Chico (Jeep only, 5 mi/8 km, an hour) and Laguna Juanacatlán

(10 mi/16 km, 2.5 rough hours—it's best to go directly from Mascota).

## Navidad

The town of Navidad, with a population of about 1,000, is more of a metropolis than either Cimarrón Chico or Yerbabuena. It basks picturesquely on the hillside above a petite green farm valley. Hillside lanes sprinkled with red tile-roofed whitewashed houses and a venerable colonial-era steepled church, dedicated to San Joaquín and Santa Ana, complete the idyllic picture.

At his store across the plaza from the church, friendly English-speaking Juan Arrizon Quintero doubles as the unofficial goodwill ambassador. As he or any of the old-timers lounging in the shade outside his store will tell you, the short supply of *terreno* (land) is a big problem here. Young people must migrate to other parts of Mexico or the United States for jobs. The Navidad mine, still operating several miles farther east, used to employ lots of local people, but now it can hire only a small number of those needing jobs.

For a wilderness camping opportunity, ask Juan about Laguna Juanacatlán Chico, whose clear 300-foot-deep (91-m-deep) waters are fine for swimming, kayaking, and trout and bass fishing.

## ◖ LAGUNA JUANACATLÁN

A block north and a block west of the Mascota town plaza, head out Calle Zaragoza by taxi, local minibus, or your own wheels to Laguna Juanacatlán (12 mi/19 km, one hour), a 7,000-foot-high (2,130-m-high) clear mountain lake framed by steep pine-tufted ridges. Even if you only plan to have lunch in the hotel restaurant and enjoy a stroll around the lake, the stunning drive is well worth the effort, providing you don't have a fear of heights. Following a good cobbled road, climb over a pine-crested ridge and descend into bucolic El Galope river valley, past rustic ranchos and rich, summer-green pastures and cornfields. The steep final 2,000-foot (610-m) ascent is a series of switchbacks; fortunately, the road was recently improved and widened, making this ascent a little easier. Once you reach the apex, the road levels out and winds through a sun-dappled evergreen forest to a lovely view of the lake. A few folks stroll its green grassy banks, small sailboats and kayaks rest by the shore, and smoke curls out of the lakefront lodge stone chimney.

Inside the ◖ **Sierra Lago Resort and Spa** (tel. 388/386-1400, toll-free Mex. tel. 01-800/832-5211, toll-free U.S./Can. tel. 877/845-3795, www.sierralago.com), the reception area leads to a spaciously handsome, beam-ceilinged, knotty-pine rustic dining room and adjacent lake-view lounge and bar. Although the whole hotel layout is luxurious, it's also unpretentiously modest in scale, blending unobtrusively within the gorgeous alpine surroundings.

The 23 accommodations, all offered only on an all-inclusive basis, divide into three categories, all deluxe: ecosuites, actually permanent, open-air tented platforms ($380 d); comfortable standard cabanas ($450 d) with room for families; and cabana suites ($550 d), roomy rustic-chic cabins. Children 4-12 stay for $40 apiece. Amenities include in-suite hot-water shower baths, big bubbling lakeside hot tub, and sauna. The suites include a whirlpool bath and are the only option with fireplaces, so opt for one of these if you plan on staying overnight during the cool winter months. In-house activities include horseback riding, mountain biking, sailing, and kayaking, and are included in the price of the room. Massage and spa treatments are available but cost extra.

High prices nothwithstanding, this spot is gorgeous and could be easily worth a splurge for lovers of both comfort and the outdoors. Remember, however, that Laguna Juanacatlán is 7,000 feet (2,130 m) above sea level and during the winter is decidedly cool, even sometimes cold. Then, a dip in the lake would feel very chilly (however, the big steaming lakeside whirlpool bath would feel very welcoming). On the other hand, summer and the drier early to mid-fall would be delightfully temperate at Laguna Juanacatlán.

## TALPA

How a petite straw figure can bring hundreds of thousands of visitors a year to lovely but remote little Talpa (pop. about 7,000, officially Talpa de Allende) is a mystery to those who've never heard the tale of the Virgin of Talpa. Back in the 1600s, the little image, believed by many to be miraculous, attracted a considerable local following. The bishop of Mascota, annoyed by those in his flock who constantly trooped to Talpa to pray to the Virgin, decided to have her transported to his Mascota church—and "jailed," some people said. But the Virgin would have none of it: The next morning she was gone, having returned to Talpa.

A few local folks brought the bishop to the outskirts of town, where they showed him small footprints in the road, heading toward Talpa. "Nonsense!" said the bishop. "The Virgin doesn't even have feet, so how could she make such footprints?" So the bishop again had the Virgin brought back to Mascota.

Determined not to be tricked again, the bishop ordered a young campesino to guard the Virgin at night. The Virgin, however, foiled the bishop once more. The young man dozed off, only to wake to the sound of footsteps leaving the church. The frightened young man looked up and saw that the Virgin was indeed gone; later, people found a new set of small footprints heading back toward Talpa.

The flabbergasted bishop finally relented. He left the Virgin in Talpa, where she, now known as the Walking Virgin, has remained ever since.

### ◖ Virgin of Talpa Basilica

For some, getting to Talpa is the best part of going there. The road from Mascota climbs up into the mountains, offering spectacular views all along the way, and then, when you reach the summit overlooking Talpa, you'll find a somewhat run-down domed chapel up a steep hill at the roadside, with a spacious parking area. From here a staircase leads to the base of the chapel, and from the base of the chapel a stair winds up and around the building nearly to the top. Another spiral staircase then takes you all

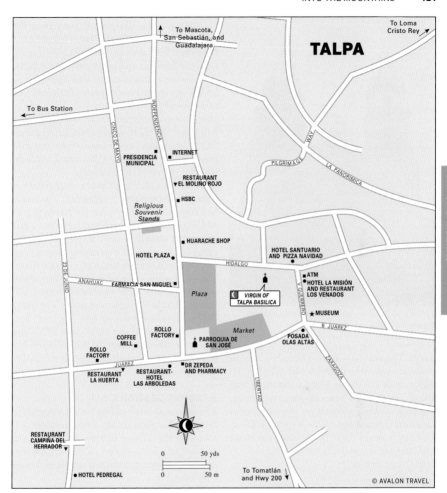

**BAY OF BANDERAS**

the way up. Amazing vistas frame a strange little altar at top. The stairs will leave you breathless, as will the views.

In the pastoral mountain-rimmed Talpa valley, all activity centers on the town square, which spreads from the stately steepled baroque cathedral. Inside, the beloved Virgin of Talpa, flanked by Joseph, Mary, and a pair of angels, occupies the place of high honor. The petite figure stands on her altar, dwarfed by her gleaming silk robe, golden crown, and radiant halo. The faithful, mostly poor folks from all parts of Mexico, stream in continuously—most walking, others hobbling (roughly hand-carved walking sticks are for sale in every religious curio shop in town), a few even crawling to the altar on their knees. Music often resounds through the tall sanctuary—either voices, solo or in choir, or instruments, often by mariachis playing mournful, stately melodies.

Head behind the cathedral to Talpa's excellent church-funded **museum** (no phone, 9am-3pm daily, donations accepted). Two floors of expertly prepared displays begin with the

Talpa's cathedral, home to the miraculous Virgin of Talpa

basics, illustrating—from a strictly Catholic point of view—the miracles and religious significance of the Virgin Mary, continuing with the three "sister" Virgins of Mexico, and description and documentation of a number of latter-day apparitions of the Virgin of Talpa. Upstairs, cases of the Virgin's gilded vestments and other devotional objects decorate the museum's airy atrium.

### Other Sights

After the museum, head to the **market,** downhill at the left (east) side of the plaza. Look over the souvenirs: small sombreros, walking sticks, flowers, and baskets all fashioned of rubbery *chicle,* the basis of chewing gum. There are several local artisans who make traditional leather sandals, huaraches, some with gum soles. They take some breaking in, but once that is accomplished, they are a comfortable option for walking. If you see a bottle filled with a yellow-orange liquid, it's probably *rompope* (rohm-POH-pay), eggnog laced with tequila.

When you feel like getting away from the crowd, climb **Loma Cristo Rey** (Hill of Christ the King), behind and to the left of the church, for some fresh air and panoramic views of the town, valley, and mountains. Back by the plaza, let the sweet perfume of guava fruit lead you to a *rollo* (ROH-yoh) factory. In front of the church, cross Independencia and head left a half block. Before the corner you'll find a shop where machines crush, heat, and stir guava pulp or other fruits until it thickens like candy, which is then sold in *rollos* (rolls).

Most days the Talpa plaza atmosphere is friendly and pleasantly uncrowded. The action heats up considerably during the *tianguis* (tee-AHN-geese) every other Saturday, when a raft of vendors come into town to set up their awnings and try to hawk everything from pirated tapes and machetes to snake oil and saucepans. This is a good location, however, to buy cheap housewares like lime squeezers, large hand juicers, tortilla warmers, and more. The Talpa hubbub boils over during four big local fiestas—February 2, March 10-19, May 10-12, and September 10-19—when the fortunate jam hotels or sleep in tents, while everyone else makes do with the sidewalks.

### Accommodations

There are a number of fine hotel choices right on the Talpa plaza. Note: Talpa hoteliers rent rooms by the number of beds, rather than the number of guests. If two of you can fit into one bed, you get the cheapest rate. It makes for cozy traveling.

The most elite choice downtown is the **Hotel La Misión** (corner of Hidalgo and Guerrero, tel. 388/385-0202), behind the cathedral. The hotel's shiny tiled lobby leads past an inviting restaurant/bar, Los Venados, to an intimate fountain and garden tucked in a sunny rear patio. Upstairs, rooms are spacious, clean, and attractively decorated in polished wood furniture and flowery bedspreads. Some of the 40 rooms have private balconies overlooking the cobbled lane below, as well as fans, hot water, and TV. Rentals run a very reasonable $23 for one bed, $28 for two beds,

## TALPA FIESTAS

Adoration of the Virgin of Talpa occurs five times during the year. The first, on February 2, coincides with the national festival of Candelaria. While everyone else in Mexico converges upon churches to get their plants, seeds, and candles blessed, Talpa people celebrate by blessing their beloved Virgin.

By far the biggest Talpa event occurs during the week before the feast of St. Joseph on March 19. A million visitors celebrate by downing tons of edible crafts, dancing in the streets, and singing mariachi serenades to the Virgin.

Merrymakers crowd in May 10-12 to celebrate the crowning of the Virgin of the Rosary, accompanied by a glittering carnival, booming fireworks, tasty regional food, and whirling folk dancers.

The prettiest and least crowded of the Talpa celebrations occurs September 10-19, concurrent with the national patriotic Fiesta de Patria. In Talpa, venerable national heroes must share acclaim with the Virgin, whom people bathe, adorn with new jewelry and silks, and parade around the plaza on a flower-petal carpet.

Pilgrims return to the basilica on October 7 for Talpa's fifth and final en masse fiesta, the traditional celebration of the Virgin of the Rosary, in which celebrants fete their beloved Virgin of Talpa with a glittering parade, booming fireworks, and a big carnival.

and $39 for three beds, except during festivals, when prices rise.

Adjacent to the Hotel La Misión stands the clean, modestly priced **Hotel Santuario** (Hidalgo 12, tel. 388/385-0046). The owners offer 38 modern, attractively furnished rooms, with hot-water shower baths, arranged around an interior patio. Get an upper-rear room for most privacy and quiet, especially during festivals. Rentals cost a reasonable $34 for one bed, $47 for two beds, and $62 for three beds; add $5 during festivals. Amenities include fans or air-conditioning (add $10) and a restaurant.

Alternatively, take a look at the relatively new **Hotel Plaza** (Independencia 20, tel. 388/385-0086), directly in front of the cathedral. Here, 33 shiny white-tiled rooms with bright new furnishings occupy two stories fronting the town plaza. Guests in the street-front rooms enjoy views of the colorful cathedral plaza hubbub below. For peace and quiet, ask for a room in the rear. Rates run about $41 for one bed, $46 for two beds, and $55 for three beds, with fans, TV, and hot water.

**Camping** is customary around Talpa, especially during festivals. Privacy, however, is not. Unless you find an isolated spot a mile or so away from town, you'll probably have to cope with a flock of curious children. Try to find a spot on the far side of the river that runs south of town.

Camping prospects are much better along the pine-shaded shoreline of **Corinches Reservoir,** near Mascota, about 10 miles (16 km) north. The principal amenities are a good *palapa* restaurant, space to picnic and/or set up a tent or park an RV, swimming, a boat ramp, and the *lobina* (largemouth bass) prized by anglers. You can see Corinches Reservoir downhill south and west of the Mascota-Talpa road. Easiest access is from downtown Mascota.

### Food

Buy supplies from the several groceries (especially Abarrotes Oasis, in front of the cathedral) along main street Independencia, or the town market on the plaza, west of the cathedral. As for restaurants, the steady flow of pilgrims supports several near the plaza.

Get a bit of graceful colonial-era atmosphere with your seafood, tacos, or *hamburguesas* at the old mansion, now **El Molino Rojo** (Red Mill) restaurant (tel. 388/385-0262, noon-10pm daily, $3-8). Find it on the main street, by the HSBC bank, a block west of the plaza. Equally serious eaters head the opposite direction—east to the end of the main street and downhill three short blocks farther (two downhill, one left)—to **Restaurant Campiña del Herrador** (23 de Junio, across from Hotel Pedregal, tel.

**BAY OF BANDERAS**

© JUSTIN HENDERSON

Talpa's plaza and cathedral

388/385-0376, 8am-10pm daily, $3-10) for
hearty country-style breakfasts, lunches, and
dinners.

**Los Venados** (corner of Hidalgo and
Guerrero, tel. 388/385-0202, 9am-5pm daily,
$3-10), the separately owned restaurant adja-
cent to the Hotel La Misión, is a sports bar, a
burger joint, and, oddly enough, an Asian restaurant offering both Chinese food and sushi
at $3-4 per piece.

The restaurant attached to the Hotel
Santuario to the side of the cathedral is now
the lively **Pizza Navidad** (Hidalgo 12, tel.
388/385-1306, 11:30am-10:30pm daily, $3-
8), with myriad pizza options and a full bar.

## Information and Services

You'll pass most of Talpa's businesses on
Independencia as you enter town from the
Mascota-Guadalajara direction.

For simple advice and remedies, consult with
Doctora Olga Valencia at her **Farmacia San
Miguel** (Independencia 16, across from the

plaza, tel. 388/385-0085, 10am-3pm and 6pm-
11pm daily). Alternatively, visit highly recommended Doctor Daniel Zepeda in his **Farmacia
La Parroquia** (at the end of Independencia,
half a block south of the plaza's southwest corner, tel. 388/385-0089, 10am-3pm and 6pm-
11pm daily). His wife speaks English.

If you need to change money, go to the
**HSBC** (tel. 388/385-0197, 8am-7pm Mon.-
Fri., 8am-3pm Sat.) or its 24-hour ATM, a
half block west of the plaza. In front of the
Hotel La Misión you'll find a small office with
several **ATMs** from different banks as well as
both the *correo* and **Telecomunicaciones,**
if you need to make a long-distance call or
send a fax.

## Getting There

**By Bus:** Talpa buses operate from a central
terminal two blocks north and three blocks
west of the plaza. Bus connection with Puerto
Vallarta via Mascota and San Sebastián is best
made by **Autotransportes Guadalajara Talpa**

souvenirs on sale in Talpa

**Mascota** (ATM, tel. 388/3850-0015, www. talpamascota.com) *rojo* buses. They customarily depart daily early mornings and afternoons, via Mascota and the La Estancia (San Sebastián) crossing. From the Puerto Vallarta end, a similar bus leaves daily early mornings and afternoons from the north side of Parque Hidalgo, two blocks north of the Hotel Rosita on the Malecón. Reserve your ticket ahead of time at the little store (tel. 322/222-4816) at the corner of Guadalupe Sánchez and Argentina, two blocks north of the plaza Hidalgo *rojo* bus stop.

ATM's *rojo* first- and second-class buses also connect Talpa with Guadalajara several times daily, arriving at both the Camionera Nueva station in Guadalajara's southeast suburb and the Camionera Vieja (tel. 333/619-7549) in downtown Guadalajara.

**Autobuses Mascota Talpa Guadalajara** (tel. 388/385-0701) *azul* buses originate in Mascota, continue to Talpa, and then to Guadalajara several times daily, arriving at the old (Camionera Antigua) terminal near the Guadalajara city center.

**By Car:** Access to Talpa from Puerto Vallarta is via Mascota. From the east side of the Mascota plaza, follow Calle Constitución north two blocks. Turn right on Calle Justo Sierra, and, a few blocks later, at the country edge of town, bear right at the signed fork to Talpa and Guadalajara. Continue about six miles (nine km) to the Talpa junction. Turn left for Guadalajara, right for Talpa, and continue along the good paved road another 8 miles (12.8 km) to Talpa. Unleaded gasoline is customarily available in Talpa at the Pemex *gasolinera* about a quarter mile into town, before you arrive at the town plaza.

A pair of alternate road routes access the Talpa-Mascota region from the south. From the Guadalajara-Barra de Navidad Highway 80, follow the signed turnoff at San Clemente. Continue 48 miles (77 km) (through Ayutla, Cuatla, and Los Volcanes) on paved (but sometimes potholed) roads northwest 44 miles (71 km) to the intersection with Highway 70. Turn left and continue another 14 miles (22 km) to a signed Talpa-Mascota junction. Turn left for Talpa (or continue straight ahead for Mascota and San Sebastián).

The other southern route—a rough, unpaved, and seemingly endless up-and-down backcountry adventure—heads from Highway 200 northeast through Tomatlán. It continues about 80 miles (130 km) via the hardscrabble hamlets of Llano Grande and La Cuesta. Figure about eight hours Tomatlán to Talpa under optimum dry conditions. I would strongly advise not attempting this route in the rainy season.

# SAYULITA AND THE RIVIERA NAYARIT

Once upon a time, not so many people made the effort to see what lies north of Puerto Vallarta along the beautiful and verdant Nayarit coastline. This has changed of late, however, as the Nayarit tourism board has been promoting "Riviera Nayarit" as a major tourist destination in Mexico. Riviera Nayarit runs from modern, upscale Nuevo Vallarta north along the coast to the

© DONNA DAY

THE RIVIERA NAYARIT

# HIGHLIGHTS

LOOK FOR ◖ TO FIND RECOMMENDED SIGHTS, ACTIVITIES, DINING, AND LODGING.

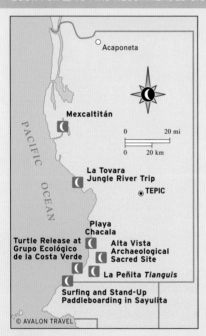

◖ **Turtle Release at Grupo Ecológico de la Costa Verde:** Get involved in helping with a turtle release when the hatchlings emerge from their nests and head down to the sea. This group in San Pancho, dedicated to turtle preservation, welcomes volunteers (page 181).

◖ **La Peñita *Tianguis*:** Spend the morning browsing wares from all over Mexico during this Thursday-morning market. Artisans from as far away as Oaxaca and Puebla come to sell handmade rugs, masks, carved bowls, and jewelry (page 193).

◖ **Alta Vista Archaeological Sacred Site:** Make the side trip to this fascinating forested site. The petroglyph-decorated trail climaxes in a magnificent natural spring and stone amphitheater (page 198).

◖ **Playa Chacala:** This strip of golden sand enfolds a petite half-moon bay. A magnificent grove provides shade, good restaurants, and fresh seafood. Nearby Playa la Caleta offers one of the best surfing waves in all of Nayarit (page 200).

◖ **La Tovara Jungle River Trip:** Along the river's winding, vine-festooned, orchid-swathed channel, enjoy close-up views of snoozing crocodiles, basking turtles, and fluttering herons and egrets (page 213).

◖ **Surfing and Stand-Up Paddleboarding in Sayulita:** Sayulita is a great place to learn how to ride waves. There are plenty of boards of all shapes and sizes available for rent and dozens of well-trained bilingual instructors. Toward the south end of the town beach, you'll find gentle, great-for-beginners surf to practice in (page 166).

◖ **Mexcaltitán:** This island-village is believed to be the fabled Aztlán homeland of the Aztec people. Stroll the automobile-free village lanes, visit the excellent historical museum, and stay at the town's modest hotel (page 225).

port city of San Blas, but for our purposes, we'll start just north of Punta Mita along the coast, at Sayulita. The beauty of coastal Nayarit—lush mountain and shoreline forests, orchard-swathed plains, and curving yellow strands of sand—is largely natural. Dotted along in coves and sheltered bays are the hidden beach towns, some lively and thriving, others tranquil and serene. Sayulita, San Francisco, Lo de Marcos, Rincón de Guayabitos, Chacala, and San Blas—each of these towns is distinct and offers different types of lodging, dining, and recreational opportunities. Whether you are looking for a quiet respite from the crowded streets and beaches of Puerto Vallarta or a non-stop beach party with hundreds of potential new friends, there's a place for you just a couple of hours away.

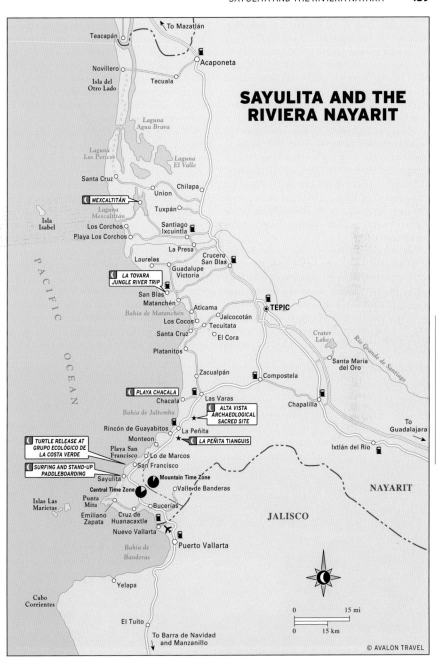

# SAYULITA AND THE RIVIERA NAYARIT

To Mazatlán

Teacapán

Acaponeta

Novillero

Isla del
Otro Lado

Tecuala

Laguna
Agua Brava

Laguna
Los Pericos

Laguna
El Valle

Santa Cruz

Chilapa

Union

MEXCALTITÁN

Laguna
Mexcaltitán

Tuxpán

Isla
Isabel

Los Corchos

Santiago
Ixcuintla

Playa Los Corchos

La Presa

Laureles

Crucero
San Blas

Guadalupe
Victoria

LA TOVARA
JUNGLE RIVER TRIP

San Blas

Matanchén

Aticama

TEPIC

Bahía de Matanchén

Los Cocos

Jalcocotán

Tecuitata

Santa Cruz

El Cora

PACIFIC

Platanitos

Crater
Lake

Río Grande de Santiago

Zacualpán

Santa María
del Oro

OCEAN

Compostela

PLAYA CHACALA

Chacala

Las Varas

Chapalilla

Bahía de Jaltemba

ALTA VISTA
ARCHAEOLOGICAL
SACRED SITE

Rincón de Guayabitos

La Peñita

TURTLE RELEASE AT
GRUPO ECOLÓGICO DE
LA COSTA VERDE

Monteon

LA PEÑITA TIANGUIS

Ixtlán del Río

Playa San
Francisco

Lo de Marcos

To
Guadalajara

SURFING AND STAND-UP
PADDLEBOARDING

San Francisco

Sayulita

Mountain Time Zone

Central Time Zone

Valle de Banderas

NAYARIT

Islas Las
Marietas

Punta
Mita

Bucerías

JALISCO

Emiliano
Zapata

Cruz de
Huanacaxtle

Nuevo Vallarta

Bahía de
Banderas

Puerto Vallarta

Yelapa

Cabo
Corrientes

0        15 mi

0        15 km

El Tuito

To Barra de Navidad
and Manzanillo

© AVALON TRAVEL

The first stop along the coast is **Sayulita,** once mostly the home of fishing families, co-conut and mango farmers, and oyster divers. You can get to Sayulita directly from Punta Mita by the former "back" road that is now, after the flood of 2010 (which took out major sections of the road), an easy-cruising two-lane blacktop—or stick to Highway 200, also nicely refinished in 2012. You can't miss the Sayulita turnoff from Highway 200, as many used to do; not with a giant Pemex gas station complete with an Oxxo store at the junction. What can one say about Pemex, or Oxxo for that matter? In Mexico, they are more perva-sive than Starbucks or McDonald's are in the United States, and they are far more garishly painted and lit.

Sayulita is now home to a decent-sized group of primarily American and Canadian part-time expats—these are the people who own the houses on the hills—and also hosts a large seasonal migration of surfers, stand-up paddle-boarders, vagabonds from the wilds of Europe and beyond, Mexican hippies, and a mixed bag of offbeat characters. During Semana Santa, Easter Week, Mexico's biggest holiday, it seems half the student body of the University of Guadalajara comes down to camp on the Sayulita beach and party all night long. The Sayuleros, Mexicans and *norteamericanos* alike, pack up and leave, or batten down their hatches and stay while the town goes wild. It's kind of fun to watch, once or twice.

While the general feel is that of a fun and funky beach town, a bohemia with waves, Sayulita has managed to go upscale at the same time. There are gourmet restaurants, high-end boutiques for clothing and jewelry, and plenty of people with serious money here—the hills are more than dotted with trophy second homes for a few hundred wealthy *norteameri-canos.* But there are also hand-to-mouth hip-pies, craftspeople, low-rent surfers, mystics, lunatics, and all manner of strange characters. Along with its natural beauty—an archetypal vision of a colorful, tranquil beach town on a perfect little bay—one of the things that makes Sayulita such a magical, welcoming, and unusual place is the mix. There's space for everybody, and as long as you mind your

view of Sayulita bay and beach from Nanzal hill

© DONNA DAY

own business and do no harm, nobody really cares what you do. The most aggressive people in town are a few of the local surfers, some of whom seem seriously annoyed that all these people have arrived in town to "steal" their waves. Purist tourists will complain that there are too many gringos, that it isn't "Mexican" enough, that everybody speaks English, and so on—and they're right. But that doesn't diminish Sayulita's charm.

A few miles farther north, **San Francisco** (or locally, San Pancho) still retains its sleepy beach-village ambience, but it is also home to an established community of well-to-do North American vacationers and retirees, old hippies and old money comfortably intermingled. Nestled between the sidewalk restaurants and Internet cafés are art galleries, upscale boutiques, and international cuisine restaurants. If Sayulita is Greenwich Village, San Pancho is Greenwich, Connecticut. A gorgeous, recently opened to the public, private golf course and a working polo field where professional matches take place serve to further enhance the monied ambience. In San Pancho, they welcome a little bit of Sayulita hippieness, but they would rather it leaves by sundown.

The magnet of **Lo de Marcos** is its wide, family-friendly beach, sheltered by headlands on both sides and bordered by a sprinkling of beach bungalows and palm-shaded RV parks and campgrounds. The same is true of **Rincón de Guayabitos,** but even more so. It's the hands-down favorite resort with Mexican families of the entire Nayarit Coast, largely for its many budget but comfortable housekeeping bungalows and tranquil, kid-friendly waves. A battalion of North American winter RV retirees have picked up the same message and stay the winter, fishing, barbecuing, and playing cards with longtime fellow returnees.

The beach list goes on: lovely **Playa Chacala,** with its creamy half-moon beach, regal palm grove, homey local lodgings, nearby classic surfing wave, and a pair of rustic-chic hotel-spas; and farther north, the broad **Bay of Matanchén,** with its beachfront hotels, trailer parks, waterfall hikes, crocodile farm, and occasional world-class surfing around the north end of the bay at Stoner's Point.

© DONNA DAY

Chacala's plaza and *playa*

Next comes **San Blas,** rich in history revealed in its ancient hilltop fortress and its restored customs house and museum downtown. In the present, San Blas has become a jumping-off point for natural adventures. These include jungle boat tours through its orchid-festooned, wildlife-rich mangrove wetland; an excursion to offshore marine life sanctuary **Isla Isabel;** and/or an overnight in **Mexcaltitán.** The "Venice of Mexico," it's the ancestral island home of the Aztec people, who wandered east from Mexcaltitán around AD 1100 and within 400 years had built one of the world's great cities and conquered Mexico.

## PLANNING YOUR TIME

You could spend as little as two days and as much as two weeks or more exploring the Nayarit Coast, depending on your interests. If you have only two days, it's best to go by tour or car, stopping at **Sayulita** or **San Francisco** for lunch and a stroll and sun on the beach, then continue north for an overnight at **Casa Pacífico** or **Mar de Jade** in Chacala. The next day, continue along the Bay of Matanchén to San Blas, for the unmissable **jungle boat tour** and lunch (four hours) at **La Tovara** spring.

With a few more days, you could add an overnight or two at Sayulita and/or San Francisco. Be sure to include a visit to the nearby **Alta Vista Sacred Site** and archaeological zone, just north of La Penita and a few miles inland.

Continuing north to San Blas, between August and December, stop by (two hours for a look, or overnight) at **Playa las Tortugas** vacation home resort and the adjacent turtle conservation center.

Spend a few nights farther north at San Blas, which you can use as an excursion hub for wildlife-watching, beach swimming, sunning, surfing, and strolling, and adventures farther afield to the **Huichol Cultural Center** in Santiago Ixcuintla and the historic and picturesque island-town of **Mexcaltitán** for perhaps an overnight.

If you simply want to chill and learn to surf or stand-up paddleboard, rent a house or a campsite in Sayulita for a week. Once there, rent a surfboard, take a lesson, and spend the week in the water and on the beach, and in the many restaurants, clubs, and bars. They're loads of fun. If you run out of money, when you're not in the water you can have a seat in the plaza and watch the endlessly entertaining Sayulita world go by.

## Getting There

**By Bus:** You can catch a bus pretty much anywhere along Highway 200 on the north side of Puerto Vallarta. Just make sure it's got Sayulita marked as its destination (if that's where you're going). Sayulita is a mile or so off the highway—a long walk on a hot day—and buses not scheduled to go there will drop you at the side of the road. If you're going farther, take a local bus or cab to the Camionera Central, a mile north of the Puerto Vallarta airport, and find a Transportes Pacífico or Estrella Blanca-affiliated northbound bus. Bus travelers heading all the way to San Blas have two options: The quickest is to ride an early Transportes Norte de Sonora bus (buy your ticket at the Estrella Blanca counter) direct to San Blas. Or you can take Transportes Pacífico's longer route uphill via Tepic; upon arrival at the Tepic station, transfer to one of the hourly Transportes Norte de Sonora buses that connect with San Blas.

**By Car:** If you're driving to Sayulita, expect to spend about 45 minutes on the road from the airport. The towns along Highway 200, including Sayulita, are easy to spot these days. Even if they are a few miles off the highway (as are Sayulita and Chacala), they all have Pemex gas stations by their Highway 200 junctions, and/ or Oxxos or other retail establishments.

**By Taxi:** You can also go directly to the Nayarit Coast after airport arrival by sharing a taxi ($55-80) to Sayulita. A *colectivo,* if available in front of the bus station, would be much cheaper. If you're traveling light, cheaper still is to go across the highway via the pedestrian bridge at the airport and catch the bus (25 pesos/less than US$2 will get you to Sayulita).

# Sayulita and Vicinity

About a half-hour ride north of Puerto Vallarta, Highway 200 bends away from the Bay of Banderas shoreline and climbs a low range of mountains. Very quickly the roadside foliage turns attractively lush, with grand, vine-draped trees that at times create a leafy green tunnel over the highway. Although not strictly a rain forest, this Nayarit coastal forest is a well-watered jungle landscape festooned with trees, shrubs, and flowering vines that provide a rich habitat for myriad animal species, both common and endangered.

Along the highway, the forest gives way to the occasional roadside village. In at least one town—such as San Ignacio—speed bumps have been strategically placed to slow everyone down so they won't miss the enterprising locals selling wares at the side of the road. On offer is everything from caged birds to bonsai trees to handmade copper pans and pots in all sizes, polished to a brilliant shine. San Ignacio and other once-quiet fishing and farming villages, both on and off the beach, have become vacation havens for mostly international travelers during the winter and Mexican vacationers during traditional holiday seasons.

Little Sayulita (pop. 800-3,000, depending on the season), 22 miles (35 km) north of the Puerto Vallarta airport, was once the kind of spot that romantics hankered for: a drowsy village on a palmy arc of sand, a hidden retreat for those who enjoy the quiet pleasures and local color of Mexico. And while Sayulita remains a sometime haven of tranquility during the low season, it becomes a high-energy town jam-packed with surfers and families during the high season.

Once only a destination for Puerto Vallarta day-trippers, Sayulita now is host to a yearly influx of second-home expats, RV retirees and youthful Americans, Canadians, Europeans, Latin Americans, and Japanese who have made Sayulita their fall-winter destination of choice. Many have opted to buy full- or part-time homes in the area, and the atmosphere

of Sayulita has grown to reflect that in the increasingly upscale boutiques and galleries, the many posh golf carts (the vehicle of choice in Sayulita), the paved streets, and so on. The plaza has been spruced up, several downtown streets have been turned into pedestrian-only promenades, and plans are afoot to bury all the power lines. In 2012 a massive but unfortunately not-very-charming arch was erected over the entrance to town, theoretically enhancing Sayulita's importance as a destination. You will not find many bargains in this little town, although a cadre of hard-core surfers and dreadlocked, pierced, and heavily tattooed hipsters—of Mexican, American, Argentinian, French, Finnish, Japanese, and every other persuasion—do manage to live on very little money here, selling jewels by day and who knows what by night. It can still be done. For those on a low budget passing through, several hostels in town make staying here on the cheap a lot easier, if you don't mind sharing a room with five or six people you don't know. And there are at least a half dozen taco restaurants, carts, and stands that will provide a full and hearty meal for a couple of bucks.

Nevertheless, any time of the year Sayulita's amenities remain: an inviting ocean that's great for swimming, bodysurfing, beginning to intermediate surfing, and fishing; colorful small-town ambience; lively nightlife if you want it; beautiful and/or lively beaches to the north and south as well as in town; and plenty of warm sun during the day and cool breezes at night.

Aside from its beauty and easy access to the international airport in Puerto Vallarta, Sayulita's popularity can in part be attributed to the excellent website, Sayulitalife.com, that entrepreneurs Ian and Kerry Hodge put together several years ago. With just about every rentable house and commercial enterprise in Sayulita listed on the site, along with plenty of fine photos and general information, Sayulitalife.com has done much to enhance the buzz and promote the town, for better or

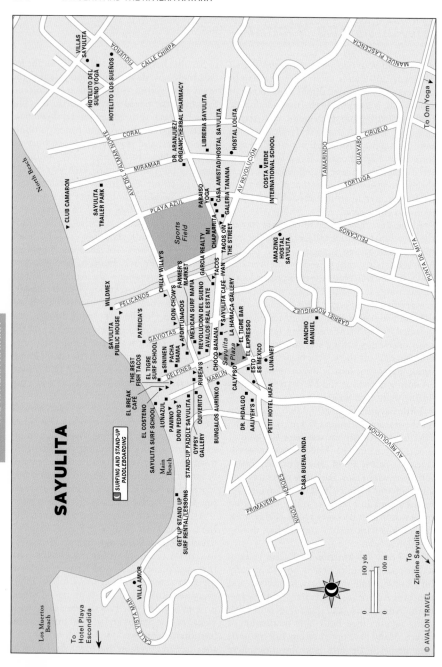

# SAYULITA

**SURFING AND STAND-UP PADDLEBOARDING**

Los Muertos Beach

To Hotel Playa Escondida

North Beach

Main Beach

CALLE VISTA MAR

VILLA AMOR

GET UP STAND UP SURF RENTAL/LESSONS

STAND-UP PADDLE SAYULITA

SAYULITA SURF SCHOOL

EL COSTENO

EL BREAK CAFÉ

DON PEDRO'S

PANINO

LUNAZUL

GYPSY GALLERY

OLIVERITO

RUBEN'S

BUNGALOS AURINKO

THE BEST FISH TACOS

EL TIGRE SURF SCHOOL

SININEN

PACHA MAMA

DELFINES

MARLIN

CHOCO BANANA

CALYPSO

DR. HIDALGO

AALIYEH'S

PETIT HOTEL HAFA

CASA BUENA ONDA

PRIMAVERA

NIÑOS HEROES

VILLAS SAYULITA

HOTELITO DEL SUEÑO YOGA

HOTELITO LOS SUEÑOS

CALLE CHIRPA

FIGUEROA

CORAL

MIRAMAR

AVE DEL PALMAR NORTE

CLUB CAMARON

SAYULITA TRAILER PARK

PLAYA AZUL

Sports Field

CHILLY WILLY'S

WILDMEX

PELICANOS

SAYULITA PUBLIC HOUSE

PATRICIA'S

GAVIOTAS

DON CHOW'S

AFORTUNADOS

MEXICAN SURF MAFIA

FARMER'S MARKET

AVALOS REAL ESTATE

REVOLUCION DEL SUEÑO

Sayulita Plaza

SAYULITA CAFÉ

LA HAMACA GALLERY

ESTO ES MEXICO

EL EXPRESSO

LUNANET

GARCIA REALTY

MI CHAPARRITA

TACOS

IVAN TACOS ON THE STREET

GALERIA TANANA

PARAISO YOGA

CASA AMISTAD/HOSTAL SAYULITA

DR. ARANJUEZ/ORGANIC/HERBAL PHARMACY

LIBRERIA SAYULITA

HOSTAL LOLITA

AV REVOLUCION

COSTA VERDE INTERNATIONAL SCHOOL

TAMARINDO

TORTUGA

PELICANOS

GUAYABO

CIRUELO

To Om Yoga

PUNTA DE MITA

MANUEL PLASCENCIA

GABRIEL RODRIGUEZ

AMAZING HOSTAL SAYULITA

RANCHO MANUEL

EL TIGRE BAR

AV REVOLUCION

To Zipline Sayulita

0    100 yds
0    100 m

© AVALON TRAVEL

downtown Sayulita, where life is a beach

worse. Sayulita has become a major destination, so much so that it is now feeding on itself: A Mexican-produced reality TV show, *Mi Vida en Sayulita,* has been attracting viewers from all across Mexico, as well as visitors from Mexico and other countries.

## BEACHES

Sayulita's "town" beach is the busy, umbrella-covered stretch between the Villa Amor hotel to the south and the river to the north. Much of this beach is almost always crowded (less so at the south end), the chairs and umbrellas are all for rent, surfboard and paddleboard rentals are everywhere, and it is, quite simply, a real "scene." It's loads of fun for partying; can be good for paddleboarding, boogie boarding, and surfing (and is great for surfing and stand-up paddleboarding lessons); and offers wonderful opportunities for people-watching. This is Sayulita's daytime circus, and it is loads of fun! Once upon a time this was a quiet, small-town beach. These days, at times it feels more like Venice Beach in LA.

If you want to take a walk or short hike and see a different beach, head south along the beach road from downtown, past the *pangas* on the beach and the Hotel Villa Amor (the road appears to be private as it passes through the hotel, but it is not), and turn left just before the last house on the road, the big one out on the rocky point called Los Arcos. The steep dirt-road hill will take you up and over, down through the town cemetery, and at the bottom to the right you'll find lovely **Playa los Muertos** (the beach of the dead), a great beach for swimming and just hanging out. The waters around the rocks just offshore to the left of the beach are good for snorkeling.

If you head north across the river from the town beach, you're on the **north beach,** which doesn't really have a formal name but is longer, cleaner, less crowded, and quieter than the downtown beach. This is a wonderful beach for early morning or sunset walks, and you just might find Erik and Odette, resident turtle keepers, doing a baby turtle release as you happen by their house, with its little Tortuga

Bar shack out front. They'll welcome your assistance in helping the hatchlings make it to the sea. The waves at the beginning (south end) of the north beach are excellent for surfing at times, but once you get beyond them, it can get quite rough when there's a big swell, so be careful, and watch out for riptides in the area in front of the trailer park. When it's calm, the water is clean and inviting, and great for swimming.

At the far end of the north beach is a beautiful house, Casa Kuesta, built into the base of the rocky headland. There are also a few trails heading back into the forest here, and if you follow one up over the headland (you can also walk around in front of it when the tide is very low), you'll come upon **Playa Malpaso,** a mile-long, usually deserted stretch of sand that terminates in another headland that marks the south end of San Pancho's beach. There is a dirt road into Malpaso from Highway 200, but few people can find it, so the beach is almost always empty except for a few wanderers or paddleboarders up from Sayulita or down from San Pancho. It's quiet, pretty, and good for swimming and paddleboarding (not surfing), except during a big swell, when the waves can get rough.

## RECREATION
### C Surfing and Stand-Up Paddleboarding

While there are better places to surf locally, or at least within 20 or 30 minutes' drive, there are few more popular than Sayulita. Sayulita's bay faces north/northwest and so takes the strong north swells of winter straight on, frequently bringing large waves November-April. The spring and fall can often be slack, surf-wise, while summer's south swells will bring great surf on occasion. In spite of the heat, summer is a good time for surfers to travel to Sayulita, as there are fewer tourists and thus fewer surfers in the water. But any surfer will tell you that surf prediction, even in the age of satellites and the Internet, is hit and miss, so you really never know what to expect until you get here, any time of year.

Surfers, take note: This is usually a small- to medium-size, not too powerful, and often very crowded wave, particularly on the right, which is the "town" wave. The left, a few hundred yards north in front of the campgrounds and trailer park, is generally less busy, and it is often a better surfing wave. It depends entirely on the size and direction of the swell. Generally speaking, Sayulita as a surf spot can be loads of fun for beginners, but not so much for serious surfers, except during a really big, powerful swell. Unfortunately there are some—only a few, but that can be all it takes—very aggressive local surfers who can make life miserable for everybody else in the water on occasion. If you consider yourself a better than average surfer, your best bet is to surf early in the morning if you want to avoid crowds—or come in the low season, when it is hotter than Hades but less crowded in the water. Or be prepared to travel—there are good, usually less-busy waves within half an hour's drive.

On the other hand, beginners will find at least a half dozen surf schools to choose from, all of them offering board rentals, lessons from really cool surfer guys and gals, and everything else you need to learn how to surf. At the south end of the town beach, in front of Don Pedro's restaurant, you'll find gentle, beginner-friendly waves almost every day. It gets crowded out there, but with soft top boards and leashes, even a crowded day is usually safe and fun, when the waves are small- or medium-size. Learning to surf in big waves is not a good idea.

Most if not all of the surf instructors in town have learned how to stand-up paddle surf as well, and they also offer paddling and paddle-surfing lessons. The advantage to stand-up paddling becomes evident when there is no surf: You can still get on a board and head out to sea, paddle around the point to the south, or at least to nearby Playa los Muertos—or even all the way north to San Pancho (the long, beautiful, and usually empty beach between the two towns is called Malpaso) if you're feeling ambitious. Stick close to shore—but stay outside the surf break—and you'll be fine. Many of the

# TOP SURF BREAKS OF THE RIVIERA NAYARIT

The Pacific coast of Mexico has been popular with traveling surfers for decades, since long before the beaches were covered with five-star hotels and condominium complexes. The empty expanses of golden beach, excellent waves of all varieties and sizes, beach camping, and cheap dining have continued to bring a seasonal crush of hobbyists, newbies, and pros during the fall and summer months, when the tourist crowds have yet to arrive for the winter and the swells are the largest. There are bigger and better waves in other parts of Mexico, but Nayarit has a fine batch of substantial, challenging breaks, with something for everyone from beginners to professional wave chasers.

**Sayulita:** Sayulita is one of the most popular places for surfing north of Punta Mita. There's a right break off a reef in front of the main beach and another faster left break north of the river mouth. To the south side of the right on the main beach, soft, shapeless but forgiving waves and a primarily sand bottom offer a great area for beginning surfers. There are year-round waves in Sayulita, and it's far from deserted. The popularity of the funky beach town means lots of competition for waves and crowded beaches, especially during the winter months. The town wave works for shortboarders and longboarders; these days there are also many stand-up paddleboarders in the lineup.

**San Francisco (San Pancho):** San Pancho makes for a great day trip if you are staying in Puerto Vallarta or somewhere along the coast. The hard break, riptides, and big waves means there are few swimmers in the water here, so surfers usually have the water to themselves. San Pancho features a close-in beach break, with potential barrels. It's better for shortboarders.

**La Caleta:** From the dock in Chacala, hire a *panga* to take you to Playa la Caleta, where you can find what is often referred to as "the best left." Surfers mostly just call this wave Chacala, and it is a good one, a long, clean left point break that takes swells from all directions. This wave is excellent for both shortboarders and longboarders. The wave is pretty well-known now, so it can get crowded, but with timing and luck, when the *panga* drops you and your friends in the water, you could be the only ones there. The beach is gorgeous, if mostly rocky, with a fine campground behind it–bring all supplies if you plan on camping, as there is nothing available here. When surfing, beware of the rocky bottom, which is covered with sea urchins.

Between Chacala and San Blas, you'll find rideable beach break waves by the river mouth just south of **Platanitos** (you can park on the bluff and paddle across the river, or approach from the south via the roads that bring you to the Las Tortugas resort area); **Santa Cruz,** where a good fast rock-bottom left breaks on most swells (just follow the streets that lead to the beach, and the wave will be right in front of you); and **Aticama,** where you'll find the wave, another rock-bottom left, directly offshore just north of the bridge in the middle of town. This spot is popular with oyster divers, so don't be surprised if you are surfing with a lot of guys in snorkeling gear with inner tubes swimming around you. All of these waves are swell-dependent, as well as being affected by wind and tidal changes.

**Matanchén Bay:** Matanchén Bay is known for having the longest ride in the world (*Guinness Book of World Records*), which takes surfers up to a mile and a half on a single wave. This break actually encompasses Matanchén Bay and another wave called Las Islitas, just beyond it. This endless wave is for real, if not that frequent, and rarely really big. But the bay is shallow a long ways out and the wave does go on for a long time, so it is a great place to take kids and beginners. Beyond Matanchén and Las Islitas, there's another cove, and beyond that cove, the legendary Stoner's Point, a wave as fickle as they come. When it does go off, it is simply a great, fast, right point break, a real roller-coaster ride and a thrill a second. You can drive most of the way in, depending on your car and the season, then walk or paddle. Alternatively, paddle across the river from the southern edge of San Blas, and then follow a short trail through the forest to the beach. The bugs here and all over the San Blas area are voracious, bloodthirsty, and nasty, so don't even think about coming here without insect repellent.

© DONNA DAY

A surfing class enters the water at Sayulita.

instructors and rental guys will happily serve as your stand-up paddleboarding guide and lifeguard for a fee.

Catch up on the local surf conditions on the Sayulita Life website (www.sayulitalife.com/sayulitasurfing), or read basic surf forecast websites such as www.surf-forecast.com, www.magicseaweed.com, and www.surfline.com, which have plenty of free information.

Surfboard, stand-up paddleboard, and boogie board rentals can be found all along the beach, from the south end past Don Pedro's all the way north to the river and beyond. There are also several shops on various streets in town. In other words, there are lots of options. What follows are a couple of favorites, based on a combination of personality, skill level, and quality and quantity of equipment. If none of these suit you, walk 20 yards down the beach or up the street.

Walking along the beach from south to north, first you'll find Eric Baraza's **Get Up Stand Up** (tel. 322/118-9992), offering surfboards, stand-up paddleboards (hereafter called

SUPs), and boogie boards for rent. Eric, who grew up in Sayulita and has been surfing and teaching all his life, also offers surfing lessons, private or group, with an emphasis on ocean awareness as well as surfing. He or one of his associates is at the kiosk 8am or 9am to 5pm or 6pm daily.

**Lunazul** (Marlin 4, tel. 329/291-2009, www.lunazulsurfing.com) also offers boogie board, surfboard, and SUP rentals, and private/group lessons. An excellent crew of instructors in surfing and SUP is always on hand on the beach in front of the Lunazul shop, across Calle Marlin from Don Pedro's restaurant. Individual lessons for 1.5 hours are $45; group lessons for 1.5 hours are $30 per person (maximum five students per instructor). Lessons include use of surfboard, rash guard, and leash for 2.5 hours. Board rentals are $20 for one day, $30 for 24 hours, and $150 per week. Lunazul has the advantage of a large selection of board rentals in every size and type.

You'll find **El Tigre's Surf School** (tel. 329/291-3267 or 322/131-8815), owned by Guillermo "El Tigre" Cadena, a former Mexican national surfing champion, on the beach at the foot of Calle Delfines, with excellent instructors in surfing and SUPping available all day, every day. Tigre also has a surf shop on the north side of the plaza, with a bar upstairs overlooking the plaza where the local surf crowd gathers and surf movies play pretty much all night long.

Brothers Sergio and Patricio Gonzalez are Sayulita-born local surfers and instructors whose **Sayulita Surf School** (tel. 322/102-1032) is located under a canopy right in the middle of the town beach. Patricio is a former national longboarding champion of Mexico; both brothers are gifted surfers and SUPpers. Sergio is fluent in English and loves teaching kids. They will take people on surf safaris for lessons at less-crowded breaks or teach right in town when the waves are right. You couldn't ask for a more upbeat and entertaining introduction to Sayulita's surfing scene that one provided by these guys. They charge around $15-20 for a board rental, and $40-50 for a lesson and board. They rep the Starboard Stand Up Paddleboard company in Sayulita, and so they have a selection of paddleboards as well as surfboards for rent.

You can also schedule lessons and/or a local surf trip through **Wildmex** (Pelicanos 7, Sayulita town beach, tel. 322/107-0601, U.S. tel. 303/242-5383, www.wildmex.com), which offers various multiday surf packages, surfing day trips, and other adventures. Two-hour private surf lessons are $55; group lessons are $40 per person, maximum four per group. Daylong surf safaris to Punta Mita breaks are $55 per person; lessons and trips include board, leash, rashguard, transportation, guiding, and instruction as necessary. Teacher Risa Mara Machuca is an excellent, patient, and entertaining instructor, with plenty of experience and knowledge of local waves and conditions. Wildmex also offers kayaking and snorkeling trips, mountain bike tours, hiking (with surf instructor and ecologist Stephen Pomeroy), and horseback riding.

**Quiverito** (Calle Marlin 12, tel. 322/171-6453, www.quiverito.com) offers a great selection of serious, high-quality surfboards for accomplished or competent surfers. Their focus is not on lessons or on beginners seeking soft tops but rather on those who know how to surf but didn't bring a board and need a good one. They've got everything from five-foot, four-inch fishes to nine-foot, two-inch single fins available for rent by the hour, day, or week. All of their vintage boards are also for sale. You can check out the stock on the website and reserve in advance online. Rentals (listed on the site in pesos, these prices are subject to currency fluctuations) range about $7.50-12 per hour, $25-35 per day, and $120-175 per week. You'll find the shop on Calle Marlin, the pedestrian-only street linking the south side of the plaza with the beach. They also do board repairs on-site and sell wax, rashguards, board shorts, and skateboards.

A little farther up the beach is **Patricia's Surfboard Rentals and Lessons** (tel. 329/291-2070). Patty Southworth has two professional-surfer sons, and her family has run Capitan Pablo's Restaurant on the beach for years. Find her at the foot of Calle Gaviotas.

## Yoga

Sayulita's other major recreational activity these days besides surfing is yoga, with retreats, schools, and yoga centers popping up all over town. At least one outfit even combines yoga and surfing: **Via Yoga** (toll-free U.S. tel. 800/603-9642, www.viayoga.com) offers six-day yoga and surfing retreats in Sayulita. These are expensive at $2,495 to $3,495 per person, but the price does include all meals and lodging at the posh Villa Amor, organized yoga and surf activities, and lessons with talented instructors. Reservations can be made through the website.

If a weeklong commitment is too much, there are many fine yoga teachers in Sayulita, and a full range of classes are available year-round (fewer options in low season). **Paraiso Yoga** (Playa Azul 21, tel. 329/291-3625 or 322/152-4296, www.paraisoyoga.com) is a yoga center on Sayulita's north side, where the gifted teacher Narayani has scheduled a number of retreats, classes, and events; she also does massage, and she even offers a couple of sweet little bungalows for rent in her quiet, verdant yoga center. Classes range in price from about $10 for a single class to $75 for a monthly pass. Punch cards are also available.

**Om Yoga** (Manuel Plascencia 81, tel. 329/291-3415, www.yogasayulita.com) is another great Sayulita yoga studio, with several teachers offering a full range of classes, retreats, and workshops in various styles and levels of yoga. Classes range in price from around $12 for drop-ins to about $75 for unlimited monthly classes. Teachers from Om will come to your rental house or hotel room to offer private 1-hour classes for $60, 1.5-hour classes for $85; $10 per extra person. Monthly rates and multiclass punch cards are also available.

**Hotelito Los Sueños** (Calle Rosalio Tapia 10, tel. 329/291-3690, www.hotelitolossue-nos.com) is a charming little budget-priced hotel on Sayulita's north side that has a full range of yoga classes and retreats. Owner Peter Achtem is a yoga aficionado, and he has several of Sayulita's finest yoga teachers on staff. Yoga classes are offered daily, and there are also specials on weeklong yoga retreats.

## Tours and Guides

If you are looking to do some diving and don't want to travel into Puerto Vallarta, you can take trips or even get your PADI certification through **Sayulita Entourage** (tel. 322/147-5893, www.sayulitaentourage.com). Experienced diver Stephane Panette offers snorkeling, whale-watching, and surfing trips, as well as diving trips and PADI certification. He and partner Roberta Commisso take their clients and students out on their 22-foot canopy-shaded motorized *panga* for trips throughout the waters off Punta Mita, where the boat is based, and the entire Banderas Bay. Their certified diver excursion includes a two-tank dive, drinks, and light lunch for $150 (maximum four persons). Their whale-watching excursion offers a guaranteed three hours on the water, snorkeling, whale-watching, light lunch, and drinks for $250 (maximum six people); for three hours on the boat without snorkeling, food, and drink, it's $200.

For fishing, surfing, and snorkeling excursions, contact local captain **Fidel Ponce Cruz** and his wife, Leticia (tel. 329/291-3563, or email through www.sayulitalife.com). Sayulita is Fidel's hometown, so he knows the best local spots. He charges about $200 for a five- to six-hour day trip.

Another excellent local fishing guide is Enrique Moeller, whose **La Morena Sportfishing Company** (cell tel. 322/229-0039, U.S. tel. 650/641-1352, kerrymoeller@hotmail.com) will take people out for a day of licensed and insured fishing in a boat smaller than a major cruiser but larger than a *panga*, with a bathroom, sink, and fridge. Enrique is completely bilingual and knows the waters of Bahía de Banderas as well as anyone in town. Meals and drinks are provided on request. Contact Enrique or his wife, Kerry, by phone or email.

**Sayulita Jose** (tel. 322/132-1004, www.sayulitajose.com) is Jose Lorenzo's fishing, surfing, and whale-watching service. Jose is one of Sayulita's original great surfers, and he's a gifted fishing boat captain as well. By gifted, I mean he knows where the fish are and is confident enough to offer a money-back guarantee if you don't catch a few. Fishing trips are $200 (maximum four people); surf trips are $50 an hour (maximum six people). Jose will go all over Punta Mita, and even all the way to Chacala if need be, to get waves.

Local **Rancho Manuel** (Gringo Hill #33, tel. 322/132-7683) offers horseback tours along shady paths through the Sayulita tropical forest and on the beach. Get tickets at the Restaurant Costeño (on the beach at the foot of Calle Delfines, tel. 329/291-3045), or at the ranch itself, about four blocks east up Calle Gaviotas, past the town plaza and the church. **Rancho Mi Chaparrita** (Manuel Rodriguez Sanchez 14, tel. 329/291-3112, www.michaparrita.com) offers horseback tours as well as ATV tours, surf trips, Marietas Islands snorkeling trips, and fishing trips. They also have a surfboard rental stand and small shop on the south end of the town beach. In addition, they operate Sayulita's only canopy zip-line tour, on a small mountain about a mile out of town. The zip line, with its 13 separate zips, is $75 for adults, $55 for kids under 12. Horseback rides are $25 for one hour, $50 for two, and ATV tours are $65 per person. All activities are scheduled several times daily.

## ENTERTAINMENT
### Nightlife

Sayulita draws so many different crowds—surfers, hippies, seasonal residents, international vagabonds—that it can be hard to characterize the nightlife. Suffice it to say that there is plenty of it, and whatever your style or taste or age, you'll find a good after-dark spot. If you don't like bars, sit on a bench in the plaza and watch the show.

On the south side of the town square a cluster of restaurants occupy the sidewalk and the first and second floors of several buildings. Up top of one is **Don Pato** (Calle Marlin, on the plaza, no phone), a serious late-night hangout for those in search of the buzz of single people, many margaritas and *cervezas,* herb in the air, and all the rest of what makes a bar scene happen. Late at night, crazy things can go on here, so be prepared. This can be a wild young crowd. Occasionally one of the local bands plays a couple of live sets, and the place absolutely rocks.

**Buddha Mar** (Calle Marlin 10, tel. 322/135-0822, www.buddhasayulita.com) is a few doors east of Don Pedro's beachfront restaurant, upstairs. It opens in the evening and stays open late, annoying many residents with the throbbing music but providing the young and the restless a place to go after midnight. The alcohol flows, the music flows, the ambient scene glows, and many a romance is ignited.

Overlooking the beach, **Don Pedro's** (Calle Marlin 2, tel. 329/291-3090) is a fine and somewhat fancy restaurant. Six nights a week it is fairly low-key unless there is an important game on the TV and there are fans in town. But every Monday brings salsa night to Don Pedro's, and Mexicans do love to salsa—especially with a live band, and a couple of handsome young dancer/surfer dudes to teach the visiting women some new steps. You can have a great time here, meet fun people, and learn to dance the salsa. This is pretty much an all ages adult scene.

The cool little wine bar **Escondido** (Calle Marlin 45A, tel. 329/291-3613), a few doors up Gringo Hill from the plaza, feels very urbane—it's like being in the city, people say. There isn't a lot of good wine available in Mexico, so if you're looking for a glass of decent pinot noir or sauvignon blanc, and some interesting, possibly even grown-up conversation, this is a good place to check out.

On the beach on the north side, in front of the campground, **Club Camaron** (Av. del Palmar 100, tel. 329/291-3373) is the ultimate tiki bar. It looks like a perfect reincarnation of a movie-set South Seas tiki bar, only it is the real thing. Up on a platform (overindulgent people fall off on occasion) with a fence made of surfboards, tables down on the sand, and the surf crashing a few yards away (the location is directly in front of the "left" surfing wave), Camaron is a rocking spot that skews a little younger than say, Don Pedro's or Escondido. Often it appears that there is more than alcohol going down.

## SHOPPING

Considering its small size, Sayulita has a surprising number of great stores with unusual and/or original stuff for sale, including clothes, jewelry, artwork, and, of course, surfboards and paddleboards. This is becoming something of a shopping destination. As a rule, in high season these shops are open from 9 or 10am until well into the evening; some take a break in the afternoon and close 2pm-4pm. Low-season hours are fewer and more intermittent.

Among the best of the handicrafts galleries—which are ubiquitous on Sayulita's busy streets—is the two-story **La Hamaca Gallery** (Av. Revolución 110, tel. 322/227-5817, 9am-8pm daily). Offerings include fine ceramics, Day of the Dead curios, and a selection of Huichol art, sales of which benefit the nonprofit Huichol Center for Cultural Survival.

The lively and unique **Revolución del Sueno** (Calle Manuel Navarrete 55, tel. 329/291-3850, www.revoluciondelsueno.com, 10am-2pm and 4pm-8pm daily, sometimes open till 9 or 10pm) is the creation of French expat Nicolea del Sueno, who has settled permanently in Sayulita and now sells clothes, furniture, jewelry, and a fine assortment of quirky stuff, all of it infused with witty verbal and visual pop art spirit overlaid atop Mexican traditional images and styles. In a small sea of Sayulita shops selling cool stuff, this one stands out for originality of vision.

The owners of **The Gypsy Gallery** (Calle Marlin 10, tel. 329/291-3385, 10am-2pm and 4pm-8pm daily, sometimes open till 9 or 10pm) wander far and wide throughout Mexico and nearby lands, rounding up great arts and crafts for sale in their store, just up from Don Pedro's restaurant. You'll find antique rugs, Day of the Dead papier-mâché figures from

THE RIVIERA NAYARIT

© JUSTIN HENDERSON

bars, boards, and boutiques in Sayulita

Patzcuaro, Guatemalan textiles, Oaxacan pottery, hand-loomed bedspreads, hand-embroidered pillow slips, hand-tooled leather bags, and hand-painted wooden bowls, plates, and trays, for starters.

The gypsy-chic French sisters (and extended family) called the Mignots, aka Les Gazelles, have established themselves as influential presences in Sayulita, with a hotel, several kids on the road to professional surfing careers, and **Pacha Mama** (Calle Delfínes 4B, tel. 329/291-3468, www.lesgazelles.com, 10am-6pm daily), their stylishly decorated, pricey clothing and jewelry store a few doors up from the beach. They've made a name for themselves selling their own quirky, sexy line of clothes and gorgeous Tahitian pearls. The pearls are indeed gorgeous. And pricey. But have a look—the store and everything in it is very pretty, indeed—and if you have some money to spend, this is a great place to spend it.

There are probably a dozen jewelry stores in Sayulita, and another two dozen talented street vendors selling jewelry from small portable stalls at the side of the street. You could do worse than shop up and down the stalls on Calle Gaviotas, where you'll find a number of tatted-up international hippies selling ethnic-looking necklaces, earrings, bracelets, and such. Some is crude, but there are sophisticated, beautifully made pieces on display, too, if you look closely. As for jewelry boutiques, along with those already mentioned there are three shops clustered on the corner of Calle Delfínes and Avenida Palmar worth checking out: Designer Kimberly Flor Keehn's **Joyeria Sol** (tel. 329/291-3502, toll-free U.S./Can. tel. 888/669-1641, www.sayulitasol.com, 10am-2pm and 4pm-8pm daily) offers her complete line of custom-made jewelry as well as the work of several other local designers. Kim has been at it since the 1980s, and her work is lovely. **Synaia Jewelry** (Calle Delfínes 8, tel. 322/108-0759, 10am-2pm and 4pm-8pm daily) features an eclectic array of silver and gold pieces influenced by Prehispanic, medieval, and Asian designs. Finally, next door to Synaia, **Debbie de la Cueva** (tel. 322/149-6295,

10am-2pm and 4pm-8pm daily) offers a range of pieces noteworthy for the use of 19th-century Venetian beads in conjunction with precious and semiprecious stones and pearls, held together in unusual forms with tiny pieces of gold. The work is delicate and distinct.

Next door to Tacos on the Street, just north of the bridge, is **Galeria Tanana** (Calle Revolución 22, tel. 329/291-3889, www.thehuicholcenter.org, 10am-8pm daily), devoted to the celebration and indeed the survival of Huichol culture, since the nonprofit store's profits go to the Huichol Center for Cultural Survival and Traditional Arts. Named for the Huichol goddess of life, the store sells all things Huichol and then some, including stunning high-end jewelry. What they sell is the real thing, since the store is a project of archaeologist/jewelry designer Susana Alvarez, an American who has spent her life studying and helping to preserve the unique Huichol culture. Having been married to a Huichol man, she has been deeply immersed in the culture. If you don't want to buy an actual art object, you can always buy a T-shirt with a gorgeous Huichol pattern expertly printed on it. Colorful, cosmological, and full of myth, these Huichol images are amazing and distinct. Alternatively, you can purchase a piece of exquisite, Huichol-inspired jewelry.

**Esto Es Mexico** (Calle Revolución across from El Expresso, just off the plaza, tel. 329/291-3928, www.sayulitalife.com/estoesmexico, 10am-8pm daily) offers some new and entertaining takes on the Day of the Dead and other Mexican traditions, as interpreted by artist/owners Belen Sandoval and Caesar Enrique Godoy. All the cool little pop art Day of the Dead paintings you see in the shop are priced to sell at about $25 bucks apiece.

Shopping in Sayulita wouldn't be complete without at least a foray into the retail realm of surfboards and stand-up paddleboards. Even if you don't have the money or interest to buy one of these large, expensive-to-travel-with objects, the stores are worth tripping through just to see what people use these days to ride waves. If you happen to be traveling and surfing in

Mexico for an extended period, buying a board is a good investment. You can always sell it before you leave or if you run out of money. The following Sayulita shops sell surfboards and/or paddleboards, plus paddles and all the rest of the gear, clothes, and stuff you need to be, or at least look like, a surfer.

Nazario Carranza's **Sininen** (Calle Delfines 4, tel. 329/291-3186, 9am-6pm daily) offers boards in all shapes and sizes, along with board shorts, bikinis, leashes, and everything else that says surf. *Sininen,* incidentally, means blue in Finnish, which is where Nazario's wife hails from.

The **Mexican Surf Mafia** (Av. del Palmar 8-d, tel. 329/291-3201 or 322/147-1080, 10am-8pm daily) is a custom board design shop with plenty of new and used boards for sale, and also clothes, paraphernalia, and skateboards. The store has a somewhat off-putting "locals-only" attitude—ironic since the guy who runs the place is from Guadalajara—but they will happily take your *norteamericano* money should you choose to buy something.

**Stand Up Paddle Sayulita** (Calle Marlin, a block up from the beach, tel. 329/291-3575, www.sayulitalife.com/supdemexico, 10am-2pm and 4pm-8pm daily) opened in 2012 and features a great selection of paddleboards and paddles from several major manufacturers. They also sell cool accessories, skateboards, and surfwear, and serve as an official retailer for GoPro cameras, those nifty little waterproof cameras you can attach to your surfboard or paddleboard and film yourself riding waves. Loads of fun. The shop also has a nice grassy backyard with a juice and coffee bar, which is a great place to hang out.

If you are looking to pick up new, used, or locally written books, stop by **Libreria Sayulita** (Miramar 17A, tel. 322/103-4703, 10am-8pm daily), a cool bookstore that also offers language lessons, Internet services, and local art. There's a nice bakery and coffee shop with an espresso/latte machine inside should you need a caffeine fix and some cake while browsing the stacks. There are semiused English-language magazines available as well.

## ACCOMMODATIONS
### Under $50
Sayulita's perennial favorite budget accommodations are the economical, clean, and comfortable (if slightly shabby) rooms at **Sayulita Trailer Park,** on the north-end beachfront. Besides the rooms ($40-50 per day, $240-300 per week), you also can opt for one of about a dozen simply but thoughtfully furnished kitchenette bungalows ($75-105 per day, $450-650 per week), four of them smack on the lovely palm-shaded beachfront ($105-150 per day, $650-900 per week). During the two weeks before Easter and December 15-31, rates rise about 20 percent, and reservations must include a minimum seven-day stay and a 50 percent deposit. Get reservations—for winter, best six months in advance—through the owners, Thies and Cristina Rohlfs, either in Mexico City (office tel. 555/390-2750, home tel. 555/572-1335, www.pacificbungalow.com) or in Sayulita directly (tel./fax 329/291-3126, Nov.-May). Rates for the trailer spaces average $18-28 depending on the size of the space. Note that many of the trailer spaces are reserved annually, for months at a stretch, by the same folks, so if you want to make a move here, move fast.

Students and others in search of supercheap lodging now have several hostel options in Sayulita. On the north side, find **Hostal Lolita** (Calle Miramar, just west of Revolución, close to the main bus stop and two blocks from the beach, tel. 322/150-6350, www.sayulitalife.com, $12 pp per night). Rooms contain three, four, or five pairs of bunk beds, with a large shared kitchen, shared bathrooms, and plenty of outside and inside gathering spaces for parties.

Also on the north side of town, Connie LaCroix's **Casa Amistad/Hostal Sayulita** (Manuel Rodriguez Sanchez 7, tel. 329/281-3804) offers both hostel and private room options in a lovely garden setting across from Sayulita's baseball field, about five minutes' walk from the beach, far enough out of town to be quiet but close enough for an easy walk in. A double room with private bath is $45 per night for two people, $10 per person for extra bodies; a hostel room (sleeps four) is $20 per bed per night. Use of surfboards, snorkeling gear, and kitchen included.

East of downtown is the **Amazing Hostel Sayulita** (Pelicanos 102, tel. 329/291-3688, www.theamazinghostelsayulita.com), which offers not only cheap lodging—$15.60 per person per day in female-only or mixed dorm room, or private rooms for $21.27 per person per day (must book room for two)—but also has free Wi-Fi, flat-screen cable TV, luggage storage, purified drinking water, and mountain bikes, kayaks, and surfboards for guest use. All this is free or supercheap, along with the swimming pool and climbing wall in the back. Their affiliation with Hosteling International means you'll save two bucks a day if you're a member.

### $50-100
On the south side of town, the sweet little **Casa Buena Onda** (Calle Niños Heroes 30, tel. 329/291-3976, www.sayulitasurfhotel.com, $50 high season, $60 holidays, $35 low season), also known as the Sayulita Surf Hotel, offers three nicely detailed rooms. Proprietors Terry and Sheryl Orr offer free Wi-Fi, breakfast coffee, pleasant terraces, surf movie nights, and board storage, and Terry will take you surfing when the swell is on. *Buena Onda* means good vibe, and that's definitely on the menu here, along with a complimentary cold beer on arrival.

Sayulita's quiet, palmy north side is primarily second-home gringo territory, with a sprinkling of Mexican families who have been in place for decades and a few small budget hotels. Perhaps the best of these hotels is **Hotelito Los Sueños** (Calle Rosalio Tapia 10, tel. 329/291-3690, www.hotelitolossuenos.com, $50-90 low season, $75-135 high), which reopened in 2011 under new ownership and after an extensive renovation (and name change). The smart, elegantly simple two-story hotel wraps around a small central courtyard with a swimming pool, and it features a smoothie bar and an outdoor yoga studio under a *palapa* on the roof, where they show weekly movies, generally with a spiritual slant, for a donation supporting local causes. Owner Peter Achtem is a yoga aficionado, and he has daily classes led by several of Sayulita's finest yoga teachers; specials on weeklong yoga retreats are also available. The hotel has 15 rooms with various bed counts, some with kitchens, and provides free bicycles, boogie boards, and surfboards for guests to use.

Also on the north side of town, the lovely **Villas Sayulita** (Calle Rosalia Tapia, tel. 329/291-3065, tel./fax 329/291-3063, www.villasayulita.com) is on a quiet street about two long blocks uphill from the beach. Owners offer about a dozen spacious kitchenette suites ($70 d), on lower and upper floors, adjacent to an invitingly intimate tropical pool patio with picnic *palapa*. The suites themselves are lovingly designed and immaculately maintained, with TV, air-conditioning, attractive rustic tile floors, deluxe modern baths, and soaring arched ceilings. Some beds are king-size, with a pullout for kids, while other rooms have two double beds. Rustically luxurious rooftop *palapa* suites ($115 d) offer panoramic views, two king beds, flat-screen TVs, and terraces with *equipale* furnishings.

Back near the town center (where it can get very noisy at night), the gorgeous *palapa*-chic ◖ **Bungalows Aurinko** (Calle Marlin, tel. 329/291-3150, www.sayulita-vacations.com) offers an excellent downtown alternative. Labor of love of its friendly owner/builder Nazario Carranza, Aurinko (sun in the Finnish language) glows with his handiwork: handcrafted natural wood bedstands and dressers, rustically luxurious whitewashed walls adorned with native arts and crafts, all beneath a handsome, towering *palapa* roof, only a block from the beach. The five one-bedroom units rent from about $81 d in high season, $65 d low. A pair of two-bedroom units go for about $127 d each in high season, $97 d low, and a gorgeous penthouse suite goes for about $106 d high season, $95 d low. All have modern bathrooms, airy patio kitchens, and ceiling fans.

If you want to stay downtown, you could do worse than Marina Garcia and Christophe Mignot's sweet **Petit Hotel Hafa** (Av. Revolución, south of the plaza, tel. 329/291-3806 or 322/779-3573, www.hotelhafasayulita.com, $50-75 d), with its Moroccan-influenced design; intimate lobby courtyard; six charming, beautifully detailed rooms; and ultracool rooftop lounge. Each room has a king or two single beds, some with an extra single. Air-conditioning is an extra $5 per night; Wi-Fi is free. Stays of fewer than two nights are $20 extra per night, while stays of longer than a week can be discounted. The hotel has an in-house boutique where, amid all the lovely stuff on offer, you'll find gorgeous pearl jewelry designed by Marina.

## Over $100

At the end of the south-side beach road, the designer cabanas of hotel **Villa Amor** (tel. 329/291-3010, fax 329/291-3018, U.S. tel. 619/291-3010, www.villaamor.com, $110-700, higher Christmas-New Year's and Easter seasons) dot the leafy headland. Villa Amor offers about 33 owner-designed architecture-as-art rustic *palapa*-chic view dwellings. Accommodations, many open-air, vary from house-size three-bedroom, 2.5-bath, full-kitchen suites down to modest but still deluxe refrigerator-and-sink studios, all enjoying vistas of Sayulita's petite bay. All have fans only, no phones, and no TV. Most beds are king- or queen-size; colors range from soft pastels to white. A possible drawback to all this luxury might be the open-air *palapa* architecture of some of the accommodations, which although inviting, might be a bit buggy and damp during summer rainy spells or chilly during midwinter cool snaps. Other drawbacks: Many people complain about the service, or lack thereof, and there are very steep stairs to many units, sometimes without adequate railings.

Nestled into the jungle and fronting its own gorgeous, isolated beach a mile south of Sayulita, **Hotel Playa Escondida** (no street address, call for directions, tel. 329/291-4748, U.S. tel. 415/259-4748, toll-free U.S./Can. tel. 888/445-0103, www.playa-escondida.com, $125-475) is one of the most charming and romantic of all hotels in Nayarit. The freestanding clusters of guest rooms and suites, each individually designed and organically linked to its site, are buried in lush, colorful plantings and feature splendid ocean, jungle, or bird canyon views. The spa and pool are lavishly romantic, and the restaurant serves gourmet cuisine for breakfast, lunch, and dinner. This is a dreamy spot (although the many squawking parrots might awaken you), perfect for a honeymoon or rekindling a romance—or getting entirely away from it all.

## Trailer Parks and Campgrounds

RV folks love the north-side **Sayulita Trailer Park** (Dec.-May tel./fax 329/291-3126, year-round fax 55/5390-2750, sayupark@prodigy. net.mx, www.pacificbungalow.com), in a big, sandy palm-shaded lot with about 36 hookups (some for rigs up to 40 feet) and some room for tents, practically right on the beach. Guests enjoy just about everything—good clean showers and toilets, electricity, drinking water, a used-book shelf, concrete pads, dump station—for about $18 for two people (one day free per week; discounts are possible for extended stays). Add about $4 per extra person. Well-behaved pets are okay. Get reservations—for winter, best six months in advance—through the owners, Thies and Cristina Rohlfs.

Trying just as hard is Sayulita's downscale campground, the gated and enclosed **Palmar del Camarón** (tel. 329/291-3373, no reservations accepted; there's always room for one more), in a big palm grove on the gorgeous palm-shadowed north-side beachfront. The environmentally conscious owner offers plenty of grassy spots for tents and smaller self-contained vans needing no hookups. Tent spaces ($5 pp) are first come, first served, with showers, toilets, and *palapas* for shelter against sun and rain. Camarón also rents rustic *palapa cabañas* ($30 d), with mosquito nets and private toilet and shower. Other extras include a beachfront *palapa* restaurant with a rocking bar, and security lockers. As you enter town from Highway 200, find it by going right on either of the first couple of paved streets (Miramar and Playa Azul) off Revolución, the

divided avenue leading into town. When you hit the beachfront road (Avenida Palmar), the campground will be close by to your left or right, and easy to find. Come Semana Santa, this is party central.

## Rental Agents

Drawn by the quiet pleasures of small-town, beachfront Mexico, a number of American, Canadian, and Mexican middle- and upper-class folks have built comfortable vacation homes in and around Sayulita and are renting them out by the week. Tamra Boltjes at **Avalos Real Estate** (tel./fax 329/291-3122, tamra@move2sayulita.com, www.move2sayulita.com), Sayulita's original real estate agency, lists such properties for rental or sale, and she knows just about every house around. For more information and listings, you may also contact their U.S. agent (tel. 805/481-7260 or toll-free fax 800/899-4167).

Alternatively, check out **Garcia Realty** (Revolución 41, tel./fax 329/291-3058, www.sayulita-garciarealty.com or www.sayulita-realestate.com), on the main street, a few doors north of the town plaza. Besides rentals, they list homes and villas for sale. Most of the houses for rent in Sayulita can be previewed online at www.sayulitalife.com and/or www.vrbo.com. When looking for a house to rent, find out if it is on a hill or not (you'll most likely need a car or a golf cart if it is); also ask about security—does it have a safe, barred windows, lockable windows and doors, and so on. While there is virtually no violent crime in Sayulita, there have been many burglaries in recent years, so these issues are not inconsequential.

## FOOD

Vegetables, groceries, and baked goods are available at Mi Tiendita by the town plaza and several other *tiendas* and *abarrotes* (snack shops) around town. Local-style food is supplied by a lineup of taco stands and carts at night, and some beachfront *palapa* restaurants.

Bountiful breakfasts, lunches, and early dinners are on offer at **Choco Banana** (on the town plaza, tel. 329/291-3051, 6am-6pm daily), with lots of hearty American-style breakfasts ($3-10), veggie and meat burgers ($5), fish fillets ($6), carrot cake ($2), and good espresso ($2-4). Don't miss out on the frozen chocolate-covered bananas or creamy, blended coffee drinks. Choco Banana does it all and remains the nerve center of Sayulita.

You'll also find great breakfasts and coffee drinks at the beachfront **El Break Café** (8am-6pm daily, evenings in high season), at the foot of Calle Delfínes; **Panino** (7am-6pm daily), a few doors up from El Break on Delfínes; and **El Expresso** (7am-6pm daily), across the plaza from Choco Banana. Halfway up Calle Delfínes between El Break and Choco Banana is a smoothie and *licuado* stand with plenty of fresh fruit and vegetable concoctions available at really great prices all day long. I recommend El Break for smoothies and views, Panino for excellent pastry, and El Expresso for great coffee.

**The Best Fish Tacos,** sold from a stand on Calle Delfínes, are not wrongly named: Laura, who runs the stand, used to have one of the great little restaurants in town, and her tacos, with grilled or fried fresh shrimp or fish, are about as tasty as can be for about a buck apiece. **Chilly Willy's,** corner of Palmar and Pelicanos, is another great budget seafood joint, with an especially good ceviche and supercheap prices.

Back on Revolución, just south of the main bridge on the right as you're heading into town, you'll find the street taco stand called **Tacos Ivan,** where they make the best *tacos pastor* in town, for about a buck apiece. Buy them plain, pile on the condiments, and make a meal. Watch out for the hotter hot sauces!

Like their "parent" restaurant in La Cruz, Sayulita's own **Tacos on the Street** (Av. Revolución 22, just north of the main bridge into downtown, tel. 322/137-4519, 6pm-10pm daily high season, hours and days vary low season) maintains the world's simplest menu—a dish of radishes and roasted jalapeño peppers to start, followed by meat and vegetarian tacos, and quesadillas made with corn or flour tortillas—but they have broken ranks with the previous generation and

added one new thing: fabulous fish tacos (on Thursday only). Otherwise, like his parents in La Cruz, Jorge Diaz and his wife, Sandrita (and baby Oceana), serve just about the best tacos in the world, with fresh grilled vegetables and great rib eye beef. There's no booze in house, but you can bring your own. The furnishings are basic plastic tables and chairs. Sandrita is a gifted baker, and the restaurant's Key lime pie, flan, and brownies are irresistible, even if you are already stuffed with tacos. Tacos are a bit over a buck apiece, same for desserts. Don't miss it.

A bit higher up the scale, a number of recommendable restaurants dot Sayulita's streets and beachfront. One of the best established is **Don Pedro's** (Calle Marlin 2, tel. 329/291-3090, 8am-11:30pm daily, $10-25), a once humble, now elegant, seafood *palapa* on the south-end beachfront. Here, the main events are the freshest catches of the day, cooked with European flair, such as mahimahi (dorado) Portofino style, and local oysters, octopus, fish, and shrimp cooked up as bouillabaisse (seafood stew). They also cater private events, such as weddings, under their private party *palapa* on the bluff overlooking the beach and sea at the south end of town.

You can get just as fresh Mexican-style seafood (fish and shrimp any style, fish tacos, and *tortas*) at neighboring **El Costeño** (tel. 329/291-3045, noon-midnight daily, $4-12), also on the Sayulita main beachfront. Don't expect speedy service, but the food is usually worth the wait. Beware of the large margarita that comes in a fishbowl-size goblet and will knock two people unconscious before they even know what hit them.

It is unfortunate that **Don Chow's Sushi Bar & Restaurant** (corner of Av. Palmar and Calle Las Gaviotas, tel. 329/291-3929, 4pm-11pm daily, $5-15) closes in summer, since it is the only restaurant in Sayulita possessed of air-conditioning, and summer is really the only time you absolutely need air-conditioning in Sayulita. However, when it is open, the sushi is good and fresh, as are the rest of the Asian fusion menu offerings, including the excellent pad thai. They have TV and are cabled up for sports at the bar (where they serve killer specialty drinks like the Rubytini), and feature live music on the patio during high season.

With its serene garden setting, sports bar TV setup, and sophisticated menu, **Los Afortunados** (Av. Palmar, btwn. Calles Gaviotas and Delfínes, tel. 322/137-9173, www.sayulitalife.com/afortunados, 5pm-11pm daily, $7-15) offers a little bit of *norteamericano* diversion right in the heart of Sayulita. Appetizers and small plates, fresh salads, and a great wine list enhance the international menu, with fresh fish and high-quality meats countered by a good selection of vegetarian entrées. The margaritas and mojitos are among the best in town, and the tequila selection is outstanding.

Great deli sandwiches are to be had at the aptly named **Ruben's** (Av. Revolución D, just off the plaza on Calle Delfínes, tel. 322/183-0692, 11am-5pm daily, sandwiches $6-10), as well as fine salads and pastas. Ruben delivers and offers everything to go. Try the Trujillo, a knockout combo of beef and vegetables on pan-toasted bread with a spicy mayo. One is enough for two.

The food's fine, but what I go for at Storm Richardson's **Sayulita Public House** (Calle Pelicanos 150-C, tel. 329/291-3712, 4pm-midnight Mon. and Wed.-Fri., noon-midnight Sat.-Sun., $4-8) is the atmosphere, the vibe, the 30 different beers on the menu, and the ambience of an old-school English pub, half a block from the beach in Sayulita. Among other standards, the menu includes a classic Philly cheesesteak sandwich, fish and chips, and taquitos. There's also occasional rock and roll in the open-air rooftop lounge.

For a more refined tropical experience, try **Calypso** (upstairs on the west side of the plaza, tel. 329/291-3704, 6pm-11pm daily, $11-22), where you can grab a cold one at the long, curved wooden bar or bring your large group for dinner under the *palapa* and watch the show in the plaza below. The portions are notoriously huge, and the menu offers a nice selection of dishes, from salads and pastas to fresh seafood

and barbecue chicken. The Capitan Ypia, for example, is a small mountain of fresh fish, mussels, and clams drenched in a great, spicy but light red sauce atop fresh pasta (about $14).

Another great addition to Sayulita's wide selection of low-cost dining options is **Aaleyah's Nachos & Wings** (Niños Heroes 2, just off the plaza, tel. 329/291-3353 or 322/150-7630, 8am-10pm Mon.-Sat., $3-10), where owner Josue Cortez and family deliver the best chicken wings and nachos in town (to call the servings generous would be an understatement), along with a good selection of Tex-Mex, Mexicalifornia, and straight-on Mexican food. There's a full bar, top-notch margaritas, and free Wi-Fi, along with a good street-side setup to watch the world go by. Josue's daughter, the restaurant's namesake, is about as charming as a kid can be, in both Spanish and English.

Owner-chef Miguel Muro of **Sayulita Cafe** (on Revolución, a block north of the plaza, tel. 329/291-3511, 1pm-11pm daily) has raised the chile relleno (stuffed chile) to a high art. He offers a quartet of delicious variations: cheese, vegetarian, tuna, or chicken ($8). Alternative options include bountiful salads ($5), barbecued ribs ($9), and T-bone steak with baked potato ($12), all served in a tranquil candlelit atmosphere, enhanced by low-volume melodies and whirring ceiling fans.

For a little self-indulgent dessert eating, try Bonnie Metzger's **Sayulita Dulces,** on Avenida Revolución a little south of the plaza. Here you can sample Bonnie's delightful sea salt caramels as well as coffee, cakes, cookies, and chocolates.

Finally, I would be terribly remiss if I failed to mention Sayulita's increasingly popular and successful **Mercado del Pueblo,** the farmers market. Created and managed by California expat Lina Weismann, the market happens every Friday during high season (November-May), and vendors sell a wonderful, colorful variety of fresh organic produce, packaged foodstuffs, and all manner of good things to eat on the spot or later at your rental home or hotel room. It's a great weekly community event with live music, lots of gossip, and a general good time. Don't miss it if you're in town on a Friday. The market is located in the Sayulita Community Culture Center on Avenida Palmar between Calles Delfínes and Gaviotas in the heart of downtown Sayulita.

## INFORMATION AND SERVICES
### Tourist Information and Communications

A number of businesses keep busy serving Sayulita's visitors. For general information, fax, and Internet connections, go to **Garcia Realty** (Revolución 41, tel./fax 329/291-3058, garciarealty@msn.com), on the main street, a few doors north of the town plaza. They also list vacation rentals and homes and villas for sale. There are several Internet cafés in town, as well as Wi-Fi at most restaurants, so getting online is never really a problem. **Lunanet,** just off the back side of the plaza on Revolución, rents computer/Internet time for about a dollar an hour.

The website **www.sayulitalife.com** amounts to a good community newspaper, chock-full of informative advertisements, from hotels and surf shops to doctors and horseback rides, plus public service announcements, maps, local news, and an events calendar to boot. Be sure and sign up for their weekly electronic newsletter, *El Sayulero* (www.elsayulero.com), as well.

### Money

There are no banks in town yet, but ATMs are everywhere. These are convenient, if suspect. In 2012 a rash of ATM rip-offs occurred, leading many people to stop using them. Although this problem has seemingly abated, the cash machines in Sayulita charge excessively high fees and limit the amount of money you can withdraw from a single account in a single day to 3,000 pesos, for which you are charged anywhere from 60 to 80 pesos here and then charged again, of course, by your own bank. Better to get your money at the airport or at a bank in Vallarta or Bucerías. Also, avoid withdrawing American dollars from the Cashola machines that offer this service, as they charge a ridiculously high markup.

## Health and Emergencies

For remedies and medical consultations, you have at least two choices. On the north side, **Doctor Richard Mendez Aranjuez** (Calle Manuel Sanchez Rodriguez, tel. 322/117-6931, 10am-2pm and 5pm-7pm Mon.-Fri.) is not only a trained and licensed MD, but also an expert acupuncturist, herbalist, and naturopath. He's willing to use antibiotics if magnets, herbs, and acupuncture don't work—or vice versa. His wife, Tanya, is an organic/naturopathic pharmacist with an office right next door. Downtown, consulting pharmacist **Roger Rios** is available at two locations: **Farmacia del Pueblo** (Av. Revolución, just north of the town plaza, tel. 333/447-0980) or at his **second pharmacy** (Av. Revolución 43, just south of the plaza, tel. 329/291-3555), which he co-owns with **Doctor Francisco Hidalgo,** whose office is next door. Both pharmacies are open 8am-11pm Monday-Saturday, 9 am-11pm Sunday, throughout the year.

## Spanish Instruction

Spanish-language lessons at levels from beginning to advanced are offered by **Costa Verde International School** (Av. Revolución 3, tel. 329/291-3222 or 329/291-3355), on the north side of town.

## Laundry

As for laundry, get yours done at the *lavandería* (Av. Revolución 9, 8am-8pm Mon.-Sat.) a block north of the river bridge.

## SAN FRANCISCO (SAN PANCHO)

The idyllic beach and drowsy country ambience of the little former mango-processing village of San Francisco (San Pancho, as locals call it, pop. about 1,000) offers yet another bundle of pleasant surprises. Exit Highway 200 at the road sign 25 miles (40 km) north of the Puerto Vallarta airport and continue straight through the town to the beach. Just before you reach the San Pancho exit (featuring the usual Pemex gas station), you'll see a large, bright red structure sprawling across the landscape on your left, with roadside flags and signage advertising a hotel, a spa, villas, casas, and other stuff. This oversized creation is the Hacienda San Pancho, the centerpiece or anchor for a major south side of San Pancho development that got halfway off the ground a few years ago and has seemingly gone into semihibernation, awaiting the next influx of easy money. In any case, within this large building, traditionally arrayed around a central courtyard, are assorted businesses—a small hotel, an espresso bar, sales offices, and a display of contemporary Cuban art that is museum quality and quite compelling. If open, this art display is worth a half hour of your time.

Meanwhile, back at the beach, the broad golden-white expanse of sand enclosed by palm-tipped green headlands extends for a half mile on both sides of the town. Big, open ocean waves (take care—there's often strong undertow) frequently pound the beach for nearly its entire length. For this reason, it is usually not good for swimming. Offshore, flocks of pelicans dive for fish while frigate birds sail

overhead. Toward the south end of town, an estuary and river mouth provide fertile feeding grounds for hundreds of waterbirds; the same river mouth creates fast, tubular sandbar surfing waves just offshore. At night during the rainy months, sea turtles come ashore to lay their egg clutches, which a determined group of volunteers protects from poachers. Beach *palapa* restaurants provide food and drinks. If you're enticed into staying, a sprinkling of good restaurants, hotels, and bed-and-breakfasts offer food and accommodations.

## Sights

San Pancho is a wonderful strolling town, especially in the evening—just walking the main street, Avenida Tercer Mundo, from end to end, from highway to beach, offers an opportunity to see most of the significant sights: galleries, cafés, restaurants, and, perhaps most interesting of all, the **Entreamigos Community Center** (Centro Comunitario Educativo, Av. Tercer Mundo 12, tel. 311/258-4377, www. entreamigos.org.mx, 9am-6pm Mon.-Fri.,

The beach in San Pancho is wide and quiet.

10am-2pm Sat.), a midsize former factory that has been transformed into a combination community education center, library, event space, theater, store (selling all kinds of cool stuff made from recycled materials), and recycling center—and it's all devoted to improving the lives of the local kids. Check the website for volunteer opportunities as well as a Spanish-language program. You'll find Entreamigos between the highway and the beach on the left side of the street, about a third of the way toward the beach.

The beach in San Pancho is wide and pretty, with rocky, palm-topped headlands bracketing both ends. While the water is frequently too rough for swimming, the sands are great for strolling, and the estuary toward the south end is a great bird-watching spot—literally hundreds of birds can be seen here, particularly in the early mornings and late afternoons. You might even spot a crocodile or two if your eyes are sharp. Contact Luis Morales at **Birding San Pancho** (Av. Tercer Mundo 28, tel. 322/139-7242) for tours of the estuary and other prime birding spots in the area.

### ◖ Grupo Ecológico de la Costa Verde

Founded in 1992, the Grupo Ecológico de la Costa Verde, headquartered in Puerto Vallarta, has been instrumental in rescuing the Puerto Vallarta region's sea turtle populations from the brink of extinction. Spurred on by a dedicated cadre of volunteers, the organization's San Pancho chapter (currently led by Frank Smith) has led the effort by working to increase the San Pancho olive ridley nesting turtle population tenfold, from about 70 to 700 active yearly nests since 1996. The San Pancho chapter (Calle America Latina 102, tel. 311/258-4100, www.project-tortuga.org) welcomes volunteers.

### Alianza Jaguar-HOJANAY Environmental Group

This worthy organization is devoted to reviving the local population of jaguars, magnificent large cats that have lived in the jungles, deserts, and mountains of Nayarit and much

of southern North America for thousands of years. Hunted near to extinction and denied their natural habitat, the jaguars have struggled; today, dedicated volunteers such as those in the Alianza are working to bring them back by helping to establish a conservatory as well as through education, population monitoring, and other methods. Contact Eric Saracho at alianzajaguar@gmail.com for information and volunteering opportunities.

## Recreation

The **La Patrona Polo Club** (Ceilán 10, tel. 311/258-4378 or 322/182-3131, www.polovallarta.com) has its home field, clubhouse, stables, and facilities in a former mango orchard in San Pancho, where matches take place weekly during the season (November-May). Polo ranks among the most expensive sports in the world, what with the maintenance and travel expenses of the polo ponies, but it is extremely challenging to play and a ball to watch, especially here, in a small beach town in Mexico. Everybody is welcome to come and watch matches and practice. The club also offers lessons in polo and equestrian technique. Check the website for various class options. The clubhouse contains a pricey gourmet restaurant and piano bar, open 5pm-10pm Thursday-Saturday in season. Practices are held at 5pm Tuesday and Thursday, while matches, which include Spanish-style dressage, live music, and other entertainments, are held at 6pm Saturday. All these schedules are in effect during the high season (November-May) only.

The formerly private **Las Huertas Golf Course** (Av. Palmas, clubhouse tel. 311/258-4521, manager tel. 322/135-0922, www.lashuertasgolfclub.com), on San Pancho's north side, is now open to the public, offering 9 holes at 3,958 yards (with elevated tees, you can play the course twice, and it feels like 18 holes). More to the point, this is an utterly exquisite course, carved out of a seaside jungle on a hillside overlooking the ocean. A small shop offers snacks and drinks—a clubhouse and a restaurant are planned—and carts are available.

THE RIVIERA NAYARIT

© JUSTIN HENDERSON

handmade goods for sale in San Pancho

Contact manager Martín Alonso Raygoza or go online to schedule a round. Fees are $35 for 9 holes, $50 for 18 holes, $10 for a shared cart for 9 holes, $20 for a shared cart for 18 holes.

## Shopping

A few arts-and-crafts gallery/shops sprinkle main street Avenida Tercer Mundo, although some of the most interesting stuff for sale is to be found at the **Entreamigos Community Center** (Centro Comunitario Educativo, Av. Tercer Mundo 12, tel. 311/258-4377, www.entreamigos.org.mx, 9am-6pm Mon.-Fri., 10am-2pm Sat.), where plastic, glass, and all sorts of recyclables have been transformed into dishes, furniture, artworks...you name it, they might have it for sale. **Galería Corazón** (tel. 311/258-4101, 9am-5pm Mon.-Sat., closed July-Sept.), across Avenida Tercer Mundo from Calandria Realty, features an eclectic assortment of locally crafted candles, ceramics, woodcrafts, textiles, and more. **Tatehuari Jewelry** (Av. Tercer Mundo 90-A, tel. 311/258-4490, www.sanpancholife.com, 9am-5pm daily) features

handcrafted silver jewelry designed by owner Susana Sanborn Tognotti and handmade by her partner, Luis Navaez Flores. The Mexican influence is subtly evident, but the designs are essentially spare, minimalist, and elegant.

On the north end of town just before the Costa Azul Resort (driving required), **Artefakto** (Calle Las Palmas 130, #2, tel. 311/258-5033, U.S. tel. 949/315-1380, www.artefakto-mx.com, open seasonally) offers a fantastic selection of antique furniture, contemporary art, antique pottery, religious artifacts, and all kinds of beautiful and intriguing objects.

## Accommodations
### IN TOWN

On a quiet, flowery side street, a venerable house was rebuilt by American owners, thus creating the **Hotel Cielo Rojo** (Red Sky) bed-and-breakfast (Calle Asia 6, tel./fax 311/258-4155, www.hotelcielorojo.com), seemingly perfect for those who appreciate quiet relaxation. A tiled entrance walkway guides visitors indoors, through an artfully decorated small lobby to an airy breakfast garden patio partially sheltered by a gracefully traditional *palapa* roof. A hot tub for guests' enjoyment is tucked on one side, perhaps a little too close to the dining area for real use.

Stairs lead to three luxuriously open upper-room stories with six spacious rooms and a larger suite, all tucked beneath a handsomely rustic top-floor *palapa*-roofed two-bedroom suite. The accommodations themselves are simply but elegantly furnished with hand-crafted wood furniture, wall arts and crafts, designer lamps, and colorful native-style handcrafted bedspreads. The exquisitely tiled bathrooms are fitted with gleaming modern-standard wash basins, toilets, and showers. The rooms (with either queen-size bed or two twins) rent for about $65 d low season, $85 d high; the larger suites (with one queen and one twin each) go for about $85 d low season, $95 d high. The top-floor two-bedroom suite goes for about $115 d low season, $150 d high; all have ceiling fans and continental breakfast included.

## NORTH OF TOWN

Travelers should be aware that the following lodging listings are on a road that leads along the coast north out of San Pancho; all are far enough from "downtown" San Pancho to require a car or taxi to get to town. There is one good restaurant not far from Costa Azul (Marplata), but otherwise it's a longish hike or a cab or car ride to dine away from your hotel or lodge.

Lovers of nature and solitude should head north of town (past the Costa Azul Adventure Resort) and continue a mile and a fraction (about 2 km) along the dirt coastal road to a signed driveway leading through the palm-tufted tropical forest. At the driveway's end is **Bungalows Lydia** (Carretera Puerto Vallarta-Tepic, Km 111, tel. 311/258-4337 or 311/258-4338, www.bungalowslydia.com or www.vrbo.com/8853), the mini Eden and life-dream-made-true of sprightly and welcoming Lydia Cisneros Mora. Her (and her sister's)

offering consists of four smallish but clean kitchenette studios ($95 low season, $105 high) and two larger one-bedroom bungalow suites (one for $130 low season, $150 high, the other for $170 low, $190 high, for up to four), with hot-water shower baths. Discounts are negotiable for longer-term rentals. Simply but thoughtfully decorated in whites and pastels, they're set in a charming oceanfront garden on a spectacularly rocky point buffeted by wild, foaming surf—the place is kept nearly bug free by the ocean breeze. There's wireless Internet but no phones or TV, and plenty of fresh air, sunsets, and animal friends—coatis, raccoons, armadillos, and squirrels (*ardillas*)—in the neighboring vine-hung tropical forest. Paths lead down to a pair of secluded beaches separated by a rocky outcropping and naturally equipped with an oceanfront tide pool whirlpool bath.

For another outdoor adventure, continue another mile past Bungalows Lydia to the secluded camping platforms at **Tailwind Outdoor** (tel. 322/100-1585, www.tailwindoutdoor.com). Here Tamara Jacobi and her family have created a luxury camping experience for those who want to experience the serene enjoyment of outdoor living. There are ecobungalows ($75 d) that offer safari tent-style camping on beautiful wooden platforms set into the hilly jungle. The platforms are completely private and offer the comforts of electricity, rustic cooking facilities, king-size beds, and mosquito nets. Hot showers are provided next to the platforms, but those who desire flush toilets will have to trek up to the main headquarters, located under a *palapa* at the top of the hillside. For those not quite ready to rough it at that level, Tailwind now offers several more enclosed casitas and *palapas* at $130-200 per night, depending on the number of people.

Guests have access to all of the facilities, including a shared kitchen and petite swimming pool. There's a wooden viewing platform for nightly sunset-watching. In the daytime, Tamara leads sea kayak and stand-up paddleboard tours in the water, hikes on land, and yoga sessions on the yoga platform; or you can

a pool in the forest at Tailwind Outdoor

ramble around the five acres on your own. A pathway leads down the hill to a small, secluded beach. The entire property sleeps up to 16 people and can be rented for $700 for families or groups. Check the Tailwind website for retreat and special event listings.

On the same road that leads north out of downtown San Pancho, but about a mile closer to town, is the **Costa Azul Adventure Resort** (Hwy. 200, Km 118, Amapas y Los Palmas, tel. 311/258-4120, fax 311/258-4099, U.S./Can. tel. 949/498-3223, toll-free U.S. tel. 800/365-7613, U.S. fax 949/498-6300, www.costaazul.com), on the beach. In-hotel activity centers around the beach and the palm-shaded pool patio and adjacent restaurant-bar. Farther afield, hotel guides lead guests (at extra cost) on kayaking, biking, surfing, and snorkeling trips, and naturalist-guided horseback rides along nearby coves, beaches, and jungle trails. I have surfing friends who come down from the States every year to stay here so their families can lounge poolside while they let the guides, who know

their way around the local surf, drive them to the best waves in the area every day.

The main hotel building, at the foot of a hillside of magnificent Colima palms, offers 18 large, comfortable suites. Uphill, sheltered beneath the palms, stand eight villas (six one-bedroom and a pair of two-bedroom). Suites in the main hotel building rent for about $120 d high season; the one-bedroom villas go for about $160 d, and the two-bedroom villas about $300, for up to six. Up to two children under 12 stay free. These rates are European plan; the resort also offers a selection of all-inclusive packages that include not only food and (nonalcoholic) drink, but also daily surf trips, which makes great sense if you are planning to surf every day. Reservations are strongly recommended, especially in the winter.

Past Costa Azul, north a block or two, turn downhill toward the beach and continue another block north to lovely, secluded **C Casa de los Obeliscos** (tel. 311/258-4315, U.S. tel. 415/233-4252, www.casaobelisco.com). Here, welcoming American owners have created their version of paradise for their guests to enjoy. They offer four supercomfortable, airy, art-and-tile decorated suites, two of them with private ocean-view patios, all overlooking a luscious hibiscus-decorated pool patio. The tropical garden setting makes for a lovely and relaxed atmosphere, and guests can enjoy snacks and drinks at the pool bar. Beach access is just across the street. Rates run $160 d low season, $175 d high ($250 Christmas-New Year's), including a big, delicious breakfast. Sorry, no children under 16 or pets. There are cats and dogs on the premises, however, so if you have allergies, be warned. Get your reservations in early (by email only: reservations@casaobelisco.com).

**RENTAL AGENTS**
For the many other available San Francisco villa, house, or apartment rentals, consult the agents at **Calandria Realty** (Av. Tercer Mundo 50, tel. 311/258-4285, www.calandriarealty.com), in front of Restaurant Ola Rica on the main street. Alternatively, you might also

consult **Feibel Real Estate** (Av. Tercer Mundo 91, tel./fax 311/258-4041, www.flfeibel.com), which also lists vacation rentals and for-sale homes. Sanpancholife.com, like Sayulitalife.com in neighboring Sayulita, is a community website that has most of the businesses and rental houses listed with comprehensive information and photographs.

## Food

The growing local community of middle-class Americans, Canadians, and Mexicans, and the trickle of Puerto Vallarta visitors, support a number of recommendable in-town eateries. In addition to the following restaurant options, both the Cielo Rojo and the Costa Azul have fine in-house restaurants, as does La Patrona Polo Club. There are also a number of excellent low-budget taco stands and chicken grills up and down the main street of San Pancho.

On Tercer Mundo in the middle of town, **La Ola Rica Restaurant and Bar** (tel. 311/258-4123, 6pm-11pm Mon.-Sat., $10-24) is recommended by nearly everyone in San Pancho. Welcoming owners Triny and Gloria offer fresh seafood, barbecued ribs, and Mexican specialties such as guajillo sizzling shrimp, chipotle mushrooms, and cream of poblano soup.

A little closer to the beach, **Café Arte** (Tercer Mundo 62, tel. 311/258-4027, 8am-11pm daily, $12) is an art-filled Italian/Chilean restaurant/art gallery/live music venue. Performances usually spill right out into the street, where passersby can order a glass of wine and enjoy whoever's playing.

Euro-tropical gourmet cuisine has arrived in San Pancho, at **Café Marplata** (Las Palmas 130, tel. 311/258-4425 or 311/258-4251, 5pm-11pm Thurs.-Tues., closed June-Sept., $10-22), near the Costa Azul Adventure Resort on the road leading north out of town. The influences are Argentine and European, with specialties such as tartare of red snapper, ma-himahi cooked with white wine, and fresh tuna seared in olive oil. The restaurant has an excellent wine list with vintages from Spain, France,

Argentina, Italy, and Mexico, and is renowned for its desserts, particularly the Belgian chocolate fondue with fresh fruits. Get there by following the signs for Bungalows Lydia and/or Costa Azul. The breezy, open-air restaurant is upstairs from the Artefakto Gallery.

**La Taza de Café** (Tercer Mundo 98, tel. 311/258-4162, 8am-3pm Wed.-Mon., $3-10) is a lovely, lively little spot in a gardenlike setting on the main street a block in from the beach. It's great for breakfast.

**The Blue Pig** (Tercer Mundo 37-A, upstairs, tel. 311/258-5042, 6pm-midnight daily) opened in 2012 to much acclaim from barbecue fans who couldn't get enough of their authentic Southern-style pulled pork, pork ribs, chicken, baked beans, and coleslaw. A band plays blues on random nights in the high season. You can get fully stuffed for about $8-12 a head.

## Health and Emergencies

San Francisco residents benefit from a modest local **general hospital** (tel. 311/258-4077), with ambulance, emergency room, and doctors on call 24 hours. Find it off the main street, to the right (north), about a quarter mile from the highway. Word is that some find this emergency room a little sketchy on sanitation, but lives have been saved here.

## LO DE MARCOS

Follow the signed Lo de Marcos turnoff 31 miles (49 km) north of the Puerto Vallarta airport (or 8 mi/13 km south of Rincón de Guayabitos). You can't miss it, with Oxxos and Pemexes on both sides of Highway 200. Continue about a mile through the town, past the pleasant central plaza to the long, sandy beach, dotted with a baker's dozen of seafood *palapa* restaurants. Playa Lo de Marcos is popular with Mexican families; on Sunday and holidays they dig into the fine golden sand and frolic in the gentle, rolling waves. The surf of the nearly level, very wide Playa Lo de Marcos is good for all aquatic sports except surfing. The south end has a rocky tide pool shelf, fine for bait casting. (Rumor has it that once in a while a good surfing wave may be found here as well.) During the clear-water late fall-winter season, scuba divers and snorkelers rent boats and head to pristine offshore Isla Islote.

## Recreation
**Cocoloco Sports** (Echeverria 24, tel. 327/275-0506) offers a full range of fishing and camping gear, as well as bikes for sale and rent. Canadian owner Corey also does bike repairs. He recommends **Mauricio** (south end on the beach, tel. 327/147-9664) as a good boat captain for anyone who wants to fish the area or go on a whale-watching trip (seasonal).

## Accommodations
There are a number of low- to mid-priced accommodations in town, some beachfront. For off-beach lodging, the best by far is **Hotel Bungalows Las Tortugas** (Echeverria 28, tel./fax 327/275-0092, $40-65 d, depending on season, for room without kitchen; with kitchens, $50-115, depending on season and number of people). The major attraction is the layout of about 18 apartments in two stories around a broad, invitingly tropical designer pool and patio, with kiddie pool and hot tub. Inside, the units, all with kitchenette, TV, dishes and utensils, and fans, are bare-bulb (bring your own lampshade), sparely but comfortably furnished, spacious, and clean. The second-floor apartments, with king-size beds, are more inviting than some others. Look at more than one before deciding. Asking rates run high, but, except during holidays and some weekends, discounts may be negotiable, so be sure to ask for a *descuento* (days-koo-AYN-toh).

For something fancier, consider the rambling **Villas and Bungalows Tlaquepaque** (Pie de Av. Luis Echeverria, tel./fax 327/275-0080, villastlaquepaque@prodigy.net.mx). Past the imposing neocolonial front gate and reception spreads a manicured, grassy park, with luxurious blue-pool patio, basketball court, soccer field, and kiddie playground, interspersed among handsome accommodation tiers. Lodgings vary from one-bedroom studios to big three-bedroom, three-bath extended-family

suites. A kiddie pool is ringed with Disney characters and a huge, playful slide structure. The grounds are colorful, spacious, and pleasant, with direct, private access to the beach. The hotel has its own trailer park and the Surf Bar El Parian.

The lodgings themselves are immaculate and handsomely decorated in white stucco, bright Spanish tiles, and traditional hand-crafted wooden furniture. A number of the studios are cozy and comfortable, with bright garden views and two double beds. Considering all the family-friendly facilities, the lower-end prices are moderate, beginning at about $33 d for the studios during the low season (Sept.-Dec. 15 and Jan.-Mar.), with breakfast sometimes included, and ranging up to $60 for two-bedroom family suites. High-season rates run from about $75 d for a room for two to $100 for a bungalow. Look at the several options before choosing. With plenty of space to run around and only a block from the beach, this is a great place for kids and large groups. Reservations are generally not necessary, except July-August, Christmas and Easter holidays, and maybe some weekends. Long-term rates are available.

If you prefer to stay closer to the sand and waves, a sprinkling of family-friendly beachfront lodgings appear promising. At **Bungalows Margarita** (Emiliano Zapata 22, tel. 327/275-0452, www.bungalowsmargarita. com), a brightly colored apartment-style complex, there is a choice of rooms ranging from ocean-view suites with kitchens that sleep up to six adults ($85 d) to rooms that sleep two ($42 d) and everything in between. There's (seasonal) air-conditioning, ceiling fans, and other creature comforts, as well as a nice beach *palapa* and barbecue area. Get there by turning left from the main town highway entrance street, at the last road before the beach.

Also on the beachfront, a block north of the main road (Echeverria), you can stay at **Villas del Rey** (U.S. tel. 425/334-6051, www.mexicobeachfrontvillas.com), where local expat artist Lonney Ford and his wife, Stacey, have created a lovely garden setting decorated with

Lonney's unusual sculptures right on the beach. The main attraction here is the enormous, spacious villa ($400/day, sleeps 10-12), which is perfect for large groups and family get-togethers. Also available are three charming studios ($80 d) and a one-bedroom ($100 d) unit. All units include a full kitchen, queen beds, ceiling fans, and wireless Internet. The villa is totally comfortable and inviting, with Lonney's quirky and entertaining sculptures—life-size Day of the Dead skeleton lady, anyone?—adding to the fun.

## TRAILER PARKS AND CAMPGROUNDS

Lo de Marcos has a number of beachfront trailer parks, popular during the winter with a regiment of American and Canadian RV retirees. Best of the bunch is the pleasant **El Caracol** trailer park and bungalow complex (P.O. Box 89, La Peñita de Jaltemba, Nayarit 63726, tel./fax 327/275-0050, http://elcaracol_mx.tripod.com). The trailer park section offers about 15 concrete-pad spaces in a palm- and banana-shaded grassy park right on the beach. Amenities include a small beachfront kiddie pool patio, all hookups, and immaculate hot-shower and toilet facilities. The spaces rent for about $22 per day, $21 per day for a month's stay, and $19 per day for a 95-day stay; add $4 per day for air-conditioning power and $5 per day per extra person. Caracol's bungalows are correspondingly well appointed. They are available with one bedroom (for up to three) or two bedrooms (for up to five), all comfortably furnished with all the comforts of Hamburg (the owner is German), including fans, optional air-conditioning, and complete kitchenettes. Daily high-season rates run $96-146 for two people in a one-bedroom bungalow, with $8 per extra person; add $8 for one-bedroom air-conditioning; $12 for two-bedroom. Long-term rates, for a three-month rental, can sometimes be negotiated to as low as $35 per day for a one-bedroom and $43 per day for a two-bedroom. Dogs are not generally welcome. It's popular, so get your reservations in early—make winter reservations in July or August.

Tent, RV camping, and bungalow lodgings are available at the trailer park **Pequeña Paraíso** (Carretera a Las Miñitas 1938, tel. 327/275-0089), beside the jungle headland at the south end of the beach. Here, the manager welcomes visitors to the spacious, palm-shaded beachside grove. Basic but clean apartments rent for about $220 per week, with kitchenettes, hot-water showers, and fans. RV spaces ($18/day, $125/wk, $465/mo) have all hookups, with showers and toilets. Dozens of grass-carpeted, palm-shaded tent spaces rent for about $5 per person per day. Stores in town nearby can furnish basic supplies. Reserve, especially during the winter.

Get to the beachfront bungalows and trailer parks by turning left just before the beach, at the foot-of-the-town main street (which leads straight from the highway past the plaza). Continue about another mile to El Caracol, on the right, and El Pequeño Paraíso, a hundred yards farther.

If those two are full, a few other trailer parks are recommendable. Best appears to be beachfront trailer park **Pretty Sunset** (tel./fax 327/275-0024 or 327/275-0055), with about 18 complete hookups ($20/day, $450/mo) in a mostly unshaded but spacious beachfront park. Another similarly equipped, but smaller, option along the same beachfront is **Trailer Park and Bungalows Huerta de Iguanas** (tel. 327/275-0089, $20).

If they're all full, you're most likely to get a tent or RV space at the huge, overflow-style **Trailer Park and Campground El Refugio** (Pie de Av. Luis Echeverria, tel./fax 327/275-0080, villastlaquepaque@prodigy.net.mx, $24/day, $525/mo), on the north end of the beach at Villas and Bungalows Tlaquepaque.

## Food

There are the usual taco stands and *fondas* to choose from in Lo de Marcos (Olivia's is acclaimed as the best of the beachfront lot), but most people dine out in nearby Guayabitos or San Francisco. In town, restaurants tend to come and go seasonally, making it difficult to offer any solid recommendations.

THE RIVIERA NAYARIT

## HIDDEN BEACHES

Continuing south along the Lo de Marcos beach road past the trailer parks, you will soon come to two small sandy beaches, **Playa las Miñitas** and **Playa el Venado**. Both of these pretty, rock-enfolded strands, especially El Venado, are likely to be crowded on the weekends but mostly empty midweek, with lots of empty *palapas,* ripe for a tent. Even if for a day, bring your swimsuit, picnic lunch, and snorkeling gear.

# Rincón de Guayabitos and La Peñita

Rincón de Guayabitos (pop. about 3,000 permanent, maybe 8,000 in winter) lies an hour's drive north of Puerto Vallarta, at the tiny south-end *rincón* (wrinkle) of the broad, mountain-rimmed Bay of Jaltemba. The full name of Rincón de Guayabitos's sister town, La Peñita (Little Rock) de Jaltemba, comes from its perch on the sandy edge of the bay.

Once upon a time, Rincón de Guayabitos (or simply Guayabitos, meaning little guavas) lived up to its diminutive name. During the 1970s, however, the government decided Rincón de Guayabitos would become both a resort and one of three places in the Puerto Vallarta region where foreigners could own property. Today Rincón de Guayabitos is a summer, Christmas, and Easter haven for Mexicans, and a winter retreat for U.S. and Canadian citizens weary of glitzy, pricey resorts.

## ORIENTATION

Guayabitos and La Peñita (pop. around 10,000) represent practically a single town. Guayabitos has the hotels and the scenic beach-village ambience, while 2 miles (3.2 km) north, La Peñita's main street, **Emiliano Zapata**, bustles with stores, restaurants, a bank, and a bus station.

Guayabitos's main street, **Avenida del Sol Nuevo,** curves lazily for about a mile parallel to the beach. During holidays and the busy winter months, it's almost like a street fair, with vendors lining the avenue and throngs of people shopping and dining. From the avenida, several short streets and *andandos* (walkways) lead to a line of *retornos* (cul-de-sacs). There are literally dozens of hotels to choose from on and within two blocks of the beach, with an emphasis on low to midrange pricing. Guayabitos might be one of the few beach resort towns where you can still get a $10 hotel room, if you shop around a bit. There are certainly $20 or $30 a day bungalows available.

## SIGHTS
### Isla Islote

Only a few miles offshore, the rock-studded humpback of Isla Islote may be seen from every spot along the bay. A flotilla of wooden glass-bottomed launches plies the Guayabitos shoreline, ready to whisk visitors across to the island. For about $20 per hour, parties of up to eight can view fish through the boat bottom and see the colonies of nesting terns, frigate birds, and boobies on Islote's guano-plastered far side. You might see dolphins playing in your boat's wake, or perhaps a pod of whales spouting and diving nearby.

### Cerro de la Santa Cruz

Some breezy afternoon, you might enjoy following the 225-step pilgrimage (May 3 and Easter) path to the summit of Cerro de la Santa Cruz (Hill of the Holy Cross). From the top of La Cruz, as it's locally known, appreciate the ocean, beach, and cloud-tipped mountain panorama of the Bay of Jaltemba. Find the trail at the south end of Guayabitos's main street, Avenida del Sol Nuevo. Turn left at the crossroads and look for the path heading uphill.

## BEACHES
### Playa Guayabitos-La Peñita

The main beach, Playa Guayabitos-La Peñita, curves 2 miles (3.2 km) north from the rocky Guayabitos headland and point, growing

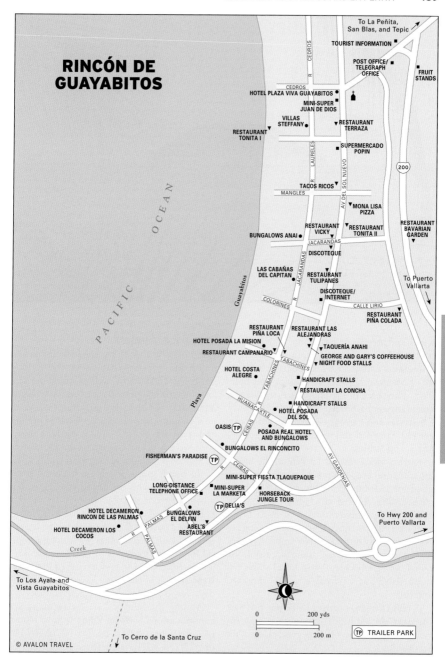

# RINCÓN DE GUAYABITOS

To La Peñita,
San Blas, and Tepic

TOURIST INFORMATION

POST OFFICE/
TELEGRAPH
OFFICE

FRUIT
STANDS

CEDROS

R. CEDROS

HOTEL PLAZA VIVA GUAYABITOS

MINI-SUPER
JUAN DE DIOS

VILLAS
STEFFANY

RESTAURANT
TONITA I

RESTAURANT
TERRAZA

R. LAURELES

SUPERMERCADO
POPIN

AV. DEL SOL NUEVO

200

TACOS RICOS

MANGLES

MONA LISA
PIZZA

RESTAURANT
VICKY

RESTAURANT
TONITA II

RESTAURANT
BAVARIAN
GARDEN

BUNGALOWS ANAI

JACARANDAS

DISCOTEQUE

LAS CABAÑAS
DEL CAPITAN

R. JACARANDAS

RESTAURANT
TULIPANES

DISCOTEQUE/
INTERNET

To Puerto
Vallarta

COLORINES

CALLE LIRIO

RESTAURANT
PIÑA COLADA

RESTAURANT
PIÑA LOCA

RESTAURANT LAS
ALEJANDRAS

HOTEL POSADA LA MISION

TAQUERÍA ANAHI

RESTAURANT CAMPANARIO

TABACHINES

GEORGE AND GARY'S COFFEEHOUSE

NIGHT FOOD STALLS

HOTEL COSTA
ALEGRE

TABACHINES

HANDICRAFT STALLS

RESTAURANT LA CONCHA

Playa

HUANACAXTLE

HANDICRAFT STALLS

HOTEL POSADA
DEL SOL

OASIS (TP)

CEIBAS

POSADA REAL HOTEL
AND BUNGALOWS

BUNGALOWS EL RINCONCITO

FISHERMAN'S PARADISE (TP)

CEIBAS

AV. GARDENIAS

MINI-SUPER FIESTA TLAQUEPAQUE

LONG-DISTANCE
TELEPHONE OFFICE

MINI-SUPER
LA MARKETA

HORSEBACK
JUNGLE TOUR

(TP) DELIA'S

HOTEL DECAMERON
RINCON DE LAS PALMAS

BUNGALOWS
EL DELFIN

R. PALMAS

ABEL'S
RESTAURANT

To Hwy 200 and
Puerto Vallarta

HOTEL DECAMERON LOS
COCOS

PALMAS

Creek

To Los Ayala and
Vista Guayabitos

OCEAN

PACIFIC

Guayabitos

To Cerro de la Santa Cruz

© AVALON TRAVEL

0     200 yds
0     200 m

(TP) TRAILER PARK

THE RIVIERA NAYARIT

© OTTO DUSBABA/DREAMSTIME.COM

Isla Islote

wider and steeper at La Peñita. The shallow south-end Guayabitos cove, lined by *palapa* restaurants and dotted with boats, is a favorite of Mexican families on Sunday and holidays. They play in the one-foot surf, ride the boats, and eat barbecued fish. During the busy Christmas and Easter holidays, the beach can get a bit crowded and messy from the people, boats, and fishing.

Farther along toward La Peñita, the beach broadens and becomes much cleaner, with surf good for swimming, bodysurfing, and boogie boarding. Afternoon winds are often brisk enough for sailing, though you must bring your own equipment. Scuba and snorkeling are good, especially during the November-May dry season, near offshore Isla Islote, accessible via rental boat from Guayabitos. Local stores sell inexpensive but serviceable masks, snorkels, and fins.

A mile (1.6 km) north of La Peñita, just past the palm-dotted headland, another long, inviting beach begins, offering good chances for surf fishing.

## Playa los Ayala

Continue south along the road about another mile to the once sleepy but now up-and-coming settlement and one-mile yellow strand of Playa los Ayala. Although local-style beachside *palapa* restaurants and bungalow accommodations are now ubiquitous, with varying levels of pricing and style, the lovely Playa los Ayala, a shortened version of the Guayabitos beach, retains its Sunday popularity among local families. All of the beach sports possible at Guayabitos are possible here, with the added advantage of a much quieter, cleaner beach.

Like Guayabitos, Los Ayala has its secluded south-end cove. Follow the path up the beach-end headland. Ten minutes' walk along a tropical forest trail leads you to the romantic little jungle-enfolded sand crescent called **Playa del Beso** (Beach of the Kiss). Except during holidays, few if any people come here.

Among the best of Los Ayala's many accommodations is **Hotel Villas Quinta Minas** (Av. del Coral 42-C, tel./fax 327/274-1141 or 327/274-1321). This three-story stack of modern kitchenette apartments enfolds an inviting beachfront pool and patio. Here, adults lounge around the small pool, while their kids frolic in a beachside kiddie pool. Upstairs, the dozen or so one-bedroom units, sleeping four, are simply but attractively furnished, with large rustic floor tiles, soft couches, white stucco walls, and shiny shower bathrooms. Low-season rentals run about $53 for up to four, except holidays and *puentes* (long weekends).

If the Quinta Minas is full, check out the Los Ayala branch of the popular Rincón de Guayabitos lodging **Bungalows el Delfín** (Av. Estero 228, tel. 327/274-0971, www.bungalowseldelfin.com, $65-90). To get there, you'll have to abandon the short section of beachfront road that is paved and head down the dirt road a ways. A few turns and you'll find it, easily enough, on the beach side of the road.

## Playa Punta Raza

Punta Raza is one of the most beautiful beaches along the coast. Tucked back down a 3-mile (4.8-km) jungle dirt road are miles of dreamy golden sand perfect for beachcombing, lazing in the sun, or frolicking in the surf. Unfortunately, developers have discovered this isolated beach and now closed the area to make way for a megaresort complex. However, there is nothing built yet, and there remains a small area where you can pull off the road; since there is no private ownership of the beaches, visitors are welcome to park and enjoy the beach. There's only space enough for a few cars, and at the moment no services are available. You will also be under the watchful eye of the security guard who staffs the guardhouse at the gate. Still, this beach is worth a visit before the road is paved and the teeming masses of tourists take over and turn El Monteón into the next Nuevo Vallarta. At the moment this seems very unlikely, but who knows?

Three miles (4.8 km) south of Guayabitos along Highway 200, turn off west at El Monteón; pass through the village and turn right at Calle Punta Raza just before the

© JUSTIN HENDERSON

**This is what passes for a crowd at Playa Punta Raza.**

pavement ends. Continue along the rough road through the creek and over the ridge north of town. At the summit, stop and feast your eyes on the valley view below, then continue down through the near-virgin jungle, barely scratched by a few poor cornfields. About a mile downhill from the summit, stop at the hillside Hotel and Restaurant Rincón del Cielo on the right.

The **Hotel and Restaurant Rincón del Cielo** affords the opportunity of enjoying an overnight at Playa Punta Raza without the effort of camping. Owner Alfonso Javier Perez has made arrangements with the beachfront developers (who have developed nothing to date) to allow his guests access to the beach and lagoon, with its many birds and rumored crocodiles, via mountain bikes. The hotel includes seven immaculate and simply but lovingly decorated rooms. Two are at the jungle's edge ($45 d), one is at the ground level in a whimsical, medieval-style stone tower ($55 d), and the others enjoy airy view perches above the surf ($65). Solar power now enhances the off-the-grid hotel with some electricity to go with the propane gas for light and refrigeration in their restaurant (which offers seafood, salads, and pasta), and candles and hurricane lanterns in the rooms. Make reservations (not usually necessary) with Alfonso at 322/168-7719.

## RECREATION

Aquatic sports are concentrated around the south end of Guayabitos beach, where launches ply the waters, offering banana (towed-tube) rides and **snorkeling** at offshore Isla Islote. Rent a **sportfishing** launch along the beach. If you want to launch your own boat, ask at the Fisherman's Paradise Trailer Park if you can use their ramp for a fee.

### Tours and Guides

A few local guides lead tours into the lush, wildlife-rich Guayabitos hinterland. Most accessible is **Indalesio Muñoz**, who leads horseback nature trail rides directly from his corral on the south end of Avenida del Sol Nuevo, across from the Hotel Bugambilias. Tariff is about $20 per person for a two-hour ride. He

is known locally as Señor Patalargo and has been around long enough to be known by all.

Highly recommended English-speaking guide **Esteban Valdivia** (home tel. 327/274-0805, Restaurant Piña Colada tel. 327/274-1211) offers more extensive tours to unusual, untouristed local sites. His itinerary can include such intriguing destinations as hidden Las Miñitas bay and beach near Lo de Marcos, Jamurca hot mineral pools, the Alta Vista Archaeological Sacred Site near Las Varas, the jungle riverboat tour to La Tovara spring in San Blas, and the sylvan volcanic Laguna Santa María, in the Sierra southeast of Tepic.

## ENTERTAINMENT
### Nightlife

Guayabitos's spot for romantics is **Vista Guayabitos** restaurant (tel. 327/274-2589, 1pm-9pm daily), on the south edge of town. Little has been spared to afford a perfect spot to enjoy a refreshment and/or snack and the breezy panoramic view of Guayabitos's curving cloud-tipped shoreline. Follow the south road to Los Ayala; at the big hilltop curve, follow the driveway on the right steeply uphill.

While Guayabitos is a bustling and energetic town during the high season, it doesn't have the nightlife options of Puerto Vallarta. A few nightspots, easily located by the noise they emanate, operate along Avenida del Sol Nuevo. There are several discos, and karaoke bars that stay open until 3am, should that late-night inspiration strike. One of the liveliest and longest-lasting nightspots is the big, booming dance club at the corner of Avenida del Sol Nuevo and Jacarandas (around 9pm-3am most nights, especially Fri. and Sat., particularly in high season). The dance club is upstairs from a karaoke bar called Nivel Zero, which keeps the same hours.

If oldies but goodies are your thing, the **Bavarian Garden** restaurant (on Hwy. 200, at the south-end signal and entrance to town, tel. 327/274-2136) offers live 1940s-1970s tunes and country music for dancing, 7pm-9pm Wednesday and Friday during the November-May high season.

## SHOPPING

### ◖ La Peñita *Tianguis*

One thing not to be missed in La Peñita is the weekly open-air markets called *tianguis*. While other areas host markets as well, the Thursday-morning market in La Peñita includes artisans from all over Mexico, some from as far away as Oaxaca and Puebla, home of Talavera pottery. The marketplace is brimming with color as the artisans display their wares on tables and spread blankets. Handwoven rugs and baskets, carved ironwood statues, gruesome and funny wooden masks—all manner of beautiful and authentic Mexican handicrafts are on offer in the square in the center of the market.

You'll see the market to your left where it starts on the south side of the main road into town about four blocks from the beach. The center square is where you will find the majority of the artisans and craftspeople. The market is usually shut down by 2pm, so make sure to get there early enough to see everything.

In addition to hand-painted wooden bowls and handmade jewelry, the *tianguis* is a great place to buy housewares like juicers, tortilla warmers, and lime squeezers. There are produce and fish vendors, as well as many taco and ceviche stands for when you get hungry. Don't miss the organic Nayarit coffee and fresh honey!

## ACCOMMODATIONS

Rincón de Guayabitos has far more hotels than any other town in Nayarit, including the state capital, Tepic. Competition keeps standards high, and prices, for the most part, moderate. During the low season (Sept.-Dec. 15), most places are more than half empty and ready to bargain. During the winter season, the livelier part of town is at the south end, where the foreigners, mostly Canadian and American RV folks, congregate.

Guayabitos has many lodgings that call themselves "bungalows." This generally implies a motel-type suite with kitchenette and less service, but it sleeps more people than most hotel rooms. For long stays or if you want to save money by cooking your own meals, bungalows can be an attractive option. Note: Virtually all of the following lodgings have a Web page on the Guayabitos general website, www.guayabitos.com.

The kindly owner of **Hotel Posada del Sol** (Av. Sol Nuevo 56, tel. 327/274-0043, fax 327/274-1319, $55), on the north side of Andando Huanacaxtle, offers 30 tastefully furnished kitchenette bungalows around a palmy garden pool patio. Best are the upper-level units, on the north side, with air-conditioning and garden-view patio-balconies. Economical long-term discounts are negotiable. This charming place, as you would expect, is very popular and full in winter with a crowd of long-time returnees. Get your reservations in early.

A good beachfront choice is the neocolonial-style **Hotel Posada La Misión** (Retorno Tabachines 6, tel./fax 327/274-0357, 327/274-0895, or 327/274-1000, www.hotelposada-lamision.com), whose centerpiece is a beach-view restaurant/bar. Extras include an inviting azure pool and patio, thoughtfully screened off from the parking. Its rooms are high-ceilinged and comfortable, except for the unimaginative bare-bulb lighting; bring your favorite bulb-clip lampshades. High-season rates range from about $65 for the smaller but comfortable economy double-bed rooms and about $108 for larger suites sleeping six, all the way up to $168 for a big kitchenette bungalow sleeping eight and $185 for one sleeping nine (all prices higher during Christmas and Easter holidays). Amenities include the good El Campanario restaurant out in front, ocean-view restaurant/bar, air-conditioning, ceiling fans, and parking; credit cards are accepted.

Among the more economical recommendable lodgings in town is the family-friendly 46-unit **Posada Real Hotel and Bungalows** (Av. Nuevo Sol and Andando Huanacaxtle, tel. 327/274-0707, toll-free Mex. tel. 01-800/714-3501, fax 327/274-0177, www.guayabitos.com.mx/posadareal), built around a cobbled parking courtyard jungle of squawking parrots and shady palms, mangoes, and bamboo. The bungalow units are on the ground floor in the shady courtyard; the hotel rooms are stacked in three plant-decorated tiers above the lobby in front. The 20 double-bed hotel rooms rent for about $50 high season, with discounts possible for longer-term stays. The 26 four-person bungalows with kitchenette rent for about $77 high season. Amenities include ceiling fans, a small pool and a kiddie pool, waterslide, racquetball, and parking; credit cards are accepted.

Right-on-the-beach **Bungalows El Rinconcito** (Retorno Ceibas s/n and Calle Ceibas, tel./fax 327/274-0229, bws_elrinconcito@hotmail.com) remains one of the best lodging buys in Guayabitos. The smallish whitewashed complex set back from the street offers large, tastefully furnished units with yellow-and-blue-tile kitchens and solid Spanish-style dark-wood chairs and beds. Its oceanside patio opens to a grassy garden overlooking the surf. The seven one-bedroom bungalows rent for about $56 high season, $44 low, with fans and parking. Three two-bedroom bungalows rent for about $75 high season, $56 low. Discounts are generally negotiable for longer-term stays.

One of the most appealing off-beach Guayabitos lodgings is **Bungalows El Delfín** (Retorno Ceibas and Andando Cocoteros, tel./fax 327/274-0385, toll-free Mex. tel. 01-800/335-3460, www.bungalowseldelfin.com), managed by friendly owners Francisco and Delia Orozco. Amenities include an intimate banana- and palm-fringed pool and patio, including recliners and umbrellas for resting and reading. Chairs on the shaded porch/walkways in front of the three room-tiers invite quiet relaxation and conversation with neighbors. A street-front café serves coffee and pizza all day long in the high season. The spacious four-person suites are large and plainly furnished, with basic stove, refrigerator, and utensils; rear laundry porches; and big tiled toilet-showers. The 23 bungalows with kitchenette sleep four and rent for about $50 d high season, $42 d low, $28 d per day for one-month rental, with ceiling fans, pool, and parking.

Just as deluxe but more spacious is the all-inclusive beachfront family-oriented **Hotel Costa Alegre** (Retorno Tabachines s/n at Calle Tabachines, tel./fax 327/274-0241, toll-free Mex. tel. 01-800/710-5683, www.costaalaegresuites.com), where the Guayabitos beach broadens. Its pluses include a big blue pool and patio on the street side and a broad, grassy ocean-view garden on the beach side. Although the rooms are adequate, most of the regiment of kitchenette bungalows are set away from the beach, with no view but the back of neighboring rooms. The most scenic choices are the several upper-tier oceanfront rooms, all with sliding glass doors leading to private sea-view balconies. Some rooms are in better repair than others; look at more than one before paying. The 30 view rooms run about $76 d all-inclusive, with discounts for children (kids under five are free); the 80 kitchenette bungalows run $68 ($440/week). Amenities include air-conditioning, pool, parking, and restaurant/bar; credit cards are accepted. Pricing specials will frequently be posted outside of the hotel.

For lots of peace and quiet in a deluxe tropical setting, the **Bungalows Anai** (Calle Jacarandas and Retorno Jacarandas, tel./fax 327/274-0245, www.suitesanai.com) is just about the best on the beach. The 12 apartments, each with private ocean-view balcony, in three separate four-unit sections, stand graciously to one side. They overlook a spacious plant-bedecked garden shaded by a magnificent grove of drowsy coconut palms. The garden leads to an ocean-view pool patio and whirlpool tub, where a few guests read, socialize, and take in the beachside scene below. Inside, the two-bedroom apartments are simply but thoughtfully furnished in natural wood, bamboo, and tile, and come with bath, three double beds, furnished kitchen, fans, air-conditioning, and TV. Rentals run about $75 for two; add about $15 for each additional person. There is a one-week minimum stay. Book your reservations early.

Set back from the road in a tropical parklike setting is **Las Cabañas del Capitan** (Retorno Jacarandas 88, tel. 327/274-0304 or 327/274-0901, www.cabanasdelcapitan.com, $85 high season, $50 low), offering quiet rooms with a rustic feel. Guests of the 28 bungalows enjoy full open-air kitchens and private balconies with views of the garden, pool, or ocean. The accommodations are done in an authentic Mexican style with tiles and wooden furniture. There are no phones or TVs in the suites, but the bedrooms have air-conditioning, and there is Wi-Fi in the public areas.

## RV Parks

All Guayabitos RV parks are customarily packed wall-to-wall most of the winter. Some old-timers have painted and marked out their spaces for years of future occupancy. The best spaces of the bunch are all booked by mid-October. And although the longtime residents are polite enough, some of them are clannish and don't go out of their way to welcome new kids on the block.

This is fortunately not true at **Delia's** (Retorno Ceibas 4, tel. 327/274-0226), Guayabitos's homiest trailer park. Friendly owner Delia Bond Valdez and her daughter Rosa Delia have around 40 spaces, but only 12 with water and power ($16/night, $425/month all year), some often unfilled even during the high season. Their place, alas, is not right on the beach, nor is it as tidy as some folks would like. On the other hand, Delia offers a little store and a long-distance phone service right next to the premises. She also rents three bungalows for about $500 a month. Spaces have all hookups (but insufficient power for a/c), showers, toilets, and room for big rigs. Pets are okay; for more than two people, there is a $5 fee per person per day. Space for camper vans costs $250/month with all hookups; tent spaces go for $10/day, $225/month.

To the north, next comes **Fisherman's Paradise Hotel and Trailer Park** (Retorno Ceibas s/n, tel. 327/274-0014, fax 327/274-0525, www.paraisodelpescador.com), which is also popular as a mango-lover's paradise. Several spreading mango trees shade the park's 33 concrete pads, and during the late spring and summer when the mangoes are ripe, you might be able to park under your own tree. Winter-season spaces rent for about $25 per day for two people, minimum 15-day rental

(or $18/day for a three-month rental), with all hookups, showers, toilets, and lovely pool and patio. Pets are okay; add $4.75 per extra person. Hotel rooms, all with Wi-Fi and kitchenettes, are available as well and start at $74 for up to four people with sea view, $58 without.

Neighboring **Trailer Park Oasis** (Retorno Ceibas s/n, Apdo. 52, tel. 327/274-0361) is among Guayabitos's most deluxe and spacious trailer parks, if a little stark. Its 19 all-concrete, partly palm-shaded spaces are wide and long enough for 40-foot rigs. Pluses include green grassy ocean-view grounds, beautiful blue beachfront pool, a fish-cleaning facility, boat ramp, a designer restaurant, and a luxury ocean-view *palapa* overlooking the beach. Spaces rent for about $26 per day, with all hookups, showers, and toilets; pets are okay.

Residents at the big **La Peñita RV Park** (P.O. Box 22, La Peñita, Nayarit 63727, Nov. 1–Apr. 30 local tel. 327/274-0996, year-round U.S. tel. 541/850-0058, year-round Can. tel. 250/244-3447, www.lapenitarvpark.com) enjoy a breezy ocean-view location 1 mile (1.6 km) north of La Peñita; watch for the big highway sign. Its 128 grassy spaces ($25/day, $600/month) are sprinkled over a shady hillside park overlooking a golden beach and bay, with all hookups; closed May-October. The many amenities include a pool, hilltop terrace club, wireless Internet, taco Tuesdays with free margaritas, hamburger night, laundry, showers and toilets, some grocery delivery, and surfing, boogie boarding, and surf fishing. Tenters are welcome for $16 per tent for two.

## FOOD
### Fruit Stands and Minimarkets
The orchard country along Highway 200 north of Puerto Vallarta offers a feast of tropical fruits. Roadside stands at Guayabitos, La Peñita, and especially at Las Varas, half an hour north, offer mounds of papayas, mangoes, melons, and pineapples in season. Watch out also for more exotic species, such as the *guanábana*, which looks like a spiny mango, but whose pulpy interior looks and smells much like its Asian cousin, the jackfruit.

A number of Guayabitos *mini-supers* supply a little bit of everything. Try **Mini-super La Marketa** (Retorno Ceibas, across from Trailer Park Villanueva, tel. 327/274-0399, 7am-8pm Mon.-Sat., 7am-2:30pm Sun.) for vegetables, a small deli, and general groceries. Competing next door is **Mini-Super Fiesta Tlaqupaque Fiesta** (tel. 327/274-0434, 8am-8pm Mon.-Sat.). On the north end of Avenida del Sol Nuevo, **Mini-super Juan de Dios** and **Supermercado Popin** (both 8am-9pm daily) opposite the church and Hotel Peñamar, respectively, stock more, including fresh baked goods.

For larger, fresher selections of everything, go to one of the big main-street *fruterías* or supermarkets in La Peñita, such as **Supermercado Lorena** on main street Emiliano Zapata, in the middle of town (tel. 327/274-0255, 8am-10pm daily).

## Cafés and Restaurants

Several Guayabitos cafés and restaurants offer good food and service during the busy winter, spring, and July-August seasons. Some, however, either close or restrict their hours during the midsummer and September-November low seasons.

By location, moving from the Guayabitos's south end, first find tidy, budget **Abel's Restaurant** *palapa* (south end of Av. del Sol Nuevo, behind Bungalows del Delfín, tel. 327/274-2030, 7am-9pm daily). Abel has been providing delicious meals for residents of Guayabitos since the 1980s. Start off your day right with a home-cooked American-style breakfast ($2-3) such as French toast, pancakes, or eggs any style. Return for lunch or dinner ($3-7), with one of Abel's hearty *burrita* or *azteca* soups, followed by a tasty meat, fish, or chicken plate.

For supper, you can't enjoy a tastier option than the family-run **Taquería Anahi** (middle of Av. del Sol Nuevo, east side, no phone, early morning-10pm daily year-round, $1-3). Here, dedicated cooks put out hearty tacos, enchiladas, spicy posole (shredded pork roast and hominy vegetable stew), and much more.

Right across the street, don't miss **George and Gary's Coffee House** (7am-9pm daily), for the best morning coffee in town. Later, drop by for a cool-down afternoon treat, such as George's mocha frappe. Master of the show is personable, knowledgeable former professor of veterinary medicine and civic leader Jorge Castuera. If there's something you want to know about Guayabitos, Jorge is the person to ask. There's an excellent selection of used paperbacks for trade here, so don't forget to bring those books you've already read.

A few doors north, the clean, local-style **Restaurant Las Alejandras** (tel. 327/274-0488, 8am-10pm daily in season, $3-7) offers good breakfasts and a general Mexican-style menu.

From Avenida del Sol Nuevo, walk a block toward the beach, to one of Guayabitos's best, the moderately priced **Campanario** (Retorno Tabachines 6 at Calle Tabachines, tel. 327/274-0357, 8am-9pm daily high season, 8am-5pm daily low, $5-12), in front of the Hotel Posada la Misión. The menu, a longtime favorite of the North American RV colony, features bountiful fresh seafood, meat, and Mexican plates; credit cards are accepted. (For a variation on a similar comfort-food theme, try equally popular **Restaurant La Piña Loca,** across the street.)

A good place to start your day is in a comfortable booth at coffee shop-style, air-conditioned **Restaurant Tulipanes** (Av. del Sol Nuevo, south corner of Jacarandas, tel. 327/274-0575, 8am-10pm daily). Pick from a long list of hearty breakfast combos ($4-5), including eggs, bacon, hash browns, hotcakes, and French toast. Return at lunch and dinner ($3-7) for guacamole ($3), soups and salads ($3), and pasta, chicken, and fish.

Similar good home-style food and service is also available farther north at **Restaurant Tonita I** (tel. 327/274-2902), on the beach in front of the Villas Steffany, and at **Restaurant Tonita II** (near the corner of Andando Colorines, 7:30am-9:30pm Mon.-Fri. in season).

If you are looking for pizza, try **Mona Lisa Pizza** (Av. del Sol Nuevo and Calle Magles, tel. 327/274-0137, 5pm-10pm, $5-8), where the specialty is thin crust, wood-fired pizza.

Also highly recommended is the **Restaurant Piña Colada** (Hwy. 200 lateral road, end of Calle Lirio, east of Av. del Sol Nuevo, tel. 327/274-1211 or 327/274-1172, $5-12), owned by friendly local guide Estaban Valdivia.

Finally, be sure not to miss Guayabitos's hands-down best restaurant, the ◖ **Bavarian Garden** (on Hwy. 200, at the south-end signal and entrance to town, tel. 327/274-2136, 5am-9pm Mon.-Sat., 8am-9pm Sun. with sumptuous morning brunch, Nov.-Easter). Here, you and probably at least a dozen winter-season (reservations recommended) diners will enjoy a feast, with entrées such as *kassler ripchen* (smoked pork chops, $10) or savory Hungarian goulash (substitute German potato pancakes for rice, $9), topped off with homemade *apfel strudel* ($3) and rich espresso. *Wunderbar!* Note: May-October low-season hours are 5am-9pm Monday-Saturday (except closed Thurs.); 8am-2pm Sunday for brunch.

## INFORMATION AND SERVICES
### Tourist Information
Nayarit State Tourism maintains an **information office** (tel. 327/274-0693, 9am-7pm Fri.-Wed.) at the north end of Avenida del Sol Nuevo, by the highway.

### Money
Pesos for your U.S. and Canadian cash are available at the **Bancomer** branch (with ATM) in La Peñita (on the highway, about three doors south of main Av. E. Zapata crossing, tel. 327/274-0237, 9am-4pm Mon.-Fri.). There are also ATMs around town; as always, be careful using them.

### Communications
Long-distance telephoning is most conveniently and economically done on public street telephones, with Ladatel phone cards, widely available in stores along Avenida del Sol Nuevo. A $5 Ladatel card will get you about 10 minutes of time to the United States or Canada on a street telephone.

Connect to the Internet at the **Internet Cafe,** open 10am-midnight daily. It's located on Avenida del Sol Nuevo, by the Juan de Dios minimarket.

### Health and Emergencies
Guayabitos has a **paramedic ambulance** (tel. 327/274-3578 or 327/274-2992) operated by the *bomberos* (firefighters) from near the tourist information office, on the north side of the north end of Avenida del Sol Nuevo. If necessary, they can take you in a hurry 14 miles (22 km) south to the small general hospital in San Francisco (tel. 311/258-4077), which offers X-ray, laboratory, gynecological, pediatric, and internal medicine consultations and services, both at regular hours (10:30am-noon and 4pm-6pm) and on 24-hour emergency call. The **Centro de Salud** public hospital run by the IMSS in La Peñita can be reached at 327/274-0150.

Alternatively, for local medical consultations in La Peñita, go to the highly recommended small, private 24-hour **Clínica Rentería** (Calle Bahia de Acapulco 8, tel. 327/274-0140, emergency cell tel. 322/205-8773). A surgeon, a gynecologist, and a general practitioner (Raul Rentería, MD) are on call there. For medical consultations, see Dr. Alfredo Rentería at his office in La Peñita (Calle Bahia de Acapulco 3, tel. 327/274-0008).

## GETTING THERE
**Transportes Pacífico** first- and second-class buses (southbound for Puerto Vallarta, and northbound for Tepic, Guadalajara, and Mazatlán) routinely stop (about twice every daylight hour, each direction) both at the main highway entrance to Guayabitos's Avenida del Sol Nuevo and at La Peñita's main Highway 200 crossing. The same is true of **Estrella Blanca** buses (Transportes Norte de Sonora), southbound to Puerto Vallarta and northbound to San Blas; and Elite, southbound to Puerto Vallarta, Manzanillo, Ixtapa-Zihuatanejo, and Acapulco, and northbound to Tepic, Guadalajara, Mazatlán, and the U.S. border.

At La Peñita, Transportes Pacífico and Estrella Blanca cooperate, sharing a pair of stations (and phone, tel. 327/274-0001) on opposite sides of the main highway crossing corner.

Also at La Peñita, a third bus line, **Primera Plus** luxury buses en route between Puerto Vallarta and Guadalajara, also stops at a separate small station next to the Transportes Pacífico, Transportes Norte de Sonora, and Elite station.

The Guayabitos coast is easily accessible by **taxi** from the Puerto Vallarta International Airport (about $60 for four people), the busy terminal for flight connections with U.S. and Mexican destinations. Buses (which you must board at the Puerto Vallarta bus station, north of the airport) and taxis cover the 39-mile (62-km) distance to Guayabitos in around an hour. Remember that if you cross over Highway 200 via the pedestrian bridge and catch the cab on the other side (or a bus), you will save a lot of money, whatever your north of Puerto Vallarta destination might be.

# The Road to San Blas

The lush 60-mile (100-km) stretch between Rincón de Guayabitos and San Blas is a Pacific Eden of flowery tropical forests and pearly, palm-shaded beaches largely unknown to the outside world. Highway 200 and the coastal bypass highway that connects at Las Varas lead travelers past leafy tropical banana and mango orchards, mangrove-edged lagoons, vine-strewn jungle, and a string of little havens—Playa El Naranjo, Chacala and Mar de Jade, Playa las Tortugas, Platanitos, Paraíso Miramar, Casa Mañana, and Las Islitas—that add sparkle to an already inviting coastline.

## PLAYA EL NARANJO

Seven miles (11 km) along Highway 200, north of Guayabitos, a signed, cobbled side road leads through Lima de Abajo village about 2.5 miles (4 km) to the gorgeous golden beach of El Naranjo (The Orange Tree). Several permanent *palapa* seafood restaurants line the beach, and a palm grove provides ample space and shade for RV parking and tent camping; a spreading mangrove lagoon beyond the grove nurtures a host of wildlife, including a few crocodiles that bask in the sun at the lagoon's edge. Bugs come out in late afternoon and evening. (Campers, be prepared with insect repellent.)

The beach itself is gloriously flat and kid friendly. About a hundred yards out in the water, rolling billows, good for beginning and intermediate surfing, break gracefully. A platoon of pelicans and frigate birds soar and

dive above the waves, while on the beach, little crabs skitter along the sand, pursued by squads of nimble shorebirds. Note that this road is pretty much impassable during the rainy season, and the beach and its seafront *palapas* close seasonally.

Among the most inviting of the dozen-odd seafood *palapas* is **Restaurant Keenia** (on the beach at Playa El Naranjo, tel. 322/294-8563, 8am-7pm daily, $3-12), run by personable, English-speaking Fidel López. He's especially proud of his *pescado sarandeado* (basted and barbecued fish).

## ◖ Alta Vista Archaeological Sacred Site

Two miles (3 km) north of the Highway 200 Playa El Naranjo turnoff (this is close to the Km 81.8 sign, 6.4 miles north of La Peñita), a right-side (east) turnoff road signed Alta Vista (the local municipality is 8 mi/12.8 km uphill) points the way to Santuario Alta Vista Archaeological Sacred Site. There you will find a *palapa* shelter, a caretaker (offer a gratuity of about $2 per person), and a half-mile self-guided trail dotted with dozens of petroglyphs that experts estimate date back at least 2,000 years.

Unlike many other such sites in Mexico, Alta Vista is still actively frequented as a holy place, known traditionally as **Chacalán** by local people. It is also frequented by some, thankfully not too many, tourists, hikers, hippies, and

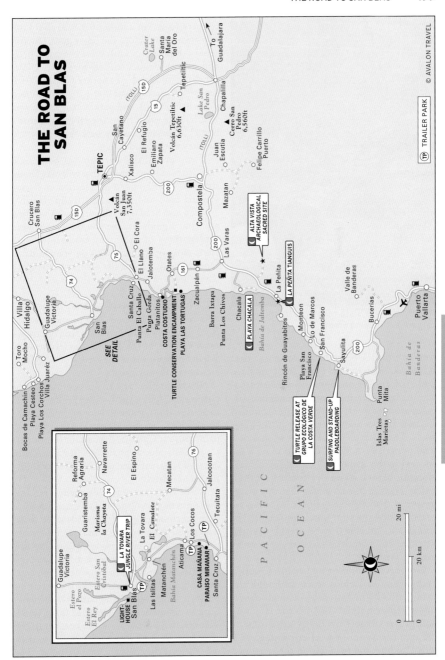

# THE ROAD TO SAN BLAS

© AVALON TRAVEL

TP TRAILER PARK

To Guadalajara

Crater Lake

Santa María del Oro

Lake San Pedro

Tepetitic

Chapalilla

(TOLL)

15D

San Cayetano

15

Cerro San Pedro 6,560ft

El Refugio

Emiliano Zapata

Volcán Tepetitic 6,630ft

Juan Escutia

Felipe Carrillo Puerto

TEPIC

Xalisco

200

Compostela

Mazatan

Crucero San Blas

15D

Volcán San Juan 7,350ft

75

El Cora

El Llano

Jalotemba

Otates

161

Las Varas

200

**ALTA VISTA ARCHAEOLOGICAL SACRED SITE**

74

Villa Hidalgo

Guadalupe Victoria

Santa Cruz

Punta El Caballo

Puga Gorda

Platanitos

**COSTA COSTUDIO**

**TURTLE CONSERVATION ENCAMPMENT**

**PLAYA LAS TORTUGAS**

Zacualpán

Chacala

Barra Ixtapa

Punta Los Chivos

La Peñita

**LA PEÑITA TIANGUIS**

Toro Mocho

Bocas de Camachin

Playa Cesteo

Playa Los Corchos

Villa Juaréz

San Blas

**SEE DETAIL**

Bahía de Jaltemba

**PLAYA CHACALA**

Rincón de Guayabitos

Monteon

Lo de Marcos

San Francisco

Valle de Banderas

Bucerías

Puerto Vallarta

Playa San Francisco

**TURTLE RELEASE AT GRUPO ECOLÓGICO DE LA COSTA VERDE**

Sayulita

200

Punta Mita

**SURFING AND STAND-UP PADDLEBOARDING**

Islas Tres Marietas

Bahía de Banderas

**THE RIVIERA NAYARIT**

P A C I F I C

O C E A N

Guadalupe Victoria

Estero el Pozo

Reforma Agraria

Navarrette

El Espino

76

74

Guaristemba

Mecatan

Jalcocotan

Marisma la Chuyota

La Tovara

El Camalote

Tecuitata

**LA TOVARA JUNGLE RIVER TRIP**

Estero San Cristóbal

San Blas

TP

Los Cocos

TP

TP

Aticama

**CASA MANANA**

**PARAISO MIRAMAR**

Santa Cruz

**LIGHT-HOUSE**

San Blas

Las Islitas

Matanchén

Bahía Matanchén

Estero El Rey

20 mi

20 km

0

0

© DONNA DAY

The hike to Alta Vista takes you up this gorgeous, tumbling creek.

families from the beach towns down the road. When you reach the end of the path, you'll see flower-adorned impromptu shrines that decorate a magnificent rock amphitheater-like cascade, studded with friendly water-rounded volcanic blocks and crystalline spring-water pools. There are plenty of places to sit under small waterfalls, in water-sculpted stone seats, and enjoy the scenery while taking an impromptu natural shower in cool, clean fresh water. There seems no doubt that this place, so special that it evokes wonder, has been revered by local folks for untold millennia. For a small fee, camping may be possible near the entrance. For more details, visit www.guayabitos.com.mx.

Get there by foot or by car (preferably a high-clearance Jeep or truck, although the road is usually in reasonable-enough condition to allow normal cars) via the Highway 200 gravel turnoff road. Pay attention, as the sign is easy to miss. After turning, go 1 mile (1.6 km) and turn left on the tree-lined

country road. Go another 0.5 mile (0.8 km) and turn right before the rebar gate. Go another 0.8 mile (1.3 km), cross the creek bed, and pass through a barbed-wire gate. Close it behind you, and go another 0.2 mile (0.3 km). Pass through another gate, go another 0.2 mile (0.3 km), and park. Chances are you will have to walk from the first right turn, but it's a pleasant country walk through ranch country, forest, and jungle.

If you prefer, there are guided horseback rides from nearby Chacala that will take about six hours (four hours to the location on horse, viewing time, and then a return trip via van). You can also head up to the town of Alta Vista and find a guide to take you on a tour, with explanations of the many mysterious and compelling petroglyphs. Put on your Indiana Jones hat—this is a really cool archaeological adventure!

## ◖ PLAYA CHACALA

Side roads off Highway 200 provide exotic, close-up glimpses of Nayarit's tangled, tropical woodland, but rarely will they lead to such a delightful surprise as the green-tufted golden crescent of Playa Chacala.

Nineteen miles (31 km) north of Rincón de Guayabitos, follow the 6-mile (9.7-km) paved road (slow down and watch for potholes as you approach the beach and town) to the great old palm grove at Chacala. Beyond the line of rustic *palapa* seafood restaurants lies a heavenly curve of sand, enfolded on both sides by palm-tipped headlands.

While there are beachside restaurants and the stores in the village, Playa Chacala doesn't have much of a nightlife; it is ideal for those who are looking for peace and quiet. Chacala used to be an excellent place for camping and RVs, but the town has eliminated all camping activities due to waste management problems. Residents have also started a clean-beach campaign, asking visitors who come on the daily caravan of tour buses to donate $2 to the cause. Volunteers routinely walk the beaches in the afternoon to remind visiting families to pack out whatever they brought onto the beach. The

© DONNA DAY

Chacala is known for its beautiful palm groves.

result is that the beach is much cleaner than it has been, especially on weekends and holidays.

A mile farther north, past Chacala village on the headland, the road ends at Playa Chacalilla, Playa Chacala's miniature twin. Due to the presence of a large, private development called Marina Chacala, access to Playa Chacalilla is now completely restricted. There is no way in to this beach except by boat. However, many of the fancy, upscale homes in Marina Chacala can be rented by the weekend or week, allowing access to the beach, beach club, and the rest of the posh stuff behind the heavily guarded gates. You just have to have the money. Contact www.casapacificachacala.com for information on available houses and rental rates. Aside from the pricey houses in Marina Chacala, the village of Chacala has dozens of bungalows, rooms for rent, small hotels, and other places to stay. Drive into town, and you'll see lodging options just about everywhere.

## Recreation

Playa Chacala's oft-gentle surf is good for close-in bodysurfing, boogie boarding, and swimming, though it's a little too close to shore for surfing. The water is generally clear enough for snorkeling off the rocks at either end of the beach. If you bring your equipment, kayaking, sailboarding, kiteboarding, and sailing are possible when the wind blows. The sheltered north-end cove is nearly always tranquil and safe, even for tiny tots. Fishing is so good that many local people make their living at it. Chacala Bay is so rich and clean that tourists sometimes eat oysters right off the rocks.

Boatmen at the dock at the bay's far north end offer excursions (figure about $35-60, depending on number of surfers, for a round-trip, including drop-off and pickup two or three hours later) to nearby **Playa la Caleta** for world-class (on occasion) surfing or **Playa las Cuevas** (the Caves) for picnicking, swimming, and snorkeling. Be prepared with your own drinks, food, and equipment, however.

Rent a bike for the day ($12) from **Bicicletas Adrian** (tel. 327/219-4116) and take a jungle

© DONNA DAY

a busy, palmy street near the beach in Chacala

ride. You can also take guided tours to the lake and other nearby scenic wonders.

Horseback rides along local jungle trails are also available from providers at the beach. Concha, owner of **Casa Concha** (tel. 327/219-4019, conchaguanahani_234@hotmail.com), offers bird- and wildlife-watching hikes. **Casa Aurora** offers boating and fishing trips with Beto (tel. 327/219-4027). **Casa Satow Bungalows** (tel. 327/219-4111) offers sea kayak rentals.

## Accommodations

◖ **Mar de Jade** (tel. 327/219-4000, toll-free U.S. tel. 800/257-0532, www.mardejade.com), the holistic-style living center at the south end of Playa Chacala, offers some distinctive accommodations. Laura del Valle, Mar de Jade's personable and dynamic physician/founder, has worked steadily since the early 1980s building living facilities and a learning center while simultaneously establishing a local health clinic. Now, Mar de Jade offers volunteer programs

for people who enjoy the tropics but want to do more than laze in the sun. A major thrust is interaction with local people. Spanish, for example, is the preferred language at the dinner table.

The semideluxe and deluxe lodgings nestled into a flowery, junglelike hillside garden complex consist of 15 suites and 12 guest rooms, each with ocean views and most with private balconies. The rooms and spacious suites are simply but elegantly decorated with designer rustic tile, rich mahogany furnishings, and cut stone. Stone pathways lead to the beachside main center, which consists of a dining room, kitchen, offices, library, and classroom overlooking the sea.

While Mar de Jade's purpose is nonprofit work that supports the neighboring community, it has nothing against visitors who *do* want to laze in the sun, beachcomb, and soak in the beachfront pool and whirlpool tub. Mar de Jade invites travelers to make reservations and stay as long as they like, for about $120 per person, double occupancy (guest room), to about $145 (suites), November-April, including three meals a day. Tax, gratuity, and alcohol are not included. Children with parents stay for about $30 each; children under six are free. Low season (May-Oct.) rates run about 25 percent less. Discounts may be negotiable for stays of three weeks or longer.

Mar de Jade still offers Spanish programs on an irregular basis, but the focus has moved on to interaction with the local community in other ways. The owners now operate an organic dairy farm in the neighborhood of Las Varas, a small farming town a few miles inland. Here, they produce organic eggs, milk, butter, and cheeses, which are used at the resort. They are also teaching local farmers about the value of organic production. Profits from this organic dairy farm are currently being used to finance a club for the poorer children of migrant and itinerant farm workers in Las Varas, providing education, child care, computer training, help with homework, and two meals a day for about 50 local children. They are also focused on microindustry,

© DONNA DAY

**Playa Chacala's southern headland is home to Mar de Jade and Majahua resorts.**

training local women in the craft of making organic fruit jams and preserves, which are packaged and sold through the resort.

Civil engineer and builder José Enrique del Valle and his wife, who own the jungle-forest parcel above Mar de Jade, have worked hard to put their land to good use. His dream-come-true, **Majahua Spa Bed and Breakfast** (tel. 327/219-4053, 327/219-4054, or 327/219-4055, www.majahua.com), now regularly receives guests. José, his wife, and his several staff members offer five luxuriously rustic and private accommodations, an open-air restaurant, and a sprinkling of spa services. The lodgings, which blend artfully into the verdant tropical-forested hillside, are all lovingly designed and hand-built of stucco and tile, with various sleeping options (that include double, king-size, and kid-size beds), modern standard baths, and beautiful views.

Accommodations vary from the La Puerta honeymoon suite just above the restaurant and move upward, through midsize double suites A and B to the airy top-level view "penthouse," La Torre, big enough for five. In the middle, a small spa section offers massage, facials, and aromatherapy. High-season (Dec. 1-May 30) rates begin at about $118 for two and run upward to about $260 for the big "penthouse" suite. All lodging prices include breakfast. Add $25 for extra guests. Two kids under 12 are free, but their breakfast is not; older children are $25 pp per day.

To get to Majahua, turn left at the beach road and pass through the gates into the large palm-grove parking area, where there is a beachfront tapas bar (and reception area). Continue along the coastline by staying to the right until you pass into another parking area. Park closest to the eastern side of the lot, and then look for the trail leading up to the hotel. The walk is short and not too difficult; however, walking shoes will make it easier. Once you check in, your luggage can be brought up by ATV.

For his more active guests, José will lead (or get a guide to lead) all-day wildlife-viewing and hiking excursions, including to a nearby extinct volcano (elev. 750 ft/228.6 m) crater lake.

José, along with the help of many others, notably Susana Escobido (owner of Casa Pacífica), have led Chacala's transition from a drowsy subsistence fishing village to a growing tourist destination. Now, with the help of many U.S. and Canadian volunteers, Chacala people, under the umbrella of the national **Techos de Mexico** (Roofs of Mexico) program (www.techosdemexico. com), have built modern-standard tourist accommodations into their homes. They invite travelers to come and stay at very reasonable rates, ranging $20-40 for two, sometimes including breakfast. Check the website for additional information including photos and prices.

Check out the website www.chacalaescape. com to reserve some of the rooms by phone, email, or online. There are plenty of options all over town. (Chacala is a small village; all of the following are within three blocks of the beach and several fresh-seafood *palapa* restaurants.) The growing list now includes: **Casa Gracia** (tel. 327/219-4021 or 327/219-4067, sescobido@aol.com, $35); **Casa Aurora** (tel. 327/219-4027 or 327/219-4067, sescobido@ aol.com, $35-45), which has four rooms, fan, sea view, and parking; **Casa Beatriz** (tel. 327/219-4005, $16), which has two rooms, fan, sea view, and parking; and **Casa Concha** (tel. 327/219-4019, conchaguanahani_234@ hotmail.com, $20-50), which has three rooms, fan, sea view, and parking.

Although not part of the Techos de Mexico, the **Hotel las Brisas** (on the beach road, tel. 327/219-4015, www.lasbrisaschacala.com) is locally owned and operated. The rooms (sheltered beneath the rustic *palapa* of a not-so-great beachfront restaurant) could be heaven for beach lovers, smack on the lovely Chacala beachfront. The 11 smallish accommodations, mostly all upstairs, are conveniently removed from the restaurant hubbub below. They are attractively decorated in pastels, with private baths, air-conditioning, cable TV, and wireless Internet. Rentals run about $57 nightly without meals included, about $115 nightly all-inclusive. Given the quality (or lack

thereof) of the restaurant, I would recommend the European plan.

Besides helping lead the Chacala community, spark plug Susana Escobido offers her own lodging, the lovely sea-view **Casa Pacífica** (tel. 327/219-4067, local Chacala cell tel. 044-327/102-0864, U.S. tel. 760/300-3908, www. casapacificachacala.com, $55-65 d high season). Choose from three invitingly comfortable modern-standard rooms with fan, hot-water shower bath, and breakfast.

## Food

There are plenty of beach *palapa* restaurants to choose from, but the best are said to be **Chico's** (first restaurant on the south end of the beach) and **Acela** (on the northern end). You'll find more or less the same type of menu at each place: lots of fresh fish, oysters and lobster, grilled meats, and full bar menus. There are probably a dozen of these restaurants lined up along the beach. Look for a crowded one if you're unsure. Crowds usually signal good, or at least cheap or passable, food.

Popular with the younger crowd is **Chac Mool** (Islas Canarias 7, tel. 327/219-4097, 8am-10pm daily, $3-15), a beachfront wine bar and café with a slightly more international approach. In addition to the usual selection of fish and shrimp dishes, they offer several wine choices and a full bar, along with coffee drinks, deli sandwiches, pastries, salads, and pizzas. They also sell locally grown and roasted organic coffee. A second Chac Mool is located at the beach club behind the gates of Marina Chacala.

## AROUND THE BAY OF MATANCHÉN

The broad Bay of Matanchén, framed by verdant mountains, sweeps northward toward San Blas, lined with an easily accessible pearly crescent of sand ripe for campers and beachcombers. Village stores, seafood *palapas,* a palmy vacation-home paradise, turtle conservation center, two beachside trailer parks, and a pair of friendly, small resorts provide the amenities for a day or a month of restful adventuring.

## Playa Las Tortugas and Turtle Conservation Center

Playa las Tortugas (Playa Las Tortugas, Las Palmeras #13, Colonia Las Fuentes, Otate, Nayarit, local administration 327/273-0543, toll-free U.S./Can. tel. 866/443-0056, email Maryanne at reservations@playalastortugas. com, www.playalastortugas.com) is a small, isolated vacation-retirement community set beneath a magnificent miles-long beachfront palm grove, about 15 miles (24 km) north of the Las Varas turnoff from Highway 200. It's the project of developer, builder, and Mexico lover Robert Hancock, whose dream is that wildlife and people can (and should) be able to coexist. Indeed, he has helped to bring that dream to reality. Since the community's beginning in 1999, the very presence of the workers, staff, residents, and visitors to Robert's minipa-radise has helped shield thousands of nesting turtles and their hatchlings from poachers and has led to a very viable yearly nesting population of about 2,000. Hancock is no longer engaged on-site, but there are currently about a dozen houses available for rent, with prices starting at $235 per day, with weekly discounts; prices are higher during high season, but are lower during turtle nesting season in the summer. Although the houses are all different, the designs—exteriors of muted earth-tone stucco beneath red-tiled roofs, interiors with lots of tile, view balconies, airy vistas, and high ceilings—are variations on a low-key, nature-friendly theme. Sizes vary, but most are modest two- or three-bedroom, two-bath layouts.

Besides lazing by the blue pool and soaking in the steaming whirlpool tub, residents and guests can enjoy their choice of beachcombing, at times good surfing off the river mouth, boogie boarding, fishing, horseback riding, kayaking, and wildlife-watching in the ocean and the adjoining mangrove estuary and lagoon. Other times, visitors can help with turtle conservation efforts at the adjacent turtle preserve and hatchery. To get in on the turtle action, arrive during the August-November 15 nesting season, when visitors are welcome to witness turtle releases around 5pm daily.

Get to Playa las Tortugas from Highway 200 via the signed left (northbound) turnoff just past the gas station at the middle of Las Varas. Continue about 8 miles (12.8 km), through Zacualpán town. After another 5 miles (8 km), pass the Otates village turnoff sign on the right, and continue another quarter mile on the main road to the signed Playa las Tortugas dirt side road, between kilometer markers 21 and 22. Turn left and continue another 6 miles (10 km) to the Playa las Tortugas entrance gate.

## Platanitos

Seventeen miles (27 km) along the coastal highway north of Las Varas, orchards and fields give way to a tropical forest at Punta Platanitos (Little Bananas), where a road leads down to a cove lined with the *pangas* and seafood *palapas* of the Platanitos village and fishing cooperative. Local folks, drawn by the yellow sand, gentle blue waves, and superfresh seafood, have for years flocked here for Sunday outings. You can do likewise, and, if you bring your own equipment, you can also enjoy surfing, kayaking to nearby hidden coves, snorkeling, and fishing from headland rocks or by boat (which, most days, you can launch from the beach). Tent or RV camping appears promising (ask if it's okay: "*¿Es bueno acampar acá?*") in the beachside shade. If you have a sturdy vehicle and a good camera, head past the large paved parking lot and make a left on the dirt track leading up the hill. Once over the rise you'll have a panoramic vista of the estuary and gorgeous blue ocean framed by the gentle swaying palms of Las Tortugas beach. Surfers can descend stairs and paddle across the river here to enjoy the often challenging sandbar/river mouth waves of the Platanitos surfing wave—not a great one, but what a beautiful spot.

## To the Bay of Matanchén and Paraíso Miramar

From Platanitos, the narrow road plunges into the forest, winding past great vine-draped trees and stands of cock-plumed Colima palms. If you glimpse green citrus fruit among the riot of leaves and flowers, you might be seeing a wild lime, or, if yellow, a guava or passion fruit dangling from its long vine. Now and then, you will pass a ponderous red-barked *papillo* tree, with its bark curling and sloughing off its great ruddy trunk and branches. The *papillo* is sometimes known as the "gringo" tree because it's always red and peeling.

The Bahía de Matanchén begins about five miles (eight km) past Platanitos, just about when you're first able to see it from the roadside—a spreading, shining vista of mountain, grove, and sea.

Continuing north, and downhill, you reach the end of Nayarit 161 at its intersection with the Tepic highway, Nayarit 76, near the twin villages of Santa Cruz and Miramar (total pop. about 1,000). Continue north about a mile (1.5 km), and you will pass through even tinier Playa Manzanilla village, where a small beachside sign marks the driveway to Paraíso Miramar.

The spacious, green bay-view park is bedecked by palms and sheltered by what appears to be the grandmother of all *higuera* trees (wild fig or banyan in India). On the cliff-bottom beach beneath the great tree, the surf rolls in gently while the blue bay, crowned by jungle ridges, curves gracefully north toward San Blas.

The owners of **Paraíso Miramar** (Carretera Costera San Blas, Km 18, tel. 323/254-9030 or 323/254-9030, http://intl.hotelparaisomiramar.com), most of whom live in Tepic, and their hardworking staff offer a little bit for everyone: six simple but clean and comfortable rooms with bath facing the bay, and behind that, grassy RV spaces with concrete pads and all hookups, and two kitchenette bungalows sleeping up to six. There are also three fully furnished two-bedroom apartments that rent nightly or by the week ($115/day or $600/wk). A small ocean-view restaurant and blue pools—swimming, kiddie, and hot tub—complete the lovely picture. Rooms rent for about $58 d, all with air-conditioning; bungalows go for about $75 for four people, $90 for six, with hot-water showers, air-conditioning, and satellite TV.

The RV area has expanded considerably,

the giant kiddie pool of Matanchén Bay

© JUSTIN HENDERSON

THE RIVIERA NAYARIT

with 48 spaces available for all sizes. These range from 16 spaces with full hookups to 12 without water or power. Rates vary depending on the type of vehicle you have, so check the website for the most recent information and to make reservations. Prices range $16-24 per day. For a week's stay, you customarily get one day free, and there are long-term discounted rates available. Camping space on a grassy lawn is also available.

## Casa Mañana

About 2.5 miles (4 km) farther north (or 8 mi/13 km south of San Blas), the diminutive shoreline retreat **Casa Mañana** (P.O. Box 49, San Blas, Nayarit 63740, tel. 323/254-9080 or 323/254-9090, toll-free Mex. tel. 01-800/202-2079, www.casa-manana.com) perches at the south end of breezy Playa los Cocos. Owned and managed by an Austrian man, Reinhardt, and his Mexican wife, Lourdes, Casa Mañana's two double-storied tiers of rooms rise over a homey, spic-and-span beach-view restaurant and pool deck and garden. Very popular with Europeans and North Americans seeking South Seas tranquility on a budget, Casa Mañana offers fishing, beachcombing, hiking, and swimming right from its palm-adorned front yard. The 26 rooms rent for about $64 d high season, $53 d low, with air-conditioning and ocean view, or $37 d high, with air-conditioning but no view. All rentals get one day free per week stay. Longer-stay discounts are negotiable, and winter reservations are strongly recommended.

If you're staying at Casa Mañana, you might look into the services of **Seven Sunsets Tours** (www.sevensunsets.com, seven_sunset_tours@shaw.ca), run by photographer-guide John Stewart and partner Ryan Graham. Their mission is to allow clients to experience the "real" Mexico via nature-friendly strolls, hikes, and horseback rides to off-the-beaten-track local sites.

## Playa los Cocos

From Casa Mañana, Playa los Cocos and its venerable palm grove stretches north past beachfront houses, a couple of very basic lodgings, and a sprinkling of beachside *palapa* restaurants.

Continuing northward, the beach, which had at one time been eroded by the occasionally heavy surf, leaving a crumbling 10-foot embankment along a mostly rocky shore, has been reclaimed. Playa los Cocos is balmy and beautiful enough to attract a winter RV colony to **Trailer Park Playa Amor** (Trailer Park Playa Amor, c/o gerente Javier López, Playa los Cocos, San Blas, Nayarit 63740, tel. 323/231-2200), which overlooks the waves right in the middle of Playa los Cocos. Besides excellent fishing, boating, boogie boarding, swimming, and potential kiteboarding, the park offers 30 grassy spaces for very reasonable prices. Rentals run about $12, $13, and $14 for small, medium, and large RVs respectively ($20 for a/c power), with all hookups, showers, and toilets; pets are okay. Tenters with no hookups pay $6. Although you can expect plenty of friendly company during the winter, reservations are not usually necessary.

## Waterfall Hikes

A number of pristine creeks tumble down boulder-strewn beds and foam over cliffs as waterfalls (*cataratas*) in the jungle above the Bay of Matanchén. Some of these are easily accessible and perfect for a day of hiking, picnicking, and swimming.

You can get to within walking distance of the waterfall near **Tecuitata** village either by car, taxi, or the Tepic-bound bus; it's five miles (eight km) out of Santa Cruz along Nayarit Highway 76. A half mile (0.8 km) uphill past the village, a sign reading Balneario Nuevo Chapultepec marks a dirt road heading downhill a half mile to a creek and a bridge. Cross over to the other side ($4 entrance fee), where you'll find a *palapa* restaurant, a hillside waterslide, and a small swimming pool.

Continue upstream along the right-hand bank of the creek for a much rarer treat. Half the fun is the sylvan jungle delights—flashing butterflies, pendulous leafy vines, gurgling little cascades—along the meandering path. The other half is at the end, where the creek spurts

© JUSTIN HENDERSON

seafood for sale at a roadside grill in Aticama

through a verdure-framed fissure and splashes into a cool, broad pool festooned with green, giant-leafed *chalata* (*taro* in Hawaii, *tapioca* in Africa). Both the pool area and the trail have several possible campsites. Bring everything, especially your water-purification kit and insect repellent. Known locally as Campamento Arroyo, it is popular with kids and women who bring their washing.

Another waterfall, the highest in the area, near the village of **El Cora,** is harder to get to, but the reward is even more spectacular. Again, on the west-east Santa Cruz-Tepic Highway 76, a negotiable dirt road to El Cora branches south just before Tecuitata. At road's end, after about five miles (eight km), you can park by a banana-loading platform. From here, the walk (less than an hour) climaxes with a steep, rugged descent to the rippling, crystal pool at the bottom of the waterfall.

While rugged adventurers may find their own way to the waterfalls, others rely upon guide **Juan "Bananas" Garcia** (tel. 323/285-0462), founder of Grupo Ecológico in San Blas.

## Playas Matanchén and Las Islitas

Playa los Cocos gives way at its north end to **Aticama** village (comprised of a few stores and beachside *palapas*), where you'll find an occasionally fun surfing wave directly offshore and just north of the bridge and river. Here the northbound shoreline road climbs a jungle headland and swoops down to the bay once again. Past a marine sciences school, the beach, a long, palm-studded sand ribbon washed by gentle rollers and dotted with beachfront *palapa* restaurants and vacation homes, curves gently northwest to the superwide and shallow giant kiddie-pool of Playa Matanchén. A left crossroad (which marks the center of Matanchén village, pop. about 300) leads past a lineup of beachfront *palapa* restaurants to Playa las Islitas, at the bay's sheltered north cove.

The beaches of Matanchén and Las Islitas are an inseparable pair. Las Islitas is dotted by little outcroppings topped by miniature jungles of swaying palms and spreading trees. If you are a very lucky surfer, you might get there on one of those rare days when a huge swell is sending

© JUSTIN HENDERSON

**Las Islitas, between Matanchén Bay and Stoner's Point**

perfect waves all the way from the outer edge of Las Islitas, or even beyond, from Stoner's Point, into the inner reaches of the bay, providing the longest wave of your life (up to 1.25 mi/2 km).

For camping, the intimate, protected curves of sand around Playa las Islitas are inviting. Check with local folks to see if it's okay to camp. There are several *palapa* restaurants awaiting the rambling surfers passing through, and the beachcombing, swimming, fishing from the rocks, shell collecting, and surfing are often good, even without the legendary Big Wave that shows up once in a decade or so. The water, however, isn't clear enough for good snorkeling. Campers should be prepared with plenty of strong insect repellent; the bugs are very hungry around here.

During surfing season (Aug.-Feb.), the Team Banana and other *palapa*-shops open up at Matanchén village and Las Islitas to rent surfboards and sell what each of them claims to be the "world's original banana bread." Try a few different banana breads; they all tasted equally sweet, wholesome, and fine to me, after

coming out of the water after a three-hour surf session on a lucky day when I got good waves at Stoner's.

## Ejido de la Palma Crocodile Farm

About three miles (five km) south of Matanchén village, a sign marks a side road to a *cocodrilario* (crocodile farm). At the end of the 2-mile (3.2-km) track (which is best navigated by truck; cars can handle it with caution when it's dry), you'll arrive at El Tanque, a spring-fed pond, home of the Ejido de la Palma crocodile farm. About 50 toothy crocs, large and small, snooze in the sun within several enclosures. Half the fun is the adjacent spring-fed freshwater lagoon, so crystal clear you can see hundreds of fish wriggling beneath the surface. Nearby, ancient trees swathed in vines and orchids tower overhead, butterflies flutter past, and turtles sun themselves on mossy logs. It's the kind of place where you'd expect a dinosaur to show up. Bring a picnic lunch (a small restaurant was under construction recently, but said construction was moving very slowly), binoculars,

a resident of the Ejido de la Palma Crocodile Farm

bird book, insect repellent, and bathing suit. You can also rent a *panga* (small boat) for a tour through the mangroves. Come early in the morning for excellent bird- and wildlife-watching. The farm did not have a phone on our last visit, but they usually open daily when one of the employees arrives. Admission is approximately $5 per person.

## San Blas and Vicinity

San Blas (pop. about 15,000) is a small town slumbering beneath a big coconut grove. Life goes on in the plaza as if San Blas has always been an ordinary Mexican village, but at one time it was anything but ordinary. During its 18th-century glory days, San Blas was Mexico's burgeoning Pacific military headquarters and port, with a population of 30,000. Ships from Spain's Pacific Rim colonies crowded its harbor, silks and gold filled its counting houses, and noble Spanish officers and their mantilla-graced ladies strolled the plaza on Sunday afternoons.

Times change, however. Politics and San Blas's pesky *jejenes* (hey-HEY-nays, invisible no-see-um biting gnats) have always conspired to deflate any temporary fortunes of San Blas. The breeding ground of the *jejenes,* a vast hinterland of mangrove marshes, may paradoxically give rise to a new, more prosperous San Blas. These thousands of acres of waterlogged mangrove jungle and savanna are a nursery home for dozens of Mexico's endangered species. This rich trove is now protected by ecologically aware governments and communities, and admired (not unlike the game parks of Africa) by increasing numbers of ecotourists.

### ORIENTATION

The overlook atop the **Cerro de San Basilio** is the best spot to orient yourself to San Blas ($1 entry fee). From this breezy point, the

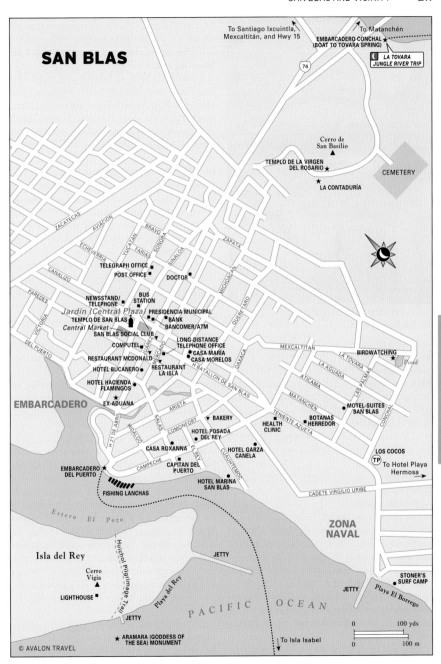

# SAN BLAS

To Santiago Ixcuintla, Mexcaltitán, and Hwy 15

To Matanchén

EMBARCADERO CONCHAL (BOAT TO TOVARA SPRING)

LA TOVARA JUNGLE RIVER TRIP

74

Cerro de San Basilio ▲

CEMETERY

TEMPLO DE LA VIRGEN DEL ROSARIO ★

LA CONTADURÍA ★

ZACATECAS

AVIACION

BRAVO

ECHEVERRIA

YUCATAN

FARIAS

SONORA

SINALOA

ZAPATA

CANALIZO

MICHOACAN

PAREDES

TELEGRAPH OFFICE

POST OFFICE

DOCTOR

QUERETARO

NEWSSTAND/ TELEPHONE

BUS STATION

*Jardín (Central Plaza)* PRESIDENCIA MUNICIPAL

VICTORIA

TEMPLO DE SAN BLAS

*Central Market*

SAN BLAS SOCIAL CLUB

BANK

BANCOMER/ATM

DEL PUERTO

COMPUTEL

JUAREZ

MERCADO

LONG-DISTANCE TELEPHONE OFFICE

CASA MARÍA

CASA MORELOS

MEXCALTITAN

LA TOVARA

BIRDWATCHING ★

RESTAURANT MCDONALD

RESTAURANT LA ISLA

OAXACA

LA AGUADA

LAS PALMAS

*Pond*

HOTEL BUCANERO

H BATALLON DE SAN BLAS

ATICAMA

HOTEL HACIENDA FLAMINGOS

EX-ADUANA ★

ARISTA

MATANCHEN

**EMBARCADERO**

H 21 DE ABRIL

SALAS

COMONFORT

HIDALGO

BAKERY ▼

TENIENTE AZUETA

BOTANAS HERREDOR ■

MOTEL-SUITES SAN BLAS ■

CONCHAL

HEALTH CLINIC

HOTEL POSADA DEL REY

CASA ROXANNA ■

EL REY

CAMPECHE

CAPITAN DEL PUERTO

HOTEL GARZA CANELA

CUAUHTEMOC

LOS COCOS

TP To Hotel Playa Hermosa

EMBARCADERO DEL PUERTO ★

FISHING LANCHAS

HOTEL MARINA SAN BLAS

CADETE VIRGILIO URIBE

*Estero El Pozo*

**ZONA NAVAL**

**Isla del Rey**

Huichol Pilgrimage Trail

Playa del Rey

JETTY

Cerro Vigia ▲

LIGHTHOUSE ■

JETTY

JETTY

STONER'S SURF CAMP ●

Playa El Borrego

P A C I F I C   O C E A N

To Isla Isabel

ARAMARA (GODDESS OF THE SEA) MONUMENT ★

0    100 yds

0    100 m

© AVALON TRAVEL

**THE RIVIERA NAYARIT**

The ruins of an 18th-century church lie atop the hill in San Blas.

palm-shaded grid of streets stretches to the sunset side of **El Pozo** estuary and the lighthouse-hill beyond it. Behind you, on the east, the mangrove-lined **San Cristóbal** river estuary meanders south to the Bay of Matanchén. Along the south shore, the crystalline white line of San Blas's main beach, **Playa el Borrego** (Sheep Beach), stretches between the two estuary mouths.

## SIGHTS
### Around Town

While you're atop the hill, take a look around the old *contaduría* counting house and fort (built in 1770), where riches were tallied and stored en route to Mexico City or to the Philippines and China. Several of the original great cannons still stand guard at the viewpoint like aging sentinels waiting for long-dead adversaries. Inside the counting house, you'll find a small museum and photo display, well worth seeing.

Behind and a bit downhill from the

weathered stone arches of the *contaduría* stand the gaping portals and towering, moss-stained belfry of the old church of **Nuestra Señora del Rosario,** built in 1769.

Downhill, historic houses and ruins dot San Blas town. The old hotels Bucanero and Hacienda Flamingos on the main street, Juárez, leading past the central plaza, preserve much of their old-world charm. Just across the street from the Hacienda Flamingos, you can admire the restored, monumental brick colonnade of the 19th-century former **Aduana,** now a cultural center. Continue west along Juárez to the El Pozo estuary. This was both the jumping-off point for colonization of the Californias and the anchorage of the silk- and porcelain-laden Manila galleons and the bullion ships from the northern mines.

**El Faro** (lighthouse) across the estuary marks the top of **Cerro Vigia,** the southern hill tip of Isla del Rey (actually a peninsula). Here, the first beacon shone during the latter third of the 18th century.

Although only a few local folks ever bother to cross over to the island, it is nevertheless an important pilgrimage site for Huichol people from the remote Nayarit and Jalisco mountains. Huichol have been gathering on the Isla del Rey for centuries to make offerings to Aramara, their goddess of the sea. A not-so-coincidental shrine to a Catholic virgin-saint stands on an offshore sea rock, visible from the beach endpoint of the Huichol pilgrimage a few hundred yards beyond the lighthouse.

Two weeks before Easter, Huichol people begin arriving by the dozens, the men decked out in flamboyant feathered hats. On the ocean beach, 10 minutes' walk straight across the island, anyone can respectfully watch them perform their rituals: elaborate marriages, feasts, and offerings of little boats laden with arrows and food, consecrated to the sea goddess to ensure good hunting and crops and many healthy children.

### Isla Isabel

Isla Isabel is a two-mile-square national park/

offshore wildlife study area 40 miles (65 km) and three hours north by boat. The cone of an extinct volcano, Isla Isabel is now home to a small government station of ecoscientists and a host of nesting boobies, frigate birds, and white-tailed tropic birds. Fish and sea mammals, especially dolphins and sometimes whales, abound in the surrounding clear waters. Although it's not a recreational area, local authorities allow serious visitors, accompanied by authorized guides, for a few days of camping, snorkeling, scuba diving, and wildlife-watching. A primitive dormitory can accommodate several people. Bring everything, including food and bedding. Contact experienced and licensed boat captain Ricardo (Pato) Murillo (tel. 323/285-1281) or equally well-qualified captain Santos Villafuente (at the Hotel Brisas del Mar, tel. 323/285-0870, cell tel. 044-311/109-1993) for arrangements and prices. Tariffs typically run $250 per day for parties of up to four people. Stormy summer and fall weather limits most Isla Isabel trips to the sunnier, calmer winter-spring season. For additional information and advice, check with manager Josefina Vasquéz at the Hotel Garza Canela front desk (Paredes 106 Sur, tel. 323/285-0112, 323/285-0307, or 323/285-0480, toll-free Mex. tel. 01-800/713-2313, fax 323/285-0308, www.garzacanela. com).

## BEACHES

San Blas's most convenient beach is **Playa el Borrego,** at the south end of Calle Cuauhtémoc about a mile south of town. With a lineup of *palapas* for food and drinks, the mile-long broad, fine-sand beach is ripe for all beach activities except snorkeling (because of the murky water). The mild offshore currents and gentle, undertow-free slope are nearly always safe for good swimming, bodysurfing, and boogie boarding. Surfing is okay here.

Shoals of shells—clams, cockles, mother-of-pearl—wash up on Borrego Beach during storms. Fishing is often good, especially when casting from the jetty and rocks at the north and south ends.

## RECREATION

### La Tovara Jungle River Trip

On the downstream side of the bridge over Estero San Cristóbal, launches-for-hire will take you up the Río Tovara, a side channel that winds about a mile downstream into the jungle.

The channel quickly narrows into a dark tree-tunnel, edged by great curtainlike swaths of mangrove roots. Big snowy *garza* (egrets) peer out from leafy branches; startled turtles slip off their soggy perches into the river, while big submerged roots, like gigantic pythons, bulge out of the inky water. Riots of luxuriant plants—white lilies, green ferns, red *romelia* orchids—hang from the trees and line the banks.

Finally you reach Tovara Springs, which well from the base of a verdant cliff. On one side, a bamboo-sheltered *palapa* restaurant serves refreshments, while on the other families picnic in a hillside pavilion. In the middle, everyone jumps in and paddles in the clear, cool water.

You can enjoy this trip either of two ways: the longer, three-hour excursion as described ($60 per boatload of 6-8) from El Conchal landing on the estuary, or the shorter version (two hours, $30 per boatload) beginning upriver at road-accessible Las Aguadas near Matanchén village. Either drive, taxi, or ride the *blanco* (white) bus or the navy blue Transportes Noreste bus.

The more leisurely three-hour trip allows more chances (especially in the early morning) to spot an ocelot, or a giant boa constrictor hanging from a limb (no kidding). Many of the boatmen are very professional; if you want to view wildlife, tell them, and they'll go more slowly and keep a sharp lookout. The crocs, however, like to appear when the sun comes out, so they are more likely to be viewed in the late morning or afternoon.

Some boatmen offer more extensive trips to less-disturbed sites deeper in the jungle. These include the Camalota spring, a branch of the Río Tovara (where a local *ejido* maintains a crocodile breeding station), and the even more remote and pristine Tepiqueñas, Los Negros, and Zoquipan lagoons in the San Cristóbal Estero's upper reaches.

In light of the possible wildlife-watching rewards, trip prices are very reasonable. For example, the very knowledgeable bird specialist Oscar Partida Hernández (Comonfort 134 Pte., tel. 323/285-0324) will guide a four-person boatload to La Tovara for about $60. If Oscar is busy, call "Chencho" Banuelos (tel. 323/285-0716) for a comparably excellent trip. More extensive options include a combined Camalota-La Tovara trip (allow 4-5 hours) for about $45 for four, or Tepiqueñas and Los Negros (6 hours, 7am departure) for about $60.

## Whale-Watching

A number of San Blas captains take visitors on less extensive, but nevertheless potentially rewarding, wildlife-viewing excursions November-April. Sightings might include humpback, gray, and sperm whales; dolphins; seals; sea lions; turtles; manta rays; and flocks of birds, including gulls, frigate birds, cormorants, boobies, terns, and much more. Guides include Pato Murillo (tel. 323/729-7944), who has an office in front of Casa Cocadas near the marina; Santos Villafuente (at the Hotel Brisas del Mar, tel. 323/285-0870, cell tel. 044-311/109-1993); and superexperienced English-speaking Tony Aguayo, who can be reached at home (tel. 323/285-0364) or at his "office," the little *palapa* to the left of the small floating boat dock at the El Pozo estuary end of Juárez. A typical five-hour excursion runs about $200 for up to six passengers.

## Bird-Watching

Although San Blas's extensive mangrove and mountain jungle hinterlands are renowned for their birds and wildlife, rewarding bird-watching can start in the early morning right at the edge of town. Follow Calle Conchal right (southeast) one block from Suites San Blas, then left (northeast) to a small pond. With binoculars, you might get some good views of local species of cormorants, flycatchers, grebes, herons, jacanas, and motmots. A copy of Peterson and Chalif's *Field Guide to Mexican Birds* or Steve Howell's *Bird-Finding Guide to Mexico* will assist in further identification.

Rewarding bird-watching is also possible on **Isla del Rey.** Bargain for a launch (from the foot of Juárez, about $4 round-trip) across to the opposite shore. Watch for wood, clapper, and Virginia rails, and boat-billed herons near the estuary shore. Then follow the track across the island (looking for warblers and a number of species of sparrows) to the beach, where you might enjoy good views of plovers, terns, Heermann's gulls, and rafts of pelicans. Bird-watching guides in the area include Mark Stackhouse (tel. 323/285-1243, http://sanblas-birding.blogspot.com), who speaks English, and Francisco Garcia (tel. 323/282-8835), who does waterfall hikes as well.

Alternatively, look around the hillside cemetery and the ruins atop **Cerro de San Basilio** for good early-morning views of hummingbirds, falcons, owls, and American redstarts.

You can include serious bird-watching with your boat trip through the mangrove channels branching from the **Estero San Cristóbal** and the **Río Tovara.** This is especially true if you obtain the services of a wildlife-sensitive guide, such as Oscar Partida (tel. 323/285-0324), "Chencho" Banuelos (tel. 323/285-0716), or Armando Santiago (tel. 323/285-0859, dolpac-arm@yahoo.com). Expect to pay about $60 for a half-day trip for four people.

In addition to the aforementioned guides, Armando Navarette (Sonora 179, no phone) offers bird-watching hikes, especially around Singayta in the foothills, where birders routinely identify 30-40 species in a two-hour adventure. Such an excursion might also include a coffee plantation visit, hiking along the old royal road to Tepic, and plenty of tropical fauna and flora, including butterflies, wildflowers, and giant vines and trees, such as ceiba, *arbolde,* and the peeling, red *papillo* tree. Armando's fee for such a trip, lasting around five hours, runs about $20 per person, plus your own or rented transportation.

Bird-watching tours and packages are another option. One of the best organized, known simply as **San Blas Birds** (www.san-blasbirds.com), lists a variety of one- to seven-day tours. The longer tours include lodging.

## EGRETS, CORMORANTS, AND ANHINGAS

In tropical San Blas, lagoon-edge mangrove trees often appear at first glance to be laden with snow. Closer inspection, however, reveals swarms of nesting white birds. Although together they appear to be a white mass, individually they belong to three species of egret—*garza* in Spanish.

Although all may seem at home, one species is a relatively new arrival to the New World. The cattle egret, *Bubulcus ibis,* wasn't seen in North America until around 1900. The smallest of egrets, it's but a foot and a half long, with a small yellow or orange bill and blackish legs and feet. Scientists suspect the bird migrated from its native Asia or Africa, where the cattle egret has foraged amid herds of cattle for millennia; the bird profits handsomely from the swarms of bugs attracted by cattle.

The other two members of Mexico's egret trio, the crystal-white snowy egret (*Egretta thula*) and the blue-gray great heron (*Casmerodius albus*) prefer to stalk fish and crabs in lagoons. You'll see them—especially the black-billed, two-foot-long snowy egret—poised in a pond, rock still, for what seems like a season, until—*pop!*—the sharp beak dives into the water and reappears with a luckless fish.

The great heron's feeding habits are similar to those of its smaller cousin, and its grand six-foot wingspan and steely blue-gray hues make it easy to recognize. At a lagoon's edge, watch quietly, and you might soon be rewarded with the magnificent sight of a great heron swooping down to land gracefully in the water.

Sharing the same watery feeding grounds are the Mexican (or olivaceous) cormorant (*Phalacrocorax olivaceous*) and its cousin the anhinga (*Anhinga anhinga*). These are often confused with loons, and they do seem a bit loony. Their necks, especially that of the anhinga—also known as "darter" or "snakebird"—sometimes bend back into a snakelike *s.* The anhinga often will swim along, submerged except for its head and neck, looking every bit like a serpent slicing through the water. Cormorants frequently nest in flocks atop mangroves and seem to have either a sense of humor or no inkling of their true identity, for if you venture too close, they'll start grunting like a chorus of pigs.

Cormorants and anhingas are as graceful in the water as they are clumsy on land. They plop along in the mud on their webbed feet, finally jumping to a rock or tree perch where, batlike, they unfold their wings to dry and preen them. Although both are about 2-3 feet in size, they're easily distinguishable: The anhinga generally appears in greater numbers and features arrays of silvery spots along the wings.

For example, three days including lodging at Hotel Posada del Rey runs around $450 per person; the same out of Hotel Garza Canela is about $650 per person.

For more details on bird-watching and hiking around San Blas, you can purchase a number of guides at the shop at Hotel Garza Canela. It also usually carries the *Checklist of Birds Found in San Blas, Nayarit* or the *Birder's Guide to San Blas,* published by San Blas Birds.

### Ecotours

For ecologically oriented tours, you might look into the services of Canadian photographer-guide John Stewart, founder of **Seven Sunset** Tours (www.sevensunsets.com), who with partner Ryan Graham works out of Casa Mañana at Playa los Cocos, several miles south of San Blas. John, Ryan, and staff like to lead their clients on ecofriendly tours to local villages, hidden beaches, waterfalls, places to bird-watch, and much more.

### ECOTOURING IN SINGAYTA

The latter-day local growth of shrimp-pond aquaculture and the associated wildlife habitat destruction has prompted action by ecoactivists in San Blas and neighboring communities, such as Singayta, five miles (eight km) east of San Blas.

Singayta villagers began taking positive

action around 2000. Since then, they have established a nursery for reintroduction of threatened native plants, a crocodile breeding farm, and an **environmental awareness center** to educate visitors and residents about the destructive reality of shrimp-pond aquaculture.

To back all this up, Singayta offers a menu of **guided ecotours and services** (www.singayta.com and www.elmanglar.com) for visitors. These include canoe trips into the mangrove wetland, walking tours, mountain bike rentals, donkey cart and horseback tours, and more. A restaurant also offers meals and refreshments. To find out more about Singayta, contact knowledgeable ecoleader and guide **Juan "Bananas" Garcia** (tel. 323/285-0462), founder of Grupo Ecológico in San Blas.

Get to Singayta by car along Tepic Highway 74, about five miles (eight km) straight east of the San Blas plaza; or, by bus, from the San Blas plaza-front bus station, by one of the hourly Tepic-bound buses.

## Walking and Jogging

The cooling late-afternoon sea breeze and the soft but firm sand of **Playa el Borrego** (south end of H. Batallón) make it the best place around town for a walk or jog. Arm yourself against *jejenes* with repellent and long pants, especially around sunset.

## Waterfall Hikes

A number of waterfalls decorate the lush jungle foothills above the Bay of Matanchén. Two of these, near Tecuitata and El Cora villages, are accessible from the Santa Cruz-Tepic Highway 76 about 10 miles (16 km) south of San Blas. The local *autobús blanco* will take you most of the way. It runs south to Santa Cruz every two hours 8:30am-4:30pm from the downtown corner of Juárez and Paredes.

While rugged adventurers may guide themselves to the waterfalls, others rely upon guides **Armando Navarette** or local ecoleader **Juan "Bananas" Garcia** (inquire at Tourist Information by the Pemex station

at the entrance to town, tel. 323/285-0271, or with Josefina Vasquéz at the Hotel Garza Canela, tel. 323/285-0112, 323/285-0307, or 323/285-0480).

## Surfing

Playa el Borrego has a good beach break when the swell and sand bar are right, but nearly all of San Blas's serious wave-riding action goes on at world-class surfing mecca **Stoner's Point,** just past Matanchén Beach. **Matanchén Bay** itself is a big, fun, entertaining right point break that goes on forever. Around the point of Las Islitas lies another cove, and beyond it, Stoner's Point. This is the real deal; though it is a notoriously fickle wave, on the right swell, tide, and wind, this is a world-class right point break. South swells are best for Matanchén and Stoner's; think April-November, and if you show up, pray for the right swell from the right direction. The sea gods here are unpredictable.

To find out more, be sure to visit **Stoner's Surf Camp** on Playa el Borrego, beach side of the entrance parking lot. Here, welcoming owner-operator Nikki Kath, besides renting boogie boards ($2/hr) and surfboards ($3/hr), offers surf lessons ($12/hr) and runs a restaurant, a hotel, and a small campground on the premises. Juan "Bananas" Garcia (tel. 323/285-0462), at his café at H. Battallón 219, also rents surfboards and boogie boards.

If you want to learn to surf, or are already a surfer and want to improve your skills, Stoner's is ready for you, with their champion instructor Jose "Pompi" Manuel Cano, who boasts a long list of awards that he began winning in 1980, at the age of eight. For much more surfing information, visit the Stoner's Surf Camp website, www.stonerssurfcamp.com.

## Sportfishing

**Tony Aguayo** (tel. 323/285-0364), **Ricardo "Pato" Murillo** (tel. 323/285-1281), and **Edgar Regalado** (tel. 323/285-1023) are all highly recommended to lead big-game deep-sea fishing excursions. Tony's "office" is the *palapa* shelter to the left of the little dock at the foot of Calle Juárez near the El Pozo estuary. Tony, Pato, and Edgar all regularly captain big-boat excursions for tough-fighting marlin, dorado, and sailfish. Their fee will run about $400 for a seven-hour expedition for up to three people, including big boat, tackle, and bait.

On the other hand, a number of other good-eating fish are not so difficult to catch. Check with Tony or other captains, such as Antonio Palmas at the Hotel Garza Canela or one of the owners of the many craft docked by the estuary shoreline at the foot of Juárez. For perhaps $150, they'll take three or four of you for a *lancha* outing, which most likely will result in four or five hefty 10-pound snapper, mackerel, tuna, or yellowtail; afterward you can ask your favorite restaurant to cook them for a feast.

During the last few days in May, San Blas hosts its long-running (30-plus years) **International Fishing Tournament.** The entrance fee runs around $600; prizes vary from automobiles to Mercury outboards and Penn International fishing rods. For more information, contact Tony Aguayo or Pato Murillo, or ask at the local tourist information office, downtown at the Presidencia Municipal.

## ENTERTAINMENT

Sleepy San Blas's entertainment is of the local, informal variety. Visitors content themselves with strolling the beach or riding the waves by day, and reading, watching TV, listening to mariachis, or dancing at a handful of clubs by night.

Owner/manager Mike McDonald works hard to keep **Mike's Place** (Juárez 36, no phone), on the second floor of his family's restaurant, the classiest club in town. He keeps the lights flashing and the small dance floor thumping with blues, Latin, and 1960s rock tunes from his own guitar, accompanied by his equally excellent drum and electronic-piano partners. Listen to live music 9pm-midnight Saturday during the summer low season, and Tuesday-Saturday during the fall-winter high

season. He usually charges a small cover; drinks are reasonably priced.

Another good option (and a good spot to meet people) is the **San Blas Social Club** bar, which sometimes offers jazz in season. Check it out at the northeast plaza corner.

A few other places require nothing more than your ears to find, such as the bar at the **Hotel Bucanero** (Calle Juárez 75, tel. 323/285-0101), where music booms seasonally.

## SHOPPING

San Blas visitors ordinarily spend little of their time shopping. Although San Blas has relatively few handicrafts sources, the shop at the **Hotel Garza Canela** (Paredes 106 Sur, tel. 323/285-0112, 323/285-0307, or 323/285-0480, toll-free Mex. tel. 01-800/713-2313, fax 323/285-0308, www.garzacanela.com, 9am-4pm daily) has arguably the finest for-sale handicrafts collections in Nayarit state.

## ACCOMMODATIONS

San Blas has several hotels, none of them huge, but all with personality. They are not likely to be full even during the high winter season (unless the surf off Mantanchén Beach runs high for an unusually long spell).

### Under $50

Soak in the full natural beach experience at San Blas's most economical accommodation, **Stoner's Surf Camp** (Playa el. Borrego, tel. 323/232-2225, www.stonerssurfcamp.com). Stay in their rustically snug bamboo-and-thatch *cabañitas,* complete with fan, mosquito net, towels, and sheets, for $10-35 d, depending on number of people, high season with shared toilets and showers. Amenities include restaurant, use of kitchen, use of surfboard ($3 for all day), and bikes for *cabaña* guests. Camping, with use of kitchen, runs $3 per person; tent rentals are available.

Slightly up the economic scale, the family-run *casa de huéspedes* (guesthouse) **Casa María** (corner of Canalizo and Michoacán, tel. 323/285-1057, $40 d) makes a reality of the old Spanish saying, *"Mi casa es su casa."* There are about 12 rooms around a homey, cluttered patio, and María offers to do everything for guests except give them baths (which she would probably do if someone got sick). It's not spic-and-span, but it's very friendly, and kitchen privileges, fans, hot-water showers, and washing machine are included.

You can also get a comfortable room at María's adjacent original guesthouse, **Casa Morelos** (108 H. Batallón, tel. 323/285-1345, $14 s, $18 d), operated by her daughter, Magdalena, who rents by drop-in only.

A block west of the plaza, the **Hotel Bucanero** (Calle Juárez 75, tel. 323/285-0101, $18 s, $26 d) appears to be living up to its name. A stanza from the "Song of the Pirate" emblazons one wall, a big stuffed crocodile bares its teeth beside the other, and a crusty sunken anchor and cannons decorate the shady patio. Despite peeling paint, the 32 rooms (with ceiling fans and hot water) retain a bit of spacious, old-world charm, with high-beamed ceilings under the ruddy roof tile. (High, circular vent windows in some rooms cannot be closed, however. Use repellent or your mosquito net.) Outside, the big pool and leafy old courtyard provide plenty of nooks for daytime snoozing and socializing. A noisy nighttime (winter-spring seasonal) bar, however, keeps most guests without earplugs jumping until about midnight.

## $50-100

Tucked on a quiet back street half a block from the sleepy El Pozo Estuary, **Casa Roxanna Bungalows** (Callejon El Rey 1, tel. 323/285-0573, www.casaroxanna.com) is a hidden gem among San Blas lodgings. Its refined amenities—manicured green lawn, blue double-laned lap pool, regal fan palms—are apparent immediately upon entering its tranquil garden compound. The four comfortable, spacious bungalows ($65 d, add $5 each additional adult), with two double beds, furnished kitchenettes, and cool air-conditioning, confirm the initial impression. Additionally, one large deluxe room and

a studio bungalow with kitchenette rent for about $55; both have air-conditioning, satellite TV, and parking. Wireless Internet is also available on-site.

At the nautical-themed **Hotel Marina San Blas** (Cuauhtémoc 109, tel. 323/285-1437, www.sanblas.com.mx), owned and operated by the same people who operate Hotel Hacienda Flamingos, a pretty tropical courtyard with circular swimming pool is the centerpiece, leading to a sandy stretch of beach where guests can relax under the *palapas* and gaze at the water. There's plenty to watch—birds, fisherfolk, boats leaving the marina—and you just might spend all day there. The 11 rooms are comfortable and offer king-size beds (some come with a king and a single), and are well appointed, continuing with the nautical theme of lighthouses and navy-striped decor. Rooms start at $96 d in high season, with a $24 charge for extra guests. Long-term rates are available for one-week or longer stays.

## $100-150

In the middle of town, three blocks west along Juárez from the plaza, the renovated ( **Hotel Hacienda Flamingos** (Juárez 105, tel. 323/285-0930, fax 323/285-0485, Mazatlán tel./fax 669/985-2727 or 669/985-5252, www.sanblas.com.mx) lives on as a splendid reminder of old San Blas. Owners have spared little in restoring this 1863 German consulate and trading house to its original graceful condition. Now, the fountain flows once more in the tranquil, tropical inner patio, furnished with period chairs and tables, and a gallery of old San Blas photos on the walls. A side door leads outside to a luxuriously elegant swimming pool and spacious garden, sprinkled with recliners, a grass-carpeted badminton court, and a croquet set ready for service. Inside, the rooms are no less than you'd expect: luxuriously airy and high-ceilinged, with elegantly simple decor, replete with Porfirian-era touches and wall art, and with baths that gleam with polished traditional-style fixtures. Year-round (except possibly Christmas and Easter holidays) rates for the 21 rooms (15 with TVs) run about $130 d.

Another San Blas jewel is the refined resort-style ◖ **Hotel Garza Canela** (Paredes 106 Sur, tel. 323/285-0112, 323/285-0307, or 323/285-0480, toll-free Mex. tel. 01-800/713-2313, fax 323/285-0308, www.garzacanela. com), tucked away at the south end of town, two blocks off Heróico Batallón. The careful management of its Vásquez family owners (Señorita Josefina Vásquez in charge) glows everywhere: manicured garden grounds, crystal-blue pool, immaculate sundeck, and centerpiece restaurant. The 45 spacious, air-conditioned rooms are tiled, tastefully furnished, and squeaky clean. Rates run about $126 d high season and $110 d low, all with a hearty breakfast, cable TV, and much more. Wireless Internet is available in the lobby. Credit cards are accepted. The family also runs a travel agency and an outstanding crafts and gift shop on the premises.

San Blas folks offer several other worthy hotel, bungalow, and apartment lodging choices. For more information, visit the excellent websites **www.sanblasmexico.com** or **www.sanblasdirectory.com.**

### Trailer Parks and Campgrounds

San Blas's only trailer park, **Los Cocos** (Teniente Azueta s/n, tel. 323/285-0055, loscocos@sanblasmexico.com), is a two-minute walk from the wide, yellow sands of Playa el Borrego. Friendly management; spacious, palm-shaded grassy grounds; pull-throughs; unusually clean showers and toilet facilities; a laundry next door; fishing; and a good air-conditioned bar with satellite TV all make this place a magnet for RVers and tenters from Mazatlán to Puerto Vallarta. The biting *jejenes* require the use of strong repellent for residents to enjoy the balmy evenings. The 110 spaces rent for about $15 per day for two people, $3 for each additional person, with all hookups, one day free per week for longer-term stays. Amenities include a bar out front open 10am-2pm daily and wireless Internet access.

The *jejenes* and occasional local toughs and Peeping Toms make **camping** on close-in Playa el Borrego a less-than-ideal possibility (although some adventurers customarily set up tents beside the beachfront *palapa* restaurants). A better option is to camp on Playa el Borrego at **Stoner's Surf Camp** for $3 per person, with kitchen privileges.

## FOOD
### Snacks, Stalls, and Markets
For basic staples and snacks, check out the fruit stands, groceries (such as **Abarrotes Flavia,** tel. 323/285-1214, 6am-9pm daily), *fondas,* and *jugerías* in and around the **Central Market** (corner of Sinaloa and H. Batallion de San Blas, 6am-2pm daily), which, incidentally, is the coolest non-air-conditioned daytime spot in town. For example, refresh yourself at **Jugos Mimi** juice stand. During the summer look for the exotic Asian jackfruit relative *yaca:* green, round, and as large as a football. Enjoy a *licuado* whipped from its deliciously mild pulp.

Late afternoons and evenings, many semipermanent street-side stands around the plaza, such as the **Taquería Las Cuatas,** at the northwest corner, by the city hall, offer tasty *antojitos* and drinks.

Get your fresh cupcakes, cookies, and crispy *bolillos* at the **panadería** (bakery) (at Comonfort and Cuauhtémoc, closed Sun.) around the uptown corner from Hotel Posada del Rey. You can get similar (but not quite so fresh) goodies at the small bakery outlet across from the plaza (corner of Juárez and Canalizo).

### Restaurants
Family-managed **Restaurant McDonald** (Juárez 36, tel. 323/285-0432, 7am-10pm daily, $3-7), half a block west of the plaza, is one of the gathering places of San Blas. Its bit-of-everything menu features soups, meat, and seafood, plus a hamburger that beats no-relation U.S. McDonald's by a mile.

As an option, step across the street to the TV-free **Wala** restaurant (tel. 323/285-0863, 8am-10pm Mon.-Sat., $3-7) for breakfast, lunch, or dinner. Its long menu of offerings—tasty salads, pastas, seafood, and fish fillets, crisply prepared and served in a simple but clean and inviting setting—will never go out of style. Everything is good; simply pick out your favorite.

Cross the adjacent corner and enter the refined marine atmosphere of **Restaurant la Isla** (Mercado, tel. 323/285-0407, 2pm-10pm Tues.-Sun., $6-10). As ceiling fans whir overhead and a guitarist strums softly in the background, the net-draped walls display a museum-load of nautical curiosities, from antique Japanese floats and Tahitian shells to New England ship models. Davy Jones notwithstanding, both local folks and visitors choose this place mainly for its good fish and shrimp entrées.

San Blas's class-act restaurant is **C El Delfín** (at Hotel Garza Canela, Cuauhtémoc 106, tel. 323/285-0112, 8am-10am and 1pm-9pm daily, $4-14). Potted tropical plants and leafy planter-dividers enhance the genteel atmosphere of this air-conditioned dining-room-in-the-round. Meticulous preparation and service, bountiful breakfasts, savory dinner soups, and fresh salad, seafood, and meat entrées keep customers returning year after year. Credit cards are accepted.

## INFORMATION AND SERVICES
### Tourist Information
San Blas has one **tourist information office** (tel. 323/285-0221, 9am-2pm and 4pm-7pm Mon.-Fri., 10am-2pm Sat.), located directly under the arch as you enter the main part of town.

Alternatively, for information, tickets, and tours, see very well-informed **Josefina Vásquez,** both the desk manager and travel agent at the Hotel Garza Canela (Paredes 106 Sur, tel. 323/285-0112, 323/285-0307, or 323/285-0480, toll-free Mex. tel. 01-800/713-2313, fax 323/285-0308, www.garzacanela.com).

### Money
**Banamex** (Juárez 36 Ote., tel. 323/285-0031,

9am-4pm Mon.-Fri.), one block east of the plaza, has a 24-hour ATM. Bancomer also has an ATM on the east side of the plaza. There is also an ATM at the Pemex gas station just as you enter town.

### Communications
The **correo** (tel. 323/285-0295, 8am-3pm Mon.-Fri., 9am-noon Sat.) and **telégrafo** (tel. 323/285-0115, 8am-2pm Mon.-Fri.) stand side by side at Sonora and Echeverria (one block behind, one block east of the plaza church).

In addition to the long-distance public phone stands that sprinkle the town, there are a number of old-fashioned *larga distancia* stores. Most prominent is the **Computel** (on Juárez, 8am-9pm daily), just west of the plaza, across from Restaurant McDonald.

Internet access without passwords or fees is available just about everywhere in San Blas. If you don't have it where you are sitting or standing, move down the street or into the next bar or café.

### Health and Emergencies
For routine remedies and nonprescription drugs, go to **Farmacia Mas Por Menos** (More For Less, Juárez 66, 8:30am-1pm and 4pm-9pm daily), across from Restaurant McDonald, who you can call to reach the pharmacy (tel. 323/285-0432).

Alternatively, go to **Farmacia Económica** (H. Batallón and Mercado, tel. 323/285-0111, 8:30am-1pm and 4:30pm-9pm Mon.-Sat., 8:30am-2pm Sun.).

For medical consultations, visit very highly recommended **Dr. Alejandro Davalos,** available at his office on Juárez (tel. 323/285-0331), corner of Farias, three blocks east of the plaza. If he's too busy, consult with general practitioner **Dr. Rene Diaz Elias,** at his Farmacia Mas Por Menos (Juárez 66, 8:30am-1pm Mon.-Sat.).

Moreover, you can go to San Blas's respectable local small hospital, the government 24-hour **Centro de Salud** (Yucatán and H. Batallón, across from the Motel Marino Inn, tel. 323/285-1207).

For **police** emergencies, contact the

headquarters (on Canalizo, tel. 323/285-0221), on the left side of and behind the Presidencia Municipal.

## Immigration and Customs

San Blas no longer has either Migración or Aduana offices. If you lose your tourist card, you'll have to go to the Secretaria de Gobernación in Tepic (Oaxaca no. 220 Sur) or, better, to Migración at the airport in Puerto Vallarta a day before you're scheduled to fly home. For customs matters, go to the Aduana in Puerto Vallarta for the necessary paperwork.

## GETTING THERE
### By Car or RV

To and from Puerto Vallarta, the highway coastal cutoff at Las Varas bypasses the slow climb up the mountain to Tepic, shortening the San Blas-Puerto Vallarta connection to about 94 miles (151 km), or about 2.5 hours.

From the east, Nayarit Highway 76 leaves Highway 15 at its signed "Miramar" turnoff at the northern edge of Tepic. The road winds downhill about 3,000 feet (1,000 m) through a jungly mountain forest to shoreline Santa Cruz and Miramar villages. It continues along the Bahía de Matanchén shoreline to San Blas, a total of 43 miles (70 km) from Tepic. Although this route generally has more shoulder than Highway 74, frequent pedestrians and occasional unexpected cattle necessitate caution.

To and from the north and east, paved roads connect San Blas to main-route National Highway 15. From the northeast, National Highway 74 winds 19 miles (31 km) downhill from its junction 161 miles (260 km) south of Mazatlán and 22 miles (35 km) north of Tepic. From its Highway 15 turnoff (marked by a Pemex gas station), Highway 74 winds through a forest of vine-draped trees and tall palms. Go slowly; the road lacks a shoulder, and cattle or people may appear unexpectedly around any blind, grass-shrouded bend.

### By Bus

From Puerto Vallarta, bus travelers have two ways to get to San Blas. Quickest is via one of the **Transportes Norte de Sonora** (tel. 323/285-0043) departures, which connect daily with San Blas. They depart from the Puerto Vallarta bus station north of the airport three times daily, at 8:30am, 12:30pm, and 3:30pm; get your ticket at the Elite-Estrella Blanca desk (tel. 322/290-1001). The buses leave San Blas for Puerto Vallarta at 7:30am, 10:30am, and 1:30pm. Fares on this bus are about $12 one way.

If you're too late for the Transportes Norte de Sonora connection, go via **Transportes Pacífico** (tel. 322/290-1008) to the Tepic bus station, where you might be early enough to catch the last of the three daily local buses that connect with San Blas, leaving Tepic on the hour every hour, run by Transportes Norte de Sonora (tel. 311/213-2315) or **Transportes Noroeste de Nayarit** (tel. 311/212-2325; go by taxi to their Tepic city-center station). The fare is about $4 each way. These buses run in both directions all day, the first one leaving San Blas at 6am and last one leaving San Blas at 8pm. Tepic to San Blas buses run on the same basic schedule; the first one leaves Tepic at 5:45am and the last one at 7:45pm.

The **San Blas bus terminal** stands adjacent to the new plaza church, corner of Calles Sinaloa and Canalizo. Transportes Norte de Sonora buses connect with Tepic many times a day (with one early departure continuing to Guadalajara).

Several daily second-class navy-blue-and-white Transportes Noroeste de Nayarit departures (about 8am and 10am) connect south with Bay of Matanchén points of Matanchén, Los Cocos, and Santa Cruz de Miramar. Other departures connect east with Tepic, and north with Santiago Ixcuintla, via intermediate points of Guadalupe Victoria and Villa Hidalgo.

A local *autobús blanco* connects San Blas south with the Bay of Matanchén points of Las Aguadas, Matanchén, Aticama, Los Cocos, and Santa Cruz. It departs from the downtown corner of Paredes and Sinaloa (a block west of the old church) four times daily, approximately every two hours between 8:30am and 4:30pm.

THE RIVIERA NAYARIT

## SANTIAGO IXCUINTLA

North of San Blas, the Nayarit coastal strip broadens into a hinterland of lush farm and marsh where, on the higher ground, rich fields of chiles, tobacco, and corn bloom, and Highway 15 conducts a nonstop procession of traffic past the major farm towns of Ruíz, Rosamorada, and Acaponeta.

But where the coastal plain nears the sea, the pace of life slows. Roads, where they exist, thread their way through a vast wetland laced with mangrove channels and decorated by diminutive fishing settlements. Through this lowland, Mexico's longest river, the Río Grande de Santiago, ends its epic five-state journey downstream, past the colorful colonial town of Santiago Ixcuintla (eeks-KOOEEN-tlah) and its historic island neighbor, **Mexcaltitán,** accessible only by boat.

Few Mexican town names are more intriguing than the name Ixcuintla. Its name derives from the Náhuatl (Aztec) word for the nearly hairless dogs that, in ancient times, were bred locally as pets and for food. Don't

miss seeing the dogs, now a whole family, at the **Centro Cultural Huichol,** donated by Nayarit Governor Huberto Delgado a few years back.

Although the town's scenic appeal is considerable, the Huichol people are *the* reason to come to Santiago Ixcuintla. Several hundred Huichol families migrate seasonally (mostly Dec.-May) from their Sierra Madre high-country homeland to work for a few dollars a day in the local tobacco fields. For many Huichol, their migration in search of money includes a serious hidden cost. In the mountains, their homes, friends, and relatives are around them, as are the familiar rituals and ceremonies they have tenaciously preserved in their centuries-long struggle against Mexicanization.

But when the Huichol come to lowland towns and cities, they often encounter the mocking laughter and hostile stares of crowds of strangers, whose Spanish language they do not understand, and whose city ways are much more alien than they appear even to foreign tourists. As strangers in a strange land, the pressure on the migrant Huichol to give up old costumes, language, and ceremonies to become like everyone else is powerful indeed.

### The Town Plaza

The Santiago Ixcuintla town plaza is a couple of blocks directly inland from the riverbank. The main town streets border the plaza: Running east-west are 20 de Noviembre on the north side and Zaragoza on the south side; Hidalgo and Allende run north-south along the east and west sides, respectively. During your stroll around the plaza, admire the pretty old church and the voluptuous Porfirian nymphs who decorate the gloriously restored bandstand. Stroll beneath the shaded porticos and the colorful market, a block west and a block north of the plaza.

### Centro Cultural Huichol

Be sure to reserve part of your time in Santiago Ixcuintla to stop by the Centro Cultural Huichol (20 de Noviembre 452, tel.

the noble cathedral of Ixcuintla

© JUSTIN HENDERSON

the elegantly wrought bandstand in Ixcuintla's plaza

323/235-1171, 9am-2pm and 4pm-8pm Mon.-Sat., www.huicholcenter.com). The immediate mission of founder Mariano Valadez, a Huichol artist and community leader, is to ensure that the Huichol people endure, with their traditions intact and growing. His instrument is the Centro Cultural Huichol—a clinic, dining hall, dormitory, library, craftsmaking shop, sale gallery, and interpretive center that provides crucial focus and support for local migratory Huichol people.

Mariano's ex-wife, Susana (who helped him found the Centro Cultural Huichol during the 1990s and more recently has opened the Galeria Tanana in Sayulita), has worked to maintain a second center, high in the mountains at Huejuquilla El Alto, Jalisco. Mariano, with the help of his local staff, continues the original mission in Santiago Ixcuintla. As well as filling vital human needs, both of these centers actively nurture the vital elements of an endangered heritage. This heritage belongs not only to the Huichol, but to the lost generations of indigenous peoples—Aleut, Yahi, Lacandones, and myriad others—who succumbed to European diseases and were massacred in innumerable fields, from Wounded Knee and the Valley of Mexico all the way to Tierra del Fuego.

Although they concentrate on the immediate needs of people, Mariano and Susana and their staffs also reach out to local, national, and international communities. For example, their Santiago Ixcuintla center's entry corridor is decorated with illustrated Huichol legends in Spanish, especially for Mexican visitors. An adjacent gallery exhibits a treasury of Huichol art for sale—yarn paintings, masks, jewelry, gourds, god's eyes—adorned with the colorful deities and animated heavenly motifs of the Huichol pantheon. You may also purchase the center's Huichol handicrafts online, via www.beadsofbeauty.net, or at La Hamaca Gallery or Galeria Tanana in Sayulita.

Get to the Santiago Ixcuintla Centro Cultural Huichol by heading away from the river, along 20 de Noviembre, the main street that borders the central plaza. Within a mile, you'll see the Centro Cultural Huichol at number 452, on the right.

You can also travel to Susana's center (call or email a week ahead of time) in person, either by charter airplane from Tepic or two days by car (via Highway 54 north from Guadalajarato Zacatecas, thence Highway 45 northwest to Fresnillo, then west via Highway 44 to Huejuquilla) to Centro Indígena Huichol (Calle Victoria 24, Huejuquilla El Alto, tel. 457/983-7054, huicholcenter@juno.com). Both the Huejuquilla and the Santiago Ixcuintla centers invite volunteers, especially those with secretarial, computer, language, and other skills, to help with projects. If you don't have the time, they also solicit donations of money and equipment.

## Accommodations and Food

If you decide on a Santiago Ixcuintla overnight, stay at the **Hotel Casino Plaza** (Arteaga and Ocampo, tel./fax 323/235-0850, 323/235-0851, or 323/235-0852, $37 d). The approximately 35 basic but clean rooms around an inner parking patio have private hot-water shower baths and air-conditioning.

For food, go to the Hotel Casino's good air-conditioned downstairs restaurant/bar or check out the hearty country food offerings of the many *fondas* (food stalls) in the town-center market.

## Information and Services

Santiago Ixcuintla is an important regional business center with a number of services. Banks, all with 24-hour ATMs, include long-hours **HSBC** (Hidalgo and Zaragoza, tel. 323/235-3401, 8am-7pm Mon.-Fri., 8am-3pm Sat.), on the south side of the plaza; **Banamex** (20 de Noviembre and Hidalgo, tel. 323/235-0053, 9am-4pm Mon.-Fri.); and **Bancomer** (20 de Noviembre and Morelos, 8:30am-4pm Mon.-Fri., 10am-2pm Sat.).

Find the *correo* (Allende 23, tel. 323/235-0214, 8:30am-3pm Mon.-Fri.) at the east side of the plaza. **Telecomunicaciones** (Zaragoza Ote. 200, tel./fax 323/235-0989, 8am-8pm Mon.-Sat.) provides telegraph, long-distance phone, and public fax.

Two grades of gasoline are customarily available at the **Pemex** station on the east-side highway (toward Highway 15) as you head out of town.

## Getting There

For bus travelers, the San Blas and Tepic bus stations are the best jumping-off places for Santiago Ixcuintla. The regional line, navy-blue-and-white Autotransportes Noroeste de Nayarit, runs a few daily buses from the San Blas and Tepic bus stations to the Santiago Ixcuintla station, where you can make connections by minibus or *colectivo* for Mexcaltitán.

With your own wheels, Santiago Ixcuintla and Mexcaltitán make an interesting off-the-beaten-track side trip from San Blas or Puerto Vallarta. Two routes are possible. From Puerto Vallarta, the simplest (but not the quickest) route is via Highway 200 to Tepic, then continuing along Highway 15, 38 miles (60 km) north of Tepic (and 16 mi/25 km north of the Highway 74-Highway 15 junction) to the signed Santiago Ixcuintla-Mexcaltitán turnoff. Within 5 miles (8 km) you'll be in Santiago Ixcuintla; Mexcaltitán is another 20 miles (32 km) beyond that. Be sure to get a very early start (or plan on an overnight en route).

Alternatively, car travelers in the mood for a little extra adventure should drive the back road that connects San Blas with Santiago Ixcuintla. The main attractions en route are the hosts of waterbirds, tobacco fields, aquaculture ponds, Huichol people in colorful local dress, and the Río Grande de Santiago, Mexico's longest river.

**Directions:** The Santiago Ixcuintla road (signed Guadalupe Victoria) heads northerly, from the eastward extension of San Blas's main street, Juárez, on the San Blas side of the Estero San Cristóbal bridge. Mark your odometer at the turnoff and continue along the paved road about 10 miles (16 km) to Guadalupe Victoria village. Follow the pavement, which curves right (east) and continues another 8 miles (13 km) to Villa Hidalgo. Keep going through the

working tools of Mexcaltitán: fishing nets and small boats

the opening of the shrimp season by staging a grand regatta, driven by friendly competition between decorated boats carrying rival images of Saints Peter and Paul.

## Sights

From either of the Mexcaltitán road's-end embarcaderos, boat workers ferry you across (about $3 pp for *colectivo,* $8 for private boat, each way) to Mexcaltitán island-village, some of whose inhabitants have never crossed the channel to the mainland. The town itself is not unlike many Mexican small towns, except more tranquil because of the absence of motor vehicles.

Mexcaltitán is prepared for visitors, however. Instituto Nacional de Arqueología y Historia (INAH) has put together an excellent **museum** (10am-2pm and 4pm-7pm Tues.-Sun., 5 pesos/ about $0.40), with several rooms of artifacts, photos, paintings, and maps describing the cultural regions of pre-Columbian Mexico. The displays climax at the museum's centerpiece exhibit, which tells the story of the Aztecs' epic migration to the Valley of Mexico from legendary Aztlán, now believed by experts to be present-day Mexcaltitán.

Outside, the proud village **church** (step inside and admire the heroic St. Peter above the altar) and city hall preside over the central plaza, from which the town streets radiate to the broad lagoon that surrounds the town.

At the watery lagoon-ends of the streets, village men set out in the late afternoon in canoes and boats for the open-ocean fishing grounds where, as night falls and kerosene lanterns are used, they attract shrimp into their nets. Occasionally during the rainy season water floods the town, and folks must navigate the streets as Venice-style canals.

## Beaches

Beachcombers might enjoy a side trip to nearby **Playa los Corchos.** If, at the junction 5 miles (8 km) west of Santiago Ixcuintla, instead of turning off for Mexcaltitán you continue straight ahead (west) for about 15 miles (24 km), you'll

town; after another five miles (eight km), turn left (north) at the signed La Presa-Santiago Ixcuintla side road. Continue to La Presa. Bear left through the village center, very quickly to the river levee, and across the new bridge, where you can see Santiago Ixcuintla across the river.

## ◖ MEXCALTITÁN

Mexcaltitán (pop. 2,000), the House of the Mexicans, represents much more than just a scenic little island town. Archaeological evidence indicates that Mexcaltitán may actually be the legendary Aztlán (Place of the Herons) from which the Aztecs, who called themselves the México (May-KSHEE-kah), in 1091, began their generations-long migration to the Valley of Mexico.

Each year on June 28 and 29, the feast days of Saints Peter and Paul, residents of Mexcaltitán and surrounding villages dress up in feathered headdresses and jaguar robes and breathe life into their tradition. They celebrate

© JUSTIN HENDERSON

THE RIVIERA NAYARIT

© JUSTIN HENDERSON

Mexcaltitán's sweet little plaza and garden

arrive at Playa los Corchos. Here, waves roll in gently from 100 yards out, leaving meringues of foam on sand speckled with little white clam shells. A few ramshackle Sunday *palapas* line the broad, wind-rippled strand.

From here you can hike or, with care, pilot your four-wheel-drive vehicle five miles (eight km) south along the beach to **Barra Asadero,** at the mouth of the Río Grande de Santiago. On the sandbar and in the adjacent river estuary, many sandpipers, pelicans, gulls, and boobies gather to feast amid the summer flood deposits of driftwood troves.

## Accommodations and Food

At the view-edge of the lagoon behind the museum stands Mexcaltitán's first official tourist lodging, the **Hotel Ruta Azteca** (tel. 323/235-6020). More like a homey guesthouse than a hotel, it has an airy rear lagoon-view patio, perfect for reading and relaxing. Its four plain, tiled rooms with bath rent for about $30 d with fans, $40 d with air-conditioning. Except for the last week in June, reservations are not

usually necessary. If you are unable to contact the hotel directly, call the town telephone operator (tel. 323/235-6077) and leave a message for the hotel.

On the town plaza opposite the church stands airy **El Camarón** seafood restaurant (although the sometimes-noisy restaurant/bar at the south-side dock has more and better food). A third option is the good **Mariscos Kika** (tel. 327/235-6054, noon-dusk daily, $4-10) seafood restaurant, visible across the lagoon from the south-side dock. Reach it by hired (or the restaurant's) boat. Its kid-friendly facilities include a pair of kiddie pools and a waterslide.

## Getting There

Mexcaltitán lies about 25 miles (32 km) by an all-weather road northwest of Santiago Ixcuintla. You get to Santiago Ixcuintla either by back road from San Blas or from Highway 15, by the Santiago Ixcuintla turnoff 38 miles (60 km) north of Tepic. About five miles (eight km) after the turnoff, you reach the town, marked by a solitary hill on the right.

The streets of Mexcaltitán have never known cars.

Just past the hill, turn right on the main street, 20 de Noviembre, which runs by the central plaza and becomes the main westbound road out of town. Continue approximately another five miles (eight km) to the signed Mexcaltitán turnoff, where you head right. You soon pass Base Aztlán, site of the Mexican experimental rocket center. The farmland then gives way to a maze of leafy mangrove-edged lagoons, home to a host of cackling, preening, and fluttering waterbirds. About 15 miles (24 km) after the turnoff, you reach the embarcadero for Mexcaltitán.

Note: Mexcaltitán is also accessible from the northeast side, from Highway 15, 136 miles (219 km) south of Mazatlán, at a signed turnoff with gas station 4 miles (6.4 km) south of Chilapa village. Initially paved, the access road changes to rough gravel for final 14 miles (22 km) through the bushy wetland, decorated by rafts of Mexican lotus lilies and flocks of preening, stalking, and fluttering egrets, herons, and cormorants, finally arriving at embarcadero La Ticha after 28 miles (45 km).

THE RIVIERA NAYARIT

# BARRA DE NAVIDAD AND THE JALISCO COAST

Those fortunate enough to travel the country between Puerto Vallarta and Barra de Navidad will fall in love with the area. Highway 200 wends its way through dense tropical landscape, thick with the vines from strangler figs and punctuated with bursts of color from flowering vines. The richness of the jungle gives way to lovely panoramic vistas of jutting volcanic hills,

© DONNA DAY

# HIGHLIGHTS

LOOK FOR ( TO FIND RECOMMENDED SIGHTS, ACTIVITIES, DINING, AND LODGING.

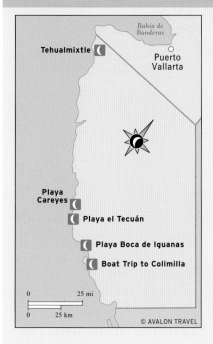

**( Tehualmixtle:** Off-highway adventurers must go to this lovely fishing hamlet in the pristine Cabo Corrientes hinterland. Snorkel, scuba dive, visit a natural hot spring, and beachcomb the golden Playa Mayto (page 236).

**( Playa Careyes:** This strand on a gorgeous half-moon bay makes for a great walk-in day trip. Beach *palapas* supply food, and local fisherfolk can take you fishing. Experienced surfers will enjoy the sometimes powerful waves (page 243).

**( Playa el Tecuán:** Public access to this de facto wild kingdom offers outdoor diversions, including advanced surfing, kayaking on the mangrove lagoon, surf fishing, and self-contained RV and tent camping (page 245).

**( Playa Boca de Iguanas:** Come for an afternoon or a week of tropical diversions, from surf fishing and beachcombing to bird- and crocodile-watching and hammock snoozing (page 247).

**( Boat Trip to Colimilla:** From Barra de Navidad, ride a boat across the mangrove-bordered expanse of Laguna de Navidad to the coastal village of Colimilla. Enjoy a cocktail before you dine on fresh seafood at one of the lagoon-front restaurants (page 255).

vast fields of pale blue agave, and orchards of mangoes and coconut palms. Rolling hills of wildflowers attract legions of butterflies and brightly colored birds. Miles of golden untouched beaches line the coast with nary a condominium or time-share salesman in sight. There are so many opportunities for exploring drowsy beach towns, walking miles of empty beaches, and for taking photographs that it's a wonder anyone ever makes it to Barra de Navidad at all.

Cabo Corrientes, Mexico's great western cape, defines the Jalisco Coast. Beginning at Puerto Vallarta, the Bay of Banderas's shoreline juts 40 miles (64 km) southwest into the Pacific, forming Cabo Corrientes. Like a

giant's great protecting chin, Cabo Corrientes regularly deflects Pacific storms past Puerto Vallarta.

South of the Cape, the coastline curves gently southeast, indented by a trio of broad beach- and islet-studded bays—Chamela, Tenacatita, and Navidad—all havens for lovers of sun, sand, and surf. Consequently, for most visitors, the Jalisco Coast's major attractions are its magnificent seclusion and outdoor beach and ocean pleasures. Topping the list are abundant fishing (freshwater, deep ocean, and surf), beachcombing, wildlife viewing, off-road adventuring, and scuba diving, snorkeling, and surfing.

For those who manage to resist the siren

THE JALISCO COAST

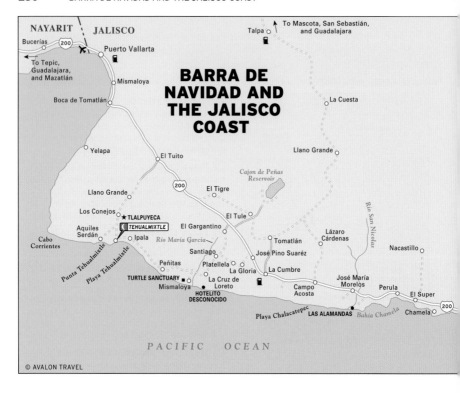

THE JALISCO COAST

song of side trips and exploration, the rewards are the twin country beach resorts of Melaque and Barra de Navidad at the Jalisco Coast's southern border. Both are lovely seaside towns with affordable lodging and dining, and a friendly atmosphere. Excepting Melaque and Barra de Navidad, the Jalisco Coast is nearly all pioneer country, with only a few villages.

Fortunately, however, everyone who travels south of Puerto Vallarta doesn't have to be a Daniel Boone. The coastal strip within a few miles of the highway has acquired some amenities—stores, trailer parks, campgrounds, hotels, and a scattering of small resorts, some humble and some posh—all enough to become well-known to Puerto Vallarta people as the Costalegre (Happy Coast).

## PLANNING YOUR TIME

If you have deep pockets or a desire to splurge, there are some incredibly posh resorts along the road to Barra. Moving from Puerto Vallarta south along the luxurious path less traveled, you might first stay at least an overnight in one of the Italian designer-chic cabanas of the **Hotelito Desconocido,** on its pristine seaside lagoon. Continue on to **Las Alamandas,** surfing resort for movie stars, moguls, and maharajas. In either case, call ahead, and, if you do make a reservation, prepare to splurge: These places are Expensive with a capital *E!*

On the other hand, for travelers seeking the moderately priced, home-grown delights of South Seas Mexico, the Costalegre offers what local people have known about for years: plenty of sun, fresh seafood, clear blue water,

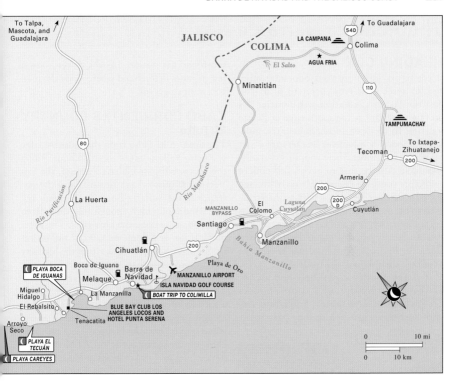

and sandy beaches, some of which stretch for miles, while others are tucked away in little rocky coves like pearls in an oyster.

From Puerto Vallarta, follow the detour into rustically pristine Cabo Corrientes country, to the bucolic **Tehualmixtle** fishing hamlet, and enjoy an idyll sharpened by the local memory of galleons, shipwrecks, and the turn-of-the-20th-century cocaine trade. Farther south, beachcomb and surf-fish the curving, sandy reach of islet-dotted **Chamela Bay** by day while lodging at a friendly local trailer park or homey hotel by night. Continue for more of the same at gorgeous **Boca de Iguana** mangrove jungle lagoon and beach, and then hop a few miles farther south to petite **La Manzanilla** beach-resort town, where a lively mix of expats and

locals have begun to transform this once sleepy pueblo into an artistic beach-lover's haven. Here you can enjoy days dining on superfresh seafood and cozy nights being lulled to sleep by the swish of the friendly La Manzanilla waves.

Whatever your style of travel, the prizes at the end of the road to Barra de Navidad are the manifold surprises of the small beach-resort towns of **Barra de Navidad** and **San Patricio-Melaque.** Here, multiple pleasures beckon: days strolling the beach, gazing out at the languid wave-washed shoreline from beneath a shady *palapa,* wildlife-watching in the broad mirror-smooth Laguna de Navidad, fishing for wild tuna and dorado, and enjoying fine fare from steaming street-front tacos to nouvelle gourmet restaurant cuisine.

THE JALISCO COAST

# The Road to Barra de Navidad

## HEADING OUT

If you're driving, note your odometer mileage (or reset your tripometer to 0) as you pass the Pemex gas station at Kilometer 214 on Highway 200 at the south edge of Puerto Vallarta. In the open southern country, mileage and roadside kilometer markers are a useful way to remember where your little paradise is hidden. Also be sure to have a full tank of gas before you leave Puerto Vallarta. Although there are far more Pemex gas stations than there used to be, on this stretch of coast gas stations are still relatively few and far between, though you can usually purchase gas in the small towns along the highway from informal *gasolineras.* You'll see their signs at the roadside.

If you're not driving, simply hop on one of the many southbound Autocamiones del Pacífico or Transportes Cihuatlán second-class buses just before they pass at the south-end gas station. Let the driver know a few minutes beforehand where along the road you want to get off.

## CABO CORRIENTES COUNTRY
### El Tuito

The drive to El Tuito from the southern edge of Puerto Vallarta takes about an hour. Along the way you'll pass Chico's Paradise, the Los Veranos Canopy Tour turnoff, and the entrance to the Vallarta Botanical Gardens before winding up high enough into the hills to find yourself among the pine trees. The town of El Tuito, at Kilometer 170 (27 mi/44 km from Puerto Vallarta), looks from the highway like nothing more than a bus stop. Most visitors pass by without even giving it a second glance. This is a pity, because El Tuito (pop. 3,500) is a friendly little colonial-era town that spreads along a long main street to a pretty town square about a mile from the highway. The cash machine on the square is the last ATM you'll see for a while, so if you're heading out into Cabo Corrientes, this is a good place to pack your wallet with pesos. There is also a tourism office with a Spanglish-speaking gentleman who'll help you figure out if the road is currently passable, and where it will take you.

El Tuito enjoys at least two claims to fame: Besides being the mezcal capital of western Jalisco, it's the jumping-off spot for the seldom-visited coastal hinterland of Cabo Corrientes, the southernmost lip of the Bay of Banderas. This is pioneer country, a land of wild beaches and sylvan forests, penetrated by only a few paved roads. Wild creatures still abound: Turtles come ashore to lay their eggs, hawks soar, and parrots swarm, and the faraway scream of the jaguar can yet be heard in the night.

The rush for the *raicilla,* as local connoisseurs call El Tuito mezcal, begins on Saturday when men crowd into town and begin upending bottles around noon, without even bothering to sit down. For a given individual, this

© JUSTIN HENDERSON

a sylvan scene on the road to Barra de Navidad

THE JALISCO COAST

© JUSTIN HENDERSON

a roadside attraction between El Tuito and Playa Mayto

cannot last too long, so the fallen are continually replaced by fresh arrivals all weekend.

Although El Tuito is famous for the *raicilla,* it is not the source. *Raicilla* comes from the sweet sap of the maguey plants, a close relative of the cactuslike century plant, which blooms once and then dies. The *ejido* (cooperative farm) of Cicatán (see-kah-TAHN), 8 miles (13 km) out along the dirt road as you head to the coast west of town, cultivates the maguey. You won't find *raicilla* outside of Jalisco, for it is made exclusively in this state.

## Along the Road to Aquiles Serdán

You can get to the coast with or without your own wheels. Road crews have paved much of the 42 kilometers (26 mi) of road that lies between El Tuito and the remote beaches of Mayto and Tehualmixtle, although extremely intense summer rains make every road on Cabo Corrientes subject to washouts. Ask around in El Tuito to find out current road conditions. If you're driving, it should be a strong, high-clearance vehicle (pickup, Jeep, very maneuverable

RV, or VW van) filled with gas; if you're not driving, currently a coast-bound bus leaves the El Tuito plaza around 2pm daily. The one-way fare is 50 pesos (about US$4). The bus leaves the coast for its daily return trip to El Tuito every morning around 7am, precise time depending on where you catch it. Destinations include Tehualmixtle, Playa Mayto, and Villa del Mar. There are also informal trips by *colectivos* and/or taxi-vans available at both ends of the trip. Or you can hitchhike; there is usually space in the back of a passing pickup, and rare indeed would be the Mexican driver unwilling to offer a ride.

Getting there along the bumpy, rutted, sometimes steep 26-mile (42-km) dirt track is half the fun of Aquiles Serdán (pop. 200). If you're driving, mark your odometer where the road takes off from the southwest corner of the El Tuito town plaza. About 8 miles (13 km) from the plaza, you'll pass through the lands of the Cicatán mezcal cooperative, marked only by a crumbling thatch house on the right. On the left, you'll soon glimpse a

## *RAICILLA:* MEXICAN MOONSHINE

*Raicilla* (rye-SEE-yah) is a homegrown version of tequila or mezcal produced only in the Jalisco region of Mexico. The moonshine heritage of *raicilla* comes from citizens making the liquor in secret to avoid the related regulations and taxes required for producing alcohol. Typically, you would find *raicilla* sold in private homes, bottled in plastic bottles or other recyclable containers.

While tequila is made from the blue agave plant, *raicilla* is made from *Agave lechuguilla*, a member of the botanical group Crenatae and commonly known as "*pata de mula*" (mule's foot). The distillation and production process is basically the same for both liquors; however, *raicilla* has a very different flavor from tequila. It's also known to be considerably more potent, sometimes with an alcohol content of up to 150 proof.

*Raicilla* has now developed enough of a following to have its own high-end distillery. Should you want to try the finest available version of this firewater, head to Cimarrón Chico, where you'll find the **Destiladora del Real,** producing the liquor in both 72-proof (*Production Limitada*) and 80-proof (*Tradicional*) versions.

field of maguey in the distance. A few dozen families (who live in the hills past the far side of the field) quietly go about their business of tending their maguey plants and extracting, fermenting, and distilling the precious sap into their renowned *raicilla.*

The road dips up and down the rest of the way, over sylvan hillsides dotted with oak (*robles*), through intimate stream valleys perfect for parking an RV or setting up a tent, and past the hardscrabble rancho-hamlets of Llano Grande (Broad Plain, 14 mi/22 km), with stores, *comedores* (places to eat), a *centro de salud,* and **Los Conejos** (The Rabbits, 19 mi/30 km). At Los Conejos, a signed road forks left five miles (eight km) to **Tlalpuyeque** hot spring and sacred site. Should you decide to head out there, obey local custom and refrain from nude bathing.

You can't get lost, because there's only one route until a few miles past Los Conejos, where a fork (23 mi/37 km) marks your approach to Aquiles Serdán. The left branch continues south a few miles to Mayto and Tehualmixtle. A mile and a half to the north along the right branch you'll arrive at the Río Tecolotlán. Aquiles Serdán stands on the far bank, across 100 yards of watery sand. Fortunately the riverbed road is concrete-bottomed, and, if it's in good repair, you can drive right across the

streambed anytime other than after a storm. If you can't drive across, roll up your pants legs and walk across, like most of the local folks do. Keep in mind that this is a trip that can't be taken in the rainy season, as there is too much water in the river. However, if you make it any other time, you can visit Aquiles Serdán, or go farther, deeper into Cabo Corrientes, and visit Naranjitos (5 mi/8 km), Playitas (9.3 mi/15 km), or Corrales (14.3 mi/23 km). These places are utterly untouristed, so prepare for an adventure.

### Aquiles Serdán

The Aquiles Serdán villagers see so few outsiders that you'll become their attraction of the week. Wave and say *hola,* buy a *refresco,* and stroll around town. After a while, the kids will stop crowding around and the adults will stop staring when they've found out that you, too, are human. By that time, someone may even have invited you into his or her tree-branch-walled, clean, dirt-floored house for some hot fish-fillet tacos, fresh tomatoes, and beans. Accept, of course.

Aquiles Serdán basks above the lily-edged river lagoon, which during the June-October rainy season usually breaks through the beach-sandbar and drains directly into the surf half a mile below the town. During the dry season,

© JUSTIN HENDERSON

Playa Mayto offers plenty of opportunity for getting away from it all.

the ocean plugs the hole in the sandbar, and the lagoon wanders lazily up the coast for a few miles. In any case, the white-sand beach is easily accessible only by boat, which you can borrow or hire at the village.

If you do, you'll have miles of untouched white sand and surf all to yourself for days of camping, beachcombing, shell collecting, surf fishing, wildlife-watching, and, if the waves permit, swimming, surfing, boogie boarding, and snorkeling. The town's two stores can provide your necessities.

Back at the fork (23 mi/37 km from the highway), continue along the left branch about 2 miles (3.2 km) through Mayto (pop. 100), which has two stores and a friendly **auto mechanic.** His name is Arias Gonzales, and his establishment is marked by a fence hung with dozens of eerie cow skulls.

A right fork just after Mayto leads a quarter mile to **Playa Mayto,** a surf fishing and beachcomber's haven where you can either park your RV or tent on the beach or stay at the excellent family-friendly beachfront **⟨ Hotel Mayto** (tel.

322/120-6206, www.mayto.com.mx, $40 pp, children $10). Amenities include eight simply furnished but clean and comfortable rooms, most with two beds; a big swimming pool; shady palm grove; green lawn; fishing tours; horses to ride; hammocks; and a restaurant. And get this: As remote as it is, they now have air-conditioning, plentiful hot water, satellite TV, and even Wi-Fi should you need to check your email! If you aren't interested in spending the night, you can make a lengthy day trip to Mayto beach and enjoy the facilities of the hotel as long as you dine at the restaurant.

Just down the road a few hundred yards is the **El Rinconcito Hotel** (tel. 322/105-7024, $25), with its air-conditioned rooms, general store, and restaurant with pool table. Owner Fernando's wife, Marisela, does the cooking, so you could honestly call it homemade.

The Mayto beach seems to stretch endlessly in the distance, and it's a wonderful place to lose yourself in your thoughts as you walk the shoreline. You will most likely be completely alone. Although the beach is pristine and

THE JALISCO COAST

THE JALISCO COAST

Summer weather in Cabo Corrientes can bring a deluge.

© JUSTIN HENDERSON

remote, the surf can get rough. There is also a sharp drop just off the beach, which can make for dangerous undertow conditions, so use precaution when swimming. When the conditions are right (depending on wind and swell), Playa Mayto can be great for kiteboarding or surfing.

## TEHUALMIXTLE

Back on the main road, continue about 1 mile (1.6 km) to another fork (at 26 mi/42 km). The right branch goes steeply up and then down a rough track to the right, which soon levels out on the cliff above the idyllic fishing cove of Tehualmixtle. Here, a headland shelters a blue nook, where a few launches float, tethered and protected from the open sea, and a small village nestles. To one side, swells wash over a submerged wreck, while an ancient moss-stained warehouse crumbles above a rocky little beach. At the end of the road downhill, a pair of beachside *palapas* invites visitors with drinks and fresh-out-of-the-water oysters, lobster, dorado, and red snapper.

**Candelario** ("Cande"), owner/operator of

the right-side *palapa,* is the moving force behind this pocket paradise. After your repast and a couple more bottles of beer for good measure, he might tell you his version of the history of this coast—stories of sunken galleons or of the days when the old warehouse stored cocaine for legal shipment to the United States, when Coca-Cola got its name from the cocaine that was added to produce "the pause that refreshes."

Nowadays, however, Tehualmixtle is almost a town, and it serves as a resting point for occasional sailors, travelers, fisherfolk, and those who enjoy the rewards of clear-water snorkeling and scuba diving around the sunken shrimp trawler and the rocky shoreline nearby. Several level spots beside the cove invite camping or RV parking. Candelario and his wife and daughters will gladly supply you with your stomach's delight of choice seafood and drinks.

Furthermore, Candelario and his family, led by friendly, outgoing English-speaking daughter Gaby (who heads the local tourism delegation), have built a small **hotel** (tel.

322/278-8708, $25 s, $30 d, $35 t). They offer four clean, simply furnished rooms with shiny white bathrooms, ocean-view windows, and ceiling fans. Additionally, they rent out a comfortable ocean-view bungalow ($45/night; discount for a one-week stay) sleeping five that's fine for groups, with a kitchenette, good bathroom, and ceiling fans.

For those who stay a few days, Candelario offers his services as a **guide** for turtle-watching (summer-fall season), fishing trips, and for equipped snorkelers and scuba divers to investigate nearby sites, especially the submerged wreck right offshore. He can also lead parties farther afield, inland a few miles, by foot or horseback, to hot spring **Tlalpuyeque,** where, years ago, a French company operated a logging concession.

## Southeast of Tehualmixtle

Returning back up the road above the cove, you'll catch a glimpse southward of the azure Bay of Tehualmixtle washing the white-sand ribbon of the Playa de Tehualmixtle. The village of **Ipala,** 3 miles (4.8 km) down the road, is supply headquarters (unleaded gasoline available) for the occasional visitors drawn by the good fishing, surfing, beachcombing, and camping prospects of the Playa de Tehualmixtle. Being on the open ocean, its waves are usually rough, especially in the afternoon. Only experienced swimmers who can judge undertow and surf should think of swimming here.

From Ipala (29 mi/47 km), you can either retrace your path back to the highway at El Tuito, or continue down the coast (where the road gets rougher before it gets better) through the hamlet and beach of **Peñitas** (36 mi/58 km), which has a few stores, beach cabanas for rent, restaurants, and an occasionally excellent surfing wave. Next you'll pass **Mismaloya** (46 mi/74 km), site of a University of Guadalajara turtle-hatching station. To get there, turn right onto the rough dirt road just before the concrete bridge over the broad Río María Garcia. From Mismaloya, return to the bridge, ford the river (during low water) 3 miles (4.8 km)

farther, and you'll soon be back in the 21st century at **Cruz de Loreto** (49 mi/79 km), equipped with many stores, sidewalks, electric lights, and phones.

After all the backcountry hard traveling, treat yourself to at least one night at luxury ecoresort ◖ **Hotelito Desconocido** (Playón de Mismaloya s/n, La Cruz de Loreto, tel. 322/281-4010, toll-free Mex. tel. 01-800/013-1313, toll-free U.S. tel. 800/851-1143, www.hotelito.com). The accommodations—deluxe (but rustically candlelit) thatched cabanas on stilts beside an idyllic lagoon, or on the deserted beach across the lagoon—rent from $625 d low season to $825 high for the least expensive, to about $1,025 for the most, with breakfast. Add $90 per person for lunch and dinner. Inquire locally for directions, or follow the signs west to the hotel at the lagoon and beach nearby. Reservations are strongly recommended.

If you decide not to stay at Hotelito Desconocido, return to Highway 200 directly from Cruz de Loreto by heading east 10 miles/16 kilometers (via Santiago and El Gargantino) to the highway at the Kilometer 133 marker, just 23 miles (37 km) south of where you started at El Tuito.

## CAJÓN DE LAS PEÑAS RESERVOIR

The lush farms of the Cabo Corrientes region owe much of their success to the Cajón de las Peñas dam, whose waters enable farmers to profit from a year-round growing season. An added bonus is the recreation—boating, fishing, swimming, camping, and hiking—the big blue lake behind the dam makes possible.

With a car, the reservoir is easy to reach. Trucks and cars are frequent, so hikers can easily thumb rides. At Highway 200 Kilometer 131, about a mile south of the Cruz de Loreto turnoff, head left (east) at a signed, paved road. After about 9 miles (14.5 km) the road forks, and you'll see several ways to go. Continue counterclockwise around the lake. Within about two miles (three km) you'll arrive at the boat-cooperative village, where several downscale *palapa* restaurants and boat landings

# SAVING TURTLES

Sea turtles were once common on Puerto Vallarta beaches. Times have changed, however. Now a determined corps of volunteers literally camps out on isolated strands, trying to save the turtles from extinction. This is a tricky business, because their poacher opponents are invariably poor, determined, and often armed. Since turtle tracks lead right to the eggs, the trick is to get there before the poachers. The turtle savers dig up the eggs and hatch them themselves, or bury them in secret locations where they hope the eggs will hatch unmolested. The reward—the sight of hundreds of new hatchlings returning to the sea—is worth the pain for this new generation of Mexican ecoactivists.

Once featured on a thousand restaurant menus from Puerto Ángel to Mazatlán, turtle meat, soup, and eggs are now illegal commodities. Though not extinct, the Mexican Pacific's three scarcest sea turtle species—green, hawksbill, and leatherback—have dwindled to a tiny fraction of their previous numbers.

The **green turtle** (*Chelonia mydas*), known locally as *tortuga verde* or *caguama*, is more black than green. Its name comes from the light-green tint of its fat. Although officially threatened, the prolific green turtle remains relatively numerous, with about 100,000 nesting females worldwide. Females can return to shore up to eight times during the year, depositing 500 eggs in a single season. When not mating or migrating, the vegetarian green turtles can be spotted most often in lagoons and bays, especially the Bay of Banderas, nipping at seaweed with their beaks. Adults, usually 3 or 4 feet (1 or 1.2 m) long and weighing 300-400 pounds (135-180 kg), are easily identified out of water by the four big plates on either side of their shells. Green-turtle meat was once prized as the main ingredient in turtle soup.

The severely endangered **hawksbill** (*Eretmochelys imbricata*), with only about 20,000 nesting females worldwide, has vanished from many Mexican Pacific beaches. Known locally as the *tortuga carey*, it was the source of both meat and the lovely translucent tortoiseshell that has been supplanted largely by plastic.

Adult *careys*, among the smaller of sea turtles, run 2-3 feet (0.6-1 m) in length and weigh 100-150 pounds (45-70 kg). Their usually brown shells are readily identified by shinglelike overlapping scales. During late summer and fall, females come ashore to lay clutches of eggs (around 100) in the sand. *Careys*, although preferring fish, mollusks, and shellfish, will eat most anything, including seaweed. When attacked, *careys* can be plucky fighters, inflicting bites with their eagle-sharp bills. Playa Teopa is one of its few nesting sites on the Mexican Pacific Coast.

You'll be fortunate indeed if you glimpse the rare **leatherback** (*Dermochelys coriacea*), the world's largest turtle. Until recent years, even experts knew little about the leatherback, *tortuga de cuero*, but now they estimate that it's severely endangered, with only about 35,000 nesting females worldwide. Tales are told of fisherfolk netting 7- or 8-foot (2- or 2.5-m) leatherbacks weighing nearly a ton apiece. If you see even a small one, you'll recognize it immediately by its back of smooth, tough skin (instead of a shell), creased with several lengthwise ridges.

Prospects are better for the more abundant (800,000 nesting females), although still endangered, **olive ridley** or *golfina* (*Lepidochelys olivacea*) turtle, which nests at a number of beaches along the Mexican Pacific coast. With a noticeably narrow head, it's one of the smallest of sea turtles, adults averaging only about 90 pounds (40 kg) and 2 feet (0.6 m) in length. Its name derives from the adult turtle's olive-green shell. Partly due to the persistence of dedicated volunteers, the olive ridley seems to be making a comeback in the Puerto Vallarta region, where there are nesting sites on the Jalisco Coast (at Playa Mismaloya, in Cabo Corrientes country, near Cruz de Loreto) and on the Nayarit Coast at San Francisco (north of Sayulita) and Playa Tortuga (north of Las Varas, on the road to San Blas). The group of volunteers at San Francisco (www.project-tortuga.org) reports more than a tenfold increase (several hundred) of nest sites since the 1990s.

provide food and recreational services for visitors. For a fee—ask at one of the restaurants, *"¿Hay una tarifa para acampar?"* ("Is there a fee to camp?")—you can usually set up a tent or park your RV under a nearby lakeside tree. Better yet, try Rancho Andrea.

**Rancho Andrea** (Calle El Dique, Domicilio Conocido, Cajon de las Penas, tel. 322/225-8294, www.ranchoandrea.com, $65, $70 with kitchenette) offers rustic cabins, cooking facilities, lake tours, fishing guides, and all else. This is the place to stop, whether you're here for a day or overnight. In addition to fishing for largemouth and/or Florida bass, you can birdwatch, water-ski, or kayak/explore the lake.

## PLAYA CHALACATEPEC

Playa Chalacatepec (chah-lah-kah-tay-PEK) lazes in the tropical sun just 6 miles (10 km) from the highway at Kilometer 88. Remarkably few people know of its charms except a handful of local youths, a few fisherfolk, and occasional families who come on Sunday outings, and the resident volunteers of the beachfront Tortuguera Verde Valle (Green Valley Turtle Encampment).

Playa Chalacatepec, with three distinct parts, has something for everyone: On the south side, a wild, arrow-straight, miles-long strand with crashing open-ocean breakers; in the middle, a low, wave-tossed rocky point; and, on the north, a long, tranquil, curving fine-sand beach. One of the few natural amenities that Playa Chalacatepec lacks is drinking water, however. Bring your own from the town back on the highway.

The north beach, shielded by the point, has gently rolling breakers good for surfing, bodysurfing, and safe swimming. Shells seasonally carpet its gradual white slope, and visitors have even left a pair of *palapa* shelters. These seem ready-made for camping by night and barbecuing fish by day with all of the driftwood lying around for the taking.

The point, Punta Chalacatepec, which separates the two beaches, is good for pole fishing on its surf-washed flanks and tide pooling in its rocky crevices.

Folks with RVs can pull off and park either along the approach road just above the beach or along tracks (beware of soft spots) downhill in the tall acacia scrub that borders the sand.

### Getting There

Just as you're entering little José María Morelos (pop. 2,000), 100 feet past the Kilometer 88 marker, turn right at the signed dirt road toward the beach at the corner. (Note the telephone booth.) If you're planning to camp, stock up with water and groceries at the stores in the town down the road, south.

The road, although steep in spots, is negotiable by passenger cars in good condition and small to medium RVs. Owners of big rigs should do a test run. On foot, the road is an easy two-hour hike—much of which probably won't be necessary because of the many passing farm pickups.

Mark your odometer at the highway. Continue over brushy hills and past fields and pastures, until Mile 5.2 (Km 8.4), where the main road veers right. Instead, continue straight ahead, over the dune, to the beach, at Mile 5.4 (Km 8.7), where the road turns left (south) and parallels the beach. Pass turtle encampment Tortuguera Verde Valle at Mile 5.9 (Km 9.5). Steer right downhill to Playa Chalacatepec at Mile 6 (Km 9.7). Several choice parking sites are available in the high brush bordering the beach (be careful of soft sand), and you may have the good company of the turtle-saving volunteers (most likely during the July-October turtle season), who would probably appreciate any help you can give them.

### LAS ALAMANDAS

After roughing it at Playa Chalacatepec, you can be pampered in the luxurious isolation of ◖ **Las Alamandas** (Quémaro, Km 83, Carretera Puerto Vallarta-Barra de Navidad, tel. 322/285-5500, toll-free U.S./Can. tel. 888/882-9616, www.alamandas.com), a deluxe 1,500-acre retreat a few miles down the road.

The small Quémaro village sign at Kilometer 83 gives no hint of the pleasant surprises that Las Alamandas conceals behind its guarded gate. Solitude and elegant simplicity seem to have been the driving concepts in the mind of Isabel Goldsmith when she acquired control of the property in the late 1980s. Although born into wealth (her grandfather was the late tin tycoon Antenor Patiño, who developed Manzanillo's renowned Las Hadas; her father was the late multimillionaire Sir James Goldsmith, who bought the small kingdom her family now owns at Cuitzmala, 25 miles south), she was not idle. Isabel converted her dream of paradise—a small, luxuriously isolated resort on an idyllic beach in Puerto Vallarta's sylvan coastal hinterland—into reality. Now, her guests (28 maximum) enjoy accommodations that vary from luxuriously simple studios to a villa sleeping six. Activities include tennis, horseback riding, bicycling, fishing, kayaking, snorkeling, and lagoon and river excursions.

The hotel's luxurious facilities—dining restaurant and veranda, bars, book and video library, sitting and reading areas, pool patio, gym, pavilions, and much more—are gracefully sprinkled throughout a plumy, grass-carpeted, beachfront palm grove. Powerful waves, good for intermediate and advanced surfing, on the south and north shoals rise about 100 yards out and break rather quickly at the creamy yellow-sand beach. With about twice as many employees as guests, the hotel's service is personal. Staff are attentive and focused on the goal of complete guest relaxation.

Daily rates range from about $370 low season ($488 high) for garden-view studios, up to about $1,499 low season ($2,070 high) for the Presidential Suite. Three meals, prepared to your order, cost about $135 more per day per person. For reservations, contact Las Alamandas directly or book through their agent, Mexico Boutique Hotels (toll-free U.S./Can. tel. 800/728-7098, www.mexicobou-tiquehotels.com).

Get there by car, taxi (about $100), bus, or rental car from the Puerto Vallarta airport via Highway 200. At the Kilometer 83 highway marker, 81 miles (130 km) south of Puerto Vallarta, turn right at the signed Quémaro

village side road. Continue about 3 miles (4.8 km) west, passing through Quémaro village, to the Alamandas gate. Don't arrive unannounced; unless you're a recognizable celebrity, the guard will not let you through the gate without a reservation in hand or unless you have made an advance appointment. Alternatively, you can arrive by charter airplane, using Las Alamandas's private airstrip. If you don't have a plane, contact a travel agent.

## CHAMELA BAY

Most longtime visitors know Jalisco's coast through Barra de Navidad and two big, beautiful beach-lined bays: Tenacatita and Chamela. Tranquil Bahía de Chamela, the most northerly of the two, is broad, blue, dotted with islands, and lined by a strip of fine honey-yellow sand.

Stretching five miles (eight km) south from the sheltering Punta Rivas headland near Perula village, Chamela Bay is open but calm. A chain of intriguingly labeled rocky *islitas*, such as Cocinas (Kitchens), Negrita (Little Black One), and Pajarera (Place of Birds), scatter the strong Pacific swells into gentle billows by the time they roll onto the beaches.

Besides its natural amenities, Chamela Bay has three bungalow complexes, one mentionable motel, two trailer parks, and an unusual "camping club." The focal point of this low-key resort area is the Kilometer 72 highway corner (88 mi/142 km from Puerto Vallarta, 46 mi/74 km to Barra de Navidad). This spot, which on many maps is incorrectly marked Chamela (actually the village at Km 63), is known simply as **"El Super"** by local people. Though the supermarket and neighboring bank have closed and are filled with the owner's dusty antique car collection, El Super nevertheless lives on in the minds of the local folks.

### Beaches and Recreation

Chamela Bay's beaches are variations on one continuous strip of sand, from Playa Rosadas in the south through Playa Chamela in the middle to Playas Fortuna and Perula at the north end.

Curving behind the sheltering headland, **Playa Perula** is the broadest and most tranquil beach of Chamela Bay. It is best for children and a snap for boat launching, swimming, and fishing from the rocks nearby. A dozen *pangas* usually line the water's edge, ready to take visitors on fishing excursions (figure $15 per hour, after bargaining) and snorkeling around the offshore islets. A line of seafood *palapas* provide food and drinks for the fisherfolk and mostly Mexican families who know and enjoy this scenic little village/cove.

**Playas Fortuna, Chamela, and Rosada:** As you head south, the beach gradually changes character. The surf roughens, the slope steepens, and the sand narrows from around 200 feet (61 m) at Perula to perhaps 100 feet (30.5 m) at the south end of the bay. Civilization also thins out. The dusty village of stores, small eateries, vacation homes, and beachfront *palapa* restaurants that line Playa Fortuna gives way to farmland and scattered houses at Playa Chamela. Two miles (3.2 km) farther on, grassy dunes above trackless sand line Playa Rosada.

The gradually varying vigor of the waves and the isolation of the beach determine the place where you can indulge your own favorite pastimes. For bodysurfing and boogie boarding, Rosada and Chamela are best, and while sailboarding is usually possible anywhere on Chamela Bay, it will be best beyond the tranquil waves at La Fortuna. For surf fishing, try casting beyond the vigorous, breaking billows of Rosada. And Rosada, being the most isolated, will be the place where you'll most likely find that shell-collection treasure you've been wishing for.

The five-mile curving strand of Chamela Bay is perfect for a morning hike from Rosada Beach. To get there, ride a Transportes Cihuatlán second-class bus to around the Kilometer 65 marker, where a dirt road heads a half mile (0.8 km) to the beach. With the sun comfortably at your back, you can walk all the way to Perula if you want, stopping for refreshments at any one of several *palapas* along the way. The firm sand of Chamela Bay beaches is likewise good for jogging, even for bicycling, provided you don't mind cleaning the sand out of the gears afterward.

## El Super Accommodations

The **Paraíso Costalegre** (Km 72, Carretera 200, Barra de Navidad-Puerto Vallarta, tel. 315/333-9778 or 315/333-9777, www.paraisocostalegre.com.mx) is a good choice, with bungalows and villas for rent. There are several options for lodging at Paraíso Costalegre, including cabins on the beach to larger villas that are excellent for families or groups. The small beachfront cabins sleep up to six people and can be had for the price of an average hotel room (in Mexico at least): $47 d low season, $58 d high. For larger groups, consider renting Villa Costalegre, which sleeps up to 10 people ($243 low season, $305 high). Although they are simple accommodations, they are clean and spacious.

Still need more space? Rent Villa Sol or Villa Luna, either of which can sleep up to 14 people under the massive *palapa* roof ($378 low season, $472 high). All of the villas have full kitchens. Other amenities besides the beach that guests can enjoy include the swimming pool, restaurant, and a phone in the office. There are no televisions or phones to interrupt your seclusion. Unfortunately, camping is no longer allowed.

Right across the lane from Paraíso Costalegre stands the **Bungalows Mayar Chamela** (Km 72, Carretera Puerto Vallarta, tel. 315/333-9711). The 18 spacious kitchenette-bungalows with fans and air-conditioning surround an attractive inner garden and a palmy banana-fringed pool and patio. Although the blue meandering pool and leafy grounds are very inviting, the bungalows themselves have suffered from neglect and appear somewhat run-down, if functional enough. Look inside three or four and make sure that everything is in working order before moving in. If so, the bungalows' pool and garden setting and the long, lovely Chamela beach just a block away might be perfect for a week or a month of tranquil relaxation. Rentals run about $44 d, $78 for four; monthly discounts are available. For reservations (usually not necessary), contact the owner, Gabriel Yáñez G. (Obregón 1425 S.L., Guadalajara, Jalisco, tel. 333/644-0044).

Note: The late summer and fall season is pretty empty on the Chamela Bay beaches. Consequently, food is scarce around Paraíso Costalegre and Bungalows Mayar Chamela. Meals, however, are available at the restaurant at the El Super corner, at a few groceries and small stores along the highway nearby, or in San Mateo village, a mile south.

## Perula Accommodations

At Kilometer 74, a sign marks a paved road to Playas Fortuna and Perula. About 2 miles (3.2 km) downhill, right on the beach, you can't miss the bright-yellow stucco **Hotel, Bungalows, and Trailer Park Playa Dorada** (Perula, Km 76, Carretera 200 Melaque-Puerto Vallarta, tel. 315/333-9710, fax 315/333-9709, www.playa-dorada.com.mx). More a motel than bungalows, its three tiers of very plain rooms and suites with kitchenettes are nearly empty except on weekends and Mexican holidays.

Playa Dorada's two saving graces, however, are the beach, which curves gracefully to the scenic little fishing nook of Perula, and its inviting palm-shaded pool and patio. The best-situated rooms are on the top floor, overlooking the ocean. The 60 attractively painted rooms sleeping two or three rent for about $53, while 15 kitchenette units sleeping four go for about $72; all include air-conditioning and parking. Discounts are customarily available for weekly rentals.

Folks who take one of the dozen trailer spaces in the bare lot across the street are welcome to lounge all day beneath the palms of the pool and patio. Spaces rent for about $18/day, $500/month, with all hookups, showers, and toilets.

It's easy to miss the low-profile **Hotel Punta Perula** (Perula, Km 76, Carretera 200, Melaque-Puerto Vallarta, tel. 315/333-9782), just one block inland from the Bungalows Playa Dorada. This homey place seems like a scene from Old Mexico (which also means it has no pool, of course), with a rustic white stucco tier of rooms enclosing a spacious green garden and venerable tufted grove. Its 14 clean, gracefully

decorated colonial-style fan-equipped rooms go for about $38 a day for two beds (except for Christmas and Easter holidays). Bargain for lower long-term rates.

Also occupying the same luscious beachfront nearby is **Red Snapper RV Park and Restaurant** (P.O. Box 42, Melaque, Jalisco 48980, tel. 315/333-9784, redsnapper@hotmail.com, $18/day, $65/wk, $250/mo), life project of friendly North American owners Harry, Carmen, and Bonnie Adams. Here, what you see is what you get: a dozen largely shadeless fenced-in spaces with all hookups (including 30 amp power), showers, toilets, washing machine, and beachfront restaurant *palapa*. Gorgeous Chamela Bay is ripe for surf or boat fishing (launch right from the beach), surfing, and kiteboarding. A 15-foot, 25-horsepower Zodiac is available for fishing. Note that the Red Snapper RV Park is seasonal and closes April-October.

## Camping

For RVs, the best spots are the trailer parks at **Paraíso Costalegre** (Km 72, Carretera 200, Barra de Navidad-Puerto Vallarta, tel. 315/333-9778 or 315/333-9777, www.paraisocostalegre.com.mx), the **Hotel, Bungalows, and Trailer Park Playa Dorada** (Perula, Km 76, Carretera 200 Melaque-Puerto Vallarta, tel. 315/333-9710, fax 315/333-9709, www.playa-dorada.com.mx), and the seasonal **Red Snapper RV Park and Restaurant** (P.O. Box 42, Melaque, Jalisco 48980, tel. 315/333-9784, redsnapper@hotmail.com).

If you can walk in, you can probably set up a tent anywhere along the bay you like. One of the best places would be the grassy dune along Playa Rosada.

**Playa Negrita,** the pristine little sand crescent that marks the southern end of Chamela Bay, offers still another picnic or camping possibility. Get there by following the dirt road angling downhill from the highway at the south end of the bridge between Kilometer 63 and Kilometer 64. Turn left at the Chamela village stores beneath the bridge, continue about 2 miles (3.2 km), and bear left to the end of the road, where a restaurant *palapa* stands at beachside. This is the southernmost of two islet-protected coves flanking the low Punta Negro headland. With clear, tranquil waters and golden-sand beaches, both coves are great for fishing from the rocks, snorkeling, sailboarding, and swimming. The gorgeous south-end beach, Playa Negrita, is offered as a campground, with plenty of room for tenting and RV parking; a friendly caretaker sometimes collects about $2.50 per day per car. On weekends and holidays the restaurant provides drinks and seafood lunches and dinners.

## Food

Groceries are available at stores near the **El Super** corner (Km 72) or in the villages of **Perula** (on the beach; turn off at Km 74), **San Mateo** (Km 70), and **Chamela** (walk north along the beach, or follow the side road, downhill, at the south end of the bridge between Km 64 and 63).

Hearty country Mexican food, hospitality, and snack groceries are available at the **Tejeban** truck stop/restaurant (tel. 315/333-9705, morning-10:30pm daily) at the El Super corner. Two popular local roadside seafood spots (8am-9pm daily, $5-10) are the **La Viuda** (The Widow, Km 64) and **Don Lupe Mariscos** (Km 63), on opposite ends of the Río Chamela bridge. They both have their own divers who go out daily for fresh fish, octopus (*pulpo*), conch, clams, oysters, and lobster.

## Information and Services

The closest bank is 34 miles (54.7 km) north at Tomatlán (turnoff at La Cumbre, Km 116). A card-operated telephone operates outside at the El Super corner, in addition to long-distance telephones inside the adjacent Tejeban restaurant and at the Centro de Salud at Pueblo Careyes, the village behind the soccer field at Kilometer 52.

Until someone resurrects the Pemex *gasolinera* at El Super, the closest unleaded gasoline is 27 miles (43 km) north at La Cumbre (Km 116) or 50 miles (80 km) south at Melaque (Km 0).

If you get sick, the closest health clinics are in Perula (Km 74, one block north of the town plaza, no phone, but a pharmacy) and at Pueblo Careyes at Kilometer 52 (medical consultations 8am-2pm daily; doctor on call around the clock for emergencies).

Local special police, known as the Policia Auxiliar del Estado, are stationed in a pink roadside house at Kilometer 46, and also in the house above the road at Kilometer 43. The local *preventiva* (municipal police) are stationed about a half mile (0.8 km) north of the El Super corner.

## PLAYA CAREYES

At Kilometer 52, just south of a small bridge and a bus stop, is a gated guard station with a sign labeled Costa Careyes. The guard, whose job is to provide security for the beach *palapa* restaurants and the houses atop the neighboring headlands, will let you park at the gate (there is space for about 10 cars) and walk in, as cars are no longer allowed into this lovely little public beach. From the gate, it's a five-minute walk to the beach. Beyond the often powerful waves (swim with caution), the intimate headland-framed bay brims with outdoor possibilities. Bird- and wildlife-watching can be quite rewarding; notice the herons, egrets, and cormorants in the lagoon just south of the dune. Fishing is good either from the beach, by boat (launch from the sheltered north end), or from the rocks on either side. Water is generally clear for snorkeling and, beyond the waves, good for kayaking. If you have no boat, no problem—the local fishing cooperative (boats beached by the food *palapa* at the north end) would be happy to take you on a fishing trip. Figure about $20 per hour, with bargaining. Afterward, they might even cook up the catch for a big afternoon dinner at their tree-shaded *palapa* restaurant, which sits behind the beach next door to the private Cocodrilo Azul restaurant. This beautiful private dining club, built atop wooden platforms in a lush garden setting, is for the use of the wealthy homeowners in the area, but it is open to the public on weekends.

As for services, **Pueblo Careyes** (inland,

behind the soccer field at Km 52) has a Centro de Salud (tel. 335/351-0170), with a pharmacy and long-distance telephone.

Access to the neighboring **Playa Teopa** is more carefully guarded. The worthy reason is to save the hatchlings of the *carey* turtles that still come ashore during the late summer and fall to lay eggs. For a closer look at Playa Teopa, you could walk south along the dunetop track, although guards might eventually stop you.

The pristine tropical deciduous woodlands that stretch for miles around Kilometer 45 are no accident. They are preserved as part of the **Fideicomiso Cuitzmala** (Cuitzmala Trust), the local kingdom of beach, headland, and forest held by the family of late multimillionaire Sir James Goldsmith. Local officials, many of whom were not privy to Sir James's grand design (which includes a sprawling sea-view mansion complex), say that a team of biologists are conducting research on the property. A ranch complex, accessible through a gate at Kilometer 45, is Fideicomiso Cuitzmala's most obvious highway-visible landmark.

## PLAYA LAS BRISAS

For a tranquil day, overnight, or weeklong beach camping and surfing adventure, consider hidden Playa las Brisas, a few miles by the dirt road (turnoff sign near Km 36) through the village of Arroyo Seco. The same name, Arroyo Seco, applies to the surf spot here—two spots really, one on each side of the headland that divides the beach. Follow the signs to Playa Chica, and en route you'll find the local surf shop, **Christianos** (tel. 315/111-0041, www.christianossurfteam. org), run by Artemio and Sandra Rosas. Bilingual Artemio spent a fair amount of time in Southern California and offers surfing lessons, surf trips, surf and boogie board rentals, and plenty of information on local waves. The pounding peaks of Playa Chica are another five minutes down the road past his shop, or backtrack to town to find your way to Playa Grande, the other surfing beach, which has generally smaller waves than Playa Chica.

About 2 miles (3.2 km) long, Playa Grande—which I refer to as Playa las Brisas here—has two distinct sections. First comes a very broad, white sandy strand decorated by pink-blossomed verbena and pounded by wild open-ocean waves. For shady tent camping or RV parking, a regal coconut grove lines the beach. Before you set up, however, you should offer a little rent to the owner/caretaker, who may soon show up on a horse. Don't be alarmed by his machete; it's for husking and cutting fallen coconuts.

To see the other half of Playa las Brisas, continue along the road past the little beachside vacation home subdivision (with a seasonal store and snack bar). You will soon reach an open-ocean beach and headland backed by a big, level, grassy dune, perfect for tent or RV camping. Take care not to get stuck in soft spots, however.

The headland borders the El Tecuán lagoon, part of the Rancho El Tecuán, whose hilltop hotel you can see on the far side of the lagoon. The lagoon is an unusually rich fish and wildlife habitat.

## Getting There

You can reach the village of Arroyo Seco, where stores can furnish supplies, 2.3 miles (3.7 km) from the highway at Kilometer 36. At the central plaza, turn left, then immediately right at the Conasupo rural store, then left again, heading up the steep dirt road. In the valley on the other side, bear right at the fork at the mango grove, and within another mile you will be in the majestic beach-bordering palm grove.

## HOTEL EL TECUÁN

Little was spared in perching the Hotel El Tecuán above its small kingdom of beach, lagoon, and palm-brushed rangeland. It was to be the centerpiece of a sprawling vacationland, with marina, golf course, and hundreds of houses and condos. The hotel was abandoned permanently and now sits unoccupied and for sale. The location was used in the Hollywood film *I Still Know What You Did Last Summer.*

Masculinity bulges out of its architecture. Its corridors are lined with massive polished tree trunks, fixed by brawny master joints to thick hand-hewn mahogany beams. The sea-view restaurant was patterned after the midships of a Manila galleon, complete with a pair of varnished tree-trunk masts reaching into the inky darkness of the night sky above. If the restaurant could only sway, the illusion would have been complete.

## Wildlife-Watching and Hiking

It is perhaps fortunate that the former hotel and its surroundings, part of the big **Rancho Tecuán,** may never be developed into a residential community. Since the land is private, public access has always been limited, allowing the rancho to become a de facto habitat-refuge for the rapidly diminishing local animal population. Wildcats, ocelots, small crocodiles, snakes, and turtles hunt in the mangroves edging the lagoon and the tangled forest that climbs the surrounding hills. The lagoon itself nurtures hosts of waterbirds and shoals of *robalo* (snook) and *pargo* (snapper).

As of this writing, visitors were still being allowed to pass along the entrance road and enjoy wildlife-watching opportunities. If such visitors tread softly, clean up after themselves, start no fires, and refrain from fishing or hunting, the present owners may continue to allow access. This would be ideal, because wildlife-watching here is superb. First, simply walk along the lagoon front below the hotel hilltop, where big white herons and egrets perch and preen in the mangroves. Don't forget your binoculars, sun hat, mosquito repellent, telephoto camera, and identification book. Try launching your own rowboat, canoe, or inflatable raft for an even more rewarding outing. Adventurous drivers can also reach the lagoon by driving all the way to the south end of Playa Las Brisas and then bearing left at the fork at the end of the dirt beach road. This easily driveable if narrow and overgrown dirt road then winds for several kilometers along the inland edge of the lagoon. There are a few spots where you can pull off and, if you have a boat, take a watery tour. Eventually the road connects with the lagoon entrance road, about half a mile in from

the gate. There are virtually no places to turn around on this road, however, so once you take the plunge, you're committed.

The environs offer plenty of jogging and walking opportunities. For starters, stroll along the lagoon-side entrance road and back (3 mi/4.8 km) or south along the beach to the Río Purificación and back (4 mi/6.4 km). Take water, mosquito repellent, sunscreen, a hat, and something to carry your beachcombing treasures in.

### ◖ Playa el Tecuán

The focal point of the long, wild, white-sand Playa el Tecuán is at the north end, where, at low tide, the lagoon's waters stream into the sea. Platoons of waterbirds—giant brown herons, snowy egrets, and squads of pelicans, ibises, and grebes—stalk and dive for fish trapped in the shallow rushing current.

On the beach nearby, the sand curves southward beneath a rocky point, where the waves strew rainbow carpets of limpet, clam, and snail shells. There the billows rise sharply, angling shoreward, often with good intermediate and advanced surfing breaks. Casual swimmers beware; the powerful surf can be dangerous.

### Getting There

The former Hotel El Tecuán is 6 miles (10 km) along a paved entrance road marked by a white lighthouse at Kilometer 33 (112 mi/181 km from Puerto Vallarta, 22 mi/35 km from Barra de Navidad).

## PLAYA TENACATITA

A developer has laid claim to this entire piece of waterfront, dispossessing numerous land, home, and business owners. There are legal challenges in the works, but meanwhile, this beach-lovers' paradise (which in the past had offered free camping on a long curve of clean white sand) is not accessible. As of this writing, access to Playa Tenacatita is now limited to a small parking area at the north end of the beach, and that access comes only after passing through a checkpoint, manned by armed guards in military uniforms who demand to

## *JEJENES:* DON'T LET NO-SEE-UMS RUIN YOUR VACATION

*Jejenes* are the vicious, invisible biting gnats that cause many tourists a great many sleepless and itchy nights. They are the unseen predators that haunt many of Mexico's prime beach locations, feasting on unsuspecting visitors (you won't find locals out and about during prime *jejene* time). The most notorious spots for *jejenes* in Nayarit and Jalisco are San Blas and Tenacatita.

Summer or winter—it doesn't matter to these pests. They are most active during the dawn and dusk hours, and no sane person should be out at those times without being slathered in DEET-laden mosquito repellent. But even DEET can't fully protect you. According to Lorena Havens and an experiment done by a very brave test subject on the **People's Guide to Mexico** website (www.peoplesguide.com), adding about 20 drops of pennyroyal oil herbal extract to your repellent (organic or commercial containing DEET) will keep the bugs at bay.

see identification. Hopefully, in the future the issues will be resolved and Tenacatita will become again what it once was. Look for updated information on the land seizure at www.tomzap.com/tenaca.html.

## BLUE BAY CLUB LOS ANGELES LOCOS

Although the Blue Bay resort chain has been operating the former Hotel Los Angeles Locos as an all-inclusive resort for several years, the curious name Los Angeles Locos (which had nothing to do with crazy people from Los Angeles) lives on in the minds of local people. Once upon a time, a rich family built an airstrip and a mansion by a lovely little beach on pristine Tenacatita Bay and began coming for vacations by private plane. The local people, who couldn't fathom why their rich neighbors would go to so much trouble and expense to come to such an out-of-the-way place, dubbed them *los ángeles locos* (the crazy angels) because they always seemed to be flying.

The beach is still lovely, and Tenacatita Bay, curving around Punta Hermanos south from Tenacatita Beach, is still pristine. Now Los Angeles Locos have made it possible for droves of sun-seeking vacationers to enjoy it en masse. Continuous music, open bar, plentiful buffets, and endless activities set the tone at Los Angeles Locos—the kind of place for folks who want a hassle-free week of fun in the sun. The guests are typically working-age couples and singles, mostly Mexicans during the summer, Canadians and some Americans during the winter. Very few children seem to be among the guests, although they are welcome.

### Recreation

Although all sports and lessons—including tennis, snorkeling, sailing, sailboarding, horseback riding, volleyball, aerobics, other exercises, and waterskiing, plus dancing, disco, and games—cost nothing extra, guests can, if they want, do nothing but soak up the sun. A relaxed attitude will probably allow you to enjoy yourself the most. Don't try to eat, drink, and do too much to make sure you get your money's worth. If you do, you're liable to arrive back home in need of a vacation.

Although people don't come to the tropics to stay inside, Los Angeles Locos's rooms are quite comfortable—completely private, in pastels and white, air-conditioned, each with cable TV, phone, and private balcony overlooking either the ocean or palmy pool and patio. There is Internet available as well, but only in the lobby.

### Information

For information and reservations, contact a travel agent or the hotel (Km 20, Carretera Federal 200, tel. 315/351-5020, toll-free Mex. tel. 01-800/713-3020, toll-free U.S. tel.

THE JALISCO COAST

800/483-7986, fax 315/351-5412, www.los-angeleslocos.com). Low-season rates for the 201 rooms and suites run a bargain-basement $84 per person per day midweek, $94 weekends, double occupancy, $126 high season. Children under 7 with parents stay free; children 7-12, $40. For a bigger, better junior suite, add about $50 per room. Prices include everything—food, drinks, entertainment—except transportation.

## Getting There

Los Angeles Locos is about four miles (six km) off Highway 200 along a signed cobbled entrance road near the Kilometer 20 marker (120 mi/194 km from Puerto Vallarta, 14 mi/23 km from Barra de Navidad, and 32 mi/51 km from the Manzanillo International Airport). If you want to simply look around the resort, don't drive up to the gate unannounced. The guard might not let you through. Instead, call ahead and make an appointment for a "tour." After your guided look-see, you have to either sign up or mosey along. The hotel doesn't accept day guests.

## Hotel Punta Serena

Part of the original Los Angeles Locos development, but separate in concept and location, is Punta Serena (through Blue Bay Club Los Angeles Locos switchboard, tel. 315/351-5020, ext. 4013 or 4011, fax 315/351-5412, www.puntaserena.com). Perched on a breezy hilltop overlooking the entire broad sweep of Tenacatita Bay, this is an adults-only romantic retreat with all meals and in-house activities included, plus a big blue ocean-view pool patio, sauna, sea-vista hot tub, gym, and clothing-optional settings. You can also enjoy all of the lively sports, discoing, and beach action of Los Angeles Locos on the beach downhill, at no extra cost. Added-cost amenities include spa services such as a native-Mexican *temescal* hot room and massage.

Paths radiate to the tile-roofed lodging units, spread over the palmy summit park like a garden of giant mushrooms. The units themselves are designer spartan, in white and blue, with modern baths, luxuriously high ceilings, and balconies with broad ocean vistas.

All-inclusive tariffs for the 70 accommodations, all with air-conditioning, run about the same as Hotel Los Angeles Locos. Directions and address are identical to Los Angeles Locos, but turn right at the signed Punta Serena entrance driveway before heading downhill to Los Angeles Locos.

## ◖ PLAYA BOCA DE IGUANAS

Plumy Playa Boca de Iguanas curves for 6 miles (9.7 km) along the tranquil inner recess of the Bay of Tenacatita. The cavernous former beachfront Hotel Bahía Tenacatita, which slumbered for years beneath the grove, is being reclaimed by the jungle and the animals that live in the nearby mangrove marsh after being destroyed in an earthquake in 1995.

The beach, however, is as enjoyable as ever: wide and level, with firm white sand good for hiking, jogging, and beachcombing. Offshore, the gently rolling waves are equally fine for bodysurfing and boogie boarding. Beds of oysters, free for those who dive for them, lie a few hundred feet offshore. A rocky outcropping at the north end invites fishing and snorkeling, while the calm water beyond the breakers invites sailboarding. Bring your own equipment.

Get to Playa Boca de Iguanas by following the signed paved road at Kilometer 17 for 1.5 miles (2.4 km).

## Accommodations

For hotel-style lodging, go to **Coconuts-by-the-Sea** (Bahía Tenacatita, tel. 315/100-8899, www.coconutsbythesea.com, $100 d low season, $125 d high). Owners Bob and Cissie Jones offer four spacious suites in a big hillside house, including full kitchens, fans, air-conditioning, uber-comfortable king-size beds, satellite TV with HBO, and hot showers with plenty of water. The house features a fantastic view of the lovely beach and bay from the hillside, verandas, hammocks, a beautiful swimming pool, and access to creamy Boca de Iguanas beach. Internet is also available. The only restaurant in Boca de Iguanas is at the resort, at the bottom of the hill. A short walk down the steep hillside will deposit guests on the resort grounds and beach. While you can walk up from the beach, road access to this property is from the entrance road to the Blue Bay Los Angeles Locos.

Second choice goes to nearby **Camping Trailer Park Boca Beach** (Km 16.5, Carretera Melaque-Puerto Vallarta, tel. 317/381-0393, fax 317/381-0342, bocabeach@hotmail.com), with about 50 camping and RV spaces shaded beneath a majestic rustling grove. Friendly owners Michel and Bertha Billot (he's French, she's Mexican) have built up their little paradise over the past couple of decades, persisting through hurricanes and at least one tidal wave. Their essentials are in place: electricity, water, showers, toilets, and about 40 spaces with sewer hookups. Much of their five acres is undeveloped and would be fine for tent campers who prefer privacy with the convenience of fresh water, a small store, and congenial company at tables beneath a rustic *palapa*. RV rates run about $17 per day, back from the beach; $26 on the beach; $500 per month for motor home, trailer, or van; including electricity for air-conditioning. Camping runs about $7 per day per group; add $3 for two kids.

A semiluxury option is available at the **Boca de Iguanas Beach Hotel** (Km. 14, Carretera 200, tel. 315/108-5490 or 314/103-4550, www. bocadeiguanas.com). The 10 rooms available at this luxury resort average $328 d low season, $409 d high for the tastefully appointed accommodations, each offering polished concrete whirlpool tub, terrace, flat-screen wall-mounted television with cable, air-conditioning, and wireless Internet. Although they are quite luxurious, these rooms do not have ocean views, and the hotel is set back in the trees well off the beach. Price includes happy hour cocktails. Beach cabanas are available as well, and the prices are somewhat lower ($220 d). The bungalows do not have air-conditioning or television.

The resort beach is beautiful and clean; however, the surf can be strong and difficult to swim in. The hotel hosts a stunning infinity pool with comfy lounge chairs for its guests.

Visitors are welcome to spend the day as long as they make a minimum purchase at the bar or restaurant.

## PLAYA LA MANZANILLA

The little fishing town of La Manzanilla (pop. 2,000) drowses at the opposite end of the same long, curving strip of sand that begins at the Boca de Iguanas trailer park. Here, the beach, Playa la Manzanilla, is as broad and flat and the waves are as gentle, but the sand is several shades darker. Probably no better fishing exists on the entire Costalegre than at La Manzanilla. A dozen seafood *palapas* on the beach manage to stay open by virtue of a trickle of foreign visitors and local weekend and holiday patronage.

Besides its gorgeous beachfront, the only other La Manzanilla sight is the town's family of toothy **crocodiles,** at the south end of main street María Asunción (as you enter the town, a block before the beach, turn right). About six individuals are usually visible, basking in the mangrove-fringed pond, waiting for handouts. The king of the heap, a 12-foot (4-m) grandfather, periodically defends his seniority by fiercely chasing off potential junior rivals.

La Manzanilla has become a haven for a small but growing community of North American expatriates and winter seekers of paradise. A growing cadre of places to stay, including a number of colorful, stunning hillside vacation rentals; restaurants; and services including fishing excursions, adventure biking, hiking, and horseback riding has appeared to cater to visitors' needs. To these eyes, this little pueblo has the makings of another Sayulita, only missing the surf. For more information on all of this ferment, visit www.tomzap.com/manza.html, www.lamanzanilla.biz, and www.lamanzanilla.info. Even better, check in with superfriendly and helpful real estate agent and information provider Ada Zuñiga (tel. 315/351-7101 or 315/107-1275, adalamanazanilla@yahoo.com, www.tenacatitabay.com) to get the lowdown on all things La Manzanillan. If she can't do what you need, she'll steer you to someone who can.

## Accommodations

### UNDER $50

A few recommendable budget hotels accommodate guests.

On the sleepy south-end beachfront edge of town, the **Hotel Puesta del Sol** (Calle Playa Blanca 94, tel./fax 315/351-5033) offers 17 basic rooms around a cool, leafy central patio where the owner has installed a small swimming pool. Low-season rates run about $22 s or d, $32 t; high-season rates are $32 s or d, $50 t. There are discounts for longer-term rentals.

One of the class-act La Manzanilla accommodations is the beautiful **Posada Tonalá** (María Asunción 75, tel./fax 315/351-5474, posadatonala@hotmail.com), life project of kindly owner/builder Alfonso Torres López. Señor López retired from his auto-parts business in Guadalajara and returned to realize his lifelong dream, to contribute to his hometown. You must at least come and look at his handiwork: the graceful teak (*granadillo*) stairway, the vines cascading on one side of the airy lobby, all topped by a uniquely lovely *palapa* roof. His rooms are immaculate and spacious, with modern shower baths and plenty of attractive tile, as well as handsome dark hand-carved furniture and colorful handmade bedspreads. There is plenty of seating on the 2nd-floor balcony and a nice collection of paperbacks and magazines for guests to enjoy. All this for only $38 s or d, $47 t, with air-conditioning, fans, and hot-water shower baths. Add about $15 during Christmas and Easter holidays. Find it on the town's main street, right in the center of town. Beds vary in comfort level, so check a few rooms before you commit.

### $50-100

Enjoy that vacation feeling with a stay at secluded sea-view **Villa Montaña** (Calle Los Angeles Locos 46), on the hillside above and behind the town. Accommodations start at $65 d low season, $139 d high; discounts are available for long-term stays. For more information and reservations, contact Dan Clarke (P.O. Box 16343, Seattle, WA 98116, tel. 206/937-3882, www.lamanzanilla.biz). This is but one of many vacation rental homes available in La Manzanilla, which contains many strikingly beautiful houses with either beachfront or hillside locations. If you want to see some other options, get in touch with real estate agent Ada Zuñiga (tel. 315/351-7101 or 315/107-1275, adalamanazanilla@yahoo.com, www.tenacatitabay.com) or check the listings on www.vrbo.com, which has a substantial number of La Manzanilla homes listed. Alternatively, visit personable Daniel Hallas's **Costalegre Properties** office on main street, María Asunción, beach side; call him in La Manzanilla at 315/351-5059; or visit his website, www.lamanzanilla.info.

Get to La Manzanilla by following the signed paved road at Kilometer 13 for 1 mile (1.6 km). The Posada Tonalá is a block farther, while Hotel Puesta del Sol is a quarter mile farther along; bear right past the town plaza for a few blocks along the beachfront street, Calle Playa Blanca. Villa Montaña is prominent on the hill, a quarter mile north of the town center. You will see many lovely new high-style houses around town and on the hills, and many are available for rent.

## Food

Two local restaurants stand out. For good comfort food, such as pizza, hamburgers, fish fillets, and Mexican plates, go to **Palapa Joe's** (María Asunción 163, tel. 315/351-5348, noon-10pm Tues.-Sat., $3-8). On the other hand, savor the breeze and the swish of the waves at **Martin's** (south end of beachfront Calle Playa Blanca, tel. 315/351-5348, 8am-10pm daily). The open-air *palapa*-style restaurant is a romantic place to dine in the evenings and can get quite crowded during the high season. Try the tortilla soup ($5) and fresh fish specials ($13). There's a full bar for all your tropical cocktail desires.

# Barra de Navidad and Melaque

The little Jalisco country beach town of Barra de Navidad (pop. 5,000), whose name literally means Bar of Christmas, has unexpectedly few saloons. However, this bar has nothing to do with alcohol; it refers to the sandbar upon which the town is built. That lowly spit of sand forms the southern perimeter of the blue Bay of Navidad, which arcs to Barra de Navidad's twin town of San Patricio Melaque (pop. 10,000), a few miles to the west.

Barra and San Patricio Melaque, locally known as Melaque (may-LAH-kay), may be twins, but they're distinct. Barra has the cobbled, shady lanes and friendly country ambience; Melaque is the metropolis of the two, with most of the stores and services, and also the best beach, long and lovely Playa Melaque.

## ORIENTATION

A sizable fraction of Barra hotels and restaurants lie on one oceanfront street named, uncommonly, after a conquistador, Miguel López de Legazpi. Barra's other main street, Veracruz, one short block inland, has most of the businesses, groceries, and small family-run eateries.

Sandwiched between Barra's two main streets is the modest block-square town plaza, known locally as the *jardín*, between the east-west streets of Michoacán and Guanajuato. At the southeast corner of the *jardín*, you'll find the town police station, post office, and a couple of ATMs.

Head south along Legazpi (take the first parking place you find if you're driving, as they are scarce) toward the steep **Cerro San Francisco** in the distance, and you will soon be on the palm-lined walkway that runs atop the famous sandbar of Barra. On the right, ocean side, the **Playa Barra de Navidad** arcs northwest to the hotels of Melaque, which spread like white pebbles along the far end of the strand. The great blue-water expanse beyond the beach, framed at both ends by jagged, rocky sea stacks, is the **Bahía de Navidad.**

Opposite the ocean, on the other side of the bar, spreads the tranquil mangrove-bordered expanse of the **Laguna de Navidad,** which forms the border with the state of Colima, whose mountains (including nearby Cerro San Francisco) loom beyond it. The lagoon's calm appearance is deceiving, for it is really an *estero* (estuary), an arm of the sea that ebbs and flows through the channel beyond the rock jetty at the end of the sandbar. Because of this natural flushing action, local folks still dump fishing waste into the Laguna de Navidad. Fortunately, new sewage plants route human waste away from the lagoon, so with care, you can usually swim safely in its inviting waters. *Do not,* however, venture too close to the lagoon mouth beyond the jetty, or you may get swept out to sea by the strong outgoing current.

On the sandbar's lagoon side, a *panga* and passenger dock hum with daytime activity. From the dock, launches ferry loads of passengers for less than half a dollar to the Colima shore, which is known as **Isla Navidad,** where an upscale hotel development has risen across the lagoon. Back in the center of town, **minibuses** enter town along Veracruz, turn left at Sinaloa by the crafts stalls, and head in the opposite direction, out of town along Mazatlán, Veracruz, and Highway 200, 3 miles (4.8 km) to Melaque.

The once-distinct villages of **San Patricio** and **Melaque** now spread as one along the Bay of Navidad's sandy northwest shore. The business district, still known locally as San Patricio (from the highway, go west two blocks toward the beach), centers around a plaza, market, and church bordering the main shopping street, López Mateos.

Continue two more blocks to beachfront Calle Gómez Farías, where a lineup of hotels, eateries, and shops cater to the vacation trade. From there, the curving strand extends toward the quiet Melaque west end, where *palapas* line a glassy, sheltered blue cove. Here, a rainbow of colored *pangas* perch upon the sand, sailboats rock gently offshore, pelicans preen and dive, and people enjoy snacks, beer, and the cooling breeze in the deep shade beneath the *palapas.*

## HISTORY

The sandbar is called Navidad because the Viceroy Antonio de Mendoza, the first and arguably the best viceroy Mexico ever had, disembarked there on December 25, 1540. The occasion was auspicious for two reasons. While it was Christmas Day, it was also notable because Don Antonio had arrived to personally put down a bloody rebellion raging through western Mexico that threatened to burn New Spain off the map. Unfortunately for the thousands of native people who were torched, hanged, or beheaded during the brutal campaign, Don Antonio's prayers on that day were soon answered. The rebellion was smothered, and the lowly sandbar was remembered as Barra de Navidad from that time forward.

A generation later, Barra de Navidad became the springboard for King Philip's efforts to make the Pacific a Spanish lake. Shipyards built on the bar launched the vessels that carried the expedition of conquistador Miguel López de Legazpi and Father André de Urdaneta in search of God and gold in the Philippines. Urdaneta came back a hero one year later, in 1565, having discovered the northern circle route, whose favorable easterly winds propelled a dozen subsequent generations of the fabled treasure-laden Manila galleon home to Mexico. By 1600, however, the Manila galleon was landing in Acapulco, which provided much quicker land transport to the capital for their priceless Asian cargoes. Barra de Navidad went to sleep and didn't wake up for more than three centuries.

Now Barra de Navidad only slumbers occasionally. The townsfolk welcome crowds of beachgoing Mexican families during national holidays, and a steady procession of North American and European budget vacationers during the winter. In the marina canals behind "downtown" Barra, around the Hotel Cabo Blanco, there are several dozen posh and pricey canal-front homes and condo projects belonging to *norteamericanos* and other expats. A substantial number of Barra properties are listed on www.vrbo.com.

## BEACHES

Although a continuous strand of medium-fine golden sand joins Barra with Melaque, it changes character and names along its gentle five-mile arc. At Barra de Navidad, where it's called **Playa de Navidad,** the beach is narrow and steep, and the waves are sometimes very rough. Those powerful swells often provide good intermediate surfing breaks adjacent to the jetty. Fishing by line or pole is also popular from the jetty rocks.

Most mornings are calm enough to make the surf safe for swimming and splashing, which, along with the fresh seafood of beachside *palapa* restaurants, make Barra a popular Sunday and holiday picnic ground for local Mexican families. Unfortunately, the relatively large number of folks walking the beach makes for slim pickings for shell collectors and beachcombers.

For a cooling midday break from the sun, drop in to one of the beachfront restaurants (such as Seamaster) at the south end of Legazpi and enjoy the bay view, the swish of the waves, and the fresh breeze streaming beneath the *palapa.*

As the beach curves northwesterly toward Melaque, the restaurants and hotels give way to dunes and pasture. At the outskirts of Melaque, civilization resumes, and the broad beach, now called **Playa Melaque,** curves gently to the west.

Continuing past the Melaque town center, a lineup of rustic *palapas* and *pangas* pulled up on the sand decorate the tranquil west-end cove, which is sheltered from the open sea behind a tier of craggy sea stacks. Here, the water clears, making for good fishing from the rocks.

### Playa Coastecomate

On another day, explore this hidden beach tucked behind the ridge rising beyond the north edge of Melaque. The dark fine-sand

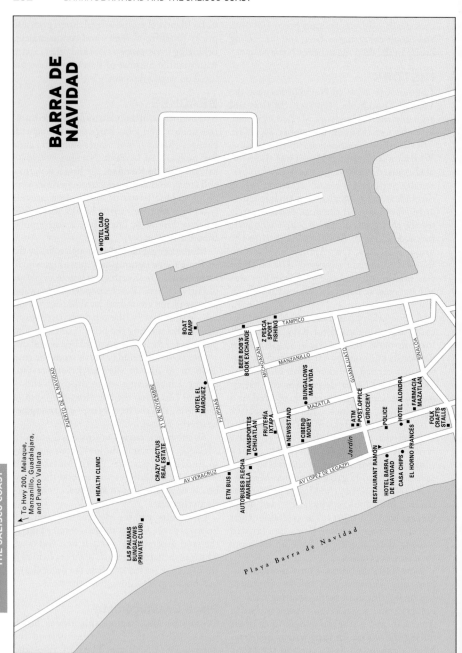

# BARRA DE NAVIDAD

HOTEL CABO BLANCO

BOAT RAMP

BEER BOB'S BOOK EXCHANGE

Z PESCA SPORT FISHING

TAMPICO

MICHOACAN

MANZANILLO

PUERTO DE LA NAVIDAD

21 DE NOVIEMBRE

HOTEL EL MARQUEZ

FILIPINAS

BUNGALOWS MAR VIDA

GUANAJUATO

HEALTH CLINIC

CRAZY CACTUS REAL ESTATE

TRANSPORTES CIHUATLAN

FRUTERIA IXTAPA

MAZATLA

NEWSSTAND

CIBER@ MONEY

ATM

POST OFFICE

GROCERY

POLICE

HOTEL ALONDRA

FARMACIA MAZATLAN

SINALOA

ETN BUS

AUTOBUSES FLECHA AMARILLA

AV VERACRUZ

*Jardín*

AV LOPEZ DE LEGAZPI

RESTAURANT RAMON

HOTEL BARRA DE NAVIDAD

CASA CHIPS

EL HORNO FRANCES

FOLK CRAFTS STALLS

To Hwy 200, Melaque,
Manzanillo, Guadalajara,
and Puerto Vallarta

LAS PALMAS
BUNGALOWS
(PRIVATE CLUB)

*Playa Barra de Navidad*

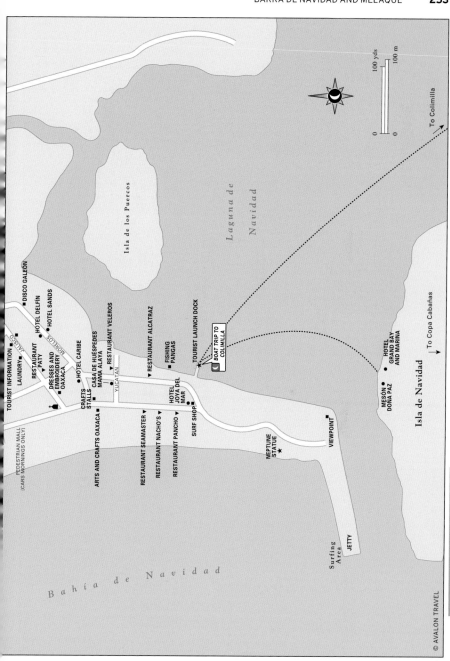

THE JALISCO COAST

© AVALON TRAVEL

100 yds
100 m

To Colimilla

Laguna de
Navidad

Isla de los Puercos

To Copa Cabañas

Isla de Navidad

DISCO GALEÓN

HOTEL DELFÍN

HOTEL SANDS

RESTAURANT VELEROS

RESTAURANT ALCATRAZ

TOURIST INFORMATION

LAUNDRY

RESTAURANT PATY

DRESSES AND EMBROIDERY OAXACA

HOTEL CARIBE

CASA DE HUESPEDES MAMA ALAYA

RESTAURANT ALCATRAZ

FISHING PANGAS

TOURIST LAUNCH DOCK

BOAT TRIP TO COLIMILLA

CRAFTS STALLS

YUCATÁN

MORELOS

JALISCO

PEDESTRIAN MALL (CARS MORNINGS ONLY)

ARTS AND CRAFTS OAXACA

RESTAURANT SEAMASTER

RESTAURANT NACHO'S

RESTAURANT PANCHO

SURF SHOP

HOTEL JOYA DEL MAR

MESON DOÑA PAZ

HOTEL GRAND BAY AND MARINA

VIEWPOINT

NEPTUNE STATUE

Surfing Area

JETTY

Bahia de Navidad

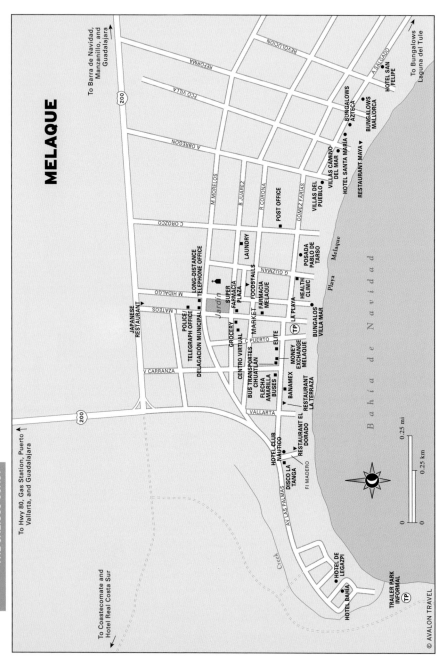

# MELAQUE

To Barra de Navidad, Manzanillo, and Guadalajara

To Hwy 80, Gas Station, Puerto Vallarta, and Guadalajara

To Coastecomate and Hotel Real Costa Sur

To Bungalows Laguna del Tule

REVOLUCION

REFORMA

FCO VILLA

A OBREGON

M MORELOS

B JUAREZ

R CORONA

GOMEZ FARIAS

C OROZCO

M HIDALGO

J MATEOS

V CARRANZA

VALLARTA

FI MADERO

AV LAS PALMAS

G GUZMAN

HOTEL SAN /FELIPE

A SALGADO

BUNGALOWS AZTECA

BUNGALOWS MALLORCA

VILLAS CAMINO DEL MAR

HOTEL SANTA MARÍA

RESTAURANT MAYA

VILLAS DEL PUEBLO

POST OFFICE

POSADA PABLO DE TARSO

HEALTH CLINIC

LA PLAYA

Playa

Melaque

Playa

FARMACIA MELAQUE

FOODSTALLS

LAUNDRY

LONG-DISTANCE TELEPHONE OFFICE

SUPER FARMACIA PLAZA

Jardín

MARKET

BUNGALOS VILLA MAR

ELITE

PUERTO

CENTRO VIRTUAL

GROCERY

POLICE/ TELEGRAPH OFFICE/ DELAGACIÓN MUNICIPAL

JAPANESE RESTAURANT

BUS TRANSPORTES CIHUATLAN FLECHA AMARILLA BUSES

MONEY EXCHANGE MELAQUE

BANAMEX

RESTAURANT LA TERRAZA

HOTEL CLUB NAUTICO

RESTAURANT EL DORADO

DISCO LA TANGA

HOTEL DE LEGAZPI

HOTEL BAHIA

TRAILER PARK INFORMAL

Bahia de Navidad

Creek

0.25 mi

0.25 km

© AVALON TRAVEL

© DONNA DAY

Barra de Navidad's promenade lies between ocean and lagoon.

beach arcs along a cove on the rampart-rimmed big blue **Bahía de Coastecomate** (kooah-stay-koh-MAH-tay). Its very gentle waves and clear waters make for excellent swimming, sailboarding, snorkeling, and fishing from the beach itself or the rocks beneath the adjacent cliffs. A number of *palapa* restaurants along the beach serve seafood and drinks.

The Coastecomate beachside village itself, home to a number of local fisherfolk and a few North Americans in permanently parked RVs, has a collection of oft-empty bungalows on the hillside, a small store, and about three times as many chickens as people.

To get there, drive or take a taxi or bus via the local minibus or Transportes Cihuatlán to the signed Melaque turnoff from Highway 200. There, a paved side road marked Hotel Real Costa Sur heads northwest into the hills, winding for 2 miles (3.2 km) over the ridge through pasture and jungle woodland to the village. If you're walking, allow an hour and take your sun hat, insect repellent, and water.

## RECREATION
### ◖ Boat Trip to Colimilla

A boat trip across the lagoon for superfresh seafood at the palm-studded village of Colimilla is a primary Barra pastime. While you sit enjoying an oyster cocktail, ceviche, or broiled whole-fish dinner, gaze out on the mangrove-enfolded glassy expanse of the Laguna de Navidad. Far away, a canoe may drift silently, while white herons quietly stalk their prey. Now and then a launch will glide in and deposit its load of visitors, or an angler will head out to sea.

One of the most pleasant Colimilla vantage spots is **La Colimilla Restaurant** (tel. 314/337-9105, 8am-8pm daily, $5-10), whose *palapa* extends into the lagoon. Take mosquito repellent, especially if you're staying for dinner. Launches routinely ferry as many as six passengers to Colimilla from the Barra lagoonside docks for about $5 round-trip. Tell them when you want to return, and they'll pick you up.

From the same Barra lagoonside dock, launches also shuttle passengers for $2.50

THE JALISCO COAST

© DONNA DAY

boats on the Barra de Navidad lagoon-side docks

round-trip across the lagoon to **Isla Navidad** and the posh resort Hotel Grand Bay, marina, vacation-home development, and golf course.

## Swimming, Surfing, and Boogie Boarding

The roughest surf on the Bahía de Navidad shoreline is closer to Barra, the most tranquil closest to Melaque. Swimming is consequently best and safest toward the Melaque end, while, in contrast, the most popular local surfing spot is where the waves rise and roll in beside the Barra jetty. Bodysurfing and boogie boarding are best somewhere in between. At least one shop in Barra, **Farmacia Zurich** (on Legazpi, south corner of Jalisco, tel. 315/355-6135), sells boogie boards, fishing poles, tackle, and lures. There is a surf shop in Barra as well, the **Barra Surf Shop** (Legazpi 46-B, no phone), with board sales and rentals, and surfing lessons. You'll find them open around 11am every day, next door to the Joya del Mar Hotel on Legazpi. If

you want to stand-up paddle, however, bring your own gear, as they have none in stock.

## Sailing, Kiteboarding, and Sailboarding

Sailing, kiteboarding, and sailboarding are best near the Melaque end of the Bay of Navidad and in the Bay of Coastecomate nearby. Bring your own equipment, however; none is available locally.

## Snorkeling and Scuba Diving

Local snorkeling is often good during the dry winter season, particularly offshore at Coastecomate, just north of Melaque. Bring your own gear, however, as the one dive shop in Barra has gone out of business. Or head over to the Grand Bay and book a trip through Nautimar, the dive shop at the hotel (tel. 315/331-0500).

The best-organized and most professional regional dive shop is **Underworld Scuba** (P.O. Box 295, Santiago, Colima 28860, tel./fax 314/333-0642 or 314/333-3678, Carlos's cell tel. 044-314/358-0327, Susan's cell tel. 044-314/358-5042, www.divemanzanillo.com or www.gomanzanillo.com/scubamex), run by Manzanillo-based Susan Dearing and her partner, NAUI-certified instructor Carlos Cuellar.

## Sportfishing

The captains of the Barra boat cooperative, **Sociedad Cooperativa de Servicios Turísticos** (Av. Veracruz 40, tel. 315/354-3792), routinely take parties on successful marlin and swordfish hunts for about $28 per hour, including bait and tackle. Ask at their lagoonside office-dock. Alternatively, you can arrange a fishing trip through highly recommended **Z Pesca** sportfishing (tel. 315/100-8505, www.zpesca.com), whose boat-dock tackle shop and office are staffed by Captain Chaparro or Captain Castillo at Tampico 71. Depending on the size of the craft, their fees run from about $200 and up. If the aforementioned aren't available, at least half a dozen gentlemen on the docks and around the edge of the lagoon offer every kind of sportfishing trip and/or tour you could

THE JALISCO COAST

© DONNA DAY

Boats deliver people from Barra de Navidad to Colimilla's restaurants, across the lagoon.

possibly dream up. Some prices: lagoon tour, $23; Melaque Bay tour, $30; Coastacomete trip/tour, $75; La Manzanilla trip/tour, $150; fishing trip, $40 per hour; 36-foot boat rental, $600; 42-foot boat rental, $700. These U.S. prices are current as of the exchange rate at this writing and are no doubt negotiable.

Fishing trips will typically net a number of large dorado, albacore, snapper, or other delicious eating fish. Local restaurants will generally cook a banquet for you and your friends if you give them the extra fish caught during such an outing.

If you'd like to enter one of a pair of annual Barra de Navidad **international fishing tournaments** (billfish, tuna, and dorado in Jan. and May; father and son/daughter tournament in Jan.), contact Captain Chaparro of Z Pesca (Tampico 71, tel. 315/100-8505, www.zpesca.com) or the tourist information office.

## Boating

If you plan on mounting your own fishing expedition, you can do it from the Barra **boat-launching ramp** (end of Av. Filipinas, 8am-4pm Mon.-Fri.) near the Hotel Cabo Blanco. The fee, about $20 per day, covers parking your boat in the canal and is payable to the boat-keeper, whose headquarters is inside the boat-yard adjacent to the ramp.

## Tennis and Golf

The **Hotel Cabo Blanco** tennis courts (tel. 315/355-5182) are customarily open for public rental for about $4 per hour. Call ahead to check. Lessons may also be available.

The plumy, breezy 18-hole **Isla Navidad Golf Course** is available to the public for a fee of around $200 per person high season, $150 low season. Call the Hotel Grand Bay (tel. 315/331-0500, www.islanavidad.com) and ask for the Club de Golf for information. Get there by regular launch from the Barra dock on the lagoon (to the Casa Club landing, about $5 round-trip). By car, turn right from Highway 200 at the Ejido La Culebra (or Isla Navidad) sign as the highway cuts through the hills at Kilometer 51 a few miles south of Barra. Follow the road about 3 miles (4.8 km) to a bridge, where the road curves right, paralleling the beach. After about 2 more miles (3.2 km), you pass through the golf course gate. After winding through the golf course another mile (1.6 km), turn right at the traffic circle at the north edge of the golf course. Continue another mile (1.6 km), between the golf course and the adjacent hillside, to the big golf clubhouse on the right. You can get detailed information on the courses and maps on the website.

## Hiking

You can do a hike between Barra and Melaque (4 mi/6.4 km either way), but if you start from Barra early in the morning, the sun will be behind you, and the sky and ocean will be at their bluest and best. Take insect repellent, sunscreen, and a hat. At either end, enjoy lunch at one of the seaside restaurants. At the Melaque end you can continue walking north to the cove on the far side of town. The trail, now

THE JALISCO COAST

swimmers in the lagoon of Barra de Navidad

© DONNA DAY

a concrete *andador* beneath the cliff, leads to spectacular wave-tossed tide pools and rugged sea rocks at the tip of the bay. At the Barra end, you can hire a launch to Colimilla for lunch or dinner. End your day by leisurely taxiing or busing back from the bus station at either end.

### Bird- and Wildlife-Watching

The wildlife-rich upper reaches of the Laguna de Navidad stretch for miles and are only a boat ride away. Besides the ordinary varieties of egrets, terns, herons, pelicans, frigate birds, boobies, ducks, and geese, patient bird-watchers can sometimes snare rainbow flash views of exotic parrots and bright tanagers and orioles.

As for other creatures, quiet, persistent observers are sometimes rewarded with mangrove-edge views of turtles, constrictors, crocodiles, coatimundis, raccoons, skunks, deer, wild pigs, ocelots, wildcats, and, very rarely, a jaguar. The sensitivity and experience of your boatman/guide is, of course, crucial to the success of any nature outing. Ask at the tourist information office in Barra or the dock-office of the **Sociedad Cooperativa de Servicios Turísticos** (Barra de Navidad, Av. Veracruz 40) on the lagoon front, or try one of the other *cooperativas;* there are several right there to choose from, with all manner of tours offered. One is **Mary Chuy Tours** (Av. Veracruz 88, tel. 315/100-3347 or 315/109-9124), with 36-and 42-foot boats available. You might also check with Tracye Ross at **Crazy Cactus** (21 de Noviembre 60, tel. 315/355-6091 or 314/357-0460, U.S. tel. 832/364-6289, crazycactusmx@yahoo.com, www.barradenavidad.com), a company that rents cars, handles real estate sales and rentals, sells insurance of all kinds, and has small storage units for rent.

### Sports Equipment Sales and Rentals

In Barra, the **Farmacia Zurich** (on Legazpi, south corner of Jalisco, tel. 315/355-8582, 9am-10pm daily) sells boogie boards, fishing poles, tackle, and lures. The **Barra Surf Shop** (Legazpi 46-B, no phone), next door to Hotel Joya del Mar, sells and rents surfboards.

# ENTERTAINMENT AND EVENTS

Most entertainments in Barra and Melaque are informal and local. **Corridas de toros** (bull-fights) are occasionally held during the winter-spring season at the bullring on Highway 200 across from the Barra turnoff. Local *vaqueros* (cowboys) sometimes display their pluck in spirited **charreadas** (Mexican-style rodeos) in neighboring country villages. Check with your hotel desk or the Barra tourist information office for details.

A small, glitzy-looking casino has opened on the road into Barra from Highway 200, for those who like to dance with the one-armed bandits. Across the road and a few hundred yards closer to town, a small water park called **Aurora Aquatica** offers the kids something a little different to do.

The big local festival occurs in Melaque during the St. Patrick's Day week of March 10-17. Events include blessing of the local fishing fleet, folk dancing, cake eating, and boxing matches.

## Nightlife

Folks enjoy the Bahía de Navidad sunset colors in Barra during the happy hours at Restaurant Seamaster, the Hotel Alondra top-floor bar, or the Casa Chips restaurant-bar, half a block south of the Hotel Barra de Navidad.

The same is true at the beachside Restaurant Maya and Restaurant Dorado at Hotel Club Náutico in Melaque. You can prepare for sunset during the afternoons (Dec.-Feb. mostly) at the very congenial 4pm-6pm happy hour around the swim-up bar at Barra's Hotel Sands. Lovers of pure tranquility, on the other hand, enjoy the breeze and sunset view from the end of Barra's rock jetty.

If discoing is your thing, starting at around 10pm huge speakers begin to thump away, lights flash, and fog oozes from the ceiling at disco **El Galeón** (tel. 315/355-5018), at the Hotel Sands in Barra (young local crowd), and at **La Tanga** (Gómez Farías, tel. 315/355-5472, 10pm-4am in season, entrance $7), across the street from Hotel Club Náutico in Melaque

(mixed younger and older, local and tourist crowd). Hours vary seasonally; call for details.

## SHOPPING

While Melaque has many stores crammed with humdrum commercial tourist curios, Barra has a few interestingly authentic sources. For example, a number of Náhuatl-speaking families from Guerrero operate small individual shops at the south end of Legazpi. Furthermore, some of the shops, near the corner of Sinaloa and Legazpi, behind the church, are minimuseums of delightful folk crafts, made mostly by *indígena* country craftspeople. Pick what you like from among hundreds—lustrous lacquerware trays from Olinalá; winsome painted pottery cats, rabbits, and fish; a battalion of wooden miniarmadillos; and glossy dark-wood swordfish from Sonora.

You can pick from an equally attractive selection two blocks south, at **Arts and Crafts of Oaxaca** (no phone, approximately 10am-8pm daily), across Legazpi diagonally southwest from the church. Besides a fetching collection of priced-to-sell Oaxacan *alebrijes, tapetes,* and masks, there is also a host of papier-mâché and pottery from Tlaquepaque and Tonalá, sombreros from Zitácuaro in Michoacán, and much more.

Across the street, a lineup of other shops, such as **Artesanías Náhuatl** (no phone, 10am-8pm daily) and **Artesanías Guerrero** (no phone, approximately 10am-8pm daily), have similarly attractive offerings, on the south end of Veracruz, near the corner of Morelos. Although bargaining is customary, don't bargain too hard. Many of these folks, far from their country villages, are strangers in a strange land. Their sometimes-meager earnings often support entire extended families back home.

## ACCOMMODATIONS

Whether on the beach or not, all Barra hotels (except the world-class Hotel Grand Bay) fall in the budget or moderate categories. Note: During fall storm season, Barra de Navidad waves sometimes hit the sand with a boom. If you're a light sleeper, best come prepared with earplugs. Otherwise, choose one of Barra's many good off-beach hotels.

In contrast to Barra de Navidad, San Patricio Melaque has many beachfront hotels. Although the majority of them, especially in the old San Patricio town center, are mediocre at best, visitors enjoy a number of well-managed comfortable, even deluxe, exceptions, especially in the quiet south-side neighborhood. All of those covered enjoy beachfront locations, although few, except those noted, accept credit cards.

## Barra Hotels
### UNDER $50

On the south end, **Casa de Huéspedes Mama Laya** (Veracruz 69, tel. 315/355-5088, $16 s, $21 d, $26 t) is one of Barra's few remaining recommendable low-budget lodgings. The grandmotherly owner (who named her hotel after her late mother) offers 14 basic rooms in an airy two-story layout overlooking the Navidad lagoon front. All rooms have two double beds, with fans and hot-water shower baths. One attractive plus is an upstairs open-air

© DONNA DAY

the Hotel Grand Bay

lagoon-view veranda with chairs and sofas for guest use.

Half a block north, the budget traveler's longtime favorite, **Casa de Huéspedes Caribe** (Sonora 15, tel. 315/355-5952, $15 s, $20 d, and $25 t), is tucked along a side street. The family owners offer their devoted following of long-term customers 11 plainly decorated barebulb but clean rooms, with twin, double, or both types of beds, all with bath and hot water. Amenities include a homey downstairs garden sitting area, and more chairs and hammocks for snoozing on an upstairs porch.

### $50-100

Return north a block, then right and east another block, where its loyal international clientele swears by the family-operated **Hotel Delfín** (Morelos 23, tel. 315/355-5068, www. hoteldelfinmx.com). Its four stories of tile-floored, balcony-corridor rooms (where curtains, unfortunately, must be drawn for privacy) are the cleanest and coziest of Barra's moderate hotels. The Delfín's tour de force, however, is the cheery patio buffet, where guests linger over the breakfast (8:30am-10:30am daily, $6) offered to all comers. Overnight guests, however, must put up with the moderate nighttime noise of the disco half a block away. For maximum sun and privacy, take one of the top-floor rooms, many of which enjoy lagoon views. The Delfín's 24 rooms rent for $49 s or d, $59 t, and $69 q, all with fans; credit cards are accepted. There are also two two-bedroom apartments available on the top floors, which can be rented for $120 per day (discounts available for long-term stays). The apartments have full kitchens and private balconies. All accommodations have access to the small pool and parking.

Right across the street, bordering the lagoon, the most charmingly tropical of Barra hotels, the drowsy old-Mexico **Hotel Sands** (Morelos 24, tel./fax 315/355-5018), offers a bit of class at moderate rates. A pair of three-story room tiers encloses an inner courtyard lined with comfortable airy sitting areas that open onto a lush green garden of leafy vines and graceful coconut palms. A right-side garden walkway leads to a panorama of Barra's colorful lineup of lagoon-front fishing launches. On the other side, past the swim-up bar, a big curving pool and outer patio lead to a grand, airy vista of the placid mangrove-bordered Laguna de Navidad.

The pool bar (happy hour 4pm-6pm daily, winter season) and the sitting areas afford inviting places to meet other travelers. The rooms, all with fans (but with slow-to-arrive hot water in some rooms—check before moving in), are clean and furnished with dark varnished wood and tile. Light sleepers should wear earplugs or book a room in the wing farthest from the disco down the street, whose music thumps away until around 2am many nights during the high season. Its 43 rooms and bungalows rent from $32 s, $48 d low season, $51 s, $65 d high (bargain for a better rate); bungalows sleeping four with kitchenette run $90 low season, $125 high. Credit cards (with a 6 percent surcharge) are accepted, and parking is available.

Return south three blocks along Veracruz (and jog half a block uphill, west) to the white-stuccoed **Hotel Joya del Mar** (Veracruz 209, tel./fax 315/355-6967, hoteljoyadelmar@yahoo. com.mx). The Mexican on-site owner offers three floors of eight simply but comfortably furnished rooms and suites, topped by a pair of suites with a view. The building's height affords upper-floor accommodations the benefit of either lagoon or ocean sunset views and cooling afternoon westerly breezes. Rooms rent from $42 s, $56 d, and $63 t to about $92 s, $105 d for the third-floor suites. Add about $10 to all rates for high season. Features include fans, air-conditioning, and nonsmoking rooms; credit cards are accepted. Make your winter reservations early.

An attractive addition to Barra's sprinkling of beachfront lodgings is **Casa Chips** (198 López de Legazpi, tel. 315/355-5555, www.casa-chips.com, or P.O. Box 882004, San Francisco, CA 94188-2004, U.S. tel. 415/671-3816), in the middle of town, tucked half a block south of the big Hotel Barra de Navidad. Here, owners have packed a lot of hotel into a small space. They offer an assortment of seven invitingly

decorated rustic-chic lodgings, ranging from double-bed rooms and one-bedroom suites all the way up to an entire deluxe two-bedroom apartment with views upstairs. All are decorated with color-coordinated bedspreads and drapes, attractive tile, and hand-hewn wood furniture. An important extra here is an airy beachfront restaurant, fine for relaxing dining, socializing, and sunset-watching. Low-season rates range from about $45-55 for the smaller accommodations up to $85 d for the largest; during high season, rates are about $65-110. Add $10 (low season) and $15 (high) per extra person. All lodgings have fans, air-conditioning, hot-water showers, television, and wireless Internet; the larger lodgings have kitchenettes.

Folks interested in tennis, boating, and/or fishing might appreciate Barra's original deluxe lodging, the stucco-and-tile four-star **Hotel Cabo Blanco** (P.O. Box 31, Barra de Navidad, Jalisco 48987, tel./fax 315/355-5103, toll-free Mex. tel. 01-800/710-5690, fax 315/355-6494, www.hotelcaboblanco.com). The 125-room low-rise complex (named after the 1970s Barra de Navidad-filmed Hollywood thriller *Cabo Blanco,* starring Charles Bronson) anchors the vacation-home development along the three marina-canals that extend about five blocks north from the Barra lagoon. Within its manicured garden-grounds, Hotel Cabo Blanco offers night-lit tennis courts, restaurants, bars, two pools, kiddie pools, and deluxe sportfishing yachts-for-hire. The deluxe pastel-decorated rooms run about $55 d, $65 with breakfast, except on holidays and some weekends; credit cards are accepted. All have air-conditioning, cable TV, and phones. Additional features include a folkloric dance show and many water sports. Bring your insect repellent; during the late afternoon and evening, mosquitoes and gnats from the nearby mangroves seem to especially enjoy the Cabo Blanco's posh ambience. All-inclusive or European plan packages are available on the website at discounted rates.

Tucked four short blocks from the beach at Barra's north end is the very worthy family-friendly three-star **Hotel El Marquez** (Calles Filipinas and Manzanillo, tel./fax

315/355-5304, www.costalegre.ca/Barra_ Hotels.htm). Inside the gate, guests enjoy about 30 comfortable semideluxe rooms around an invitingly intimate inner pool patio. Rates begin at about $48 d low season, $60 d high, with air-conditioning ($10 extra), kiddie play-ground, and parking. Wireless Internet and televisions are also provided in all of the rooms.

If the Marquez is full, try similarly comfort-able but smaller three-star neighbor **Bungalows Mar Vida** (Mazatlán 168, tel. 315/355-5911, fax 315/355-5349, www.vrbo.com/58088), one block west and one block south. Friendly owner and real estate agent Marsha Ewing Hernandez asks $55 d year-round for the bungalow with kitchenette and $50 d for her comfortable, semideluxe rooms sans kitchen, with air-con-ditioning and small pool patio.

Right in the middle of town, located securely a block away from Barra's sometimes destruc-tive surf, is the block-square five-story **Hotel la Alondra** (Calle Sinaloa 16, tel. 315/355-8372, 315/355-8373, or 315/355-8305, hotellaalon-dra@yahoo.com.mx, www.alondrahotel.com). Commercial shops, adjacent to the small lobby, occupy the downstairs floor. Upstairs, guests enjoy three floors of 54 (40 double rooms, 4 junior suites, and 10 suites) light, airy accom-modations, some with private ocean-view bal-conies. All are attractively decorated in pastel blue-and-orange bedspreads and curtains, and offer double, queen-, or king-size bed options. Low-season rates run about $75 d for rooms with one (although king-size) bed, $106 d for two double beds, and $180 for the larger and fancier junior suites. Corresponding high-sea-son prices are $85, $120, and $220. A fifth-floor panoramic-view restaurant, beachfront swimming pool with view, and swim-up bar are available for guest relaxation and sunset-watching. Boat tours are arranged through the front desk, and guests can take a ride through the lagoon or bay for about $30 per person.

The second of Barra's two recommend-able beachfront lodgings is the white, stucco, three-story **Hotel Barra de Navidad** (Av. L. de Legazpi 250, tel. 315/355-5122, fax 315/355-5303, www.hotelbarradenavidad.com), on the beach side of the town plaza. Guests in the seaside upper two floors of comfortable semideluxe rooms enjoy palm-fringed ocean vistas from private balconies. A shady, plant-decorated interior courtyard and inviting pool and patio on one side and the good Bananas Restaurant upstairs complete the compact but attractive picture. Rates for the 60 rooms run about $75 s, $82 d, and $90 t, all with air-con-ditioning. Ask for one of the sunnier, quieter, ocean-view rooms. Credit cards are accepted.

## OVER $100

Across the lagoon on Isla Navidad is Barra's ecologically correct (as in solar-powered) **Coco Cabañas** (Km 8.2, on the road between Hwy. 200 and Isla Navidad, tel. 335/004-2686 or 315/100-0441, U.S. tel. 281/205-4100, www. cococabanas.com), perched on pristine and breezy Playa los Cocos, a couple of miles south of Barra de Navidad. This is clearly a place for those who enjoy solitude. There are no tele-phones or cable TV in the rooms, but there is a great, reasonably priced restaurant; miles of luscious beach to explore; and a pool that meanders in front of the rustic cabanas. There is wireless Internet as well as a television with cable available in the restaurant just in case you can't bear to be away from technology.

The cabanas can sleep as many as four adults and two kids—two adults downstairs in a sofa bed, kids on a moveable foam mattress, and two more adults in a king-size bed in an up-stairs loft. There are hot showers and fans in-side and hammocks in front for your daily siesta. Rates run $80 d low season, $125 d high; add $5 per extra person. The surf can get very rough at the beach here, so expert swimmers or waders only. There's been considerable de-velopment on Isla Navidad, but hopefully Coco Cabañas will remain a rustic haven amid the condos and new hotels that are currently under construction.

Nearby, in complete contrast, stands Barra's plushest hotel by far, the class-act **Hotel Grand Bay** (P.O. Box 20, Barra de Navidad, Jalisco 48987, tel. 315/331-0500, fax 315/355-0560, www.islanavidad.com), a short boat ride to the Isla Navidad development across the lagoon. Builders spared little expense to create the appearance of a *gran época* resort. The 198 rooms are elaborately furnished with marble floors, French-provincial furniture reproductions, and Italian jade-hued marble bathroom sinks. Accommodations include spacious "superior" rooms, for about $200 d (except holidays and some weekends); master suites, from about $390 d; and grand four-room executive suites that include their own steam rooms, from about $1,200. Amenities include three elegant restaurants, tennis, volleyball, children's club, marina, and an exceptional oceanfront golf course. You won't run out of things to do during your stay. The centerpiece of the hotel are the three ground-floor pools (there are other pools hidden on various floors, too; half the fun is exploring the place to find them), which cascade into one another through waterfalls and waterslides. A small hot tub under the gazebo is popular in the cool winter evenings. There are lagoonside sun beds and hammocks under shady palms if you prefer a more natural setting. Plentiful online promotions with better rates are available, so have a look at the website before making your reservations.

The owners of the Hotel Grand Bay also offer a more private, personal option, the **Mesón Doña Paz** (tel. 315/337-9002 or 315/337-9000, fax 314/337-9015, www.mesondonapaz.com), a boutique "hotel within the hotel," located within the resort complex. Originally built as the owners' private manor house (which they now use only at Christmas), the Mesón Doña Paz is a maharaja's mansion of spacious, superluxurious suites, elegantly decorated in the marble French provincial mode of the neighboring Hotel Grand Bay. The load of conveniences includes elaborate telephone-equipped bathrooms (with separate rooms for tubs and showers), airy private patios with views, an exclusive restaurant, dining veranda, bar, pool, Jacuzzi, and boat landing. Upstairs, a regal penthouse-view salon, perfect for executive meetings (up to about 50 people), adds an attractive business-friendly option. Rates, beginning at $180 d (about $310 holidays and

some weekends) and going up to $390 ($540) for junior suites and $560 ($680) for master suites, are reasonable considering the luxurious exclusive facilities. Reserve for Mesón Doña Paz directly.

Note: Security is tight at Hotel Grand Bay and Mesón Doña Paz. Guards at the hotel's lagoonside boat dock (and the separate Mesón Doña Paz dock) only allow entrance to guests and prospective guests. If you want to look around, you have to be accompanied by an in-house guide. Call the desk beforehand for an appointment. You can also drive around to the hotel along Isla Navidad if you have a vehicle.

## South of Town Melaque Hotels

Most of Melaque's recommendable hotels lie in the quiet south-of-town neighborhood.

### UNDER $50

Melaque's best-buy budget lodging is the **Hotel Santa María** (Abel Salgado 85, tel. 315/355-5677, fax 315/355-5553). Long popular with cost-conscious Canadians and Americans in winter, the Santa María's 46 accommodations, all one-bedroom kitchenette apartments, are arranged in two motel-style wings around an invitingly green and tranquil inner patio. All are close enough to the water for the waves to lull guests to sleep. Units vary; uppers are brighter, so look at a few before you move in. All-season prices for the spartan but generally tidy apartments begin at about $32 d per day, $180/week, $365/month, with TV, fans, hot-water showers, and pleasantly sunny beach-front pool patio.

North a few blocks, closer to the town center, is the well-kept colonial-chic **Posada Pablo de Tarso** (Av. Gómez Farías 408, tel./ fax 315/355-5707 or 315/355-5717), named after the apostle Paul of Tarsus. Guests enjoy many attractive details, including art-decorated walls, hand-carved bedsteads and doors, and a flowery beachside pool and patio. The main drawback to all this lies in the motel-style corridor layout, which requires guests to pull the dark drapes for privacy. Year-round rates for the 27 rooms and bungalows begin at about $45 d

($25 daily rate for one-month rental), except possibly for some holidays; a kitchen in the unit raises the tariff to about $85 d. All have fan, air-conditioning, TV, and phones. You may also reserve with their Guadalajara office (tel./fax 333/811-5262 or 333/811-4273).

Priced at about $26 per night for two people, the beachfront **Bungalows Villamar** (Calle Hidalgo 1, tel. 315/355-5005, bungalowsvillamar@prodigy.net.mx) is another great Melaque budget option. The tidy little property includes six one-bedroom units, two two-bedroom units, and four great RV sites overlooking the beach (the latter renting for $300 per month). The small but comfortable rooms all have fully equipped kitchens, tiled patios, TV, Wi-Fi, air-conditioning, and fans. Friendly manager Roberto Zepeda is fluent in English and will gladly steer you to the restaurants, activities, and sights Melaque and Barra have to offer.

### $50-100

Classy in its unique way is the [C] **Villas Camino del Mar** (Calle Francisco Villa, corner Abel Salgado, tel. 315/355-5207, fax 315/355-5498, www.villascaminodelmar.com.mx). A few signs in the humble beach neighborhood about a quarter mile on the Barra side of the Melaque town center furnish the only clue that this gem of a lodging hides at the beach end of a bumpy Melaque street. (Note: The owners have added an annex across the street, which, although inviting, crams in more accommodations in a smaller space than the original building. Specifically ask for a room in the original building in your reservation request.) A five-story white stucco monument draped with fluted neoclassical columns and hanging pedestals, the original Villas Camino del Mar hotel offers a lodging assortment from simple double rooms and deluxe suites with kitchenettes to a rambling penthouse. The upper three levels have sweeping ocean views, while the lower two overlook an elegant blue pool and patio bar and shady beachside palm grove. The clientele is split between Mexican middle-class families who come for weekends year-round and quiet Canadian and American couples who come to soak up the winter sun for weeks and months on end. Reserve early, especially for the winter. Rates for the 37 rooms and suites run as little as $49 ($43 per day for a week, $34 per day for a month) for small but comfortable ocean-view rooms for two; $79 ($71 per day weekly, $55 per day monthly) for a studio with kitchenette; $95 ($85 per day weekly, $66 per day monthly) for a medium one-bedroom with two queen beds and kitchenette; and $120 ($108 per day weekly, $88 per day monthly) for a deluxe two-bedroom, two-bath suite with kitchen; all with fans only. All rates are discounted 10 percent during low occupancy (usually May-June and Sept.-Nov.).

Camino del Mar's nearby upscale **Villas Alvanelly,** set in a spacious, grassy beachfront compound with its own pool, offers much more luxury and space. The nine one- and two-bedroom kitchenette apartments go for $95-135 (a one-week rental gets an 8 percent discount; one month 30 percent). Reserve early, through Villas Camino del Mar (tel. 315/355-5207, fax 315/355-5498, www.villascaminodelmar.com.mx).

Close by, the sky-blue-and-white **Bungalows Azteca** (P.O. Box 57, San Patricio Melaque, Jalisco 48980, tel./fax 315/355-5150, www.bungalowsazteca.com) auto court-style cottages line both sides of a cobbled driveway courtyard garden that spreads to a lazy beachfront pool patio. The 14 spacious kitchenette cottages, in one-bedroom or three-bedroom versions, are plainly furnished but clean. The nine one-bedroom units rent for about $55 per day low season and $65 per day high. The five three-bedrooms rent for about $150 per day low and $160 per day high. Get your reservation in early, especially for the winter.

Less than a block south, the open, parklike grounds, spacious blue pool with kiddie pools, and beachside palm garden of the **Bungalows Mayorca** (Abel Salgado 133, Colonia Villa Obregón, tel./fax 315/355-5219, bungalowsmayorca@prodigy.net.mx, www.tomzap.com/mayorca.html) invite unhurried outdoor relaxation. Its stacked, Motel 6-style layout, attractively draped with tropical greenery, has aged gracefully. Groups and families used to providing their own atmosphere find the kitchens and spacious (but dark) rooms of the Bungalows Mayorca appealing. The 21 two-bedroom bungalows, all with air-conditioning and TV, rent for about $60 d, $230 per week, $890 per month low season ($76, $330, and $1,020 high). If you're in the mood for a splurge, ask for one of their three beachfront suites, with balconies with views and whirlpool tubs, for about 20 percent additional.

## North of Town Melaque Hotels

A sprinkling of hotels in the sleepy Melaque north-end neighborhood offer comfortable accommodations at budget to moderate rates.

### UNDER $50

One of the tidiest is the ◖ **Hotel Bahía** (Calle Legazpi 5, tel./fax 315/355-6894, www3.telus. net/public/a7a84441/hotelbahia), just half a block off the beach, presided over by kindly owner/managers Evelia and Rafael Galvez Moreno. The hotel's 21 rooms and two kitchenette bungalows line a pair of two-floor tiers that enclose a lovely inner patio, a pool, a second patio off to one side, and an airy upstairs veranda, all fine for relaxing and socializing. The rooms, although smallish, are spic-and-span and attractively decorated with flowery curtains and matching bedspreads. A common kitchen is available downstairs for guest use. Room rates run from about $36 (for 1-4) low season to about $45 high; bungalows are about $55. All include TV, fans, hot-water showers, and filtered drinking water.

The neighboring homey, downscale-modern white-stucco **Hotel de Legazpi** (Av. de las Palmas 3, tel./fax 315/355-5397, hoteldelegazpi@prodigy.net.mx) offers relaxing vacation options right on the beachfront. A number of the hotel's spacious, clean, and comfortable beachside rooms have balconies with palmy ocean and sunset views. Downstairs are a small restaurant and a rear-court pool and patio. The hotel's beachside entrance leads through a jungly front garden straight to the idyllic Melaque west-end sand crescent. Here,

good times bloom among an informal club of longtime winter returnees beneath the *palapas* of the popular La Sirenita, Cabo Blanco, and Viva María restaurants. The hotel's 18 fan-only rooms (two with kitchenette) rent for $30 s or d, $35 t (low season), and $39 s, $44 d, $49 t (high), with hot-water shower baths.

### $50-100

If you prefer hotel high-rise ambience with privacy, a sea-view balcony, and a disco (weekends and holidays) next door, you can have it right on the beach at the **Hotel Club Náutico** (Av. Gómez Farías 1A, tel. 315/355-5770 or 315/355-5766, fax 315/355-5239, www.hotelclubnautico.com). The 40 simply but attractively decorated rooms, in blue, pastels, and white, angle toward the ocean in sunset-view tiers above a smallish pool and patio. The upper-floor rooms nearest the beach are likely to be quieter and have the best views. The hotel also has a good beachside restaurant, whose huge *palapa* captures the cool afternoon sea breeze and frames the blue waters of the Bay of Navidad. The hotel's main drawback is lack of exterior space, being sandwiched into a long, narrow beachfront lot. Rentals run about $70 d, $84 t; add about 30 percent during Christmas and Easter holidays. Ask for a discount during times of low occupancy. Features include air-conditioning, TV, and phones. Credit cards are accepted.

## Apartments, Houses, and Long-Term Rentals

If you're planning on a stay longer than a few weeks, you'll get more for your money if you can find a long-term house or apartment rental. Check out the good **Vacation Rentals by Owner** website (www.vrbo.com), which lists a number of Barra rental choices as of this writing. Alternatively, contact longtime real estate agent Tracye Ross at **Crazy Cactus Real Estate** (21 de Noviembre 60, tel./fax 315/355-6091 or 314/357-0460, U.S. tel. 832/364-6289, crazycactusmx@yahoo.com, www. casademarco.com), in Barra, or Marsha Ewing Hernandez, operator of **Mar Vida Real Estate** (tel. 315/355-5911, fax 315/355-5349, marsha-hernandez@yahoo.com).

## Trailer Parks and Campgrounds

Barra-Melaque's best trailer park is **La Playa** (Av. Gómez Farías 250, tel. 315/355-5065), right on the beach in downtown Melaque. Although the park is a bit cramped and mostly shadeless, longtimers nevertheless get their winter reservations in early for the choice beach spaces. The better-than-average facilities include a small store, fish-cleaning sinks, showers, toilets, and all hookups. The water is brackish—drink bottled. Boat launching is usually easy on the sheltered beach nearby. La Playa's 45 spaces rent for about $19 per day, $110 per week, or $355 per month.

Scores of winter returnees enjoy Melaque's north-end shoreline **informal RV park-campground,** with room for about 50 rigs and tents, operated by the Ejido Emiliano Zapata community. The cliff-bottom lot spreads above a calm rocky cove, ripe for swimming, snorkeling, and sailboarding. Other extras include super fishing and a sweeping view of the entire Bay of Navidad. All spaces are usually filled by Christmas and remain that way until March. The people are friendly, the price ($3 per tent or $5 per RV per day, $15/wk, $70/mo, small garbage collection fee, collected by the *ejido* folks) is certainly right, and the beer and water trucks arrive regularly throughout the winter season. Please dump your waste in sanitary facilities while staying here; continued pollution of the cove by irresponsible occupants in the past has led to complaints. Get there by the dirt road that continues from Avenida del Palmar, at the northwest end of Melaque.

A complex called **Bungalows Laguna del Tule** (Calle Topacio 231, tel. 315/355-5395 or 315/355-7241, www.lagunadeltulebunga-lows.com) occupies the southernmost end of the Melaque beachfront, just north of Barra. The complex includes 61 hotel rooms and bungalows, and 40 RV spaces; all face either the lagoon or the beach. (Don't forget the bug repellent.) The hotel rooms and bungalows are light and airy, with comfortable wooden furniture; bright, functional kitchens in the bungalows; and some seriously flashy finishes inside and out, including bright fabrics and art over the beds that looks about ready to jump off the wall. Then there's the hotel itself, with elaborate domes and stacked columns everywhere, and a swim-up bar in the large pool overlooking the sands of Melaque's beach. It's a pretty gaudy package, but it's definitely priced for families: hotel rooms with two double beds, refrigerator, TV, and lagoon views go for $30 low season, $50 high; bungalows sleeping 4-16 (yes, the big ones have up to eight beds) go for $38-123, depending on the size and season. The 40 RV spaces ($550/mo) come with water, power, and pool privileges.

Wilderness campers will enjoy **Playa los Cocos,** the miles-long golden sand beach south of Barra de Navidad that borders the ocean side of the Isla Navidad golf course. Playa los Cocos has an intimate hidden north-end sandy cove, perfect for an overnight or a few barefoot days of bird-watching, shell collecting, beach-combing, and dreaming around your driftwood campfire. The restaurants at the village of Colimilla or the stores (by launch across the lagoon) in Barra are available for food and water. Mosquitoes come out around sunset. Bring plenty of good repellent and a mosquito-proof tent.

The easiest way to get to Playa los Cocos is by hiring a launch at the Barra de Navidad lagoon front that will drop you off right on the Playa los Cocos beach. You can also go by hiring a taxi from Barra de Navidad, or by your own car from Highway 200. From Barra de Navidad, head south on Highway 200 a few miles to the signed Isla Navidad right turnoff. Continue through the golf course, bearing left, toward the ocean, to the golf course's northwest corner and an oceanfront parking lot at the beach.

## FOOD
### Breakfast, Snacks, and Stalls

An excellent way to start your Barra day is at the intimate *palapa*-shaded patio of the **Hotel Delfín** (Av. Morelos 23, tel. 315/357-0068,

8:30am-10:30am daily, $6). While you dish yourself fruit and pour your coffee from its little countertop buffet, the cook fixes your choice of breakfast options, from savory eggs and omelets to French toast and luscious, tender banana pancakes. Alternatively, in Barra, for an equally satisfying breakfast ($3-6), go to the ocean-view restaurant **Bananas** (tel. 315/355-5122, 8am-noon daily), upstairs at the Hotel Barra de Navidad.

Plenty of good daytime eating in Melaque goes on at the lineup of small permanent *fondas* ($2-4) in the alley that runs south from Avenida Hidalgo, half a block toward the beach from the southwest plaza corner. You can't go wrong with *fonda* food, as long as it's made right in front of you and served piping hot.

For evening light meals and snacks, Barra has plenty of options. Here, families seem to fall into two categories: those who sell food to sidewalk passersby and those who enjoy their offerings. The three blocks of Avenida Veracruz from Morelos to the city *jardín* (park) are dotted with tables that residents nightly load with hearty, economical food offerings, from tacos *de lengua* (tongue) and pork tamales to *pozole Guadalajara* and chiles rellenos ($1-3). The wholesomeness of their menus is evidenced by their devoted followings of longtime neighbor and tourist customers.

If you are looking for a nice deli sandwich or some French pastries, you can't miss **El Horno Francés** (Lepazpi 125, next to the Hotel al Alondra pool, tel. 315/355-0050,), where everything is baked fresh each morning. A case of sumptuous pies and croissants will tempt you. or grab an espresso and cookie to go.

## Barra Restaurants

One local family has built its sidewalk culinary skills into a thriving Barra storefront business: the **Restaurant Paty** (corner of Veracruz and Jalisco, tel. 315/355-5907, 8am-11pm daily, $2-5). It offers the traditional menu of Mexican *antojitos*—tacos, quesadillas, tostadas—plus roast beef, chicken, and very tasty posole. For a variation, try expatriate favorite **Pizzeria Yvette** (Jalisco 56, tel.

315/355-5918, 10:30am-11:30pm daily, $4-12), a few doors away.

Among Barra's favorite eateries is the **Restaurant Ramón** (Legazpi 260, tel. 315/355-6435, 7am-11pm daily, $5-12), across the street from the Hotel Barra de Navidad. Completely unpretentious and making the most of the usual list of international and Mexican specialties, friendly owner/chef Ramón and his hardworking staff continue to build their already sizable following. Choose whatever you like—chicken, fish, chiles rellenos, guacamole, spaghetti—and you'll most likely be pleased. Meals include gratis salsa and chips to start, hearty portions, and often a healthy side of cooked veggies on your plate.

One of Barra's most entertainingly scenic restaurants is **Veleros** (Veracruz 64, tel. 315/355-5907, noon-10pm daily, $7-15), right on the lagoon. If you happen to visit Barra during the full moon, don't miss watching its shimmering reflection from the restaurant *palapa* as it rises over the mangrove-bordered expanse. An additional Veleros bonus is the fascinating school of darting, swirling fish attracted by the spotlight shining on the water. Finally comes the food, which you can select from a menu of carefully prepared and served shrimp, lobster, octopus, chicken, and steak entrées. The brochettes are especially popular. Credit cards are accepted.

Alternatively, for a singularly romantic option, try refined lagoon-front **Restaurant Alcatraz** (Veracruz 12, tel. 315/355-7041, noon-10pm daily, $8-20), named by friendly owners Sergio and Susana Aguilar for the native lily that grows only in the Mexican altiplano. (It is nevertheless very common in California gardens.) Susana, who manages the restaurant, offers a delicious menu including soups and salads, meats, fish fillets, shrimp, and lobster. During winter high season, reservations are recommended.

Shift your scene one block away, to the **Restaurant Seamaster** (López de Legazpi 140, no phone, 8am-11pm daily, $6-10), on the beach side of the sandbar, where guests enjoy a refreshing sea breeze every afternoon and a happy-hour sunset every evening. Besides superfresh seafood selections, Seamaster features savory barbecued chicken and rib plates, and a nice cocktail list.

**Restaurant Pancho** (Legazpi 53, tel. 315/355-5176, 8am-8pm daily, $6-10), a few doors away, is one of Barra's original *palapas*, which old-timers can remember from the days when *all* Barra restaurants were *palapas.* The reputation for superfresh seafood, built up by the original (but now late) Pancho, who saw lots of changes in the old sandbar in his 80-odd years, is now continued by his wife and son.

Don't miss the shrimp cocktail ($8) at **Casa Chips Restaurant,** also known as **Marlena's** (Legazpi 198, tel. 315/355-5555, 11am-11pm Tues.-Sun.), which comes in a massive goblet filled with vegetables and broth, served hot. It's one of the best this author has ever had. If you are still hungry, there are lots of other delicious menu items to choose from, like the pineapple shrimp ($14).

## Melaque Restaurants

In Melaque, jazz and nouvelle cuisine first arrived at ◖ **Restaurant Maya** (in the alley at the foot of south-side Calle Obregón, 6pm-11pm Tues.-Sat., brunch 10:30am-2pm Sun.), favorite of a loyal cadre of American and Canadian vacationers and expatriates. Its private sheltered garden and the murmur of the Melaque surf set the stage, while the music and the food provide the shadow and act. For example, start out with a Maya Martini ($4); continue with curried fish cakes ($5); follow up with linguine with pesto, cream, and prawns ($14); and finish off with the chef's dessert creation of the day ($5). Winter high-season reservations are highly recommended.

**Restaurant el Dorado** (Calle Gómez Farías 1A, tel. 315/355-5770, 8am-11pm daily, $8-20), under the big beachside *palapa* in front of the Hotel Club Náutico, provides a cool, breezy place to enjoy the beach scene during breakfast or lunch; it's also a great sunset-watching spot for cocktails and dinner. Fresh seafood is the centerpiece, but the menu also includes ribs,

burgers, and chicken. Service is crisp, and the specialties are carefully prepared. Credit cards are accepted.

## Fruit, Vegetable, and Grocery Stores

There are no large markets, traditional or modern, in Barra. However, a few minimarkets and *fruterías* stock basic supplies. Best is probably **Frutería Ixtapa** (northeast corner of Veracruz and Michoacán, tel. 315/355-6443, 8am-10pm Mon.-Sat.). Drop by and find out the produce delivery day, so you can get it when it's fresh.

In Melaque, nearly all grocery and fruit shopping takes place at the **central market** or at several good stores on main street López Mateos, which runs away from the beach past the west side of the central plaza.

## INFORMATION AND SERVICES
## Tourist Information

The small Barra-Melaque regional office of the **Jalisco Department of Tourism** (Jalisco 67, tel./fax 315/355-5100, www.costalegre.com) is tucked near the east end of Jalisco across the street from the Terraza upstairs bar. Staff distributes maps and literature and answers questions during office hours (9am-5pm Mon.-Fri., 9am-2pm Sat.). The office is a good source of information about local civic and ecological issues and organizations.

## Publications

The Barra **newsstand** (corner of Veracruz and Michoacán, 7am-10pm daily) may seasonally stock some English-language newspapers and magazines.

Perhaps the best English-language lending library in all of the Mexican Pacific is **Beer Bob's Book Exchange** (Calle Tampico, btwn. Pilipinas and Michoacán), on a Barra back street. Many hundreds of vintage paperbacks, free for borrowing or exchange, fill the shelves. Chief librarian and Scrabble devotee Bob (a retired counselor for the California Youth Authority) manages his little gem of an establishment just for the fun of it. "It's not a store," he says. Just drop your old titles in the box and take away the equivalent from his well-organized collection. If you have nothing to exchange, simply return whatever you borrow before you leave town.

In Melaque, the **Librería Saifer** (on the southwest corner of the central plaza, by the church, 9am-3pm and 5pm-10pm daily) stocks the *Miami Herald.*

## Money

Although Barra has no bank, it does have a couple of ATMs at the Barra southeast plaza corner. Melaque does have a bank, **Banamex** (tel. 315/355-5217, 9am-4pm Mon.-Fri., 10am-2pm Sat.), with ATM, across the street and half a block north of the main bus station. Barra's friendliest money exchange is **Ciber@Money** (Veracruz 212, tel. 315/355-6177, 9am-6pm Mon.-Sat.).

## Communications

Barra and Melaque each have a small *correo.* The **Barra post office** (8am-3pm Mon.-Fri.) is on Veracruz, south side of the town *jardín.*

The **Melaque post office** (Clemente Orozco 13, btwn. G. Farías and Corona, tel. 315/355-5230, 8am-3pm Mon.-Fri.) is three blocks south of the plaza, a block and a half from the beach.

In Barra, go to friendly **Ciber@Money** (Veracruz 212, tel. 315/355-6177, 9am-6pm Mon.-Sat.) for public telephone, Internet access, and money exchange. Internet access in Barra is the rule, not the exception, these days, so you will not have a problem finding the Web.

## Health and Emergencies

In Barra, the government **Centro de Salud** (corner of Veracruz and Puerto de La Navidad, tel. 315/355-6220), four blocks north of the town plaza, has a doctor 24 hours a day. The **Melaque Centro de Salud** (Calle Gordiano Guzman 10, tel. 315/355-5880), off the main beachside street Gómez Farías two blocks from the trailer park, also offers access to a doctor 24 hours a day.

In a medical emergency, call for a Red Cross (Cruz Roja) **ambulance** (tel. 315/355-2300) to whisk you to the well-equipped hospitals in Manzanillo.

Otherwise, for over-the-counter remedies, in Barra, go to **Farmacia Zurich** (on Legazpi, tel. 315/355-6135), across from the church, at the south corner of Jalisco; or in Melaque, try **Super Farmacia Plaza** (on López Mateos, tel. 315/355-5167), at the northwest corner of the town plaza.

The **Barra police** (Veracruz 179, tel. 315/355-5399) are on 24-hour duty at the city office adjacent to the *jardín.*

For the **Melaque police**, either call (tel. 315/355-5080) or go to the headquarters behind the plaza-front *delegación municipal* (municipal agency) at the plaza corner of L. Mateos and Morelos.

## Laundry

Barra and Melaque visitors enjoy the services of a number of *lavanderías.* In Barra, try **Lavandería Jardín** (Jalisco 69, tel. 315/355-6135, 9am-2pm and 4pm-7pm Mon.-Fri., 9am-noon Sat.), next to the *turismo.* In Melaque, step one block east (parallel to the beach) along Juárez from the plaza, to **Lavandería Frances** (Juarez 49-A, no phone, 8am-8pm Mon.-Sat.).

## GETTING THERE
## By Air

Barra de Navidad is air accessible either through **Puerto Vallarta Airport** or the **Manzanillo Airport,** only 19 miles (30 km) south of Barra-Melaque. While the Puerto Vallarta connection has the advantage of many more flights, transfers to the south coast are time-consuming. If you can afford it, the quickest option from Puerto Vallarta is to rent a car. Alternatively, ride a local bus or hire a taxi from the airport to the new central bus station, north of the airport. There, catch a bus, preferably **Autocamiones del Pacífico** (tel. 322/290-0716) or Flecha Amarilla's luxury service **Primera Plus** (tel. 322/221-0994) to Barra or Melaque (three hours).

On the other hand, arrival via the

Manzanillo airport, half an hour from Barra-Melaque, is much more direct, provided that good connections are obtainable through the relatively few carriers that serve the airport.

### MANZANILLO AIRPORT FLIGHTS

**U.S. Airways** (www.usairways.com) flights connect with Phoenix during the winter-spring season, weekend flights only. For reservations, call the airline via the U.S. toll-free number (tel. 800/428-4322).

**Aeromar Airlines** flights connect daily with Mexico City, where many U.S. connections are available. For reservations and flight information, contact its airport office (tel. 314/333-0151 or 314/334-0532) or the Manzanillo downtown office (tel. 314/334-8356 or 314/334-8355, toll-free Mex. tel. 01-800/237-6627).

**Alaska Airlines** (toll-free U.S. tel. direct from Mexico 01-800/426-0333) flights connect daily with Los Angeles; **Magnicharter** airlines connects directly with Mexico City.

**United Airlines** (www.united.com) has a daily flight out of Houston that connects in Mexico City.

**Delta Airlines** (toll-free U.S. tel. 800/241-4141, www.delta.com) offers flights out of Atlanta, Dallas, and Los Angeles, with a connection in Mexico City.

### AIRPORT ARRIVAL AND DEPARTURE

The terminal, although small for an international destination, does have a money exchange counter, open 10am-6pm daily. It also has a few gift shops for last-minute purchases, snack stands, a good restaurant upstairs, some car rentals, and a *buzón* (mailbox) just outside the front entrance. It has no hotel booking service, however, so you should arrive with a hotel reservation, or you'll be at the mercy of taxi drivers who love to collect fat commissions on your first-night hotel tariff. Upon departure, be sure to save enough cash to pay the approximate $12 **departure tax** (if your ticket doesn't already include it).

After the usually rapid immigration and customs checks, independent arrivees have their choice of a car rental or taxi tickets from a booth just outside the arrival gate. *Colectivos* head for Barra de Navidad and other northern points seasonally only. Taxis, however, will take three passengers to Barra or Melaque for about $34 total; to El Tamarindo, $52; Blue Bay Club Los Angeles Locos, $54; Chamela-El Super, $84; or Las Alamandas, $120. *Colectivo* tickets run about $10-12 per person to any Manzanillo hotel, while a *taxi especial* runs about $25-34, depending on destination.

No public buses serve the Manzanillo airport. Strong, mobile travelers on tight budgets could save pesos by hitching or hiking the three miles to Highway 200 and flagging down one of the frequent north- or southbound second-class buses (fare about $2 to Barra or Manzanillo). Don't try it at night, however.

As for airport **car rentals,** you have a choice of Alamo (tel. 314/333-0611, fax 314/333-1140, alamomanzanillo@prodigy.net.mx), Hertz (tel. 314/333-3191, 314/333-3141, or 314/333-3142), Thrifty (tel. 314/334-3282 or 314/334-3292, autzs@prodigy.net.mx), and Budget (tel./fax 314/333-1445 or 314/334-2270, budgetmzo@prodigy.net.mx). Unless you don't mind paying upward of $50 per day, shop around for your car rental by calling the company's U.S. and Canada toll-free numbers at home *before* you leave.

Don't lose your tourist card; if somehow you do, arrive early enough to get a replacement (bring proof of arrival date, such as air ticket or copy of the lost document) at the Manzanillo airport *migración* (tel. 315/335-3689 or 315/335-3690).

## By Car or RV

Three highway routes access Barra de Navidad: from the north via Puerto Vallarta, from the south via Manzanillo, and from the northeast via Guadalajara.

From Puerto Vallarta, Mexican National Highway 200 is all asphalt and in good condition (except for some potholes) along its 134-mile (216-km) stretch to Barra de Navidad. Traffic is generally light; it may slow a bit as the highway climbs the 2,400-foot (732-m) Sierra Cuale summit near El Tuito south of

Puerto Vallarta, but the light traffic and good road make passing safely possible. Allow about three hours for this very scenic trip. Bring a good camera, as there are many spots for photo opportunities.

From Manzanillo, the 38-mile (61-km) stretch of Highway 200 is nearly all countryside and all level. It's a snap in under an hour.

The longer, but quicker and easier, Barra de Navidad-Guadalajara road connection runs through Manzanillo along *autopistas* (superhighways) 54D, 110, and 200D. In Guadalajara, start out at the Minerva Circle (at the intersection of Av. López Mateos and Guadalajara west-side Av. Vallarta). Mark your odometer and follow Avenida López Mateos south. After about 10 miles (32 km), at Guadalajara's country edge, continue, following the signs for Colima that direct you along the four-lane combined Mexican National Highways 15, 54, and 80 heading southwest. At 19 miles (30 km) from the Minerva Circle, as Highway 15 splits right for Morelia and Mexico City, continue straight ahead, following the signs for Colima and Barra de Navidad. Very soon, follow the Highway 80/Highway 54D right fork for Barra de Navidad-Colima. Two miles (3.2 km) farther, follow the Highway 54D branch left toward Colima. Continue on Highway 54D straight ahead for about two hours, bypassing Colima. About 10 miles (32 km) south of Colima, Highway 54D changes, continuing as Highway 110 expressway. At Tecoman, Highway 110 becomes Highway 200D expressway, which you follow another hour, bypassing Manzanillo (via the Manzanillo Highway 200 *cuota* bypass) all the way to Barra de Navidad. Easy grades allow a leisurely 55 mph (90 kph) most of the way for this 192-mile (311-km) trip. Allow about 4.5 hours, either direction.

The same is not true of the winding, two-lane, 181-mile (291-km) Highway 80 route between Barra de Navidad and Guadalajara. Start out from the Minerva Circle, as previously described, but south of the city, instead of forking left on Highway 54D to Colima, continue straight ahead on Highway 80 toward Barra de Navidad. The narrow, two-lane road continues through a dozen little towns, over three mountain ranges, and around curves for another 160 miles (258 km) to Melaque and Barra de Navidad. To be safe, allow about six hours of driving time uphill to Guadalajara, five hours in the opposite direction.

## By Bus

Several regional bus lines cooperate in connecting Barra and Melaque north with Puerto Vallarta; south with Cihuatlán, Manzanillo, Colima, Playa Azul, Zihuatanejo, and Acapulco; and northeast with Guadalajara, via Highway 80, and Morelia and Mexico City, via the expressway. They arrive and leave so often (about every half hour during the day) from the three little Barra de Navidad stations, clustered on Avenida Veracruz a block and a half north past the central plaza, that they're practically indistinguishable.

Of the various companies, affiliated lines **Transportes Cihuatlán** and **Autocamiones del Pacífico** (tel. 315/355-5200) provide the most options: Super-first-class Primera Plus buses connect (several per day) with Guadalajara, Manzanillo, and Puerto Vallarta, and they also offer at least a dozen second-class buses per day in all three directions. These often stop anywhere along the road if passengers wave them down.

Across the street, other lines, affiliated with bus giant **Flecha Amarilla,** provide similar services, including a different Primera Plus luxury-class service to Manzanillo, Puerto Vallarta, Guadalajara, and León, out of its separate station (Veracruz 269, tel. 315/355-6111), across and half a block up the street.

Also, next door to Flecha Amarilla, **ETN,** or Enlaces Transportes Nacionales (tel. 315/355-8400), buses leave from a small air-conditioned station to connect with Manzanillo, Colima, Morelia, and Mexico City.

With the exception of Elite, which stops only in Melaque, all the buses that stop in Barra also stop in Melaque; all Autocamiones del Pacífico and Transportes Cihuatlán buses stop at the Melaque main terminal, **Central de**

**Autobuses** (on Gómez Farías at V. Carranza, tel. 315/355-5003, open 24 hours daily).

In Melaque, **Flecha Amarilla** maintains its own fancy new air-conditioned station (tel. 315/355-6110) across the street, where you can ride its luxury-class Primera Plus buses, in addition to regular second-class Autobuses Costalegre, north to Puerto Vallarta, south to Manzanillo, and with expanded service to Guadalajara, León, and Mexico City.

One line, first-class **Elite,** does not stop in Barra. It maintains its own little Melaque station (Gómez Farías 257, tel. 315/355-5177) a block south of the main station, across from the Melaque Trailer Park. From there, Elite connects by first-class express north (two daily departures) all the way to Puerto Vallarta, Mazatlán, and Tijuana, and south (two daily departures) to Manzanillo, Zihuatanejo, and Acapulco.

Note: All Barra de Navidad and Melaque bus departures are *salidas de paso,* meaning they originate somewhere else. Although seating cannot be ascertained until the bus arrives, seats are generally available, except during the crowded Christmas and Easter holidays.

# BACKGROUND

## The Land

The sun-drenched resort of Puerto Vallarta (pop. 256,000) and its surrounding region owe their prosperity to their most fortunate location, where gentle Pacific breezes meet the parade of majestic volcanic peaks marching west from central Mexico.

Breeze-borne moisture, trickling down mineral-rich volcanic slopes, has nurtured civilizations for millennia in the highland valleys around Tepic and Guadalajara, the state capitals of Nayarit and Jalisco. Running from Lake Chapala, just south of Guadalajara, the waters plunge into the mile-deep canyon of Mexico's longest river, the Río Grande de Santiago (known as the Río Lerma upstream of the lake). They finally return to the ocean, nourishing the teeming aquatic life of the river's estuary just north of

San Blas, Nayarit, two hours' drive north of Puerto Vallarta.

Within sight of Puerto Vallarta rise the jagged mountain ranges of the Sierra Vallejo and the Sierra Cuale. The runoff from these peaks becomes the Río Ameca, which sustains a lush patchwork of fruit, corn, and sugarcane that decorates the broad valley bottom. The Ameca meets the ocean just north of the Puerto Vallarta town limits. There, myriad sea creatures seek the river's nourishment at the Puerto Vallarta shoreline, the innermost recess of the Bay of Banderas, Mexico's broadest and deepest bay.

On the map of the Puerto Vallarta region, the Bay of Banderas appears gouged from the coast by some vengeful Aztec god (perhaps in retribution for the Spanish conquest) with a single 20-mile-wide swipe of his giant hand, just sparing the city of Puerto Vallarta.

Time, however, appears to have healed that great imaginary cataclysm. The rugged Sierra Vallejo to the north and Sierra Cuale to the south have acquired green coats of jungly forest on their slopes, and sand has accumulated on the great arc of the Bay of Banderas. There, a diadem of palmy resort towns—Punta Mita, Cruz de Huanacaxtle, Bucerías, Mismaloya, Boca de Tomatlán, and Yelapa—decorates the bay to the north and south of town. In the mountains that rise literally from Puerto Vallarta's city streets, the idyllic colonial-era villages of San Sebastián, Mascota, and Talpa nestle in verdant valleys only 20 minutes away by light plane.

Farther afield, smaller bays dotted with pearly strands, sleepy villages, and small resorts adorn the coastline north and south of the Bay of Banderas. To the south, beyond the pine- and oak-studded Sierra Lagunillas summit, stretch the blue reaches of the bays of Chamela, Tenacatita, and, finally, Navidad, at the Jalisco-Colima state border. There, the downscale little resort of Barra de Navidad drowses beside its wildlife-rich lagoon.

To the north of the Bay of Banderas stretches the vine-strewn Nayarit Coast, where the broad inlets of Jaltemba and Matanchén curve past the formerly sleepy winter havens of Sayulita, Rincón de Guayabitos, and San Blas. From there, a mangrove marshland extends past the historic Mexcaltitán island-village to the jungly Río Cañas at the Nayarit-Sinaloa border.

## CLIMATE

Nature has graced the Puerto Vallarta region with a microclimate tapestry. Although rainfall, winds, and mountains introduce pleasant local variations, elevation provides the broad brush. The entire coastal strip where frost never bites (including the mountain slopes and plateaus up to 4,000 or 5,000 ft/1,200-1,500 m) luxuriates in the tropics.

The seashore is a land of perpetual summer. Winter days are typically warm and rainless, peaking at 80-85°F (27-30°C) and dropping to 55-65°F (16-18°C) by midnight.

Increasing elevation gradually decreases both heat and humidity. In the valley of Tepic (elev. 3,000 ft/900 m), you can expect warm, dry winter days of 75-80°F (24-27°C) and cooler nights around 50-60°F (10-15°C). Days will usually be balmy and springlike, climbing to around 75°F (24°C) by noon, with nights dropping to a temperate 40-50°F (5-10°C); pack a sweater or light jacket.

May, before the rains, is often the warmest month in the entire Puerto Vallarta region. Summer days on Puerto Vallarta beaches are very warm, humid, and sometimes rainy. July, August, and September forenoons are typically bright, warming to the high 80s (around 32°C). By afternoon, however, clouds often gather and bring short, sometimes heavy, showers. By late afternoon the clouds part, the sun dries the pavements, and the tropical breeze is just right for enjoying a sparkling Puerto Vallarta sunset. Tepic summers are delightful, with afternoons in the 80s (27-32°C) and balmy evenings in the 70s (21-26°C), perfect for strolling.

# Flora

Abundant sun and summer rains nurture the vegetation of the Puerto Vallarta region. At roadside spots, spiny bromeliads, pendulous passion fruits, and giant serpentine vines luxuriate, beckoning to admirers. Now and then visitors may stop, attracted by something remarkable, such as a riot of flowers blooming from apparently dead branches or what looks like grapefruit sprouting from the trunk of a roadside tree. More often, travelers pass by the long stretches of thickets, jungles, and marshes without stopping; however, a little knowledge of what to expect can blossom into recognition and discovery, transforming the humdrum into the extraordinary.

## VEGETATION ZONES

Mexico's diverse landscape and fickle rainfall have sculpted its wide range of plant forms. Botanists recognize at least 14 major Mexican vegetation zones, 7 of which occur in the Puerto Vallarta region.

Directly along the coastal highway, you often pass long sections of three of these zones: savanna, thorn forest, and tropical deciduous forest.

### Savanna

Great swaths of pasturelike savanna stretch along Highway 15 in Nayarit north of Tepic. In its natural state, savanna often appears as a palm-dotted sea of grass—green and marshy during the rainy summer, dry and brown by late winter.

Although grass rules the savanna, palms give it character. Most familiar is the **coconut,** or *cocotero* (*Cocos nucifera*)—the world's most useful tree—used for everything from lumber to candy. Coconut palms line the beaches and climb the hillsides—drooping, slanting, rustling, and swaying in the breeze like troupes of hula dancers. Less familiar, but with as much personality, is the Mexican **fan palm,** or *palma real* (*Sabal mexicana*), festooned with black fruit and spread flat like a senorita's fan.

The savanna's list goes on: the grapefruit-like fruit on the trunk and branches identify the **gourd tree,** or *calabaza* (*Crescentia alata*). The mature gourds, brown and hard, have been carved into *jícaros* (cups for drinking chocolate) for millennia.

Orange-size pumpkinlike gourds mark the **sand box tree,** or *jabillo* (*Hura polyandra*), so named because they once served as desktop boxes full of sand for drying ink. The Aztecs, however, called it the exploding tree, because the ripe gourds burst their seeds forth with a bang like a firecracker.

The waterlogged seaward edge of the savanna nurtures forests of the **red mangrove,** or *mangle colorado* (*Rhizophora mangle*), short trees that seem to stand in the water on stilts. Their new roots grow downward from above; a time-lapse photo would show them marching, as if on stilts, into the lagoon.

### Thorn Forest

Lower rainfall leads to the hardier growth of the thorn forest—domain of the pea family—the **legumes** marked in late winter and spring by bursts of red, yellow, pink, and white flowers. Look closely at the blossoms, and you will see they resemble the familiar wild sweet pea of North America. Even when the blossoms are gone, you can identify them by seed pods that hang from the branches. Local folks call them by many names. These include the **tabachín,** the scarlet Mexican bird of paradise; and its close relative the **flamboyán,** or **royal poinciana,** an import from Africa, where it's called the flame tree.

Other spectacular members of the pea family include the bright-yellow **abejón,** which blooms nearly year-round, and the **coapinol,** marked by hosts of white blooms (Mar.-July) and large dark-brown pods. Not only colorful but useful is the **fishfuddle,** with pink flowers and long pods, from which fisherfolk derive a fish-stunning poison.

More abundant (although not so noticeable)

# VEGETATION ZONES

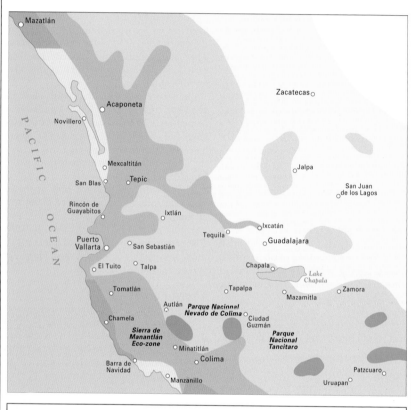

Mazatlán

Zacatecas

Acaponeta

Novillero

PACIFIC

Mexcaltitán

Tepic

San Blas

Jalpa

San Juan
de los Lagos

OCEAN

Rincón de
Guayabitos

Ixtlán

Puerto
Vallarta

San Sebastián

Ixcatán

Tequila

Guadalajara

El Tuito    Talpa

Chapala

Lake
Chapala

Tomatlán

Tapalpa

Mazamitla

Zamora

Chamela

Autlán    *Parque Nacional
Nevado de Colima*

Ciudad
Guzmán

*Sierra de
Manantlán
Eco-zone*

*Parque
Nacional
Tancitaro*

Minatitlán

Colima

Barra de
Navidad

Patzcuaro

Manzanillo

Uruapan

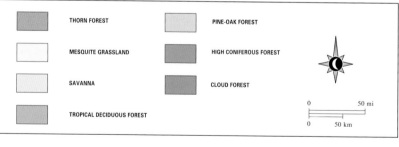

| | | | |
|---|---|---|---|
| THORN FOREST | | PINE-OAK FOREST | |
| MESQUITE GRASSLAND | | HIGH CONIFEROUS FOREST | |
| SAVANNA | | CLOUD FOREST | |
| TROPICAL DECIDUOUS FOREST | | | |

0          50 mi

0      50 km

© JUSTIN HENDERSON

This tree on Isla Río Cuale is a massive tangle of ancient roots and limbs.

are the legumes' cousins, the **acacias** and **mimosas.** Long swaths of thorn forest grow right to the coastal highway and side-road pavements, so that the road appears tunnel-like through a tangle of brushy acacia trees. Pull completely off the road for a look, and you will spot the small yellow flower balls, ferny leaves, and long, narrow pods of the **boat spine acacia,** or *quisache tempamo* (*Acacia cochliacantha*). Take care, however, around the acacias; some of the long-thorned varieties harbor nectar-feeding, biting ants.

Perhaps the most dramatic member of the thorn community is the **morning glory tree,** or *palo blanco* (*Ipomoea aborescens*), which announces the winter dry season by a festoon of white trumpets atop its crown of seemingly dead branches.

The Mexican penchant for making fun of death shows in the alternate name for *palo del muerto,* or the tree of the dead. It is also called *palo bobo* (fool tree) in some locales, because folks believe if you take a drink from a stream near its foot, you will go crazy.

The cactus are among the thorn forest's sturdiest and most spectacular inhabitants. Occasional specimens of the spectacular **candelabra cactus,** or *candelabro* (*Stenocereus weberi*), spread as much as 40 feet (12 m) tall and wide.

## Tropical Deciduous Forest

In rainier areas, the thorn forest grades into tropical deciduous forest. This is the "friendly" or "short-tree" forest, blanketed by a tangle of summer-green leaves that fall in the dry winter to reveal thickets of branches. Some trees show bright fall reds and yellows, later blossoming with brilliant flowers—spider lily, cardinal sage, pink trumpet, poppylike yellowsilk (*pomposhuti*), and mouse-killer (*mata ratón*), which swirl in the spring wind like cherry-blossom blizzards.

The tropical deciduous forest is a lush jungle coat swathing much of the coastal Puerto Vallarta region. It is especially lush in the mountains above San Blas and along the low summit of Highway 200 over the Sierra Vallejo north of Puerto Vallarta. Where the mountains rush directly down to the sea, the forest appears to spill right over the headland into the ocean. Vine-strewn thickets overhang the highway like the edges of a lost prehistoric world, where at any moment you expect a dinosaur to rear up. The biological realities here are nearly as exotic. A four-foot-long green iguana, looking every bit as primitive as a dinosaur, slithers across the pavement. Beside the road, a spreading, solitary **strangler fig** (*Ficus padifolia*) stands, draped with hairy, hanging air roots (which, in time, plant themselves in the ground and support the branches). Its Mexican name, *matapalo* (killer tree), is gruesomely accurate, for strangler figs often entwine themselves in death embraces with less aggressive tree-victims.

Much more benign is my favorite in the tropical deciduous forest: the **Colima palm** (*Orbignya guayacule*), or *guaycoyul* or *cohune,* which means magnificent. Capped by a proud cock plume, it presides over the forest singly or in great, graceful swaying groves atop sea cliffs. Its nuts, harvested like small coconuts, yield oil and animal fodder.

Excursions by Jeep or foot along shaded off-highway tracks through the tropical deciduous forest can bestow delightful jungle scenes; however, unwary travelers must watch out for the poison oak-like **mala mujer** (evil woman) tree. The oil on its large five-fingered leaves can cause an itchy rash.

## Pine-Oak Forest

Along the upland highways (notably at the Sierra Cuale summit of Highway 200 south from Puerto Vallarta, and at high stretches of National Highway 80 between Barra de Navidad and Guadalajara), the tropical forest gives way to temperate pine-oak forest, the Puerto Vallarta region's most extensive vegetation zone. Here, many of Mexico's 112 oak and 39 pine species thrive. Oval two-inch cones and foot-long drooping needles (three to a cluster) make the **pino triste,** or sad pine (*Pinus lumholtzii*), appear in severe need of water. Unlike many of Mexico's pines, it produces neither good lumber nor much turpentine, although it *is* prized by guitar makers for its wood.

Much more regal in bearing and more commercially important are the tall pines, **Chihuahua pine** (*Pinus chihuahuana*) and **Chinese pine** (*Pinus leiophylla*). Both reddish-barked with yellow wood, they resemble the ponderosa pine of the western United States. You can tell them apart by their needles: The Chihuahua pine (*pino prieto*) has three to a cluster, while the Chinese pine (*pino chino*) has five.

Pines often grow in stands mixed with **oaks,** which occur in two broad classifications—*encino* (evergreen, small-leafed) and *roble* (deciduous, large-leafed)—both much like the oaks that dot California hills and valleys. Clustered on their branches and scattered in the shade, *bellotas* (acorns) distinctly mark them as oaks.

## Mesquite Grassland

Although much of the mesquite grassland of the Puerto Vallarta region has been tamed into farmland, a number of its more interesting plants do grow in the more arid districts, notably on the Jalisco Coast, not far south of the town of El Tuito.

Among the mesquite grassland's most interesting species is the **maguey** (mah-GAY), or century plant, so-called because it's said to bloom once, then die, after 100 years of growth—although its lifespan is usually closer to 50 years. The maguey and its cactus-like relatives (such as the very useful **mezcal, lechugilla,** and **sisal,** all of the genus *Agave*), each grow as a roselike cluster of leathery, long, pointed gray-green leaves, from which a single flower stalk eventually blooms.

Century plants themselves, which can grow as large as several feet tall and wide, thrive either wild or in cultivated fields in ranks and files like a botanical army on parade. These fields, prominently visible from National Highway 15 west of Guadalajara, are eventually harvested, the leaves crushed, fermented, and distilled into fiery 80-proof liquor known locally as *raicilla,* some of the most renowned of which is made near the town of El Tuito.

Watch for the mesquite grassland's **candelilla** (*Euphorbia antisyphillitica*), an odd cousin of the poinsettia, also a Mexico native. In contrast to the poinsettia, the *candelilla* resembles a tall (two- to three-foot) candle, with small white flowers scattered upward along its single vertical stem. Abundant wax on the many pencil-size stalks that curve upward from the base is useful for anything from polishing your shoes to lubricating your car's distributor.

Equally exotic is the *Jatropha dioica,* called the **sangre de dragón** (blood of the dragon), which also grows in a single meaty stem, but with two-inch-long lobed leaves with small white flowers. Break off a stem and out oozes a clear sap, which soon turns bloodred.

## Cloud Forest
Adventurous visitors who travel to certain remote, dewy mountainsides above 7,000 feet (2,000 m) can explore the plant and wildlife community of the cloud forest. The Sierra Manantlán, a roadless de facto wilderness southeast of Autlán, Jalisco, preserves such a habitat. There, abundant cool fog nourishes forests of glacial-epoch remnant flora: tree ferns and lichen-draped pines and oaks above a mossy carpet of orchids, bromeliads, and begonias.

## High Coniferous Forest
The Puerto Vallarta region's rarest, least-accessible vegetation zone is the high coniferous forest, which swathes the slopes of lofty peaks, notably the Nevado de Colima (elev. 14,220 ft/4,325 m), on the Jalisco-Colima border. This pristine green alpine island, accessible only on horseback or by foot, nurtures stands of magnificent pines and spruce, laced by grassy meadows, similar to the higher Rocky Mountain slopes in the United States and Canada. Reigning over the lesser species is the regal **Montezuma pine** (*Pinus montezumae*), distinguished by its long, pendulous cones and rough, ruddy bark, reminiscent of the sugar pine of the western United States.

# Fauna

Despite continued habitat destruction—forests logged, wetlands filled, and savannas plowed—great swaths of the Puerto Vallarta region still abound with wildlife. Common in the temperate pine-oak forest highlands are mammals familiar to U.S. residents—such as mountain lion (puma), coyote, fox (*zorro*), rabbit (*conejo*), and quail (*codorniz*).

However, the tropical coastal forests and savannas are home to fascinating species seen only in zoos north of the border. The reality of this dawns on travelers when they glimpse something exotic, such as raucous, screeching swarms of small green parrots rising from the roadside, or a coati nosing in the sand just a few feet away from them at the forested edge of an isolated beach.

Population pressures have nevertheless decreased wild habitats, endangering many previously abundant animal species. If you are lucky, you may find a tracker who can lead you to a band of now-rare reddish-brown **spider monkeys** (*monos*) raiding a wild fruit tree. And deep in the mountain vastness, you may be led to a view of the endangered striped cat, the **ocelot** (*tigrillo*), or its smaller relative, the **margay**. On such an excursion, if you are really fortunate, you may hear the "chesty" roar or catch a glimpse of a jaguar, the fabled *el tigre.*

## MAMMALS
### Jaguars
"Each hill has its own *tigre,*" a Mexican proverb says. With black spots spread over a tan coat, stretching 5 feet (1.5 m) and weighing 200 pounds (90 kg), the typical jaguar resembles a muscular spotted leopard. Although hunted since prehistory, and now endangered, the jaguar lives on in the Puerto Vallarta region, where it hunts along thickly forested stream bottoms

and foothills. Unlike the mountain lion, the jaguar will eat any game. Jaguars have even been known to wait patiently for fish in rivers and to stalk beaches for turtle and egg dinners. If they have a favorite food, it is probably the piglike wild peccary (*jabalí*). Experienced hunters agree that no two jaguars will have the same prey in their stomachs.

Although humans have died of wounds inflicted by cornered jaguars, there is little or no hard evidence that they eat humans, despite legends to the contrary.

### Armadillos, Coatis, and Bats

Armadillos are cat-size mammals that act and look like opossums but carry reptilian-like shells. If you see one, remain still, and it may walk right up and sniff your foot before it recognizes you and scuttles back into the woods.

A common inhabitant of the tropics is the raccoonlike coati (*tejón, pisote*). In the wild, coatis like shady stream banks, often congregating in large troops of 15-30 individuals. They are identified by their short brown or tan fur, small round ears, long nose, and straight, vertically held tail. With their endearing and inquisitive nature, coatis are often kept as pets; the first coati you see may be one on a string offered for sale at a local market.

Mexican bats (*murciélagos*) are widespread, with at least 126 species (compared to 37 in the United States). In Mexico, as everywhere, bats are feared and misunderstood. As sunset approaches, many species come out of their hiding places and flit through the air in search of insects. Most people, sitting outside enjoying the early evening, will mistake their darting silhouettes for those of birds, who, except for owls, do not generally fly at night.

Bats are often locally called *vampiros,* even though only three relatively rare Mexican species actually feed on the blood of mammals—nearly always cattle—and of birds.

The many nonvampire Mexican bats carry their vampire cousins' odious reputation with forbearance. They go about their good works, pollinating flowers, clearing the air of pesky gnats and mosquitoes, ridding cornfields of mice, and dropping seeds, thereby restoring forests.

## BIRDS

The coastal lagoons of the Puerto Vallarta region lie astride the Pacific flyway, one of the Americas' major north-south paths for migrating waterfowl. Many of the familiar American and Canadian species, including pintail, gadwall, baldpate, shoveler, redhead, and scaup, arrive October-January, when their numbers will have swollen into the millions. They settle near food and cover—even at the borders of cornfields, to the frustration of farmers.

Besides the migrants, swarms of resident species—**herons** and **egrets** (*garzas*), cormorant-like **anhingas, lily-walkers** (*jacanas*), and hundreds more—stalk, nest, and preen in the same lagoons.

Few spots are better for observing seabirds than the beaches of the Puerto Vallarta region. Brown **pelicans** and black-and-white frigate birds are among the prime actors. When a flock of pelicans spots a school of their favorite fish, they go about their routine deliberately. Singly or in pairs, they circle and plummet into the waves to come up, more often than not, with fish in their gullets. Each bird then bobs and floats over the swells for a minute or two, seeming to wait for its dozen or so fellow pelicans to take their turns. This continues until they've bagged a dinner of 10-15 fish apiece.

**Frigate birds,** the scavengers par excellence of the Puerto Vallarta region, often profit by the labor of the teams of fishermen who haul in nets of fish on village beaches. After the fishermen auction off the choice morsels of perch, tuna, red snapper, octopus, or shrimp to merchants, and the local villagers have scavenged everything else edible, the motley residue of small fish, sea snakes, skates, squid, slugs, and sharks is thrown to a screeching flock of frigate birds.

The sprawling, wild mangrove wetland near San Blas, 100 miles north of Puerto Vallarta, nurtures a trove of wildlife, especially birds, ripe for viewing on foot near the town, or by guided boat tours.

© JUSTIN HENDERSON

Parrots roam wild and are kept as pets in many Vallarta businesses and households.

## REPTILES AND AMPHIBIANS
### Snakes, Gila Monsters, and Crocodiles

Mexico has 460-odd snake species, the vast majority shy and nonpoisonous; they will generally get out of your way if you give plenty of warning. In Mexico, as everywhere, poisonous snakes have been largely eradicated in city and tourist areas. In brush or jungle areas, carry a stick or a machete and beat the bushes ahead of you while watching where you put your feet. When hiking or rock climbing in the country, don't put your hand in niches you can't see.

You might even see a snake underwater while swimming offshore at an isolated Bay of Banderas beach. The **yellow-bellied sea snake** (*Pelamis platurus*) grows to about 2 feet (0.6 m) and, although rare and shy, can inflict fatal bites. If you see a yellow-and-black snake underwater, get away, pronto. (Some eels, which resemble snakes but have gills like fish and inhabit rocky crevices, can inflict nonpoisonous bites and should also be avoided.)

The Mexican land counterpart of the *Pelamis platurus* is the **coral snake** (*coralillo*), which occurs as about two dozen species, all with multicolored bright bands that always include red. Although relatively rare, small, and shy, coral snakes occasionally inflict serious, sometimes fatal, bites.

More aggressive and generally more dangerous is the Mexican **rattlesnake** (*cascabel*) and its viper relative, the **fer-de-lance** (*Bothrops atrox*). About the same in size (to 6 ft/2 m) and appearance as the rattlesnake, the fer-de-lance is known by various local names, such as *nauyaca, cuatro narices, palanca,* and *barba amarilla.* It is potentially more hazardous than the rattlesnake because it lacks a warning rattle.

The Gila monster (confined in Mexico to northern Sonora) and its southern tropical relative, the yellow-spotted black **escorpión** (*Heloderma horridum*), are the world's only poisonous lizards. Despite its beaded skin and menacing, fleshy appearance, the *escorpión* bites only when severely provoked; even then, its venom is rarely, if ever, fatal.

The **crocodile** (*cocodrilo* or *caimán*), once prized for its meat and hide, came close to vanishing in Mexican Pacific lagoons until the government took steps to ensure its survival; it's now officially protected. A few isolated breeding populations live on in the wild, while government and private hatcheries (for example, in San Blas) are breeding more for the eventual repopulation of lagoons where crocodiles once were common.

Two crocodile species occur in the Puerto Vallarta region. The true crocodile, *Crocodilus acutus,* has a narrower snout than its local cousin, *Caiman crocodilus fuscus,* a type of alligator (*lagarto*). Although past individuals have been recorded at up to 15 feet (4.5 m) long (see the stuffed specimen upstairs at the Tepic anthropology and history museum, or in the Hotel Bucanero lobby in San Blas), wild native crocodiles are usually young and 2 feet (0.6 m) or less in length.

### Turtles

The story of Mexican sea turtles is similar to

that of crocodiles: They once swarmed ashore on Puerto Vallarta regional beaches to lay their eggs. Prized for their meat, eggs, hide, and shell, the turtle population was severely devastated. The good news is that, now officially protected, Mexican sea turtle numbers are beginning to recover their nesting numbers in some locations.

Of the four locally occurring species, the endangered olive ridley turtle (*Lepidochelys olivacea*), or *golfina,* is by far the most common. The smallest and among the most widespread of the world's sea turtles, *golfinas* flock ashore at a number of Puerto Vallarta-region beaches, notably Playa San Francisco on the Nayarit Coast, and Playa Mismaloya, near La Cruz de Loreto, on the southern Jalisco Coast. At these and many other Mexican Pacific locations, determined groups of volunteers camp out on isolated beaches during the summer and fall in order to save and incubate turtle eggs, for the final reward of watching the safe return of hundreds, and hopefully someday thousands, of turtle hatchlings to the sea.

Also present in some numbers along the Puerto Vallarta regional coastline is the green turtle (*Chelonia mydas*), or *tortuga negra* (black turtle), as it's known in Mexico. From tour boats, green turtles can sometimes be seen grazing on sea grass offshore in the Bay of Banderas.

## FISH AND MARINE MAMMALS

Shoals of fish abound in Puerto Vallarta's waters. Four billfish species are found in deep-sea grounds several miles offshore: **swordfish, sailfish,** and **blue** and **black marlin.** All are spirited fighters, though the sailfish and marlin are generally the toughest to bring in. The blue marlin is the biggest of the four; in the past, 10-foot (3-m) specimens weighing more than 1,000 pounds (450 kg) were brought in at Pacific Coast marinas. Lately, 4 feet (1.2 m) and 200 pounds (90 kg) for a marlin and 100 pounds (45 kg) for a sailfish are more typical. Progressive captains now encourage victorious anglers to return these magnificent "tigers of the sea" (especially the sinewy sailfish and blue marlin, which make for poor eating) to the deep after they've won the battle.

Billfish are not the only prizes of the sea, however. Serious fish lovers also seek varieties of tunalike **jack,** such as **yellowtail, Pacific amberjack, pompano, jack crevalle,** and the tenacious **roosterfish,** named for the "comb" atop its head. These, and the **yellowfin tuna, mackerel,** and **dorado** (which Hawaiians call mahimahi), are among the delicacies sought in Puerto Vallarta waters.

Accessible from small boats offshore and by casting from shoreline rocks are varieties of **snapper** (*huachinango, pargo*) and **sea bass** (*cabrilla*). Closer to shore, **croaker, mullet,** and **jewfish** can be found foraging along sandy bottoms and in rocky crevices.

**Sharks** and **rays** inhabit nearly all depths, with smaller fry venturing into beach shallows and lagoons. Huge **Pacific manta rays** appear to be frolicking, their great wings flapping like birds, not far off Puerto Vallarta shores. Just beyond the waves, local fisherfolk bring in **hammerhead, thresher,** and **leopard sharks.**

Also common is the **stingray,** which can inflict a painful wound with its barbed tail. Experienced swimmers and waders avoid injury by both shuffling (rather than stepping) and watching their feet in shallow waters with sandy bottoms.

## Sea Lions, Porpoises, and Whales

Although seen in much greater numbers in Baja California's colder waters, fur-bearing species, such as seals and sea lions, do occasionally hunt in the tropical waters and bask on the sands of island beaches off the Puerto Vallarta coast. Due to the rigid government protections that have been enforced for a generation, their numbers appear to be increasing.

The **California Gulf porpoise**—*delfin* or *vaquita* (little cow)—once very numerous, is now rare. The smallest member of the whale family, it rarely exceeds 5 feet (1.5 m). Hopefully, if conservation plans are successful, its playful diving and jumping antics will again be observable from Puerto Vallarta-based tour and fishing boats.

Although the **California gray whale** has a migration pattern extending only to the southern tip of Baja California, occasional pods stray farther south, where deep-sea anglers and cruise- and tour-boat passengers see them in deep waters offshore.

Larger whale (*ballena*) species, such as the **humpback** and **blue whale,** appear to enjoy tropical waters even more, ranging the north Pacific tropics from Puerto Vallarta west to Hawaii and beyond.

Offshore islands, such as the nearby Marietas and María Isabel (accessible from San Blas), and the Revillagigedo (ray-vee-yah-hee-HAY-doh) 300 miles (480 km) due west of Puerto Vallarta, offer prime viewing grounds for Mexico's aquatic fauna.

# History

Once upon a time, perhaps as early as 50,000 years ago, the first bands of hunters, perhaps following great game herds, crossed from Siberia to the American continent. For thousands of years they drifted southward, many of them eventually settling in the lush highland valleys of Mexico.

Much later, perhaps around 5000 BC, and in what would later be called Mexico, these early people began gathering and grinding the seeds of a hardy grass that required only the summer rains to thrive. After generations of selective breeding, this grain, called *teocentli* (sacred seed, which we call maize or corn), led to prosperity.

## EARLY MEXICAN CIVILIZATIONS

With abundant food, settlements grew, and leisure classes arose—artists, architects, warriors, and ruler-priests—who had time to think and create. With a calendar, they harnessed the constant wheel of the firmament to life on earth, defining the days to plant, harvest, feast, travel, and trade. Eventually grand cities arose.

### Teotihuacán

Teotihuacán, with a population of perhaps 250,000 around the time of Christ, was one of the world's great metropolises. Its epic monuments still stand not far north of Mexico City: The towering Pyramid of the Sun at the terminal of a grand, 150-foot-wide (152-m-wide) ceremonial avenue faces a great Pyramid of the Moon. Along the avenue sprawls a monumental temple-court surrounded by scowling, reptilian effigies of Quetzalcoatl, the feathered serpent god of gods.

Teotihuacán crumbled mysteriously around AD 650, leaving a host of former vassal states to tussle among themselves. These included Xochicalco, not far south of present-day Mexico City. Freed from tribute to Teotihuacán, Xochicalco flourished.

### The Living Quetzalcoatl

Xochicalco's wise men tutored a young noble who was to become a living legend. In AD 947, Topiltzín (literally, Our Prince) was born. He advanced astronomy, agriculture, and architecture and founded the city-state of Tula in AD 968, north of old Teotihuacán.

Contrary to the times, Topiltzín opposed human sacrifice; he taught that tortillas and butterflies, not human hearts, were the food of Quetzalcoatl. After his two decades of benign rule, Topiltzín's name became so revered that the people began to know him as the living Quetzalcoatl, the plumed serpent-god incarnate. Bloodthirsty local priests, lusting for human victims, tricked him with alcohol, however; Topiltzín awoke groggily one morning in bed with his sister. Devastated by shame, Quetzalcoatl banished himself. He headed east from Tula with a band of retainers in AD 987, vowing that he would return during the anniversary of his birth year, Ce Acatl. Legends

© JUSTIN HENDERSON

an ancient petroglyph on display on Isla Río Cuale

say he sailed across the eastern sea and rose to heaven as the morning star.

## The Aztecs

The civilization that Topiltzín founded, known to historians as the Toltec (People of Tula), was eventually eclipsed by others. These included the Aztecs, a collection of seven aggressive immigrant subtribes. Migrating around AD 1350 from the mysterious western land of Aztlán into the lake-filled valley that Mexico City now occupies, the Aztecs survived by being forced to fight for every piece of ground they occupied. Within a century, the Aztecs' dominant tribe, whose members called themselves the México, had clawed its way to dominion over the Valley of Mexico. With the tribute labor that their emperors extracted from local vassal tribes, the México built a magnificent capital, Tenochtitlán, on an island in the middle of the valley-lake. From there, Aztec armies, not unlike Roman legions, marched out and subdued kingdoms for hundreds of miles in all directions. They returned with the spoils of conquest: gold, brilliant feathers, precious jewels, and captives, whom they sacrificed by the thousands as food for their gods.

Among those gods they feared was Quetzalcoatl, who, legends said, was bearded and fair skinned. It was a remarkable coincidence, therefore, that the bearded, fair-skinned Castilian Hernán Cortés landed on Mexico's eastern coast on April 22, 1519, during the year of Ce Acatl, exactly when Topiltzín, the Living Quetzalcoatl, had vowed he would return.

## THE CONQUEST

Although a generation had elapsed since Columbus founded Spain's West Indian colonies, returns had been meager. Scarcity of gold and of native workers, most of whom had fallen victim to European diseases, turned adventurous Spanish eyes westward once again, toward rumored riches beyond the setting sun.

Preliminary excursions piqued Spanish interest, and Hernán Cortés was commissioned by the Spanish governor, Diego Velázquez, to explore further.

Cortés, then only 34, had left his base of Cuba in February 1519 with an expedition of 11 small ships, 550 men, 16 horses, and a few small cannon. By the time he landed in Mexico, he was burdened by a rebellious crew. His men, mostly soldiers of fortune hearing stories of the great Aztec empire west beyond the mountains, had realized the impossible odds they faced and become restive.

Cortés, however, cut short any thoughts of mutiny by burning his ships. As he led his grumbling but resigned band of adventurers toward the Aztec capital of Tenochtitlán, Cortés played Quetzalcoatl to the hilt, awing local chiefs. Coaxed by Doña Marina, Cortés's native translator and mistress, local chiefs began to add their warrior-armies to Cortés's march against their Aztec overlords.

## Moctezuma, Lord of Tenochtitlán

Once inside the walls of Tenochtitlán, the Aztecs' Venice-like island-city, the Spaniards were dazzled by gardens of animals, gold, and palaces, and a great pyramid-enclosed square where tens of thousands of people bartered goods gathered from all over the empire. Tenochtitlán, with perhaps a quarter of a million people, was the grand capital of an empire more than equal to any in Europe at the time.

However, Moctezuma, the lord of that empire, was frozen by fear and foreboding, unsure if these figures truly represented the return of Quetzalcoatl. He quickly found himself hostage to Cortés, and then died a few months later, during a riot against Spanish greed and brutality. On July 1, 1520, on what came to be called *noche triste* (the sad night), the besieged Cortés and his men broke out, fleeing for their lives along a lake causeway from Tenochtitlán, carrying Moctezuma's treasure. Many of them drowned beneath their burdens of gold booty, while the survivors hacked a bloody retreat through thousands of screaming Aztec warriors to safety on the lakeshore.

A year later, reinforced by a small fleet of armed sailboats and 100,000 Indian allies, Cortés retook Tenochtitlán. The stubborn defenders, led by Cuauhtémoc, Moctezuma's nephew, fell by the tens of thousands beneath a smoking hail of Spanish grapeshot. The Aztecs refused to surrender, forcing Cortés to destroy the city to take it.

The triumphant conquistador soon rebuilt Tenochtitlán in the Spanish image; Cortés's cathedral and main public buildings—the present *zócalo* or central square of Mexico City—still rest upon the foundations of Moctezuma's pyramids.

## NEW SPAIN

With the Valley of Mexico firmly in his grip, Cortés sent his lieutenants south, north, and west to extend the limits of his domain, which eventually expanded to more than a dozenfold the size of old Spain. In a letter to his king, Charles V, Cortés christened his empire "New Spain of the Ocean Sea."

## MALINCHE

If it hadn't been for **Doña Marina** (whom he received as a gift from a local chief), Cortés may have become a mere historical footnote. Doña Marina, speaking both Spanish and native tongues, soon became Cortés's interpreter, go-between, and negotiator. She persuaded a number of important chiefs to ally themselves with Cortés against the Aztecs. Smart and opportunistic, Doña Marina was a crucial strategist in Cortés's deadly game of divide and conquer. She eventually bore Cortés a son and lived in honor and riches for many years, profiting greatly from the Spaniards' exploitation of the Mexicans.

Latter-day Mexicans do not honor her by the gentle title of Doña Marina, however. They call her Malinche, after the volcano—the ugly, treacherous scar on the Mexican landscape—and curse her as the female Judas who betrayed her country to the Spanish. *Malinchismo* has become known as the tendency to love things foreign and hate things Mexican.

## The Missionaries

While the conquistadores subjugated the Mexicans, missionaries began arriving to teach, heal, and baptize them. A dozen Franciscan brothers impressed natives and conquistadores alike by trekking the entire 300-mile stony path from Veracruz to Mexico City in 1523. Missionary authorities generally enjoyed a sympathetic ear from Charles V and his successors, who earnestly pursued Spain's Christian mission, especially when it dovetailed with their political and economic goals.

## The King Takes Control

Increasingly after 1525, the crown, through the Council of the Indies, began to wrest power away from Cortés and his conquistador lieutenants, many of whom had been granted rights of *encomienda:* taxes and labor of an indigenous district. From the king's point of view, tribute pesos collected by *encomenderos* from their native serfs reduced the gold that would otherwise flow to the crown. Moreover, many *encomenderos* callously enslaved and sold their native wards for quick profit. Such abuses, coupled with European introduced diseases, began to reduce the native Mexican population at an alarming rate.

The king and his councillors, realizing that without their local labor force New Spain would vanish, acted decisively, instituting new laws and a powerful viceroy to enforce them.

Don Antonio de Mendoza, the new viceroy, arrived in 1535. He wasted no time, first getting rid of the renegade opportunist and Cortés's enemy Nuño de Guzmán, whose private army, under the banner of conquest, had been laying waste to a broad belt of western Mexico, including the modern Puerto Vallarta region states of Nayarit and Jalisco. During his five-year rampage, Guzmán nevertheless managed to found the Puerto Vallarta region towns of Guadalajara, Tepic, and Compostela.

## Hernán Cortés, the Marqués del Valle de Oaxaca

Cortés, meanwhile, had done very well for himself. He was one of Spain's richest men, with the title of Marqués del Valle de Oaxaca. He received 80,000 gold pesos a year from hundreds of thousands of native Mexican subjects on 25,000 square miles from the Valley of Mexico through the present states of Morelos, Guerrero, and Oaxaca.

Cortés continued tirelessly on a dozen projects: an expedition to Honduras; a young wife whom he brought back from Spain; a palace (which still stands) in Cuernavaca; sugar mills; and dozens of churches, city halls, and presidios. He supervised the exploits of his conquistador-lieutenants: Francisco Orozco and Pedro de Alvarado went south to subdue the Zapotecs and Mixtecs in Oaxaca, while Cortés's nephew, Francisco de Cortés de Buenaventura, explored and christened the valley—Valle de las Banderas—where Puerto Vallarta stands today. Meanwhile, Cortés was in Acapulco building ships to explore the Pacific. In 1535, Cortés led an expedition to the Gulf of California (hence the Sea of Cortez) in a dreary six-month search for treasure around La Paz.

## Cortés's Monument

Disheartened by his failures and discouraged with Mendoza's interference, Cortés returned to Spain. Mired by lawsuits, a small war, and his daughter's marital troubles, he fell ill and died in 1547. Cortés's remains, according to his will, were eventually laid to rest in a vault at the Hospital de Jesús, which he had founded in Mexico City.

Since latter-day Mexican politics preclude memorials to the Spanish conquest, no monument anywhere in Mexico commemorates Cortés's achievements. His monument, historians note, is Mexico itself.

## COLONIAL MEXICO

In 1542, the Council of the Indies, through Viceroy Mendoza, promulgated its liberal New Laws of the Indies. They rested on high moral ground: The only Christian justification for New Spain was the souls and welfare of the indigenous people. Slavery was outlawed, and the colonists' *encomienda* rights over land and the Indians were to eventually revert to the crown.

Despite near rebellion by the colonists, Mendoza and his successors kept the lid on New Spain. Although some *encomenderos* held their privileges into the 18th century, chattel slavery of native Mexicans was abolished in New Spain 300 years before Lincoln's Emancipation Proclamation.

Peace reigned in Mexico for 10 generations. Viceroys came, served, and went; settlers put down roots; friars built country churches; and the conquistadores' rich heirs played while the natives worked.

## The Church

The church, however, moderated the Mexicans' toil. On feast days, the natives would dress up, parade their patron saint, drink pulque, and ooh and aah at the fireworks.

The church nevertheless profited from the status quo. The biblical tithe—one-tenth of everything earned—filled clerical coffers. By 1800, the church owned half of Mexico.

Moreover, both the clergy and the military were doubly privileged. They enjoyed the right of *fuero* (exemption from civil law) and could be prosecuted only by ecclesiastical or military courts.

## Trade and Commerce

In trade and commerce, New Spain existed for the benefit of the mother country. Foreign trade through Mexico was completely prohibited. As a result, colonists had to pay dearly for often-shoddy Spanish manufactures. The Casa de Contratación (the royal trade regulators) always ensured the colony's yearly payment deficit would be made up by bullion shipments from Mexican mines, from which the crown raked 10 percent off the top.

Despite its faults, New Spain was, by most contemporary measures, prospering in 1800. The native labor force was both docile and growing, and the galleons carried increasing tonnages of silver and gold to Spain. The authorities, however, failed to recognize that Mexico had changed in 300 years.

## Criollos, the New Mexicans

Nearly three centuries of colonial rule gave rise to a burgeoning population of more than a million *criollos*—Mexican-born European descendants of Spanish colonists, many rich and educated—to whom power was denied.

High government, church, and military office had always been the preserve of a tiny minority of *peninsulares*—whites born in Spain. *Criollos* could only watch in disgust as unlettered, unskilled *peninsulares,* derisively called *gachupines* (wearers of spurs), were boosted to authority over them.

Although the *criollos* stood high above the mestizo, *indígena,* and *negro* underclasses, that seemed little compensation for the false smiles, deep bows, and costly bribes that *gachupines* demanded.

## Mestizos, Indígenas, and African Mexicans

Upper-class luxury existed by virtue of the sweat of Mexico's mestizo, *indígena* (native or indigenous), and *negro* laborers and servants. African slaves were imported in large numbers during the 17th century after typhus, smallpox, and measles epidemics had wiped out most of the *indígena* population. Although the African Mexicans contributed significantly (crafts, healing arts, dance, music, drums, and marimba), they had arrived last and experienced discrimination from everyone.

# INDEPENDENCE

The chance for change came during the aftermath of the French invasion of Spain in 1808, when Napoléon Bonaparte replaced King Ferdinand VII with his brother Joseph on the Spanish throne. Most *peninsulares* backed the king; most *criollos,* however, inspired by the example of the recent American and French revolutions, talked and dreamed of independence. One such group, urged on by a firebrand parish priest, acted.

## El Grito de Dolores

"*¡Viva México!* Death to the *gachupines!*" **Father Miguel Hidalgo,** shouting his impassioned *grito*

## POPULATION CHANGES IN NEW SPAIN

**Peninsulares**

- Early Colonial (1570): 6,600
- Late Colonial (1810): 15,000

**Criollos**

- Early Colonial (1570): 11,000
- Late Colonial (1810): 1,100,000

**Mestizos**

- Early Colonial (1570): 2,400
- Late Colonial (1810): 704,000

**Indígenas**

- Early Colonial (1570): 3,340,000
- Late Colonial (1810): 3,700,000

**Negros**

- Early Colonial (1570): 22,000
- Late Colonial (1810): 630,000

from the church balcony in the Guanajuato town of Dolores on September 16, 1810, ignited action. A mostly *indígena,* machete-wielding army of 20,000 coalesced around Hidalgo and his compatriots, Ignacio Allende and Juan Aldama. Their ragtag force raged out of control through the Bajío, massacring hated *gachupines* and pillaging their homes.

Hidalgo advanced on Mexico City but, unnerved by stiff royalist resistance, retreated and regrouped around Guadalajara. His rebels, whose numbers had swollen to 80,000, were no match for a disciplined, 6,000-strong royalist force. On January 17, 1811, Hidalgo (now "Generalisimo") fled north toward the United States but was soon apprehended, defrocked, and executed. His head and those of his comrades hung from the walls of the Guanajuato granary for 10 years in compensation for the slaughter of 138 *gachupines* by Hidalgo's army.

### The 10-Year Struggle

Others carried on, however. A mestizo former student of Hidalgo, **José María Morelos,** led a revolutionary shadow government in the present states of Guerrero and Oaxaca for four years until he was apprehended and executed in December 1815.

Morelos's compatriot, **Vicente Guerrero,** continued the fight, joining forces with *criollo* royalist Brigadier **Agustín de Iturbide.** Their

Plan de Iguala promised "Three Guarantees"— the renowned Trigarantes: Independence, Catholicism, and Equality—which their army (commanded by Iturbide) would enforce. On September 21, 1821, Iturbide rode triumphantly into Mexico City at the head of his army of Trigarantes. Mexico was independent at last.

Independence, however, solved little except to expel the *peninsulares.* With an illiterate populace and no experience in self-government, Mexicans began a tragic 40-year love affair with a fantasy: the general on the white horse, the gold-braided hero who could save them from themselves.

### The Rise and Fall of Agustín I

Iturbide, crowned Emperor Agustín I by the bishop of Guadalajara on July 21, 1822, soon lost his charisma. In a pattern that became sadly predictable for generations of topsy-turvy Mexican politics, an ambitious garrison commander issued a *pronunciamiento* or declaration of rebellion against him; old revolutionary heroes endorsed a plan to install a republic. Iturbide, his braid tattered and brass tarnished, abdicated in February 1823.

**Antonio López de Santa Anna,** the eager 28-year-old military commander of Veracruz, whose *pronunciamiento* had pushed Iturbide from his white horse, maneuvered to gradually replace him. Meanwhile, throughout the late

1820s the government teetered on the edge of disaster as the presidency bounced between liberal and conservative hands six times in three years. During the last of these upheavals, Santa Anna jumped to prominence by defeating an abortive Spanish attempt at counterrevolution at Tampico in 1829. "The Victor of Tampico," people called Santa Anna.

## The Disastrous Era of Santa Anna

In 1833, the government was bankrupt; mobs demanded the ouster of conservative President Anastasio Bustamante, who had executed the rebellious old revolutionary hero Vicente Guerrero. Santa Anna issued a *pronunciamiento* against Bustamante; Congress obliged, elevating Santa Anna to "Liberator of the Republic" and naming him president in March 1833.

Santa Anna would pop in and out of the presidency like a jack-in-the-box 10 more times before 1855. First, he foolishly lost Texas to rebellious Anglo settlers in 1836; then he lost his leg (which was buried with full military honors) fighting the emperor of France.

Santa Anna's greatest debacle, however, was to declare war on the United States with just 1,839 pesos in the treasury. With his forces poised to defend Mexico City against a relatively small 10,000-man American invasion force, Santa Anna inexplicably withdrew. United States Marines surged into the "Halls of Montezuma," Chapultepec Castle, where Mexico's six beloved Niños Héroes cadets fell in the losing cause on September 13, 1847.

In the subsequent treaty of Guadalupe Hidalgo, Mexico lost nearly half of its territory—the present states of New Mexico, Arizona, California, Nevada, Utah, and Colorado—to the United States. Mexicans have never forgotten; they have looked upon gringos with a combination of awe, envy, admiration, and disgust ever since.

For Santa Anna, however, enough was not enough. Called back as president for the last and 11th time in 1853, Santa Anna financed his final extravagances by selling off a part of southern New Mexico and Arizona for $10 million in what was known as the Gadsden Purchase.

## REFORM, CIVIL WAR, AND INTERVENTION

Mexican leaders finally saw the light and exiled Santa Anna forever. While conservatives searched for a king to replace Santa Anna, liberals plunged ahead with three controversial reform laws: the Ley Juárez, Ley Lerdo, and Ley Iglesias. These *reformas,* augmented by a new Constitution of 1857, directly attacked the privilege and power of Mexico's landlords, clergy, and generals. They abolished *fueros* (the separate military and church courts), reduced huge landed estates, and stripped the church of its excess property and power.

Conservative generals, priests, *hacendados* (landholders), and their mestizo and *indígena* followers revolted. The resulting War of the Reform (not unlike the U.S. Civil War) ravaged the countryside for three long years until the victorious liberal army paraded triumphantly in Mexico City on New Year's Day 1861.

### Juárez and Maximilian

Benito Juárez, the leading *reformista,* had won the day. Like his contemporary Abraham Lincoln, Juárez, of pure Zapotec Indian blood, overcame his humble origins to become a lawyer, a champion of justice, and the president who held his country together during a terrible civil war. Like Lincoln, Juárez had little time to savor his triumph.

Imperial France invaded Mexico in January 1862, initiating the bloody five-year imperialist struggle, infamously known as the **French Intervention.** After two costly years, the French pushed Juárez's liberal army into the hills and installed the king whom Mexican conservatives thought the country needed. Austrian Archduke Maximilian and his wife, Carlota, the very models of modern Catholic monarchs, were crowned emperor and empress of Mexico in June 1864.

The naive Emperor Maximilian I was surprised that some of his subjects resented his presence. Meanwhile, Juárez refused to yield, stubbornly performing his constitutional duties in a somber black carriage one jump ahead of the French occupying army. The climax came in May 1867, when the liberal forces besieged and defeated Maximilian's army at Querétaro. Juárez, giving no quarter, sternly ordered Maximilian's execution by firing squad on June 19, 1867.

## RECONSTRUCTION AND THE PORFIRIATO

Juárez worked day and night at the double task of reconstruction and reform. He won reelection but died, exhausted, on July 18, 1872.

The death of Juárez, the stoic partisan of reform, signaled hope to Mexico's conservatives. They soon got their wish: General **Don Porfirio Díaz,** the "Coming Man," was elected president in 1876, initiating the **Porfiriato,** the long, virtually imperial, rule of Porfirio Díaz.

### Pax Porfiriana

Don Porfirio is often remembered wistfully, as old Italians remember Mussolini: "He was a bit rough, but, dammit, at least he made the trains run on time."

Although Porfirio Díaz's humble Oaxaca mestizo origins were not unlike Juárez's, Díaz was not a democrat: When he was a general, his officers took no captives; when he was president, his country police, the *rurales,* shot prisoners in the act of "trying to escape."

Order and progress, in that sequence, ruled Mexico for 34 years. Foreign investment flowed into the country; new railroads brought the products of shiny factories, mines, and farms to modernized Gulf and Pacific ports. Mexico balanced its budget, repaid foreign debt, and became a respected member of the family of nations.

The human price was high. Don Porfirio allowed more than 100 million acres—one-fifth of Mexico's land area (including most of the arable land)—to fall into the hands of his friends and foreigners. Poor Mexicans suffered the most. By 1910, 90 percent of the *indígenas* had lost their traditional communal land. In the spring of 1910, a smug, now-cultured, and elderly Don Porfirio anticipated with relish the centennial of Hidalgo's Grito de Dolores.

## REVOLUTION AND STABILIZATION
### ¡No Reelección!

Porfirio Díaz himself had first campaigned on the slogan. It expressed the idea that the president should step down after one term. Although Díaz had stepped down once in 1880, he had gotten himself reelected for 26 consecutive years. In 1910, **Francisco I. Madero,** a short, squeaky-voiced son of rich landowners, opposed Díaz under the same banner.

Although Díaz had jailed him before the election, Madero refused to quit campaigning. From a safe platform in the United States, he called for a revolution to begin on November 20, 1910.

### Villa and Zapata

Not much happened, but soon the millions of poor Mexicans who had been going to bed hungry began to stir. In Chihuahua, followers of Francisco (Pancho) Villa, an erstwhile ranch hand, miner, peddler, and cattle rustler, began attacking the *rurales,* dynamiting railroads, and raiding towns. Meanwhile, in the south, horse trader, farmer, and minor official Emiliano Zapata and his *indígena* guerrillas were terrorizing rich *hacendados* and forcibly recovering stolen ancestral village lands. Zapata's movement gained steam and by May had taken the Morelos state capital, Cuernavaca. Meanwhile, Madero crossed the Río Grande and joined with Villa's forces, who took Ciudad Juárez.

The *federales,* government army troops, began deserting in droves, and on May 25, 1911, Díaz submitted his resignation.

As Madero's deputy, **General Victoriano Huerta,** put Díaz on his ship of exile in Veracruz, Díaz confided, "Madero has unleashed a tiger. Now let's see if he can control it."

### The Fighting Continues

Emiliano Zapata, it turned out, was the tiger Madero had unleashed. Meeting with Madero in Mexico City, Zapata fumed over Madero's go-slow approach to the "agrarian problem," as Madero termed it. By November, Zapata had denounced Madero. *"¡Tierra y Libertad!"* ("Land and Liberty!") the Zapatistas cried, as Madero's support faded. The army in Mexico City rebelled; Huerta forced Madero to resign on February 18, 1913, put him under house arrest, and then had him murdered four days later.

The rum-swilling Huerta ruled like a Chicago mobster; general rebellion, led by the "Big Four"—Villa, Álvaro Obregón, and Venustiano Carranza in the north, and Zapata in the south—soon broke out. Pressed by the rebels and refused U.S. recognition, Huerta fled into exile in July 1914.

## The Constitution of 1917

Fighting sputtered on for three years as authority seesawed between revolutionary factions. Finally Carranza, whose forces ended up controlling most of the country by 1917, got a convention together in Querétaro to formulate political and social goals. The resulting Constitution of 1917, while restating most ideas of the *reformistas'* 1857 constitution, additionally prescribed a single four-year presidential term, labor reform, and subordinated private ownership to public interest. Every village had a right to communal *ejido* land, and subsoil wealth could never be sold away to the highest bidder.

The Constitution of 1917 was a revolutionary expression of national aspirations and, in retrospect, represented a social and political agenda for the entire 20th century. In modified form, it has lasted to the present day.

## Obregón Stabilizes Mexico

On December 1, 1920, General Álvaro Obregón legally assumed the presidency of a Mexico still bleeding from 10 years of civil war. Although a seasoned revolutionary, Obregón was also a pragmatist who recognized peace was necessary to implement the goals of the revolution. In four years, his government pacified local uprisings, disarmed a swarm of warlords,

executed hundreds of *bandidos,* obtained U.S. diplomatic recognition, assuaged the worst fears of the clergy and landowners, and began land reform.

All this set the stage for the work of **Plutarco Elías Calles,** Obregón's Minister of Gobernación (Interior) and handpicked successor, who won the 1924 election. Aided by peace, Mexico returned to a semblance of prosperity. Calles brought the army under civilian control, balanced the budget, and shifted Mexico's social revolution into high gear. New clinics vaccinated millions against smallpox, new dams irrigated thousands of previously dry acres, and campesinos received millions of acres of redistributed land.

By single-mindedly enforcing the proagrarian, pro-labor, and anticlerical articles of the 1917 constitution, Calles made many influential enemies. Infuriated by the government's confiscation of church property, closing of monasteries, and deportation of hundreds of foreign priests and nuns, the clergy refused to perform marriages, baptisms, and last rites. As members of the Cristero movement, militant Catholics crying *"¡Viva Cristo Rey!"* armed themselves, torching public schools and government property and murdering hundreds of innocent bystanders.

Simultaneously, Calles threatened foreign oil companies, demanding they exchange their titles for 50-year leases. A moderate Mexican supreme court decision over the oil issue and the skillful arbitration of U.S. Ambassador Dwight Morrow smoothed over both the oil and church troubles by the end of Calles's term.

Calles, who started out brimming with revolutionary fervor and populist zeal, became increasingly conservative and dictatorial. Although he bowed out peaceably in favor of Obregón (the constitution had been amended to allow one six-year nonsuccessive term), Obregón was assassinated two weeks after his election in 1928. Calles continued to rule for six more years through three puppet-presidents: Emilio Portes Gil (1928-1930), Pascual Ortíz Rubio (1930-1932), and Abelardo Rodríguez (1932-1934).

For the 14 years since 1920, the revolution had first waxed, then waned. With a cash surplus in 1930, Mexico skidded into debt as the Great Depression deepened and Calles and his cronies lined their pockets. In blessing his minister of war, General Lázaro Cárdenas, for the 1934 presidential election, Calles expected more of the same.

## Lázaro Cárdenas, President of the People

The 40-year-old Cárdenas, former governor of Michoacán, immediately set his own agenda, however. He worked tirelessly to fulfill the social prescriptions of the revolution. As morning-coated diplomats fretted, waiting in his outer office, Cárdenas ushered in delegations of campesinos and factory workers, and sympathetically listened to their petitions.

In his six years of rule, Cárdenas moved public education and health forward on a broad front, supported strong labor unions, and redistributed 49 million acres of farmland, more than any president before or since.

Cárdenas's resolute enforcement of the constitution's Artículo 123 brought him the most renown. Under this pro-labor law, the government turned over a host of private companies to employee ownership and, on March 18, 1938, expropriated all foreign oil corporations.

In retrospect, the oil corporations, most of which were British, were not blameless. They had sorely neglected the wages, health, and welfare of their workers while ruthlessly taking the law into their own hands with private police forces. Although Standard Oil cried foul, U.S. president Franklin Roosevelt did not intervene. Through negotiation and due process, the U.S. companies eventually were compensated with $24 million, plus interest. In the wake of the expropriation, President Cárdenas created Petróleos Mexicanos (Pemex), the national oil corporation that continues to run all Mexican oil and gas operations.

## Manuel Ávila Camacho

Manuel Ávila Camacho, elected in 1940, was the last revolutionary general to be president of Mexico. His administration ushered in a gradual shift of Mexican politics, government, and foreign policy as Mexico allied itself with the U.S. cause during World War II. Foreign tourism, initially promoted by the Cárdenas administration, ballooned. Good feelings surged as Franklin Roosevelt became the first U.S. president to officially cross the Río Grande when he met with Camacho in Monterrey in April 1943.

In both word and deed, moderation and evolution guided President Camacho's policies. "*Soy creente*" ("I am a believer"), he declared to the Catholics of Mexico as he worked earnestly to bridge Mexico's serious church-state schism. Land-policy emphasis shifted from redistribution to utilization as new dams and canals irrigated hundreds of thousands of previously arid acres. On one hand, Camacho established IMSS (Instituto Mexicano de Seguro Social), and on the other, he trimmed the power of labor unions.

As World War II moved toward its 1945 conclusion, both the United States and Mexico were enjoying the benefits of four years of governmental and military cooperation and mutual trade in the form of a mountain of strategic minerals that had moved north in exchange for a similar mountain of U.S. manufactures that moved south.

## CONTEMPORARY MEXICO
### The Mature Revolution

During the decades after World War II, beginning with moderate president **Miguel Alemán** (1946-1952), Mexican politicians gradually honed their skills of consensus and compromise as their middle-aged revolution bubbled along under liberal presidents and sputtered haltingly under conservatives. Doctrine required of all politicians, regardless of stripe, that they be "revolutionary" enough to be included beneath the banner of the PRI (Partido Revolucionario Institucional—the Institutional Revolutionary Party), Mexico's dominant political party.

**Adolfo Ruíz Cortínes,** Alemán's secretary of the interior, was elected overwhelmingly in 1952. He fought the corruption that had crept into government under his predecessor, continued land reform, increased agricultural production, built new ports, eradicated malaria, and opened a number of automobile assembly plants.

Despite concerns that women would vote for conservatives, the millions of women who had fought and died in the Revolution, had served in state governments, and even led military units were finally given their due. Under the Ruíz Cortínes administration, women gained the right to vote in national elections in 1953.

Women, voting for the first time in a national election, helped to keep the PRI in power by electing liberal **Adolfo López Mateos** in 1958. Resembling Lázaro Cárdenas in social policy, López Mateos redistributed 40 million acres of farmland, forced automakers to use 60 percent domestic components, built thousands of new schools, and distributed hundreds of millions of new textbooks. *"La electricidad es nuestra"* ("Electricity is ours"), Mateos declared as he nationalized foreign power companies in 1962.

Despite his left-leaning social agenda, unions were restive under López Mateos. Protesting inflation, workers struck; the government retaliated, arresting Demetrios Vallejo, the railway union head, and renowned muralist David Siqueiros, former Communist Party secretary.

Despite the troubles, López Mateos climaxed his presidency gracefully in 1964 as he opened the celebrated National Museum of Anthropology, appropriately located in Chapultepec Park, where the Aztecs had first settled 20 generations earlier.

In 1964, as several times before, the outgoing president's interior secretary succeeded his former chief. Dour, conservative **Gustavo Díaz Ordaz** immediately clashed with liberals, labor, and students. The pot boiled over just before the 1968 Mexico City Olympics. Reacting to a student rebellion, the army occupied the National University; shortly afterward, on October 2, government forces opened fire with machine guns on a downtown protest, killing and wounding hundreds of demonstrators.

## Maquiladoras

Despite its serious internal troubles, and complaints when Mexico gave Vietnam War resisters asylum as political refugees, Mexico's relations with the United States were cordial. President Lyndon Johnson visited and unveiled a statue of Abraham Lincoln in Mexico City. Later, Díaz Ordaz met with President Richard Nixon in Puerto Vallarta.

Meanwhile, bilateral negotiations produced the **Border Industrialization Program.** Within a 12-mile strip south of the U.S.-Mexico border, foreign companies could assemble parts into finished goods and export them without any duties on either side. Within a dozen years, a swarm of such plants, called maquiladoras, were humming as hundreds of thousands of Mexican workers assembled and exported billions of dollars' worth of consumer goods—electronics, clothes, furniture, pharmaceuticals, and toys—worldwide.

Concurrently, in Mexico's interior, Díaz Ordaz pushed Mexico's industrialization ahead full steam. Foreign money financed hundreds of new plants and factories. Primary among these was the giant Las Truchas steel plant at the new industrial port and town of Lázaro Cárdenas at the Pacific mouth of the Río Balsas.

Discovery, in 1974, of gigantic new oil and gas reserves along Mexico's Gulf coast added fuel to Mexico's already rapid industrial expansion. During the late 1970s and early 1980s, billions in foreign investment, lured by Mexico's oil earnings, financed other major developments—factories, hotels, power plants, roads, airports—all over the country.

## Economic Trouble of the 1980s

The negative side to these expensive projects was the huge debt required to finance them. President **Luis Echeverria Álvarez** (1970-1976), diverted by his interest in international affairs, passed Mexico's burgeoning financial deficit to his successor, **José López Portillo.** As feared by some experts, a world petroleum glut during the early 1980s burst Mexico's ballooning oil bubble and plunged the country into financial crisis. When the 1982 interest came due on its foreign debt, Mexico's largest holding company couldn't pay the $2.3 billion owed. The peso plummeted more than five-fold, to 150 per U.S. dollar. At the same time, prices doubled every year. With capital fleeing to foreign banks, López Portillo took the radical step of nationalizing the banks, which had the perverse effect of making a bad situation worse, as Mexican credit dried up.

But by the mid-1980s, President **Miguel de la Madrid** (1982-1988) was straining to get Mexico's economic house in order. He sliced government and raised taxes, asking rich and poor alike to tighten their belts. Despite getting foreign bankers to reschedule Mexico's debt, de la Madrid couldn't stop inflation. Prices sky-rocketed as the peso deflated to 2,500 per U.S. dollar, becoming one of the world's most devalued currencies by 1988.

## Salinas de Gortari and NAFTA

Public disgust with official corruption led to significant opposition during the 1988 presidential election. Millionaire businessman Manuel Clothier ran as the candidate of PAN, the right-leaning National Action Party, and Cuauhtemoc Cárdenas—the son and heir of socialist president Lázaro Cárdenas—left the PRI to run as candidate for the dissident National Democratic Front. Harvard-educated technocrat Carlos Salinas de Gortari was selected by the PRI.

Despite open fraud and voter intimidation, Cárdenas was far ahead in the vote count on election night when a mysterious computer crash, followed by a fire in election headquarters, left the election in doubt for the first time. All three candidates claimed victory. Congress eventually claimed Salinas won the election, but only by barely half of the vote, the worst ever for a PRI president. The election was, however, a breakthrough in democratization, creating two viable opposition parties, conservative PAN, and the leftist Revolutionary Democratic Party (PRD), an outgrowth of the Cárdenas coalition movement.

Salinas, however, was widely hailed abroad as Mexico's "Coming Man" of the 1990s. Selling off the nationalized banks, the telephone company, and the national airline were seen as necessary steps to modernizing the economy. His major achievement—despite significant national opposition—was the North American Free Trade Agreement (NAFTA), negotiated in 1992 by him, U.S. president George H. W. Bush, and Canadian prime minister Brian Mulrooney.

## Rebellion, Political Assassination, and Reconciliation

On the very day in early January 1994 that NAFTA took effect, rebellion broke out in the poor, remote state of Chiapas. A small but well-disciplined campesino force calling itself Ejército Zapatista Liberación Nacional (Zapatista National Liberation Army—EZLN—or "Zapatistas") captured a number of provincial towns and held the former governor of Chiapas hostage.

To further complicate matters, Mexico's already tense 1994 drama veered toward tragedy. While Salinas de Gortari's chief negotiator, Manuel Camacho Solis, was attempting to iron out a settlement with the Zapatista rebels, PRI presidential candidate Luis Donaldo Colosio, Salinas's handpicked successor, was gunned down just months before the August balloting. However, instead of disintegrating, the nation united in grief; opposition candidates eulogized their fallen former opponent and later earnestly engaged his replacement, stolid technocrat **Ernesto Zedillo,** in Mexico's first presidential election debate.

In a closely watched election unmarred by irregularities, Zedillo piled up a solid plurality against his PAN and PRD opponents. By perpetuating the PRI's 65-year hold on the presidency, the electorate had again opted for the PRI's familiar although imperfect middle-aged revolution.

## New Crisis, New Recovery

Zedillo, however, had little time to savor his victory. Right away he had to face the consequences of his predecessor's shabby fiscal policies. Less than a month after he took office, the peso crashed, losing a third of its value just before Christmas 1994. A month later, Mexican financial institutions, their dollar debt having nearly doubled in a month, were in danger of defaulting on their obligations to international investors. To stave off a worldwide financial panic, U.S. president Clinton, in February 1995, secured an unprecedented multibillion-dollar loan package for Mexico, guaranteed by U.S. and international institutions.

Although disaster was temporarily averted, the cure for the country's ills was another painful round of inflation and belt tightening for poor Mexicans. During 1995, inflation soared; more and more families became unable to purchase staple foods and basic medicines. Malnutrition and a resurgence of diseases of the developing world, such as cholera and dengue fever, menaced the countryside. Compounding rural woes, NAFTA regulations spelled the end of farm subsidies. Millions fled the countryside for the cities, for the maquiladoras along the United States border, or into the United States itself.

At the same time, Mexico's equally serious political ills seemed to defy cure. Raul Salinas de Gortari, an important PRI party official and the former president's brother, was arrested for money laundering and political assassination. As popular sentiment began to implicate Carlos Salinas de Gortari himself, the former president fled Mexico, living in Cuba and Ireland for many years.

Mexican democracy got a much-needed boost when notorious Guerrero governor Ruben Figueroa, who had tried to cover up a bloody massacre of campesinos by police with a bogus videotape, was forced from office. At the same time, the Zedillo government gained momentum in addressing the Zapatistas' grievances in Chiapas, even as it decreased federal military presence, built new rural electrification networks, and refurbished health clinics. Moreover, Mexico's economy began to improve. By mid-1996, inflation had slowed to a 20 percent annual rate, investment dollars were flowing back into Mexico, the peso had stabilized at about 7.5 to the U.S. dollar, and Mexico had paid back half the borrowed U.S. bailout money.

## Zedillo's Political Reforms

In the political arena, although the justice system generally left much to be desired, a pair of unprecedented events signaled an increasingly open political system. In the 1997 congressional elections, voters elected a host of opposition candidates, depriving the PRI of an absolute congressional majority for the first time since 1929. A year later, in early 1998, Mexicans were participating in their country's first primary elections—in which voters, instead of politicians, chose party candidates.

Although President Zedillo had had a rough ride, he entered the twilight of his 1994-2000 term able to take credit for an improved economy, some genuine political reforms, and relative peace in the countryside. The election of 2000 revealed, however, that the Mexican people were not satisfied.

## End of an Era: Vicente Fox Unseats the PRI

During 1998 and 1999 the focal point of opposition to the PRI's three-generation rule had been shifting to relative newcomer Vicente Fox, former president of Coca-Cola Mexico and clean former PAN governor of Guanajuato.

Fox, who had announced his candidacy for president two years before the election, seemed an unlikely challenger. After all, the minority PAN had always been the party of wealthy businessmen and the conservative Catholic right. But blunt-talking, six-foot-five Fox, who sometimes campaigned in vaquero boots and a 10-gallon cowboy hat, preached populist themes of coalition building and "inclusion." He backed up his talk by carrying his campaign to hardscrabble city barrios, dirt-poor country villages, and traditional outsider groups, such as Jews.

In a relatively orderly and fair July 2, 2000, election, Fox decisively defeated his PRI opponent Fernando Labastida, 42 percent to 38 percent, while PRD candidate Cárdenas polled a feeble 17 percent. Fox's win also swept a PAN plurality (223/209/57) into the 500-seat Chamber of Deputies lower house (although the Senate remained PRI dominated).

Nevertheless, in pushing the PRI from the all-powerful presidency after 71 consecutive years of domination, Fox had ushered Mexico into a new, more democratic era.

Despite stinging criticism from his own ranks, President Zedillo, whom historians were already praising as the real hero behind Mexico's new democracy, made an unprecedentedly early appeal for all Mexicans to unite behind Fox.

On the eve of his December 1, 2000, inauguration, Mexicans awaited Fox's speech with hopeful anticipation. Although acknowledging that he couldn't completely reverse 71 years of PRI entrenchment in his one six-year term, he vowed to ride a crest of reform by revamping the tax system and reducing poverty by 30 percent, creating a million new jobs a year through new private investment in electricity and oil production, and forming a new common market with Latin America, the United States, and Canada.

He promised, moreover, to secure justice for all by a much-needed reform of police, the federal attorney general, and the army. Potentially most difficult of all was Fox's call for the formation of an unprecedented congressional Transparency Commission to investigate a generation of past grievances, including the 1968 massacre of student demonstrators and the assassinations of Cardinal Posada Ocampo in 1993 and presidential candidate Luis Donaldo Colosio in 1994.

## Vicente Fox, President of Mexico

Wasting little time getting started, President Fox first headed to Chiapas to confer with indigenous community leaders. Along the way, he shut down Chiapas military bases and removed dozens of military roadblocks. Back in Mexico City, he sent the long-delayed **peace plan,** including the **indigenous bill of rights,** to Congress. Zapatista rebels responded by journeying en masse from Chiapas to Mexico City, where, in their black masks, they addressed Congress, arguing for indigenous rights. Although by mid-2001 Congress had passed a modified version of the negotiated settlement, and the majority of states had ratified the required constitutional amendment, indigenous leaders condemned the legislation plan as watered down and unacceptable, while proponents claimed it was the best possible compromise between the Zapatista demands and the existing Mexican constitution.

Furthermore, Fox continued to pry open the door to democracy in Mexico. In May 2002, he signed Mexico's first **freedom of information act,** entitling citizens to timely copies of all public documents from federal agencies. Moreover, Fox's long-promised **Transparency Commission** was taking shape. In July 2002, federal attorneys took extraordinary action, questioning a list of 74 former government officials, including ex-president Luis Echeverria, about their roles in government transgressions, notably political murders and the University of Mexico massacres during the 1960s and 1970s.

But Mexico's economy, reflecting the U.S. economic slowdown, began to sour in 2001, losing half a million jobs and cutting annual growth to 2.5 percent, down from the 4.5 percent that the government had predicted. Furthermore, a so-called Towelgate furor (in which aides had purchased dozens of $400 towels for the presidential mansion) weakened Fox's squeaky-clean image.

During 2002 and 2003, the Mexican economy continued its lackluster performance, increasing public dissatisfaction. In the July 7, 2003, congressional elections, voters took their frustrations out on the PAN and gave its plurality in the Chamber of Deputies to the PRI. When the dust settled, the PRI total had risen to 225 seats, while the PAN had slipped to 153. The biggest winner, however, was the PRD, which gained more than 40 seats, to a total of about 100.

The best news of 2004 was not political, but economic. The Mexican economy, reflecting that of the United States, began to recover, expanding at a moderate (if not robust) rate of about 4 percent, while exports to the United States also increased.

By mid-2005, despite only modest political gains and with Vicente Fox's term mostly spent, critics were increasingly claiming that he was a lame-duck president who had run out of time to accomplish what he promised. But Fox, despite a hostile congress that almost continuously blocked his legislative proposals, could claim some solid accomplishments. During his first five years, he had pushed through significant gains in indigenous rights, national reconciliation and government transparency, drug enforcement, social security reform, housing, and education. Moreover, in addition to nurturing a recovering economy, Fox had undeniably kept exports robust, kept the peso strong against the dollar, and had clamped the lid on inflation.

So in the twilight of Fox's term, in early 2006, although the typical Mexican man and woman on the street acknowledged that he had not delivered on his promises to completely remake the economy and political system, most still believed that unseating the PRI was good for Mexico, and they acknowledged that even Fox couldn't be expected to completely undo in 6 years what 71 years of PRI dominance had created.

## The Election of 2006 and Its Aftermath

During the first half of 2006, as Vicente Fox was winding down his presidency, Mexicans were occupied by the campaign to elect his successor. Over Vicente Fox's objections, PAN voters chose Harvard-educated former energy secretary Felipe Calderón, a leading light of President Fox's cabinet who also enjoyed clerical and reactionary support within his party. Robert Madrazo, the PRI chair, carried the banner for what appeared to be a resurgent party. Most headlines went to the PRD candidate, the mercurial leftist-populist Andres Manuel López Obrador, former mayor of Mexico City.

When it appeared that López Obrador would sweep the PRD into the presidency, an unprecedented media and political campaign was launched to undercut his popularity. PAN attempted to have López Obrador arrested and disqualified for office on the basis of a minor eminent domain case in Mexico City, and advertising campaigns accused López Obrador of everything from being an admirer of Hitler to being a secret Presbyterian. But, after a half year of mudslinging and angry debates over the major election issues of drug-related mayhem, killings and kidnappings, police and judicial corruption and inefficiency, and lack of jobs for impoverished workers, Madrazo's initial popularity faded, narrowing the contest to a bitter neck-and-neck race between Calderón and López Obrador.

On Sunday, July 2, 2006, 42 million Mexicans cast their ballots. Unofficial returns indicated that voters had awarded Calderón a paper-thin plurality. Four days later, after all returns were certified, the Federal Electoral Institute announced the official vote tally: only about 22 percent for Madrazo, with the remaining lion's share divided nearly evenly, with 38.7 percent going to López Obrador and 39.3 percent for Calderón. This result, the Federal Electoral Institute ruled, was too close to declare a winner without a recount.

Besides the close López Obrador-Calderón vote, the election results revealed much more. Not only were the 32 electoral entities (31 states and the Federal District) divided equally, with 16 going for López Obrador and 16 for Calderón, the vote also reflected a nearly complete north-south political schism, with virtually all of the 16 PAN-majority states forming a solid northern bloc, while the 16 PRD-voting states did the same in the south. Furthermore, the election appeared to signal a collapse of PRI power; with no state (nor the Federal District) giving either a majority or a plurality to Madrazo.

When elections officials decided any irregularities were too minor to investigate, a howl of protest came from López Obrador and his PRD followers after the election results were announced. They claimed the PAN had stolen the election. They jammed the Federal Electoral Institute with lawsuits, alleging a host of irregularities and ballot-stuffing incidents, and demanding a complete recount of all 42 million ballots. They yelled, marched, blocked Mexico City's Paseo de la Reforma, and camped in the Zócalo.

After weeks of hearing the PRD and PAN arguments about ballot fraud, the Federal Election Institute announced a recount of a limited number of questionable ballots, all from Calderón-majority states. The Supreme Election Tribunal, a panel of federal judges, found the recount only shifted a few thousand votes away from Calderón and declared him the winner by a mere 240,000 votes.

López Obrador and his supporters screamed foul even louder and threatened to ignore Calderón and/or block his presidency. On September 16, Mexican Independence Day, López Obrador convened in the Mexico City Zócalo hundreds of thousands of his supporters that declared him the legitimate president. In the succeeding days, the PRD delegates and their congressional allies prevented the president of Mexico, for the first time in history, from delivering his annual state of the union address.

Negative reporting on the PRD tactics—in the halls of Congress and on the streets—led to a drop in support for the López Obrador position. National polls showed that more than two-thirds of Mexicans disapproved of the protest. By October, many of the PRD's leaders agreed, further isolating the López Obrador camp to a minority position, even within the PRD.

An important result of the 2006 election, initially overshadowed by the intense struggle over the presidential vote, but potentially crucial, was the federal legislative vote, which indicated PAN showed a slight majority in voter preference and much stronger support for the PRD than was suspected. Under Mexico's proportional representation system, this gave PAN 206/127/106 over the PRD and PRI, respectively, in the 500-seat federal Chamber of Deputies, and 52/29/33 in the 128-seat Senate, with the remainder of seats scattered among minor parties.

With no single party able to overwhelm the opposition, Felipe Calderón had to compromise with opposition leaders to accomplish any of his legislative goals. A new tax code largely reflected the presidential plan, while a radical goal to privatize the state oil company, Pemex, was scaled back because of PRI and PRD opposition. Although most presidential goals reflected PAN's probusiness, pro-NAFTA ideas, the legislative results borrowed considerably from the liberal-populist agenda of López Obrador and the PRD.

## The Calderón Presidency, the Drug War, and the Election of 2012

Felipe Calderón's inauguration on December 1, 2006, was the shortest in recent memory. Threatened by interference by unruly PRD legislators, Calderón, accompanied by Vicente Fox, entered the national congressional chamber through a back door, took the oath of office, gave a short speech, and left quickly.

During the next few months, however, Calderón showed that he was a president to be reckoned with. Having campaigned on the promise of a "hard hand" toward insecurity, he took immediate action against protesters in the state of Oaxaca, arresting demonstration leaders and putting military units in the streets. Ironically, or by design, this benefited the sitting PRI governor, who was the target of the initial protests. Despite mounting violence and an alarmingly high death toll among soldiers and police officials, a nationwide assault on drug traffickers was widely praised.

Even opposition critics agreed that Calderón was off to a good start. By mid-March 2007, his national approval rating had soared to 58 percent. Despite the early popularity of the tax reforms and anticrime initiatives, serious challenges remained. Poverty was estimated at 40 percent. Mexican factories had been challenged by Asian competitors, especially those from nations with weak labor laws, like China. Lack of jobs, exacerbated by the violent "war" between narcotics traders and the military, had forced millions of Mexicans north of the border.

The drug war within Mexico, between the military and various cartels, and among the cartels themselves, has turned parts of Mexico, primarily close to the U.S. border but in other regions as well, into some of the most dangerous places in the world. It has wreaked havoc on Mexico's tourism industry, although most of the popular destinations, such as Puerto Vallarta and Cancún, remain safe. Mazatlán, on the other hand, is now off-limits to many visitors, and, like Acapulco, is no longer on cruise ship itineraries. These changes are due to random acts of primarily accidental violence against tourists—but calling such incidents "unfortunate accidents" does little to change the perception. For tourists, cities such as Mazatlán and Acapulco are probably no less safe than, say, Los Angeles or Miami, but perception is everything here, and many Americans—not so much Canadians or Europeans—are simply afraid to come to Mexico. Thus far Puerto Vallarta on the west coast and Cancún on the Caribbean are doing all right, if not attracting the same numbers of tourists as they were a few years ago.

Whether Calderón's aggressive tactics in fighting this drug war will bring positive long-term results is still unclear, but the murder rate in Mexico spiraled upward during his term. Among the candidates who ran to replace him, there was a quiet consensus that perhaps it might be better to leave the cartels alone. This, of course, is unacceptable to the United States. (However, it shouldn't be forgotten that the market for the drugs lies in the United States, and the guns Mexican criminals are using to fight this war are manufactured in the United States. The country bears a huge measure of responsibility.) Some Mexican people are also in a quandary on the subject. To allow the drug lords to operate with impunity is unacceptable, but so, too, is the murder rate that this war has generated.

Calderón's presidency was to a great degree overwhelmed by this single issue, at least in the eyes of the world. Coupled with the swine flu epidemic of 2009, the drug war drove a stake into the heart of one of the country's most important industries: tourism. This is a tragedy, for Mexico is one of the most physically beautiful and culturally rich countries in the world.

The new president, Enrique Peña Nieto, of the PRI, was elected in the summer of 2012 in a cloud of suspicion; many people believe the election was manipulated illegally to put the PRI back in business as usual. The president, born in 1966, is more or less a blank slate, with not much history or political experience to analyze, although there are those who claim he is in the pocket of the drug cartels or the U.S. government. The history of Mexican elections being what it is, these suspicions are understandable. However, Peña Nieto is now in office, and time will tell what changes he will bring. Ultimately, the big question is how he will deal with the cartels. While Calderón went after them aggressively, his approach did not slow the trade, lessen their influence and power, or affect the number of drug abusers—but it did raise the murder rate alarmingly.

# Economy and Government

## THE MEXICAN ECONOMY
### Post-Revolutionary Gains

By many measures, Mexico's 20th-century revolution appears to have succeeded. Since 1910, illiteracy has plunged from 80 percent to under 8 percent, life expectancy has risen from 30 years to over 76, infant mortality has dropped from a whopping 40 percent to under 2 percent, and, in terms of caloric intake, average Mexicans are eating about twice as much as their forebears at the turn of the 20th century.

Decades of near-continuous economic growth account for rising Mexican living standards. The Mexican economy has rebounded from its last two recessions because of plentiful natural resources, notably oil and metals;

diversified manufacturing, such as cars, steel, and petrochemicals; steadily increasing tourism (which has suffered mightily in recent years due to the drug wars); exports of fruits, vegetables, and cattle; and its large and willing low-wage workforce.

Recent Mexican governments, moreover, have skillfully exploited Mexico's economic strengths. The Border Industrialization Program that led to millions of jobs in thousands of border maquiladoras has spread all over the country, especially to Monterrey, Mexico City, Guadalajara, and Puerto Vallarta itself. Tourism, Puerto Vallarta's strongest job creator for years, grew even stronger during 2005, when Puerto Vallarta drew more foreign visitors than any other Mexican beach destination. In the years since, however, tourism has leveled off and even fallen, relative to the boom years of the 1990s and into the 2000s. This is in part due to Mexico's internal problems, but some of the blame rests north of the border, where there is simply not as much money to go around. Americans are less well off now than they were 10 years ago, and so they travel less.

However, medical tourism is now bringing huge economic benefits to Mexico, as the cost of medical care has spiraled out of control in the United States. Estimates are that this has added 5-7 percent to Mexico's GDP in the past few years. Numerous world-class hospitals are under construction to keep up with the demand.

The number of American and Canadian people choosing to live permanently in Mexico—drawn by good weather, beautiful land, and the low cost of living—has been increasing steadily in spite of the bad press. As of 2012 there were two million Canadian and American property owners in Mexico, and that number is expected to reach six million by 2027.

In Mexico as a whole, the country's increased manufacturing output has produced manifold economic benefits, including reduced dependency on oil exports and burgeoning foreign trade. Consequently, Mexico has become a net exporter of goods and services to the United States, its largest trading partner. In 2001,

however, the U.S. economic slowdown decreased demand for Mexican products; consequently Mexico lost more than half a million jobs, forcing economic growth down to a weak 2.5 percent for 2001. Nevertheless, the slower growth resulted in neither significant inflation nor weakening of the peso, and by late 2004, the Mexican gross domestic product was again rising at a healthy annual rate of about 5 percent.

But, during 2004 and 2005, despite high prices for its oil, rock-bottom inflation, large payments of money from Mexicans working in the United States, and a balanced budget, the Mexican economy still didn't produce the million jobs a year it needed to keep up with population increase. Although some of the sluggishness could be blamed on the hurricane that devastated Cancún in fall 2005, most experts agree that Mexico's largest economic problem is lack of ability to compete, especially with respect to Asian countries—notably China, which floods Mexico with low-cost goods while Mexico sells very little to China in return. A serious marker of all this appeared in 2004, when China replaced Mexico as the United States's second-largest import source, jumping to about 14 percent of U.S. imports, compared to Mexico, at around 10 percent.

Fortunately, 2006 painted a much brighter economic picture. Nearly all economic experts agreed with the pronouncement that the Mexican economy was "firing on all cylinders." Virtually all of Mexican economic indicators rose sharply, from the annual growth rate (more than 5 percent for the first half year), pushed upward by a 50 percent increase in car production and the high price of Mexico's exported oil, both of which lifted exports to the United States by 22 percent to record levels. Moreover, on the domestic side, wages were up by more than 4 percent, coupled with both the fortunate low inflation and low interest rates.

All of this good economic news bodes well for what many experts suggest: that Mexico, in order to breathe permanent new life into its economy, needs fundamental structural reforms, such as more flexible labor rules, more effective tax collection (hardly anyone pays any income tax), and more private investment to modernize the energy and oil industries.

In recent years, along with tourism beginning to come back to life, some U.S.-based manufacturing industries that had fled to Asia, including auto parts and electronics, have found that reduced shipping costs more than compensate for lower Asian wages (which are on the rise anyway); additionally, an increasingly well-educated work force has nurtured the growth of an emerging high-tech sector in cities such as Querétaro and Guadalajara.

## Long-Term Economic Challenges

Despite huge gains, Mexico's Revolution of 1910 is nevertheless incomplete. Improved public health, education, income, and opportunity have barely outdistanced Mexico's population, which increased from 15 million to over 113 million from 1910 to 2010. For example, although the illiteracy rate has decreased, the actual number of Mexican people who can't read, about 10 million, has remained fairly constant since 1910.

Moreover, the land reform program, once thought to be a Mexican cure-all, has long been a disappointment. The *ejidos* of which Emiliano Zapata dreamed have become mostly symbolic. The communal fields are typically small and unirrigated. *Ejido* land, formerly constitutionally prohibited from being sold, has not traditionally served as collateral for bank loans. Capital for irrigation networks, fertilizers, and harvesting machines is consequently lacking. Communal farms are typically inefficient; the average Mexican field produces about *one-quarter* as much corn per acre as a U.S. farm. Mexico must accordingly use its precious oil-dollar surplus to import millions of tons of corn—originally indigenous to Mexico—annually.

The triple scourge of overpopulation, lack of arable land, and low farm income has driven millions of campesino families to seek better lives in Mexico's cities and the United States. Since 1910, Mexico has evolved from a largely rural country where 70 percent of the population lived on farms to an urban nation where 70 percent of the population lives in cities. Fully one-fifth of Mexico's people now lives in Mexico City.

Nevertheless, the future appears bright for many privately owned and managed Mexican farms, concentrated largely in the northern border states. Exceptionally productive, they typically work hundreds or thousands of irrigated acres of crops, such as tomatoes, lettuce, chiles, wheat, corn, tobacco, cotton, fruits, alfalfa, chickens, and cattle, just like their counterparts across the border in California, New Mexico, Arizona, and Texas.

Staples—wheat for bread, corn for tortillas, milk, and cooking oil—are all imported and consequently expensive for the typical working-class Mexican family, which must spend half or more of its income (typically $500 per month) for food. Recent inflation has compounded the problem, particularly for the millions of families on the bottom half of Mexico's economic ladder.

Although average gross domestic product figures for Mexico—about $10,000 per capita compared to more than $40,000 for the United States—place it above nearly all other developing countries, averages, when applied to Mexico, mean little. A primary socioeconomic reality of Mexican history remains: The richest one-fifth of Mexican families earns about 10 times the income of the poorest one-fifth. A relative handful of people own a large hunk of Mexico, and they don't seem inclined to share much of it with the less fortunate. As for the poor, the typical Mexican family in the bottom one-third income bracket often owns neither car nor refrigerator, and the children typically do not finish elementary school.

## GOVERNMENT AND POLITICS
### The Constitution of 1917

Mexico's governmental system is rooted in the Constitution of 1917, which incorporated many of the features of its reformist predecessor of 1857. The 1917 document, with amendments, remains in force. Although drafted at the behest of conservative revolutionary Venustiano

Carranza by his handpicked Querétaro "Constitucionalista" Congress, it was greatly influenced by Álvaro Obregón and generally ignored by Carranza during his subsequent three-year presidential term.

Although many articles resemble those of its U.S. model, the Constitution of 1917 contains provisions developed directly from Mexican experience. Article 27 addresses the question of land. Private property rights are qualified by societal need, subsoil rights are public property, and foreigners and corporations are severely restricted in land ownership. Although the 1917 constitution declared *ejido* land inviolate, 1994 amendments allow, under certain circumstances, the sale or use of communal land as loan security.

Article 23 severely restricts church powers. In declaring that "places of worship are the property of the nation," it stripped churches of all title to real estate, without compensation. Article 5 and Article 130 banned religious orders, expelled foreign clergy, and denied priests and ministers all political rights, including voting, holding office, and even criticizing the government. Most of these restrictions were dropped in 1994. Churches can own property, provided it is only for religious use, and run schools as long as they follow the national curriculum. Priests and ministers are allowed to vote but are ineligible for public office.

Article 123 establishes the rights of labor: to organize, bargain collectively, strike, work a maximum eight-hour day, and receive a minimum wage. Women are to receive equal pay for equal work and be given a month's paid leave for childbearing. Article 123 also establishes social security plans for sickness, unemployment, pensions, and death. Attempts by the Calderón administration to weaken the amendment were beaten back by PRD and PRI opposition, and changing this article is not currently on the agenda of the new president.

On paper, Mexico's constitutional government structures appear much like their U.S. prototypes: a federal presidency, a two-house

© JUSTIN HENDERSON

The plaza, or town square, often provides the most immediate connection to the democratic process in Mexico.

Congress, and a Supreme Court, with their counterparts in each of the 32 states. Political parties field candidates, and all citizens vote by secret ballot.

Mexico's presidents, however, have traditionally enjoyed greater powers than their U.S. counterparts. They need not seek legislative approval for many cabinet appointments, can suspend constitutional rights under a state of siege, can initiate legislation, veto all or parts of bills, refuse to execute laws, and replace state officers. The federal government, moreover, retains nearly all taxing authority, relegating the states to a role of merely administering federal programs.

Although ideally providing for separation of powers, the Constitution of 1917 subordinates both the legislative and judicial branches, with the courts being the weakest of all. The Supreme Court, for example, can only, with repeated deliberation, decide upon the constitutionality of legislation. Five separate individuals must file successful petitions for writs *amparo* (protection) on a single point of law in order to affect constitutional precedent. The court system is being reformed at this time. Several legal changes, involving the rights of the accused and the structure of courtroom procedure, are at the forefront of a movement to strengthen the judiciary's role in Mexican life.

## Democratizing Mexican Politics

Reforms in Mexico's stable but top-heavy "Institutional Revolution" came only gradually. After the repression during the 1968 Olympics, and especially after the 1985 Mexico City earthquake, the people began giving up on the one dominant party's ability to improve their lives, and—despite a cynical belief reflected by one outstanding PRI leader of the time, "a politician who is poor is a poor politician"— movements toward justice and pluralism slowly took form.

During the subsequent dozen years, minority parties increasingly elected candidates to state and federal office. Although none captured a majority of any state legislature, the strongest non-PRI parties, such as the conservative

pro-Catholic Partido Acción Nacional (PAN, or National Action Party) and the liberal-left Partido Revolucionario Democratico (PRD) elected governors. In 1986, minority parties were given federal legislative seats, up to a maximum of 20, for winning a minimum of 2.5 percent of the national presidential vote. In the 1994 election, minority parties received public campaign financing, depending upon their fraction of the vote.

After 1994, President Zedillo oversaw a series of reforms—appointing opposition party members to his cabinet, seeking congressional approval for important foreign policy measures, and, most importantly, separating the government from the party that radically altered the political and social landscape.

## A New Mexican Revolution

One of Zedillo's most statesmanlike acts came in 2000, when he refused to intervene in the election of his successor, Vicente Fox. Fox, the first opposition candidate to win the presidency since the Revolution, promised a "new revolution" for Mexico, laying out an ambitious program calling for reducing poverty by 30 percent, a million new jobs a year, and free trade between Mexico and the rest of Latin America, as well as with Canada and the United States. He promised to reform the police, the army, and the judiciary, as well as establish a "transparency commission" to look into abuses of the past. However, other than his goal of concluding a treaty with the Zapatistas, very little of Fox's promises ever came to fruition.

Vicente Fox had been a business executive (president of Coca-Cola's Latin American division) before entering politics, and though he was a symbol of the new, democratic Mexico, he was also a victim of it. Not used to making compromises, he was unable to work with the largely opposition Congress, and few of his legislative proposals made it into law. And, like the PRI leaders before him, he wanted to handpick his successor. His own choice was rejected by his party's voters in the primaries, and—having broken the unofficial barrier to a changing of the party in control of the presidency—the

© JUSTIN HENDERSON

government seal

voters appeared to be opting for Mexico City's PRD leader, Andres Manuel López Obrador.

Fox unwisely enmeshed himself in the 2006 election, finally won by a very narrow margin by PAN's Felipe Calderón. Calderón's "hard-hand" approach to law and order came at the cost of Fox's reputation as having been tough on crime. As the war on narcotics traffickers wore on, Mexican opinion makers, including the Roman Catholic hierarchy, have questioned whether the antinarcotics actions are worth the cost in human lives, the reported human rights abuses, and the neglect of equally pressing concerns like global warming, agricultural development, and financial stability. Finally, foreign reports on the drug war have damaged Mexico's reputation as a secure tourist destination—unfairly, most observers believe. The drug war's critics, and even former president Calderón himself, have pointed out that it is narcotics buyers (and gun sellers) in the United States that fuel the criminal enterprises.

On the positive side, Calderón did show more flexibility in working with his congressional opposition, accepting massive changes to proposals, and scaling back his party's ideological commitments to "free trade" as Mexico faces the challenges of a changing economy. Having been through its own financial crisis during the early 1990s, Mexico's financial stability is less threatened than that of other nations in the hemisphere, and a relatively stable political and social climate, open to peaceful, radical change, promises to smooth the path to a more democratic, more open society as Mexico celebrated the bicentennial of its War of Independence and the centennial of the first modern Revolution.

The inauguration of Enrique Peña Nieto at the end of November 2012, marks the beginning of a new era. Thus far, Peña Nieto has attempted to recast the discussion of Mexico to one of positives rather than negatives, talking not about winning or losing the drug war but rather emphasizing the expanding middle class and the expanding number of well-trained college graduates who are being hired into high-tech industries in cities like Guadalajara and Querétaro. The Obama administration has acknowledged the fact that many of Mexico's problems are driven by the U.S. demand for drugs, and has, to some extent, shown a willingness to rethink the discussion as well. Again, time will tell, as will moves to legalize various personal-use drugs on both sides of the border (personal-use quantities of marijuana are now legal in Mexico, Washington State, and Colorado).

# People and Culture

Let a broad wooden chopping block represent Mexico; imagine hacking it with a sharp cleaver until it is grooved and pocked. That fractured surface resembles Mexico's central highlands, where most Mexicans, divided from each other by high mountains and yawning barrancas, have lived since before history.

The Mexicans' deep divisions, in large measure, led to their downfall at the hands of the Spanish conquistadores. The Aztec empire that Hernán Cortés conquered was a vast but fragmented collection of tribes. Speaking more than 100 mutually alien languages, those original Mexicans viewed each other suspiciously, as barely human barbarians from strange lands beyond the mountains. And even today the lines Mexicans draw between themselves—of caste, class, race, wealth—are the result, to a significant degree, of the realities of their mutual isolation.

## POPULATION

The Spanish colonial government and the Roman Catholic religion provided the glue that through 400 years has welded Mexico's fragmented people into a burgeoning nation-state. Mexico's population, more than 113 million by the year 2010, increased during the 1990s, but at a rate diminished to about half that of previous decades. Increased birth control and emigration largely account for the slowdown.

Mexico's population has not always been increasing. Historians estimate that European diseases, largely measles and smallpox, wiped out a tragic 95 percent of the *indígena* population within a few generations after Cortés stepped ashore in 1519. The Mexican population dwindled from an estimated 20 million at the eve of the conquest to a mere 1 million inhabitants by 1600. It wasn't until 1950, more than four centuries after Cortés, that Mexico's population recovered to its preconquest level of 20 million.

## Mestizos, *Indígenas*, *Criollos*, and African Mexicans

Although by 1950 Mexico's population had recovered, it was completely transformed. The mestizo, a Spanish-speaking person of mixed blood, had replaced the pure Native American, the *indígena* (een-DEE-hay-nah), as the typical Mexican.

The trend continues. Perhaps three out of four Mexicans would identify themselves as mestizo: that class whose part-European blood elevates them, in the Mexican mind, to the level of *gente de razón* (people of reason or right). And there's the rub. The *indígenas* (or, mistakenly but much more commonly, Indians), by the usual measurements of income, health, or education, squat at the bottom of the Mexican social ladder.

The typical *indígena* family lives in a small adobe house in a remote valley, subsisting on corn, beans, and vegetables from its small, unirrigated *milpa* (cornfield). They usually have chickens, a few pigs, and sometimes a cow, but no electricity; their few hundred dollars a year in cash income isn't enough to buy even a small refrigerator, much less a truck.

The usual mestizo family, on the other hand, enjoys most modern benefits. They typically own a modest concrete house in town. Their furnishings, simple by developed-world standards, will often include an electric refrigerator, washing machine, propane stove, television, and car or truck. The children go to school every day, and the eldest son sometimes looks forward to college.

Sizable *negro* communities, descendants of 18th-century African slaves, live in the Gulf states and along the Guerrero-Oaxaca Pacific coastline. Last to arrive, the *negros* experience discrimination at the hands of everyone else and are integrating very slowly into the mestizo mainstream.

Above the mestizos, a small *criollo* (Mexican-born white) minority, a few percent of the total population, inherits the privileges—wealth, education, and political power—of its colonial Spanish ancestors.

## THE *INDÍGENAS*

Although anthropologists and census takers classify them according to language groups (such as Huichol, Náhuatl, and Cora), *indígenas* generally identify themselves as residents of a particular locality rather than by language or ethnic grouping. And although, as a group, they are referred to as *indígenas,* individuals are generally uncomfortable being labeled as such.

While the mestizos are the emergent self-conscious majority class, the *indígenas,* as during colonial times, remain the invisible people of Mexico. They are politically conservative, socially traditional, and tied to the land. On market day, the typical *indígena* family might make the trip into town. They bag tomatoes, squash, or peppers, and tie up a few chickens or a pig. The rickety country bus will often be full, and the mestizo driver may wave them away, giving preference to his friends, leaving them to make their way on foot.

Their lot, nevertheless, has been slowly improving. *Indígena* families now almost always have access to a local school and a clinic. Improved health has led to a large increase in their population. Official census figures, however, are probably low. *Indígenas* are traditionally suspicious of government people, and census takers, however conscientious, seldom speak the local language.

Recent figures, however, indicate that 8 percent of Mexicans are *indígenas*—that is, they speak one of Mexico's 50-odd native languages. Of these, a quarter speak no Spanish at all. These fractions are changing only slowly. Many *indígenas* prefer the old ways. If present trends continue, the year 2019, 500 years after the Spanish arrival, will mark the return of the Mexican indigenous population to the preconquest level of 20 million.

### *Indígena* Language Groups

The Maya speakers of Yucatán and the aggregate of the Náhuatl (Aztec language) speakers of the central plateau are Mexico's most numerous *indígena* groups, totaling roughly three million (one million Maya, two million Nahua).

Official figures, which show that the Puerto Vallarta region's indigenous population amounts to a mere 1 percent of the total, are misleading. Official counts do not measure the droves of transient folks—migrants and new arrivals—who sleep in vehicles, in shantytowns, behind their crafts stalls, and with friends and relatives. Although they are officially invisible, you will see them in Puerto Vallarta, walking along the beach, for example, laden with their for-sale fruit or handicrafts—men often in sombreros and scruffy jeans, women often in homemade full-skirted dresses with aprons much like your great-great-grandmother may have worn.

Immigrants in their own country, they flock to cities and tourist resorts from hardscrabble rural areas of the poorest states, often Michoacán, Guerrero, and Oaxaca. Although of pure native blood, they will not acknowledge it or will even be insulted if you ask them if they are *indígenas.* It would be more polite to ask them where they're from. If from Michoacán, they'll often speak Tarasco (more courteously, say Purépecha: poo-RAY-pay-chah); if from Guerrero, the answer will often be Náhuatl, Tlapaneco, or Amuzgo. Oaxaca folks, on the other hand, will probably be fluent in a dialect of either Zapotec or Mixtec. If not one of these, then it might be Amuzgo, Chatino, Trique, Chontal, or any one of a dozen others from Oaxaca's crazy quilt of language.

As immigrants always have, they come seeking opportunity. If you're interested in what they're selling, bargain with humor. And if you err, let it be on the generous side. They are proud, honorable people who prefer to walk away from a sale rather than to lose their dignity.

### The Huichol and Cora

In contrast to the migrants from the south, the Huichol and their northerly neighbors, the Cora, are native to the Puerto Vallarta region. Isolated and resistant to Mexicanization, about 20,000 Huichol (and half as many Cora) farm, raise cattle, and hunt high in their Sierra Madre homeland, which extends northerly and easterly from the foothills north of Tepic. Although the Cora's traditional territory intermixes with the Huichol's at its southern limit, it also spreads northward, between the foothills and the 6,000-foot-high (1,830-m-high) Sierra Occidental valleys, to the Nayarit-Durango border.

The Huichol, more than all *indígena* groups, have preserved their colorful dress and religious practices. Huichol religious use of hallucinogenic peyote and the men's rainbow-tinted feathered hats and clothes are renowned. Tepic, San Blas, and especially Santiago Ixcuintla north of Puerto Vallarta are the most important and easily accessible Huichol centers. In both Puerto Vallarta and Tepic, several stores specialize in the Huichol's colorful religious crafts. Santiago Ixcuintla has a Huichol handicrafts store and community center, and San Blas is an important pilgrimage site where Huichol gather, especially around Easter, for weddings and to pay homage to the sea goddess, Aramara.

While not so well-known as the Huichol's, the Cora's traditions also remain essentially preserved. These include use of peyote in the worship of pre-Christian deities, such as the fertility gods Grandfather Sun and Grandmother Moon, earth mother Tatei, and the heroic monster killer Brother Morning Star. Although many Cora have migrated to the Nayarit lowland towns, such as Acaponeta, Rosamorada, Tuxpan, and Ruíz along Highway 15, they return for festivals to their mountain homeland villages that center around remote Jesús María, about 128 rough mountain kilometers (79.5 mi) from Ruíz. The most notable festivals occur January 1-5 (inauguration of the Cora governor) and Semana Santa (the week before Easter).

## Dress

Country markets are where you're most likely to see people in traditional dress. There, some elderly men still wear the white cottons that blend Spanish and native styles. Absolutely necessary for men is the Spanish-origin straw sombrero (literally, shade maker) on their heads, loose white cotton shirt and pants, and leather huaraches on their feet.

Women's dress, by contrast, is more colorful. It can include a *huipil* (long, sleeveless dress) embroidered in bright floral and animal motifs, and a handwoven *enredo* (wraparound skirt that identifies the wearer with a locality). A *faja* (waist sash) and, in winter, a *quechquémitl* (shoulder cape) complete the ensemble.

## RELIGION

"God and gold" was the two-pronged mission of the conquistadores. Most of them concentrated on gold, while missionaries tried to shift the emphasis to God. They were famously successful; more than 90 percent of Mexicans profess to be Catholics.

Catholicism, spreading its doctrine of equality of all persons before God and incorporating native gods into the church rituals, eventually brought the *indígenas* into the fold. Within 100 years, nearly all native Mexicans had accepted the new religion, which raised the universal God of humankind over local tribal deities.

### The Virgin of Guadalupe

Conversion of the *indígenas* was sparked by the vision of Juan Diego, a humble farmer. On the hill of Tepayac north of Mexico City in 1531, Juan Diego saw what he described as a brown-skinned version of the Virgin Mary enclosed in a dazzling aura of light. She told him to build a shrine in her memory on that spot, where the Aztecs had long worshipped their earth mother, Tonantzín. Juan Diego's Virgin told him to go to the cathedral and relay her instruction to Archbishop Zumárraga.

The archbishop, as expected, turned his nose up at Juan Diego's story. The vision returned, however, and this time Juan Diego's Virgin realized that a miracle was necessary. She ordered him to pick some roses at the spot where she had first appeared to him (a true miracle, since roses had been previously unknown in the vicinity) and take them to the archbishop.

Juan Diego wrapped the roses in his rude fiber cape, returned to the cathedral, and placed the wrapped roses at the archbishop's feet. When he opened the offering, Zumárraga gasped: Imprinted on the cape was an image of the Virgin herself—proof positive of a genuine miracle.

In the centuries since Juan Diego, the brown Virgin—La Virgen Morena, or Nuestra Señora la Virgen de Guadalupe—has blended native and Catholic elements into something uniquely Mexican. In doing so, she has become the virtual patroness of Mexico, the beloved symbol of Mexico for *indígenas,* mestizos, *negros,* and *criollos* alike.

**Pope John Paul II,** in the summer of 2002, journeyed to Mexico to perform a historic gesture. On July 31, before millions of joyous faithful, the frail aging pontiff elevated Juan Diego to sainthood, thus making him Latin America's first indigenous person to be so honored.

With few exceptions, every Puerto Vallarta regional town and village celebrates the cherished memory of the Virgin of Guadalupe on December 12. This celebration, however joyful, is but one of the many fiestas that Mexicans, especially the *indígenas,* live for. Each village holds its local fiesta in honor of its patron saint, who is often a thinly veiled sit-in for a local preconquest deity. Themes appear Spanish—Christians vs. Moors, devils vs. priests—but the native element is strong, sometimes dominant.

## FESTIVALS AND HOLIDAYS

Mexicans love a party. Urban families watch the calendar for midweek national holidays that create a *puente* or bridge to the weekend and allow them to squeeze in a three- to five-day minivacation. Visitors should likewise watch the calendar. Such holidays (especially Christmas and Semana Santa, pre-Easter week) mean packed buses, roads, and hotels, especially around the Puerto Vallarta region's beach resorts.

Campesinos, on the other hand, await their local saint's or holy day. The name of the locality often provides the clue. For example, in

Santa Cruz del Miramar, near San Blas, expect a celebration on May 3, El Día de la Santa Cruz (Day of the Holy Cross). People dress up in their traditional best, sell their wares and produce in a street fair, join a procession, get tipsy, and dance in the plaza.

The following calendar lists national and notable Puerto Vallarta-region holidays and festivals. Local festival dates may vary by a few days; check with a local travel agent or government tourism office if you're planning to attend. (However, if you just happen to be where one of these is going on, get out of your car or bus and join in!)

- Jan. 1: **New Year's Day** (*¡Feliz Año Nuevo!;* national holiday)
- Jan. 1-5: **Inauguration** of the Cora governor in Jesús María, Nayarit (Cora indigenous dances and ceremonies)
- Jan. 6: **Día de los Reyes** (Day of the Kings; traditional gift exchange)
- Jan. 12: **Día de Nuestra Señora de Guadalupe,** in El Tuito, Jalisco, an hour's drive south of Puerto Vallarta (local festival of the Virgin of Guadalupe one month after Puerto Vallarta: parade, music, evening Mass, and carnival)
- Jan. 17: **Día de San Antonio Abad** (decorating and blessing animals)
- Jan. 20-Feb. 2: **Fiesta of the Virgin of Candelaria,** in San Juan de los Lagos, Jalisco (hundreds of thousands from all over Mexico honor the Virgin with parades, dances depicting Christians vs. Moors, rodeos, cockfights, fireworks, and much more)
- Feb. 1-3: **Festival of the Sea,** in San Blas, Nayarit (dancing, horse races, and competitions)
- Feb. 2: **Día de Candelaria** (blessing of plants, seeds, and candles; procession; and bullfights)
- Feb. 5: **Constitution Day** (national holiday commemorating the Constitutions of 1857 and 1917)
- Feb. 24: **Flag Day** (national holiday)

- Late Feb.: During the four days before Ash Wednesday, usually in late February, many towns stage **Carnaval** (Mardi Gras) extravaganzas
- Mar. 11-19: Week before the **Day of St. Joseph** in Talpa, Jalisco (food; edible crafts made of colored *chicle,* or chewing gum; dancing; bands; and mariachi serenades to the Virgin of Talpa)
- Mar. 18-Apr. 4: Grand **ceramics and handicrafts fair,** in Tonalá (Guadalajara), Jalisco
- Mar. 19: **Día de San José** (Day of St. Joseph)
- Mar. 21: **Birthday of Benito Juárez,** the revered "Lincoln of Mexico" (national holiday)
- Late Mar. or Apr. (the Sunday preceding Easter Sunday): **Fiesta de Ramos** (Palm Sunday), in Sayula, Jalisco (on Hwy. 54 south of Guadalajara; local crafts fair, food, dancing, mariachis)
- Apr.: **Semana Santa** (pre-Easter Holy Week, culminating in Domingo Gloria, Easter Sunday national holiday)
- Apr. 18-30: Big **country fair** in Tepatitlán, Jalisco (on Hwy. 80 northeast of Guadalajara; many livestock and agricultural displays and competitions, regional food, rodeos, and traditional dances)
- May 1: **Labor Day** (national holiday)
- May (1st and 3rd Wed.): **Fiesta of the Virgin of Ocotlán,** in Ocotlán, Jalisco (on Lake Chapala; religious processions, dancing, fireworks, regional food)
- May 3: **Día de la Santa Cruz** (Day of the Holy Cross, especially in Santa Cruz de Miramar, Nayarit, and Mascota, Jalisco)
- May 3-15: **Fiesta of St. Isador the Farmer,** in Tepic, Nayarit (blessing of seeds, animals, and water; agricultural displays and competitions; and dancing)
- May 5: **Cinco de Mayo** (defeat of the French at Puebla in 1862; national holiday)
- May 10: **Mother's Day** (national holiday)
- May 10-12: **Fiesta of the Coronation of the Virgin of the Rosary,** in Talpa, Jalisco (processions, fireworks, regional food, crafts, and dances)
- June 24: **Día de San Juan Bautista** (Day of St. John the Baptist; fairs and religious festivals, playful dunking of people in water)
- June 28-29: **Regatta,** in Mexcaltitán, Nayarit (friendly rivalry between boats carrying images of St. Peter and St. Paul to celebrate opening of the shrimp season)
- June 29: **Día de San Pablo y San Pedro** (Day of St. Peter and St. Paul)
- Sept. 14: **Charro Day** (Cowboy Day; held all over Mexico; rodeos, or *charreadas*)
- Sept. 16: **Independence Day** (national holiday; mayors everywhere reenact Father Hidalgo's 1810 Grito de Dolores from city hall balconies on the night of September 15)
- Oct. 4: **Día de San Francisco** (Day of St. Francis)
- Oct. 12: **Día de la Raza** (national holiday commemorating the union of the races; known as Columbus Day in the United States)
- Oct. (last Sun.): **Día de Cristo Rey,** especially in Ixtlán del Río, Nayarit (Day of Christ the King; "Quetzal y Azteca" and "La Pluma" *indígena* dances, horse races, processions, and food)
- Nov. 1: **Día de Todos Santos** (All Souls' Day, in honor of the souls of children; the departed descend from Heaven to eat sugar skeletons, skulls, and treats on family altars)
- Nov. 2: **Día de los Muertos** (Day of the Dead, in honor of ancestors; families visit cemeteries and decorate graves with flowers and favorite food of the deceased)
- Nov. 20: **Revolution Day** (anniversary of the revolution of 1910-1917; national holiday)
- Dec. 1: **Inauguration Day** (national government changes hands every six years: 2012, 2018, 2024, etc.)
- Dec. 8: **Día de la Purísima Concepción** (Day of the Immaculate Conception)

- Dec. 12: **Día de Nuestra Señora de Guadalupe** (Festival of the Virgin of Guadalupe, patron of Mexico; processions, music, and dancing nationwide, especially celebrated around the church in downtown Puerto Vallarta)
- Dec. 16-24: **Christmas Week** (week of *posadas* and piñatas; midnight Mass on Christmas Eve)
- Dec. 25: **Christmas Day** (*¡Feliz Navidad!*; Christmas trees and gift exchange; national holiday)
- Dec. 31: **New Year's Eve**

# Arts and Crafts

Mexico is so stuffed with lovely, reasonably priced handicrafts or *artesanías* (ar-tay-sah-NEE-ahs) that many crafts devotees, if given the option, might choose Mexico over Heaven. A sizable fraction of Mexican families still depend upon the sale of homespun items—clothing, utensils, furniture, forest herbs, religious offerings, adornments, toys, musical instruments—which either they or their neighbors make at home. Many craft traditions reach back thousands of years, to the beginnings of Mexican civilization. The work of generations of artisans has, in many instances, resulted in finery so prized that whole villages devote themselves to the manufacture of a single class of goods.

Although few handicrafts are actually manufactured in Puerto Vallarta, fine examples of virtually all of the following are available in Puerto Vallarta's many well-stocked handicrafts shops and galleries.

## BASKETRY AND WOVEN CRAFTS

Weaving straw, palm fronds, and reeds is among the oldest of Mexican handicraft traditions. Mat- and basket-weaving methods and designs 5,000 years old survive to the present day. All over Mexico, people weave *petates* (palm-frond mats) that vacationers use to stretch out on the beach and that locals use for everything, from keeping tortillas warm to shielding babies from the sun. Along the coast, you might see a woman or child waiting for a bus or even walking down the street while weaving white palm leaf strands into a coiled basket. Later, you may see a similar basket, embellished with a bright animal—parrot, burro, or even Snoopy—for sale in the market.

Like the origami paper folders of Japan, folks who live around Lake Pátzcuaro have taken basket weaving to its ultimate form by crafting virtually everything—from toy turtles and Christmas bells to butterfly mobiles and serving spoons—from the reeds they gather along the lakeshore.

Hatmaking has likewise attained high refinement in Mexico. Workers in Sahuayo, Michoacán (near the southeast shore of Lake Chapala) make especially fine sombreros. Due east across Mexico, in Becal, Campeche, workers fashion Panama hats, called *jipis* (HEE-pees), so fine, soft, and flexible you can stuff one into your pants pocket without damage.

## CLOTHING AND EMBROIDERY

Although **traje** (ancestral tribal dress) has nearly vanished in Mexico's large cities, significant numbers of Mexican women make and wear it. Such traditional styles are still common in remote districts of the Puerto Vallarta region and in the states of Michoacán, Guerrero, Oaxaca, Chiapas, and Yucatán. Most favored is the **huipil**—a long, square-shouldered short- to midsleeved full dress, often hand-embroidered with animal and floral designs. Among the most treasured are *huipiles* from Oaxaca, especially from San Pedro de Amusgos (Amusgo tribe; white cotton, embroidered with abstract colored animal and floral motifs), San Andrés Chicahuatxtla (Trique tribe; white cotton, richly embroidered red stripes, interwoven with

# SHOP SMART

## WHAT TO BUY

Although bargains abound in Mexico, savvy shoppers are selective. Steep import and luxury taxes drive up the prices of foreign-made goods such as cameras, computers, sports equipment, and English-language books. Instead, concentrate your shopping on locally made items: leather, jewelry, cotton resort wear, Mexican-made designer clothes, and the galaxy of handicrafts for which Mexico is renowned.

## HANDICRAFTS

Many hundreds of factories, mostly of the family-run cottage variety, in Guadalajara and its renowned suburban villages of Tlaquepaque and Tonalá, are among Mexico's prolific handicrafts sources, nurturing vibrant traditions rooted in the pre-Columbian past. This rich cornucopia spills over to Puerto Vallarta, where shoppers enjoy a bountiful selection that also includes other national Mexican sources. These, along with a kaleidoscope of offerings from the local art colony, fill sidewalks, stalls, and shops all over town.

## HOW TO BUY

**Credit cards,** such as Visa, MasterCard, and, to a lesser extent, American Express, are widely honored in the hotels, crafts shops, and boutiques that cater to foreign tourists. Although convenient, such shops' offerings will be generally higher priced than those of stores in the older downtown districts that depend more on local trade. Local shops sometimes offer discounts for cash purchases or add the fees they are charged by credit card companies to the price of whatever you're buying.

**Bargaining** will stretch your money even further. It comes with the territory in Mexico and needn't be a hassle. On the contrary, if done with humor and moderation, bargaining can be an enjoyable way to meet Mexican people and gain their respect, and even friendship.

The local crafts market is where bargaining is most intense. For starters, try offering half the asking price. From there on, it's all psychology: You have to content yourself with not needing to have the item. Otherwise,

you're sunk; the vendor will sense your need and stand fast. After a few minutes of good-humored bantering, ask for *el último precio* (the final price), which, if it's close, may be just the bargain you've been looking for.

## BUYING SILVER AND GOLD JEWELRY

Silver and gold jewelry, the finest of which is crafted in Taxco, Guerrero, Guadalajara, and Guanajuato, fills many Puerto Vallarta-region shops. Pure silver (sent from processing mills in the north of Mexico to be worked in Taxco shops) is rarely sold because it's too soft—it's nearly always alloyed with 7.5 percent copper to increase its durability. Such pieces, identical in composition to sterling silver, should have ".925," together with the initials of the manufacturer, stamped on their back sides. Other, less-common grades, such as "800 fine" (80 percent silver), should also be stamped.

If silver is not stamped with the degree of purity, it probably contains no silver at all and is an alloy of copper, zinc, and nickel, known by the generic label "alpaca," or "German," silver. Once, after haggling over the purity and prices of his offerings, a street vendor handed me a shiny handful and said, "Go to a jeweler and have them tested. If they're not real, keep them." Calling his bluff, I took them to a jeweler, who applied a dab of hydrochloric acid (commonly available as muriatic acid) to each piece. Tiny telltale bubbles of hydrogen revealed the cheapness of the merchandise, which I returned the next day to the vendor.

Some shops price sterling silver jewelry simply by weighing, which typically translates to about $1 per gram. If you want to find out if the price is fair, ask the shopkeeper to weigh it for you.

People prize pure gold partly because, unlike silver, it does not tarnish. Gold, nevertheless, is rarely sold pure (24 karat); for durability, it is alloyed with copper. Typical purities, such as 18 karat (75 percent) or 14 karat (58 percent), should be stamped on the pieces. If not, chances are they contain no gold at all.

greens, blues, and yellows, and hung with colored ribbons), and Yalalag (Zapotec tribe; white cotton, with bright flowers embroidered along two or four vertical seams and distinctive colored tassels hanging down the back). Beyond Oaxaca, Maya *huipiles* are also highly desired. They are usually made of white cotton and embellished with brilliant machine-embroidered flowers around the neck and shoulders, front and back.

Shoppers sometimes can buy other less-common types of *traje* accessories, such as a **quechquémitl** (shoulder cape), often made of wool and worn as an overgarment in winter. The **enredo** (literally, tangled) wraparound skirt enfolds the waist and legs like a sarong. Mixtec women in Oaxaca's warm south coastal region around Pinotepa Nacional (west of Puerto Escondido) commonly wear the *enredo,* known locally as the **pozahuanco** (poh-sah-oo-AHN-koh), below the waist and, when at home, go bare-breasted. When wearing her *pozahuanco* in public, a Mixtec woman usually ties a **mandil,** a wide calico apron, across her front. Women weave the best *pozahuancos* at home, using cotton thread dyed a light purple with secretions of tide pool-harvested snails, *Purpura patula pansa,* and silk dyed deep red with cochineal, extracted from the dried bodies of a locally cultivated scale insect, *Dactylopius coccus.*

Colonial Spanish styles have blended with native *traje* to produce a wider class of dress, known generally as **ropa típica.** Fetching embroidered *blusas* (blouses), *rebozos* (shawls), and *vestidos* (dresses) fill boutique racks and market stalls throughout the Mexican Pacific. Among the most handsome is the so-called **Oaxaca wedding dress,** in white cotton with a crochet-trimmed riot of diminutive flowers hand-stitched about the neck and yoke. Some of the finest examples are made in Antonino Castillo Velasco village, in the Valley of Oaxaca.

Unlike the women, only a very small population of Mexican men—members of remote groups, such as Huichol, Cora, Tepehuan, and Tarahumara in the northwest, and Maya and Lacandón in the southeast—wear *traje.*

Nevertheless, shops offer some fine men's *ropa típica,* such as serapes, decorated wool blankets with a hole or slit for the head, worn during northern or highland winters, or guayaberas, hip-length pleated tropical dress shirts.

Fine **bordado** (embroidery) embellishes much traditional Mexican clothing, *manteles* (tablecloths), and *servilletas* (napkins). As everywhere, women define the art of embroidery. Although some still work by hand at home, cheaper machine-made needlework is more commonly available in shops.

## Leather

The Puerto Vallarta region abounds in for-sale leather goods that, if not manufactured locally, are shipped from the renowned leather centers. These include Guadalajara, Mazatlán, and Oaxaca for sandals and huaraches, and León and Guanajuato for shoes, boots, and saddles. For unique and custom-designed articles, you'll probably have to confine your shopping to the pricier stores; for more usual though still attractive leather items such as purses, wallets, belts, coats, and boots, veteran shoppers find bargains at the Mercado Municipal in Puerto Vallarta.

## FURNITURE

Although furniture is usually too bulky to carry back home with your airline luggage, low Mexican prices make it possible for you to ship your purchases home and enjoy beautiful, unusual pieces for half the price, including transport, you would pay—even if you could find them—outside Mexico.

A number of classes of furniture (*muebles,* moo-AY-blays) are crafted in villages near the sources of raw materials: notably, wood, rattan, bamboo, or wrought iron.

Sometimes it seems as if every house in Mexico is furnished with **colonial-style furniture,** the basic design for much of it dating at least to the Middle Ages. Although many variations exist, most colonial-style furniture is heavily built. Table and chair legs are massive, usually lathe turned; chair backs are customarily arrow straight and often vertical. Although usually brown varnished, colonial-style tables, chairs, and chests sometimes shine with inlaid wood or tile, or animal and flower designs. Family shops turn out good furniture, usually in the country highlands, where suitable wood is available. Products from shops in and around Guadalajara (Tlaquepaque and Tonalá), Lake Pátzcuaro (especially Tzintzuntzán), and Taxco and Olinalá, Guerrero, are among the most renowned.

**Equipal,** a very distinctive and widespread class of Mexican furniture, is made of leather, usually brownish pigskin or cowhide, stretched over wood frames. Factories center mostly in Guadalajara and nearby Tlaquepaque and Tonalá villages.

It is interesting that **lacquered furniture,** in both process and design, has much in common with lacquerware produced half a world away in China. The origin of Mexican lacquerware presents an intriguing mystery. What is certain, however, is that it predated the conquest and was originally practiced only in the Pacific states of Guerrero and Michoacán. Persistent legends of pre-Columbian coastal contact with Chinese traders give weight to the speculation, shared by a number of experts, that the Chinese may have taught the lacquerware art to the Mexicans many centuries before the conquest.

Today, artisan families in and around Pátzcuaro, Michoacán, and Olinalá, Guerrero, carry on the tradition. The process, which at its finest resembles cloisonné manufacture, involves carving and painting intricate floral and animal designs, followed by repeated layerings of lacquer, clay, and sometimes gold and silver to produce satiny, jewel-like surfaces.

A sprinkling of villages produce furniture made of plant fiber, such as reeds, raffia, and bamboo. In some cases, entire communities, such as Ihuatzio (near Pátzcuaro, Michoacán) and Villa Victoria (Mexico state, west of Toluca), have long harvested the bounty of local lakes and marshes as the basis for their products.

**Wrought iron,** produced and worked according to Spanish tradition, is used to produce tables, chairs, and benches. Ruggedly fashioned in a riot of baroque scrollwork, it often decorates garden and patio settings. Several colonial cities, notably San Miguel de Allende, Toluca, and Guanajuato, are wrought-iron manufacturing centers.

## GLASS AND STONEWORK

Glass manufacture, unknown in pre-Columbian times, was introduced by the Spanish. Today, the tradition continues in factories throughout Mexico that turn out mountains of **burbuja** (boor-BOO-hah)—bubbled glass tumblers, goblets, plates, and pitchers, usually in blue or green. Finer glass is manufactured, notably in Guadalajara (in suburban Tlaquepaque and Tonalá villages), where you can watch artisans blow glass into a number of shapes—often paper-thin balls—in red, green, and blue.

Mexican artisans work stone, usually near sources of supply. Puebla, Mexico's major onyx (**ónix,** OH-neeks) source, is the manufacturing center for the galaxy of mostly rough-hewn, cream-colored items, from animal charms and chess pieces to beads and desk sets, which crowd curio-shop shelves all over the country. **Cantera,** a pinkish stone, quarried near Pátzcuaro and Oaxaca, is used similarly.

For a keepsake from a truly ancient Mexican tradition, don't forget the hollowed-out stone **metate** (may-TAH-tay), a corn-grinding basin, or the three-legged **molcajete** (mohl-kah-HAY-tay), a mortar for grinding chiles.

## HUICHOL ART

Huichol art evolved from the charms that Huichol shamans crafted to empower them during their hazardous pilgrimages to their peyote-rich sacred land of Wirikuta. To the original items—mostly **devotional arrows, yarn cicuri** (see-KOO-ree—god's eyes), and **decorated gourds** for collecting peyote—have been added colorful **cuadras** (yarn paintings) and **bead masks.**

*Cuadras,* made of synthetic yarns pressed into beeswax on a plywood backing, traditionally depict plant and animal spirits, the main actors of the Huichol cosmos. Bead

## HAGGLING 101

Mexico is the land of negotiations. Nearly everything, from hotel rooms to trinkets, can be negotiated to a lower price. If you come from a country where haggling in stores and hotels is uncommon, the United States, for example, this can produce a mixed bag of reactions. Some people prefer to just pay the inflated asking price right away to avoid having to haggle. Others only shop where there is no haggling, like grocery stores and shopping malls. If you aren't an experienced haggler, attempts can produce anxiety, a feeling of doing something "wrong," or simply the sneaking suspicion that even though you got the price down, you still didn't get a good deal. Here are some tips to make haggling a little easier.

First, have the right attitude. Your goal is not to get the absolute lowest, rock-bottom price but to get a fair price; fair to you and to the seller. It should be friendly, not aggressive. Remember that the people of Mexico make significantly less than a minimum-wage worker in the United States. To them, 10 pesos—roughly US$0.80–is a big deal. Don't bother haggling over items that only cost a few dollars unless you want a volume discount.

Starting at the asking price, counteroffer less than you actually want to pay, but don't go nuts. In popular tourist areas like the artisan market in Puerto Vallarta, you can safely start at 40 percent of the asking price without offending anyone. Again, it's not about getting the lowest price. Don't make an insulting offer of $1 for a hand-carved wooden mask. Shop around and see what the asking price is in a variety of places before you make your purchases.

Be prepared to walk away. If the seller won't negotiate to a reasonable price, be assured that nearby is someone who will. The simple act of turning to walk away can prompt acceptance of your last offer or a better, final offer from the seller. In other cases, if it's something you cannot live without, you may just have to pay the seller's price. However, in an ideal situation, both the buyer and the seller will reach a happy midpoint, each feeling like they got a decent deal.

The bottom line is that if you feel you got a good deal, then you did.

---

masks likewise blend the major elements of the Huichol worldview into an eerie human likeness, often of Grandmother Earth (Tatei Nakawe).

Although Huichol men do not actually manufacture their headwear, they do decorate them. They take ordinary sombreros and embellish them into Mexico's most flamboyant hats, flowing with bright ribbons, feathers, and fringes of colorful wool balls.

Many commercial outlets, especially in Puerto Vallarta (and even commercial Christmas catalogs in the United States), now offer made-for-tourists Huichol goods. However, discriminating collectors find the finer examples nearer the source. Visit the Huichol Cultural Center in Santiago Ixcuintla, the long-established Huichol outlet shops in Tepic, the Galeria Tanana in Sayulita, and the more exclusive Puerto Vallarta shops.

## JEWELRY

Gold and silver were once the basis for Mexico's wealth. Her Spanish conquerors plundered a mountain of gold—religious offerings, necklaces, pendants, rings, bracelets—masterfully crafted by a legion of native metalsmiths and jewelers. Unfortunately, much of that indigenous tradition was lost because the Spanish denied access to precious metals to the Mexicans for generations while they introduced Spanish methods. Nevertheless, a small goldworking tradition survived the dislocations of the 1810-1821 War of Independence and the 1910-1917 revolution. Silver crafting, moribund during the 1800s, was revived in Taxco, Guerrero, principally through the efforts of architect/artist William Spratling, working with the local community.

Today, spurred by the tourist boom,

jewelry making thrives in Mexico. Taxco, where dozens of enterprises—guilds, families, cooperatives—produce sparkling silver and gold adornments, is the acknowledged center. Many Puerto Vallarta regional shops sell fine Taxco products—shimmering butterflies, birds, jaguars, serpents, turtles, fish—reflecting pre-Columbian tradition. Taxco-made pieces, mostly in silver, vary from humble but good-looking trinkets to candelabras and place settings for a dozen, sometimes embellished with turquoise, garnet, coral, lapis, jade, and, in exceptional cases, emeralds, rubies, and diamonds.

## METALWORK

Bright copper, brass, and tinware; sturdy ironwork; and razor-sharp knives and machetes are made in a number of regional centers. **Copperware,** from jugs, cups, and plates to candlesticks—and even the town lampposts and bandstand—all come from Santa Clara del Cobre, a few miles south of Pátzcuaro, Michoacán.

Although not the source of **brass** itself, Tonalá, in Guadalajara's eastern suburbs, is the place where brass is most abundant and beautiful, appearing as menageries of brilliant, fetching birds and animals, sometimes embellished with shiny nickel highlights.

Several Oaxaca family factories turn out piles of fine **cutlery**—knives, swords, and machetes—scrolled **cast-iron grillwork,** and a swarm of bright **tinware,** or *hojalata* (oh-hah-LAH-tah), mirror frames, masks, and glittering Christmas decorations.

Be sure not to miss the miniature **milagros,** one of Mexico's most charming forms of metalwork. Usually made of brass, they are of homely shapes—a horse, dog, or baby, or an arm, head, or foot—which, accompanied by a prayer, the faithful pin to the garment of their favorite saint, whom they hope will intercede to cure an ailment or fulfill a wish. Look for them at pilgrimage basilicas, such as Zapopan (suburban Guadalajara), Talpa (mountains east of Puerto Vallarta), and San Juan de los Lagos, northeast of Guadalajara.

## PAPER AND PAPIER-MÂCHÉ

Papier-mâché has become a high art in Tonalá, Jalisco, where a swarm of birds, cats, frogs, giraffes, and other animal figurines are meticulously crafted by building up repeated layers of glued paper. The result—sanded, brilliantly varnished, and polished—resembles fine sculpture rather than the humble newspaper from which it was fashioned.

Other paper goods you shouldn't overlook include piñatas (durable, inexpensive, and as Mexican as you can get), available in every town market; colorful decorative cutout banners (string overhead at your home fiesta) from San Salvador Huixcolotla, Puebla; and **amate,** wild fig tree bark paintings in animal and flower motifs, from Xalitla and Ameyaltepec, Guerrero.

## POTTERY AND CERAMICS

Although Mexican pottery tradition is as diverse as the country itself, some varieties stand out. Among the most prized is the so-called **Talavera** (or Majolica), the best of which is made by a few family-run factories in Puebla. The name Talavera originates from the Spanish town of the same name, from which the tradition migrated to Mexico; before that it originated on the Spanish Mediterranean island of Majorca (thus Majolica) from a combination of still older Arabic, Chinese, and African ceramic styles. Shapes include plates, bowls, jugs, and pitchers, hand painted and hard fired in intricate bright yellow, orange, blue, and green floral designs. So few shops make true Talavera these days that other cheaper lookalike grades, made around Guanajuato, are more common, selling for as little as a tenth of the price of the genuine article.

More practical and nearly as prized is hand-painted, high-fired **stoneware** from Tonalá in Guadalajara's eastern suburbs. Although made in many shapes and sizes, such stoneware is often available in complete place settings. Decorations are usually in abstract floral and animal designs, hand painted over a reddish clay base.

From the same tradition come the famous *bruñido* pottery animals of Tonalá. Round, smooth, and cuddly as ceramic can be, the Tonalá animals—very commonly doves and ducks, but also cats and dogs and sometimes even armadillos, frogs, and snakes—each seem to embody the essence of their species.

Some of the most charming Mexican pottery, made from a ruddy low-fired clay and crafted following pre-Columbian traditions, comes from western Mexico, especially Colima. Charming figurines in timeless human poses—flute-playing musicians, dozing grandmothers, fidgeting babies, loving couples—and animals, especially Colima's famous **playful dogs,** decorate the shelves of a sprinkling of shops.

The southern states of Guerrero and Oaxaca are both centers of a vibrant pottery tradition. Humble but very attractive are the unglazed, brightly painted animals—cats, ducks, fish, and many others—that folks bring to Puerto Vallarta centers from their family village workshops.

Much more acclaimed are certain types of pottery from the valley surrounding the city of Oaxaca. The village of Atzompa is famous for its tan, green-glazed clay pots, dishes, and bowls. Nearby San Bártolo Coyotepec village has acquired even more renown for its **black pottery** (*barro negro*), sold all over the world. Doña Rosa, now deceased, pioneered the crafting of big round pots without using a potter's wheel. Now made in many more shapes by Doña Rosa's descendants, the pottery's exquisite silvery black sheen is produced by the reduction (reduced air) method of firing, which removes oxygen from the clay's red (ferric) iron oxide, converting it to black ferrous oxide.

Although most latter-day Mexican potters have become aware of the **health dangers of lead pigments,** some for-sale pottery may still contain lead. The hazard comes from low-fired pottery in which the lead pigments have not been firmly melted into the surface glaze. In such cases, acids in foods such as lemons, vinegar, and tomatoes dissolve the lead pigments, which, when ingested in sufficient quantities, will result in lead poisoning. In general, the hardest, shiniest pottery, which has been twice fired—such as the high-quality Tlaquepaque stoneware used for place settings—is the safest.

## WOOD CARVING AND MUSICAL INSTRUMENTS
### Masks
Spanish and native Mexican traditions have blended to produce a multitude of masks—some strange, some lovely, some scary, some endearing, all interesting. The tradition flourishes in the strongly indigenous southern Pacific states of Michoacán, Guerrero, Oaxaca, and Chiapas, where campesinos gear up all year for the village festivals—especially Semana Santa, early December (Virgin of Guadalupe), and the festival of the local patron, whether it be San José, San Pedro, San Pablo, Santa María, Santa Barbara, or one of a host of others. Every local fair has its favored dances, such as the Dance of the Conquest, the Christians and Moors, the Old Men, or the Tiger, in which masked villagers act out age-old allegories of fidelity, sacrifice, faith, struggle, sin, and redemption.

Although masks are made of many materials—from stone and ebony to coconut husks and paper—wood, where available, is the medium of choice. For the entire year, mask makers cut, carve, sand, and paint to ensure that each participant will be properly disguised for the festival.

The popularity of masks has led to an entire made-for-tourists mask industry of mass-produced duplicates, many cleverly antiqued. Examine the goods carefully; if the price is high, don't buy unless you're convinced it's a real antique.

### Alebrijes
Tourist demand has made zany wooden animals, or *alebrijes* (ah-lay-BREE-hays), a Oaxaca growth industry. Virtually every family in the Valley of Oaxaca villages of Arrazola and San Martin Tilcajete runs a factory studio. There,

piles of soft copal wood, which men carve and women finish and intricately paint, become whimsical giraffes, dogs, cats, iguanas, gargoyles, dragons, and most of the possible permutations in between. The farther from the source you get, the higher the *alebrije* price becomes; what costs $5 in Arrazola will probably run about $10 in Puerto Vallarta and $30 in the United States or Canada.

Also commonly available wooden items are the charming colorfully painted fish carved mainly in the Pacific coastal state of Guerrero, and the burnished, dark hardwood animal and fish sculptures of desert ironwood from the state of Sonora.

## Musical Instruments

Most of Mexico's guitars are made in Paracho, Michoacán (southeast of Lake Chapala, 50 miles north of Uruapan). There, scores of cottage factories turn out guitars, violins, mandolins, *viruelas,* ukuleles, and a dozen more variations every day. They vary widely in quality, so look carefully before you buy. Make sure that the wood is well cured and dry; damp, unripe wood instruments are more susceptible to warping and cracking.

## WOOLEN WOVEN GOODS

Mexico's finest wool weavings come from Teotitlán del Valle, in the Valley of Oaxaca, less than an hour's drive east of Oaxaca city. The weaving tradition, carried on by Teotitlán's Zapotec-speaking families, dates back at least 2,000 years. Many families still carry on the arduous process, making everything from scratch. They gather the dyes from wild plants and the bodies of insects and sea snails. They hand wash, card, spin, and dye the wool, and even travel to remote mountain springs to gather water. The results, they say, *vale la pena* (are worth the pain): intensely colored, tightly woven carpets, rugs, and wall hangings, known in Mexico as *tapetes,* that retain their brilliance for generations.

Rougher, more loosely woven blankets, jackets, and serapes come from other areas, notably mountain regions, especially around San Cristóbal de las Casas, in Chiapas, and Lake Pátzcuaro, in Michoacán.

# ESSENTIALS

## Getting There

### BY AIR
#### From the United States and Canada
The vast majority of travelers reach Puerto Vallarta by air. Flights are frequent and reasonably priced, although the airlines have cut back on the number of flights in recent years, and in some cases raised prices. Competition sometimes shaves tariffs to as low as $275 for a Puerto Vallarta low-season round-trip from the departure gateways of San Francisco, Los Angeles, Denver, Dallas, Phoenix, or Houston. Air travelers can save lots of money by shopping around. Don't be bashful about asking for the cheapest price. Make it clear to the airline or travel agent that you're interested in a bargain. Ask the right questions: Are there special-incentive, advance-payment, night, midweek, tour-package, or charter fares? Peruse the ads in the

Sunday newspaper travel section for bargain-oriented travel agencies. Check airline and bargain-oriented travel websites, such as www.orbitz.com, www.expedia.com, and www.travelocity.com.

Although some agents charge booking fees and don't like discounted tickets because their fee depends on a percentage of ticket price, many will nevertheless work hard to get you a bargain, especially if you book an entire air-hotel package with them.

Although only a sprinkling of airlines fly directly to Puerto Vallarta from the northern United States and Canada, many charters do. In locales near Vancouver, Calgary, Ottawa, Toronto, Montréal, Minneapolis, Chicago, Detroit, Cleveland, and New York, consult a travel agent for charter flight options. Be aware that charter reservations, which often require fixed departure and return dates and provide minimal cancellation refunds, decrease your flexibility. If available charter choices are unsatisfactory, then you might choose to begin your vacation with a connecting flight to one of the Puerto Vallarta gateways of San Francisco, Los Angeles, San Diego, Denver, Phoenix, Dallas, Houston, Atlanta, Chicago, San Jose, or Oakland.

### From Europe, Latin America, and Australia

A few airlines fly across the Atlantic directly to Mexico City, where easy Puerto Vallarta connections are available via VivaAerobus, Copa, and Aeroméxico. These include **Lufthansa,** which connects directly from Frankfurt, and **Aeroméxico,** which connects directly from Paris and Madrid.

From Latin America, **Aeroméxico** connects directly with Mexico City, customarily with São Paulo, Brazil; Santiago, Chile; Lima, Peru; Buenos Aires, Argentina; and Bogota, Colombia. They also connect directly with Guatemala City, San Jose in Costa Rica, San Pedro Sula in Honduras, and San Salvador in El Salvador. A number of other Latin American carriers also fly directly to Mexico City.

Very few flights cross the Pacific directly to Mexico, but **Japan Airlines** connects Tokyo to Mexico City via Los Angeles or Dallas. More commonly, travelers from Australasia transfer at New York, Chicago, Dallas, San Francisco, or Los Angeles for Puerto Vallarta.

### BY BUS

As air travel rules in the United States, bus travel rules in Mexico. Hundreds of sleek, first-class bus lines such as Elite, Turistar, Futura, Transportes Pacífico, and White Star (Estrella Blanca) depart the border daily, headed for the Puerto Vallarta region.

Since North American bus lines ordinarily terminate just north of the Mexican border, you must usually disembark and continue on foot across the border to the Mexican immigration office (*migración*). There, after having filled out the necessary but very simple paperwork, you can walk outside and bargain with one of the local taxis to drive you the few miles to the *camionera central* (central bus station).

First-class bus service in Mexico is much cheaper and more frequent than in the United States. Tickets for comparable trips in Mexico cost a fraction (around $80 for a 1,000-mile trip, compared with about $120 in the United States).

In Mexico, as on U.S. buses, you often have to take it as you find it. *Asientos reservados* (seat reservations), *boletos* (tickets), and information must generally be obtained in person at the bus station, and credit cards and travelers checks are not often accepted. Nor are reserved bus tickets typically refundable, so don't miss the bus. On the other hand, plenty of buses roll south almost continually.

### Bus Routes to Puerto Vallarta

**From California and the western United States,** cross the border to Tijuana, Mexicali, or Nogales, where you can ride one of at least three bus lines along the Pacific coast route (National Highway 15) south to Puerto Vallarta by Estrella Blanca (via its subsidiaries, Elite, Transportes Norte de Sonora, or Turistar) or independents Transportes Pacífico or Transportes y Autobuses del Pacífico (TAP).

A few Estrella Blanca and Transportes

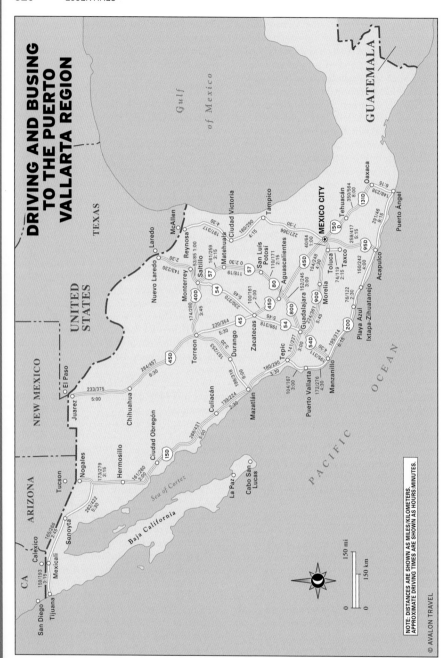

# DRIVING AND BUSING TO THE PUERTO VALLARTA REGION

NOTE: DISTANCES ARE SHOWN AS MILES/KILOMETERS.
APPROXIMATE DRIVING TIMES ARE SHOWN AS HOURS:MINUTES.

© AVALON TRAVEL

Pacífico departures may go all the way from the border to Puerto Vallarta. Otherwise, you will have to change buses at Mazatlán or Tepic, depending on your connection. Allow a full day and a bit more (about 30 hours), depending upon connections, for the trip. Carry liquids and food (which might be only minimally available en route) with you.

**From the midwestern United States,** cross the border from El Paso to Juárez and head for Mazatlán by way of Chihuahua and Durango by either Estrella Blanca (via subsidiaries Transportes Chihuahuenses or super-first-class Turistar) or independent Ómnibus de Mexico. Both Transportes Chihuahuenses and Turistar usually offer a few daily departures direct to Mazatlán. Otherwise, transfer at Durango to a Mazatlán-bound bus and continue south to Puerto Vallarta as described earlier.

**From the southeastern and eastern United States,** cross the border at Laredo to Nuevo Laredo and ride Transportes Norte de Sonora or Turistar direct to Mazatlán, or to Durango. At Durango, transfer to a Mazatlán bus, where you can continue south to Puerto Vallarta, as described previously.

**From the central or eastern United States,** it may be more convenient to ride a bus from the border direct to Guadalajara, where you can easily transfer to one of many buses bound for Puerto Vallarta.

## BY CAR OR RV

If you're adventurous and like going to out-of-the-way places, but you still want to have all the comforts of home, you may enjoy driving your own car or RV to Puerto Vallarta. On the other hand, consideration of cost, risk, wear on both you and your vehicle, and the congestion hassles in towns may change your mind.

### Mexican Car Insurance

Mexico does not recognize foreign insurance. When you drive into Mexico, Mexican auto insurance is at least as important as your passport. At the busier crossings, you can get it at insurance "drive-ins" just north of the border. The many Mexican auto insurance companies are government regulated; their numbers keep prices and services competitive.

**Sanborn's Mexico Insurance** (2009 S. 10th Street, McAllen, TX 78503, tel. 956/686-3601, toll-free U.S. tel. 800/222-0158, www.sanbornsinsurance.com), one of the best-known agencies, certainly seems to be trying hardest. It offers a number of books and services, including the *Recreational Guide to Mexico,* a good road map, "smile-by-mile" *Travelog* guide to "every highway in Mexico," hotel discounts, and more. Much of this is available to members of Sanborn's Sombrero Club.

Alternatively, look into **Vagabundos del Mar** (toll-free U.S. tel. 800/474-2252, www.vagabundos.com), an RV-oriented Mexico travel club offering memberships that include a newsletter, caravanning opportunities, discounts, insurance, and much more.

Mexican car insurance runs from a bare-bones rate of about $8 a day for minimal $10,000/$50,000 (property damage/medical payments) coverage to a more typical $15 a day for more complete $20,000/$100,000 coverage. On the same scale, insurance for a $50,000 RV and equipment runs about $35 a day. These daily rates decrease sharply for six-month or one-year policies, which run from about $200 for the minimum to $400-1,600 for complete, high-end coverage.

If you get broken glass, personal effects, and legal expenses coverage with these rates, you're lucky. Mexican policies don't usually cover them.

You should get something for your money, however. The deductibles should be no more than $300-500, the public liability/medical payments should be about double the legal minimum ($25,000 maximum payment for property damage, $25,000 maximum medical payments per person, and $50,000 maximum total medical payments per accident), and you should be able to get your car fixed in the United States and receive payment in U.S. dollars for losses. If not, shop around.

### A Note of Caution

Although *bandidos* no longer menace Mexican

roads (but loose burros, horses, and cattle still do), be cautious in the infamous marijuana- and opium-growing region of Sinaloa state north of Mazatlán. It's best not to stray from Highway 15 between Culiacán and Mazatlán or from Highway 40 between Mazatlán and Durango. Curious tourists have been assaulted in the hinterlands adjacent to these roads. In general, *norteamericanos* on the road are advised to more or less hurry through northern Baja and northern Mexico in general. The occasional kidnapping and/or random, "collateral damage" type incident does occur—let's not kid ourselves—but these incidents are few and far between. Perhaps tourists cannot go off the beaten track in northern Mexico like they could in safer times, but there are literally thousands of Americans who drive through Mexico every year without incident.

## The Green Angels

The Green Angels have answered many motoring tourists' prayers in Mexico. Bilingual teams of two, trained in auto repair and first aid, help distressed tourists along main highways. They patrol fixed stretches of road twice daily by truck. To make sure they stop to help, pull completely off the highway and raise your hood. You may want to hail a passing trucker to call them for you (Mexico emergency number 078 for the tourism hotline, or 01-800/903-9200).

If for some reason you have to leave your vehicle on the roadside, don't leave it unattended. Hire a local teenager or adult to watch it for you. Unattended vehicles on Mexican highways are quickly stricken by a mysterious disease, the symptom of which is rapid loss of vital parts.

## Mexican Gasoline

Pemex, short for Petróleos Mexicanos, the government oil monopoly, markets diesel fuel and two grades of gasoline, both unleaded: 92-octane premium and 89-octane Magna. Magna (MAHG-nah) is good gas, yielding performance similar to that of U.S.-style "regular" or "super-unleaded" gasoline. It runs about $0.75 per liter (about $2.85 per gallon).

On main highways, Pemex makes sure that major stations (spaced typically about 20 mi/32 km apart) stock Magna. There has been a huge upsurge in the number of Pemex stations in recent years, so the fear of running out of gas is much diminished. However, when traveling long distances in Mexico, it's a good rule of thumb to fill up whenever you get under half full.

## Gas Station Thievery

When stopping at the *gasolinera,* make sure that your cameras, purses, and other movable items are out of reach. Also, make sure that your car has a lockable gas cap. If not, insist on pumping the gas yourself, or be superwatchful as you pull up to the gas pump. Make certain that the pump reads zero before the attendant pumps the gas.

## A Healthy Car

Preventive measures spell good health for both you and your car. Get that tune-up (or that long-delayed overhaul) *before,* rather than after, you leave. Also, carry a stock of spare parts, which will be more difficult to get and more expensive in Mexico than at home. Carry an extra tire or two, a few cans of motor oil and octane enhancer, oil and gas filters, fan belts, spark plugs, tune-up kit, points, and fuses. Be prepared with basic tools and supplies, such as screwdrivers; pliers, including vise grip; lug wrench; jack; adjustable wrenches; tire pump and patches; tire pressure gauge; steel wire; and electrical tape. For breakdowns and emergencies, carry a folding shovel, a Husky rope or chain, a gasoline can, and flares.

## Car Repairs in Mexico

The American big three—General Motors, Ford, and Chrysler—as well as Nissan and Volkswagen are represented by extensive dealer networks in Mexico. (Newcomers Toyota and Honda are less so, and you're more likely to find them in major metro areas.) Getting your car or truck serviced at such agencies is straightforward. While parts will probably be higher in price, shop rates run about one-third of U.S.

prices, so repairs will generally come out to about half the prices back home.

The same is not true for repairing other makes, however. Mexico has only a light sprinkling of foreign-make car dealers. Consequently, it is difficult if not impossible to find officially certified mechanics for Japanese or European makes other than Volkswagen.

Although computerization of engines has complicated matters, many clever Mexican independent mechanics can fix any car that comes their way. Their humble *talleres mecánicos* (tah-YER-ays may-KAH-nee-kohs), or repair shops, dot town and village roadsides everywhere.

Although most mechanics are honest, beware of unscrupulous operators who try to collect double or triple their original estimate. If you don't speak Spanish, find someone who can assist you in negotiations. *Always* get a written cost estimate, including needed parts and labor, even if you have to write it yourself. Make sure the mechanic understands, then ask him to sign it before he starts work. Although this may be a hassle, it might save you a much nastier hassle later. Labor at small, independent repair shops should run $10-20 per hour. The most common repair you're likely to need is a simple tire patch, which should run less than $5 at the typical (and very common) roadside *llantera* (tire repair shop). For more information, and for entertaining anecdotes of car and RV travel in Mexico, consult Carl Franz's *The People's Guide to Mexico.*

## Mordidas (Bribes)

The usual meeting ground of the visitor and Mexican police is in the visitor's car on a highway or downtown street. To the tourist, such an encounter may seem to be mild harassment by the police, accompanied by vague threats of going to the police station or impounding the car for such-and-such a violation. The tourist often goes on to say, "It was all right, though...We paid him $20, and he went away.... Mexican cops sure are crooked, aren't they?"

And, I suppose, if people want to go bribing their way through Mexico, that's their business. But calling Mexican cops crooked isn't exactly fair. Police, like most everyone else in Mexico, have to scratch for a living, and they have found that many tourists are willing to slip them a $20 bill for nothing. Rather than crooked, I would call them hungry and opportunistic.

Instead of paying a bribe, do what I've done a dozen times: Remain cool, and if you're really guilty of an infraction, calmly say, "Ticket, please." (*"Boleto, por favor."*) After a minute or two of stalling, and no cash appearing, the officer most likely will not bother with a ticket but will wave you on with only a warning. If, on the other hand, the officer does write you a ticket, he will probably keep your driver's license, which you will be able to retrieve at the *presidencia municipal* (city hall) the next day in exchange for paying your fine.

If you rent a car at the airport in Puerto Vallarta and head north, do not start out by rushing up the stretch of highway just outside the airport—this is a notorious speed trap, with *transitos* (local traffic cops) just waiting for excited, newly arrived vacationing gringos to speed past.

## Crossing the Border

Squeezing through border bottlenecks during peak holidays and rush hours can be time-consuming. Avoid crossing 7am-9am and 4:30pm-6:30pm.

## Highway Routes from the United States

If you've decided to drive to Puerto Vallarta, you have your choice of three general routes. At safe highway speeds, each of these routes requires a minimum of about 24 hours of driving time. Maximize comfort and safety by following the broad toll (*cuota*) expressways that often parallel the old, narrow nontoll (*libre*) routes. Despite the increased cost (about $60 for a car, more than double that for a motor home), the *cuota* expressways will save you at least a day's driving time (and the extra food and hotel tariffs) and wear and tear on both your vehicle and your nerves. Most folks allow three full south-of-the-border driving days to Puerto Vallarta, but it can be done in less.

**From the U.S. Pacific Coast and west,** follow National Highway 15 (called 15D as the toll expressway) from the border at Nogales, Sonora, an hour's drive south of Tucson, Arizona. Highway 15D continues southward smoothly, leading you through cactus-studded mountains and valleys, which turn into green lush farmland and tropical coastal plain and forest by the time you arrive in Mazatlán. Watch for the *periféricos* and truck routes that guide you past the congested downtowns of Hermosillo, Guaymas, Ciudad Obregón, Los Mochis, and Culiacán. The *cuota,* for the most part, now bypasses the cities, so you don't need to work very hard at avoiding them. Between these centers, you speed along via *cuota* expressway all the way to Mazatlán. If you prefer not to pay the high tolls, stick to the old *libre* highway. Hazards, bumps, and slow going might force you to reconsider, however.

From Mazatlán, continue along the new multilane *cuota* to Tepic, where Highways 15 and 15D fork left (east) to Guadalajara and Highway 200 heads south to Puerto Vallarta and beyond.

If, however, you're driving to Puerto Vallarta **from the central United States,** cross the border at El Paso to Ciudad Juárez, Chihuahua. There, National Highway 45D, the new *cuota* multilane expressway, leads you southward through high, dry plains past the cities of Chihuahua and Jiménez, where you continue by expressway Highway 49 to Gómez Palacio-Torreón. There, proceed southwest toward Durango, via expressway Highway 40D. At Durango, head west along the winding but spectacular two-lane trans-Sierra National Highway 40, which intersects National Highway 15 just south of Mazatlán. From there, continue south as already described. This road from Durango to Mazatlán should not under any circumstances be driven at night or in bad weather conditions. There are literally hundreds of switchbacks, and way too many large trucks with aggressive, impatient drivers. This is a spectacular drive better taken

under optimum conditions. After driving it once, I was told by several people that it has been ranked among the top 10 most dangerous stretches of road in the world—hence the nickname the Devil's Backbone. As an alternative, consider continuing south from Torreón to Zacatecas, and then southwest to Guadalajara. From Guadalara it's an easy spin on the *cuota* to Compostela and then down Highway 200 to Puerto Vallarta.

Folks heading to western Pacific Mexico **from the eastern and southeastern United States** should cross the border from Laredo, Texas, to Nuevo Laredo. From there, you can follow either the National Highway 85 (*libre*) route or the new Highway 85D *cuota* road, which continues, bypassing Monterrey, where you proceed via expressway Highway 40D all the way to Saltillo. At Saltillo, keep going westward on Highway 40 or expressway 40D, through Torreón to Durango. Continue via the two-lane Highway 40 over the Pacific crest all the way to National Highway 15, just south of Mazatlán. Continue southward as described earlier (or choose the alternative described earlier).

## BY TRAIN

Privatization has put an end to most passenger train service in Mexico, with the exception of the **Copper Canyon** scenic route. One of the few remaining passenger train rides in Mexico typically begins with a bus trip or flight south to Chihuahua, where you board the Chihuahua-Pacific Railway train and ride west along the renowned Copper Canyon (Barranca del Cobre) route to the Pacific. Only finished during the early 1960s, this route traverses the spectacular canyon-land home of the Tarahumara people. At times along the winding 406-mile (654-km) route, your rail car seems to teeter at the very edge of the labyrinthine Barranca del Cobre, a canyon so deep that its climate varies from Canadian at the top to tropical jungle at the bottom.

The railway-stop village of Creel, with a few stores and hotels and a Tarahumara mission, is the major jumping-off point for trips into the canyon. For a treat, reserve a stay en route to Puerto Vallarta at the Sierra Lodge (call Yolanda in the United States at 360/588-1290 or Martha Elena Carbajal in Chihuahua at 01-800/830-8325, www.coppercanyonlodges.com) in Creel. From there, the canyon beckons: Explore the village, enjoy panoramic views, observe mountain wildlife, and breathe pine-scented mountain air. Farther afield, you can hike to a hot spring or spend a few days exploring the canyon bottom itself, with overnights at the Riverside Lodge in the rustic village of Batopilas.

## Copper Canyon Tours

Some agencies arrange unusually good Copper Canyon rail tours. Among the best is Baja-based **Copper Canyon Travel** (154 Terrasol, Av. Solmar, Cabo San Lucas, Baja California Sur, C.P. 23450, tel. 624/143-4400 or 624/178-0413, www.canyontravel.com), which employs its own resident guides. Trips range from small-group, rail-based sightseeing and birding/ natural history tours to customized wilderness rail-Jeep-backpacking adventures.

**Nature Treks** (P.O. Box 542, Bryantville, MA 02327, tel. 781/789-8127, www.nature-treks.net) offers a birding tour of the canyon as well as a six-day hike with pack burros and experienced Mexican and Tarahumara guides into some of the more remote areas of the canyon. All trips begin with the spectacular Copper Canyon train trip from Los Mochis on the coast.

## BY FERRY

An alternative route to Puerto Vallarta is by ferry from the southern tip of Baja California. Bus travelers should cross the border at Tijuana or Mexicali and ride **Autobuses Blanca Coordinados** (ABC, Tijuana local tel. 664/621-2424, toll-free Mex. tel. 01-800/025-0222, www.abc.com.mx) through the long desert to La Paz (about 20 hours). Car travelers also cross at Tijuana or Mexicali and follow good two-lane Mexico National Highway 1, a long 900 miles (1,500 km) south to La Paz.

At La Paz (a pleasant, midsize Mexican fishing port and busy resort destination, although it's usually very hot in the late spring and summer), you have your choice of two ferry crossings. **Baja Ferries** (at the La Paz ferry dock, toll-free Mex. tel. 01-800/337-7437, from U.S. dial direct 01152-612/125-6324, fax 01152-612/123-0504, www.bajaferries.com.mx) ferries passengers and vehicles between La Paz and Topolobampo, near Los Mochis in northern Sinaloa (rates are one-way: about $60 per adult, kids $30, cars about $85, motor homes about double), and between La Paz and Mazatlán ($68, $34, and $170 respectively) in southern Sinaloa. Note: If you're planning on continuing south to Puerto Vallarta, you should probably opt for the Mazatlán crossing. Although it won't save you much time (since the bus or your vehicle travels much faster than the ferry), you might save the price of a hotel room and highway tolls (or bus fare).

The La Paz-Topolobampo run goes via the excellent Italian-built 1,000-passenger *California Star*. As of this writing, it leaves La Paz Monday-Friday at 2:30pm, Saturday at 11pm, and takes 6.5 hours. The La Paz-Mazatlán run, on the older *Mazatlan Star*, leaves La Paz Tuesday and Thursday at 6pm and Sunday at 5pm, and takes 18 hours. Although seats are provided, you may want to reserve one of their clean cabins with beds and private toilet (about $60 for a cabin). Ferry facilities on both runs include bar, lounge, and restaurant, but pets are not allowed, and passengers are not allowed to stay in their vehicles during the crossing. MasterCard and Visa are accepted for payment.

Reservations are recommended at all times and are a must during the supercrowded Christmas and Easter holidays. You can make reservations either through the website www.bajaferries.com or directly at any of the many reservations/ticket-sales offices that the website lists. Of all of these, the most useful would probably be their U.S. agent, **Native Trails** (613 Queretaro, El Paso, TX 79912-2210, tel. 915/833-3107, fax 915/585-7027), or the La Paz sales office, which has English-speaking agents (corner of Isabel la Catolica and Navarro, tel.

612/125-7443, toll-free Mex. tel. 01-800/122-1414, fax 612/125-7444).

Although greatly improved in recent years, Baja ferry service is subject to change. Be sure to check by phone or Internet for the newest ferry information before making the long desert trip south to La Paz.

## ORGANIZED TOURS

For travelers on a tight time budget, prearranged tour packages can provide a hassle-free option for sampling the attractions of Puerto Vallarta and its surrounding region. If, however, you prefer a self-paced vacation or desire thrift over convenience, you should probably defer tour arrangements until after arrival. Many Puerto Vallarta agencies are as close as your hotel telephone or front-lobby tour desk and can customize a tour for you. Options vary from city highlight tours and bay snorkeling adventures to safaris through San Blas's wildlife-rich mangrove jungle.

### Cruises and Sailboats

North-of-the-border travel agents will typically have a stack of cruise brochures that include Puerto Vallarta on their itineraries. People who enjoy being pampered with lots of food and ready-made entertainment (and who don't mind paying for it) can have great fun on cruises. Accommodations on a typical 10-day winter cruise (which would include a day or two in Puerto Vallarta) can run as little as $75 per day per person, double occupancy, to as much as $1,000 or more.

If, however, you want to get to know Mexico and the local people, a cruise is not for you. Onboard food and entertainment is the main event of a cruise; shore sightseeing excursions, which cost extra, are a sideshow.

Sailboats, on the other hand, offer an entirely different kind of sea route to Puerto Vallarta. **Ocean Voyages** (1709 Bridgeway, Sausalito, CA 94965, tel. 415/332-4681, toll-free U.S. tel. 800/299-4444, fax 415/332-7460, www.oceanvoyages.com), a California-based agency, arranges passage on a number of sail and motor vessels that regularly depart to the Puerto Vallarta region from Pacific ports such as San Diego, Los Angeles, San Francisco, and Vancouver. It offers custom itineraries and flexible arrangements that can vary from complete Puerto Vallarta round-trip voyages to weeklong coastal idylls between Puerto Vallarta and other Pacific ports of call. Some captains allow passengers to save money by signing on as crew.

### Special-Interest Tours

Some tour and study programs include in-depth activities centered around arts and crafts, language and culture, people-to-people contact, wildlife-watching, ecology, or off-the-beaten-track adventuring. Outstanding among them are programs by University of Guadalajara, Field Guides, Oceanic Society, Elderhostel, Mar de Jade, and Rancho El Charro.

In Puerto Vallarta, the **University of Guadalajara** (www.cepe.udg.mx) maintains excellent study programs for visitors, through its **Centro de Estudios Para Extranjeros (CEPE)** (Study Center for Foreigners). Their extensive offering ranges from beginning Spanish language to advanced history, politics, literature, and art. Housing options include homestays with local families.

**Mar de Jade** (tel. 327/219-4000, toll-free U.S. tel. 800/257-0532, www.mardejade.com), a holistic-style living center at Playa Chacala, about 50 miles (80 km) north of Puerto Vallarta, offers unique people-to-people work-study opportunities. These include Spanish-language study at Mar de Jade's rustic beach study-center and assisting at its organic dairy farm in Las Varas town nearby. It also offers accommodations and macrobiotic meals for travelers who would want to do nothing more than stay a few days and enjoy Mar de Jade's lovely tropical ambience.

Naturalists enjoy the excellent **Field Guides** (toll-free U.S./Can. tel. 800/728-4953, fax 512/263-0117, www.fieldguides.com) San Blas and Sinaloa Highlands bird-watching tour, centered in bird-rich San Blas and climbing up to 7,000 feet (2,134 m) in the northeastern Sinaloa. This tour takes in high pine forest species at one end, and the lush, bird-filled San Blas estuary at the other.

The remote lagoons and islands of Baja California, about 200 miles (300 km) due west of Mazatlán, nurture a trove of marine and onshore wildlife. Such sanctuaries are ongoing destinations of **Oceanic Society** (30 Sir Francis Drake Blvd., P.O. Box 437, Ross, CA 94957, tel. 415/256-9604, toll-free U.S. tel. 800/326-7491, www.oceanicsociety.org) winter expedition-tours around La Paz, Baja California. Tours are priced at $2,375 per person and cover several islands and shorelines on both the Baja California Pacific and Gulf of California coasts. Activities include about one week of marine mammal-watching, snorkeling, bird-watching, and ecoexploring, both on- and offshore.

The Oceanic Society trip might make an exciting overture or finale to your Puerto Vallarta adventure. You can connect with the Oceanic Society's Baja California (La Paz-Los Cabos) jumping-off points via airlines' (Aeroméxico, Alaska, Frontier) mainland (Mazatlán/Guadalajara/Puerto Vallarta) destinations.

A Puerto Vallarta ranch, **Rancho El Charro** (Francisco Villa 895, Fracc. Las Gaviotas, tel. 322/224-0114, www.ranchoelcharro.com.mx), organizes naturalist-led horseback treks in the mountains near Puerto Vallarta. Tours run several days and include guided backcountry horseback riding, exploring antique colonial villages, camping out on the trail, swimming, hearty dining, and cozy, relaxing evenings at a rustic hacienda. Tariffs begin at about $875 per person.

# Getting Around

## BY AIR

The Puerto Vallarta region's four major jet airports are in Puerto Vallarta, Guadalajara, Manzanillo, and Tepic. Both scheduled and charter airlines connect these points with a number of national destinations, such as Mexico City, Mazatlán, Acapulco, La Paz, and Los Cabos. Although much pricier than first-class bus tickets, Mexican domestic airfares are on par with U.S. prices. If you're planning on lots of in-Mexico flying, upon arrival get the airlines' handy (although rapidly changeable) *itinerarios de vuelo* (flight schedules) at the airport.

Mexican airlines have operating peculiarities that result from their tight budgets. Don't miss a flight; you will likely lose half the ticket price. Adjusting your flight date may cost 25 percent of the ticket price. Get to the airport at least an hour ahead of time. Last-minute passengers are often bumped in favor of early-bird wait-listers. Conversely, go to the airport and get in line if you must catch a flight that the airlines claim is full—you might get on anyway. Keep your luggage small so you can carry it on. Lost-luggage victims receive scant compensation in Mexico.

Although the Puerto Vallarta-Guadalajara air connection is a good option, flying between most other Puerto Vallarta regional destinations is much less convenient than riding the bus.

## BY BUS

The passenger bus is the king of the Mexican road. Several lines connect major destinations in the Puerto Vallarta region, both with each other and with the rest of Mexico.

### Classes of Buses

Three distinct levels of intercity service—luxury-class, first-class, and second-class—are generally available. **Luxury-class** (called something like "Primera Plus" or "Ejecutivo" depending upon the line) service speeds passengers between the major destinations of Puerto Vallarta, Tepic, and Barra de Navidad, with few stops en route. In exchange for relatively high fares (about $25 for Puerto Vallarta-Tepic, for example), passengers enjoy rapid passage and airline-style amenities: plush reclining seats, a (usually) clean toilet, air-conditioning, onboard video, and an aisle attendant.

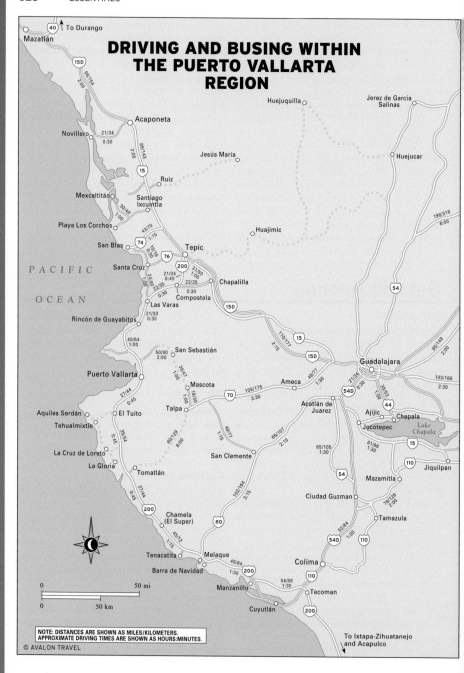

# DRIVING AND BUSING WITHIN THE PUERTO VALLARTA REGION

To Durango

Mazatlán

Novillero

Acaponeta

Jesús María

Huejuquilla

Jerez de Garcia Salinas

Huejucar

Ruiz

Mexcaltitán

Santiago Ixcuintla

Playa Los Corchos

San Blas

Tepic

Huajimic

Santa Cruz

Chapalilla

Las Varas

Compostela

Rincón de Guayabitos

San Sebastián

PACIFIC OCEAN

Puerto Vallarta

Mascota

Ameca

Guadalajara

Aquiles Serdán

El Tuito

Talpa

Acatlán de Juarez

Ajijic

Chapala

Tehualmixtle

Jocotepec

Lake Chapala

La Cruz de Loreto

San Clemente

La Gloria

Tomatlán

Jiquilpan

Mazamitla

Chamela (El Super)

Ciudad Guzman

Tamazula

Tenacatita

Melaque

Colima

Barra de Navidad

Manzanillo

Tecoman

Cuyutlán

To Ixtapa-Zihuatanejo and Acapulco

0    50 mi

0    50 km

NOTE: DISTANCES ARE SHOWN AS MILES/KILOMETERS.
APPROXIMATE DRIVING TIMES ARE SHOWN AS HOURS:MINUTES.

© AVALON TRAVEL

*Map labels:* 45, 54, 45, Zacatecas, 49, 45D, San Luis Potosí, 70, 80, 70, Aguascalientes, 54/87 1:30, Ojuelos de Jalisco, 37/60 1:00, 45D, 45, 252/405 5:00, Lagos de Moreno, 80D, 28/45 1:00, 80, San Juan de Los Lagos, León, 110, 63/102 1:45, Silao, Guanajuato, To Mexico City, 45D, Irapuato, 90, 61/98 1:45, La Piedad de Cabadas, 33/53 0:45, 43, 38/61 1:00, 15, Zamora, 15D, 48/77 1:15, 15, 92/148 2:30, Morelia, To Mexico City, 15, Paracho, 24/38 0:45, 39/62 1:30, Pátzcuaro, 120, 42/67 1:15, Uruapan, 37, To Playa Azul and Ixtapa-Zihuatanejo, © AVALON TRAVEL

Although less luxurious, but for about two-thirds the price, **first-class** (*primera clase*) service is frequent and always includes reserved seating. Additionally, passengers enjoy soft reclining seats and air-conditioning (if it's working). Besides regular stops at or near most towns and villages en route, first-class bus drivers, if requested, will usually stop and let you off anywhere along the road.

**Second-class** (*clase ordinario*) seating is unreserved. In outlying parts of the Puerto Vallarta region, there is even a class of bus beneath second class, but given the condition of many second-class buses, it seems as if third-class buses wouldn't run at all. Such buses are the stuff of travelers' legends: The recycled old GMC, Ford, and Dodge school buses that stop everywhere and carry everyone and everything to even the smallest villages tucked away in the far mountains. As long as there is any kind of a road, the bus will most likely go there.

Now and then you'll read a newspaper story of a country bus that went over a cliff somewhere in Mexico, killing the driver and a dozen unfortunate souls. The same newspapers, however, never bother to mention the half-million safe passengers for whom the same bus provided trips during its 15 years of service before the accident.

Second-class buses are not for travelers with weak knees or stomachs. Often, you will initially have to stand, cramped in the aisle, in a crowd of campesinos. They are warm-hearted but poor people, so don't tempt them with open, dangling purses or wallets bulging in back pockets. Stow your money safely away. After a while, you will be able to sit down. Such privilege, however, comes with obligation, such as holding an old woman's bulging bag of carrots or a toddler on your lap. But if you accept your burden with humor and equanimity, who knows what favors and blessings may flow to you in return.

## Tickets, Seating, and Baggage

Mexican bus lines do not usually publish schedules or fares. Simply ask someone who knows (such as your hotel desk clerk) or call (or ask

Local travel in a place like Yelapa can require a mule and a saddle.

(*medio*) of the bus. The rear seats are often occupied by smokers, drunks, and rowdies. At night, you will sleep better on the right side (*lado derecho*), away from the glare of oncoming traffic lights.

Baggage is generally secure on Mexican buses. Label it, however. Overhead racks are generally too cramped to accommodate airline-size carry-ons. Carry a small bag with your money and irreplaceables on your person; pack clothes and less-essentials in your checked luggage. For peace of mind, watch the handler put your checked baggage on the bus and watch to make sure it is not mistakenly taken off the bus at intermediate stops.

If your baggage gets misplaced, remain calm. Bus employees are generally competent and conscientious. If you are patient, recovering your luggage will become a matter of honor for many of them. Baggage handlers are at the bottom of the pay scale; a tip for their mostly thankless job is very much appreciated.

On long trips, carry food, beverages, and toilet paper. Station food may be dubious, and the sanitary facilities may be ill maintained.

If you are waiting for a first-class bus at an intermediate *salida de paso* (passing station), you have to trust to luck that there will be an empty seat. If not, your best option may be to ride a more frequent second-class bus.

## BY CAR
### Rental Car
Car and Jeep rentals are an increasingly popular transportation option in Puerto Vallarta. They offer mobility and independence for local sightseeing and beach excursions. In the Puerto Vallarta, Tepic, and Manzanillo (Barra de Navidad) airports, the gang's all there: Hertz, National, Avis, Budget, Thrifty, Alamo, Dollar, and several local outfits. They require drivers to have a valid driver's license, passport, and major credit card, and may require a minimum age of 25. Some local companies do not accept credit cards but do offer lower rates in return.

Base prices of international agencies such as Hertz, National, and Avis are not cheap. With a 17 percent value-added tax and mandatory

someone to call) the bus station. Few travel agents handle bus tickets. If you don't want to spend the time to get a reserved ticket yourself, hire someone trustworthy to do it for you. Another option is to get to the bus station early enough on your traveling day to ensure that you'll get a bus to your destination.

Although some lines accept credit cards and issue computer-printed tickets at their major stations, most reserved bus tickets are sold for cash and are handwritten, with a specific seat number (*número de asiento*) on the back. If you miss the bus, you lose your money. Furthermore, airline-style automated reservations systems have not yet arrived at many Mexican bus stations. Consequently, you can generally buy reserved tickets only at the local departure (*salida local*) station. (An agent in Puerto Vallarta, for example, may not be able to reserve you a ticket on a bus that originates in Tepic, 100 miles up the road.)

Request a reserved seat, if possible, with numbers 1-25 in the front (*delante*) to middle

insurance, rentals run more than in the United States. The cheapest possible rental car, usually a used stick-shift VW Beetle, runs $40-60 per day or $250-450 per week, depending on location and season. Prices are highest during Christmas and pre-Easter weeks. Before departure, use the international agencies' toll-free numbers and websites for availability, prices, and reservations. During nonpeak seasons, you may save lots of pesos by waiting until arrival and renting a car through a local agency. Shop around, starting with the agent in your hotel lobby or with the local Yellow Pages (under *"Automoviles, Renta de"*).

**Car insurance** that covers property damage, public liability, and medical payments is an absolute must (and required by law) with your rental car. If you get into an accident without insurance, you will be in deep trouble and probably be sent to jail. Narrow, rough roads and animals grazing at roadside make driving in Mexico more hazardous than back home.

## Taxi

The high prices of rental cars make taxis a useful option for local excursions. Cars are luxuries, not necessities, for most Mexican families. Travelers might profit from the Mexican money-saving practice of piling everyone in a taxi for a Sunday outing. You may find that an all-day taxi and driver—who, besides relieving you of driving, will become your impromptu guide—will cost less than a rental car.

The magic word for saving money by taxi is *colectivo:* a taxi you share with other travelers. The first place you'll practice getting a taxi will be at the airport, where *colectivo* tickets are routinely sold from booths at the terminal door.

If, however, you want a private taxi, ask for a *taxi especial,* which will cost about three or four times the individual tariff for a *colectivo.*

Your airport experience will prepare you for in-town taxis, which rarely have meters. *You must establish the price before getting in.* Bargaining comes with the territory in Mexico, so don't shrink from it, even though it seems a hassle. If you get into a taxi without an agreed-upon price, you're letting yourself in for a more serious and potentially nasty hassle later. If your driver's price is too high, he'll probably come to his senses as soon as you hail another taxi.

After a few days, getting taxis around town will be a cinch. You'll find that you don't have to take the more expensive taxis lined up in your hotel driveway. If the price isn't right, walk toward the street and hail a regular taxi.

In town, if you can't find a taxi, it may be because they are waiting for riders at the local stand, called a taxi *sitio.* Ask someone to direct you to it: *"Excúseme. ¿Dónde está el sitio de taxi, por favor?"* ("Excuse me. Where is the taxi stand, please?")

## Hitchhiking

Although hitchhiking is legal in Mexico, most everyone agrees that it's not the safest mode of transport. If you're unsure, don't do it. Continual hitchhiking does not make for a healthy travel diet, nor should you hitchhike at night.

The recipe for trouble-free hitchhiking requires equal measures of luck, savvy, and technique. The best places to catch rides are where people are arriving and leaving anyway, such as bus stops, highway intersections, gas stations, RV parks, and the highway out of town.

Male-female hitchhiking partnerships seem to net the most rides, although it is technically illegal for women to ride in commercial trucks. The more gear you and your partner have, the fewer rides you will get. Pickup and flatbed truck owners often pick up passengers for pay. Before hopping onto the truck bed, ask how much the ride will cost.

# Visas and Officialdom

For U.S. and Canadian citizens, entry by air into Mexico for a few weeks could hardly be easier. Airline attendants hand out tourist cards (*tarjetas turísticas*) en route, and officers make them official by glancing at passports and stamping the cards at the immigration gate. Business travel permits for 30 days or fewer are handled by the same simple procedures. Moreover, Mexican authorities no longer require payment for a land-entry tourist permit, which has simplified entry by bus and car.

There are some simple entry requirements, however. Mexican immigration officials require that all entering U.S. citizens 15 years old or over must present proper identification—either a valid U.S. passport or original birth certificate (or notarized copy). Naturalized citizens must show naturalization papers, a laminated naturalization card, or a valid U.S. passport. Although you can enter Mexico without a passport, you'll still need to bring one, as it is required for reentry into the United States.

Canadian citizens must also show a valid passport or original birth certificate. Nationals of other countries (especially those such as Hong Kong, which issue more than one type of passport) may be subject to different or additional regulations. For advice, consult your regional Mexico Tourism Board office or consulate. For more Mexico-entry details, contact the Mexico Tourism Board (toll-free U.S./Can. tel. 800/44-MEXICO or 800/446-3942) or your closest Mexico Tourism Board office.

## DON'T LOSE YOUR TOURIST CARD

If you do, present your passport at the police station and get an official police report detailing your loss. Take the report to the nearest federal *migración* office (at the Puerto Vallarta, Manzanillo, and Guadalajara airports) or *oficina de turismo* (in Puerto Vallarta, Guadalajara, Tepic, San Blas, Rincón de Guayabitos, and Barra de Navidad) and ask for a duplicate tourist card. Savvy travelers carry copies of their passports, tourist cards, car permits, and Mexican auto-insurance policies, while leaving the originals in a hotel safe-deposit box.

For more complicated cases, get your tourist card early enough to allow you to consider the options. Tourist cards can be issued for multiple entries and a maximum validity of 180 days; photos are often required. If you don't request multiple entry or the maximum (*el máximo*) time, your card will probably be stamped single entry, valid for some shorter period, such as 90 days. If you are not sure how long you'll stay in Mexico, request the maximum (180 days is the absolute maximum for a tourist card; long-term foreign residents routinely make semiannual "border runs" for new tourist cards).

## STUDENT AND BUSINESS VISAS

A visa is a notation stamped and signed on your passport showing the number of days and entries allowable for your trip. Apply for a student visa at the consulate nearest your home well in advance of your departure; the same is true if you require a business visa of longer than 30 days. One-year renewable student visas are available (sometimes with considerable red tape). An ordinary 180-day tourist card may be the easiest option, if you can manage it.

## YOUR PASSPORT

Your passport (or birth or naturalization certificate) is your positive proof of national identity; without it, your status in any foreign country is in doubt. Don't leave home without one. U.S. citizens may obtain passports (allow 4-6 weeks) at local post offices. For-fee private passport agencies can speed this process and get you a passport within a week, maybe less.

## ENTRY FOR CHILDREN

Children under the age of 15 can be included on their parents' tourist cards, but complications occur if the children (by reason of illness, for example) cannot leave Mexico with both parents. Parents can avoid such red tape by getting a passport and a Mexican tourist card for each of their children.

In addition to passport or birth certificate, minors (under age 18) entering Mexico without parents or legal guardians must present a notarized letter of permission signed by both parents or legal guardians. Even if accompanied by one parent, a notarized letter from the other must be presented. Divorce or death certificates must also be presented, when applicable. Airlines will require the name, address, and telephone number of the person meeting unaccompanied minors upon arrival in Mexico.

Puerto Vallarta travelers should hurdle all such possible delays far ahead of time in the cool calm of their local Mexican consulate rather than the hot, hurried atmosphere of a border or airport immigration station.

## ENTRY FOR PETS

A pile of red tape can delay the entry of dogs, cats, and other pets into Mexico, or it could be smooth as silk. Be prepared with veterinary-stamped health and rabies certificates for each animal, and keep the animals in sturdy crates during travel. Contact your regional Mexico Tourism Board (toll-free U.S./Can. tel. 800/44-MEXICO or 800/446-3942, www.visitmexico.com) for assistance. Changes in rules banned pets from passenger cabins for a while in 2012, but this was seemingly rescinded later in the year. Be sure and look into this if you are bringing a pet and want to make certain he or she can ride in the cabin with you.

## CAR PERMITS

If you drive to Mexico, you will need a permit for your car. Upon entry into Mexico, be ready with originals and copies of your proof-of-ownership or registration papers (state title certificate, registration, or notarized bill of sale), current license plates, and current driver's license. The auto permit fee runs about $27, payable only by non-Mexican-bank MasterCard, Visa, or American Express credit cards. (The credit-card-only requirement discourages those who sell or abandon U.S.-registered cars in Mexico without paying customs duties.) Credit cards must bear the same name as the vehicle proof-of-ownership papers.

The resulting car permit becomes part of the owner's tourist card and receives the same length of validity. Vehicles registered in the name of an organization or person other than the driver must be accompanied by a notarized affidavit authorizing the driver to use the car in Mexico for a specific time.

Border officials generally allow you to carry or tow additional motorized vehicles (motorcycle, another car, large boat) into Mexico but will probably require separate documentation and fee for each vehicle. If a Mexican official desires to inspect your trailer or RV, go through it with him.

Accessories, such as a small trailer, small boat, CB radio, or outboard motor, may be noted on the car permit and must leave Mexico with the car.

For updates and details on documentation required for taking your car into Mexico, contact the Mexico Tourism Board in the United States (toll-free U.S. tel. 800/446-3942, www.visitmexico.com). For more details on motor vehicle entry and what you may bring in your baggage to Mexico, consult the AAA (American Automobile Association) *Mexico TravelBook.*

Since Mexico does not recognize foreign automobile insurance, you *must* buy **Mexican car insurance.**

## CROSSING THE BORDER AND RETURNING HOME

Squeezing through border bottlenecks during peak holidays and rush hours can be time-consuming. Avoid crossing 7am-9am and 4:30pm-6:30pm. If you can manage it, cross instead during late-night or early-morning hours. Furthermore, the U.S. Customs and Border Patrol maintains an informative border crossing page. Visit www.bhp.gov, and click the "Border Wait Times" link on the right side.

Just before **returning** across the border with your car, park and have an *aduana* (customs) official *remove and cancel the holographic* *identity sticker that you received on entry.* If possible, get a *recibo* (receipt) or some kind of verification that it's been *cancelado* (canceled). Tourists have been fined hundreds of dollars for inadvertently carrying uncanceled car-entry stickers on their windshields.

At the same time, return all other Mexican permits, such as tourist cards and hunting and fishing licenses. Also, be prepared for Mexico exit inspection, especially for cultural artifacts and works of art, which may require exit permits. Certain religious and pre-Columbian artifacts, legally the property of the Mexican government, cannot be taken from the country.

If you entered Mexico with your car, you cannot legally leave without it except by permission from local customs authorities, usually the Aduana (Customs House) or the Oficina Federal de Hacienda (Federal Treasury Office).

All returnees are subject to **U.S. immigration and customs inspection.** These inspections have become much more time-consuming since September 11, 2001. The biggest change is that **all U.S. citizens must present a valid U.S. passport in order to reenter the United States.** On a good day, the wait amounts to about an hour. The worst bottlenecks are at the big border crossings, especially Tijuana and, to a lesser extent, Mexicali, Nogales, Ciudad Juárez, Laredo, and Brownsville.

U.S. law allows a fixed value (at present $400) of duty-free goods per returnee. This may include no more than one liter of alcoholic spirits, 200 cigarettes, and 100 cigars. A flat 10 percent duty will be applied to the first $1,000 (fair retail value; save your receipts) in excess of your $800 exemption. You may, however, mail packages (up to $50 value each) of gifts duty free to friends and relatives in the United States. Make sure to clearly write "unsolicited gift" and a list of the value and contents on the outside of the package. Perfumes (over $5), alcoholic beverages, and tobacco may not be included in such packages.

Improve the security of such mailed packages by sending them by Mexpost class, similar to U.S. Express Mail service. Even better (but much more expensive), send them by DHL international couriers, which maintains offices in Puerto Vallarta, Tepic, and Manzanillo. DHL also has satellite offices in the Bahía de Banderas area, including one in Mezcales north of Puerto Vallarta.

Be forewarned, however, that having friends and family mail you items while in Mexico carries more risk, depending on the contents. Clothes, CDs, DVDs, and other valuable American goods tend to "disappear" long before the package ever reaches you. When a package does arrive carrying goods from the United States, it is usually accompanied by an exorbitant tariff as well.

For more information on U.S. customs regulations important to travelers abroad, write for a copy of the useful pamphlet *Know Before You Go,* from the U.S. Customs Service (1300 Pennsylvania Ave., Washington, DC 20229, tel. 202/354-1000, www.cbp.gov). You can also order the pamphlet by phone or download it from their website (click on "Travel" at the bottom of the home page, then click on "Know Before You Go").

Additional U.S. rules prohibit importation of certain fruits, vegetables, and domestic animal and endangered wildlife products. Certain live animal species, such as **parrots,** may be brought into the United States, subject to 30-day agricultural quarantine upon arrival, at the owner's expense. The U.S. Customs Service's *Know Before You Go* pamphlet provides more details on agricultural product and live animal importation.

For more information on the importation of endangered wildlife products, contact the Fish and Wildlife Service (1849 C St. NW, Washington, DC 20240, tel. 202/208-4717, www.fws.gov).

# Sports and Recreation

It's easy to understand why most vacationers come to Puerto Vallarta to stay on the beach. And these days, they don't simply confine themselves to Playa de Oro, the golden Puerto Vallarta luxury hotel strand. Increasing numbers are venturing out and discovering the entire Puerto Vallarta region's quieter resorts. Beginning in the north, on the lush Nayarit Coast, are sleepy San Blas and Rincón de Guayabitos; farther south, the crystal sands of Bucerías decorate the northern arc of the Bay of Banderas, while south past Puerto Vallarta are tiny Boca de Tomatlán and Yelapa, nestling at the Bay of Banderas's jungly southern edge. Beyond that, south of the pine-clad Sierra Lagunillas crest, lie the gemlike bays of Chamela, Careyes, and Tenacatita; and past that, the homey country resorts of Melaque and Barra de Navidad bask on the Costa Alegre (Happy Coast) of southern Jalisco.

The shoreline offers more than resorts, however. Visitors are increasingly seeking rustic paradises where they can lay out a picnic or even set up camp and enjoy the solitude, wildlife, and fishing opportunities of a score of breezy little beach hideaways.

The 300-odd miles of the Puerto Vallarta coastal region offer visitors their pick of shorelines, which vary from mangrove-edged lagoons and algae-adorned tide pools to shoals of pebbles and sands of many shades and consistencies.

Sand makes the beach, and the Puerto Vallarta region has plenty—from dark, warm mica to cool, velvety white coral. Some beaches drop steeply to turbulent, close-in surf, fine for fishing. Others are level, with gentle, rolling breakers made for surfing and swimming.

Beaches are fascinating for the surprises they yield. Puerto Vallarta-area beaches, especially the hidden strands near resorts and the dozens of miles of wilderness beaches and tide pools, yield treasure troves of shells and flotsam and jetsam for those who enjoy looking for them. Beachcombing is more rewarding during the summer storm season, when big waves deposit acres of shells—conchs, scallops, clams, combs of Venus, whelks, limpets, olives, cowries, starfish, and sand dollars. It's illegal to remove seashells, however, so remember to leave them for others to enjoy.

During the summer-fall rainy season, beaches near river mouths (notably Río Santiago north of San Blas and the Río Purificación near Tenacatita) are outdoor galleries of fantastic wind- and water-sculpted snags and giant logs deposited by the downstream flood.

## WILDLIFE-WATCHING

Wildlife-watchers should keep quiet and always be on the alert. Animal survival depends on their seeing you before you see them. Occasional spectacular offshore sights, such as whales, porpoises, and manta rays, or an onshore giant constrictor, beached squid, crocodile (*caimán*), or even jaguar looking for turtle eggs, are the reward of those prepared to recognize them. Don't forget your binoculars and your *Bird-Finding Guide to Mexico*.

Although wildlife-watching is likely to be rewarding for the prepared everywhere in the Puerto Vallarta region, the lush mangrove lagoons around San Blas are special. For even casual nature enthusiasts, the La Tovara jungle-river trip is a must.

## FISHING

The Puerto Vallarta region offers many excellent fishing opportunities. Sportspeople routinely bring in dozens of species from among the more than 600 that abound in Mexican Pacific waters.

### Surf Fishing

Good fishing beaches away from the immediate resort areas will typically be uncrowded, with only a few local folks (mostly fishing with nets) and fewer visitors. Mexicans do little rod-and-reel sportfishing. Most either make their living from fishing or do none at all. Although some for-sale fishing equipment is available, sportfishing equipment is both expensive and hard to get. Plan to bring your own, including hooks, lures, line, and weights.

A good general information source before you leave home is a local bait-and-tackle shop. Tell the folks there where you're going, and they'll often know the best lures and bait to use and what fish you can expect to catch with them.

In any case, the cleaner the water, the more interesting your catch. On a good day, your reward might be one or more *sierras, cabrillas,* porgies, or pompanos pulled from the Puerto Vallarta surf.

You can't have everything, however. Foreigners cannot legally take Mexican abalone, coral, lobster, clams, rock bass, sea fans, seashells, shrimp, or turtles. Neither are they supposed to buy them directly from fishermen.

## Deep-Sea Fishing

Puerto Vallarta, Barra de Navidad, and San Blas captains operate dozens of excellent big charter boats. Rental generally includes a 30- to 40-foot boat and crew for a full or half day, plus equipment and bait for 2-6 people, not including food or drinks. The charter price depends upon the season. During the high Christmas-New Year's and before-Easter seasons, reservations are mandatory, and a Puerto Vallarta boat can run $600 per day or a lot more depending on the size of the charter. Off-season rates, which depend strongly on your bargaining ability, can cost as little as half the high-season rate. For high-season charter boat reservations, contact an experienced agency several weeks before departure.

## Other Boat-Rental Options

Renting an entire big boat is not your only choice. High-season business is sometimes so brisk at Puerto Vallarta that agencies can fill up boats by booking individuals, who typically pay $70 per person.

*Pangas,* outboard launches seating 4-6, are available on the beaches for as little as $50, depending on the season. Once, in Barra de Navidad, four of my friends went out in a *panga*

all day, had a great time, and came back with a boatload of big tuna, jack, and mackerel. A restaurant cooked them as a banquet for a dozen of us in exchange for the extra fish. I discovered for the first time how heavenly fresh *sierra veracruzana* can taste.

If you or a friend speaks a bit of Spanish, you can bargain for a *panga* right on the beach in Puerto Vallarta or at a dozen other seaside villages such as San Blas, Rincón de Guayabitos, Sayulita, Punta Mita, Cruz de Huanacaxtle, Bucerías, Mismaloya, Boca de Tomatlán, Chamela, Careyes, Tenacatita, La Manzanilla, Melaque, and Barra de Navidad.

## Bringing Your Own Boat

If you're going to do lots of fishing, your own boat may be your most flexible and economical option. One big advantage is you can go to the many excellent fishing grounds that the charter boats do not frequent. Keep your boat license up-to-date, your equipment simple, and your eyes peeled and ears open for local regulations and customs, plus tide, wind, and fishing information.

## Fishing Licenses and Boat Permits

Anyone 16 or older who is either fishing or riding in a fishing boat in Mexico is required to have a fishing license. Although Mexican fishing licenses are obtainable from certain travel and insurance agents or at government fishing offices in Puerto Vallarta, San Blas, and Barra de Navidad, save yourself time and trouble by getting both your fishing licenses and boat permits by mail ahead of time from the Mexican Department of Fisheries (Oficina de Pesca, 2550 5th Ave., Suite 15, San Diego, CA 92103-6622, tel. 619/233-4324, fax 619/233-0344, www.swr.nmfs.noaa.gov/alisth.htm). Call to request applications, which they can supply by mail, fax, or email. Fees are reasonable but depend upon the period of validity and the fluctuating exchange rate. On the application, fill in the names (exactly as they appear on passports) of the people requesting licenses. Include a cashier's check or a money order for the exact amount, along with a stamped, self-addressed envelope.

## WATER SPORTS

Swimming, surfing, sailboarding, kiteboarding, snorkeling, scuba diving, kayaking, sailing, and personal watercraft-riding are the Puerto Vallarta region's water sports of choice.

### Safety First

Viewed from Puerto Vallarta beaches, the Pacific Ocean usually lives up to its name. Many protected inlets, safe for child's play, dot the coastline. Unsheltered shorelines, on the other hand, can be deceiving. Smooth water in the calm morning often changes to choppy in the afternoon; calm ripples that lap the shore in March can grow to hurricane-driven walls of water in November. Such storms can wash away sand, temporarily changing a wide, gently sloping beach into a steep one plagued by turbulent waves and treacherous currents.

Undertow, whirlpools, crosscurrents, and occasional oversized waves can make ocean swimming a fast-lane adventure. Getting unexpectedly swept out to sea or hammered onto the beach bottom by a surprise breaker are potential hazards.

*Never* attempt serious swimming when tipsy or full of food; never swim alone where someone can't see you. Always swim beyond big breakers (which come in sets of several, usually climaxed by a huge one, which breaks highest and farthest from the beach). If you happen to get caught in the path of such a wave, avoid it by *diving directly toward and under it,* letting it roll harmlessly over you. If you are unavoidably swept up in a whirling, crashing breaker, try to roll and tumble with it, as football players tumble, to avoid injury.

Look out for other irritations and hazards. Now and then, particularly during the late spring months, swimmers get a nettlelike (but usually harmless, unless you have an allergy) jellyfish sting. Certain types of jellyfish stings, such as those from the blue man o' wars, with

riding the waves in the evening light at the beach of Barra de Navidad

long stinging tendrils, can be extremely painful and, in rare cases, fatal. Be careful around coral reefs and beds of sea urchins; corals can sting (like jellyfish), and you can additionally get infections from coral cuts and sea-urchin spines. *Shuffle* along sandy bottoms, especially during cool winter months, to scare away stingrays before stepping on one. If you're unlucky, its venomous tail spines may inflict a painful wound.

## Snorkeling and Scuba Diving

A number of clear-water sites await snorkelers and scuba divers. North of the Bay of Banderas, Isla Islote, just offshore from Rincón de Guayabitos, is an enjoyable site for snorkelers. Accessible from the Bay of Banderas itself are Islas Marietas, off north-shore Punta Mita, and the famous Los Arcos rocks off Mismaloya. Additionally, tour boats regularly take snorkelers to small coves near Playa las Ánimas and Playa Quimixto on the Bay of Banderas's verdant southern shore. Adventurous snorkelers and divers go farther afield to explore the wreck at Tehualmixtle on the pristine Cabo Corrientes coast past the Bay of Banderas's southern lip. Beyond that, rock-studded bays, such as gemlike Bahía Careyes and Tenacatita, invite snorkelers and divers to explore their clear waters.

Veteran divers usually arrive during the dry winter and early spring when river outflows are mere trickles, leaving offshore waters clear. In Puerto Vallarta, a number of professional dive shops rent equipment, provide lessons and guides, and transport divers to choice sites.

While beginners can usually do well with rented equipment, serious snorkelers and divers bring their own gear. This should include wetsuits in winter, when many swimmers feel cold after more than an unprotected half hour in the water. For anything deeper than a 30- to 40-foot dive in the winter, you will be most comfortable in a 7 ml wetsuit and hood. It gets quite chilly below the thermocline.

## Sailing, Surfing, Sailboarding, Kiteboarding, and Kayaking

With its endless miles of Pacific coast offering point breaks, beach breaks, and reef breaks, Mexico is considered by many to the number one country in the world for surfing. The waves are always good somewhere in Mexico, for there are hundreds of surf spots facing south, west, and north, assuring that there most likely good waves breaking.

Point breaks such as Stoner's, south of San Blas, and El Faro, at Punta Mita, offer world-class waves when the swell is coming from the right direction: usually south is best at Stoner's, north by northwest at El Faro. Puerto Escondido, farther south, offers the famed "Mexican Pipeline," with its backbreaking, board-breaking barrels. There are countless other breaks with great waves all up and down the coast. Look at any surf forecasting site, and you'll see dozens of listings for Mexico.

For intermediates and beginners, the Puerto Vallarta vicinity offers a number of good spots. These include Sayulita, La Lancha just east of Punta Mita, and Anclote, at Punta Mita.

Kayakers and nonsurfing paddleboarders, by contrast, require more tranquil waters, and they will find plenty of calm, flat-water days in Banderas Bay. Kiteboarders and sailboarders have discovered that the wind blows strong and steady on the ocean off Bucerías almost every afternoon.

With the price of traveling with a surfboard or paddleboard going through the roof, many shops all over Mexico now offer a wide selection of rental gear for surfers of every skill level. There are good rental shops in Sayulita, Punta Mita, Chacala, and Bucerías, in the Puerto Vallarta area.

## Waterskiing, Parasailing, and Personal Watercraft

The Puerto Vallarta hotel beachfronts of northside Playa de Oro and, to a lesser extent, Playa los Muertos, on the south side, have long been centers for waterskiing, parasailing, and personal watercraft-riding. In parasailing, a motorboat pulls while a parachute lifts you, like a soaring gull, high over the ocean. After 5 or 10 minutes it deposits you—usually gently—back

surfboards and *pangas:* two ways to play in Jalisco and Nayarit

© JUSTIN HENDERSON

on the sand. This is fun, once, for 10 minutes. Then you wonder why you are up there.

Jet Ski boats (also called WaveRunners or personal watercraft) are like snowmobiles except that they operate on water, where, with a little practice, beginners can quickly learn to whiz over the waves. Although many luxury resort hotels provide experienced crews and equipment for Jet Ski enthusiasts, crowded conditions increase the hazard to both participants and swimmers. You, as the patron, are paying plenty for the privilege; you have a right to expect that your providers and crew are well equipped, sober, and cautious. You also have to be aware of the fact that you are making a lot of noise, polluting the water, and irritating everyone within 500 yards of your machine. However, these personal watercraft are also useful for water rescues in dangerous surf conditions.

## BEACH BUGGIES AND ATVS
Some visitors enjoy racing along the beach and rolling over dunes in beach buggies and ATVs

(all-terrain vehicles, called *motos* in Mexico)—balloon-tired three-wheeled motor scooters. While certain resort rental agencies cater to the growing use of such vehicles, limits are in order. Of all the proliferating high-horsepower beach pastimes, these, along with Jet Skis, are the most intrusive. Noise and gasoline pollution, injuries to operators and bystanders, and the scattering of wildlife and destruction of their habitats have led to the restriction of dune buggies and ATVs on Puerto Vallarta-region beaches. If you see anyone other than a policeman riding an ATV on the beach, rest assured that he or she is doing so illegally, and don't hesitate to say something.

## TENNIS AND GOLF
Puerto Vallarta visitors can enjoy a number of excellent private courts and courses. In Puerto Vallarta itself, golfers have their pick of the Marina course in town, the Vista Vallarta course inland from town, The Tigre course in Nuevo Vallarta, and the Los Flamingos course several miles north of the airport. There are

also several world-class courses at Punta Mita and a gorgeous nine-hole course in San Pancho. Likewise, south of Puerto Vallarta, you can enjoy a pair of fabulously exclusive golf courses: the exotically scenic golf course in the jungle at El Tamarindo, and the breezy palm-tufted course at Isla Navidad resort near Barra de Navidad.

As for tennis, many resort hotels in Puerto Vallarta and Nuevo Vallarta have tennis courts. Other smaller hotels in Rincón de Guayabitos, Cruz de Huanacaxtle, Mismaloya, Careyes, Tenacatita, Los Angeles Locos, Tamarindo, Melaque, and Barra de Navidad also have courts.

No public golf or tennis courts exist in the Puerto Vallarta region, but many hotels and private clubs allow for-fee use by the general public. If you plan to play a lot of golf or tennis, you're best to stay at one of the many hotels with access to these courts and courses.

Use of hotel tennis courts is sometimes, but not always, included in your hotel tariff. If not, fees will run upward of $5 per hour. Golf greens fees, which begin at about $75 for 18 holes, are always extra.

## BULLFIGHTING

It is said there are two occasions for which Mexicans arrive on time: funerals and bullfights.

Bullfighting is a recreation, not a sport. The bull is outnumbered seven to one, and the outcome is never in doubt. Even if the matador (literally, killer) fails in his duty, his assistants will entice the bull away and slaughter it in private beneath the stands.

### La Corrida de Toros

Moreover, Mexicans don't call it a "bullfight"; it's the *corrida de toros,* during which six bulls are customarily slaughtered, beginning at 5pm (4pm in the winter) on Wednesdays. After the beginning parade, featuring the matador and his helpers, the picadores and the banderilleros, the first bull rushes into the ring in a cloud of dust. Clockwork *tercios* (thirds) define the ritual: The first, the *puyazos* (stabs), requires that two picadores on horseback thrust lances into the bull's shoulders, weakening it. During the second *tercio,* the banderilleros dodge the bull's horns to stick three long, streamered darts into its shoulders.

Trumpets announce the third *tercio* and the appearance of the matador. The bull—weak, confused, and angry—is ready for the finish. The matador struts, holding the red cape, daring the bull to charge. Form now becomes everything. The expert matador takes complete control of the bull, which rushes at the cape, past its ramrod-erect opponent. For charge after charge, the matador works the bull to exactly the right spot in the ring—in front of the judges, a lovely señorita, or perhaps the governor—where the matador mercifully delivers the precision *estocada* (killing sword thrust) deep into the drooping neck of the defeated bull.

Benito Juárez, as governor during the 1850s, outlawed bullfights in Oaxaca. In his honor, they remain so, making Oaxaca unique among Mexican states.

The Puerto Vallarta bullring is just north of the Maritime Terminal and the Galerias Vallarta shopping mall, on the east side of Highway 200. Bullfights are scheduled for Wednesday evenings.

# Accommodations

The Puerto Vallarta region has many hundreds of lodgings to suit every style and pocketbook: world-class resorts, small beachside hotels, comfortable apartments and condos, homey *casas de huéspedes* (guesthouses), palmy trailer parks, and dozens of miles of pristine beaches, potentially ripe for tent or RV camping. The high seasons—when reservations are generally required—run from mid-December to March, during Easter week, and during the month of August.

The hundreds of accommodations described in the destination chapters of this guide are positive recommendations—checked out in detail—solid options from which you can pick according to your taste and purse.

## Hotel Rates

The rates listed in this guide are U.S. dollar equivalents of peso prices, 17 percent taxes included, as quoted by the hotel management at the time of writing.

In Puerto Vallarta, hotel rates depend strongly upon inflation and season. To cancel the effect of the relatively steep Mexican inflation, rates are reported in U.S. dollars (although, when settling your hotel bill, you will nearly always save money by insisting on **paying in pesos**). To further increase accuracy, estimated low- and high-season rates are quoted whenever possible.

## Saving Money

At any time other than the superhigh Christmas and Easter seasons, you can often get at least one or two free days with a one-week stay. Promotional packages available during slack seasons may include free extras such as breakfast, a car rental, a boat tour, or a sports rental. A travel agent or travel website can be of great help in shopping around for such bargains.

You nearly always save additional money if you deal in pesos only. Insist on both booking your lodging for an agreed price in pesos and paying the resulting hotel bill in the same pesos, rather than dollars. The reason is that dollar rates quoted by hotels are often based on the hotel desk exchange rate, which is customarily about 5 percent, or even as much 15 percent, less than bank rates. For example, if the clerk tells you your hotel bill is $1,000, instead of handing over the dollars, ask the clerk how much it is in pesos. Using the desk conversion rate, he or she might say something like 9,000 pesos (considerably less than the 10,000 pesos that the bank might typically give for your $1,000). Pay the 9,000 pesos or have the clerk mark 9,000 pesos on your credit card slip, and save yourself $100.

For stays of more than a week or two, you'll save money and add comfort with an **apartment or condominium** rental. Monthly rates range $500-1,500 (less than half the comparable hotel per diem rate) for comfortable one-bedroom furnished kitchenette units, often including resort amenities such as pool and sundeck, beach club, and private balcony with a view.

Airlines regularly offer **air-hotel packages** that may save you lots of pesos, especially if you're planning on staying at an upscale ($100 or more) hotel. These deals, which seldom extend to moderately priced lodgings, customarily require that you depart for Puerto Vallarta through certain gateway cities, which depend on the airline. Accommodations are usually (but not exclusively) in luxury resorts. If you live near one of these gateways, it may pay to consult the airlines.

## GUESTHOUSES AND LOCAL HOTELS

Puerto Vallarta, like many coastal resorts, began as an old town that expanded into a new *zona hotelera,* where big hotels rise along a golden strand of beach. In the old town, surrounded by the piquant smells, sights, and charms of old Mexico, are the family-managed *casas de huéspedes* and smaller hotels, often arranged around sunny, plant-festooned inner patios.

Such lodgings vary from scruffy to spic-and-span, and from humble to distinguished. At minimum, you can expect a plain room, a shared toilet, a hot-water shower, and plenty of atmosphere for your money. Rates typically run $15-40, depending upon season and amenities. Discounts for long-term stays are often available. Such family-run, small hostelries are rarely near the beach, unlike many of the medium and larger older hotels.

### Medium and Larger Older-Style Hotels

These hotels make up a large fraction of the recommendations of this guide. Many veteran travelers find it hard to understand why people come to Mexico and spend $200 or more a day for a hotel room when good alternatives are available for as little as $35.

Many such hostelries are the once-grand first-class hotels established long before their towering international-class neighbors mushroomed along the beach. You can generally expect a clean, large (but not deluxe) room with bath and toilet, and even sometimes a private beach-view balcony. Although they often share the same velvety sand and golden sunsets as their more expensive neighbors, such hotels usually lack the costly international-standard amenities—air-conditioning, cable TV, direct-dial phones, tennis courts, exercise gyms, and golf access—of the big resorts. Their guests, however, enjoy surprisingly good service, good food, and a native ambience more charming and personal than that of many of their five-star neighbors.

Booking these hotels is straightforward. All of them may be dialed direct (from the United States, dial 011-52, then the local area code and number), and, like the big resorts, many even have toll-free U.S. and Canadian information and reservation numbers.

## INTERNATIONAL-CLASS HOTELS

The Puerto Vallarta region offers many beautiful, well-managed international-class resort hotels in Puerto Vallarta and Nuevo Vallarta. A number of others dot the pristine southern Jalisco coastline between Puerto Vallarta and Barra de Navidad. Most are in Puerto Vallarta, however, where they line the Bay of Banderas's crystal strand north of the old town.

The resorts' plush amenities, moreover, need not be overly expensive. During the right time of year, you can vacation at many of the big-name spots—Sheraton, Westin, NH Krystal, Fiesta Americana, Holiday Inn—for surprisingly little. While high-season tariffs ordinarily run $100-300, low-season (May-Nov., and to a lesser degree, Jan. 6-Feb. 1) packages and promotions can cut these prices significantly. Shop around for savings via your Sunday newspaper travel section, through travel agents, and by calling the hotels directly at their toll-free numbers.

© MSNANCY/ISTOCKPHOTO

hotels on Playa los Muertos, in Puerto Vallarta

## Other Luxury Options

Puerto Vallarta-region visitors enjoy a pair of increasingly common variations on the international-class hotel theme. One of these is the **all-inclusive resort** that offers all lodging, food and beverages, and entertainment (usually with plenty for kids to do) included at one price. High-season tariffs customarily run $100-150 per person, double occupancy ($70-100 low season). In some of the newer, higher-end all-inclusives, such as the Riu Palace and the Grand Velas, the tariffs can run into the hundreds of dollars per person. Kids stay for half price or less. This choice appeals to folks who like company and prefer a hassle-free week of fun in the sun on a beautiful beach. On the other hand, don't choose an all-inclusive resort if you want to do lots of outside local exploring, entertaining, and wining and dining downtown. At least a dozen such all-inclusive resort hotels are in operation, nearly all on Puerto Vallarta and Nuevo Vallarta beaches.

The other increasingly common international-class hotel variation is the small- to midsize **boutique hotel.** Although only a handful are located in Puerto Vallarta itself, several have opened on splendidly isolated beaches sprinkled north and south along the Jalisco and Nayarit Coasts. Most lodgings in this category have fewer than 20 rooms, and all have gorgeous locations and a plethora of deluxe amenities and services, including at least one fine restaurant and bar. Rates customarily run $200 and up for two.

## GAY-FRIENDLY HOTELS

Gay and lesbian visitors have enjoyed increasing acceptance in Puerto Vallarta for a generation, and now the vast majority of Puerto Vallarta hotels could be termed gay friendly. Moreover, a number of lodgings welcome gay visitors by advertising in the excellent *Gay Guide Vallarta* magazine (or online at www. gayguidevallarta.com). Many gay-welcoming hotels, bed-and-breakfasts, apartments, and condominium complexes, most of which are gay owned, sprinkle the Zona Románica, long popular with a legion of savvy long-time Puerto Vallarta visitors, both straight and gay.

## APARTMENTS, BUNGALOWS, CONDOMINIUMS, AND VILLAS

For longer stays, many Puerto Vallarta visitors prefer the convenience and economy of an apartment or condominium or the luxurious comfort of a villa vacation rental. Choices vary, from spartan studios to deluxe beachfront suites and rambling homes big enough for entire extended families. Prices depend strongly upon season and amenities, ranging from about $500 per month for the cheapest to at least 10 times that for the most luxurious. If you don't mind living a bit inland and either taking the bus or driving, you can find a variety of furnished and unfurnished apartments and houses in neighborhoods like Las Juntas and Pitillal for a fraction of what you would pay in downtown Puerto Vallarta. Things might be a bit more rustic, but you are sure to make friends with the locals and learn a lot more about the culture than you would in a condo complex with other Americans or Canadians. In these more rural areas, expect prices to be more in the $250-350 range for a monthly rental. To find available rentals, check out the **Mano a Mano** classified listings, which are available every Thursday morning at newsstands and your local OXXO. You can also check their website for current listings at www.manoa-mano.com.mx.

At the low end, you can expect a clean, furnished apartment within several blocks of the beach, with kitchen and regular maid service. More luxurious condos, which rent for about $500 per week, are typically high-rise ocean-view suites with hotel-style desk services and resort amenities such as pool, hot tub, sundeck, and beach-level restaurant. Villas vary from moderately upscale homes to sky's-the-limit beach-view mansions blooming with built-in designer luxuries, private pools and beaches, tennis courts, gardeners, cooks, and maids.

In contrast to Puerto Vallarta, owners in country beach resorts such as Bucerías, Rincón de Guayabitos, and Barra de Navidad call their apartment-style accommodations **bungalows.** This generally implies a motel-type kitchenette-suite with less service, though it's more spacious and more suitable for families than a hotel room. For long stays by the beach, when you want to save money by cooking your own meals, such an accommodation might be ideal.

Back in town, many of Puerto Vallarta's best-buy *apartmentos* (ah-part-MAYN-tohs) and *condominios* (cohn-doh-MEE-nee-ohs) are in the colorful Olas Altas old-town district. They are often rented on the spot or reserved by writing or phoning the individual owners or local managers. (Look on the local Craigslist page, http://pv.craigslist.org, under "Vacation Rentals.")

Nevertheless, a number of agents in Puerto Vallarta manage and rent vacation lodgings, including **Bayside Properties** (Rodolfo Gómez 111, tel. 322/222-8148, fax 322/223-0898, www.baysidepropertiespv.com), in the heart of the Olas Altas district, as well as south-of-Cuale rental agencies **Tropicasa Realty** (Pulpito 145A, corner of Olas Altas, tel. 322/222-6505, fax 322/222-2555, www.tropicasa.com) and **Tango Rentals** (tel. 322/224-7398, U.S./Can. tel. 310/401-6752, toll-free tel. 888/433-9057, www.tangorentals.com).

Even more vacation rental homes and condos, many of them moderately priced, in the Jalisco and Nayarit small coastal towns of Barra de Navidad, Melaque, and La Manzanilla, south of Puerto Vallarta; and Bucerías, Punta Mita, Sayulita, San Francisco, and Rincón de Guayabitos, north of Puerto Vallarta, are accessible both through websites or by local rental agents. One of the best websites is the big (but easily useable) worldwide site **Vacation Rentals By Owner** (www.vrbo.com), which lists many Puerto Vallarta-region vacation rentals, from budget to upscale, including color photographs. Other good rental websites are www.choice1.com and www.mexconnect.com.

More expensive Puerto Vallarta condo and villa rentals are quite easy to locate. They're sprinkled everywhere, from the marina on the north side to the Conchas Chinas ocean-view hillside on the southern edge of town. All the local Puerto Vallarta agents rent them. A number of U.S.-based agencies do the same through toll-free information and reservations numbers. For example, try **Villas de Oro Vacation Rentals** (638 Scotland Dr., Santa Rosa, CA 95409, toll-free U.S. tel. 800/638-4552 or 800/898-4552, www.villasdeoro.com), **Villas of Mexico** (P.O. Box 3906, Chico, CA 95927, toll-free U.S. tel. 800/456-3133, www.villasofmexico.com), and **Villa World** (4230 Orchard Lake Rd., Suite 3, Orchard Lake, MI 48323, toll-free U.S. tel. 800/521-2980 or toll-free Can. tel. 800/453-8719, www.villaworld.com).

Another good vacation-rental source is the Sunday travel section of a major metropolitan daily newspaper, such as the *Los Angeles Times* and the *San Francisco Chronicle,* which routinely list Puerto Vallarta vacation rentals. National real estate networks, such as Century 21, also rent Puerto Vallarta properties (or can recommend someone who does).

You may also want to consider using the services of a home-exchange agency, such as www.homeexchange.com, whereby you swap homes with someone in Puerto Vallarta for a contracted time period. Travelers who like to meet new people can try couch surfing in the home of a resident at www.couchsurfing.com.

## Closing the Deal

Prudence should guide your vacation rental decision making. Before paying a deposit on a sight-unseen rental, ask for satisfied customer testimonials and photographs of the property you are considering. As with all rentals, don't pay anything until you have approved a written contract describing the rental and what's included (such as inclusive dates, linens, towels, dishes and utensils, maid service, view, pool, taxes, and transportation from the airport) for the specified sum. Put down as little advance payment as possible, preferably with a credit card, to secure your reservation. If you do have a problem with your rental when you arrive, resolve the situation immediately and do not

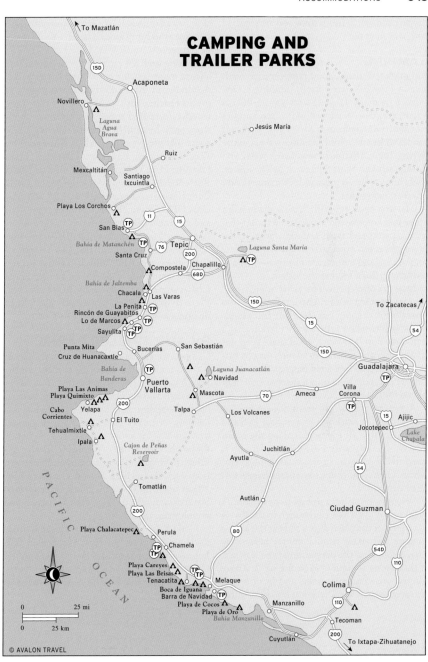

# CAMPING AND TRAILER PARKS

To Mazatlán

Acaponeta

Novillero

Laguna Agua Brava

Jesús María

Ruiz

Mexcaltitán

Santiago Ixcuintla

Playa Los Corchos

San Blas

Bahía de Matanchén

Santa Cruz

Tepic

Laguna Santa María

Compostela

Chapalilla

Bahía de Jaltemba

Chacala

Las Varas

La Peñita

Rincón de Guayabitos

Lo de Marcos

Sayulita

Punta Mita

Cruz de Huanacaxtle

Bucerías

San Sebastián

Bahía de Banderas

Puerto Vallarta

Laguna Juanacatlán

Navidad

Mascota

Ameca

Villa Corona

Guadalajara

Playa Las Animas

Playa Quimixto

Yelapa

Talpa

Los Volcanes

Jocotepec

Ajijic

Lake Chapala

Cabo Corrientes

Tehualmixtle

El Tuito

Ipala

Cajon de Peñas Reservoir

Juchitlán

Ayutla

Tomatlán

Autlán

Ciudad Guzman

PACIFIC OCEAN

Playa Chalacatepec

Perula

Chamela

Playa Careyes

Playa Las Brisas

Tenacatita

Boca de Iguana

Barra de Navidad

Playa de Cocos

Playa de Oro

Melaque

Manzanillo

Bahía Manzanillo

Colima

Tecoman

Cuyutlán

To Ixtapa-Zihuatanejo

To Zacatecas

0        25 mi

0        25 km

© AVALON TRAVEL

pay any additional funds until you are satisfied with the outcome.

## CAMPING

Although few, if any, good campsites are available in Puerto Vallarta itself, camping is customary at many favored sites in the Puerto Vallarta region. Mexican middle-class families crowd certain choice strands—those with soft sand and gentle, child-friendly waves—only during the Christmas-New Year's week and during Semana Santa, the week before Easter. Most other times, tenters and RV campers find beaches uncrowded.

The best spots typically have a shady palm grove for camping and a *palapa* restaurant that serves drinks and fresh seafood. *Heads up for falling coconuts,* especially in the wind. Costs for parking and tenting are minimal—usually only the price of food at the restaurant.

Days are often perfect for swimming, strolling, and fishing, and nights are balmy—too warm for a sleeping bag, but fine for a hammock (which allows the air circulation that a tent does not). However, good tents keep out mosquitoes and other pests, which may be further discouraged by a good bug repellent. Tents can get hot, requiring only a sheet or very light blanket for sleeping cover.

As for camping on isolated beaches, opinions vary, from dire warnings of *bandidos* to bland assurances that all is peaceful along the coast. The truth is somewhere in between. Trouble is most likely to occur in the vicinity of towns, where a few local thugs sometimes harass isolated campers.

When scouting out a private place to camp, a good rule is to arrive early enough in the day to get a feel for the place. Buy a soda at the *palapa* or store and take a stroll along the beach. Say *"Buenos días"* to the people along the way; ask if the fishing is good (*"¿Pesca buena?"*). Above all, use your common sense and intuition. If the people seem friendly, ask if it's *seguro* (safe).

If so, ask permission: *"¿Es bueno acampar acá?"* ("Is it okay to camp around here?") You'll rarely be refused.

Tenting and RV parking are permitted for a fee at many beachfront RV and trailer parks. A number of other informal spots, mostly at pretty beaches with no facilities, await those travelers prepared to venture from the well-worn path. Moving from north to south, likely spots include Novillero; Playa Borrego (San Blas); Matanchén Bay; Playa Platanitos; Playa Chacala; Playa El Naranjo; La Peñita (at Motel Russell); Laguna Santa María de Oro (at Koala Bungalows and Trailer Park, inland, south of Tepic); Playa Punta Raza; Laguna Juanacatlán and Corinches Reservoir (both in the mountains near Mascota); Playa Destiladeras; Playa las Ánimas, Playa Quimixto, and Yelapa (all three boat-accessible only); Tehualmixtle; Ipala; Cajón de Peñas reservoir; Playa Chalacatepec; Chamela Bay; Playa Careyes; Playa las Brisas; Playa Tenacatita; Playa Boca de Iguana; Melaque; and Playa de Cocos.

## RV AND TRAILER PARKS

Campers who prefer company to isolation stay in RV and trailer parks. About 20 of them dot the Puerto Vallarta region's beaches from San Blas to Barra de Navidad. The most luxurious have all hookups and dozens of amenities, including restaurants, recreation rooms, and swimming pools; the humblest are simple palm-edged lots beside the beach. Virtually all of them have good swimming, fishing, and beachcombing. Prices run from a few dollars for a tent space to about $18-26 per night including air-conditioning power. Significant discounts are available for weekly and monthly rentals.

Good RV and trailer parks are located (from north to south) at San Blas, Matanchén Bay, Laguna Santa María, La Peñita, Rincón de Guayabitos, Lo de Marco, Sayulita, Puerto Vallarta, Chamela Bay, Boca de Iguana, and Melaque.

# Food

Some travel to Puerto Vallarta for the food. True Mexican food is old-fashioned, home-style fare requiring many hours of loving preparation. Such food is short on meat and long on corn, beans, rice, tomatoes, onions, eggs, and cheese.

Mexican food is the unique product of thousands of years of native tradition. It is based on corn—*teocentli,* the Aztec "holy food"—called *maíz* (mah-EES) by present-day Mexicans. In the past, a Mexican woman spent much of her time grinding and preparing corn: soaking the grain in lime water, which swells the kernels and removes the tough seed-coat, then grinding the bloated seeds into meal on a stone metate. Finally, she patted the meal into tortillas and cooked them on a hot, baked-mud griddle, a *comal* (KOH-mahl).

Sages (men, no doubt) wistfully imagined that gentle pat-pat-pat of women all over Mexico to be the heartbeat of Mexico, which they feared would cease when women stopped making tortillas. Fewer women these days make tortillas by hand. The gentle pat-pat-pat has been replaced by the whir and rattle of the automatic tortilla-making machine in myriad *tortillerías,* where women and girls line up for their family's daily kilo-stack of tortillas.

Tortillas are to the Mexicans what rice is to the Chinese and bread is to the French. Mexican food is invariably some mixture of sauce, meat, beans, cheese, and vegetables wrapped in a tortilla, which becomes the culinary be-all: the food, the dish, and the utensil wrapped into one. If a Mexican man has nothing to wrap in his lunchtime tortilla, he will content himself by rolling a thin filling of salsa (*chile* sauce) in it.

## HOT OR NOT?

Much food served in Mexico is not "Mexican." Eating habits, as most other customs, depend upon social class. Upwardly mobile Mexicans typically shun the corn-based *indígena* fare in favor of the European-style food of the Spanish colonial elite: chops, steaks, cutlets, fish, clams, omelets, soups, pasta, rice, and potatoes.

Such fare is often as bland as Des Moines on a summer Sunday afternoon. *No picante*—not spicy—is how the Mexicans describe bland food. *Caliente,* the Spanish adjective for hot (as in hot water), does not, in contrast to English usage, imply spicy, or *picante.*

## VEGETARIAN FARE

Strictly vegetarian cooking is the exception in Mexico, as are macrobiotic restaurants, health-food stores, and organic produce. Meat is such a delicacy for most Mexicans that they can't understand why people would give it up voluntarily. If vegetable lovers can manage with corn, beans, cheese, eggs, *legumbres* (vegetables), and fruit, and not be bothered by a bit of pork fat (*manteca de cerdo*), Mexican cooking will suit them fine. On the other hand, if pork fat bothers you, ask for your food *sin manteca* (without lard).

In the more metropolitan Puerto Vallarta, there are excellent vegetarian restaurants, and many other establishments routinely offer several veggie options on the menu.

## SEAFOOD

Early chroniclers wrote that Aztec emperor Moctezuma employed a platoon of runners to bring fresh fish 300 miles from the sea every day to his court. Around Puerto Vallarta, fresh seafood is fortunately much more available from dozens of shoreline establishments, varying from humble beach *palapas* to luxury hotel restaurants.

Seafood is literally here for the taking, although less so than in the past. In the summer on the beach at Puerto Vallarta, fish and squid have been known to swarm so thickly in the surf that tourists pulled them out barehanded. Nowadays, with such bounty usually lacking, villagers up and down the coast use small nets to retrieve enough fish for supper,

# CATCH OF THE DAY

A bounty of fish darts, swarms, jumps, and wriggles in the Puerto Vallarta region's surf, reefs, lagoons, and offshore depths. While many make delicious dinners (especially dorado for fillets, *sierra* for ceviche, and *huachinango* for grilled whole fish), others are tough (sailfish), bony (bonefish), and even poisonous (puffers). Some grow to half-ton giants (marlin, grouper), while others are diminutive reef grazers (parrot fish, damselfish, angelfish) whose bright colors delight snorkelers and divers. Here's a sampling of what you might find underwater or on your dinner plate:

**albacore** (*albacora, atún*): tunalike, 2-4 feet in size; blue; found in deep waters; excellent taste

**angelfish** (*ángel*): one foot; yellow, orange, blue; reef fish*

**barracuda** (*barracuda, picuda*): two feet; brown; deep waters; good taste

**black marlin** (*marlin negro*): six feet; blue-black; deep waters; good taste

**blue marlin** (*marlin azul*): eight feet; blue; deep waters; poor taste

**bobo** (*barbudo*): one foot; blue, yellow; found in surf; fair taste

**bonefish** (*macabi*): one foot; blue or silver; found inshore; poor taste

**bonito** (*bonito*): tunalike, two feet; black; deep waters; good taste

**butterfly fish** (*muñeca*): six inches; black, yellow; reef fish*

**chub** (*chopa*): one foot; gray; reef fish; good taste

**croaker** (*corvina*): two feet; brownish; found along inshore bottoms; rare and protected

**damselfish** (*castañeta*): four inches; brown, blue, orange; reef fish*

**dolphinfish, mahimahi, dorado:** three feet; green, gold; deep waters; good taste

**grouper** (*garopa*): three feet; brown, rust; found offshore and in reefs; good taste

**grunt** (*burro*): eight inches; black, gray; found in rocks, reefs*

**jack** (*toro*): 1-2 feet; bluish-gray; offshore; good taste

**mackerel** (*sierra*): two feet; gray with gold spots; offshore; good taste

**mullet** (*lisa*): two feet; gray; found in sandy bays; good taste

**needlefish** (*agujón*): three feet; blue-black; deep waters; good taste

**Pacific porgy** (*pez de pluma*): 1-2 feet; tan; found along sandy shores; good taste

**parrot fish** (*perico, pez loro*): one foot; green, pink, blue, orange; reef fish*

**pompano** (*pómpano*): one foot; gray; inshore bottoms; excellent taste

**puffer** (*botete*): eight inches; brown; inshore; poisonous

**red snapper** (*huachinango, pargo*): 1-2 feet; reddish pink; deep waters; excellent taste

**roosterfish** (*pez gallo*): three feet; black, blue; deep waters; excellent taste

**sailfish** (*pez vela*): five feet; blue-black; deep waters; poor taste

**sardine** (*sardina*): eight inches; blue-black; offshore; good taste

**sea bass** (*cabrilla*): 1-2 feet; brown, ruddy; reef and rock crevices; good taste

**shark** (*tiburón*): 2-10 feet; black to blue; in- and offshore; good taste

**snook** (*robalo*): 2-3 feet; black-brown; found in brackish lagoons; excellent taste

**spadefish** (*chambo*): one foot; black-silver; found along sandy bottoms; reef fish*

**swordfish** (*pez espada*): five feet; black to blue; deep waters; good taste

**triggerfish** (*pez puerco*): 1-2 feet; blue, rust, brown, black; reef fish; excellent taste

**wahoo** (*peto, guahu*): 2-5 feet; green to blue; deep waters; excellent taste

**yellowfin tuna** (*atún amarilla*): 2-5 feet; blue, yellow; deep waters; excellent taste

**yellowtail** (*jurel*): 2-4 feet; blue, yellow; offshore; excellent taste

*generally too small to be considered edible

## CHOCOLATL

The refreshing drink *chocolatl* enjoyed by Aztec nobility is a remote but distinct relative of the chocolate consumed today by hundreds of millions of people. It was once so precious that chocolate beans were a common medium of exchange in preconquest Mexico. In those days a mere dozen cacao beans could command a present value of upward of $100 in goods or services. Counterfeiting was rife—entrepreneurs tried to create *chocolatl* from anything, including avocado seeds. Moreover, *chocolatl* was thought to be so potent an aphrodisiac and hallucinogen that its use was denied, under penalty of death, to commoners.

Although intrigued, Europeans were put off by the bitter taste of *chocolatl*. Around 1600, a whole shipload of chocolate beans was jettisoned at sea by English privateers who, having captured a Spanish galleon, mistook its cargo for goat dung.

The French soon made *chocolatl* easier to stomach by powdering it; the British added milk; and finally, the Swiss, of Nestlé fame, cashed in with chocolate candy. The world hasn't been the same since.

Though *chocolatl* found its way to Europe, it never left Mexico, where hot chocolate, whipped frothy with a wooden-ringed *molinillo* (little mill), is more common now than in Aztec times. In Mexico chocolate is more than mere dessert: Used to spice the tangy moles of southern Mexico, it's virtually a national food.

while communal teams haul in big netfuls of silvery, wriggling fry for sale right on the beach.

Puerto Vallarta seafood prices reflect high worldwide demand, even at the humblest seaside *palapa*. The freshness and variety, however, make the typical dishes bargains at any price. Buying fresh and cooking it yourself can save you quite a bit. If you are cooking in your condo, for example, you can expect to pay, at the time of this writing, approximately $10 for a kilo (2.2 lbs) of shrimp.

## BREAD AND PASTRIES

Excellent locally baked bread is a delightful surprise to many first-time Puerto Vallarta visitors. Small bakeries everywhere put out trays of hot, crisp-crusted *bolillos* (rolls) and sweet *panes dulces* (pastries). The pastries vary from simple cakes, muffins, cookies, and doughnuts to fancy fruit-filled turnovers and puffs. Half the fun occurs before the eating: perusing the goodies, tongs in hand, and picking out the most scrumptious. With your favorite dozen or two finally selected, you take your tray to the cashier, who deftly bags everything up and collects a few pesos ($2-3) for your entire mouthwatering selection.

## FRUITS AND JUICES

Squeezed vegetable and fruit juices, *jugos* (HOO-gohs), are among the widely available thousand delights of Puerto Vallarta. Among the many establishments—restaurants, cafés, and *loncherías*—willing to supply you with your favorite *jugo*, the *jugerías* (juice bars) are the most fun. Colorful fruit piles mark *jugerías*. If you don't immediately spot your favorite fruit, ask; it might be hidden in the refrigerator.

Besides your choice of pure juice, *jugerías* will often serve *licuados*. Into the juice, they whip powdered milk, your favorite flavoring, and sugar to taste for a creamy afternoon pick-me-up or evening dessert. One big favorite is a cool banana-chocolate *licuado*, which comes out tasting like a milk shake (minus the calories).

## ALCOHOLIC DRINKS

The Aztecs sacrificed anyone caught drinking alcohol without permission. The later, more lenient, Spanish attitude toward getting *borracho* (soused) has led to a thriving Mexican renaissance of native alcoholic beverages: tequila, mezcal, Kahlúa, pulque, and *aguardiente*. Tequila and mezcal, distilled

© JUSTIN HENDERSON

Vallarta hilltop dining can require its own mode of transportation.

from the fermented juice of the maguey, originated in Oaxaca, where the best are still made. Quality tequila (named after the Guadalajara-area distillery town) and mezcal come 76 proof (38 percent alcohol) and up. A small white worm, endemic to the maguey, is customarily added to each bottle of factory mezcal for authenticity.

Pulque, although also made from the sap of the maguey, is locally brewed to a lower alcohol content between that of beer and wine. The brewing houses are sacrosanct preserves, circumscribed by traditions that exclude women and outsiders. The brew, said to be full of nutrients, is sold to local *pulquerías* and drunk immediately. If you are ever invited into a *pulquería,* it is an honor you cannot refuse.

*Aguardiente,* by contrast, is the notorious fiery Mexican "white lightning," a locally distilled dirt-cheap ticket to oblivion for poor Mexican men.

While pulque comes from age-old Indian tradition, beer is the beverage of modern mestizo Mexico. Full-bodied and tastier than "light" U.S. counterparts, Mexican beer enjoys an enviable reputation.

Those visitors who indulge usually know their favorite among the many brands, from light to dark: Superior, Corona, Pacífico, Tecate (served with lime), Carta Blanca, Modelo, Dos Equis, Bohemia, Tres Equis, and Negro Modelo. Nochebuena, a hearty dark brew, becomes available only around Christmas.

Mexicans have yet to develop much of a taste for *vino tinto* or *vino blanco* (red or white table wine), although some domestic wines (such as the Baja California labels Cetto and Domecq, and the boutique Monte Xanic) are at least good, and sometimes excellent. There is also a decent sparkling wine, similar to champagne, called **Chambrule,** which you can purchase at any liquor store or supermarket for about $7. Most of the major supermarkets now stock imported wines from Chile, Spain, Argentina, California, and France. The selections aren't amazing, but they are substantial.

## RESTAURANTS, LONCHERÍAS, AND FONDAS

In Mexico, a *restaurante* (rays-tah-oo-RAHN-tay) generally implies a fairly fancy joint, with prices to match. The food and atmosphere, however, may be more to your liking at other types of eateries (in approximate descending order of formality and price): *comedor* (dining room), *cafetería* (coffee shop), *cenaduría* (light supper only, from about 6pm), *fonda* (permanent food stall), *lonchería* (breakfast and sandwich counter), *jugería* (juice and sandwich bar), and *taquería* (often, but not always, a street stand).

# Conduct and Customs

Mexico is an old-fashioned country where people value traditional ideals of honesty, fidelity, and piety. Crime rates are low; visitors are often safer in Mexico than in their home cities.

Even though four generations have elapsed since Pancho Villa raided the U.S. border, the image of a Mexico bristling with *bandidos* persists. And similarly for Mexicans' view of those north of the border: Despite the century and a half since the *yanquis* invaded Mexico City and took half their country, the communal Mexican psyche still views gringos (and, by association, all white foreigners) with revulsion, jealousy, and wonder.

Fortunately, the Mexican love-hate affair with foreigners does not usually apply to individual visitors. Your friendly "*buenos días*" ("good morning") or "*por favor*" ("please"), when appropriate, is always appreciated, whether in the market, the gas station, or the hotel. The shy smile you will most likely receive in return will be your small, but not insignificant, reward.

### TIPPING

Without their droves of visitors, Mexican people would be even poorer. Deflation of the peso, while it makes prices low for outsiders, makes it rough for Mexican families to get by. The help at your hotel typically get paid only a few dollars a day. They depend on tips to make the difference between dire and bearable poverty. Give the *camarista* (chambermaid) and floor attendant 20 pesos every day or two. And whenever uncertain of what to tip, it will probably mean a lot to someone—maybe a whole family—if you err on the generous side.

In restaurants and bars, Mexican tipping customs are similar to those in the United States: Tip waiters, waitresses, and bartenders about 15 percent for satisfactory service.

Unlike the United States, it is not customary to tip the taxi drivers unless they go above and beyond, such as wrangling heaps of luggage or giving you a tour. However, the baggers at the supermarket, mostly school-age children and the elderly, work only for tips, so every peso counts. Tip them with your change or about five pesos per trip to the store. Gas station attendants similarly get tips. Gas stations are full-service and usually include at least a windshield wash. Attendants will check your oil and tire pressure, and perform other tasks upon request. Tip them a few pesos for the trouble.

### SAFE CONDUCT

Your own behavior, despite low crime statistics, largely determines your safety in Mexico. For women traveling solo, it is important to realize that the double standard is alive and well in Mexico. Dress and behave modestly, and you will most likely avoid embarrassment. Whenever possible, stay in the company of friends or acquaintances; find companions for beach, sightseeing, and shopping excursions. Ignore strange men's solicitations and overtures. A Mexican man on the prowl will invent the sappiest romantic overtures to snare a gringa. He will often interpret anything but a firm "no" as a "maybe," and a "maybe" as a "yes."

For male visitors, alcohol often leads to trouble. Avoid bars and cantinas; if, given Mexico's

# MACHISMO

An issue that seems to affect many Mexican men, machismo is a sometimes-reckless obsession to prove one's masculinity, to show how macho you are. Men of many nationalities share the instinct to prove themselves (Japan's Bushido samurai code is one example).

When confronted by a Mexican braggart, male visitors should remain careful and controlled. If your opponent is yelling, stay cool, speak softly, and withdraw as soon as possible. On the highway, be courteous and unprovoking—don't use your car to spar with a macho driver. Drinking often leads to problems. It's best to stay out of bars or cantinas unless you're prepared to deal with the macho consequences. Polite refusal of a drink may be taken as a challenge. If you visit a bar with Mexican friends or acquaintances, you may be heading for a no-win choice between a drunken all-night *borrachera* (binge) or an insult to the honor of your friends by refusing.

For women, machismo requires even more cautious behavior. In Mexico, women's liberation is long in coming. Few women hold positions of power in business or politics. One woman, Rosa Luz Alegría, did attain the rank of minister of tourism during the former Portillo administration; she was the president's mistress.

Female visitors can follow the example of their Mexican sisters by making a habit of going out in the company of friends or acquaintances, especially at night. Many Mexican men believe an unaccompanied woman wants to be picked up. Ignore their offers; any response, even refusal, might be taken as an encouraging sign. If, on the other hand, there is a Mexican man whom you'd genuinely like to meet, the traditional way is an arranged introduction through family or friends.

Mexican families, as a source of protection and friendship, should not be overlooked—especially on the beach or in the park, where, among the gaggle of kids, grandparents, aunts, and cousins, there's room for one more.

excellent beers, you can't abstain completely, at least maintain soft-spoken self-control in the face of challenges from macho drunks.

The sense of security one feels while downtown in Vallarta can lead to a false sense of imperviousness. Avoid flashing large amounts of cash and expensive watches or cameras. Do not, unless you wish to see the inside of an authentic Mexican prison, attempt to buy drugs. Unfortunate "accidents" have happened when hard-partying tourists have invited strangers back to their hotel rooms for sex or drugs. Just use common sense and be aware of your surroundings.

Of particular note to women, be very aware, especially in situations like booze cruises, of consuming anything you didn't actually see prepared. Like in the United States, roofies and other date-rape drugs have been slipped to unsuspecting tourists (often single women). Keep your drink with you at all times, even when you visit the restroom, and do not accept drinks from strangers.

## SOCIALLY RESPONSIBLE TRAVEL AND ECOTOURISM

Latter-day jet travel has brought droves of vacationing tourists to developing countries largely unprepared for the consequences. As the visitors' numbers swell, power grids black out, sewers overflow, and roads crack under the strain of accommodating more and larger hotels, restaurants, cars, buses, and airports.

Worse yet, armies of vacationers drive up local prices and begin to change native customs. While visions of tourists as sources of fast money replace traditions of hospitality, television wipes out folk entertainment, Coke and Pepsi substitute for fruit drinks, and prostitution and drugs flourish.

Some travelers have said enough is enough and are forming organizations to encourage visitors to travel with increased sensitivity to native people and customs. They have developed travelers' codes of ethics and guidelines that encourage visitors to stay at local-style accommodations, use local transportation, and seek alternative vacations and tours, such as language-study and cultural programs and people-to-people work projects.

A number of especially active socially responsible travel groups sponsor tours all over the world, including some in the Puerto Vallarta region. These include organizations such as **Green Tortoise** (www.greentortoise. com) and **Green Globe** (www.greenglobe. org), both of which run tours that visit the Puerto Vallarta region. For more alternatives, visit the umbrella website www.sociallyresponsible.org.

# Tips for Travelers

## BRINGING THE KIDS

Children are treasured like gifts from heaven in Mexico. Traveling with kids will ensure your welcome most everywhere. On the beach, take extra precautions to make sure they are protected from the sun.

A sick child is no fun for anyone. Fortunately, clinics and good doctors are available even in small towns. When in need, ask a storekeeper or a pharmacist, "*¿Dónde hay un doctor, por favor?*" (¿DOHN-day eye oon doc-TOHR por fah-VOHR?) In most cases, within five minutes you will be in the waiting room of the local physician or hospital.

Children who do not prefer typical Mexican fare can easily be fed with always-available eggs, cheese, *hamburguesas,* milk, oatmeal, corn flakes, bananas, cakes, and cookies.

Your children will generally have more fun if they have a little previous knowledge of Mexico and a stake in the trip. For example, help them select some library picture books and magazines so they'll know where they're going and what to expect, or give them responsibility for packing and carrying their own small travel bag.

Be sure to mention your children's ages when making air reservations; child discounts of 50 percent or more are often available. Also, if you can arrange to go on an uncrowded flight, you can stretch out and rest on the empty seats.

For more details on traveling with children, check out *Adventuring with Children* by Nan Jeffrey.

## TRAVEL FOR PEOPLE WITH DISABILITIES

Mexican airlines and hotels are becoming increasingly aware of the needs of travelers with disabilities. Open, street-level lobbies and large, wheelchair-accessible elevators and rooms are available in most Puerto Vallarta resort hotels. Most street-corner curbs accommodate wheelchairs.

U.S. law forbids travel discrimination against otherwise qualified people with disabilities. As long as your disability is stable and not liable to deteriorate during passage, you can expect to be treated like any passenger with special needs.

Make reservations far ahead of departure and ask your agent to inform your airline of your needs, such as boarding wheelchair or in-flight oxygen. Be early at the gate to take advantage of the preboarding call.

For many helpful details to smooth your trip, get a copy of *Survival Strategies for Going Abroad* by Laura Hershey, published in 2005 by **Mobility International USA** (132 E. Broadway, Suite 343, Eugene, OR 97401, tel. 541/343-1284 voice/TDD, fax 541/343-6812, www. miusa.org). Mobility International is a valuable resource for many disabled lovers of Mexico, for it encourages disabled travelers with a gold mine of information and literature, and can provide them with valuable Mexico connections. They publish a regular newsletter and offer information and referrals for international exchanges and homestays.

Similarly, **Partners of the Americas** (1424

K St. NW, Suite 700, Washington, DC 20005, tel. 202/628-3300, toll-free U.S. tel. 800/322-7844, fax 202/628-3306, www.partners.net), with chapters in 45 U.S. states, works to improve understanding of disabilities and facilities in Mexico and Latin America. It maintains communications with local organizations and individuals whom disabled travelers may contact at their destinations.

Be aware that most of the streets in Puerto Vallarta are cobblestone, often with high sidewalks accessible only by stairs. Tourist attractions, restaurants, and shops may not be wheelchair accessible, so be sure to call in advance.

## GAY AND LESBIAN TRAVELERS

Puerto Vallarta has a particular draw for national and international gay and lesbian travelers for a number of reasons, among them the strong support system within the local community that goes beyond nightlife and beaches. Certainly Puerto Vallarta doesn't match Mexico City in terms of organization within the gay community, as it tends to attract more vacationers than residents, and there is no gay and lesbian center per se. Nevertheless, a strong gay community has existed here as early as the 1970s, but in the last decade, numerous gay-owned businesses have opened and, more importantly, are unabashed about their gay friendliness. For more information, take a look at www.gayguidevallarta.com for tips on activities, venues, and more. In addition, most of the websites of the gay-friendly real estate agents include interesting facts and figures. Pick up the gay-friendly bimonthly, bilingual *Bay Vallarta* as an additional option for events for foreigners as well as nationals, and other culture, art, music, and sports activities.

Locals have always adopted the "live and let live" attitude about Vallarta's nightlife, and they tend to be respectful as long as restraint is practiced in public. It's important, however, not to lose sight of the fact that there are locals who may not be open to shows of public affection between same-sex couples. Also be aware

that during this time of rapid growth in Puerto Vallarta, many people you might assume are locals are not locals at all, but come from other areas in Mexico, some of which are not as liberal or as used to turning a blind eye.

Beyond the town of Puerto Vallarta, you can expect to find open and friendly people throughout the Bay of Banderas. In some of the smaller towns, however, it's not that they won't be as friendly, but their curiosity at seeing foreign-appearing visitors may get the better of them. Their actions are not necessarily aggressive—just curious. As always, speaking Spanish will be helpful.

As laws in Mexico are in the process of change (several states have voted to accept same-sex relationships and allow legal rights and benefits), those very changes may occasionally spark reactions. Resort towns are usually more open in that the population tends to be more aware not only of differences but of the economic importance of tourism. Be aware that nudity is not officially allowed on beaches in Mexico.

With regard to safety, most visitors should avoid areas that are unlit at night, whether in the Zona Romántica or elsewhere. Be aware that young men sometimes try to attract the interested foreigner with the intention of mugging or worse. If you've had too much to drink, don't open yourself to trouble. Tell your friends where you're going or who you're planning to go with. And if you've met someone special during your vacation, be sure to protect yourself by wearing a condom as well as maintaining your common sense at all times—even after that third (who's counting!) margarita.

## SENIOR TRAVELERS

Age, according to Mark Twain, is a question of mind over matter: If you don't mind, it doesn't matter. Mexico is a country where whole extended families, from babies to great-grandparents, live together. Elderly travelers will benefit from the respect and understanding Mexicans accord to older people. Besides these encouragements, consider the number of retirees already in havens in Puerto Vallarta; the Nayarit coastal towns of Bucerías, Sayulita, and San Francisco; and nearby centers of Guadalajara and Lake Chapala.

Certain organizations support senior travel. Leading the field is **Elderhostel** (11 Ave. de Lafayette, Boston, MA 02111-1746, toll-free U.S. tel. 877/426-8056, www.elderhostel. org). Elderhostel invites folks over 50 to join their extensive U.S. and international program of special tours, study, homestays, and people-to-people travel itineraries. Contact them for their free catalogs.

A number of newsletters publicize senior vacation and retirement opportunities. Among the best is the **Mexico File** monthly newsletter, which, besides featuring pithy stories by Mexico travelers and news updates, offers an opportunity-packed classified section of Mexico rentals, publications, services, and much more. Subscribe ($39/year) through Simmonds Publications (5580 La Jolla Blvd. #306, La Jolla, CA 92037, tel./fax 858/456-4419, toll-free U.S. tel. 800/563-9345 [voice mail], www.mexicofile.com).

Some books publicize senior travel opportunities. One of the pithiest is *Unbelievably Good Deals and Great Adventures You Can't Have Unless You're Over 50,* by Joan Rattner Heilman, published by McGraw Hill (2003). Its 200 pages are packed with details of how to get bargains on cruises, tours, car rentals, lodgings, and much, much more.

For seniors with online access (as close as your neighborhood library these days), the **Internet** is a treasure trove of senior-oriented travel information. For example, the **Transitions Abroad** site, www.transitionsabroad.com, offers a gold mine of a subsite (www.transitionsabroad.com/listings/travel/senior), with a load of useful resources centering around senior traveling and living abroad.

# Health and Safety

## STAYING HEALTHY

In Puerto Vallarta, just as everywhere, prevention is the best remedy for illness. For those visitors who confine their travel to the beaten path, a few basic common-sense precautions will ensure vacation enjoyment.

Resist the temptation to dive headlong into Mexico. It's no wonder that people get sick—broiling in the sun, gobbling peppery food, guzzling beer and margaritas, then discoing half the night—all in their first 24 hours. An alternative is to give your body time to adjust. Travelers often arrive tired and dehydrated from travel and heat. During the first few days, drink plenty of bottled water and juice, and take siestas.

### Immunizations and Precautions

A good physician can recommend the proper preventatives for your Puerto Vallarta trip. If you are going to stay pretty much in town, your doctor will probably suggest little more than updating your basic typhoid, diphtheria-tetanus, hepatitis, and polio shots.

For camping or trekking in remote tropical areas—below 4,000 feet or 1,200 meters—doctors often recommend a gamma-globulin shot against hepatitis A and a schedule of chloroquine pills against malaria. While in backcountry areas, use other measures to discourage mosquitoes—and fleas, flies, ticks, no-see-ums, "kissing bugs," and other tropical pesties—from biting you. Common precautions include sleeping under mosquito netting, burning *espirales mosquito* (mosquito coils), and rubbing on plenty of pure DEET (n,n-diethyl-meta-toluamide) "jungle juice," mixed in equal parts with rubbing (70 percent isopropyl) alcohol. Although supereffective, 100 percent DEET dries and irritates the skin.

### Sunburn

For sunburn protection, use a good sunscreen with a sun protection factor (SPF) rated 15 or more, which will reduce burning rays to one-fifteenth or less of direct sunlight. Better still, take a shady siesta-break from the sun during the most hazardous midday hours. If you do get burned, applying your sunburn lotion (or one of the "caine" creams) after the fact usually decreases the pain and speeds healing. The UV index in Mexico is much higher than in northern countries, so even if you aren't used to using high SPF sunscreen and keeping track of your sun time, it is very wise to do so here.

## Safe Water and Food

Although municipalities have made great strides in sanitation, food and water are still potential sources of germs in some parts of the Puerto Vallarta region. Although the water is probably safe most everywhere, except in a few upcountry localities, it's still probably best to drink bottled water only. Hotels, whose success depends vitally on their customers' health, generally provide *agua purificada* (purified bottled water). If, for any reason, the available water is of doubtful quality, add a water purifier, such as Potable Aqua brand (get it at a camping goods stores before departure), or a few drops per quart of water of *blanqueador* (household chlorine bleach) or *yodo* (tincture of iodine) from the pharmacy.

Pure bottled water, soft drinks, beer, and fresh fruit juices are so widely available that it is easy to avoid tap water, especially in restaurants. Ice and *paletas* (iced juice-on-a-stick) may be risky, especially in small towns.

Washing hands before eating in a restaurant is a time-honored Mexican ritual that visitors should religiously follow. The humblest Mexican eatery will generally provide a basin to *lavar las manos* (wash the hands). If it doesn't, don't eat there.

Hot, cooked food is generally safe, as are peeled fruits and vegetables. These days milk and cheese in Mexico are generally processed under sanitary conditions and sold pasteurized (ask, "*¿Pasteurizado?*") and are typically safe. Mexican ice cream used to be both bad tasting and of dubious safety, but national brands available in supermarkets are so much

improved that it's no longer necessary to resist ice cream while in town.

In recent years, much cleaner public water and increased hygiene awareness have made salads—once shunned by Mexico travelers—generally safe to eat in tourist-frequented Puerto Vallarta cafés and restaurants. Nevertheless, lettuce and cabbage, particularly in country villages, are more likely to be contaminated than tomatoes, carrots, cucumbers, onions, and green peppers. In any case, you can try dousing your salad in vinegar (*vinagre*) or plenty of sliced lime (*limón*) juice, the acidity of which kills some but not all bacteria.

## First-Aid Kit

In the tropics, ordinary cuts and insect bites are more prone to infection and should receive immediate first aid. A first-aid kit with aspirin, rubbing alcohol, hydrogen peroxide, water-purifying tablets, household chlorine bleach or iodine for water purifying, swabs, bandages, gauze, adhesive tape, Ace bandage, chamomile (*manzanilla*) tea bags for upset stomachs, Pepto-Bismol, acidophilus tablets, antibiotic ointment, hydrocortisone cream, mosquito repellent, knife, and good tweezers is a good precaution for any traveler and mandatory for campers.

## HEALTH PROBLEMS
### Traveler's Diarrhea

Traveler's diarrhea (known in Southeast Asia as "Bali Belly" and in Mexico as turista or "Montezuma's Revenge") sometimes persists, even among prudent vacationers. You can suffer turista for a week after simply traveling from California to Philadelphia or New York. Doctors say the familiar symptoms of runny bowels, nausea, and sour stomach result from normal local bacterial strains to which newcomers' systems need time to adjust. Unfortunately, the dehydration and fatigue from heat and travel reduce your body's natural defenses and sometimes lead to a persistent cycle of sickness at a time when you least want it.

Time-tested protective measures can help

your body either prevent or break this cycle. Many doctors and veteran travelers swear by Pepto-Bismol for soothing sore stomachs and stopping diarrhea. Acidophilus, the bacteria found in yogurt, is widely available in the United States in tablets and aids digestion. Warm *manzanilla* (chamomile) tea, used widely in Mexico (and by Peter Rabbit's mother), provides liquid and calms upset stomachs. Temporarily avoid coffee and alcohol, drink plenty of *manzanilla* tea, and eat bananas and rice for a few meals until your tummy can take regular food.

Although powerful antibiotics and antidiarrhea medications such as Lomotil and Imodium are readily available over *farmacia* counters, they may involve serious side effects and should not be taken in the absence of medical advice. If in doubt, consult a doctor.

## Chagas' Disease and Dengue Fever

Chagas' disease, spread by the "kissing" (or, more appropriately, "assassin") bug, is a potential hazard in the Mexican tropics. Known locally as a *vinchuca,* the triangular-headed, three-quarter-inch (two-cm) brown insect, identifiable by its yellow-striped abdomen, often drops upon its sleeping victims from the thatched ceiling of a rural house at night. Its bite is followed by swelling, fever, and weakness, and can lead to heart failure if left untreated. Application of drugs at an early stage can, however, clear the patient of the trypanosome parasites that infect the bloodstream and vital organs. See a doctor immediately if you believe you're infected.

Most of the precautions against malaria-bearing mosquitoes also apply to dengue fever, which does occur (although uncommonly) in outlying tropical areas of Mexico. The culprit here is a virus carried by the mosquito species *Aedes aegypti.* Symptoms are acute fever, with chills, sweating, and muscle aches—hence the nickname bonebreak fever. A red, diffuse rash frequently results, which may later peel. Symptoms abate after about five days, but fatigue may persist. A particularly serious, but

fortunately rare, form, called dengue hemorrhagic fever, can be fatal. This usually occurs when a person gets the disease a second time. Although no vaccines or preventatives, other than deterring mosquitoes, exist, you should nevertheless see a doctor immediately for IV hydration.

For more good tropical preventative information, get a copy of the excellent pamphlet distributed by the **International Association for Medical Advice to Travelers** (IAMAT, 1623 Military Rd. #279, Niagara Falls, NY 14304-1745, tel. 716/754-4883; in Canada at 40 Regal Rd., Guelph, ON N1K 1B5, tel. 519/836-0102, or 1287 St. Clair Ave. W., Toronto, ON M6E 1B8, tel. 416/652-0137; www.iamat.org), *How to Protect Yourself Against Malaria,* which includes worldwide malaria risk and communicable disease charts.

## Scorpions and Snakes

While camping or staying in a *palapa* or other rustic accommodation, watch for scorpions, especially in your shoes, which you should shake out every morning. Scorpion stings and snakebites are rarely fatal to an adult, unless you happen to be allergic to the venom. Watch for shortness of breath and rapid heartbeat, and get to a doctor immediately. Even without an allergy, scorpion stings can be very serious for a child or a pet. Get the victim to a doctor (or vet, depending on the patient) calmly but quickly.

## Sea Creatures

While snorkeling or surfing, you may suffer a coral scratch or jellyfish sting. Experts advise you to wash the afflicted area with ocean water and pour alcohol (rubbing alcohol or tequila) over the wound, then apply hydrocortisone cream (available from the *farmacia*).

Injuries from sea urchin spines and stingray barbs are painful and can be serious. Physicians recommend similar first aid for both: Remove the spines or barbs by hand or with tweezers, then soak the injury in as-hot-as-possible fresh water to weaken the toxins and provide relief. Another method is to rinse the area with an antibacterial solution—rubbing alcohol, vinegar, wine, or ammonia diluted with water. If none are available, the same effect may be achieved with urine, either your own or someone else's in your party. Get medical help immediately.

## Tattoos

All health hazards don't come from the wild. A number of Mexico travelers have complained of complications from black henna tattoos. When enhanced by the chemical dye PPD, the henna can result in an itchy rash that can lead to scarring. It's best to play it safe: If you must have a vacation tattoo, get it at an established, professional shop.

## MEDICAL CARE

For medical advice and treatment, let your hotel (or if you're camping, the closest *farmacia*) refer you to a good doctor, clinic, or hospital. Mexican doctors, especially in small- and medium-size towns, practice like private doctors in the United States and Canada once did before health insurance, liability, and group practice. They will come to you if you request it, and they often keep their doors open even after regular hours. Fees are usually reasonable.

You will receive generally good treatment at the many local hospitals in the Puerto Vallarta region. If you must have an English-speaking, American-trained doctor, the **International Association for Medical Advice to Travelers** (IAMAT, 1623 Military Rd. #279, Niagara Falls, NY 14304-1745, tel. 716/754-4883; in Canada at 40 Regal Rd., Guelph, ON N1K 1B5, tel. 519/836-0102, or 1287 St. Clair Ave. W., Toronto, ON M6E 1B8, tel. 416/652-0137; www.iamat.org) publishes an updated booklet of qualified member physicians, some of whom practice in Puerto Vallarta. IAMAT also distributes a very detailed *How to Protect Yourself Against Malaria* guide, with worldwide malaria risk and communicable disease charts.

For more useful information on health and safety in Mexico, consult Dr. Robert H. Page and Dr. Curtis P. Page's *Mexico: Health and Safety Travel Guide* (Med to Go Books, 2004), or Dirk Schroeder's *Staying Healthy*

*in Asia, Africa, and Latin America* (Avalon Travel Publishing, 2000). With the skyrocketing cost of almost everything medical in the United States, Puerto Vallarta has become a major destination for medical tourism. There are a number of major surgeries as well as cosmetic surgeries and dental operations that can be performed for a fraction of the cost in the United States. As a result of this demand, there are many highly trained English-speaking specialist doctors in Puerto Vallarta, and you will have no trouble finding one there. However, in smaller outlying towns they may be more difficult to come by.

There are hyperbaric chambers available in Puerto Vallarta for decompression sickness should you suffer from a dive accident. Ask a local dive shop for the emergency information if you plan on diving without a local guide or tour group (not recommended).

## THE LAW AND POLICE

While Mexican authorities are tolerant of alcohol, they are decidedly intolerant of other substances such as marijuana, psychedelics, cocaine, and heroin. Getting caught with such drugs in Mexico usually leads to swift and severe results. However, possession of personal-use quantities of marijuana—up to 5 grams—was legalized in Mexico in 2009.

Nude sunbathing is both illegal in public and offensive to Mexicans. Confine your nudism to very private locations. Even in towns like Sayulita, where the bikinis can get microscopically small, you will not see nudity or even toplessness. It is immodest and illegal.

Although it has been happening with decreasing frequency, traffic police in Puerto Vallarta sometimes seem to watch foreign cars with eagle eyes. Officers seem to inhabit busy intersections and one-way streets, waiting for confused tourists to make a wrong move. If they whistle you over, stop immediately, or you will really get into hot water. If guilty, say *"Lo siento"* ("I'm sorry") and be cooperative. Although the officer probably won't mention

# IS IT SAFE?

Mexico has received a tremendous amount of negative coverage in the U.S. news. The majority of this has focused on the violent and public war among the narcotics traffickers and also with the military and police. Many people, especially those who have never been to Mexico or do not visit regularly, wonder if it is still safe to travel there.

I live in Sayulita, a town utterly dependent on tourism, so perhaps this heightens one's willingness to ignore the things that are wrong. In this case, however, when I say this is a safe town in a safe region, I am not being misleading. Nayarit and Jalisco, aside from some troubles in Tepic, are very safe areas.

That said, there are a couple of things to be aware of in this part of Mexico. One is ATM fraud, a rampant problem as of this writing, and the other is nonviolent but pervasive burglary, of rental houses and apartments and hotel rooms in Sayulita, and elsewhere in the region as well. So if you come, some vigilance is necessary. If you rent a place, use the safe, keep the doors locked, and don't leave things out in the open. When you use an ATM, don't let anyone approach you for any reason.

The majority of the violent crimes in Mexico take place along the Mexico-America border, and although there have been tragic instances of innocents being caught in the crossfire, the majority of casualties remain drug dealers and those trying to catch them or kill them. Puerto Vallarta and many other areas have a strong vested interest in maintaining a safe and hospitable atmosphere as the entire livelihood of the people and city itself lies within the tourism industry. While the increased military presence may frighten some people, the armed police are actually there to lend an air of security, not intimidation—unless that intimidation is of would-be rabble-rousers.

As many residents and frequent visitors will attest, there is still a very low crime rate in Puerto Vallarta, especially when compared with a U.S. city of comparable size and socioeconomic background. The majority of crimes are nuisance crimes: vandalism, pickpocketing, and simple burglary (usually of unattended belongings that can present an irresistible temptation to some).

By far, the biggest dangers to out-of-town visitors remain sunburn, overimbibing, jellyfish stings, and other typical vacation woes. But do lock your stuff up, and use ATMs with care.

it, he or she is usually hoping that you'll cough up a $20 *mordida* (bribe) for the privilege of driving away.

Don't do it. Although he may hint at confiscating your car, calmly ask for an official *boleto* (written traffic ticket, if you're guilty) in exchange for your driver's license (make sure you have a copy), which the officer will probably keep if he writes a ticket. If after a few minutes no money appears, the officer will most likely give you back your driver's license rather than go to the trouble of writing the ticket. If not, the worst that will usually happen is you will have to go to the *presidencia municipal* (city hall) the next morning and pay the $10 to a clerk in exchange for your driver's license.

# PEDESTRIAN AND DRIVING HAZARDS

Although Puerto Vallarta's cobbled pavements and "holey" sidewalks won't land you in jail, one of them might send you to the hospital if you don't watch your step, especially at night. "Pedestrian beware" is especially good advice on Mexican streets, where it is rumored that some drivers speed up rather than slow down when they spot a tourist stepping off the curb. Falling coconuts, especially frequent on windy days, constitute an additional hazard to unwary campers and beachgoers.

Driving Mexican country roads, where slow trucks and carts block lanes, campesinos stroll the shoulders, and horses, burros, and cattle wander at will, is hazardous—doubly so at night. Closed roads, dangerous shoulders, and washed-out bridges may or may not have a sign warning motorists, so it's best to drive in unfamiliar areas only during the daytime and keep your eyes peeled for hazards.

# Information and Services

## MONEY
### The Peso: Down and Up
Overnight in early 1993, the Mexican government shifted its monetary decimal point three places and created the "new" peso, which was trading at around 13 pesos to the U.S. dollar as of this writing and has ranged between 10 and 14 to the dollar for the past five years. Since the peso value sometimes changes rapidly, U.S. dollars have become a much more stable indicator of Mexican prices; for this reason they are used in this guide to report prices. You should, nevertheless, always use pesos to pay for everything in Mexico.

Since the introduction of the new peso, the centavo (one-hundredth of a new peso) has

The streets of Puerto Vallarta's Old Town are full of lively restaurants, bars, and stores.

reappeared, in coins of 5, 10, 20, and 50 centavos. Incidentally, the dollar sign, "$," also marks Mexican pesos. Peso coins (*monedas*) in denominations of 1, 2, 5, 10, and 20 pesos, and bills in denominations of 20, 50, 100, 200, and 500 pesos, are common. When you are exchanging money, ask for some small bills. A 500-peso note, while common at the bank, may look awfully big to a small shopkeeper, who might be hard-pressed to change it.

### Banks, ATMs, and Money-Exchange Offices
Mexican banks, like their North American counterparts, have lengthened their business hours. Your best choice is usually a branch of the Hong Kong-Shanghai Banking Corporation (HSBC) bank, which maintains very long hours: often 8am-7pm Monday-Saturday. Banamex (Banco Nacional de Mexico), generally the most popular with local people, usually posts the best in-town dollar exchange rate in its lobbies; for example: *Tipo de cambio: venta 10.615, compra 10.820,* which means the bank will sell pesos to you at the rate of 10.615 per dollar and buy them back for 10.820 per dollar.

ATMs (automated teller machines, *cajeros automáticos,* kah-HAY-rohs ahoo-toh-MAH-tee-kohs) are rapidly becoming the money source of choice in Mexico. Virtually every bank has a 24-hour ATM, accessible (with proper PIN identification code) by a swarm of U.S. and Canadian credit and ATM cards. Note: Some Mexican bank ATMs may "eat" your ATM card if you don't retrieve it within about 15 seconds of completing your transaction. Retrieve your card *immediately* after getting your cash. There has also been a rash of stolen PINs all over Mexico in recent years. Do not let anyone "help" you with an ATM, and look around when using one to make sure there are no hidden cameras or anything else suspicious in the booth with you. Many people recommend only using ATMs inside banks, so ubiquitous has the problem become.

Although one-time bank charges, typically about $3, for ATM cash remain small, the pesos you can usually get from a single card is limited to about $3,000 in some machines and $5,000 in others (about US$240 and US$400, respectively, as of this writing) or less per day. But since the ATM charge is generally a fixed fee regardless of the amount you withdraw, you will save money by withdrawing the maximum available in a single transaction.

Even without an ATM card, you don't have to go to the trouble of waiting in long bank service lines. Opt for a less-crowded bank, such as Bancomer, Banco Serfín, HSBC bank, or a private *casa de cambio* (money-exchange office). Such offices are often most convenient, offering long hours and faster service than the banks for a fee (as little as $0.50 or as much as $3 per $100).

## Keeping Your Money Safe

Travelers checks, formerly the traditional prescription for safe money abroad, are no longer in general use in Puerto Vallarta. The American Express office is long gone.

In Puerto Vallarta, as everywhere, thieves circulate among the tourists. Keep valuables in your hotel *caja de seguridad* (security box). If you don't particularly trust the desk clerk, carry what you cannot afford to lose in a money belt. Pickpockets love crowded markets, buses, and airport terminals, where they can slip a wallet out of a back pocket or dangling purse in a blink of an eye. Guard against this by carrying your wallet in your front pocket, and your purse, waist pouch, and daypack (which clever crooks can sometimes slit open) on your front side.

Don't attract thieves by displaying wads of money or flashy jewelry. Don't get sloppy drunk; if so, you may become a pushover for a determined thief.

Don't leave valuables unattended on the beach; share security duties with trustworthy-looking neighbors, or leave a secure bag with a shopkeeper nearby.

## Credit Cards

Credit cards, such as Visa, MasterCard, and to a lesser extent American Express and Discover, are generally honored in the hotels, restaurants, handicrafts shops, and boutiques that cater to foreign tourists. You will generally get better bargains, however, in shops that depend on local trade and do not so readily accept credit cards. Such shops sometimes offer discounts for cash sales or tack the credit card company charges onto the retail price.

Whatever the circumstance, your travel money will usually go much further in Puerto Vallarta than back home if you pay attention. If you stay strictly in high-end tourist zones, you'll pay American prices. However, if you get off that treadmill, even with the national 17 percent ("value added," or IVA) sales tax, local lodging, food, and transportation prices will often seem like bargains compared to what you're accustomed to at home. Outside of the pricey high-rise beachfront strips, pleasant, palmy hotel room rates often run $40 or less.

# COMMUNICATIONS
## Using Mexican Telephones

Along with increasingly reliable landline service in most of Mexico, almost everybody has a cell phone in the Vallarta area. However, service can be spotty on occasion, and if a number doesn't get through, you may have to redial it more than once. When someone answers (usually "*Bueno*"), be especially courteous. If your Spanish is rusty, say, "*¿Por favor, habla inglés?*" (¿POR fah-VOR, AH-blah een-GLAYS?) If you want to speak to a particular person (such as María), ask, "*¿María se encuentra?*" (¿mah-REE-ah SAY ayn-koo-AYN-trah?)

Since November 2001, when telephone numbers were standardized, Mexican phones operate pretty much the same as in the United States and Canada. In Puerto Vallarta, for example, a complete telephone number is generally written like this: 322/221-4709. As in the United States, the "322" denotes the telephone area code (*lada*, LAH-dah), and the 221-4709 is the number that you dial locally. If you want to dial this number long-distance (*larga distancia*), first dial "01" (like "1" in the United States), then 322/221-4709. All Mexican telephone numbers, with only three exceptions, begin with a three-digit *lada*, followed by a seven-digit local number. (The exceptions are Monterrey, Guadalajara, and Mexico City, which have two-digit *ladas* and eight-digit local numbers. The Mexico City *lada* is 55; Guadalajara's is 33, and Monterrey's is 81. (For example, a complete Guadalajara phone number would read 33/6897-2253.)

In Puerto Vallarta-region towns and cities, direct long-distance dialing is the rule—from hotels, public phone booths, and efficient private *larga distancia* telephone offices. The cheapest, often most convenient way to call is by buying and using a public-telephone Ladatel card. Buy them in 20-, 30-, 50-, and 100-peso denominations at the many outlets—minimarkets, pharmacies, liquor stores—that display the blue-and-yellow Ladatel sign. Area codes change as you move north from Vallarta, so make sure you are aware of the area code in whatever town you might be calling to or from. Also, when you are calling a Mexican cell phone from a Mexican landline, you need to dial 045 ahead of the area code. There are several tricks like this to using phones in Mexico—you'll have to learn the ones specific to your type of phone and location.

## Calling Mexico and Calling Home

To call Mexico direct from the United States, first dial 011 (for international access), then 52 (for Mexico), followed by the Mexican area code and local number.

For station-to-station calls to the United States from Mexico, dial 001 plus the area code and the local number. For calls to other countries, ask your hotel desk clerk or see the easy-to-follow directions in the local Mexican telephone directory.

Another convenient way (although a much more expensive one) to call home is via your personal telephone credit card. Contact your U.S. long-distance operator by dialing 001-800/462-4240 for AT&T, 001-800/674-7000 for Verizon, or 001-800/877-8000 for Sprint.

Yet another (although very expensive) way of calling home is collect. You can do this in one of two ways. Simply dial 09 for the local English-speaking international operator, or dial the aforementioned AT&T, Verizon, and Sprint numbers.

*Beware* of certain private "To Call Long Distance to the U.S.A. Collect and Credit Card" telephones installed prominently in airports, tourist hotels, and shops. Tariffs on these phones often run as high as $10 per minute (with a three-minute minimum), for a total of $30 whether you talk three minutes or not. Always ask the operator for the rate, and if it's too high, buy a $3 Ladatel card that will give you about six minutes to the United States or Canada.

In smaller towns, you must often do your long-distance phoning in the *larga distancia* (local phone office). Typically staffed by a young woman and often connected to a café, the *larga distancia* becomes an informal community social center as people pass the time waiting for their phone connections.

Obviously, Voice Over Internet Protocol (VOIP) calling through companies such as Vonage, and computer phoning via Skype, have changed the rules for international calling. If you are in a hotel with Wi-Fi, chances are you can Skype.

## Post, Telegraph, and Internet Access

Mexican **correos** (post offices) operate similarly, but more slowly and less securely, than their counterparts in other parts of the world. Mail services usually include *lista de correo* (general delivery; address letters "*a/c lista de correo*"), *servicios filatelicas* (philatelic services), *por avión* (airmail), *giros* (postal money orders), and Mexpost secure and fast delivery service, usually from separate Mexpost offices.

Mexican ordinary mail is sadly unreliable and pathetically slow. If, for mailings within Mexico, you must have security, use the efficient, reformed government Mexpost (like U.S. Express Mail) service. For international mailings, check the local Yellow Pages for widely available DHL courier service.

**Telégrafos** (telegraph offices), usually near the post office, send and receive *telegramas* (telegrams) and *giros*. Telecomunicaciones or Telecom, high-tech telegraph offices, add telephone and public fax to the available services.

**Internet** service, including personal email access, has arrived in the Puerto Vallarta region's towns. Internet cafés are a dime a dozen, especially in up-to-date Puerto Vallarta, Sayulita, Rincón de Guayabitos, Tepic, and Barra de Navidad. Online service rates run about $1-2 per hour or less. Most hotels are also online, and if you can't get online in your room, you probably can in the lobby or bar.

## WEIGHTS AND MEASURES

Mexican electric power is supplied at U.S.-standard 110 volts, 60 cycles. Plugs and sockets are generally two-pronged, nonpolar (like the pre-1970s U.S. ones). Bring adapters if you're going to use appliances with polar two-pronged or three-pronged plugs. (A two-pronged polar plug has different-size prongs, one of which is too large to plug into an old-fashioned nonpolar socket.)

The Puerto Vallarta region is split between **two time zones.** The time zone border, formerly at the Río Ameca just north of the Puerto Vallarta airport, was moved farther north in 2011 and is now located by the turnoff to Lo de Marcos at the northern border of the Bahía de Banderas municipality, which is more or less equivalent to a county line in the United States. So San Blas and Chacala are now one hour earlier than Sayulita, but Sayulita is the same as Puerto Vallarta.

Mexican businesses and government offices sometimes use the 24-hour system to tell time. Thus, a business that posts its hours as 0800-1700 is open 8am-5pm. When speaking, however, people customarily use the 12-hour system.

# RESOURCES

## Glossary

Many of the following words have a socio-historical meaning; others you will not find in the usual English-Spanish dictionary.

**abarrotería:** grocery store

**alcalde:** mayor or municipal judge

**alfarería:** pottery

**andando:** walkway or strolling path

**antojitos:** native Mexican snacks, such as tamales, chiles rellenos, tacos, and enchiladas

**artesanías:** handicrafts, as distinguished from artesano—a person who makes handicrafts

**audiencia:** one of the royal executive-judicial panels sent to rule Mexico during the 16th century

**ayuntamiento:** either the town council or the building where it meets

**bandidos:** bandits or outlaws

**bienes raices:** literally, good roots, but popularly, real estate

**birria:** goat, pork, or lamb stew, in spiced tomato broth, especially typical of Jalisco

**boleto:** ticket, boarding pass

**caballero:** literally, horseman, but popularly, gentleman

**cabercera:** head town of a municipal district, or headquarters in general

**cabrón:** literally a cuckold, but more commonly, bastard, rat, or SOB; sometimes used affectionately

**cacique:** chief or boss

**camionera:** bus station

**campesino:** country person; farm worker

**canasta:** basket of woven reeds, with handle

**casa de huéspedes:** guesthouse, usually operated in a family home

**caudillo:** dictator or political chief

**charro, charra:** gentleman cowboy or cowgirl

**chingar:** literally, to rape, but is also the universal Spanish f-word, the equivalent of screw in English

**churrigueresque:** Spanish baroque architectural style incorporated into many Mexican colonial churches, named after José Churriguera (1665-1725)

**científicos:** literally, scientists, but applied to President Porfirio Díaz's technocratic advisers

**cofradia:** Catholic fraternal service association, either male or female, mainly in charge of financing and organizing religious festivals

**colectivo:** a shared public taxi or minibus that picks up and deposits passengers along a designated route

**colegio:** preparatory school or junior college

**colonia:** suburban subdivision; satellite of a larger city

**Conasupo:** government store that sells basic foods at subsidized prices

**correo:** post office

**criollo:** person of all-Spanish descent born in the New World

**cuadra:** a rectangular work of art, usually a painting

**Cuaresma:** Lent

**curandero(a):** indigenous medicine man or woman

**damas:** ladies, as in ladies' room

**Domingo de Ramos:** Palm Sunday

**ejido:** a constitutional, government-sponsored form of community, with shared land ownership and cooperative decision making

**encomienda:** colonial award of tribute from a designated indigenous district

**estación ferrocarril:** railroad station

**farmacia:** pharmacy or drugstore

**finca:** farm

**fonda:** food stall or small restaurant, often in a traditional market complex

**fraccionamiento:** city sector or subdivision

**fuero:** the former right of clergy to be tried in separate ecclesiastical courts

**gachupín:** literally, one who wear spurs; a derogatory term for a Spanish-born colonial

**gasolinera:** gasoline station

**gente de razón:** literally, people of reason; whites and mestizos in colonial Mexico

**gringo:** once-derogatory but now commonly used term for North American whites

**grito:** impassioned cry, as in Hidalgo's Grito de Dolores

**hacienda:** large landed estate; also the government treasury

**hidalgo:** nobleman/woman; called honorifically by "Don" or "Doña"

**indígena:** indigenous or aboriginal inhabitant of all-native descent who speaks his or her native tongue; commonly, but incorrectly, an Indian (*indio*)

**jejenes:** no-see-um biting gnats, especially around San Blas, Nayarit

**judiciales:** the federal or state "judicial," or investigative police, best known to motorists for their highway checkpoint inspections

**jugería:** stall or small restaurant providing a large array of squeezed vegetable and fruit *jugos* (juices)

**juzgado:** the hoosegow or jail

**larga distancia:** long-distance telephone service, or the *caseta* (booth) where it's provided

**licencado:** academic degree (abbr. Lic.) approximately equivalent to a bachelor's degree

**lonchería:** small lunch counter, usually serving juices, sandwiches, and *antojitos* (Mexican snacks)

**machismo; macho:** exaggerated sense of maleness; person who holds such a sense of himself

**mestizo:** person of mixed European/indigenous descent

**milpa:** native farm plot, usually of corn, squash, and beans

**mordida:** slang for bribe; literally, little bite

**palapa:** thatched-roof structure, often open and shading a restaurant

**panga:** outboard launch (*lancha*)

**Pemex:** acronym for Petróleos Mexicanos, Mexico's national oil corporation

**peninsulares:** the Spanish-born ruling colonial elite

**peón:** a poor wage earner, usually a country native

**plan:** political manifesto, usually by a leader or group consolidating or seeking power

**Porfiriato:** the 34-year (1876-1910) ruling period of president-dictator Porfirio Díaz

**pozole:** stew of hominy in broth, usually topped by shredded pork, cabbage, and diced onion; called posole in English

**presidencia municipal:** the headquarters, like a U.S. city or county hall, of a Mexican *municipio,* countylike local governmental unit

**preventiva:** municipal police

**pronunciamiento:** declaration of rebellion by an insurgent leader

**pueblo:** town or people

**quinta:** a villa or country house

**quinto:** the royal "fifth" tax on treasure and precious metals

**retorno:** cul-de-sac

**rurales:** former federal country police force created to fight *bandidos*

**Semana Santa:** pre-Easter holy week

**Tapatío, Tapatía:** a label referring to anyone or anything from Guadalajara or Jalisco

**taxi especial:** private taxi, as distinguished from *taxi colectivo,* or shared taxi

**Telégrafo:** telegraph office, lately converting to high-tech Telecomunicaciones, or Telecom, offering telegraph, telephone, and public fax services

**vaquero:** cowboy

**vecinidad:** neighborhood

**yanqui:** Yankee

**zócalo:** town plaza or central square

## ABBREVIATIONS

**Av.:** *avenida* (avenue)
**Blv.:** *bulevar* (boulevard)
**Calz.:** *calzada* (thoroughfare, main road)
**Fco.:** Francisco (proper name, as in "Fco. Villa")

**Fracc.:** *fraccionamiento* (subdivision)
**Nte.:** *norte* (north)
**Ote.:** *oriente* (east)
**Pte.:** *poniente* (west)
**s/n:** *sin número* (no street number)

# Spanish Phrasebook

Your Mexican adventure will be more fun if you use a little Spanish. Mexican folks, although they may smile at your funny accent, will appreciate your halting efforts to break the ice and transform yourself from a foreigner to a potential friend.

Spanish commonly uses 30 letters—the familiar English 26, plus four straightforward additions: ch, ll, ñ, and rr.

## PRONUNCIATION

Once you learn them, Spanish pronunciation rules—in contrast to English—don't change. Spanish vowels generally sound softer than in English. (*Note:* The capitalized syllables below receive stronger accents.)

### Vowels

**a** like ah, as in "hah": *agua* AH-gooah (water), *pan* PAHN (bread), and *casa* CAH-sah (house)

**e** like ay, as in "may": *mesa* MAY-sah (table), *tela* TAY-lah (cloth), and *de* DAY (of, from)

**i** like ee, as in "need": *diez* dee-AYZ (ten), *comida* ko-MEE-dah (meal), and *fin* FEEN (end)

**o** like oh, as in "go": *peso* PAY-soh (weight), *ocho* OH-choh (eight), and *poco* POH-koh (a bit)

**u** like oo, as in "cool": *uno* OO-noh (one), *cuarto* KOOAHR-toh (room), and *usted* oos-TAYD (you); when it follows a "q" the **u** is silent; when it follows an "h" or has an umlaut, it's pronounced like "w"

### Consonants

**b, d, f, k, l, m, n, p, q, s, t, v, w, x, y, z, and ch** pronounced almost as in English; **h** occurs, but is silent—not pronounced at all

**c** like k, as in "keep": *cuarto* KOOAR-toh (room), Tepic tay-PEEK (capital of Nayarit state); when it precedes "e" or "i," pronounce **c** like s, as in "sit": *cerveza* sayr-VAY-sah (beer), *encima* ayn-SEE-mah (atop)

**g** like g, as in "gift" when it precedes "a," "o," "u," or a consonant: *gato* GAH-toh (cat), *hago* AH-goh (I do, make); otherwise, pronounce **g** like h, as in "hat": *giro* HEE-roh (money order), *gente* HAYN-tay (people)

**j** like h, as in "has": *Jueves* HOOAY-vays (Thursday), *mejor* may-HOR (better)

**ll** like y, as in "yes": *toalla* toh-AH-yah (towel), *ellos* AY-yohs (they, them)

**ñ** like ny, as in "canyon": *año* AH-nyo (year), *señor* SAY-nyor (Mr., sir)

**r** is lightly trilled, with tongue at the roof of your mouth like a very light English d, as in "ready": *pero* PAY-doh (but), *tres* TDAYS (three), *cuatro* KOOAH-tdoh (four)

**rr** like a Spanish r, but with much more emphasis and trill. Let your tongue flap. Practice with *burro* (donkey), *carretera* (highway), and Carrillo (proper name), then really let go with *ferrocarril* (railroad)

*Note:* The single small but common exception to all of the above is the pronunciation of Spanish **y** when it's being used as the Spanish word for "and," as in *Ron y Kathy*. In such case, pronounce it like the English ee, as in "keep": Ron "ee" Kathy (Ron and Kathy).

### Accent

The rule for accent, the relative stress given to syllables within a given word, is straightforward. If a word ends in a vowel, an "n," or an "s," accent the next-to-last syllable; if not, accent the last syllable.

Pronounce *gracias* GRAH-seeahs (thank you),

*orden* OHR-dayn (order), and *carretera* kah-ray-TAY-rah (highway) with stress on the next-to-last syllable.

Otherwise, accent the last syllable: *venir* vay-NEER (to come), *ferrocarril* fay-roh-cah-REEL (railroad), and *edad* ay-DAHD (age).

**Exceptions** to the accent rule are always marked with an accent sign: (á, é, í, ó, or ú), such as *teléfono* tay-LAY-foh-noh (telephone), *jabón* hah-BON (soap), and *rápido* RAH-pee-doh (rapid).

## BASIC AND COURTEOUS EXPRESSIONS

Most Spanish-speaking people consider formalities important. Whenever approaching anyone for information or some other reason, do not forget the appropriate salutation—good morning, good evening, etc. Standing alone, the greeting *hola* (hello) can sound brusque.

**Hello.** *Hola.*
**Good morning.** *Buenos días.*
**Good afternoon.** *Buenas tardes.*
**Good evening.** *Buenas noches.*
**How are you?** *¿Cómo está usted?*
**Very well, thank you.** *Muy bien, gracias.*
**Okay; good.** *Bien.*
**Not okay; bad.** *Mal or feo.*
**So-so.** *Más o menos.*
**And you?** *¿Y usted?*
**Thank you.** *Gracias.*
**Thank you very much.** *Muchas gracias.*
**You're very kind.** *Muy amable.*
**You're welcome.** *De nada.*
**Goodbye.** *Adios.*
**See you later.** *Hasta luego.*
**please** *por favor*
**yes** *sí*
**no** *no*
**I don't know.** *No sé.*
**Just a moment, please.** *Momentito, por favor.*
**Excuse me, please (when you're trying to get attention).** *Disculpe or Con permiso.*
**Excuse me (when you've made a boo-boo).** *Lo siento.*
**Pleased to meet you.** *Mucho gusto.*
**Do you speak English?** *¿Habla usted inglés?*

**Is English spoken here? (Does anyone here speak English?)** *¿Se habla inglés?*
**I don't speak Spanish well.** *No hablo bien el español.*
**I don't understand.** *No entiendo.*
**How do you say... in Spanish?** *¿Cómo se dice... en español?*
**What is your name?** *¿Cómo se llama usted?*
**My name is...** *Me llamo...*
**Would you like...** *¿Quisiera usted...*
**Let's go to...** *Vamos a...*

## TERMS OF ADDRESS

When in doubt, use the formal *usted* (you) as a form of address.

**I** *yo*
**you (formal)** *usted*
**you (familiar)** *tu*
**he/him** *él*
**she/her** *ella*
**we/us** *nosotros*
**you (plural)** *ustedes*
**they/them** *ellos* (all males or mixed gender); *ellas* (all females)
**Mr., sir** *señor*
**Mrs., madam** *señora*
**miss, young lady** *señorita*
**wife** *esposa*
**husband** *esposo*
**friend** *amigo* (male); *amiga* (female)
**sweetheart** *novio* (male); *novia* (female)
**son; daughter** *hijo; hija*
**brother; sister** *hermano; hermana*
**father; mother** *padre; madre*
**grandfather; grandmother** *abuelo; abuela*

## TRANSPORTATION

**Where is...?** *¿Dónde está...?*
**How far is it to...?** *¿A cuánto está...?*
**from... to...** *de... a...*
**How many blocks?** *¿Cuántas cuadras?*
**Where (Which) is the way to...?** *¿Dónde está el camino a...?*
**the bus station** *la terminal de autobuses*
**the bus stop** *la parada de autobuses*
**Where is this bus going?** *¿Adónde va este autobús?*
**the taxi stand** *la parada de taxis*

**the train station**  *la estación de ferrocarril*
**the boat**  *el barco*
**the launch**  *lancha; tiburonera*
**the dock**  *el muelle*
**the airport**  *el aeropuerto*
**I'd like a ticket to...**  *Quisiera un boleto a...*
**first (second) class**  *primera (segunda) clase*
**roundtrip**  *ida y vuelta*
**reservation**  *reservación*
**baggage**  *equipaje*
**Stop here, please.**  *Pare aquí, por favor.*
**the entrance**  *la entrada*
**the exit**  *la salida*
**the ticket office**  *la oficina de boletos*
**(very) near; far**  *(muy) cerca; lejos*
**to; toward**  *a*
**by; through**  *por*
**from**  *de*
**the right**  *la derecha*
**the left**  *la izquierda*
**straight ahead**  *derecho; directo*
**in front**  *en frente*
**beside**  *al lado*
**behind**  *atrás*
**the corner**  *la esquina*
**the stoplight**  *la semáforo*
**a turn**  *una vuelta*
**right here**  *aquí*
**somewhere around here**  *por acá*
**right there**  *allí*
**somewhere around there**  *por allá*
**road**  *el camino*
**street; boulevard**  *calle; bulevar*
**block**  *la cuadra*
**highway**  *carretera*
**kilometer**  *kilómetro*
**bridge; toll**  *puente; cuota*
**address**  *dirección*
**north; south**  *norte; sur*
**east; west**  *oriente (este); poniente (oeste)*

## ACCOMMODATIONS

**hotel**  *hotel*
**Is there a room?**  *¿Hay cuarto?*
**May I (may we) see it?**  *¿Puedo (podemos) verlo?*
**What is the rate?**  *¿Cuál es el precio?*
**Is that your best rate?**  *¿Es su mejor precio?*

**Is there something cheaper?**  *¿Hay algo más económico?*
**a single room**  *un cuarto sencillo*
**a double room**  *un cuarto doble*
**double bed**  *cama matrimonial*
**twin beds**  *camas gemelas*
**with private bath**  *con baño*
**hot water**  *agua caliente*
**shower**  *ducha*
**towels**  *toallas*
**soap**  *jabón*
**toilet paper**  *papel higiénico*
**blanket**  *frazada; manta*
**sheets**  *sábanas*
**air-conditioned**  *aire acondicionado*
**fan**  *abanico; ventilador*
**key**  *llave*
**manager**  *gerente*

## FOOD

**I'm hungry**  *Tengo hambre.*
**I'm thirsty.**  *Tengo sed.*
**menu**  *carta; menú*
**order**  *orden*
**glass**  *vaso*
**fork**  *tenedor*
**knife**  *cuchillo*
**spoon**  *cuchara*
**napkin**  *servilleta*
**soft drink**  *refresco*
**coffee**  *café*
**tea**  *té*
**drinking water**  *agua pura; agua potable*
**bottled carbonated water**  *agua mineral*
**bottled uncarbonated water**  *agua sin gas*
**beer**  *cerveza*
**wine**  *vino*
**milk**  *leche*
**juice**  *jugo*
**cream**  *crema*
**sugar**  *azúcar*
**cheese**  *queso*
**snack**  *antojo; botana*
**breakfast**  *desayuno*
**lunch**  *almuerzo*
**daily lunch special**  *comida corrida* (or *el menú del día* depending on region)

**dinner** *comida* (often eaten in late afternoon); *cena* (a late-night snack)
**the check** *la cuenta*
**eggs** *huevos*
**bread** *pan*
**salad** *ensalada*
**fruit** *fruta*
**mango** *mango*
**watermelon** *sandía*
**papaya** *papaya*
**banana** *plátano*
**apple** *manzana*
**orange** *naranja*
**lime** *limón*
**fish** *pescado*
**shellfish** *mariscos*
**shrimp** *camarones*
**meat (without)** *(sin) carne*
**chicken** *pollo*
**pork** *puerco*
**beef; steak** *res; bistec*
**bacon; ham** *tocino; jamón*
**fried** *frito*
**roasted** *asada*
**barbecue; barbecued** *barbacoa; al carbón*

## SHOPPING

**money** *dinero*
**money-exchange bureau** *casa de cambio*
**I would like to exchange travelers checks.** *Quisiera cambiar cheques de viajero.*
**What is the exchange rate?** *¿Cuál es el tipo de cambio?*
**How much is the commission?** *¿Cuánto cuesta la comisión?*
**Do you accept credit cards?** *¿Aceptan tarjetas de crédito?*
**money order** *giro*
**How much does it cost?** *¿Cuánto cuesta?*
**What is your final price?** *¿Cuál es su último precio?*
**expensive** *caro*
**cheap** *barato; económico*
**more** *más*
**less** *menos*
**a little** *un poco*
**too much** *demasiado*

## HEALTH

**Help me please.** *Ayúdeme por favor.*
**I am ill.** *Estoy enfermo.*
**Call a doctor.** *Llame un doctor.*
**Take me to...** *Lléveme a...*
**hospital** *hospital; sanatorio*
**drugstore** *farmacia*
**pain** *dolor*
**fever** *fiebre*
**headache** *dolor de cabeza*
**stomach ache** *dolor de estómago*
**burn** *quemadura*
**cramp** *calambre*
**nausea** *náusea*
**vomiting** *vomitar*
**medicine** *medicina*
**antibiotic** *antibiótico*
**pill; tablet** *pastilla*
**aspirin** *aspirina*
**ointment; cream** *pomada; crema*
**bandage** *venda*
**cotton** *algodón*
**sanitary napkins** use brand name, e.g., Kotex
**birth control pills** *pastillas anticonceptivas*
**contraceptive foam** *espuma anticonceptiva*
**condoms** *preservativos; condones*
**toothbrush** *cepilla dental*
**dental floss** *hilo dental*
**toothpaste** *crema dental*
**dentist** *dentista*
**toothache** *dolor de muelas*

## POST OFFICE AND COMMUNICATIONS

**long-distance telephone** *teléfono larga distancia*
**I would like to call...** *Quisiera llamar a...*
**collect** *por cobrar*
**station to station** *a quien contesta*
**person to person** *persona a persona*
**credit card** *tarjeta de crédito*
**post office** *correo*
**general delivery** *lista de correo*
**letter** *carta*
**stamp** *estampilla, timbre*
**postcard** *tarjeta*
**aerogram** *aerograma*
**air mail** *correo aereo*

**registered**  registrado
**money order**  giro
**package; box**  paquete; caja
**string; tape**  cuerda; cinta

## AT THE BORDER

**border**  frontera
**customs**  aduana
**immigration**  migración
**tourist card**  tarjeta de turista
**inspection**  inspección; revisión
**passport**  pasaporte
**profession**  profesión
**marital status**  estado civil
**single**  soltero
**married; divorced**  casado; divorciado
**widowed**  viudado
**insurance**  seguros
**title**  título
**driver's license**  licencia de manejar

## AT THE GAS STATION

**gas station**  gasolinera
**gasoline**  gasolina
**unleaded**  sin plomo
**full, please**  lleno, por favor
**tire**  llanta
**tire repair shop**  vulcanizadora
**air**  aire
**water**  agua
**oil (change)**  aceite (cambio)
**grease**  grasa
**My... doesn't work.**  Mi... no sirve.
**battery**  batería
**radiator**  radiador
**alternator**  alternador
**generator**  generador
**tow truck**  grúa
**repair shop**  taller mecánico
**tune-up**  afinación
**auto parts store**  refaccionería

## VERBS

Verbs are the key to getting along in Spanish. They employ mostly predictable forms and come in three classes, which end in ar, er, and ir, respectively:

**to buy**  comprar
**I buy, you (he, she, it) buys**  compro, compra
**we buy, you (they) buy**  compramos, compran

**to eat**  comer
**I eat, you (he, she, it) eats**  como, come
**we eat, you (they) eat**  comemos, comen

**to climb**  subir
**I climb, you (he, she, it) climbs**  subo, sube
**we climb, you (they) climb**  subimos, suben

Here are more (with irregularities indicated):

**to do or make**  hacer (regular except for hago, I do or make)
**to go**  ir (very irregular: voy, va, vamos, van)
**to go (walk)**  andar
**to love**  amar
**to work**  trabajar
**to want**  desear, querer
**to need**  necesitar
**to read**  leer
**to write**  escribir
**to repair**  reparar
**to stop**  parar
**to get off (the bus)**  bajar
**to arrive**  llegar
**to stay (remain)**  quedar
**to stay (lodge)**  hospedar
**to leave**  salir (regular except for salgo, I leave)
**to look at**  mirar
**to look for**  buscar
**to give**  dar (regular except for doy, I give)
**to carry**  llevar
**to have**  tener (irregular but important: tengo, tiene, tenemos, tienen)
**to come**  venir (similarly irregular: vengo, viene, venimos, vienen)

Spanish has two forms of "to be":

**to be**  estar (regular except for estoy, I am)
**to be**  ser (very irregular: soy, es, somos, son)

Use estar when speaking of location or a temporary state of being: "I am at home." "Estoy en casa." "I'm sick." "Estoy enfermo." Use ser

for a permanent state of being: "I am a doctor."
"*Soy doctora.*"

## NUMBERS

**zero** *cero*
**one** *uno*
**two** *dos*
**three** *tres*
**four** *cuatro*
**five** *cinco*
**six** *seis*
**seven** *siete*
**eight** *ocho*
**nine** *nueve*
**10** *diez*
**11** *once*
**12** *doce*
**13** *trece*
**14** *catorce*
**15** *quince*
**16** *dieciseis*
**17** *diecisiete*
**18** *dieciocho*
**19** *diecinueve*
**20** *veinte*
**21** *veinte y uno* or *veintiuno*
**30** *treinta*
**40** *cuarenta*
**50** *cincuenta*
**60** *sesenta*
**70** *setenta*
**80** *ochenta*
**90** *noventa*
**100** *ciento*
**101** *ciento y uno* or *cientiuno*
**200** *doscientos*
**500** *quinientos*
**1,000** *mil*
**10,000** *diez mil*
**100,000** *cien mil*
**1,000,000** *millón*
**one half** *medio*

**one third** *un tercio*
**one fourth** *un cuarto*

## TIME

**What time is it?** *¿Qué hora es?*
**It's one o'clock.** *Es la una.*
**It's three in the afternoon.** *Son las tres de la tarde.*
**It's 4am** *Son las cuatro de la mañana.*
**six-thirty** *seis y media*
**a quarter till eleven** *un cuarto para las once*
**a quarter past five** *las cinco y cuarto*
**an hour** *una hora*

## DAYS AND MONTHS

**Monday** *lunes*
**Tuesday** *martes*
**Wednesday** *miércoles*
**Thursday** *jueves*
**Friday** *viernes*
**Saturday** *sábado*
**Sunday** *domingo*
**today** *hoy*
**tomorrow** *mañana*
**yesterday** *ayer*
**January** *enero*
**February** *febrero*
**March** *marzo*
**April** *abril*
**May** *mayo*
**June** *junio*
**July** *julio*
**August** *agosto*
**September** *septiembre*
**October** *octubre*
**November** *noviembre*
**December** *diciembre*
**a week** *una semana*
**a month** *un mes*
**after** *después*
**before** *antes*

# Suggested Reading

Some of these books are informative, others are entertaining, and all of them will increase your understanding of both Puerto Vallarta and Mexico. Virtually all of these will be easier to find at home than in Puerto Vallarta. Although many of them are classics and out of print, www.amazon.com, www.barnesandnoble.com, and libraries have used copies. Take some along on your trip. If you find others that are especially noteworthy, let us know. Happy reading.

## HISTORY AND ARCHAEOLOGY

Calderón de la Barca, Fanny. *Life in Mexico, with New Material from the Author's Journals.* Edited by H. T. and M. H. Fisher. New York: Doubleday, 1966. An update of the brilliant, humorous, and celebrated original 1913 book by the Scottish wife of the Spanish ambassador to Mexico.

Casasola, Gustavo. *Seis Siglos de Historia Gráfica de Mexico (Six Centuries of Mexican Graphic History).* Mexico City: Editorial Gustavo Casasola, 1978. Six fascinating volumes of Mexican history in pictures, from 1325 to the 1970s.

Collis, Maurice. *Cortés and Montezuma.* New York: New Directions Publishing Corp., 1999. A reprint of a 1954 classic piece of well-researched storytelling. Collis traces Cortés's conquest of Mexico through the defeat of his chief opponent, Aztec emperor Montezuma. He uses contemporary eyewitnesses—notably Bernal Díaz de Castillo—to revivify one of history's greatest dramas.

Cortés, Hernán. *Letters from Mexico.* Translated by Anthony Pagden. New Haven: Yale University Press, 1986. Cortés's five long letters to his king, in which he describes contemporary Mexico in fascinating detail, including, notably, the remarkably sophisticated life of the Aztecs at the time of the conquest.

Davies, Nigel. *Ancient Kingdoms of Mexico.* London: Penguin Books, 1990. An authoritative history of the foundations of Mexican civilization. Clearly traces the evolution of Mexico's five successive worlds—Olmec, Teotihuacán, Toltec, Aztec, and finally Spanish—that set the stage for present-day Mexico.

Díaz del Castillo, Bernal. *The Discovery and Conquest of Mexico.* Translated by Albert Idell. London: Routledge (of Taylor and Francis Group), 2005. A soldier's still-fresh tale of the conquest from the Spanish viewpoint.

Garfias, Luis. *The Mexican Revolution.* Mexico City: Panorama Editorial, 1985. A concise Mexican version of the 1910-1917 Mexican revolution, the crucible of present-day Mexico.

Grabman, Richard. *Gods, Gachupines and Gringos.* Mazatlán: Editorial Mazatlan, 2008. An excellent people's history of Mexico by historian Richard Grabman. Colorful and engaging enough to capture the attention of people who would normally eschew a history book. A must-read for anyone looking for a fascinating walk through Mexico's history and culture.

Gugliotta, Bobette. *Women of Mexico.* Encino, CA: Floricanto Press, 1989. Lively legends, tales, and biographies of remarkable Mexican women, from Zapotec princesses to Independence heroines.

León-Portilla, Miguel. *The Broken Spears: The Aztec Account of the Conquest of Mexico.* New York: Beacon Press, 1992. Provides an interesting contrast to Díaz del Castillo's account.

Meyer, Michael, and William Sherman. *The Course of Mexican History*. New York: Oxford University Press, 2003. An insightful 700-plus-page college textbook in paperback. A bargain, especially if you can get it used.

Novas, Himlice. *Everything You Need to Know About Latino History*. New York: Plume Books (Penguin Group), 1994. Chicanos, Latin rhythm, La Raza, the Treaty of Guadalupe Hidalgo, and much more, interpreted from an authoritative Latino point of view.

Reed, John. *Insurgent Mexico*. New York: International Publisher's Co., 1994. Republication of 1914 original. Fast-moving, but not unbiased, description of the 1910 Mexican revolution by the journalist famed for his reporting of the subsequent 1917 Russian revolution. Reed, memorialized by the Soviets, was resurrected in the 1981 film biography *Reds*.

Ridley, Jasper. *Maximilian and Juárez*. New York: Ticknor and Fields, 1999. This authoritative historical biography breathes new life into one of Mexico's great ironic tragedies, a drama that pitted the native Zapotec "Lincoln of Mexico" against the dreamy, idealistic Archduke Maximilian of Austria-Hungary. Despite their common liberal ideas, they were drawn into a bloody no-quarter struggle that set the Old World against the New, ending in Maximilian's execution and the subsequent insanity of his wife, Carlota. The United States emerged as a power to be reckoned with in world affairs.

Ruíz, Ramon Eduardo. *Triumphs and Tragedy: A History of the Mexican People*. New York: W. W. Norton, Inc., 1992. A pithy, anecdote-filled history of Mexico from an authoritative Mexican American perspective.

Simpson, Lesley Bird. *Many Mexicos*. Berkeley: The University of California Press, 1960. A much-reprinted, fascinating broad-brush version of Mexican history.

Townsend, Richard, et al. *Ancient West Mexico: Art and Archaeology of the Unknown Past*. New York: W. W. Norton, 1998. This magnificent coffee-table volume, with lovely photos and authoritative text, reveals the little-known culture being uncovered at Guachimontones and other sites, notably the "bottle tombs" in the Tequila valley west of Guadalajara. Dozens of fine images illuminate a high culture of sculptural and ceramic art, depicting everything from warriors, ball players, and acrobats to loving couples, animals, and sacred rituals.

## UNIQUE GUIDE AND TIP BOOKS

American Automobile Association. *Mexico TravelBook*. Heathrow, FL: American Automobile Association, 2003. Short, sweet summaries of major Mexican tourist destinations and sights. Also includes information on fiestas, accommodations, restaurants, and a wealth of information relevant to car travel in Mexico. Available in bookstores, or free to AAA members at affiliate offices.

Burton, Tony. *Western Mexico, A Traveler's Treasury*. St. Augustine, FL: Perception Press, 2001. A well-researched and lovingly written and illustrated guide to dozens of fascinating places to visit, both well-known and out of the way, in Michoacán, Jalisco, and Nayarit.

Church, Mike, and Terri Church. *Traveler's Guide to Mexican Camping*. Kirkland, WA: Rolling Homes Press, 2005. This is an unusually thorough guide to trailer parks all over Mexico, with much coverage of the Pacific Coast in general and the Guadalajara region in particular. Detailed maps guide you accurately to each trailer park cited, and clear descriptions tell you what to expect. The book also provides very helpful information on car travel in Mexico, including details of insurance, border crossing, highway safety, car repairs, and much more.

Franz, Carl. *The People's Guide to Mexico.* 14th ed. Berkeley, CA: Avalon Travel, 2012. The bible of Mexico travel; chock-full of entertaining anecdotes and indispensable information on the joys and pitfalls of independent economy travel in Mexico.

Graham, Scott. *Handle with Care.* Chicago: The Noble Press, 1991. Should you accept a meal from a family who lives in a grass house? This insightful guide answers this and hundreds of other tough questions for persons who want to travel responsibly in the developing world.

Guilford, Judith. *The Packing Book.* Berkeley, CA: Ten Speed Press, 2006. The secrets of the carry-on traveler, or how to make everything you carry do double and triple duty. All for the sake of convenience, mobility, economy, and comfort.

Howells, John, and Don Merwin. *Choose Mexico.* Guilford, CT: The Globe Pequot Press, 2005. A pair of experienced Mexico residents provide a wealth of astute counsel about the important questions—health, finance, home ownership, work, driving, legalities—of long-term travel, residence, and retirement in Mexico. Includes a specific section on Puerto Vallarta.

Meade, Julie Doherty. *Living Abroad in Mexico.* 2nd ed. Berkeley, CA: Avalon Travel, 2012. A handy package of traveler's tools for living like a local in Mexico. Provides much general background and some specific details on settling (and perhaps making a living) in one of a number of Mexico's prime expatriate living areas, such as Mexico City, Guadalajara, Lake Chapala, Puerto Vallarta, and San Miguel de Allende.

Werner, David. *Where There Is No Doctor.* Palo Alto, CA: Hesperian Foundation, 2006. How to keep well in the tropical backcountry.

Whipperman, Bruce. *Moon Pacific Mexico.* 8th ed. Emeryville, CA: Avalon Travel, 2007. A wealth of information for traveling the Pacific Coast route, through Mazatlán, Guadalajara, Puerto Vallarta, Ixtapa-Zihuatanejo, Acapulco, and Oaxaca.

## SPECIALTY TRAVEL GUIDES

Annand, Douglass R. *The Wheelchair Traveler.* Milford, NH: Self-published, 1990. Step-by-step guide for planning a vacation. Accessible information on air travel, cruises, ground transportation, selecting the right hotel, what questions to ask, solutions to problems that may arise, and accessibility to many wonderful destinations in the United States and Mexico.

Jeffrey, Nan. *Adventuring with Children.* Ashland, MA: Avalon House Publishing, 1995. This unusually detailed classic starts where most travel-with-children books end. It contains, besides a wealth of information and practical strategies for general travel with children, specific chapters on how you can adventure—trek, kayak, river raft, camp, bicycle, and much more—successfully with the kids in tow.

## FICTION

Bolaño, Roberto. *The Savage Detectives.* English translation by Natasha Wimmer. New York: Farrar, Straus, and Giroux, 2007. Chilean exile novelist Bolaño wrote two novels of contemporary Mexico, *The Savage Detectives* and *2666.* This book chronicles the life and times of aspiring Mexican poet Juan García Madero, member of a gang of Mexico City poets who call themselves the Visceral Realists. The first and last sections are about Madero; the center is a polyphonic history of the so-called Visceral Realists over 20 years. The whole thing is a crazy, absurdist, amusing, and tragic tale of modern-day Mexican intellectuals. Bolaño died in 2003 at the age of 50.

Bolaño, Roberto. *2666*. English translation by Natasha Wimmer. New York: Farrar, Straus, and Giroux, 2008. Bolaño's last published novel, this book explores 20th-century degeneration through a wide array of characters, locations, and time periods, but the most compelling story is about the unsolved serial murders of hundreds of women in and around Ciudad Juárez in northern Mexico. It is not a pretty story, but this book, as profoundly sad and depressing as it is, is an undeniable work of genius—and in it, the author reclaims the lives and identities of dozens of women who died brutally and anonymously at the hands of a still-unknown killer.

Bowen, David, and Juan A. Ascencio. *Pyramids of Glass*. San Antonio: Corona Publishing Co., 1994. Two-dozen-odd stories that lead the reader along a monthlong journey through the bedrooms, the barracks, the cafés, and streets of present-day Mexico.

Boyle, T. C. *The Tortilla Curtain*. New York: Penguin-Putnam; Vancouver: Raincoast Books, 1996. A chance intersection of the lives of two couples—one affluent and liberal Southern Californians, the other poor homeless illegal immigrants—forces all to come to grips with the real price of the American Dream.

De la Cruz, Sor Juana Inez. *Poems, Protest, and a Dream*. New York: Penguin, 1997. Masterful translation of collection of love and religious poems by the celebrated pioneer (1651-1695) Mexican nun-feminist.

Doerr, Harriet. *Consider This, Señor*. New York: Harcourt Brace, 1993. Four expatriates tough it out in a Mexican small town, adapting to the excesses—blazing sun; driving rain; vast, untrammeled landscapes—and interacting with the local folks, while the local folks observe them with a mixture of fascination and tolerance.

Fuentes, Carlos. *Where the Air Is Clear*. New York: Farrar, Straus, and Giroux, 1971. The seminal work of Mexico's celebrated novelist.

Fuentes, Carlos. *The Years with Laura Díaz*. Translated by Alfred MacAdam. New York: Farrar, Straus, and Giroux, 2000. A panorama of Mexico from Independence to the 21st century, through the eyes of one woman, Laura Díaz, and her great-grandson, the author. One reviewer said that she "...as a Mexican woman, would like to celebrate Carlos Fuentes; it is worthy of applause that a man who has seen, observed, analyzed, and criticized the great occurrences of the century now has a woman, Laura Díaz, speak for him."

Jennings, Gary. *Aztec*. New York: Forge Books, 1997. Beautifully researched and written monumental tale of lust, compassion, love, and death in preconquest Mexico.

Nickles, Sara, ed. *Escape to Mexico*. San Francisco: Chronicle Books, 2002. A carefully selected anthology of 20-odd stories of Mexico by renowned authors, from Steven Crane and W. Somerset Maugham to Anaïs Nin and David Lida, who all found inspiration, refuge, adventure, and much more in Mexico.

Peters, Daniel. *The Luck of Huemac*. New York: Random House, 1981. An Aztec noble family's tale of war, famine, sorcery, heroism, treachery, love, and finally disaster and death in the Valley of Mexico.

Rulfo, Juan. *The Burning Plain*. Austin: University of Texas Press, 1967. A celebrated Guadalajara author tells stories of people torn between the old and new in Mexico.

Rulfo, Juan. *Pedro Páramo*. New York: Grove Press, 1994. Rulfo's acknowledged masterpiece, originally published in 1955, established his renown. The author, thinly disguised as the protagonist, Juan Preciado, fulfills his mother's dying request by returning to his shadowy Jalisco hometown, Comala, in search of this father. Although Preciado discovers that his father, Pedro Páramo (whose surname implies "wasteland"), is long dead, Preciado's search resurrects his father's restless spirit, which recounts its horrific life tale of massacre, rape, and incest.

Traven, B. *The Treasure of the Sierra Madre.* New York: Hill and Wang, 1967. Campesinos, *federales,* gringos, and *indígenas* all figure in this modern morality tale set in Mexico's rugged outback. The most famous of the mysterious author's many novels of oppression and justice set in Mexico's jungles.

Villaseñor, Victor. *Rain of Gold.* New York: Delta Books (Bantam, Doubleday, and Dell), 1991. The moving, best-selling epic of the author's family's gritty travails. From humble rural beginnings in the Copper Canyon, they flee revolution and certain death, struggling through parched northern deserts to sprawling border refugee camps. From there they migrate to relative safety and an eventual modicum of happiness in Southern California.

## PEOPLE AND CULTURE

Berrin, Kathleen. *The Art of the Huichol Indians.* New York: Harry N. Abrams, 1978. Lovely, large photographs and text by a symposium of experts provide a good interpretive introduction to Huichol art and culture.

Castillo, Ana. *Goddess of the Americas.* New York: Riverhead Books, 1996. Here, a noted author has selected from the works of seven interpreters of Mesoamerican female deities, whose visions range as far and wide as Sex Goddess, the Broken-Hearted, the Subversive, and the Warrior Queen.

Collings, Peter R. *The Huichol Puerto Vallarta.* Available from the author in Puerto Vallarta (at Casa Isabel, 257 Allende, Puerto Vallarta, 48300, huicholbks@hotmail.com) or

antiquarian booksellers (such as Bolerium Books in San Francisco, toll-free U.S. tel. 800/326-6353, www.bolerium.com). In a series of precious photos gathered over years of living among them, the author details the life and rituals of present-day Huichol people.

Haden, Judith Cooper, and Matthew Jaffe. *Oaxaca, the Spirit of Mexico.* New York: Workman Publishing, Artisan, 2002. Simply the loveliest, most sensitively photographed and crafted coffee-table book of Mexico photography yet produced. Photos by Haden, text by Jaffe.

Lewis, Oscar. *Children of Sánchez.* New York: Random House Vintage Books, 1979. Poverty and strength in the Mexican underclass, sympathetically described and interpreted by renowned sociologist Lewis.

Medina, Sylvia López. *Cantora.* New York: Ballantine Books, 1992. Fascinated by the stories of her grandmother, aunt, and mother, the author seeks her own center by discovering a past that she thought she wanted to forget.

Meyerhoff, Barbara. *Peyote Hunt: The Sacred Journey of the Huichol Indians.* Ithaca, NY: Cornell University Press, 1974. A description and interpretation of the Huichol's religious use of mind-bending natural hallucinogens.

Montes de Oca, Catalina. *Puerto Vallarta, My Memories.* Translated by Laura McCullough. Puerto Vallarta: University of Guadalajara, 2002. A longtime Puerto Vallartan breathes life into the early history and old times in Puerto Vallarta as she remembers them, from her arrival as a child in 1918 to the present.

Palmer, Colin A. *Slaves of the White God: Blacks in Mexico, 1570-1650.* Cambridge, MA: Harvard University Press, 1976. A scholarly study of why and how Spanish authorities imported African slaves into America and how they were used afterward.

Replete with poignant details, taken from Spanish and Mexican archives, describing how the Africans struggled from bondage to eventual freedom.

Riding, Alan. *Distant Neighbors: A Portrait of the Mexicans.* New York: Random House Vintage Books, 1989. Rare insights into Mexico and Mexicans.

Toor, Frances (1890-1956). *A Treasury of Mexican Folkways.* New York: Bonanaza, 1988. First published 1947 by Crown Books. An illustrated encyclopedia of vanishing Mexicana—costumes, religion, fiestas, burial practices, customs, legends—compiled during the celebrated author's 35-year residence in Mexico.

Wauchope, Robert, ed. *Handbook of Middle American Indians.* Vols. 7 and 8. Austin: University of Texas Press, 1969. Authoritative surveys of important Indian-speaking groups in northern and central (vol. 8) and southern (vol. 7) Mexico.

## FLORA AND FAUNA

Goodson, Gar. *Fishes of the Pacific Coast.* Stanford, CA: Stanford University Press, 1988. Over 500 beautifully detailed color drawings highlight this pocket version of all you ever wanted to know about the ocean's fishes (including common Spanish names) from Alaska to Peru.

Howell, Steve N. G. *Bird-Finding Guide to Mexico.* Ithaca, NY: Cornell University Press, 1999. A unique, portable guide for folks who really want to see birds in Mexico. Unlike other bird books, this authoritative guide has dozens of clear maps and lists of birds seen at sites all over Mexico. Pacific sites include Mazatlán, San Blas, Puerto Vallarta, El Tuito, Manzanillo, Oaxaca, and many more. Use this book along with Howell and Webb's *A Guide to the Birds of Mexico and Northern Central America.*

Howell, Steve N. G., and Sophie Webb. *A Guide to the Birds of Mexico and Northern Central America.* Oxford: Oxford University Press, 1995. All the serious bird-watcher needs to know about Mexico's rich species treasury. Includes authoritative habitat maps and 70 excellent color plates that detail the males and females of around 1,500 species.

Leopold, Starker. *Wildlife of Mexico.* Berkeley: University of California Press, 1959. Classic, illustrated layperson's survey of common Mexican mammals and birds.

Mason, Charles T., Jr., and Patricia B. Mason. *Handbook of Mexican Roadside Flora.* Tucson: University of Arizona Press, 1987. Authoritative identification guide, with line illustrations, of all the plants you're likely to see in the Puerto Vallarta region.

Morris, Percy A. *A Field Guide to Pacific Coast Shells.* Boston: Houghton Mifflin, 1974. The complete beachcomber's Pacific shell guide.

Pesman, M. Walter. *Meet Flora Mexicana.* Globe, AZ: D. S. King, 1962. Now out of print. Delightful anecdotes and illustrations of hundreds of common Mexican plants.

Peterson, Roger Tory, and Edward L. Chalif. *Field Guide to Mexican Birds.* Boston: Houghton Mifflin, 1999. With hundreds of Peterson's crisp color drawings, this is a must for serious bird-watchers and vacationers interested in the life that teems in the Puerto Vallarta region's beaches, jungles, lakes, and lagoons.

Wright, N. Pelham. *A Guide to Mexican Mammals and Reptiles.* Mexico City: Minutiae Mexicana, 1989. Pocket-edition lore, history, descriptions, and pictures of commonly seen Mexican animals.

## ART, ARCHITECTURE, AND CRAFTS

Baird, Joseph. *The Churches of Mexico 1530-1810*. Berkeley: University of California Press, 1962. Mexican colonial architecture and art, illustrated and interpreted.

Cordrey, Donald, and Dorothy Cordrey. *Mexican Indian Costumes*. Austin: University of Texas Press, 1968. A lovingly photographed, written, and illustrated classic on Mexican Indians and their dress, emphasizing textiles.

Covarrubias, Miguel. *Indian Art of Mexico and Central America*. New York: Knopf, 1957. A timeless work by the renowned interpreter of *indígena* art and design.

Martínez Penaloza, Porfirio. *Popular Arts of Mexico*. Mexico City: Editorial Panorama, 1981. An excellent, authoritative pocket-size exposition of Mexican art.

Mullen, Robert James. *Architecture and Its Sculpture in Viceregal Mexico*. Austin: University of Texas Press, 1997. The essential work of Mexican colonial-era cathedrals and churches. In this lovingly written and illustrated life work, Mullen breathes new vitality into New Spain's preciously glorious colonial architectural legacy.

Sayer, Chloë. *Arts and Crafts of Mexico*. San Francisco: Chronicle Books, 1990. All you ever wanted to know about your favorite Mexican crafts, from papier-mâché to pottery and toys to Taxco silver. Beautifully illustrated with traditional etchings and David Lavender's crisp black-and-white and color photographs.

# Internet Resources

## GENERAL MEXICO

### Go To Mexico
**www.go2mexico.com**
A broad, well-organized commercial site that covers, among others, the Mexican Pacific destinations of Mazatlán, Puerto Vallarta, Ixtapa-Zihuatanejo, Acapulco, Huatulco, Oaxaca, Guadalajara, and Manzanillo (including current weather reports).

### MexConnect
**www.mexconnect.com**
An extensive Mexico site with dozens upon dozens of subheadings and links, especially helpful for folks thinking of traveling, working, living, or retiring in Mexico.

### Mexico Desconocido
**www.mexicodesconocido.com.mx**
The site of the excellent magazine *Mexico Desconocido* (Undiscovered Mexico), which mostly features stories of unusual and off-the-beaten-track destinations, many in the Puerto Vallarta region. Accesses a large library of past articles that are not unlike a Mexican version of *National Geographic Traveler*. Click the small "English" button at the top to translate. Excellent, hard-to-find information, with good English translation.

### Mexico Tourism Board
**www.visitmexico.com**
The official website of the public-private Mexico Tourism Board; a good general site for official information, such as entry requirements. It has lots of summarily informative subheadings, not unlike an abbreviated guidebook.

### MexOnline
**www.mexonline.com**
Very extensive, well-organized site with many subheadings and links to Mexico's large and medium destinations, and even some small destinations. The Puerto Vallarta section is typical, with manifold links, including many accommodations, from budget to luxury. Excellent.

**The People's Guide to Mexico**
**www.peoplesguide.com**
Website of the popular *People's Guide to Mexico.* Carl Franz and Lorena Havens answer reader questions and blog about travel throughout Mexico.

**www.planeta.com**
Life project of Latin America's dean of ecotourism, Ron Mader, who furnishes a comprehensive clearinghouse of everything ecologically correct, from rescuing turtle eggs in Jalisco to preserving cloud forests in Peru. Contains dozens of subheadings competently linked for maximum speed. For example, check out the Mexico travel directory for ecojourneys, maps, information networks, parks, regional guides, and a mountain more.

## ACCOMMODATIONS
**Choice One**
**www.choice1.com**
A potentially useful site for picking a vacation rental house, condo, or villa, with information and reservations links to individual owners. Prices vary from moderate to luxurious. Coverage extends to a number of regional towns, including Puerto Vallarta and the neighboring coast (Bucerías, Sayulita, San Francisco).

**Couchsurfing**
**www.couchsurfing.com**
A site that connects those with a couch to surf with people who wish to surf a couch. Of course, not all available accommodations are actual couches. Quite a few people have guest rooms and other facilities available.

**www.homexchange.com**
**www.homeforexchange.com**
Sites for temporarily trading your home with someone else in dozens of places in the world, including a total of about two dozen Puerto Vallarta listings on each site.

**VRBO (Vacation Rentals by Owner)**
**www.vrbo.com**
A superuseful site for folks looking for hard-to-find vacation rentals by owner. Although this site covers nearly the whole world, it has dense Puerto Vallarta region coverage, with hundreds of vacation rental listings in Puerto Vallarta and regional towns and villages, from the Bay of Banderas north to San Blas, and south to Barra de Navidad.

## DESTINATIONS
### Puerto Vallarta
**Craigslist Puerto Vallarta**
**http://pv.es.craigslist.com.mx**
Puerto Vallarta version of the popular Craigslist website. Includes rentals, jobs, personals, for sale ads, and more.

**Mano a Mano**
**www.manoamano.com.mx**
Website of the very popular Puerto Vallarta classifieds newspaper that comes out every Thursday morning. Mostly in Spanish, but it does include some English listings. Great resource for rentals and housewares.

**www.pvmirror.com**
Thoughtful and up-to-date Puerto Vallarta news magazine with lots of information on what's new in places to stay, eat, shop, invest, and much more.

**www.puertovallarta.net**
Wow! All you need to prepare for your Puerto Vallarta vacation. Contains a wealth of details in dozens of competently linked subheadings, such as hotels, both humble and grand (but mostly grand); car rentals; adventure tours; and on and on. Nearly every tourism service provider in Puerto Vallarta seems to be on board.

**Vallarta Tribune**
**www.vallartatribune.com**
Online website of one of Puerto Vallarta's two English-language newspapers. Current edition is usually available for PDF download.

**www.virtualvallarta.com**
The website of *Vallarta Lifestyles* magazine. Like its parent magazine, it's strong in things upscale, such as boutiques, expensive restaurants, and condo sales and rentals.

## Nayarit Coast
**Discover Nayarit**
**www.discovernayarit.com**
Local website with a variety of articles and useful information pertaining to Nayarit. Primary focus is on real estate sales and rentals.

**www.sanblasdirectory.com**
Unique low-impact ecotourism-oriented site with links to rustic local accommodations, ecotours, things to do in nature, artwork, real estate, and more.

**www.sanblasmexico.com**
Small but informative site with details on what to do and links to where to stay, where to eat, and more in San Blas.

**www.sayulitalife.com**
Excellent site with seemingly everything you need to know about the up-and-coming pocket paradise of Sayulita. Coverage includes vacation rentals by owner, hotels, real estate, restaurants, services, shopping, surfing, massage, and much more.

**www.sanpancholife.com**
Like its sister site Sayulitalife.com, Sanpancholife.com covers everything you need to know about the town of San Francisco, locally known as San Pancho, including vacation rentals, hotels, restaurants, recreational opportunities, shopping, and much more.

**www.visitsanblas.com**
Another ecotourism-oriented site, but with quite a bit of typical-tourist-oriented information, including what's new around town and links to modest lodgings, budget tips, beaches, surfing, nightlife, and more.

## Jalisco Coast
**www.costalegre.ca**
Unusually detailed site (even with authentic sounds) with lots of up-to-date lodging, restaurant, beach, tour, service, and other information. Coverage includes not only Barra de Navidad and Melaque, but a swarm of small beaches and villages along the coast all the way north to Perula.

**www.tomzap.com**
Competent, straightforward commercial site (but with lots of useful background content) that covers parts of Jalisco, Colima, and Oaxaca. Especially good coverage of the small beaches and villages, and Barra de Navidad and Melaque, on the Jalisco Coast.

## SPECIALTY TRAVEL
**www.discoveryvallarta.com**
The best and most complete gay Puerto Vallarta website, with dozens of search categories, such as hotels, restaurants, bars, tours, art galleries, shopping, and vacation rentals, with many links to associated websites. They even have a good lesbian section, with information about lesbian-friendly hotels and services in Sayulita, Yelapa, Bucerías, Paco's Paradise, and more.

**Elderhostel**
**www.elderhostel.org**
Site of Boston-based Elderhostel, Inc., with a sizable selection of ongoing Mexico study tours.

**www.gayguidevallarta.com**
Online version of the excellent *Gay Guide to Vallarta* magazine, stuffed with links to many gay-friendly lodgings, clubs, bars, galleries, services, and much more.

**Mobility International**
**www.miusa.org**
Site of Mobility International, wonderfully organized and complete, with a flock of travel services for travelers with disabilities, including many people-to-people connections in Mexico.

**Purple Roofs**
**www.purpleroofs.com**
One of the best general gay travel websites is maintained by San Francisco-based Web travel agency Purple Roofs. It offers, for example, details of about 20 gay-friendly Puerto Vallarta hotels, in addition to a wealth of gay-friendly travel-oriented links worldwide.

## TRAVEL INSURANCE

**www.sanbornsinsurance.com**
Site of the longtime, very reliable Mexico auto insurance agency, with the only north-of-the-border adjustment procedure. Get your quote online, join the Sombrero Club, order their many useful publications, and get tips for crossing the border by car.

**www.travelguard.com**
Very good for travel insurance and other services.

**www.travelinsure.com**
Site offering comprehensive travel insurance policies for individuals and groups worldwide. In business since 1973, the company offers student health, medical, trip cancellation, business travel, and a number of other types of insurance for travelers.

# Index

# List of Maps

# Acknowledgments

As the most recent rewriter and updater of this book, I'd like to thank Bruce Whipperman, author of the previous editions, for his thorough, entertaining, and informative research and background work; and Robin Noelle, for her additions to Bruce's original work. From a personal point of view, thanks to all the people on the many roads who showed me the way. And especially thanks to Donna Day and Jade Henderson, my family, who let me talk them into moving down here. Thanks to Donna as well for her photographic contributions. *¡Viva México!*

—Justin Henderson

# www.moon.com

DESTINATIONS | ACTIVITIES | BLOGS | MAPS | BOOKS

**MOON.COM** is ready to help plan your next trip! Filled with fresh trip ideas and strategies, author interviews, informative travel blogs, a detailed map library, and descriptions of all the Moon guidebooks, Moon.com is all you need to get out and explore the world—or even places in your own backyard. While at Moon.com, sign up for our monthly e-newsletter for updates on new releases, travel tips, and expert advice from our on-the-go Moon authors. As always, when you travel with Moon, expect an experience that is uncommon and truly unique.

KEEP UP WITH MOON:  f  🐦  📌

# MAP SYMBOLS

| | | | | | | | |
|---|---|---|---|---|---|---|---|
| ≡≡≡ | Expressway | 【 | Highlight | ✗ | Airfield | ⌕ | Golf Course |
| ═══ | Primary Road | ○ | City/Town | ✈ | Airport | P | Parking Area |
| ═══ | Secondary Road | ◉ | State Capital | ▲ | Mountain | ≜ | Archaeological Site |
| ═══ | Unpaved Road | ⊛ | National Capital | ✦ | Unique Natural Feature | ♦ | Church |
| - - - - | Trail | ★ | Point of Interest | | | ◘ | Gas Station |
| ········· | Ferry | • | Accommodation | 🌊 | Waterfall | ⌒ | Glacier |
| ⊶⊶⊶ | Railroad | ▼ | Restaurant/Bar | ▲ | Park | ⌇ | Mangrove |
| ═══ | Pedestrian Walkway | ■ | Other Location | ❶ | Trailhead | | Reef |
| ⊞⊞⊞ | Stairs | ⋀ | Campground | ⛷ | Skiing Area | | Swamp |

# CONVERSION TABLES

°C = (°F - 32) / 1.8
°F = (°C x 1.8) + 32
1 inch = 2.54 centimeters (cm)
1 foot = 0.304 meters (m)
1 yard = 0.914 meters
1 mile = 1.6093 kilometers (km)
1 km = 0.6214 miles
1 fathom = 1.8288 m
1 chain = 20.1168 m
1 furlong = 201.168 m
1 acre = 0.4047 hectares
1 sq km = 100 hectares
1 sq mile = 2.59 square km
1 ounce = 28.35 grams
1 pound = 0.4536 kilograms
1 short ton = 0.90718 metric ton
1 short ton = 2,000 pounds
1 long ton = 1.016 metric tons
1 long ton = 2,240 pounds
1 metric ton = 1,000 kilograms
1 quart = 0.94635 liters
1 US gallon = 3.7854 liters
1 Imperial gallon = 4.5459 liters
1 nautical mile = 1.852 km

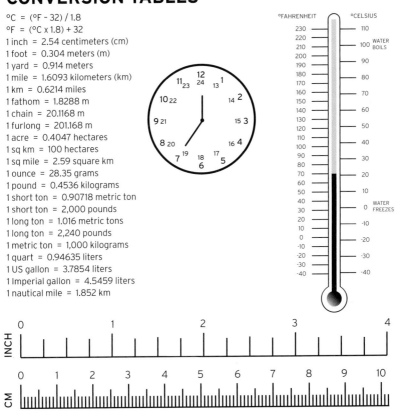

**MOON PUERTO VALLARTA**

Avalon Travel
a member of the Perseus Books Group
1700 Fourth Street
Berkeley, CA 94710, USA
www.moon.com

Editor and Series Manager: Kathryn Ettinger
Copy Editor: Justine Rathbun
Graphics and Production Coordinator: Lucie Ericksen
Cover Designer: Lucie Ericksen
Map Editor: Mike Morgenfeld
Cartographers: Kaitlin Jaffe and Paige Enoch
Indexer: Greg Jewett

ISBN-13: 978-1-61238-515-0
ISSN: 1533-4198

Printing History
1st Edition – 1995
9th Edition – August 2013
5 4 3 2 1

Text © 2013 by Bruce Whipperman & Avalon Travel.
Maps © 2013 by Avalon Travel.
All rights reserved.

Front cover photo: Mother and child walking on a beach through palm shadows, Puerto Vallarta © Mark D Callanan/GettyImages
Title page photo: Dames of the Dead © Donna Day
Other front matter photos: pages 6 bottom, 7, 8, 10-12, 14, 17, 18, 21: © Donna Day; page 6 inset: © 123rf.com; pages 4, 5, 13, 15, 20, 22-24: © Justin Henderson

Printed in China by RR Donnelley

## KEEPING CURRENT

If you have a favorite gem you'd like to see included in the next edition, or see anything that needs updating, clarification, or correction, please drop us a line. Send your comments via email to feedback@moon.com, or use the address above.